also by chris salewicz

REDEMPTION SONG

the ballad of

JOE STRUMMER

Faber and Faber, Inc.

An affiliate of Farrar, Straus and Giroux

New York

REDEMPTION SONG

chris salewicz

FABER AND FABER, INC.
An affiliate of Farrar, Straus and Giroux
19 Union Square West, New York 10003

Originally published in different form in 2006 by
HarperCollins*Entertainment*, Great Britain, as *Redemption Song:*
The Authorised Biography of Joe Strummer
Published in the United States by Faber and Faber, Inc.
First American edition, 2007

Library of Congress Cataloging-in-Publication Data
Salewicz, Chris.
    Redemption song : the ballad of Joe Strummer / Chris Salewicz.—1st
    American ed.
        p.   cm.
    Includes index.
    ISBN-13: 978-0-571-21178-4 (hardcover : alk. paper)
    ISBN-10: 0-571-21178-X (hardcover : alk. paper)
    1. Strummer, Joe.   2. Rock musicians—England—Biography.   I. Title.

ML420   S918S25 2007
782.42166092—dc22
[B]
                                                              2006039106

Designed by Cassandra J. Pappas

www.fsgbooks.com

10 9 8 7 6 5 4 3 2 1

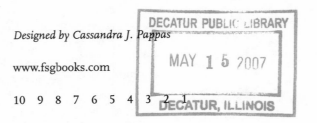
Frontispiece: Joe Strummer in Japan, 1982. (Sho Kikuchi)

roots of heathen

No heritage or culture
Imagined empires at our feet
The tribe beats upon the bench
A country shadowed in defeat

They sing twelve tribes of Israel
But not here in Punkertown
Gray and white I am a heathen
My people have no chosen crown

Waving bibles soaked in petrol
My leaders burn our shantytown
They slam that bible on the pulpit
Grinding only poor men down

Liars talk of purity
They dream the super-race
I give my Scots-Armenian laugh
Into his Indu-Saxon face

But when power is turned to hunger
And scientists will tire of war
When money no longer has a number
We will see what prophets saw

—JOE STRUMMER

contents

REDEMPTION SONG

1

straight to heaven

2002

This is how I heard about Joe's death: Don Letts, the Rastafarian film director who had made all the Clash videos, called me at around 9:30 on the evening of December 22, 2002.

"I've got to tell you, Chris: Joe's died—of a heart attack."

"Oh-fuckin'-hell-Oh-fuckin'-hell-Oh-fuckin'-hell" was all I could say.

I poured a large glass of rum and stuck Don's documentary about the group, *Westway to the World*, in the VCR. I called up Mick Jones, who in between sobs was his usual funny self, telling me how glad he was he'd played with Joe at the benefit for the Fire Brigades Union five weeks before.

"I don't even know what religion he was," Mick said.

"Some kind of Scottish low-church Presbyterian," I suggested.

"Church of Beer, probably," laughed Mick, tearfully.

I went to bed late, and although I hardly slept I didn't get up until around 9:30. At around 9:55 the phone rang: ITN News. Could they interview me for the 10:00 bulletin? I sat down on the sofa and made some quick sound-bite-sized notes. I'm not even sure what I said. The phone rang again: *The Independent* wanted me to write an obituary, a long one, two thousand words, by four o'clock. I started up the computer, opening up my assorted Strummer files, pulling out quotes and phrases. Then the phone rang once more: ITN News again. Could they send a car for me to be on the 12:30 news? Call me back in a minute, I said: I need to work out whether I can do it—the obituary is what counts most. I put the phone down. Someone's got to do this for Joe, I thought, but I don't want to blow the obit by doing too much. I called Joe's home in Somerset and left a message of condolence for Lucinda, his widow.

By the time the car came for me at half past eleven, I'd got a good amount done. As it always does, the TV stuff took much longer than it was meant to—they wanted to record something more for the evening news. It was 2:00 p.m. before I was home again. I still had a lot to do. But somehow time stretched, giving me many more minutes an hour than I might have expected. I e-mailed the obituary through at ten minutes to four. This is what I wrote:

 he job of being Joe Strummer, spokesman for the punk generation and front man for the Clash, never sat easily with the former John Mellor. Always prepared to give of himself to his fans, he still felt a weight of responsibility on his shoulders that often made him crave anonymity, as much as the natural performer within him needed the spotlight.

But when—after a hiatus of almost a decade and a half—he returned to recording and performing with his new group the Mescaleros in 1999, it was business as usual: seemingly the same huge amounts of energy, passion and heart-on-sleeve belief that were his trademark with the Clash and that drew a worldwide audience for him and the group. After a show the dressing room or backstage bar still would be crammed with fans and friends as Joe held forth on the issues of the day, in his preferred role of pub philosopher and articulate rabble-rouser for the dispossessed. (But even here was the endless paradox of Joe Strummer: he could argue the case for Yorkshire pitworkers or homeless Latinos in Los Angeles, but if obliged to reveal himself through any interior observation, he would generally freeze. Even other members of the Clash would complain about his hopelessness at soul-baring.)

Yet when he played a show at London's 100 Club two years ago, he was so exhausted afterward that he had to lie down on the floor of the dressing room: his Mescaleros' set included a good percentage of Clash songs, and you worried that the frenetic speed at which they were performed would test the health of a man approaching his fiftieth birthday. In an irony that

Joe Strummer no doubt would have appreciated, his death last Sunday afternoon came not from the stock rock 'n' roll killers of drugs, drink or travel accidents, but after taking his dog for a walk at his home in Somerset: sitting down on a chair in his kitchen, he suffered a fatal heart attack. [I later learned it was in his living room, and it was "dogs," not "dog."]

Neither of his parents had lived to a ripe old age. Joe Strummer, who earned his sobriquet from his crunchy rhythm guitar style, was born in Ankara, Turkey, in 1952 to a career diplomat. Christened John Graham Mellor, he was sent at the age of ten [nine] to a lesser public [i.e., private] school, the City of London Freemen's School at Ashstead Park in Surrey. He had already lived in Cairo, Mexico City ("I remember the 1956 earthquake vividly; running to hide behind a brick wall, which was the worst thing to do," he once told me) and Bonn. Strummer's father's profession of career diplomat didn't arise from any position of privilege—quite the opposite, in fact. "He was a self-made man, and we could never get on," said Strummer. "He couldn't understand why I was last in every class at school. He didn't understand there were different shapes to every piece of wood, different grains to people. I don't blame him, because all he knew was that he pulled himself out of it by studying really hard."

All the same, such a background was not especially appropriate in the mid-1970s punk world of supposed working-class heroes, which may explain why Strummer always seemed even more anarchic than his contemporaries. Mick Jones, like Strummer a former art-school student, discovered Joe when he was singing with squat-rock R&B group, the 101'ers, and poached him for a group he was forming called the Clash, becoming his songwriting partner: matched to Jones's zeitgeist musical arrangements, Strummer's lyrics were the words of a satirical poet, and often hilariously funny—one of his first creative contributions on linking up with Mick Jones was to change the title of a love song called "I'm So Bored with You" to "I'm So Bored with the USA." Verbal non sequiturs were a specialty: his gasped aside of "vacuum cleaner sucks up budgie" at the end of "Magnificent Seven," inspired by a newspaper headline on the studio floor, is one of the funniest lines in rock 'n' roll.

Strummer had one brother, David, who was eighteen months older than himself. By the time he reached sixteen, the younger boy had become accustomed to his brother's far-right leanings—he had joined the National Front—and to the fact that he was obsessed, "in a cheap paperback way," with the occult. Was it this unpleasant cocktail that led David to commit suicide? Whatever, it was clearly a cathartic moment for his younger brother: Joe Strummer often seemed overhung by a mood of mild depression, a constant struggle.

After dropping out of Central School of Art ("after about a week," [he lied about this]), he threw himself into the alternative world of squatting. Moving for a time to Wales, he spent one Christmas on acid listening to Big Youth's *Screaming Target* classic and so discovered reggae. One of the main themes propagated by the Clash was the rise of a multicultural Britain; in the group's early music reggae rhythms jostled with an almost puritan sense of rock 'n' roll heritage; as the group progressed, it osmosed and absorbed Latin, blues and early hiphop sounds, with Strummer's never-less-than-heartfelt lyrics making him a modern-day protest singer, in a tradition stretching back to Woody Guthrie.

Positive light to the darkness of the Sex Pistols, the Clash released an incendiary, eponymously titled first album in 1977, the year of punk, a Top Ten hit. With Strummer at the helm, the group toured incessantly: at a show that year at the University of Leeds, he delivered the customary diatribe of the times: "No Elvis, Beatles or Rolling Stones . . . but John Lennon rules, OK?" he barked, revealing a principal influence and hero of his own. The next year, after a night spent at a reggae concert, he wrote what he himself felt was his finest song, "White Man in Hammersmith Palais," a blues-ballad that opened up the musical gates for the future of the group. In that song, however, was contained the seeds of a paradox that would become more and more uncomfortable for Strummer: one line spoke of "new groups . . . turning rebellion into money." Through writing such outsider lyrics, he became a millionaire; his problem was one common to many radical figureheads: how do you remain a folk hero when you have succeeded in your aim and are no longer the underdog? Touring the country that summer of 1978, the group's concerts were shot for a feature film, *Rude Boy*, directed by David Mingay and Jack Hazan. "He already seemed to be suffering terribly from the notion of being Joe Strummer," said Mingay. "He wasn't exactly lying back and having a great time. Joe was always full of contradictions, one of which was that he managed to be both ultra-British and anti-British at the same time."

With *London Calling*, their third album, the group achieved commercial

American success. *Sandinista!*, a sprawling three-record set, followed. When it became clear that the album was commercial folly, Joe Strummer demanded the return of their original manager, Bernard Rhodes, a business colleague of Malcolm McLaren and someone with whom Mick Jones had always had an awkward relationship. With Rhodes's sense of wily situationism powering the group, the potential disaster of *Sandinista!* was turned into a triumph after the group played sixteen nights at Bond's in New York's Times Square. The group were the toast of the town, and only a big commercial hit stood between them and superstardom.

That came in 1982 with *Combat Rock*, a huge international success, selling five million copies. Strummer bought a substantial terrace house in London's Notting Hill, yet seemed to feel obliged to justify this possession by explaining that it reminded him of the houses in which he used to squat. By 1983, the Clash had begun to disintegrate; first, heroin-addicted drummer Topper Headon was replaced; then, extraordinarily, Mick Jones was fired, Strummer having gone along with Rhodes's perversely iconoclastic desire to get rid of the founder of the group. New members were brought in, but the Clash finally fizzled out in 1986.

Strummer's sense of guilt over the sacking of Jones developed to a point of almost clinical complexity. In the late summer of 1985 he asked me to go for a drink with him. After much alcohol had been consumed, he suddenly announced: "I've got a big problem: Mick was right about Bernie [Rhodes]." He had finally realized he had been manipulated. He caught a plane to the Bahamas, where Mick Jones was on holiday: an ounce of grass in his hand, he sought out the guitarist's hotel, and presented him with this tribute, asking to get the Clash back together. But it was too late: Jones had already formed a new group, Big Audio Dynamite; although Joe Strummer ended up coproducing BAD's second album, his own plans came to nothing.

A familiar figure on the streets and in the bars of Notting Hill, Joe Strummer was mired—as he later admitted to me—in depression. He tried acting, with a passable role in Alex Cox's *Straight to Hell* (1987), and a minor part in the same director's *Walker* (1987), for which he also wrote the music; he made a much more significant impression in 1989, playing an English Elvis-like rocker in Jim Jarmusch's *Mystery Train*. That same year he released an impressive solo album, *Earthquake Weather*, and toured. But apart from briefly filling in as singer with the Pogues, he was hardly heard of again. For a time Tim Clark, who now manages Robbie Williams, attempted to guide his career. "He was obviously in bad shape," Clark told me. "He'd turn up for meetings the worse for wear. You could see he was going through a bad time, but you also felt there was probably no one he could really talk to about it."

After moving out of Notting Hill to a house in Hampshire—he had become worried about his two daughters, he said, after one of them found a syringe in a West London playground—he subsequently split up with his long-term partner Gaby [Salter]. Remarrying in 1995, to Lucinda Tait, and moving to Bridgwater in Somerset, Joe seemed to find a relative peace. He formed the Mescaleros and began recording again, releasing two excellent albums, *Rock Art and the X-Ray Style* (1999) and *Global a Go-Go* (2001), that title a reflection of his interests in world music, about which he presented a regular show on the BBC's World Service. Strummer was once again touring, incessantly and on a worldwide basis: he was playing to sold-out audiences, with a set that contained a large amount of Clash material. "All that's happening for me now is just a chancer's bluff," he told me in 1999. "This is my Indian summer . . . I learned that fame is an illusion and everything about it is just a joke. I'm far more dangerous now, because I don't care at all."

One of Joe Strummer's last concerts was at Acton Town Hall last month, a benefit for the Fire Brigades Union. Andy Gilchrist, the leader of the FBU, was apparently politicized after seeing the Clash perform a "Rock Against Racism" concert in Hackney in 1978, and had asked Strummer if he would play the Acton show. That night Mick Jones joined him onstage, the first time they had performed live together since Jones had been so unfairly booted out of the Clash. "I nearly didn't go. I'm glad I did," said the guitarist, the poetry of that reunion clear to him.

Bitterly critical that the present Labour government has betrayed many of its former ideals, Joe Strummer was delighted at the show for the firemen; a smile came over his face at the idea that, if only tangentially, his former group was still capable of causing discomfort for those in power. His death, however, comes as a deep shock. After considerable time in the wilderness, Joe Strummer seemed to have reinvented himself as a kind of Johnny Cash–like elder statesman of British rock 'n' roll, a much-loved artist and everyman figure. "I still thought he'd be doing this in thirty years time," said his friend the film director Don Letts.

2

r.i.punk

2002

Christmas Day 2002. Driving through South London, I am wondering whether Joe Strummer had known how much people loved him. Pulling up at traffic lights, I glance to my left; there, spray-painted across a building in large scarlet letters, seems to be some sort of answer to my meditations: JOE STRUMMER R.I.PUNK. I call Mick Jones and leave a message, telling him what I'd seen. Joe's funeral, eight days after he died, polarized all my thoughts and feelings. The following day I wrote this:

Monday, December 30, 2002

The sky is a slab of dark, gravestone gray; rain belts down in bucketfuls, leaving enormous pools of water on the roadside: Thomas Hardy funeral weather. Ready for the funeral's 2:00 p.m. kickoff, I find myself at the entrance to the West London Crematorium on Harrow Road. A voice calls to me from one of the parked cars: it is Chrissie Hynde with Jeannette Lee (formerly of PIL, now co–managing director of Rough Trade, a punk-era girlfriend of Joe). Chrissie is clearly in a bad state. "Not great," she answers my question.

On the main driveway I bump straight into the music journalist Charles Shaar Murray and Anna Chen, his girlfriend: he looks fraught. It is pouring with rain. I take a half-spliff out of my jacket pocket and light it, take a few tokes and hand it to Charlie. Out of the hundreds of hours I had spent with Joe I don't think I had been with him on a single occasion when marijuana had not been consumed, so it seems appropriate, even important, to get in the right frame of mind to be with him again.

The spliff is still burning when I see massed ranks of uniformed men. Not police, but firemen, two ranks of a dozen, standing to attention in Joe's honor. With Charlie and Anna, I walk between them. Standing under the shelter of a window arch I see Bob Gruen, the photographer, and walk over to him. We hug. Then Chrissie and Jeannette arrive; Jeannette and I hug. Soon Don Letts also arrives. I roll him a cigarette.

Suddenly it seems time to walk inside the building, into the main vestibule. That's where everyone has been waiting. I see Jim Jarmusch, who directed Joe in *Mystery Train*; Clash road manager Johnny Greene; and—next to him—the stick-thin, Stan Laurel–like figure of Topper Headon. We hug; there is a lot of hugging today. Against the wall I see an acoustic guitar, covered in white roses, really beautiful. In its hollowed-out center is a message: R.I.P. JOE STRUMMER HEAVEN CALLING 1952–2002. A large boom box, next to it, is similarly covered in white roses. All the seats in the chapel are full. I find a gap against the rear wall. A lot of people are sniffling.

Then the sound of bagpipes sails in through the door, lengthily, growing nearer. (Later I learn that the music is "The Mist-Covered Mountains of Home," also played at the funeral of John F. Kennedy.) At last Joe's coffin slowly comes in, held aloft by half a dozen pallbearers. It is placed down at the far end of the chapel. Keith Allen, the actor and comedian, steps forward and positions a cowboy hat on top of it. There's a big sticker on the nearest end: QUESTION AUTHORITY, it reads, then in smaller letters, "Ask Me Anything." Next to it is a smaller sticker: "Vinyl Rules." On the sides of the coffin are more messages: "Get In, Hold On, Sit Down, Shut Up" and "Musicians Can't Dance." Around the end wall of the chapel are flags of all nations. More people are ushered in, like the kids Joe would make sure got through the stage door at Clash gigs, until the place is crammed. In the crush I catch a glimpse of Lucinda, Joe's beautiful widow: she carries herself with immense dignity but—hardly surprisingly—has an aura of almost indescribable grief, pain and shock. People are standing right up by the coffin. The aisle is packed: suddenly a tall blonde, looking half-gorgeous, a Macbeth witch, is pushed through the throng, to kneel on the stone floor at the front of the aisle—it's not until later on that I realize this is Courtney Love.

The service begins. I don't know who the emcee is, a man in his late fifties, a vague cross between Gene Hackman and Woody Allen. He's good, tells us how much love we are all part of, stresses how honored we are that our lives were so touched by Joe, says that he's never seen a bigger turnout for a funeral. (There is a sound system outside, relaying the proceedings to the several hundred people now there.) Then he says we'll hear the first piece of music, and we should turn our meditations on Joe: it is "White Man in Hammersmith Palais."

Paul Simonon gets up to speak. He tells a story about how when the Clash first formed in 1976, he and Joe had been in Portobello Road, discussing the merits of mirror shades, as worn by Jimmy Cliff in *The Harder They Come*. If anyone showed you any aggression while you were wearing such a pair, Joe decided, then their anger would be reflected back at them. Immediately he stepped into a store that sold such sunglasses. Paul didn't follow: he was completely broke, having been kicked off social security benefits; Joe, however, had just cashed that week's social security check. He came out of the store wearing his brand-new mirror shades. Then they set off to beat the tube fare to Rehearsal Rehearsals in Camden. As they walked toward Ladbroke Grove tube station, Joe dug into his pocket. "Here," he said, "I bought you a pair too." Although Joe was now completely broke and with no money to eat for three days, he'd helped out his mate. This story increases the collective tear in the chapel.

Maeri, a female cousin, gets up to speak. Joe's mother had been a farmer's daughter, who became a nurse and met Joe's father in India during the war. Joe's dad liked to have a great time: a real rebel himself, it seems, not at all the posh diplomat he has been made out to be, a man who pulled himself up by his bootstraps. We are told a story about Joe as a ten-year-old at a family gathering: he is told that he can go anywhere but "the barn"; immediately he wants to know where "the barn" is. Then another cousin, Anna, reads a poem, in English, by the Gaelic poet Sorley MacLean.

Dick Rude, an old friend of Joe from L.A. who has been making a documentary about the Mescaleros, speaks. Keith Allen reads out the lyrics of a song about Nelson Mandela, part of an AIDS charity project for South Africa organized by Bono of U2, that Joe had just finished writing. A Joe demo tape, just him and a guitar, a slow blueslike song, is played. And the Mescaleros tune "From Willesden to Cricklewood." The emcee suggests that as we file past the coffin to leave, we say a few words to Joe. "Wandering Star" begins to play. "See you later, Joe," someone says. Yeah, see you later, Joe.

After the extraordinary tension that has built up to the funeral since Joe's death eight days ago—my sleep is disturbed and troubled the night before the service—it feels like a release when the service concludes. (I have felt Joe around ever since he passed on: Gaby, his former long-term partner, has felt the same thing, she tells me on the phone the previous Friday, and I tell her that a mystic friend of mine has spoken of Joe "ascending" very clearly—according to Buddhism, there is a period of forty-eight days following a death before the soul returns in another form; Gaby feels the same, saying she feels he is very at peace; job done, on to the next incarnation. Until someone reminds me, I have forgotten that Gaby has had plenty of experience of death, her brother having committed suicide while she was still with Joe—as his brother did.) Somehow I expect almost a party atmosphere outside the chapel, with the sound system maybe blaring out some Studio One. But everyone is wandering around in a daze. The wake is being held at the Paradise bar in nearby Kensal Rise.

Outside the Paradise a bloke in a suit and black tie asks if I have any change so he can park his car. He looks familiar; it is Terry Chimes, the original Clash drummer, who had resigned from the group after making the first album, leaving the way open for Topper Headon. Terry is now a famed chiropractor, giving seminars on the subject.

The bar is packed with people and a gray atmosphere of grief. I see Lucinda and hold her for a moment. Simultaneously she feels as frail as a feather and as strong as an oak beam. But she is clearly floating in trauma. I tell her how sorry I am, and as I speak my words feel inadequate and pathetic. From a stage at one end speakers are batting out reggae. The pair of pretty barmaids are struggling with the crush. I am handed a beer, which I down, pushed into a corner. I see a woman with a familiar face: Marcia, the wife of Jem Finer, effectively leader of the Pogues—I used to enjoy spending time with them at evenings and parties at Joe's house when he still lived in Notting Hill. I am incredibly flattered by what she says to me. She says: "Joe always used to say that you were the only journalist he trusted. And he said he loved you as a friend. He really loved you." I am unbelievably touched by this. I want to talk to her more, but she is clearly looking for someone. I nearly burst into tears when what she has said fully registers with me. (I'm not unusual in being in such a state: all around me I see men putting their hands to their eyes, sobbing for a few moments.) Later Jem Finer, Marcia with him, deliberately seeks me out and tells me this again.

Next to the cloakroom I find a couple of more rooms, where food has been laid out. I grab a plate: smoked salmon, feta cheese salad, pasta—good nosh. And sitting down I find a middle-aged woman, Sheena Yeats, Joe's cousin. She's very Scottish, however: "Well, this is the best funeral I've ever been to," she burrs, with a smile. "Joe would have really appreciated it." She tells me how Joe had been up to Scotland a month ago, to a wedding, and that he had been in touch with everyone in his family recently. She reminds me that Joe's mum, Anna, had passed on in January 1987. "Although he chose to call himself Joe, because it was such an everyman name, his real name was John, a name with the common touch," she explains.

Bob Gruen tells me how Joe had been in New York a couple of months ago, in some bar, leading the assembled throng in revelry and having a great time. Seated nearby is Gerry Harrington, a Los Angeles agent who had guided Joe's career when he was working on *Walker* and *Mystery Train* and releasing 1989's *Earthquake Weather*. Joe had written a song for Johnny Cash last April, at Gerry's house in L.A., entitled "Long Shadow": Gerry plays it for me on an iPod, an extraordinary valedictory work that could have been about Joe himself, with lines about crawling up the mountain to the top.

I talk to Rat Scabies, former drummer with the Damned. He tells me he and Joe had been working together in 1995 on the soundtrack of *Grosse Pointe Blank*, but that they fell out over that hoary old rock 'n' roll chestnut—money. "I was stupid," he admits. "I thought I knew everything from playing with the Damned. But working with Joe was like an entirely new education. He understood how to trust his instincts and go with them every time. I couldn't believe how fast he worked."

I run into Mick Jones. He puts his arms around me and kisses me on the cheek. We hold each other. He tells me how he'd loved the message I'd left on his voice mail after seeing the JOE STRUMMER R.I.PUNK graffito on

Christmas Day; it had touched Mick as deeply as it touched me. He tells me how great the Fire Brigades Union have been, and that the police have behaved similarly. At the Chapel of Rest where Joe had been laid in Somerset a sound system had blared out 24/7. When the police came round in response to complaints from neighbors, and were told it was Joe who was lying there, instead of telling them they must turn down the music, they responded by placing a permanent two-man unit outside the chapel: a Great Briton getting a fitting honor guard, an irony Joe would have appreciated as his mourning bredren consumed several pounds of herb.

Pearl Harbor, Paul Simonon's ex-wife, is there, talking to Joe Ely, the Texan rockabilly star who had often played with the Clash. She tells me how this trip has brought closure for her by bringing her back to what, she admits, was the happiest time in her life.

A moment later Tricia—Mrs. Simonon—comes over as Pearl departs and proceeds to tell me how the absent Clash manager Bernie Rhodes had been contacted and invited to come to the funeral, but after the usual overlengthy conversation it was impossible to discover what Bernie really felt or thought. "It seemed that he was more intent on getting on to the next agenda, which was that he desperately wanted to be invited to the Rock and Roll Hall of Fame induction for the Clash next March. What he didn't realize was that it was already decided that he would be invited."

"I always had a soft spot for Joe," Bernie later told me. "But I couldn't go to the funeral because I didn't like the people he was hanging around with."

Joe and Mick had both wanted a re-formed Clash to play at the Rock and Roll Hall of Fame induction. But the one refusenik? Paul Simonon, painter of Notting Hill. Trish admits that the last communication Paul had from Joe was on the morning that he died. Joe sent Paul a fax—he loved faxes, hated e-mails—saying, "You should try it—it could be fun." Paul, however, was adamant that the group shouldn't re-form for the show.

Next I find myself in a long conversation with Jim Jarmusch's partner, Sara Driver, who commissioned Joe to write the music for *When Pigs Fly*, a film she made in 1993, starring Marianne Faithfull, which had only a limited release after business problems, and with Bob Gruen's wife, Elizabeth. Jim is sitting next to us, deep in conversation with Cosmic Tim, a mutual friend of Joe and myself, from completely separate angles of entry. I had walked into the main upstairs bar as Cosmic Tim was standing on the stage

Never too computer-literate, Joe wrote on a typewriter to the
end. *(Lucinda Mellor)*

with a microphone. It was the usual stuff that had gained him his sobriquet, and I groaned inwardly. "And this man Baba had been to the mountains of Tibet and lived there for twenty-five years, meditating." Other
people in the packed crowd were groaning too. ("Get on with it.") But then
Cosmic Tim turned it around: "And one day when he returned to London,
I was walking down Portobello Road with Baba when I see Joe walking
toward us. I cross the road, and Baba and Joe look at each other. Suddenly,

Baba calls out, 'Woody!' [Joe's nickname from the 101'ers]. And Joe looks up and shouts, 'Baba!'" According to Tim, Baba and Joe had known each other at art school. At length Sara, Elizabeth and I discuss the state of depression in which Joe was regularly mired, and that most of the tributes to him that day are utterly omitting. Sara says that Jim used to refer to him as "Big Chief Thundercloud." She also tells me that Joe had an enormous crisis when he was on tour in the States singing with the Pogues: he had fallen deeply in love with a girl and wanted to leave Gaby for her. Although he didn't at the time, in some ways it was the end of his relationship with the mother of his children. (This was a period when I remember Joe seemed even more in turmoil than usual, an air of great anger about him.)

The party is thinning out a little. It is eleven o'clock. I've got a slight headache. I leave and walk down to Ladbroke Grove tube station with Flea, Mick's guitar roadie, and get home around midnight. I fall asleep on the sofa.

3

indian summer

1999

November 7, 1999

In a shrinelike case in the seedily glitzy foyer of Las Vegas's Hard Rock casino stands a guitar once owned by Elvis Presley. "What would Elvis think?" groans Joe Strummer, here to play a show on his first solo tour in ten years. This distress seems a trifle exaggerated, as though Strummer is trying to force himself into the character of a forty-seven-year-old bad boy rocker. "This case is only Plexiglas: we could smash it open and have the guitar out of there before anyone noticed," he continues. Is this a confrontational posture he feels he should adopt in his job of Last Active Punk Star?

The frozen grins on the faces of those around him—his wife, an old friend from San Francisco, myself—suggest this is not what we want to hear: there seems a certain anxiety among us that, to prove his point, Strummer might carry out his threat, and that within seconds we will be shot to death by security guards. Thankfully, a fan approaches him for an autograph, the moment passes and he makes his way backstage for his performance.

As a stage act, the reputation of the Clash was almost unsurpassed. Championed by many as the most exciting live rock 'n' roll group ever, there's recently been the release of a concert album, accompanied by Don Letts's documentary *Westway to the World*. If ever there was a time to jump-start his solo career, this was it. Strummer seized the moment: he released an excellent album, *Rock Art and the X-Ray Style*, and took off on a seemingly endless tour, which is how I come to find him in Las Vegas.

Standing with him at the Hard Rock casino's central bar at four in the morning after many postshow drinks, I tell him I'd had the impression that for years he had been going through an ongoing minor nervous breakdown. He balks at this, but initially will admit to having been locked into a state of long-term depression: "When people have nervous breakdowns, they really flip out. We shouldn't treat them flippantly. It was more like depression, miserable-old-gitness."

How long were you depressed for?

"About five minutes. Until I had a spliff."

A moment later he tries to wriggle out of even this admission: "I'm not claiming to have been depressed. All I'll allow is that I didn't have any confidence and I thought the whole show was over: you can wear your brain out—like on a knife-sharpening stone, run it until it shatters—and I just wanted to have some of it left."

Assisted by his now four-year-old marriage to Lucinda, his second wife, Strummer seems to have found a relative peace; Lucinda is credited by many around him with pulling him out of his malaise.

Christened John Mellor ("without an 's' on the end, unfortunately: if there was, I'd have pulled more women," he said, referring to the game-keeper's surname in *Lady Chatterley's Lover*), he was born in Ankara. The musician's grandparents had worked as management on the colonial railway network in India. "My father was a smart dude: he won a scholarship to a good school, then won another scholarship to university. When the war broke out, he joined the Indian army. My mother and father met in a casualty ward in India—she was working in the nursing battalion. After the war he joined the civil service at a lowly rank."

Strummer's earliest memory was of his brother, who was eighteen months older, "giving me a digestive biscuit in the pram." He still is unable to assess what it was that led David to commit suicide. "Who knows? You can't say, can you?"

Clearly this would have seemed a crucial, motivating catalyst in the life of the person who became Joe Strummer. How did it affect him? "I don't know how it affects people. It's a terrible thing for parents." He pauses for a very long time, until it becomes evident that this is all he is prepared to offer.

If it hadn't been for punk, what on earth would have happened to Joe? He didn't last too long at art school. After that, the only upward career move he seemed to have made was when he decided to stop being a busker's money collector and to become a street entertainer himself—but even that worried him, he tells me, because he thought it might prove too difficult. It was this that led to him playing with the 101'ers, from which he was poached to become the Clash's singer. "There is a part of Joe that is a real loser," says Jon Savage, author of *England's Dreaming*, the definitive account of the punk era. "That's what he was in his days as a squatter. And it's that that comes across in his vocals, which was why people could identify with them so much."

I tell Joe that Kosmo Vinyl, the unlikely named "creative director" of the Clash, once said to me that if it hadn't been for punk the singer would have ended up a tramp.

"Yeah," he agrees, without a moment's thought. "When I was a kid I knew that I was never going to make it in the thrusting executive world. I love picking stuff out of skips [dumpsters]. A few bum records and I'll be away with my shopping trolley."

I ask Joe Strummer what he learned from his years in the wilderness. "Any pimple-encrusted kid can jump up and become king of the rock 'n' roll world," he says, voicing something to which he has clearly given much thought. "But when you're a young man like that you really do glow in the light of everyone's attention. It becomes a sustaining part of your life—which is something that is rotten to the core: you cannot have that as a crutch, because one day you're going to be over. So obviously I learned that fame is an illusion and everything about it is just a joke.

"I don't give a damn anymore. I've learned not to take it seriously—that's what I've learned. And I've also learned that because what you do is sort of interesting, doesn't mean you're any better than anyone else: after all, we're not exactly devising new forms of protein. If they say, 'Release this record because otherwise your career is finished,' and I don't want them to, then I just won't do it. I'm far more dangerous now, because I don't care at all."

stepping out of babylon (one more time)

2003 (1952–1957)

Moving at a fast pace, Paul Simonon and I are cutting along a narrow rocky mud path that splits the wet grass on this high stretch of Scottish flatland. In a soaking spray of fine rain we have been climbing for twenty minutes. But the moment that we had stepped onto this level plateau the downpour stopped: damp odors and mysterious scents are all that saturate us now. In the dagger-cold water of a lochan, we stash two cans of beer for our return journey. On the far bank a frog croaks irregularly.

Lusher and even more magical than its much larger, bleaker neighbor of Skye, this is the remote Inner Hebrides island of Raasay, up toward the northern tip of its thirteen-mile length. Thanks to an abiding impression of all-pervading strangeness, however, we feel we could as easily be on the other side of the moon as on the far northwestern periphery of Europe. But you can't avoid that feeling of being out on the edge. For miles around there are no other human beings, only a vast, amorphous silence, the soundtrack to the grayish blue wild mountain scenery that juts around us; you can almost hear the clouds clashing on the highland rock and rustling on the purple heather.

As we push on, each turn of a corner seems to brings a new microclimate, announced by a gasp of angular wind, like a message from a spirit: now the cloud cover is dashed away and a crisp blue sky sets in relief the Cuillin Hills, Skye's looming mountain peaks, a few miles across the Sound of Raasay; in this sudden sunlight the sea turns azure, the rough breakers crackling and glistening. After our steep, wet, upward hike, the flat stretch has come as a relief. We don't know there is a far more arduous climb still to come: finally perched on a rock cairn at the top of that tough ascent, we can see both east and west coasts of the isle of Raasay, three miles apart.

Tough, gritty, awkward, dangerous, an astonishing terrain of primal, pure, mysterious beauty . . . It is little surprise that one of the descendants of Raasay—John Graham Mellor, known to those outside his blood family as Joe Strummer—has many of the same qualities as the island itself. Although he'd marked it in his diary for the summer of 2003, Joe himself never made it to Raasay; in the years immediately preceding his death, he had been making a conscious effort to reacquaint himself with the Scottish roots on his mother's side, an effort to redeem the previous thirty or so years when he admitted he had neglected this part of his past. "I've been a terrible Scotsman, but I'm going to be better," Joe said to his cousin Alasdair Gillies at the wedding of their cousin George in Bonar Bridge, three weeks before he died.

To the east, across the deepest inshore water in Britain, sits the mainland of Scotland and the mountain peaks of the Applecross peninsula, rising to over two thousand feet and tipped by streaks of white quartzite. Opposite it, down toward the Raasay shoreline, lies our destination. Paul Simonon and I are here to find the earliest known home of Joe Strummer's Scottish ancestors: the rocky, heathery, hilly path we are following, which at times we have to hang on to with our fingertips, is the same one that Joe's grandmother Jane Mackenzie would have taken to school. Donald Gilliejesus ("servant of Jesus"), a stone mason, from near Mallaig on the Scottish mainland, arrived to repair Raasay House, destroyed by English redcoats after Bonnie Prince Charlie hid on the island in 1746 following the Jacobite rebellion against the English crown. The house at Umachan was built in the early 1850s after the Gillieses fled from the "clearances"—the savage requisitioning of smallholdings by landowners—on the south of Raasay. Built by Angus Gillies, the great-grandson of Donald, it was inherited by his son Alastair Gillies. The second of Alastair's ten children was Jane—Joe's grandmother—born in 1883.

We head sharply down, across a lazy burn, past further cairns of stone. On our right there is what appears to be a natural amphitheater, and a clearly evident ancient burial mound rising out of the green-brown terrain. Finally we are standing amid waist-high bracken on a precipitous ledge, looking down on where we have been told Umachan should be. Between us we have distributed Paul's canvases, paints and an easel, which have become a burden: we hide them in some undergrowth. Paul, something of a gourmet, tells me how in London he had popped into Bentley's Oyster Bar in Swallow Street for a dozen oysters and a bottle of Chablis while buying the hiking shoes he's wearing; it's a long way from heating up flour-water poster-paste on a saw to eat, as Paul did in the early days of the Clash at Rehearsal Rehearsals. But a nourished belly and well-shod feet can only mark us out as the useless city slickers we are: we can find no trace of the home of Joe Strummer's ancestor.

At a quarter to one, lunchtime on Friday, September 12, 2003, my phone rings. It is Paul Simonon. "I think you'd better pack your bag, Chris. On Sunday I'm going up to Raasay off the Isle of Skye to do a painting of the house Joe's grandmother used to live in. You should come with me."

The Herald has commissioned Paul to paint a landscape of Rebel Wood, the forest on the Isle of Skye dedicated to Joe Strummer. Paul Simonon is one of the two members of the Clash to have carved out a nonmusical career; returning to his original love of painting, and utilizing contacts he made along the way as a member of such a prestigious group, he has made a name and money as a figurative painter. Paul has agreed to paint the wood, but also will supply what he believes is a better idea: a picture of the ruined house in Umachan on Raasay. Iain Gillies, Joe's cousin, had told us about these ruins.

As I am to discover, our expedition forms part of an experience that will bring some form of ending to the former Clash bass player for the thor-

oughly unexpected death of his former lead singer. During our time together, Paul emphasizes on several occasions that Joe was his brother, "my
older brother."

E very August film director Don Letts and his wife, Grace, throw a garden barbecue at their Queen's Park home as a sort of refuge for the
over-forties and under-tens from the Notting Hill carnival taking place a
mile or so to the south. At the event in 2003, eighteen days before he made
that Friday lunchtime call to me to come up to Scotland, I'd last seen Paul
Simonon. The smaller 1976 Notting Hill carnival, when black youths and
police had violently clashed beneath the Westway (an elevated highway
leading out of London to the west) in front of Joe Strummer and Paul Simonon, had inspired "White Riot," one of the most contentious songs in
the Clash's canon of work, a tune that at first—before people understood
that its lyrics expressed the envy of white outsiders that black kids could so
successfully rebel against the forces of law and order—led to suspicions
that the group had a fascist political agenda. The 1976 event and the Westway became part of Clash mythology.

In the early days of the group Paul had always seemed shy. In 2001,
however, when I had written the text for a picture book about the Clash by
Bob Gruen, the New York photographer, I had been surprised by a change
that had overcome the group's former bass player; as Gruen and I went
through hundreds of photographs with each of the group members, he was
by far the most articulate. Mick was as warm as ever, but his comments
were more jokey and less specific; and although Joe had insisted to Gruen
that I should write the text for his book, he surprised me by being the worst
of the three interview subjects. Perhaps the photographs, which encapsu-
lated almost the entire span of the career of the Clash, drew up too many
memories; he ended up by saying he would write captions himself—and
never did. Global a Go-Go, his second CD with the Mescaleros, was being
readied for release and Joe was exhaustively—the only way he knew how to
do anything—promoting it; I could feel tension from Lucinda, on the couple of occasions when I rang up and spoke to her, trying to press Joe to
come up with some text. A couple of months later, in the upstairs office that
served as a dressing room at the HMV megastore on London's Oxford

Street, where Joe and the Mescaleros had just aired the new *Global a Go-Go* songs to a full house, he came up and apologized to me for not having come up with the goods.

"It's fine," I said, telling him I'd used quotes he'd given me over the years. "I know you had a lot on your plate, and we came up with something anyway."

"But you shouldn't let down your mates." He shook his head at himself.

Anyway, in Don Letts's back garden it dawned on me that—contrary to everything that you might have expected in 1977—even before Joe's passing Paul had become the spokesman and historian of the Clash. At Don's home that August evening he was especially communicative and open and seemed to feel an urge to talk about the group.

P aul Gustave Simonon was born on December 15, 1955, to Gustave Antoine Simonon and Elaine Florence Braithwaite. Gustave, who preferred to call himself Anthony, was a twenty-year-old soldier who later opened a bookshop; Elaine worked at Brixton Library. As happened to Mick Jones, Paul's bohemian parents split up when he was eight; he and his brother were taken to Italy when he was about ten, where they lived for six months in Siena, and six months in Rome. There his mother took him to see all the latest spaghetti westerns—not just Sergio Leone, but all the *Django* films also. In London, Paul moved to live with his father in Notting Hill. His father, once an ardent Roman Catholic churchgoer, joined the Communist Party: "Suddenly we're being told we're not going to church anymore. I'm being sent off to stuff leaflets for the Communist Party through people's letter boxes in Ladbroke Grove. You can imagine what it was like: all these rough Irish or West Indians, hanging out on the steps, and I'm coming up to their letter boxes: 'What's that you're putting through there?' 'Oh, it's just something about the Communist Party.' Then I figured out, if my dad was such a passionate Communist, how come he was sitting at home and sending me off to do this?"

"The Clash was a bit like the Communist Party," Paul free-associates, drawing up mention of manager Bernie Rhodes, "with Bernie as Stalin. We were his playthings. Bernie is a total original, it's impossible to pin down exactly what he is—he's absolutely unique.

"What happened to Topper," he brings up the subject of the firing in 1982 of Topper Headon, "was that Mick, Joe and myself had an absolute belief in what we were setting out to do, and Topper came along later, when our attitudes were already set in stone. It's like Topper said in Don's documentary, *Westway to the World*, he thought he'd play with the Clash for a bit and use it as a stepping-stone for the rest of his career. He had a different attitude to it all.

"But the Clash really was made up of Mick with his rock-star attitudes, Joe with his hippie beliefs and me. And I was out there on my own: I wasn't caught up in anything. I didn't even really have any friends, only Nigel Dixon from the rockabilly group Whirlwind.

"I was angry at the time when it all came to a halt. It seemed such a waste. But now I'm glad we stopped at a point when we were about to be mega-huge and enormously rich. I'm glad we never re-formed. We proved we could come through it all. None of us were casualties, even though we came close to it. We came out the other side and survived, and people still love our music. Twelve-year-olds love the Clash now, so we must have done something right."

U p on Raasay, Paul and I return to the site of Umachan with a guide, the ranger who looks after Rebel Wood. In fact, we had been right all along about the location of the settlement. The ranger shows us how we should have gone backward along a trail to go forward, a lesson in Highland zen. When we finally round a sheer mountain cliff and find Umachan a hundred yards in front of us, a lonely and haunting place, a tiny hamlet of eight homes. On the scurrying high winds a golden eagle sails past us, its wings seeming to wave to us from the solitude in the sky, before it disappears behind a headland.

Among the ruins that have been reduced almost to rubble since the settlement was abandoned during the 1930s, Angus Gillies's house is still standing, although its heather roof is long gone. A sturdy building, it is clearly the largest of those in the settlement, with an intact chimney gable and upper window. In the fireplace, Paul places a gift to it, a copy of the *Clash on Broadway* boxed set, which sits like an icon amid the rubble. There are two rooms on the ground floor—the smaller room was used for keeping livestock warm in winter. In the late September sun the building's pink

sandstone is warm, vibrating with pulses of energy. The house is held together with lime mortar—beach sand—which allows moisture to be absorbed. Above it is a small, flat pasture. In front, toward the sea, a hundred
yards below, is a walled-off yard, where kale and potatoes were grown to
supplement the salt herring that was the staple diet of the islands. Out of
the rear wall grows a red-berried rowan tree, which according to legend
keeps away such bad spirits as witches. This is the house where Joe's grandmother Jane lived.

Paul Simonon immediately sets up his easel and starts work, slipping
off his jeans jacket and his shoes, which have been giving him blisters. As
he stands painting in his white V-neck T-shirt, gray Levi's 501s and bare
feet, Paul seems to be method-painting, swaying and rocking and feeling
with the elements. He always paints standing, physically getting into it. "I
act as a conduit: it's not really me painting. I just stand there and something goes on, and it ends up on the canvas," he says.

In the sunlight the view across the sea of the mainland and the Applecross mountains is awesome. A lone yacht plows the water, edging the
coastline, bounced back almost vertically by each crashing wave, a warning.
Suddenly the weather changes. Thick, dark gray clouds gust across the
mountaintops. The view vanishes as we are engulfed in a haze of instant
mist. It starts to piss down: thick, drenching rain. Struggling with the billowing wind, Paul even more assiduously straps his canvas to the easel.

The only spot in the roofless house to give any rain protection is in
the shadow of the gable. When his canvas is running with rainwater, Paul
brings it down to the house and slips it into the fireplace. Our guide produces a flask of malt whisky, mint tea, chocolate cake; we also consume
a Joe Strummer Memorial Spliff. Our conversation veers to the practical: where did Joe's ancestors keep the house whisky still, common to
every Highland croft? Paul reveals that in his mid-teens he and his father
had gone on holiday to Skye, hitchhiking the seven hundred miles from
London.

When the downpour eases, Paul picks up his canvas and steps back out
again into the blustery fray. But the elements are simply too extreme for any
more work. Again, he stashes his canvas in the fireplace, next to the Clash
boxed set, turning the painted side away from the wind and rain. On the
back, in red paint, he adds a warning note: *Back later! Paul!*

F or travelers heading up the east coast of Scotland, Bonar Bridge, birth-place of Joe's mother, Anna Mackenzie, was the crossing point over the Kyle of Sutherland—looking at the map it is the last significant inden-tation on the coastline. Nestling on the north bank of the estuary, the east of the area still hosts the ancient woodland planted by James IV to replace the oak forest that had been decimated in the fourteenth and fifteenth cen-turies by the village's iron foundry. Five miles from Bonar Bridge is Skibo Castle, the scene in 2000 of the wedding of Madonna to Guy Ritchie; at the handyman shop in Bonar Bridge the stepladders were all sold out, having been bought by paparazzi trying to snap pictures over the wall of the castle. At Spinning Dale, on the edge of Bonar Bridge, the actor James Robertson Justice lived overlooking the water; when Joe's aunt Jenny worked for him there was a certain amount of local gossip after he was once alleged to have pinched her on the bottom. Nearby is the battlefield at which the Marquis of Montrose was defeated in 1650, forcing the later Charles II of England to accept the Scots' demands for Presbyterianism if he was also to be accepted as King of Scotland; the ethos of Presbyterianism runs strongly in Bonar Bridge. A further battle affected Joe's family history: after Cullo-den, which marked the defeat of the Jacobite army in 1746, four brothers from the Mackenzie clan hid in this remote corner from the savage reprisals.

When speaking to any of Joe's Scottish relatives, I sometimes feel I am wandering in a fog of confusion: the same Christian names recur through-out the generations, but to compound my bewilderment the Gillies rela-tives I met weren't always related to Joe's grandmother Jane Gillies. When Jane moved to Bonar Bridge at the start of the twentieth century, she mar-ried David Mackenzie; Jane did not pass on until Joe was fourteen. The Mackenzies form a large extended family. Anna Mackenzie, who was born January 13, 1915, and married Ron Mellor in 1949, was one of nine broth-ers and sisters. At the wake I spoke to Sheena Yeats, one of Joe's eighteen cousins.

It was amid the wood-paneled surrounds of Carbisdale Castle that, three weeks before he died, Joe Strummer spent his last night at Bonar Bridge—on November 30, 2002, St. Andrew's Night, at the wedding banquet of cousin George to his partner, Fiona. Folded in his pocket Joe had a copy of the family tree that his cousin Anna Gillies had drawn up. From time to time he would put down his ever-present can of cider and pull out the chart as another of his countless relatives hove into view; and he would show his willowy blonde wife, Lucinda, how this person fit into his life.

Joe and Lucinda had rented a car at Inverness train station. Disdaining to take the new, faster motorway, he had driven over the highland route of the Struie, which he loved for its wildness and fabulous views of the Dornoch firth, past the inn on the road that is open all night and which serves soup and haggis until seven in the morning. "That's the only way you can come," he would say. Arriving in Bonar Bridge that afternoon he and Luce had taken a room at a pub to rest up: "He seemed so healthy, so debonair, relaxed, healthy and fit, and young," said Alasdair Gillies, who was five years younger. "I remember saying, 'You look younger than me.'" "He was in good shape," confirmed his aunt Jessie, his mother's younger sister, and the only surviving female among her siblings. Aunt Jenny, who had been married to the late David Mackenzie, one of Joe's mother's three younger brothers, thought Joe looked "terribly tired," but she added "they hadn't eaten and were starving."

At the wedding party at the Carbisdale Castle Joe was fascinated by the traditional Scottish melodies of the Carach Showband, and spent time talking with the piper. He was distressed to find that an LP sleeve of the Bonar Bridge Pipe Band, on which the cover photograph showed the musicians posing outside the castle, contained no record inside it: writing down its details, he vowed to trace the LP and get hold of a copy. "Unfortunately he didn't have time," said Alasdair.

Fiona, George's bride, and two of her friends sang unaccompanied versions of Gaelic songs at the party. "I looked over at Joe and he was in tears," recalled Alasdair. "A few minutes later he was saying, 'Wouldn't it be great if you could get twelve of those tunes and put them on a CD. You don't get songs like that now: they last forever.'" Lucinda had mentioned that in New York on Tartan Day the previous April Joe had insisted on marching all the way up Fifth Avenue, determined to see the pipe bands, and again he had been so moved that tears had run down his face. To the amusement of some of his relatives, Joe and Luce danced their own, not very accurate versions of the Highland "Skip the Reel."

The following day, Joe visited a property called West Airdens, a farm with a startling view that belonged to his aunt Jessie and her shepherd husband, Ken, an extraordinary house that seemed magical to Joe. When he learned that Jessie and her husband had decided it was time to move down to Bonar Bridge, Joe made an instant decision: "Let's buy it now, all of us, all the cousins." "'For each according to his means,' he said," Alasdair remembered, "quoting Marx. I said, 'What would Engels say?' And he laughed. 'What would Jessie say?' I wondered. 'She'll be up for it,' said Joe. Then it was five p.m., and he had to go the station."

Joe was already a day late. He had to be in Rockfield studio in South Wales, where he was to record his next album with the Mescaleros. But he had learned something that was strongly drawing him back to Bonar Bridge: that day, December 1, was the birthday of Uncle John Mackenzie, his mother's brother and the man Joe always called "the original punk rocker." As he grew older, Joe Strummer felt close to all his Bonar Bridge relatives, but Uncle John held a special meaning for him and touched his heart. Johnny Mellor was even christened after Uncle John. "In a perfect world, I wouldn't go home," he stated. "Uncle John told me he's seventy-seven today. In a perfect world I'd go to the local pub for the evening. Maybe I could go back tomorrow." "He knew he had to go," said Alasdair, "but he didn't want to. But at the last minute, he said, 'I'd better go. In a perfect world, I'd stay. But this is not a perfect world.'" (When we call round, Uncle John pours us each "a wee dram" of the Irish whisky that Joe had dispatched up to him as a birthday gift as soon as he arrived at Rockfield.)

Minutes into Joe and Luce's hourlong drive to Inverness station, he phoned Alasdair, fired up with enthusiasm, reminding him they had to buy the house. Moments later he called again, repeating this insistence, and— filled with the emotion of the weekend—reminding his cousin he would waste no time in tracking down the LP by the Bonar Bridge Pipe Band. "The Bonar Bridge magnetism holds you: you don't want to go back to the city. On his last visit Joe exhibited all the symptoms of that condition. Then he phoned me at the station, saying he had made it, and we'd sort out the house. 'Love to all,' he said. And that was the last time I saw him. The next thing I knew I got a call from Amanda Temple, the wife of Julien Temple, the film director, who lived near him in Somerset, three weeks later.

"But those two days we were with him, I felt he'd reached a new level, reconciled both his father's side and his mother's [low-church] Highland stuff. He was being restored to his rightful place in the bosom of the family, onward and upward. And it was very hard to bear, when he died."

S itting in his favorite armchair by the window of the living room in the sturdy family Carnmhor farm, Uncle John speaks with the same lilting Highlands accent that Joe's mother, Anna, never lost. "Johnny first came here when he was under a year. They were just back from Turkey, and came up by train." At one moment on the first of these fortnight-long visits to Bonar Bridge, the toddler Johnny Mellor was found standing at the top of Carnmhor's steep stairs, shouting in Turkish for someone to carry him down them as there was no banister. Upstairs at Carnmhor, the bedroom in which John and his brother, David, stayed had big brass bedsteads, hard mattresses and bolsters. The two boys were always collectively referred to by the family as David-and-Johnny, like fish 'n' chips, or Morecambe-and-Wise, or—perhaps more appositely—like rock 'n' roll.

With his young nephew, Uncle John Mackenzie shared certain characteristics which only increased as Johnny matured into the figure of Joe Strummer. In his almost Australian aboriginal tendency to go "walkabout," Uncle John predicted behavior that many people connected with Joe were obliged to accept: the most public example of this was his famous vanishing act in 1982 before a Clash U.S. tour. Uncle John had that same ability to disappear. In the early 1940s, "Bonnie John"—as he was known in his youth—vanished for several weeks. Assuming he was dead, Jane Mackenzie, his mother, went to bed for a fortnight. Eventually he was discovered in Inverness.

After that first visit to Bonar Bridge it was seven years ("a long while," said John, with sadness in his voice) before the Mellor family returned to Anna's home. On each of the annual visits his family paid to Bonar Bridge between 1960 and 1963, Johnny Mellor liked nothing better than running after Uncle John and his tractor. "David was about nine, Johnny was about seven," John remembered of that next visit. "Johnny was a very cheery, happy boy. He would just wander around the place. He was very fond of being outside. He was a young boy full of life. He did a painting of cowboys and Indians, which we hung up on the wall." That painting, a precursor of a theme around which much of Joe's later drawing and painting was based, hung on the hallway wall at Carnmhor for many years.

David, Johnny's older brother, was "much quieter," remembered Uncle John. "Johnny used to wander around with me when I was working. I had cattle and sheep: he was always watching them with me. He'd help with what he called the 'hoos coo,' milking it. I never saw him play a guitar. I heard his music often. I saw them on the TV as well. They were oot of my mind altogether—the young people liked them." But he remembered a surprise phone call from Joe in Japan in 1982: "He was just blathering away. 'I'm looking for a job, teaching rock 'n' roll,' he said to me, joking of course.

"He was here for a long while on the Sunday with his wife," said Uncle John. "He was very reluctant leaving. If anyone had said two words to him he'd have stayed. He said, 'I'm bringing my two daughters up in the summertime.' But it never came to pass."

The Mellor family's next visit, in the summer of 1960, marked the first time that Alasdair's brother Iain met Johnny. From their home in Glasgow, the Gillies family—with Joe's four cousins Iain, Anna, Alasdair and Rona—had also gone up to Bonar Bridge, as they did every year without fail, and both families were crammed into Carnmhor. With Johnny, Iain would play in the barn, swinging on the rope and rolling on the piles of corn. Together they caught newts from the stream in jam jars, releasing those still left alive. In a pillbox concrete bunker on the farm they discovered leftover boot polish. "We probably showed off too much that we thought we were from somewhere else. Johnny seemed to me to be very lively, funny and inventive. David was quiet. I recall Johnny being the organizer and the one who dictated the plans for our games and general mischief making. He was a bit pugnacious and always insouciant. On the first day we met at the croft, Johnny started a pebble-throwing fight. It was Johnny and David versus me. I was two years younger than Johnny and three younger than David, so I was a bit concerned at first. As the stone throwing got more vicious I could tell that David's heart wasn't really in it, and it tailed off into a draw. Johnny said, 'We won that battle, didn't we, Dave?' In retrospect, I think, to gee David up, give him succour." The lines of battle, claimed Anna, were drawn between the Scots and the English. "Because I was a girl I wasn't even recruited for that," she complained.

"In the living room at the farm," said Iain, "he recited some scurrilous rhyme that he knew, the subject matter of which concerned coating the crack of a female bottom with jam. He knew all the words and to my six-year-old mind it was very funny, slightly shocking, but exhilarating." Clearly by that age Johnny was indicating the mischievous humor within him that would remain all his life. But he was also revealing a slight tendency to bully, an aspect of himself that also never entirely went away. "On another occasion at Carnmhor," Iain recalled, "he convinced me that it would be a great idea to completely strip my sister Anna, who was about five, of all her clothes and hide them upstairs in our Uncle John's closet— nobody would ever find them in there, he said. Anna came downstairs and made her grand naked entrance."

"I can remember going down the three steps," said Anna, "where Aunt Anna was drying clothes, and there was a tremendous hullabaloo. They couldn't find my clothes, which were hidden in Uncle John's room."

Each Sunday morning the adults would take themselves and any girls about the house to endure the tedious sermonizing of Mr. McDonald at church. On one of these occasions Johnny and Iain, who had quickly become partners in crime, decided to provide an entertaining homecoming greeting for Anna. Taking her favorite doll, they suspended it upside down in the lobby. She was most distressed. "It was all blamed on Johnny," she said. "I was immediately aware," added Iain, "that for all my six years of worldly experience, cousin Johnny was unlike anyone I had met so far."

It was on one of those trips between 1960 and 1963 that Johnny's family broke their journey up from London by staying for a couple of days with the Gillies family in Glasgow. In Bonar Bridge itself, "Johnny decided," said Iain, "that since we were going on a two-mile walk to visit our relatives and the road would take us past a gypsy encampment, that we would need to be fully armed to repel any attack. Johnny told me to explain the seriousness of the situation to my parents; he would do the same with his, and therefore our parents were bound to provide us with the funds for weapons. There was much adult laughter but they complied, and we bought shiny, one-shilling penknives at the local newsagent's. I remember Johnny and I debating whose knife had the most style and panache." Johnny and Iain managed to arrive without having to draw their weapons.

Anna Mackenzie was born on January 13, 1915, the second child of David and Jane Mackenzie and their first daughter. After attending local schools, she opted for a career in nursing, one of the few choices open for women from families with limited means and one that accorded well with the Presbyterian need to fulfill one's societal duty. Anna's older brother, David, had died of peritonitis as a young man. Anna herself was imbued with characteristic Mackenzie qualities: "self-reliant, uncomplaining, serene, stoic, ironic, shrewd, determined, engaging, solicitous, and quietly aware of the vicissitudes of life," thought Iain Gillies. She was also beautiful.

Moving to Aberdeen, 120 miles south of Bonar Bridge, Anna received her training at Forester Hill hospital. Fifteen years older than her sister Jessie, she was nursing before Jessie had even gone to school. After Aberdeen, Anna went to Stob Hill hospital on the northeast edge of Glasgow, moving into nearby lodgings. Anna was promoted to Sister, or head nurse, a position with much responsibility for one still in her early twenties, a clear indication of her abilities.

At Stob Hill she met Adam Girvan, a male nurse from Ayrshire. Twice when she traveled home to Bonar Bridge he was with her. In 1940 they were married.

But as World War II had begun the previous year, Anna Girvan, as she now was, joined the Queen Alexandra Nursing Service; meanwhile, her husband went into the Royal Army Medical Corps. Although they had expected to do service together, Adam Girvan was sent to Egypt, while Anna went to India. It was three years before she again saw her husband.

Stationed at a large army hospital in Lucknow in northern India, this woman from the north of Scotland suffered from the climate. "The heat disagreed with her severely," said her sister Jessie. Struck down with appendicitis, which must have triggered memories of the death of her older brother, David, she was successfully operated on. Then she was sent to recuperate in the cooler weather higher up in the hills. "In the hospital where she stayed she had a great view of the Himalayas."

There, while lancing a boil for him, she met a lieutenant in an artillery regiment in the Indian army named Ronald Mellor, who had been called up into the armed forces in 1942.

R onald Mellor was born in Lucknow on December 8, 1916. He was the youngest of four children; Phyllis, Fred and Ouina came before him. His father was Frederick Adolph Mellor, who had married Muriel St. Editha Johannes; half-Armenian and half-English, she was a governess to a wealthy Indian family. There was a large population of Armenians in Lucknow. Frederick Adolph Mellor was one of five sons of Frederick William Mellor and Eugenie Daniels, a German Jewess, who had married during the Boer War when his father lived in East Budleigh in Devon. Shortly afterward they moved to India. The family home in Lucknow was named Jahangirabad Mansion. Later Frederick William Mellor returned to East Budleigh, where he bought a row of cottages that he rented out. His son Bernhardt came to East Budleigh and married the local postmistress. Phyllis, Bernhardt's daughter, still lives there.

Muriel Johannes was one of three daughters of Agnes Eleanor Greenway and a Mr. Johannes: her two sisters were Dorothy and Marian. After the early death of her Armenian father, Muriel's mother, Agnes, got remarried, to a Mr. Spiers, with whom she had two more daughters, Mary and Maggie.

Frederick Adolph Mellor, Joe's grandfather, worked in a senior administrative position for the Indian railway, but died of pleurisy in 1917, when Ronald was still a baby. Following his death his widow married George Chalk, who became Ronald Mellor's stepfather, but Chalk disappeared to South Africa. Joe's grandmother Muriel Mellor, however, was not without her problems. A social whirl was inherent to the colonial norm in India; excessive drinking was an accepted part of that world, and she was an alcoholic, taking out her drunken rages on her children. Gerry King, a former teacher who lives in Brighton, is the daughter of Phyllis, the eldest of Ron's siblings: "I was told that the mother was alcoholic, and used to beat them up. So my mother protected all four of them, and they used to hide from her." In 1927 Muriel Mellor died, largely because of her addiction to drink. (In 1999 Joe Strummer told me that both his grandparents on his father's side had been killed in an Indian railway accident. When I learned what the truth was, I suspected him of some Bob Dylan– or Jim Morrison–like obfuscation of his past. But no, said Gaby, the mother of his two children: "Joe really thought that was the truth. All the information that came down to him about his father's life in India was so befuddled, and he was always trying to find out what the real history was.") Joe's father, Ronald Mellor, and his brother and two sisters were then brought up by their grandmother Agnes Spiers, although Mary, her daughter, took a keen interest in helping to raise the children. "Ronald was the favorite with his half-aunt Mary," said Jonathan Macfarland, another cousin on Joe's father's side. Ronald and Fred were educated at La Martinière College in Dilkusha Road in Lucknow, a revered Indian school. After La Martinière Ronald Mellor moved on to the University of Lucknow.

After Mrs. Adam Girvan met Lieutenant Ronald Mellor, they fell in love. Ron, who by the end of the war had been promoted to major, was great company: funny, sensitive, intelligent and articulate; his Indian upbringing and racial mix made him seem unusual to the woman with a pure Highlands bloodline. "Ron was very exotic, and I can see why Anna was captivated," thought Rona, Alasdair Gillies's twin sister. Anna's heart was touched by the subtly lingering sense of sadness that Ron had carried with him ever since the death of his difficult mother; some felt that the fact that he couldn't even remember his father accounted for his faint otherworldly air of permanent bewilderment.

They decided to make their lives together. But there was a problem: Anna was still married. Divorce in those days was very rare, and not in the vocabulary of the Bonar Bridge Mackenzies. All the same, Anna communicated her intentions to Adam Girvan. When she returned to the United Kingdom at the end of the war, they divorced: Anna discovered that as soon as Girvan had learned of her relationship with Ron Mellor, he had cleaned out their joint bank account.

"I remember my father wasn't very pleased about the divorce," said her sister Jessie. "But Mum didn't say much." But would you have expected her to? As Jessie pointed out, "You didn't even talk about pregnancy. Granny was very, very strict." Anna went up to Bonar Bridge and made peace with her parents. In that Highland way of keeping intimate matters close to the chest, the divorce was kept secret from everyone, including her children. "My mum told me Anna had been married before, but she never told my dad," Rona said, describing a typical piece of Mackenzie behavior. "I wasn't surprised about it—things happen," said Uncle John, customarily phlegmatic. Joe didn't learn about it until he was in the Clash. "I've just found out that my mum was married before," he said, tickled. "She seems to have been a bit of a goer."

Ron Mellor made his way to London, and took a job in the Foreign Office as a clerical officer; considered highly prestigious, the F.O. only admitted candidates considered highfliers; they were subjected to a supposedly rigorous security check. Soon Ron and Anna were married: in a picture of Ron and Anna on their wedding day, October 22, 1949, his caddish Clark Gable–thin mustache and double-breasted suit give him the appearance of an archetypal Terry Thomas marriage wrecker—which, in a way, he was. The newlyweds moved into a top-floor flat, up four flights of stairs, at 22 Sussex Gardens in the seedy area of Paddington. They lived there for two years. Meanwhile, Anna took a post as Sister at one of the largest hospitals in London, St. George's by Hyde Park Corner.

Ron traveled to the Foreign Office in Whitehall every day, studying the intricacies of sending and decoding messages, which would earn him the job of cipher clerk, a role whose top-secret nature was only emphasized by the growing Cold War. In the manner of those employed in such positions, he laid down a smoke screen by describing himself to his relatives as "third secretary to the third undersecretary."

David Nicholas Mellor was born on March 17, 1951, in Nairobi, Kenya, Ron Mellor's first overseas posting. Soon Ronald Mellor was transferred to Ankara in Turkey. For unclear reasons, the Mellor family had been in Germany immediately prior to this move to Ankara. Booked on the Orient Express from Paris to Istanbul, they traveled from Germany to the French capital by road. Running late, Ron telephoned ahead: employing diplomatic protocol, he managed to delay the departure of this prestigious train, and Anna told her younger son about running down the platform under the eyes of the waiting passengers.

In Ankara on August 21, 1952, Anna Mellor gave birth to her second son, John Graham Mellor. Brought up with Turkish help around the family home, he learned a pidgin form of the language.

Ron Mellor's skills at coding and decoding messages did not go unappreciated by the powers that be. He was transferred to the British embassy in Cairo, which was paying close attention to the zealous proclamations of Gamal Abdel Nasser, the Egyptian leader, soon to bring about the Suez Crisis with his nationalizing of the vital canal. In this John Le Carré world the Mellor family moved into a house vacated by a diplomat named Donald Maclean and his wife, Melinda—Anna complained about Melinda's terrible taste in curtains and had them replaced. Ron Mellor would regularly have lunch, which invariably consisted of little more than a bottle of vodka, with a close friend of Maclean called Kim Philby. Maclean and Philby, along with Guy Burgess, would defect to the Soviet Union; the trio of intellectuals had been working for Moscow. Interestingly, as the years progressed, Ron Mellor revealed himself more and more to be almost Marxist in political philosophy, an undisguised leaning that might seem surprising for someone working at such a level.

The social whirl of diplomatic functions meant, as it did for many of the embassy staff, that alcohol became a staple of Ron and Anna Mellor's diets. Ron was always partial to a gin and tonic, and was fastidious that it was served with a slice of lemon. Anna had a wardrobe of cocktail dresses, and forced herself to learn bridge, which she secretly detested. "But that was what you had to do as an embassy wife," pointed out Maeri, another of Joe's Mackenzie cousins. Anna would laugh scathingly to her sisters about a publication called *Diplomatic Wives*, the in-house magazine of embassy spouses. "Anna wouldn't complain. She wasn't the complaining type. But I don't think she liked Cairo," said her sister Jessie. As they grew older her two sons, David and John, learned to serve drinks and cutely play the parts of junior waiters. A story that attained the status of legend within the Mackenzie family told of how when the boys were taken by Anna Mellor to get a haircut in Cairo, Johnny wriggled so much that it incensed the Arab barber to the point where he had to stick his head under a tap to cool down.

In 1956, two months before the invasion of Suez by British and French troops, Ron Mellor was transferred again, to Mexico City. Of all Ron's overseas postings, this was where Anna was happiest; in a photograph of her with her two sons in Mexico City she wears curved Sophia Loren–like sunglasses that emphasize her film-star beauty: she looks impossibly glamorous, rather like the sort of girl you would find backstage at a Clash gig. As though to underline his wife's sophistication, Ron bought a boat-size 1948 Cadillac in which to transport his family.

Not long after they had arrived in Mexico City, the area was struck by a devastating series of earthquakes. One night while they were having dinner the lights started swinging back and forth; Ron and Anna ran out of the house carrying David and John and sat in the middle of the lawn away from any swaying structures. When the tremors seemed to have ceased, Anna attempted to bring some calm and normality back into the boys' lives by giving them a bath. Suddenly the water started to slop from side to side as the tremors returned. That night Ron and Anna moved the boys' beds into their room, so they could all die together.

It was in Mexico City that Ron Mellor developed an ulcer; and he was troubled by the altitude. In 1957 the Mellor family was shipped back to London.

$$\overline{\underline{5}}$$

be true to your school (like you would to your girl)

1957-1964

Before 1957 was over, the Mellor family again was on the move overseas: Ron was posted to work with the British embassy in Bonn, the
capital of West Germany. "I was eight when I came back to England, after
Germany," Joe Strummer told me, forty years later. "Germany was frightening, man: it was only ten years after the war, and what do you think the
young kids were doing? They were still fighting the Germans, obviously.
We lived in Bonn on a housing estate filled with foreign legation families.
The German youth knew there was a bunch of foreigners there, and it was
kind of terrifying. We'd been told by the other kids that if Germans saw us
they would beat us up. So be on your toes. And we were [very] young."

Aware of the need for some kind of stability in the lives of his family,
Ron Mellor decided that he must establish a permanent home in England,
his adopted country—particularly for his sons, who lost a new circle of
friends with every overseas move. One consequence of this seemed to be

Johnny's almost acute sense of self-reliance and self-awareness. But for David, Ron and Anna's elder son, the constant breakup of friendships, accompanied by that nagging wonder of whether everyone would always disappear from his life with such sudden ease, seemed to be having a negative effect: increasingly quiet, he often seemed lost in thought. This struck a nerve with Ron: his memories of his own traumatic childhood would rise when confronted by the hushed sense of "otherness" that floated about David. In turn, it was hard for sensitive David to be unaffected by the way this unhappy childhood was so deeply etched in his father's being; it was as though they were infecting each other with indeterminate but undeniable suffering. Yet David showed no evidence of Ron Mellor's tendency toward volatile mood swings. "Ron loved being able to just reminisce," said Gerry King, Joe's cousin, remembering her visits to the Mellors. "But he would go into moroseness. I felt it once or twice—some pity about him. I think he'd had such a sad life, really."

Back in London in 1959 for what he knew would be a three-year stint in Whitehall, Ron Mellor made a down payment on a three-bedroom single-story house just outside Croydon in the southeast of London. The property, at 15 Court Farm Road in Upper Warlingham in Surrey, was being sold for £3,500, cheap even by property prices of the day, a reflection of its doll's-house size. A cul-de-sac, Court Farm Road wound round the side of a steep hill that formed one side of a valley that sloped down to the main road. Located on a corner of Court Farm Road, No. 15 was the last of four identical bungalows, built in the 1930s and—partially due to their hillside perch—having something of the appearance of Swiss mountain chalets, a look that distinguished them all the more from the larger detached and semi-detached houses that made up the rest of the street.

When the Mellor family moved into the bungalow, David and Johnny were sent to the local state primary school in nearby Whyteleafe. Joe Strummer would later seem to dismiss the home bought by his father as "a bungalow in south Croydon." But this is exactly what it was; for once he was not disguising his past. Presumably dictated to by the maxim that location is everything, Ron Mellor had bought what was essentially a miniature version of the adjacent properties in the neighborhood. In fact, it was typical of English houses built in the 1930s, and—as did much of Britain at the beginning of the 1960s—it still had the flavor of that decade. Through the black-and-white front door was a corridor: to the left was Ron and Anna's bedroom. Opposite, on the right-hand side, was a small kitchen whose window faced the road; farther along on the left was David's bedroom and the bathroom; and on the right was the sitting room and Johnny's small bedroom. "They never spent a lot of time worrying about pretty carpets or furniture. It was just kind of bricks and mortar and that's where they were," said a visitor. On display at 15 Court Farm Road were exotic artifacts gathered at Ron's various international ports of call: bongo drums, a wooden framed camel's saddle, ottomans made of Persian leather. Although a television did not appear at first, there was a large radio of the type later featured on the sleeve of the "London Calling" single. "My parents weren't musical at all," Joe later told Mal Peachy. "They had sort of cancan records, from the Folies Bergère, and that was about it. Maybe a few show tunes like *Oklahoma!*, that sort of thing. I remember hearing *Children's Favourites* [a request show broadcast at nine every Saturday morning] on the BBC, things like 'Sixteen Tons' by Tennessee Ernie Ford."

Visitors would sometimes feel the house seemed run-down—the diplomat and his wife, after all, had been used to servants and had lost the habit of home maintenance. Although slightly shabby, 15 Court Farm Road was an extremely comfortable house. But the sense of alienation in the area was reflected inside it. "I think Ron and Anna lived this very weird, isolated life," Gerry King remembered of a visit there in the late 1960s. "You could imagine them in the times of the Raj, as though he had been posted to some obscure place in India, and they are there, sipping their sherry, and going on to whisky. That sort of thing: a feeling of not being real. But there was something very wonderful and lovely about them both. And Uncle Ron also had that gentleness. I felt that he didn't cope with reality well. But he was a lovely man." Yet Ron and Anna's loneliness was not surprising: like their sons, Ron and Anna had suffered disappearing diplomatic service relationships, and had few friends in London.

Living at 54 Oakley Road, some five hundred yards from 15 Court Farm Road, was the Evans family. Richard, the youngest child, was a few months younger than David Mellor and a year older than Johnny Mellor. Soon after the Mellor family had moved into their new home, the Evanses and Mellors met—the boys all attended Whyteleafe primary school. "It's just a village primary at the bottom of the hill. That's where I went. That must've been where we met." The two families became close; Richard quickly came to regard David Mellor as his best friend. "It was Johnny-and-David, a kind of Scottish thing. 'Johnny'—that's what his mother always called him. David is nine, I'm nine. He's very quiet, very withdrawn, but there's something very comfortable about being with him. And I would literally sit there with him not saying anything for half an hour and it was OK, you didn't have to. He was my mate, my best mate. But all three of us played together."

Hardly a day would go by when Richard Evans was not over at the Mellor house: "My recollection of it was that I was always there and it was always a very warm house. . . . The door was always open. My parents were really security conscious: our house had been burgled. But Anna was not, they never locked the door. Yet they never got robbed. Maybe it was just the atmosphere of the place. But it was always an open house."

Anna's engaging and welcoming personality meant that Richard very quickly grew close to her ("hugely"), and she took on the role of a surrogate aunt. "I was closer to her than I was to my own mother, emotionally. It was Anna I spoke to about my issues, my successes and failures. No disrespect to my mum, who was hugely strong in other ways, but it was Anna who was the emotional pillow or rock or whatever. She was tiny, just over five feet, but one of those people who is physically diminutive but whose heart is huge. She was very quiet, and whenever you went there there was always a cup of tea or sandwiches. She'd be fussing around, making you feel comfortable, and would have just made a cake or whatever. She was constantly caring for you. I'm absolutely sure—and it was one of the great joys of Joe—that he had his mother's huge generosity."

As a teenager, Johnny Mellor was in increasing conflict with his father, playing out the classic struggle between a father and the son who wants to find his own course in life. To Iain Gillies Johnny once glumly described Ron Mellor as being like "an old bear in a bad mood." Richard Evans agreed: "Like a bear. Sometimes quite angry. You walked around him and weren't quite sure how it was going to be. If he was purring, it was OK, you could have a really good time with him. But if he was growling you just got the hell out of there. I think Joe and David were wary of him too. There was a weird juxtaposition between the downy-faced mother, with really soft skin, and the dad. I think that's how they got along."

As Johnny Mellor grew into Joe Strummer, he displayed considerable behavioral similarities to his father, rendering the earlier conflict between them even more archetypal. "Joe and I had this big gap from around the time of the Clash until the last three years of his life, one of about twenty years," said Richard. "The first thing I noticed when I saw Joe as a grown man was, 'Fuck, he's got his dad's eyes.' His dad's eyes were always quite wild and quite irritated-looking, quite red, as though he needed to have an eye bath. The eyelids were almost separated from the eyeball. Joe's were the same. It was bizarre, because I looked at Joe as a forty-seven-year-old man, and I went straight back to his dad. His dad was wild-eyed and erratic.

"Joe's dad was very critical. God knows why he was in the diplomatic corps. He'd rant about inequality. There's something in there that didn't add up—as a child I was wary of him. He was a diplomat, but not diplomatic. He was passionate, full of conviction: he was a socialist. That's Joe's political aspect—came from his dad. Somehow that doesn't fit. If you looked at the man, this was not a sharp-suited, smooth-talking diplomat. He was passionate and volatile. He was also exciting—there was an attraction to the man. You can see what that was for Anna: the international lifestyle, but also that the man was mysterious. It could be beautiful or it could be harmful.

"There was a huge positiveness about Joe, an energy, that everybody liked. I found myself more and more attracted away from David toward Joe, his younger brother. Being a year younger is an issue as a nine-year-old. But I felt drawn toward Joe, as everybody did. He was just a good person, he had a wonderful capacity to just make you feel better about everything. If he had a good idea—'Let's do this or that'—somehow he turned it into your idea. He'd be the one saying, 'Great idea, I wish I'd thought about that.' You're going, 'Did I think of it? Oh, brilliant.' He had that huge ability to make people feel much better about themselves. It was remarkable: at eight years old he had that. It was nothing to do with the Clash: he just had that gift."

It was a gift, however, that was about to be sorely tested, at the new school that Ron and Anna Mellor had chosen for their two sons, City of London Freemen's School in Ashtead in Surrey, twenty miles southwest of Upper Warlingham.

The school had been founded in 1854 as the City of London Freemen's Orphan School. In 1926 the Corporation of London moved the school into the country and it reopened in Ashtead Park in Surrey, a gorgeous estate of fifty-seven acres of landscaped grounds, approached by an avenue of lime trees. You might think that the idea of being sent to a school established to educate parentless children would have struck a sad chord within Johnny Mellor: he spoke later of how he felt abandoned by Ron and Anna when he was sent to CLFS as a boarding pupil, their solution to the dilemma of how the overseas postings were affecting the boys' education. After the light discipline at Whyteleafe, CLFS would prove traumatic for both the Mellor boys; Johnny Mellor would never really come to terms with having been sent away to boarding school by his parents and he never forgave them for the wound created by this apparent desertion in his childhood. So great had that hurt been that, according to Gaby, Joe's long-term partner, he was still berating his mother about sending him to CLFS as she lay dying in a cancer hospice twenty-five years later. Part of him felt that his entire life would have been different if he had not been sent there—though that experience was a formative one for the person he was eventually to become.

But naturally Johnny was not showing any indication of such emotion on his first visit to the school. "Loudmouth!" was Paul Buck's very first impression of John Mellor when he saw him at the entrance examination. Of all the fifty or so students at the exam, aged between eight and ten, the short-trousered John Mellor—one of the youngest and smallest present—seemed the only candidate unbowed by the exam worries: he didn't seem to be taking it seriously, laughing and making cracks. "I just remember him as being a kid who wasn't bowed by having to take an exam—which can be daunting for a nine-year-old."

At the beginning of September 1961, dressed in the navy blue blazers that bore the CLFS coat of arms on the badge pocket, the red-and-blue striped ties of the school neatly knotted at the collars of their white shirts, the regulation blue caps pulled down over their freshly shorn hair, David and Johnny Mellor bade farewell to their parents. Johnny was just nine—because of where his birthday fell he was almost always the youngest in his year—and David ten and a half. Later, in the days of punk, when such a skewed background counted, Joe would claim he had failed the school's entrance examination and was accepted only because he had a sibling who was already there. This was not true. Because City of London Freemen's was a public school,* however, this led his punk peers to snipe at Joe. Joe never fell back on an easy excuse: that his place at the school was a perk of

*For reasons too complex to comprehend, an English public school is the exact opposite: it is a private school, with all the implied elitism of such institutions.

John Mellor in his regulation school uniform.
(*Pablo Labritain*)

Ron's job. The Foreign Office paid for David and John Mellor's school fees, an acknowledgment of the need for some stability in a diplomat's peripatetic life. (Part of Ron's employment package was summer-holiday plane tickets for the boys to wherever he was stationed; Ron and Anna would add to this themselves with fares paid out for their sons to visit them every Christmas holiday.) There were a number of boys and girls at CLFS whose parents were diplomats or in the military, 10 percent of the school's four hundred pupils; but there were many more day students than boarders, which added to the boarders' sense of embattled remoteness; unusually for a British boarding school, CLFS was also coeducational.

Later Joe Strummer recalled his years at CLFS guardedly and defensively, not even mentioning its name until October 1981, when he revealed it in an interview with Paul Rambali in *NME*. To Caroline Coon he lied for a *Melody Maker* article in 1976 that the school had been "in Yorkshire." "I went on my ninth birthday"—in fact it was a couple of weeks after his birthday—"into a weird Dickensian Victorian world with sub-corridors under sub-basements, one lightbulb every hundred yards, and people coming down 'em beating wooden coat hangers on our heads," he told *NME*'s Lucy O'Brien in 1986. Paul Buck, who was in the same boarding house as John Mellor, confirmed this. "Joe spoke of dark corridors, and basements, and he wasn't exaggerating. When we started we used to spend most of our time in a dark basement corridor in our boarding house mucking about. There was a recreation room, at the top of the building, very cold and uncomfortable. You didn't go up there because if the seniors needed to get anybody to do anything they'd go straight there. So we preferred the corridor."

"On the first day," Joe Strummer said in an interview with *Record Mirror* in 1977, "I was surrounded and taken to the bathroom where I was confronted by a bath full of used toilet paper. I had to either get in or get beaten up. I got beaten up." In a *Melody Maker* article written in 1979 by Chris Bohn, he continued this theme: "I was a dwarf when I was younger, grew to my normal size later on. But before then I had to fight my way through school."

During his first year at CLFS, the nine-year-old Johnny Mellor tried to run away from the school with another boy. "We got about five miles before a teacher found us. I remember being taken back to school and the vice-headmaster came out and shouted at us for not wearing our caps. I was thinking, 'You idiot. Do you really think we're going to run away with our caps on?' I just couldn't believe it."

Years later Sara Driver, the American film director, told me how she saw Joe behaving at the end of the 1980s: "He was very much wallowing in darkness and talking about growing up and being beaten up at public school when he was a kid and how rough that was." As time went by Joe worked out a standard line on his school days: "I had to become a bully to survive."

Paul Buck dismisses this self-assessment: "He wasn't a bully. He was full of life and very funny." Nor, he says, was John Mellor a participant in the fights that are often a feature of coexisting adolescent boys. "I might have forgotten or maybe I wasn't there, but it certainly wasn't 'Oh, Mellor's in a fight again.' No way. He was boisterous but he wasn't dominant. He was one of us."

As though making a statement to Ron and Anna Powell, Johnny Mellor refused to participate in schoolwork for much of his time at CLFS; his mystification at having been taken away from his parents seemed to have created a befuddlement of stubbornness that simply did not allow him to find any interest in his studies; he had had an exciting and exotic family life which overnight had stopped: why? Like a punishment, he would never post the letter to his parents that he was compelled to write once a week. The self-confident persona seen by Paul Buck at that entrance exam was a front, something that the quietly sensitive and sometimes easily hurt

Johnny Mellor had learned as a social art on the diplomatic cocktail circuit. When Gaby Salter went through Ron Mellor's papers at 15 Court Farm Road, she found that almost every year until the sixth form the headmaster had written to Johnny's father, apologizing for the school's failure to make any headway with his academic progress—he flunked his GCE O-levels, and had to repeat a year in the fifth form.*

Although Paul Buck was a year behind John Mellor, the boy—who also had an older brother at the school—was to become one of his closest friends, a relationship that continued into the early days of the Clash. "He was his best friend," the writer Peter Silverton, friends with both of them, confirms of Buck's relationship to Joe. "I saw him and thought, 'Oh, I remember you at that entrance exam,'" said Paul Buck, who formed a double-act with John Mellor, bound together by an absurdist view of life and a common love of music. "I remember getting on with him all through school. We were as thick as thieves." At first, John would be referred to—as were all junior boys in the school—by his surname, Mellor, frequently contorted into the jokey *Mee*-lor.

But how did the other Mellor boy, whose personality seemed the diametric opposite of his younger brother's, fit into this dog-eat-dog world? "My brother and I were sent to school," Joe Strummer told Mal Peachy for Don Letts's *Westway to the World* documentary, "and it was a little strange in my case because my brother was very shy. He was the opposite of me—I mean the complete and utter opposite. The running joke in school was that he hadn't said a word all term—which was more or less true. He was really shy, and I was the opposite, like a big-mouthed ringleader up to no good.

"I often think about my parents," he continued, "and how I must have felt about it, because being sent away and seeing them only once a year, it was rather weird. [He leaves out the Christmas trips here.] When you're a child you just deal with what you have to deal with, and it really changed my

---

*In the British education system, fifth form refers to the tenth year of secondary schooling. GCE O-level is short for General Certificate of Education, Ordinary Level, and refers to exams taken during the fifth form. Passing the O-levels is mandatory before being able to take the A-levels, which are more specialized exams, consisting of only three or four subjects. A-levels are taken in the sixth form, an optional two years of additional schooling, split into lower and upper sixth, which a student can take to prepare for university. Although the A-levels are not specifically university entrance exams, it is not possible to go on to further education at university or art college without satisfactory—or, in the case of some establishments, outstanding—A-level results.

life because I realized I just had to forget about my parents in order to keep my head above water in this situation. When you're a kid you go straight to the heart of the matter. There's no procrastination. I mean, I feel bad now because I was a bad son to them. When they came back to eventually live in England, I'd never go to see them, and I feel bad about that.

"I would say that going to school in a place like that you became independent. You didn't expect anybody to do anything for you. And that was a big part of punk: do the damn thing yourself and don't expect anything from anybody."

The boy boarders were lodged in four dormitories, according to age. For the younger boys bedtimes were strict: they had to be in bed by 7:30. The seniors did not have an official bedtime. The junior dormitory, where John Mellor first slept, lodged ten boys and two prefects (student monitors). The dormitory had fifteen-foot-high windows, from which the more adventurous pupils, like Mellor, would climb out onto the building's flat roof.

Life for CLFS boarders was regimented: day students had to arrive at 8:45 a.m. for assembly, held in the main hall, which doubled as dining room; by then the boarders already had gathered for "Boarders' Assembly," at which they had to account for what they would do at the end of that day's lessons, which started at 9:00. Games or homework were all that were on offer. "We usually put down games, as this would get us out of the school buildings," said Adrian Greaves, who had joined the school the year after Johnny Mellor, also as a boarder. While a "grub," as younger boys were known, John Mellor wore short trousers for two years and was so diminutive in stature that he was known as "little Johnny Mellor." At first he remained in the fantasy world of small boys in which role-playing games are a norm; in the grounds of the school Adrian Greaves remembered Johnny and himself making "tiny villages of mud huts with twig people. He was very normal—bright, enthusiastic and mixed well." As a member of the school's Boy Scout troop, Johnny Mellor learned to put up a tent and sleep outdoors, a skill he would later harness to enhance his love of the festival outdoor life; his woodworking classes gave him the skills to throw together lean-tos and small sheds. Adrian Greaves recalled how even as a grub

Johnny would immerse himself in the world of art that had led to the cowboy painting that hung on the wall at Carnmhor: "Johnny was very good at drawing. I can remember as early as 1962 him drawing cartoon strips on long rolls of paper. They were good stories, cowboy and Indian stuff. Certainly I didn't expect him to be a musician. He would often be in the art room. I think the art teacher had a lot of time for him."

In 1962 Ron Mellor had been given another overseas posting, to Tehran, the capital of Persia, a Muslim state ruled in a feudal manner by the king-like Shah, whose family had been installed by American oil interests. Ron and Anna drove down to CLFS and spent a Saturday afternoon with their sons, explaining where they would be living for the next two years. In the interview he gave to Caroline Coon in November 1976, Joe vented at the notion of boarding school: "It's easier, isn't it? I mean, it gets kids out of the way. And I'm really glad I went, because my dad's a bastard. I shudder to think what would have happened if I hadn't gone to boarding school. I only saw him once a year. If I'd seen him all the time, I'd probably have murdered him by now. He was very strict."

The "old bear" had plenty of spirit, however. He decided that he and Anna would get to Persia by driving, taking the boys with them during the summer holiday. In Tehran Ron and Anna lived in an embassy compound. But Anna was not at all taken with the country. "She didn't like Tehran," said her sister Jessie. "She said she had been spat at in the street. The locals didn't like her walking out on her own." Unfortunately for Anna, Ron was stationed in Tehran for almost four years. During school holidays and even for the half-term break, she would often return to Britain. The next time that David and John went to Persia, they flew. Arriving in a taxi at their parents' residence, they climbed out of the vehicle to pay their driver, at which point he drove off, stealing their luggage. John Mellor thought this was hilarious, spluttering as he recounted the story back at school.

In 1963 John Mellor and Adrian Greaves appeared together onstage at a school drama evening; previously, John had performed in an ensemble, playing recorder onstage at the age of ten. Inspired by the satire craze of the time, the evening's performance took current television advertisements and twisted them into skits. At the carol service that Christmas, Johnny and Adrian sang "In the Deep Midwinter" to the tune of "Twist and Shout," a recent hit for the Beatles.

John (right) and David Mellor (left) share a donkey ride in Tehran with an unknown friend. *(Phyllis Netherway)*

By the autumn of 1963, in the locker room and in the showers after games, Johnny Mellor, Adrian Greaves and their cohorts would join in off-key spontaneous renditions of a song that had swept the country late that summer, "She Loves You" by the Beatles. "We'd all sing along to 'She loves you, yeah, yeah, yeah,'" remembered Paul Buck. "The first record I bought would have been probably 'I Want to Hold Your Hand' by the Beatles," said Joe Strummer of the follow-up to "She Loves You." Throughout Britain the image of the Fab Four was ubiquitous by the end of that year; and at CLFS John Mellor's illustrative skills played a small part. "He had a job drawing the Beatles on the covers of everyone's notebook," said Buck. "And he'd get the guitars the right way round." Plugging earphones into their tinny transistor radios, the boarders would listen in bed to the newest pop sounds on Radio Luxembourg's evening English service, sailing through the airwaves and clouds of static from the Continent; this was especially popular on Thursday nights, to drown out the weekly bell-ringing practice in the nearby church. There was greater listening choice after Easter 1964 and the launch of Radio Caroline, from a converted fishing boat anchored outside the three-mile limit of the British legal restrictions, pumping out the British "beat boom" nonstop; soon Caroline's twenty-four-hour pop service, a symbol of rebellion for teenagers against the staid BBC, was joined by a flotilla of competitors, including Radio London, Radio City and Swinging Radio England, whose name alone defined the cultural change taking place. On Sunday afternoons the boarders could watch the ATV pop program *Thank Your Lucky Stars*, hosted by Brian Matthew. "That's the first time I saw the Stones, way down the bill on *Thank Your Lucky Stars* in the sort of dead-end slot, singing 'Come On' by Chuck Berry," Joe told Mal Peachy. "And we just flipped when we saw it: the whole school was sort of gathered in the day room to watch it and we didn't need anyone to tell us this was the new thing. We all flipped, and likewise with the Beatles. In fact, I can't imagine how we would've got through being at that school without that explosion going off in London: the Beatles, the Stones, the Yardbirds, the Kinks. Without that rock explosion, I don't think we would have been able to stand it. It just got us through. Every Friday a new great record. We couldn't have survived without that music, definitely. We were very young at the time this really happened, and the older boys would bring in the records and on Saturdays they'd let them play them on this huge radiogram [phonograph] that had speakers all over the hall."

But it was not the Beatles or other avatars of the "beat boom" who inspired Johnny Mellor to become obsessive about popular music. This came through the California group who became great rivals to the Liverpool quartet, the Beach Boys. "Johnny came back to school one term with a copy of a Beach Boys greatest hits compilation. It knocked him and me out," says Paul Buck. John Mellor tried to grow his hair as long as he could, which was not very long at all, tucking it behind his ears to avoid the attention of teachers.

The boarders' communal room, a small, badly heated square space intended for the reading of improving books and serious newspapers, also contained a Grundig mono record player and a large tube radio, both put to purposeful use by Johnny Mellor and his cohorts. Another contemporary, Andy Ward, recalls hearing "Little Red Rooster" by the Rolling Stones blasting out of the window, Johnny Mellor silhouetted in the frame as he mimed exaggeratedly to the Stones' cover of the blues classic.

In 1988 Joe Strummer told the *NME*'s Sean O'Hagan that one record had changed his life, the Rolling Stones' "Not Fade Away," which came out in February 1964, about a year before "Little Red Rooster": "'Not Fade Away' sounded like the road to freedom! *Seriously*. It said, 'LIVE! ENJOY LIFE! FUCK CHARTERED ACCOUNTANCY!'" Later he expanded on this: "I remember hearing 'Not Fade Away' by the Rolling Stones coming out of this huge wooden radio in the day room. Very loud—they always kept it on very loud. And I remember walking into the room and that's the moment I thought, 'This is something else! This is completely opposite all the other stuff we're having to suffer here.' It was really a brutal situation. That's the moment I think I decided here is at least a gap in the clouds, or here's a light shining. And that's the moment I think I fell for music. I think I made a subconscious decision to only follow music forever."

Although Johnny Mellor was a willing participant in the annual school dances, held in the dining hall, this was the extent of the boy's musical education: "I was nonmusical all my childhood. I wasn't in any choir, didn't learn any instrument, couldn't be more completely away from the music. But we were fervent listeners and it was only after I left school that I began to think that I could actually play. I mean, I had a big problem with getting over that, which is why I called myself Joe Strummer. Because I can still only play six strings or none, and not all the fiddly bits. That was part of my makeup, that it was really impossible to play music, and so when I managed to get some chords together I was [delighted]. That's all I ever wanted to do: play chords. Jimi Hendrix said that if you can't play rhythm guitar you can't play lead, and I think he's right, but I haven't got to the lead guitar playing. But, still, rhythm guitar playing is an art."

Anne Day, who was two years behind him, insists John Mellor *was* a member of the fifteen-strong school choir who sang in St. Giles church on Sunday mornings—Mellor also seems to forget his ability with the recorder. There were advantages to being a choir member. "You had about half an hour's start on everyone in going over to the church and having a sneaky cigarette if you were in the choir," she said.

One abiding memory of life at City of London Freemen's for Adrian Greaves was the appearance in 1964 of him and John Mellor "as woodland sprites in *The Merry Wives of Windsor*: it was just an excuse to get off school. He was very keen on amateur dramatics. Especially from around fifteen upward." The plays would be staged in the Ashtead Peace Memorial Hall, off Ashtead High Street, and parents would be invited—though Johnny Mellor's could never attend.

6

blue apples

1965-1969

When the Mellor boys went out to Tehran in the summer of 1965, Johnny came across a Chuck Berry EP that included Berry's version of a song that Johnny thought was a Beatles original. "I remember putting on Chuck Berry's 'Rock and Roll Music' and comparing it to the Beatles and being a bit surprised that they hadn't written it," Joe said. Discovering that both the Beatles and the Rolling Stones spoke openly of their allegiance to American rhythm and blues, Johnny Mellor, who had just turned thirteen, further investigated Berry's music when he returned to the United Kingdom, also discovering the unique shuffling sound of Bo Diddley, and promptly fell in love.

After a brief stint back in London, in 1966 Ron was promoted to second secretary of information and dispatched to Blantyre, Malawi, in southern Africa, where he and Anna would spend the next two years. In Malawi, Johnny discovered the BBC World Service, which kept him in touch with the new big releases. He was also very interested in the local Malawian musicians. A stamp in his passport also shows a visit to Rhodesia. "Ron and Anna quite liked Malawi," said Jessie. "But then independence came and they came back to England, pretty much for good. They used to say that

Johnny had really liked Malawi. But David found it somehow troubling and unsettling."

In memories of Johnny Mellor at CLFS, an etiolated, almost spectral figure stands off to one side, indistinct, passive and vague. It is David Mellor. At CLFS the younger Mellor boy spent little time with his elder sibling. Later, according to Gaby Salter, he had regrets over this. But no one really seems to have any sense at all of David Mellor, even those who shared living accommodations with him. "Although we were in the same boarding house for two years, we hardly spoke at all," admitted David Bardsley. "Dave Mellor was very quiet, very shy, very introverted—the complete opposite to John. I suspect David was put upon by the world in general." "David was in my elder brother's year," Andy Ward told me. "He was floppy-fringed and quiet, although he wasn't someone who was bullied. But no one remembers much about him."

In the cloistered bowels of the British Museum, where he now works as a clock conservator, Paul Buck produces a photograph of David Mellor; my heart leaps as he hands it to me, as though I have made a great find. But the teenage boy in the photograph seems shrouded in gloom and so indistinct as to be almost transparent; his image is so imprecise that he looks like a ghost, or at least a man who isn't there. My elation vanishes and instead a chill runs through me. In a set of five photographs of the Mellors at Court Farm Road in 1965, the mystery is repeated: in three of them, taken as the family works in the back garden, David is turned away from the camera— all you see is an anonymous back. In the one picture of the two boys with Anna and Ron, Johnny squats between his parents, while David stands, leaning off to one side of Anna. In the printing process a tiny blue smudge has appeared in his right eye, like a tear, a portent.

"I do have to agree with what most people say about David Mellor," considered Adrian Greaves. "I didn't talk to him much at first. He was a nice chap, but you had to initiate the conversation. He seemed very calm but very shy." They both read the works of Cyril Henry Hoskins, who wrote, he claimed, under the direction of the spirit of a deceased lama, Lobsang Rampa. A mishmash of occult, theosophical and metaphysical speculation dressed up in a Tibetan robe, his books read like adventure stories, and enjoyed great popularity during the 1960s. David Mellor devoured them. In 1999 Joe Strummer mentioned to me his brother's fondness for bodice-ripper black magic novels like those of Dennis Wheatley. But would he have included Lobsang Rampa among the occult works that fascinated David Mellor in what Joe referred to as "a cheap paperback way"?

The interests of the younger Mellor boy were also broadening. When he was fifteen, studying for his O-level GCEs in the fifth form, John Mellor was a member of the school's rugby team, playing in the line, either as a winger or a three-quarter, a reflection of the stamina that he would later show on-stage and which was already evident in his ability at cross-country running: he was developing into one of the most accomplished long-distance ath-letes in the school. Perhaps he should have devoted more time to his stud-ies. When he took his O-levels in July 1968, he passed only four subjects, English literature and history (scraping by on both with the lowest accept-able grade, a 6, the equivalent of 45 to 50 percent), art (one grade higher), and a more respectable grade 3—60 to 65 percent—in English language; in the November retakes that year, he added a grade 6 in economics and pub-lic affairs, giving him a total of five O-levels, the minimum requirement to go to college.

By the time "Strawberry Fields Forever" and "Penny Lane" were re-leased as a double A-side in February 1967, John Mellor's fondness for the Beatles had evaporated. Now he hungrily devoured both the latest "under-ground rock" music and its early blues progenitors, much of it from revered DJ John Peel's late-night *Perfumed Garden* show on Radio London; every week Johnny read *Melody Maker* from cover to cover, the former jazz-based music weekly having reinvented itself to find a new readership with long articles about "serious" album artists. Like many other adolescent boys in Britain, he was immersing himself in blues music, although—as with most of his contemporaries—at first it was a case of white-men-sing-the-blues: John Mellor incessantly played an iconic LP of the time, John Mayall's 1966 *Blues Breakers* album, featuring Britain's first guitar hero, Eric Clapton. Soon he was seeking out the available American imports by Robert Johnson, the godfather of rural blues, as well as records by the British-based American blues artists Sonny Terry and Brownie McGhee. He was already in awe of the work of another American expatriate, Jimi Hendrix. When Clapton quit the Mayall group to form Cream with Jack Bruce and Ginger Baker, John Mellor bought all their releases. Other records became part of his daily diet: the iconoclastic first album by the Velvet Underground, Blood, Sweat and Tears' *Child Is Father to the Man* and, the next year, the first album by Led Zeppelin.

Secreted away in their Surrey school, the boarders were not entirely removed from the modern world. There was, for example, that access to a television set: "We got a special dispensation," remembered fellow diplomat's son Ken Powell, "to watch *The Frost Show* when the Stones performed 'Sympathy for the Devil.'" On Saturday evenings they were permitted to watch whichever film—usually a war movie or western—was being screened. "Joe and I were allowed one night to watch *Psycho*. I can remember being terrified in this cavernous room. I can also recall how I once brought back from Cape Town—where my father had been posted—this shark's tooth that I would wear around my neck. The next thing I saw he was wearing it. And then I reacquired it. He saw this, and a week later he reacquired it. Then I did. This went on for possibly a year. We never discussed it." The shark's tooth drew attention to Johnny's own teeth. He refused to ever clean them, or visit a dentist. "I've decided," he announced, "to let them fall out, then get false ones. It'll save time."

Intriguingly, at this zenith of apartheid, Johnny Mellor never questioned Ken Powell about the political situation in South Africa. "We weren't big into social commentary—it was more girls and music," said Adrian Greaves. "But Johnny Mellor did have a poster up saying, 'I'm Backing Out of Britain.'" This poster, a twist on Prime Minister Harold Wilson's "I'm Backing Britain" campaign, was fixed to the wall of the study that Greaves by now shared with Mellor and Paul Buck. The psychedelic poster images of the Beatles that formed part of the British packaging of *The White Album* also adorned the study's walls after the record's release in autumn 1968. Whatever his thoughts on the collective output of John Lennon's group, Johnny Mellor was taken with the man himself, the "difficult" Beatle forever firing off his judgments on injustice or his thoughts on great rock 'n' roll, his hip attitudinizing filtered through a patchouli-oil-stained cloak of state-of-the-art psychobabble. The study's facilities included a mono record player, "a portable plastic thing, with a speaker in the lid," recalled Paul Buck, who remembered the affection that he and Mellor had for Elmer Gantry's *Velvet Opera* and for Frank Zappa's protégé Captain Beefheart and His Magic Band, who had been championed by John Peel when his *Safe as Milk* album was released in 1967. By the time he was in the sixth form John

Mellor had suffered a personality change, not necessarily for the better. "He had become a distinct Dramatic Society arty type, a bit Marlon Brando–like, a sneer to his lip, no respect for convention," remembered Adrian Greaves. "When he was around eighteen I found him rather obnoxious. He and Paul Buck got on well, because they were both sneerers." Greaves remembered Paul Buck and John Mellor falling for the urban myth about banana skins. They dried some over a Bunsen burner then attempted to smoke them in an effort to get high, to no discernible effect.

In 1968 a brief scandal had billowed through the school when a girl had been expelled for possession of a small lump of hashish. John Mellor became partial to smoking joints whenever he possibly could—he and Ken Powell had gotten high that year before they went to their first rock concert, the American blues revivalists Canned Heat, at the Fairfield Hall in Croydon. Richard Evans also remembered going with Johnny Mellor to the same venue to see a show by the group Free.

"Messing about in the study at school, everything seemed to relate to music," said Powell. "John would play a game in which he would mime different artists. Two of these I can remember distinctly: he put his hands over his head like an onion-shaped dome, and then he put them out again, as though they were shimmering like water. Who is he referring to? Taj Mahal, of course! Then he mimed some very humble, Uriah Heep–like behavior, and then tapped his bum—the Humblebums, which was Billy Connolly's group."

During the school summer holidays the next year Johnny Mellor, Ken Powell and Paul Buck went to the Jazz and Blues Festival held at Plumpton racetrack just north of Brighton, on the south coast. Among the other jazz and blues acts on the bill were those avatars of progressive rock, King Crimson and Yes, as well as Family, featuring the bleating vocals and manic performance of Roger Chapman, long a favorite of Johnny Mellor. "We slept on the racetrack in sleeping bags," remembered Ken Powell. "The festival ran for three days. We ate lentils from the Hare Krishna tent: we were hardly the types to take food with us."

That summer was eventful for Johnny Mellor. Richard Evans had long noted Johnny's skills as a visual artist, endlessly drawing and doodling. "He was good, a hugely talented cartoonist. Cartoons were his thing—he had that creativity to do Gerald Scarfe–type satire. Even when very young he had a political awareness in what he was drawing." Several of his friends and relatives assumed this was the direction in which Johnny Mellor would pursue a career. Increasingly influenced by pop art and notions of surrealism, as well as by the consumption of cannabis and occasional LSD trips, the younger Mellor boy would sometimes disappear into creative flights of fancy. One of the most imaginative of these, which created a major furor at 15 Court Farm Road, was when—assisted by Richard Evans—he took a can of blue paint into the garden and painted all the apples on the trees blue. "His father went mad. But we thought it was great. We spent days over this, painting blue emulsion on these apples." Before Ron Mellor discovered what his son had done, Johnny took photographs of the trees; later he included them as an example of his work in his application to art school.

By now Richard Evans was known more regularly as "Dick the Shit"; the sobriquet was not a character assessment, as "shit" was a contemporary term for pot. After taking his O-levels, Dick the Shit had left school, joining a computer company in Croydon. He had just enough money to buy the cheapest available "wreck of a car," a black Austin A40. Wouldn't it be a good idea to paint the vehicle a more interesting color? suggested Johnny Mellor. "When he said that, I thought of going to the shop and picking out something like metallic silver. But Joe wasn't having any of that. He was on a different planet." Johnny had a better idea: that they use up the rest of the gallon of blue emulsion he had bought to paint the apples; to add some variety he produced more paint, white emulsion this time. "We literally just threw this paint over the car. It went rippling down it, in a Gaudí-esque pattern. We painted in the windows like round TV screens. So now I had this blue-and-white car. Joe signed it, on the front, just above the windshield."

That summer Pink Floyd played a free concert in London's Hyde Park. The pair of Upper Warlingham boys drove up to it in the blue-and-white Austin. "We didn't bother parking, we just drove over the grass and got out of it. It was like art, we just left it," recalled Richard Evans. Predictably stoned, they were heading home across the King's Road and over Albert Bridge when the car's unusual paint scheme drew the attention of a police vehicle. "A policeman says to Joe, 'We can do this the easy way or the difficult way. Where's the acid?' We had no acid, but they did have dope. Joe says, 'OK, officer, it's a fair cop [deal]. It's in the battery.' They searched us and the car, but they never found the hash."

At the end of those 1969 school holidays the Isle of Wight festival was held. This epic event had Bob Dylan topping an extraordinary bill, including the Who, and attracted an audience of a quarter of a million. Johnny went with Dick the Shit in the psychedelic Austin. "We went to the Isle of Wight a week before, like the way Joe would go to Glastonbury later," said Richard Evans. "And we stayed there afterward. We lived there for at least two weeks, building a little camp. It was great." The Isle of Wight festival marked Johnny Mellor's first long-term immersion in an alternative existence. He found that he liked it. And the next year, which featured an equally stellar bill, culminating in the last performance in Britain by Jimi Hendrix, he and Dick the Shit went back again. This time the musical extravaganza ended in a state of near-anarchy as the Ladbroke Grove agit-prop hippie group Hawkwind established an alternative festival on a hill overlooking the site. Johnny Mellor liked that even more: Hawkwind became for a long time one of his favorite groups.

Late in 1969 Ron and Anna Mellor returned to Britain from their posting in Malawi. From then on Ron, who was now fifty-three, would travel daily up to the Foreign Office in Whitehall: in the 1970 New Year's Day honors list he was prestigiously named a Member of the Order of the British Empire. That Christmas of 1969 Johnny Mellor persuaded Ron and Anna to let him throw a party at 15 Court Farm Road, the only one he held there. The event turned out to be a little different from the social events with which his parents had been familiar at overseas diplomatic functions. Their son photocopied invitations describing how to get to the Mellor family home. Like any apprehensive host he was concerned that the event go smoothly. Anxiously he wrote to Paul Buck, who had left CLFS the previous summer, at his home in East Sussex. He'd invited ninety people, he told his friend, before getting to the heart of his worries: "'How long does it take to drink a pint of beer? About ten minutes,' he said. So he's imagining the whole party running dry in ten minutes. It didn't."

"By 8:30 in the evening no one was left standing," said Ken Powell, "not because of alcohol or other substances, but because of romantic inclinations. People were all over each other: there wasn't a single space on the couch, or on the floor." Ron and Anna kept discreetly out of the way, until at the end of the evening there was some disagreement between Ron and his younger son. "I remember at the end," said Paul Buck, "his father wasn't happy about something, and Joe said, 'Yeah, well it's my pigeon now,* isn't it?' I can remember that phrase, because I hadn't heard it before."

Earlier that year Adrian Greaves had also thrown a party. By now Joe had a steady girlfriend at CLFS, "a lovely girl called Melanie Meakins, with curly black hair and freckles and fresh skin, who was younger than him." Johnny Mellor spent his entire time at the party in the garden, snuggled up with Melanie inside the tent he had pitched that afternoon. "Sexual relationships were mainly between the boarders," said Ken Powell. "You didn't have any parental control. And there would be people you were close to, with hormones running around. A highly charged and exciting situation. Nice, really. We were all in heat." Johnny Mellor told his friends that he lost his virginity on another weekend visit to Adrian Greaves's parents' house. (It is not clear whether or not this was with Melanie.)

In the summer of 1969, when Johnny Mellor was still sixteen, he had gone with his family to the wedding of Stephen Macfarland, a cousin on his father's side. The Macfarlands lived in Acton in West London. Another guest at the wedding was Gerry King, another paternal cousin, a pretty girl: "John was there, and I had never met him before. He was about sixteen, and I was about twenty-four. We were chatting, and hit it off. We spent the whole wedding day together. In the evening, after all the other guests had left, we all stayed together behind at Stephen's, all the young people. I really, really liked him. I could feel his charisma. I could feel that he was different. He told me about all his dreams, that he was really going to do something with his life—though he didn't say what. He seemed very restless, and he was very articulate. At the end he gave me a coral necklace that he had with him."

At the wedding reception John Mellor learned that his cousin Jonathan Macfarland had been to school with the Who's Pete Townshend, and that an early version of the Who had even played in the basement of the house in which the wedding reception was held; Jonathan showed his cousin an acoustic guitar he owned, on which he said Townshend had occasionally played. Johnny Mellor took the guitar back to school and tried out rudimentary chords, notably those of Cream's version of blues master Willie Dixon's

*"It's my thing."

Sixteen-year-old Johnny Mellor, at the wedding of his cousin Stephen
Macfarland. Anna Mellor, his mother, is on his left. *(Gerry King)*

"Spoonful"; although Paul Buck made a bass guitar in woodwork, and
would attempt to play with Johnny in their joint study, the Mellor boy was
defeated by the need for assiduous practice. But he acquired another "instrument," a feature of his corner of the CLFS study, a portable typewriter,
an unusual possession for an English schoolboy: in later life a portable
typewriter would often accompany him. Its acquisition at this stage could
be an indication that he saw some form of writing as his future.

John Mellor spent the summer of 1969 suitably fueled on pints of bitter
and small buys of Lebanese hash, with Paul Buck and two of his friends,
Steve White and Pete Silverton, cruising the pubs and lanes of Sussex and
Kent in Steve's Vauxhall Viva van, close to Pete's hometown of Tunbridge
Wells, looking for parties and girls. "It was always good fun," remembered
White, "going to these parties where you'd end up staying for three or four
days, lying around in gardens and fields, especially after The Man had come

up from Hastings with the gear." (Another friend, Andy Secombe, recalls, "I remember fetching up in a field in Betchworth in Surrey—I've no idea why—at about two a.m., and Joe was jumping up and down with a Party 7 beer can and being very 'lit up.'") "I've no visual memory of what Joe looked like when I first met him," said Silverton, "except his hair was long. We all had long hair. This was the late 1960s. But I can remember him writing and doodling in this curled way, with his left hand. He and Paul Buck would in-cessantly play 'Gloria' by Them, as though it was the only record in the world."

Like his new crew of compadres, Johnny Mellor was attired in the uni-form of the day: flared jeans and denim jackets, worn with colored, often check shirts and reasonably tight crew-neck sweaters; an army surplus greatcoat was considered highly fashionable, as was a secondhand fur coat, preferably moth-eaten: Johnny Mellor went out of his way to acquire one of these.

Significantly, both Steve White and Pete Silverton remembered Johnny Mellor's being introduced to them as "Woody." "Paul Buck was known as Pablo then," added Silverton. "He didn't suddenly become Pablo Labritain in the days of punk—that was something that was going on since he was sixteen." Later, Paul Buck—Pablo, as he still prefers to be known—gave me an explanation, suggesting Steve and Pete might be slightly inaccurate. "All Captain Beefheart's Magic Band changed their names. So we did. My name was Pablo, and he was Woolly Census. Next time I saw him after he'd left school, he said 'No, no: I'm Woody now.' It was just kids' stuff."

In the mythology of Joe Strummer, his "Woody" nickname has always been said to be a tribute to folksinger Woody Guthrie, which Joe was happy to go along with—but there seems to have been a much simpler, rather less romantic explanation. It's easy to see how "Woolly" could mutate to the more direct "Woody"—to Pablo, Johnny Mellor wrote letters signed "Wood." Such nicknaming is an everyday feature of public school life, almost part of a rite of passage in which pupils are given a new identity—as Johnny be-came "*Mee*-lor," for example.

Years later, in 1999, Pete Silverton bumped into Joe Strummer in a pub in Primrose Hill. "He started telling stories about when I first knew him, which he remembered in great detail, but I don't. Many of these involved drug taking in teenage years and police raiding parties—that sort of normal thing. Specifically, he remembered a party at which I convinced the police that nothing untoward was taking place while being totally off my head. Joe remembered that I explained very logically and convincingly to the police there was nothing going on out of the ordinary despite the fact that Pablo was in the bath with his girlfriend. Perhaps that was why the police pro-longed the interview, on the grounds that there was a naked woman in the place."

With Woody, Pablo and Steve White, Pete Silverton gate-crashed parties throughout the summer of 1969. It was, he said, "the kind of area where you count the staircases: most of the parties we went to were in two-staircase houses. None of us were rich, but we went to rich girls' homes on the edge of the country. We were always welcome gate-crashers, but also al-ways over in the corner with the drugs. There was lots of hash around, lots of acid." The consumption of drugs, in fact, seemed to take precedence over sex. "There was not a high level of sexual activity," according to Pete Silver-ton. "A bit, but not a lot. It was more people having sex with their girl-friends, and even then not everybody."

I mentioned to Silverton that in the opinion of Adrian Greaves Johnny Mellor had by this time become sardonic and sneering, an attitude in which he shared companionship with Paul Buck. "That explains how they fit in with our circle. In our circle they were warm, generous people. There was a sense of superiority among all of us of being the coolest people around."

In class behind Johnny at CLFS was Anne, or Annie, Day, from an army family based in Germany. By the time Annie got to know John in the school choir, he was in the sixth form and known as either "Woody" or—another nickname—"Johnny Red." Annie Day became a "sort of girlfriend" of Johnny Mellor: "We snogged a bit, but we weren't full on." Perhaps the state of his teeth held him back: "When he kissed you he didn't quite open his mouth. He was always really embarrassed about his teeth." There was a considerable age gap between Annie Day and Johnny Mellor; as he ma-tured into the character of Joe Strummer, this became a pattern.

"We clicked. We just got on well. I think what really cemented our friendship was that every Wednesday afternoon at school, every single class did games. I was excused from games pretty much the whole of the summer. Instead of Joe doing games, he was given free range to use the art department whenever he liked: he was in the upper sixth, doing his art A-level, so he used to spend all his time in the art room. At the time he was doing a twenty-seven-foot-long painting, and I became his artist's assistant. I thought he was a really talented artist. I had a conversation with him where I said: 'You are going to be really famous and I think you will be famous for your art.'"

For the Christmas celebrations in his final year at CLFS, Johnny Mellor did a series of pop-art-style, comic-strip-like paintings which were put up on display in the school's dining hall. In the manner of Roy Lichtenstein, whose work was widely popular, he adorned them with speech bubbles bearing such Marvel-type utterances as "BIFF!" and "POW!" These did not meet with the approval of Michael Kemp, the headmaster. The paintings were approved for public consumption only after each caption had been altered to the more seasonal "Happy Christmas!"

I n the Lent edition of *The Ashteadian* ("The Journal of City of London Freemen's School"), in his last year at the school, "J. G. Mellor" is listed as one of the nine boys and eight girls who are school prefects. On page 10, beneath the heading of "Dramatic Society," there is a brief appeal: "Again I would like to make a strong plea for material, in the form of songs, sketches or jokes which should be handed into the prefects' room," signed, "JOHN MELLOR (*Chairman*)." Elsewhere, John Mellor is listed as "School cross-country running champion"; surprisingly, as he was hardly the tallest of competitors, on Sports Day he also won the high jump. But his approach to school games was flexible; he picked the volleyball teams on the basis of whomever he felt like hanging out and talking with, perfunctorily playing the game whenever teachers turned up.

On Saturday nights he would put on entertainments, "off-the-wall things," according to Ken Powell. One such evening was clearly influenced by a parody of *The Sound of Music* regularly performed by the then highly popular Bonzo Dog Doo-Dah Band. It proved inspirational for Andy Secombe: "I'd never seen anything like it: it was really fantastic, hysterically funny." Adrian Greaves recalls Johnny Mellor appearing alongside him in a production of Oscar Wilde's *The Importance of Being Earnest*. "He also had a small role in Sandy Wilson's *Free as Air*, with one line, 'Dinner is served,' delivered in a French accent."

In *Reaction: The School Poetry Magazine*, Number 1 ("A selection of the poems from *Reaction* will be printed weekly in the *Leatherhead Advertiser*," the reader is advised), published early in his final year at CLFS, John Mellor has written a poem entitled "Drunken Dreams"—aptly enough, one might think with the benefit of hindsight. It is short, only four lines long, and telling: "And the pebbles fight each other as rocks / And my father bends among them / Two hands outstretching shouting up to me / Not that I can hear."

In his obituary of Joe in *The Washington Post*, Desson Thomson, a writer on the paper, recalled his years spent at CLFS. John Mellor, Thomson recalled, was very unlike the other prefects at the school. He had "a fantastic, surrealistic and absurd sense of humor." "Prefects never gave us the time of day, except to beat us or force us to polish their shoes. John Mellor was the one with the implied twinkle. Always playing pranks, mind games. Not as cruel as the others. Always funny. I suddenly remember that he once wore a T-shirt with a heart on it. It said: 'In case of emergency, tear out.'. . . 'Thomson, you're in for the high jump,' he thundered one night, after catching me talking in the dormitory after lights out. I was shaking. Even Mellor could be like the rest of them, at times. This was going to hurt. Solemnly, he made me stand in front of my bed. Withdrew a leather slipper from his foot and told me . . . to jump over my bed. End of punishment." And every single night John Mellor would make the eleven-year-old Desson Thomson sing the Rolling Stones' "Off the Hook." "He made me recite the names of the band members. Who plays bass? Bill Wyman, I told him. What about the drummer? Charlie Watts. Right, he said. Who's your favorite band? The Rolling Stones! Not the poxy Beatles."

7

the magic vest

1970–1971

Toward the end of the 1960s the ever-withdrawn David Mellor began to assert his identity in an unexpected way. An extreme inner change in his personality was externally expressed in the visual world he erected around him. When Richard Evans went round to 15 Court Farm Road not long after David's eighteenth birthday, he was very surprised: "I went into his bedroom and David had completely changed it. It had been just a normal boy's room and now it had Nazi pictures all around it, swastikas and images of Hitler: he had become extremely extreme. Very strange. It seemed to happen in about a day. He'd gone off on this extreme tangent." Perhaps as a rebellion against the fervor of left-wing revolutionary thought, and Ron Mellor's socialism, David Mellor had joined the National Front, the radical right-wing British political party. "That was the point at which both Joe and I were aware something was going on we didn't understand. At that point I felt closer to Joe than to David. But what was going on with David, I just didn't understand."

David Mellor left CLFS in July 1969; to the consternation of his family and Richard Evans, he had decided to become a chiropodist, treating foot ailments such as corns and bunions. "It made no sense. But he insisted.

And off he went to college in London." "David was studying chiropody, Johnny was going to be a cartoonist," Iain Gillies was told. That September, David Mellor moved up to London into a hostel on Tottenham Court Road in the West End.

Toward the end of his first year at chiropody college he severed contact with his parents and brother. His mother believed him to be in the grip of depression, which she attributed to anxiety over exams. Johnny Mellor was very concerned for his elder brother. Many an artist is given the dubious blessing of a gift that can be defined simply as intuitive or—more complex and loaded—"psychic"; one theory insists this is the consequence of early trauma and that such predictive insight is an inbuilt defense mechanism. By the early summer of 1970 Johnny Mellor had a presentiment that something about his brother was not right. Then the Mellor family learned that David had been missing from his hostel for a week. Deeply worried, Johnny Mellor set off with Richard Evans to find his brother. They scoured their old play-haunts, especially a nearby abandoned World War II airfield, sprinkled with wartime pillboxes like the one that sits at the gate to Carnmhor. "At that point Joe and I became twins. All I remember is that we knew something had happened to David. At the airfield was this pillbox, with a rusty old door, it's dark and dank. We went in but found nothing."

On July 31, 1970, David Mellor was found dead on a bench on an island in a lake in Regent's Park, not far from the hostel in which he was staying. The cause of death was given as aspirin poisoning, following the ingestion of a hundred tablets. The verdict was suicide.

David's self-inflicted death cast a pall of depression over the remainder of Ron and Anna Mellor's lives. Johnny was equally afflicted. He said the worst day of his life was when he had to identify the body of his brother, which had lain undiscovered in the park for three days. Surviving members of families in which suicide has occurred are frequently haunted by the fear that it runs in the family—that one day they too might take their own lives.

On two occasions I spoke to Joe Strummer about the death of David. I felt a professional need to do this, to get something on the record about what seemed a cathartic moment in his life. But each time I asked him, I wished that I hadn't, so great was Joe's recoil into himself, every defense mechanism instantly raised, the atmosphere suddenly spiky. The first time was in his hotel room in Aberdeen in July 1978, where he was on tour with the Clash. Then he admitted that David's death "happened at a pretty crucial time in my life . . . He was such a nervous guy that he couldn't bring himself to talk at all. Couldn't speak to anyone. In fact, I think him committing suicide was a really brave thing to do. For him, certainly. Even though it was a total cop-out."

Over twenty-one years later, in November 1999 in Las Vegas, I tried again—I sincerely felt that the death of David must have been such a great issue in his life that there had to be more to learn about it, especially as Joe had just admitted to me that for years he'd been in a state of depression. Joe told me he was sixteen when David died, and that his brother had been in the National Front.

"And it just did his head in?"

"Well, I don't know if that did. Who knows? You can't say, can you? But I don't think it was being in the NF that did his head in."

"Was your brother's suicide a catalyst? How did it affect you?"

"I don't know how it affects people. It's a terrible thing for parents."

That was it: Joe paused for a long, long time—I couldn't tell whether he was being deeply thoughtful, or indicating the end of this line of questioning.

Richard Evans says that he and Johnny never once talked about the death of David. Paul Buck says it was the same with him. People around Johnny describe his response as having been, essentially, *no* response. Evans, however, feels there was a discernible shift in his friend: "I think he . . . maybe he did change a bit, but only in terms of *more focused.*" This would hardly be surprising: tragedy in the family often acts as a spur for other members. "All I know is that within a year Joe had gone to Central School of Art. We're still reeling from David, and Joe went off to Central."

Johnny Mellor's response to David's death was no different from that of his parents: for them it became an unmentionable subject, an indication of the terrible grief and shock that they were suffering. As we know, the Mackenzies were always very "close" when it came to family secrets, and Anna, though grief-stricken beyond belief, toed the familiar line, Ron going along with her. Anna's family in Scotland had noted that in 1970 the Mellors hadn't been in touch, failing to send their habitual Christmas cards. "As a small boy and later, I remember my mother reading out the greetings from the Mellors' annual Christmas card, always from somewhere far away and overseas," said Iain Gillies. "I enjoyed this seasonal ritual. My mother was puzzled that we had not received a Christmas card from the Mellors in December 1970."

It wasn't until over two months later, when Iain Gillies hitchhiked down to London to check out an art school he was thinking of attending, that the story came out. "I went to London to apply to St. Martin's School of Art in early March 1971. I hadn't seen Aunt Anna and Uncle Ron and cousins David and Johnny in seven or eight years and I wanted to reconnect with them. In the midafternoon of the ninth of March I went to their house and found no one at home. Their neighbor asked me what I wanted. I told her who I was and she said I'd better come across to her house.

"On her front step I mentioned that Uncle Ron and Aunt Anna had two sons, my cousins. 'They've only got one son now,' she said. I asked what she was talking about. In a very dramatic and hushed voice she said, 'David . . . he took his life.' Those exact words. She invited me into her house where I sat stunned for maybe an hour or so, my mind flicking back to my memories of David. For a few moments I thought she might be deranged and was making this up. Eventually Ron arrived home.

"Ron was welcoming. As we went into his house Ron said that his neighbor was very kind but I should not start thinking they're all like that. Meaning, I suppose, the population of the Home Counties. Ron and I sat in the living room. He surmised very quickly that I had been told about David. We then left to collect Anna from her nursing job at the local hospital.

"Anna was surprised to see me. She was friendly and said it was a welcome surprise to have me visit. She told me they'd been in contact with David a few days before he died, saying they were going to meet him somewhere in London, but he called to say he had to return to his hostel to pick up a bag. Their meeting didn't take place. Within five to ten minutes Anna said she couldn't talk about it anymore. It was indeed a difficult time. I felt very sad for them and all of us. They told me what John was doing. Aunt Anna and Uncle Ron had some charmingly detailed *naïf* paintings that Johnny had done in Malawi. They said Johnny had enjoyed being there and meeting the people who lived in the mud hut dwellings that were in his paintings. Uncle Ron told me that David had found Malawi to be 'troubling.' I stayed the night in David's old bedroom, which had remained as David had left it. I stayed awake far into the night."

R on and Anna Mellor's ghastly difficulties over David did not end there. Acting with its characteristic blend of insensitivity and profound hypocrisy about the death of one of its parishioners, the local Anglican church at first refused to bury David because he had committed the sin of suicide. "Anna had to fight to get David buried," remembered Richard Evans. "Eventually he was buried in Warlingham." Along with Keith Wellsted, a friend of Johnny Mellor with whom he would sometimes stay at half-term at his parents' home in Suffolk, Ken Powell from CLFS went to the funeral with Johnny to offer support. Some twenty or so mourners were present. "I'm sure it affected him, but he wasn't in pieces," said Ken. "Whereas Joe was quite ebullient, his brother wasn't. I can remember going to the house after the funeral, thinking how dreadful it must be for his parents. At the house the sadness was all-pervading."

Iain Gillies told me Joe had shown him David's suicide note: "It was the evening of Anna's funeral that Joe and I went up to the loft at Court Farm Road. He passed me a few things to look at and then a piece of folded paper. It was David's suicide note. I had not known of its existence and I was very surprised at Joe showing it to me. I read it silently, sighed, and handed it back to him. Neither of us said a word about it. We went back downstairs. Thinking back to that day, when I was first sitting alone with Uncle Ron in his living room, he did say something about David leaving a note. By the time Joe showed it to me, sixteen years later, I had forgotten about this and also presumed, perhaps naïvely, that it would have been destroyed. I was asked not to repeat its contents."

Two weeks after David's suicide, his younger brother went on an already planned holiday with Paul Buck. You can imagine the hushed, tearful conversations between the desperate Ron and Anna: "Best for him to get out of the house, let's try and let things get back to normal."

Johnny Mellor had booked two "berths" for four nights, beginning on August 13, 1970, for one pound at a camping site near Newhaven in East Sussex. "He rang me up and he said his brother had committed suicide and I was shocked," said Paul Buck. "I think he just wanted to blank it out. He didn't really talk about it on that camping trip. Except for one time he came back to the tent and he said, 'I've just washed with my dead brother's soap.' I don't know whether he felt guilty or not."

The two teenagers had a nice time on their camping trip, hitchhiking the sixty or so miles to the south coast and extending the four days for another three. ("We weren't that grown up because I rang my mum and asked if she minded if we stayed a bit longer.") Yet Paul Buck was aware of the shadow of death that loomed over the holiday: "Certainly at the time he was in denial. They turned their backs on what had happened to David, but not in a callous way. While we were there, all the time we heard this Joni Mitchell line, 'You don't know what you've got 'til it's gone,' from 'Big Yellow Taxi.' That bothered him."

There is a picture Paul has of Johnny on the shoreline, looking pleasantly miserable, seeing the irony of the mistake he has just made: he has run into the sea, straight into a submerged boulder, and banged his shin. There's another one with a nameless pretty girl who had been at CLFS and happened to be staying at the campsite. Johnny and Paul had a little hash with them, and in the evenings they'd go out drinking and try to pick up girls.

It's fair to wonder if Joe took on some of his brother's distant qualities after David committed suicide. Siblings of the deceased frequently assume

Johnny "Woody" Mellor outside a shop in Horam, East Sussex, in 1970. *(Pablo Labritain)*

something of their late sibling's former role. So it is almost certain that whoever Joe was before David died, he had a bit of his brother in him afterward; and at the same time, the death of David caused Joe to lose a large part of himself.

Moreover, considering the extent to which David Mellor was influenced by the National Front and Nazism, is it any surprise that Joe Strummer should have turned so resolutely against fascism? From the time in 1978 that the Clash appeared at the "Rock Against Racism" concert in Victoria Park, before an audience of eighty thousand people, their front man was almost indelibly associated with the side of punk rock that had disassociated itself from those flirtations with swastikas espoused by Sid Vicious and Siouxsie Sioux. Joe changed that image of punk, becoming rather righteous in his role of tragic, vulnerable spokesman.

Although it could hardly compensate for the tragedy Johnny Mellor and his parents had undergone, at least there was some good news that summer.

Although his progress in his A-level exams had been as stumbling as when he had taken his O-levels, Johnny had been accepted on the strength of his portfolio for a foundation course at Central School of Art and Design in Southampton Row in central London, by Holborn underground station— a more prestigious school than his original choices, Norwich and Stourbridge. His ambition was still to be a cartoonist, though at school he had declared he wanted to "be in advertising." John Mellor's course at Central began on September 7, 1970: it was less than six weeks since the sudden death of his brother, and one must presume he was in a state of shock. At the instigation of his grieving parents, anxious that their surviving son should have some sort of support system during his further education, he moved into Ralph West residence hall in Worfield Street by Battersea Park. On his first day at Central he learned that his place at the art school positioned him as a member of an elite group: there had been more than four hundred applicants for the sixty places available in the so-called "Foundation Year," which introduced students to the disciplines of art school, preparing them for a degree course at a college of their choice. That Johnny Mellor had succeeded in getting into Central was a tribute to his talent as an artist.

Being in a fresh environment, he attempted to metamorphose into some sort of semi-adult new being, announcing to everyone he met at Central that his name was Woody. No one called him John or Johnny or even

"Woolly," or was confused that he was no longer known as that. Attracted by the cut of his jib, another new student, a girl called Deborah Kartun, overheard him in conversation with a boy who introduced himself as Ollie. "My name's Woody," he said to him. When Deborah started talking to Johnny, he said, "My name's not really Woody: I made it up—but that name 'Ollie' sounded so stupid." "At Central," said Deborah, "he was quite extraordinary. It was evident from the first moment I met him there: he was always at the center of things."

On his first day at the art college, in the vast studio room where the "fresher" students collected nervously to meet up, Woody Mellor encountered another new student, a girl named Helen Cherry. "On the first day we made friends," she said. In what would become increasingly typical of him, Johnny was drawn to her because of her eccentric, quirky personality; although her striking prettiness was probably also an attraction: tall and lanky, Helen Cherry would swan through Central in sweeping long dresses. Later that first term John Mellor and Helen Cherry worked together on a cartoon that was published in the college newspaper. Considering what he had so recently endured with David, its theme was telling: "It was about this bloke," she said, "who fell in love with a picture of a [stewardess] on a poster on the tube. And then in a state of depression he thinks he can find her by jumping on the tube line—and dies." Yet at no point during Woody's time at Central was there any mention of David Mellor, that other depression sufferer, and what had happened to him. Another Foundation Year student, Celia Pyke, said Woody's demeanor was such that until I told her about it she had had no knowledge at all of the tragedy: "My impression was that he wasn't somebody who had anything hanging over him. He was so lovely, so funny, so charismatic. A girl I'd met had told me to watch out for him when I got to Central. She said he was one of her best friends—I think she'd been at school with him—and that he was not only a really great person but that he was someone who would do something really great." (Later at Central, Celia would discover one aspect of Woody's greatness— that he was "a really great snogger.")

Helen Cherry had been born only days before Woody Mellor, on August 10. "When he first met me and found out that I was born in 1952, that seemed to be a definite advantage to being his friend: 'It's a really special year!' He had funny little phobias about things. Sometimes in a group of

National Council for Diplomas in Art and Design

Application/Registration Form
for Admission to a Course leading to
the Diploma in Art and Design 1971

Registration No. 1925

For Office use

_____

Fine Art

_____

Graphic Design

_____

Three-Dimensional Design

_____

Textiles/Fashion

Full names as on birth certificate (surname first)

MELLOR John Graham

Home address and telephone number

15 COURT FARM ROAD
WARLINGHAM SURREY
WARL 2108

Address during term if different from above

~~15 WORFIELD ST~~
~~BATTERSEA S.W.11~~   18, Ashgrove
Palmers Green
London N.13

Date of birth
21 AUGUST 1952

Age on 1st October next
19 years old

Married or Single
SINGLE

Nationality
BRITISH

Passport-size photograph

Name and address of parent or guardian

R.R.MELLOR 15 COURT FARM ROAD
WARLINGHAM SURREY

Names of two Colleges in order of preference

1. Norwich School of Art
2. Stourbridge College of Art

Indicate below the area of study of your choice stating the chief study where appropriate

Fine Art	~~Graphic Design~~	~~Three-Dimensional Design~~	~~Textiles/Fashion~~
1			

Local Education Authority to whom you are applying for an award

SURREY COUNTY COUNCIL

Any other scholarships, grants or bursaries held or have been awarded for any previous course. Give details
and awarding authority

SENIOR GRANT FOR FOUNDATION COURSE 1970—71. SURREY C.C

FORM APP.1.

Johnny's completed art-school application form. *(Deborah van der Beek, née Kartun)*

people he'd need to pick on somebody: I felt that was a downer side of his character. But he was a very lively, warm person, and really good fun, a laugh a minute. We'd never walk down the street: we'd have to run. He'd say, 'We'll be old when we can't run down streets. We must run down streets and skip. It'll be the end of us if we walk.' A very vibrant personality."

When Iain Gillies came down to London in March 1971 for his interview at art school, he immediately got a sense of his cousin's life in the residence hall. "He let me—illegally—crash in his room at Ralph West. We collaborated on some artworks in his room. There was paint, glue, cardboard, broken glass and other assorted detritus stuck and smeared over most of the floor. He seemed to approve of this at first, but then to my surprise he decided I was making too much mess and he terminated the art projects." (Iain was so untidy that he nearly got Johnny thrown out of his room.)

"At Ralph West," continued his cousin, "he had a picture or two of Jimi Hendrix stuck on his wall, along with the date of Hendrix's death. He said that Hendrix was his favorite. He also told me that he'd been to the Isle of Wight pop festival. He was very enthusiastic about it and had written out a reminiscence for either a school or college project. He had a few, short, absurdist poems he had written lying around in his room. One poem was called 'I'm Going to Getcha': 'I'm going to getcha / You can run into the garage.'"

In an evident effort to mark out an identity for himself, Woody would carry a small, battered suitcase with him everywhere that he went; as well as his work materials for the day, it also contained various items of sentimental value: a bus ticket from his favorite bus ride, for example, and the stub from the most enjoyable cigarette he had smoked. But this seems to have been the full extent of any personality that he carried around. One student, Carol Roundhill, remembered him being dressed in clothes only on the very periphery of fashionability: "too short corduroy trousers, a sleeveless knitted pullover, and a short-sleeved shirt and big shoes. He used to swap things: he had a shirt of mine he used to wear, a little short-sleeved athletic shirt from my grammar school." Helen Cherry found him another secondhand fur coat, of the sort affected by some student boys aspiring vaguely at hipness, a look by now a little out-of-date. Carol Roundhill's initial impression of Woody Mellor, in fact, was that "he was like a lot of boys: he wasn't that attractive. He had very dry skin, very curly hair and dandruff.

He struck me as a little lost. It seemed to me sad that someone would move to London and live where he was—although there were a bunch of boys from Central in the same place. He reminded me of one of Peter Pan's lost boys. The other boys were very focused. Most came from public school and were very self-assured: lots of them knew what they wanted to do before they'd even done the course. But he definitely didn't. Yet he was really, really friendly. Everybody really loved him. He didn't have any false exterior and was totally approachable. He wasn't at all ambitious. I'm amazed he did get it together in the end to work out his talent, because he didn't seem that bothered at all at art school. He seemed to be in the wrong place."

Joe Strummer later was characteristically thoroughly dismissive of his time at Central. "Well, if you're in the position I was, there's only one answer to what you're going to do after school, and that is art school, the last resort of malingerers and bluffers and people who don't want to work basically," he declared to Mal Peachy, with what you may feel is something akin to false modesty. "I applied to join Central art school, in Southampton Row, and I was amazed when I got in. And then when I [got there] I realized that all the lecturers were lechers . . . and they had chosen twenty-nine girls and ten blokes to make up the complement of forty [sic]. I just got in there as one of the ten blokes that they needed to make it look not so bad. They had chosen—obviously—twenty-nine of the most attractive applicants from the female sex, and then they spent all year hitting on them. And that was art school."

"Maybe it would have been better for him if he'd done fine art, or if he had been able to work out his own ideas," considered Carol Roundhill, on the same course. "In the graphics studio the work you had to do was very prescriptive, not very creative. It was literally learning how to make letters of the alphabet. It wasn't his thing." This was not what Helen Cherry saw as being the experience of Woody Mellor at Central. "A lot of the information about Joe's life at Central isn't correct—that he was pushed out of art school, or that he dropped out. He didn't: he really enjoyed his first year at art college. He liked it!" "He really loved being at Central," confirmed Iain Gillies.

The college's éminences grises seemed not only to like him, but to appreciate his work. One of the tutors at Central was Derek Boshier, a pop artist of considerable renown—he appears, dancing the twist, in *Pop Goes the Easel*, a Ken Russell documentary about pop art. Boshier "was very friendly with the girl students. He used to get off with them, though," added Carol Roundhill, "not with me." You also wonder if he might not have been a model for the type of rock-star artist that Woody became as Joe Strummer, when he was not disinclined to behave in a similar manner. Woody and Derek got on well. "Derek Boshier was a very sensitive and intuitive man, and he was very sympathetic and friendly toward Woody, particularly friendly with him," said Carol.

Derek was a Trotskyite. "I connected with Woody over politics," he recalled, indicating that the mood of the times, and perhaps Ron Mellor's incessant left-wing rants, had finally found a sympathetic home in the soul of Woody Mellor. "The atmosphere then was very open to politics. The courses I taught were always mind-opening, not academic. I was into appropriation, a big art movement of the time: for example, I asked my students [a previous one was Caroline Coon, who by now was a doyenne of the hippie underground and ran Release, a charity that provided legal assistance for people who had been busted for drugs] to get hold of a map of the London underground and replace the stations with people's faces or images that seemed appropriate.

"When I knew him, he was called Woody. He was a good worker. He had this sort of white man's Afro haircut, not too long, and was a jeans and sweater sort of person. I was aware that there had been something troubling in his past." Derek insists that Woody would often do his own thing, bringing a guitar with him to art college, no doubt the one he had been given by his cousin the previous year: "He'd sit there with a guitar, playing things like 'Blowin' in the Wind,' during the morning break. He was a huge fan of Bob Dylan. Sometimes it would be hard to get him back to work after that."

"Doing his own thing" included Woody Mellor's extracurricular activities while at college, specifically smoking joints on the building's roof. ("I think he was more into smoking hash than I realized," said Carol Roundhill. "I used to carry it for him, in case he was stopped and searched." Iain Gillies recalled trudging round Surrey lanes near Ron and Anna's house with Woody: "'This must be the definition of impossibility,' he said to me. 'Trying to score dope at midnight in Warlingham on Christmas Eve.'")

Once he absented himself for a couple of days from the college: this followed a visit to the cinema to see Arthur Penn's *Little Big Man*, in which Dustin Hoffman plays an ancient Cheyenne Indian, recounting his days of the Old West. The epic film purported to be an accurate portrayal of Native American life and was both a commercial and artistic success. It had a deep effect on Woody Mellor. Along with another Central student called Simon Winks, he purloined a set of Helen Cherry's Caran d'Ache pastels. With them they adorned their faces with Cheyenne-like war-paint markings. So attired, with blankets draped around their shoulders, they went and sat cross-legged on small rugs or in the grass opposite the Houses of Parliament. "They did that for a couple of days," remembered Helen.

As the subject matter of his cartoons clearly demonstrated, Woody Mellor was very taken with the romance of the American West, and especially with the lifestyle of the natives. In 1991, when he stepped in to briefly replace Shane MacGowan as singer with the Pogues, he told me some of his reasons for temporarily joining the Irish group: "I like to make instant decisions, and go the whole hog with them. Because when I was young I remember reading about the Cherokees. I read some book about Indians, and one sentence was that when a Cherokee is faced with a decision he always takes the more reckless alternative. That briefly flashed through my mind, and I thought, 'Go for it. What's life for but to make reckless decisions?'"

"There was always that whole Red Indian, earthy, camping thing he was into," considered Helen Cherry, "and how that was a more normal way of life, and that we should be living more like Red Indians. There was his admiration for Indian ghost dancing, for instance: if you put this magic vest on, you won't get shot! He did live life a bit like that."

For a time Woody Mellor remained in touch with Ken Powell from CLFS. They would meet up in central London and go to pubs or the cinema, often to see art films—Eisenstein's *The Battleship Potemkin* was one. Ken Powell was surprised when Woody led him to the Plaza Cinema in the Haymarket to see *Paint Your Wagon*, the comedy western musical written by Paddy Chayefsky that starred Lee Marvin and Clint Eastwood; Marvin's performance of the song "Wanderin' Star" was the final tune played at Joe's funeral, thirty-two years later.

Music was not something that Johnny Mellor claimed as a career choice. Carol Roundhill never had any reason to think he might end up as

The back of an envelope addressed by John Mellor to his schoolfriend
Anne Day. *(Anne Day)*

a musician. "A writer, or a lyric writer, I thought. I don't know about the actual music side of it." The doodles and sketches he would endlessly come up
with she thought to be "very *Catcher in the Rye* stuff, always relating to himself, just quirky, childish, witty, funny stuff. He stood out as being quirky
and funny. I think he was very in touch with himself. He didn't put on any
acts or try and impress anyone ever, he just didn't mind letting it all hang out
and revealing himself. That was what was so attractive about him."

But Woody already may have been harboring secret musical ambitions.
If he was bringing his guitar with him into class, it would suggest that
somewhere within him he had decided on his direction. That Christmas he
saw Andy Secombe, who by now was in his last year at CLFS. Andy had become the drummer in a band but had tired of it. "I bumped into John, and
he said he'd swap the drum kit for something: 'What are you into?' I said I
was getting interested in photography. He said, 'You can have my Minolta
SLP camera. I'll take the drum kit.' So I drove over in my Mini with the
drum kit to his parents' house. But we fumbled and dropped the camera on
the concrete outside the house. Miraculously it still worked. But he was
deeply embarrassed about it. 'Does the camera still work?' he'd ask me
every time I saw him."

The death of David Mellor had distressed Richard Evans, bringing home the pointlessness of the job he'd blundered into. Abruptly one day he quit: "And I walk out the door onto this industrial estate, and Joe's sitting on the wall. He shouldn't be here: he's in London, at Central, and he's sitting on this wall. And I said, 'Johnny, what the fuck are you doing?' And he said, 'Oh, I came to see you. I thought you were in trouble. Come with me.' Off we went." Richard moved into Ralph West, sleeping on the floor for two or three weeks and even joining Johnny Mellor for classes at Central, tucking himself away in the back row.

As the year progressed at Central School of Art, Woody Mellor continued to make his mark. "Not in artistic terms," said Helen Cherry, "not in terms of producing much work, definitely he didn't. But in terms of personality everybody knew him, though some thought he was an egotist." Carol Roundhill added, "He was everybody's friend. I thought I was very close to him, but I went to a Central reunion later, and then a lot of people were claiming to be very close to him."

Having tired of the constraints of their respective student housing by the end of the first term, Woody, Helen Cherry, Simon Winks, who had sat with Woody as an American Indian opposite Parliament, and Eric Drennen, also at Central, did what many students do and rented a cheap property together. A suitable address was found at 18 Ash Grove, in Wood Green in North London. Richard Evans took a room. Clive Timperley, a guitarist who had a day job working for an insurance firm, also moved in.

And there was another lodger. Interlinked with what she perceived as Woody's indubitable charisma, Deborah Kartun, who had met him on that first day at Central, was impressed that he had spent time in Africa: she thought this to be most sophisticated. For his part, the boy from a bungalow in Upper Warlingham found her background to be equally urbane: educated at King Alfred's, a progressive coeducational school off Hampstead Heath near her Highgate home, Deborah, blonde, bespectacled and the same height as Woody Mellor, had a Communist father who was foreign editor of *The Daily Worker*. "Woody wanted revolution," she said, "although that was the mood of the times. It was all very unspecific—none of us were at all politically sophisticated. We were both so naïve."

In the second term at Central they had begun to become close. "It was very gradual," she said. "I was splitting up with this guy who had been having a nervous breakdown—he helped me through that. At first Woody and I just became friends—he could be good friends with women. I hardly dared think I might go out with him—he was at the center of everything that was happening. Gradually we got together. At first I'd vaguely gone out with a friend of his, Tim Talent, but that was to get close to Woody."

When Woody found the house in Ash Grove in Wood Green "around April or May of '71," Deborah, who had been born a month before him, moved in with him. He told Deborah about what had happened to his brother: "He just said [David] had trouble communicating, but there was an implication that he might have been gay. Because you're young you didn't realize how enormous a thing like the suicide of a family member might be. He was probably still in shock. And his poor parents, when we went down to see them that summer of 1971 and had Sunday lunch with them . . . I had no idea they might be in mourning. There was no alcohol, and it was rather formal, like Sunday lunches were in those days—I was terrified."

The extracurricular activities at the Ash Grove house led Woody to re-name it "Vomit Heights," although not necessarily because of the effects of alcohol consumed. "There wasn't that much drinking," said Helen. "A lot of dope, and sometimes some acid." "It was very suburban," remembered Richard. "The poor bastard who was the neighbor had these people move in next door, which must have been a bloody disaster for him. He was getting all these sleepless nights because these hippies have moved in. We would still be ranting and raving at three in the morning."

"At Ash Grove," confirmed Deborah Kartun, "we were nightmare ten-ants. We played music loudly until four a.m. One morning Woody went out and put all his transistor radios in the garden and started banging dustbins to keep us awake. But we were all too stoned to get out of bed."

At Ash Grove, said Helen, was when she really got to know Woody Mel-lor: "Joe was like a big mischievous child. He was a great personality to live with, and he used to have a lot of pillow fights with me. We also used to arm-wrestle: even though I was a girl, because I was doing sculpture I could easily push his arm down. I could always win on arms. We had quite a bois-terous relationship. But he would never hurt me, it was just very close. There was a lot of hugging, a lot of touching."

When Woody Mellor mutated into Joe Strummer, this tactile aspect of his personality was always very apparent. In fact, among all of the Clash there seemed to be a ceaseless need to express empathy through physical contact: a flick of the finger on the arm to emphasize a point; a lightly bunched fist to the shoulder to underline the punchline of a joke; a touch to the back of the neck to express sympathy. Such un-English behavior extended to Woody's diet as well. "He did say that his favorite family dish was curry," said Helen Cherry. "He always went on about his mother's curry—and it wasn't that natural for someone like him to really love curry. I felt there had been a certain strictness around Woody that he was always trying to press against and throw out of the window, a bit of a strict household. His father seemed an elderly gentleman, with a very nice posture and white hair—very middle class." I pointed out to Helen that Ron Mellor was then only in his midfifties: "Really? He seemed to me like a pensioner. I think he was very proud of Woody, though.

"When I went to stay there, his dad said to both of us, what did we want to make of ourselves, and Woody said, 'I want to be a rock 'n' roll star.' His dad said, 'After one year of art college you want to do this?' He said to me, 'What do you want to do?' I said, 'I just want to run through long grass.' He said, 'That's not much of an ambition, my lady.' The father didn't really like these wild things that we said we were going to do with our lives in our late teens: he thought we had our heads right up in the clouds." Clearly, Woody Mellor's expression of an ambition to become "a rock 'n' roll star" seems noteworthy. Not only is this the first announcement of any such idea, but he is telling it to his father.

One of Helen Cherry's tutors at Central ran an organization called Action Space, a kind of peripatetic playgroup for deprived children, which traveled around London. It was, said Helen Cherry, "arty sculptural stuff. There was a group of us that went around with inflatables, being stupid and dressing up for children. It was some of the first inflatable work that was done in playgrounds. Our tutor used to use students as cheap assistants. Joe used to sometimes come along."

At one such event, at West End Green in the hardly deprived area of Hampstead, a game of "imaginary cricket" was organized for the benefit of the children who came along to watch. Essentially this consisted of the Action Space students miming a game of cricket, like the mimed game of tennis in which a group of London students participate at the end of Antonioni's 1966 film *Blow-up*, a staple work of art-house cinema that was almost a way of thinking about how to live in London. A visitor to this quasi-happening was one Tymon Dogg.

Two years older than Woody Mellor, the Liverpudlian Tymon had been something of a teenage musical prodigy: a multi-instrumentalist, he was already on his way to becoming a masterly violin player. Very shortly Woody would consider him as something of a mentor. He had even had a record released on the Apple label, founded by the Beatles; but when he realized that they wanted to market him as a singles artist, Tymon stuck to his principles and walked out on his deal.

Tymon ended up living at 18 Ash Grove. He was making a living of sorts by busking and playing the occasional small gig, and saw Joe's interest. "He would turn up, if I was doing something in some poxy folk gig. There was a crypt in the basement of St. Martin's church in Trafalgar Square where they had folk gigs. I went down there to try out a few new songs. I remember seeing this car coming into Trafalgar Square, and the door opening, and Woody rolling out like a tumbleweed. 'Hi, Tymon, when are you going on?'" Deborah Kartun insisted that 18 Ash Grove "was named Vomit Heights after this reggaelike song he and Tymon wrote together that had this line 'Chuck it in a bucket.'"

As the academic year progressed at Central School of Art, Woody Mellor had continued to study, but not enthusiastically. "I realized they weren't teaching us anything," he told Mal Peachy. "They were teaching us to make arty little marks on paper. They weren't teaching us to draw an object, they were teaching us how to make a drawing that looked like we knew how to draw the object. And then we got hold of acid, and started to take acid, and then it looked even more transparent. And that was it, really: I had to peel off and it was either work for a living or play music."

Iain Gillies, who would shortly enter Glasgow School of Art, had noticed that his cousin was already cynical about formal art training by the time he visited him in March 1971. "I remember at Ralph West I mentioned the term 'negative space.' Woody was scornful of this type of thing. He said, 'Huh, that's the sort of shit they talk about at art college.' I don't think he liked art being dissected and he didn't want to know about technique: he just wanted it to flow and be spontaneous. Maybe dope and acid had also increased his disenchantment with institutionalized 'art.' Tymon said that Woody had used one of Tymon's drawings in his end-of-

Foundation-Year show at the Central School of Art, a doodle of a horse smoking a cigarette. I think most of Woody's show was in this vein and the professors didn't see the joke."

Richard Evans remembered another aspect of Woody's end-of-Foundation-Year show: "He went into the ladies loos and got all the used Tampaxes for a collage, and that was the last straw. Whether he got kicked out or not I'm not sure. But the essence of Joe was always eight years old."

To an extent Deborah Kartun had to share him with the other women friends he had during this time, like Helen Cherry—although she insists that theirs was not a sexual relationship: "He also had a lot of genuine women friends who he valued. I've never had a man be a friend with me the way he was when we were living in Ash Grove—just really there for you. He was quite sympathetic."

"I'd done terribly in my Foundation Year," said Deborah Kartun, "so I went to Cambridge, which did a two-year course, and went into the second Foundation Year there. It was really old-fashioned, the opposite of Central where everything was conceptual. Woody would come up at weekends or I'd go down to London to Ridley Road. We were still very much girlfriend and boyfriend."

"Woody" Mellor—as he now was—with Deborah Kartun, his art-school love. *(Pablo Labritain)*

Woody Mellor was secretly distressed that he and Deborah were not together all the time. He wrote to Annie Day: "Last time you told me you had had a romance upset but I expect you got over that. Remember: NEVER GET HUNG UP ABOUT ANYTHING!"

"Woody was a truly exceptional person," said Deborah Kartun. "He could be very endearing. But he could also be very nasty to people. On the other hand, I could be horrible to him. He announced quite early on that he was going to be a famous pop star. It must have been when I was at Cambridge. He wrote to me on lavatory paper telling me this. But when we were near the end I would be horrible about this: 'You're never going to be a famous pop star.' This was because I really thought he couldn't achieve it. I was disparaging toward him about going down what I thought was the wrong road: I thought he should stick to art. And I was also worried for him: I thought it seemed such a hard life. At the time I think he was briefly working as a dust [garbage] man."

8

the bad shoplifter
goes gravedigging

1971-1974

In the summer of 1971 the second Glastonbury festival took place, with a very special guest. Michael Eavis, a dairy farmer on whose land the festival was held, was contacted by the devotees of the Guru Maharaj Ji and his Divine Light Mission: "We've got God in town: can we bring him to the festival?" "It was very odd," Eavis told the writer Mick Brown for his book *The Spiritual Tourist*. "Somebody said God had arrived and could we put him onstage, and my thought was: Well, the festival's for everybody really, so why not? By the time he went onstage everybody in the audience was completely stoned out of their minds, and you could hear this ripple going around, 'Wow! That's God!' Then he started preaching against drugs, which I think everybody there found a bit disconcerting." Guru Maharaj Ji, a pudgy-faced thirteen-year-old Indian boy, had been whisked down to Glastonbury in a Rolls-Royce rented to honor him by those who were already his followers.

Maharaj Ji's unique selling point was the promise of "inner peace" through the practice of meditation techniques known as "Knowledge." As this is also a term for the rigorous training undertaken by London taxi drivers, I can never hear the term in a Maharaj Ji context without visualizing fleets of black cabs. Maharaj Ji now lives in some splendor near Zuma beach, north of Malibu, in southern California.

That 1971 Glastonbury festival was the moment at which the Divine Light Mission planted itself in the (un)consciousness of potential followers in the United Kingdom. One of them was Woody Mellor, who was at the festival. Helen Cherry said: "Like me, Joe got into Guru Maharaj Ji and we used to go to that a lot." I recall telling Joe Strummer during the time of punk how I'd once done a course in Transcendental Meditation and him surprising me by replying, "Yeah, I did something like that."

This interest in Maharaj Ji was not a fleeting craze for Woody Mellor. For over a year the Eastern religion filtered ceaselessly through to his brain via the habitual haze of marijuana smoke around him: the following year Iain Gillies visited Woody at his new flat, on Ridley Road in Harlesden, and his cousin asked Iain the question, "Who are you Scots into?" "I said I liked the artist Egon Schiele and Dylan Thomas. Woody pointed to a poster on the wall of Guru Maharaj Ji: 'We're into him. We think he's cool.'" This revelation of his cousin's mystical leanings startled Iain: "I said, 'You're into him?'" The next day Iain came across Woody in the kitchen explaining to someone how to rob a nearby bank.

It's natural to wonder if Woody Mellor's fascination with Guru Maharaj Ji could have been a consequence of the death of David. Tragedy often obliges those left in its wake to seek answers in some form of religious figurehead. But it's also possible that Woody was simply infected with the ubiquitous mystical spirit of the times.

Richard "Dick the Shit" Evans also became an adherent of Maharaj Ji. "Helen had a huge spiritual side to her. I think we got sucked in. I learned a lot of things, like breathing techniques, that I still use today. There would be emphasis on things like, 'I want you to think of nothing,' and you just can't. Woody and I did it for about a year. It suddenly occurred to us that it wasn't that interesting."

Woody was not "fanatical" about the Divine Light Mission, Helen Cherry said, but would certainly meditate for the requisite hour every day. "Guru Maharaj Ji had a big function in Central Hall, in central London, the first public meeting in London. Joe saw him, but I don't think he met him personally. He would hang around the ashram in North London a bit, but not as much as me." Deborah Kartun did not approve or participate in this allegiance to Maharaj Ji: "I'd been brought up in an atheist family."

Something else had happened to Woody Mellor at that Glastonbury festival. During the set by Arthur Brown, the self-proclaimed "God of Hellfire," a rooster named Hector had flown up and perched himself atop an imposing crucifix, part of the stage dressing, at the very moment it was about to be set alight during Brown's performance highlight of his hit song "Fire." Hector was almost instantly incinerated, the ultimate fast food. From that moment on Woody became a vegetarian: he decorated a soap tin for Helen with drawings and the adage: "We love to eat nuts and honey." Shortly afterward, returning home from a party toward breakfast time, Woody Mellor picked up a pint of milk that had just been delivered to a doorstep and was promptly arrested by a passing policeman: in court the next morning he was fined a few pounds, earning a criminal record for petty theft. Did this lead to a certain amount of musing on the nature of drinking cow's milk? Soon he announced to all and sundry that the drinking of milk was a con by the Milk Marketing Board: "He thought milk was very bad for you," said Helen. "He felt that people should have never been persuading children in the 1950s to drink milk." He maintained this view for the rest of his life.

With almost painful slowness, Woody Mellor began to angle himself in the direction of the career choice he had expressed to his father. The arrival of Tymon Dogg at 18 Ash Grove, along with the presence of the accomplished guitarist Clive Timperley, had proved inspirational. "I remember Joe singing this chorus, 'I'm going to be sick / I wanna puke up in a bucket of water,' and trying to play it on Tymon's ukulele," said Helen.

Soon their time at Vomit Heights was at an end. "Ash Grove was falling apart after we'd lived there for a year," said Helen. "There was a bit of damage: there had been so much dancing at one party the kitchen ceiling had come down, and Tymon somehow destroyed the garden." It was time to move.

In September 1971 the Vomit Heights crowd moved into a second-floor, three-bedroom flat at 34 Ridley Road, Harlesden, rented from an Irish couple; with occasional exceptions, Woody's subsequent London addresses would draw closer and closer to Notting Hill until he was living in the area proper. For some reason, Woody Mellor always insisted that his new address was in Willesden, although that is at least a mile to the north. Was this because Harlesden was considered an almost unmentionably rough area, an underclass immigrant district locked away into its own world because it was so badly served by public transport? Helen lived there with her boyfriend Robert Basey; Woody shared a room with Kit Buckler, a friend from Ralph West who had booked the groups at his own college—when Kit moved out, he was replaced by Dick the Shit; a Frenchman had the third bedroom, little more than a box; and Tymon Dogg slept in the living room.

It was not a great time for Woody Mellor. No longer receiving a government grant as a student at Central, he was frequently virtually destitute. He had sunk to the ocean floor of life: the dank, threatening district of Harlesden was a long way mentally from the landscaped lawns of the City of London Freemen's School, or the quaint village life of Upper Warlingham. Woody was, said Helen, "very lost at the end of the art college year," although his spirits were still underpinned by his devotions to Guru Maharaj Ji. He briefly worked laying carpets, following this with apartment-cleaning jobs. He attempted to start a painting and decorating business called HIC, which stood for Head in the Clouds, but this attempt at business stalled almost from its inception.

Iain Gillies came to stay a few times, and he and Woody would stay up all night: "On a couple of occasions, as I was making my way to bed at eight in the morning, Joe would say that he had to go off to do a flat-cleaning job."

In a letter to Annie Day, Woody gives his impression of the district in which he is living: "This pad is in a pretty GRIM area like goods [freight] yards etc etc Oh yeah loads of spades* like this." He has illustrated this thought with a distinctly politically incorrect cartoon of a black man wearing a sweater emblazoned with the slogan OOGA BOOGA, dancing in front of a house that bears the number 34. Out of the top window peers a character with a question mark emerging from the top of his head, who you assume can only be the letter's signatory—in this instance "Johnny Red." Stuck next to the cartoon black guy is a celebrated frame from the then renowned underground comic strip "The Fabulous Furry Freak Brothers," in which the

---

*It is worth noting that in hip circles of the time in Britain to call black people "spades" was considered a sort of cool political correctness.

stoned hero holds a handful of joints and is mouthing the speech bubble, "Well, as we all know, DOPE will get you through times of NO MONEY better than MONEY will get you through times of NO DOPE!"

Poverty meant that Woody would occasionally stoop to shoplifting, at which he was not very good. "One time," said Helen, "we were in this bakery, and I could tell that he was going to go for this mince pie. He ordered some bread and as this poor woman turned round to get it, he stole this mince pie off the top of the counter and put it into the big dirty old fur coat that he had. But he'd forgotten that it had no pocket in it, and so this mince pie came tumbling out by his foot on the floor, and the woman spotted it. It was so embarrassing that I just couldn't stop laughing as we followed him out of the door, trailing crumbs behind him. He was just no good as a thief, made a complete [mess] of it. He hadn't thought it out at all. He was better at dressing up as a poor boy and putting it on for the greengrocer, he was quite good at that.

"He was a very sincere person, and you were very lucky if you had him as a friend, because he had an energy, a spark. Sometimes we'd spend whole evenings by getting out a piece of wallpaper and having drawing fights. We'd have battles: he'd imagine something and he'd draw it, and say, 'This is coming to get you.' I'd have to do a drawing back to put his men down and send in another missile. I remember him getting hold of one of my sketchbooks and starting in felt-tip in the corner 'This Is Gonad': it was all about this poor chap called Gonad. He was very good at starting some of the titles, but the endings . . . no, he didn't get a lot of endings."

On visits to his parents, John Mellor would gloss over the hand-to-mouth existence he was living. "Woody tried to reassure his father that he was on the correct career path by announcing that he had secured a desk job," said Iain Gillies. "A few seconds later he added that he would be sweeping up for a Warlingham cabinetmaker. Ron thought that this was very funny."

In a letter sent to Paul Buck in December 1971, Woody included a centerfold poster of Led Zeppelin singer Robert Plant—whose first albums he had loved at CLFS—from the weekly music paper Sounds. He had satirically improved the picture of this archetypal rock god, including a speech bubble that read, "Look at me, I'm wonderful," and adding drawings of holes in the singer's arm with one word appended to them: "heroin." The letter contains instructions for a then current urban myth about a method

☆ ☆ TOP FLOOR 34 RIDLEY Rd N.W.10

Ψ Apre muchos gracious por vo lettre, yes really good, when you eventually get
, lets sus out when I can meet you. Maybe a day out or summat,
know. When I last wrote to you I was probably cleaning flats. Well
given that up now, and its now PAINTING & DECORATING firme.
called Fart, me and 2 other guys are trying to get together a Rip-off
of Painters. At the moment me + Fart are working with another guy
he's splitting in about 2 weeks so we fancy setting up on our own.
is a little mad since I know fuck all about painting a
m, Fart knows a little, but not really amounting to
ing proffesional I will wait till you get back
chool before I send this as it might
so you in germany How are doing
- time you told me you had a a
unce upset but I expect you got over
Remember, NEVER GET HUNG UP ABOUT ANYTHING!
thats what BUS. I've sussed out
2 years, and its pretty those.
tell me when you can get out and I'll come down
meet you or maybe you come up here. This pad
a pretty GRIM area like goods yards etc eft
yeah Loads of spardes ⟶

CROW

PENGIN

Woody's missive to Anne Day from 34 Ridley Road. Soon he would be physically ejected from the property. *(Anne Day)*

of getting high, on a par with—but probably much more dangerous than—their efforts to smoke banana skins at CLFS: it consisted of boiling toadstools in red wine, the drinking of which was alleged to promote an interesting trip. "I don't know: I'm afraid," he admitted in his letter. "But there's plenty of guinea pigs here. I had a haircut last Monday, hope you're still in this room 8 of yours, otherwise you are not going to get this poster. Why don't you come up? Love the Wood Bird."

By early spring of 1972 Woody had begun to accompany Tymon Dogg down to the West End on his busking expeditions in the tiled corridors of the London tube system. They would hit the underground in the late evening, "when we judged everyone in town was drunk." At first Woody Mellor simply acted as Tymon's "bottler," his money collector; their regular pitch was at Green Park, where the Piccadilly and Victoria lines converge. "That's how I got into playing, following Tymon Dogg around in the London underground and first collecting money for him like a Mississippi bluesman apprentice." Then Woody moved up in the world: "I bought a ukulele, 'cos I figured that had to be easier than a guitar, having only four strings." The instrument, for which he paid £2.99, came from a Shaftesbury Avenue music shop: "I began to learn Chuck Berry songs on the ukulele, and go out on my own, down in the London underground." One night when Tymon Dogg decided to try his luck one stop up the Victoria line at Oxford Circus, he left Woody at Green Park with his ukulele. "The train emptied at one end of the corridor. One second the corridor was empty, the next it was packed with people streaming through. It was like, now or never, playing to this full house. That was the first time I remember performing on my own." Realizing how crucial it was to grab the attention of his prospective audience in seconds, an attitude he developed in the future, Woody came up with a repertoire of Chuck Berry songs: "Once I was playing 'Sweet Little Sixteen' on the ukulele and an American happened to walk past and he stopped in front of me and went, 'I don't believe it, I can't believe it,' and he began smacking his forehead, and staggering around, and nearly fainting, and I stopped playing and said, 'What? What?' And he went, 'You're playing Chuck Berry on a ukulele!' And I hadn't considered it to be odd at all. I only started to think it was a bit odd after this American had, like he was nearly banging his head on the subway wall with the ridiculousness of it. And so I just carried on with that, and eventually I got a guitar."

Then they were evicted from their flat. The Irish landlady's displeasure with her tenants seems to have been based on a number of factors that had equal weighting; but they mainly focused on the fact that Woody had taken in a mentally ill black homeless man, giving him his bed.

Helen Cherry has a certain sympathy with the response of the landlords: "I mean, we did make a terrible mess of 34 Ridley Road, and they could probably see that this was all a bit anarchic. 'What is going on in our place? So they kicked us out really badly. They just turned up, let them-

selves in and started dragging people down the stairs and putting everything in black bags and throwing it out of windows. They were larger than
we were, and took everyone by surprise. My boyfriend was dragged down
the steps. All our stuff was just thrown out in bags." "We were paying rent,"
said Dick the Shit, "but the landlord and his wife came up, with a couple of
Irish mates, and they physically threw all our stuff out of the house, onto
the road." After being manhandled down the stairs and pushed out of the
house, Woody stood on the pavement in a state of shock, absolutely
stunned that this had happened.

The effect of this eviction, at the end of April 1972, was for Woody's
shocked stupefaction to almost immediately transform into furious anger.
It strongly politicized his view of the property-owning classes, even though
his landlord oppressors were working-class Irish. "I've been fucked up the
arse by the capitalist system," he later told *Sounds*. "Me, personally. I've had
the police teaming up with landlords, beating me up, kicking me downstairs, all illegally, while I've been waving Section 22 of the Rent Act 1965 at
them. I've watched 'em smash all my records up, just because there was a
black man in the house. And that's your lovely capitalist way of life: 'I own
this, and you fuck off out of it!'"

Luckily for Helen Cherry and Tymon Dogg, Helen's parents had a flat
they used in London in Miles Buildings, a five-story tenement walk-up between Church Street and Bell Street, close to where the beginning of the
Westway crosses Edgware Road. It wasn't available right away, however, and
the Ridley Road collective first moved in with Dave and Gail in their two-
room flat. "They'd put down a bed in their living room. But there would be
three or four of us. I remember once even sleeping at the end of their bed.
They were very generous and giving," said Helen.

Dave Goodall, a Jewish Marxist from Manchester who smoked ceaseless
quantities of hash but could always be relied upon to come up with food or
supplies of electricity, would join with Tymon Dogg in forming the two
biggest influences at this time on Woody Mellor; whereas Tymon informed
Woody's musical education, Dave was at the heart of his political instruc-
tion. Coming after the unpleasant eviction from Ridley Road, Dave found
in Woody a candidate ripe for schooling in the possibilities of more radical
means of accommodation. "There was a hierarchy of articulateness," said
Gill Calvert, a cousin of Gail Goodall, "and Joe wasn't necessarily at the top

of it." He also was not that certain about himself. "I remember having a conversation with him in Dave and Gail's place," said Helen Cherry, "and him saying very seriously, 'Look, I want to be a guitarist, but maybe I can't be because I should have been starting at thirteen or fourteen. I can't just pick it up now. I'm not going to be good enough.' And my saying, 'No, go for it, if that's what you really want to do.'"

As though to drive home Dave Goodall's lessons about the iniquities of the property-owning classes, there was no real room in his and Gail's apartment, and any lodgers had to crash where they could until Gail and Dave got up in the morning—at which point Woody was always the swiftest to take their bed. In a postcard to Annie Day, dated "May 1972," with an address given only as "Warrington Lane," he tells her of his problems: "I have been evicted so don't send no letters to 34 Ridley Road. At the moment I'm hitching to Wales planning to stay there. Just been to Bickershaw Festival, it rained a lot but had a pretty good time. I'll send you my new address when I've got one or if not I'll write in 2 weeks. Writing this with 1 hand standing up. Love John."

"Between my visits in Easter 1972 to Ridley Road and summer 1972 to Edgware Road, he had started busking in the tube with Tymon," remembered Iain Gillies. "He had his ukulele at Edgware Road, but he had plans to play some serious guitar, first left-handed and then right-handed. I said something to him about him being left-handed and he said, 'Don't worry, 'cos my left hand's on the fret and it's shit hot . . .'"

Once the guitar arrived, Dick the Shit accompanied Woody on a couple of busking expeditions. "I bought this bass, so we were kind of playing: we were just learning how to do it. I used to tune his guitar for him, 'cause he couldn't physically do it. When we were busking together all Joe could play was 'Johnny B. Goode,' with a twang in his voice. I had a huge issue about this. I'd say, 'We've got to play something else. We're just frauds: all we can play is half a dozen chords—it's just appalling.' He just said, 'Look, they're just walking through. Nobody every hears the second song!' He was absolutely right. He didn't give a shit. I did, but he was right."

"Tymon and Woody went off to Holland to do some busking," said Iain. "But they were back in London within a day or so, having been deported as undesirables. Woody suggested that they could try again after disguising their instruments as bags of golf clubs."

Woody Mellor was still pretty much financially destitute. Later he told Gaby Salter that at this stage of his life he was often driven to scavenging around the rotting fruit and vegetables discarded in the gutters of Soho's Berwick Street market to find something to eat. ("Around that time," said Iain Gillies, "Aunt Anna told me, 'We let John have a little money.' Those exact words. So he had a little allowance at this 'financially destitute' time.") But soon an episode occurred on the London underground that disturbed Woody enough for him to decide to abandon busking altogether as a career choice. While he was performing on his patch at Oxford Circus, a loud-speaker blasted out above his head, commanding him to stop playing and advising him that the Transport Police had been dispatched to arrest him. As he told Paul Morley in *NME*, "This guy walked past, and I screamed at him, 'Can you hear that? This is 1984!' And he gave me a funny look, and rushed off. I thought, 'Ah, fuck it,' and packed it in."

At this point, early in the summer of 1972, several of the former Ridley Road collective also said "Ah, fuck it" to London. The father of a friend owned a farm outside Blandford Forum in Dorset, 140 miles west of Lon-don and for the last nine or so months Woody and his friends from Ridley Road, with the addition of Deborah Kartun, would frequently hitchhike down there for a few days' respite from London. But now, because of their lack of permanent accommodation in London, a planned "weekend in Dorset" turned into a stay of two months. As, according to Dick the Shit, "there was all sorts of sex, drugs and rock 'n' roll" going on, a blind eye needed to be turned by the farm owner, who happened to be the local jus-tice of the peace. The fact that an Indian tepee, in which Woody frequently slept, had been set up by the visitors on his grounds was no doubt consid-ered only an aesthetic embellishment. Deborah Kartun joined him there for the duration: "The tepee, which we shared, was really tiny. It wasn't one of those hardcore hippie tepees, it was one from a child's toyshop."

When Deborah went away for a couple of weeks on a family holiday, Woody wrote to her in a letter that fully expresses his tender feelings for her:

Dear Debbie,

My arms and legs are aching and there is straw in my hair. I have been working all day on this farm—it's really good work because its [sic] "in time with the seasons" if you know what I mean.

I just got [*sic*] your letter . . . it was *lovely*. I really enjoyed reading it, and it put me in a good mood. I hope you don't look like that drawing! Oh yeah last night we were all standing around after work getting paid when who should drive up but Ken Turner! Later on when we passed around the joints he got pissed off a bit and left. I can imagine the house and fields and woods from when we went there last time. I can see you wandering about like this.

I really would like to be with you—two weeks isn't long at all, but I'm a bit better off than you because I've got something to do re work but you're on holiday.

Love

Love

Love

Woody XXX

I LOVE YOU

But from the bottom of his heart Joe also cared for and loved his male friends. "Drug cocktails" were such a specialty of the house that Dick the Shit began to develop what Woody Mellor considered to be a dependency on amphetamines. "He solved that problem for me by sitting me down in a room and repeatedly playing Canned Heat's 'Speed Kills.' He was being a real friend, and sorted that out for me."

The assembled collective made ends meet by haphazardly laboring on the farm. "We made a life-sized replica of Stonehenge out of straw bales. We all got severe bollockings [severely chewed out] for that," said Dick.

But the last straw was when Helen Cherry went down to answer the door to the postman with no clothes on. "He runs back to the village and announces, 'There's sex, drugs and rock 'n' roll up there.' We all got kicked out. Joe went back to town."

For her part Deborah Kartun went off to Cardiff School of Art & Design, to begin a three-year degree course in ceramics. "That was when I dumped Woody. I had to split up with him: he was dropping out quite seriously, and doing a lot of speed and acid. He was becoming quite wild, and was difficult to live with—you'd make an arrangement and he'd turn up four days late.

"But I don't know if he realized I adored him. But we were both acting parts very much, part of that art-school thing. You know how he always acted. I remember he went to an early Gilbert and George show, and was

Woody's loving cartoon of Deborah Kartun.
(Deborah van der Beek, née Kartun)

bowled over by it. We went to a fancy-dress party where I dressed up as a vampire tough woman, gorgeous fifties dress, but with plastic vampire teeth. He got very upset.

"But the acting thread ran through everything all of us did: it was play-acting, like children, all a continuation of dressing up as kids. Even his cowboys and Indians thing was part of this conceptual approach to life."

But Woody Mellor had friends at the art school in Newport, a few miles from where Deborah was studying in Cardiff.

In November 1972 he wrote to Annie Day from Upper Warlingham, at what in hindsight we may see as a pivotal point in his life. Although he writes on a greeting card that bears the image of a blue elephant—shooting flowers out of its trunk—under the light of a full moon in a floral jungle, he packs both sides with his neat italic script; the envelope is postmarked "Croydon Surrey, 10:45 a.m., 15 Nov. 1972," and he has appended the phrase "Tutti Fruti Mail Service" by the stamp.

Dear Anne I'm doin' a cartoon strip at the moment called "GONAD SLEEPS IN LATRINES." I have to because in a flash moment I said I'd do it for the college I used to go to's magazine. This girl was supposed to do it but she couldn't be arsed [bothered] and I saw a chance to get my famous character in print but now in the early hours of the morning I begin to weary and the cigarette smoke drifts into my eyes but with a few tons of SELF CONTROL I should finish in about 3 hours. I'm down at my parents home for the weekend and tomorrow I'm going back to London, then on Wednesday I'm going down the M4 to Newport in Wales. I've decided to settle down there HA-HA for a while at least. The stinking press of humanity drives me from London. I wonder how yer college education is getting on. What are you learning anyway? Will you accept belated thanks for that last letter of yours? Cut your hair? I've just had mine done. I wanted it Futuristic so at the moment its like the Queen's. Last week I had a great rocknroll quiff but it takes a lot of sweat to keep it like that. Maybe I gotta use Brylcreem again. I'm playing the guitar a lot now and I'm goin down Newport to practice and get shit hot. May take a year or too [sic]. Well now, you got any young men chasing you? It might make life more interesting but NEVER believe a word they say. What do you think of the picture on the front? I got it because it looks just like a bad copy of ROUSSEAU which I suppose it is. Some of that guy's paintings are really OK. Do you know that one with a tiger asleep in a desert with a full moon? Its [sic] my favorite, makes you want to cry if you're drunk. And I think he was a bank clerk during the day and doing these really weird pictures at night. I got a real NIGHT scene set up here at the moment with Radio Lux just turned up dead faint so you can hardly hear the guy say "DATELINE—friendship, love and EVEN marriage"! I'm sittin at my drum kit with a drawing board on the snare drum and a spotlight on the side Tom Tom because it's the only "table" available but I have to be careful not to tap the bass drum pedals when some rock n roll comes on because it will wake the P. and M. In one of your letters you say you were listening to the Doors, well funny you should say that because I've been living with a guy whose nuts on the Doors and he puts on "Riders of the Storm" and I've been thinking it's real good because before I didn't reckon on them. "LA Woman" that's good too. It's a pity Jim Morrison died he was OK. Have you heard "Runnin Blue"? That's neat. Ah Kid Jensen [the Radio Luxembourg disc jockey] puts on the crummy records! I'm staying with a friend when I get to Newport but when I get a place I'll send you the address straight off OK? I was goin to draw you a souvenir picture of Gonad but I can't now. All my lovin John. PS. You heard Buddy Holly? Keep well XXX

Of course, the most interesting information in this revealing missive is John Mellor's announcement of his ability with the guitar: "I'm playing the guitar a lot now and I'm goin . . . get shit hot. May take a year or too." Clearly he had decided to pursue music with complete dedication.

"I ended up in Wales, after I had served my apprenticeship with Tymon Dogg, and there didn't seem to be any way of making a living in London or surviving," Joe said to Mal Peachy. "I followed a girl to Cardiff Art School, who I'd known in London, and she told me that she wasn't interested, and I started to hitch back to London, and the first town you come to is Newport in South Wales . . . And then I got a job in the graveyard, got a room, crashed my way into art school, although I wasn't at the art school, into the art-school rock band, and that was really great to learn your chops with some really kind people who let me sleep on the floor at first, and yeah that gave me a whole heap of help."

The "really kind people" were Gill Calvert, Gail Goodall's cousin, and her boyfriend, Mickey Foote. Mickey Foote had got into Newport art school "by accident," said Gill. "He drove someone else down for an interview and got in. He was very talented." There was also a practical reality about this move, as Joe later told his friend Keith Allen: "I went there because there wasn't any room in London. That's why I went there. I was sleeping on someone's floor, for a few months, in their kitchen, in a two-room flat, and you outstay your welcome. And I had a girlfriend at Cardiff art college. So I thought I'd hitch down there and rekindle the romance. And I hitched down to Cardiff and she told me to shove off. And so I started to hitch back and the first stop off was Newport, and I had some friends there at Newport, 'cause these were all people I'd met at the Foundation Year in London at Central. And I hadn't made it into any other course so I was kind of on the lam."

"Suddenly," said Gill Calvert, "Joe turned up in the corridor of Newport College of Art, a massive public building, with his guitar on his back, and that was that. He was standing there, and I was very surprised. He wasn't into [Maharaj Ji] anymore. Helen Cherry says he walked around at Central with a white sheet on. But when he came down to Newport he wasn't into religion. He left all that behind him. He came with that guitar on his back and Divine Light wasn't going to do it for him."

Woody Mellor had come down to stay with a friend from Central School of Art named Forbes Leishman, now a student at Newport. We get a glimpse of his life in Newport from a letter that he sent to Paul Buck:

So I'm living in Newport Mon[mouthshire]. I'm sending you a letter and want to buy you a guitar. £10—yeah. You are getting a bass before you get a car. I don't have my room here, but my address is Wood c/o Sir Forbes Freshman, 18 North Street, Newport, Wales. Forbes is the guy I'm staying with in Newport and I want to do this all winter: chasing women and playing guitar. Maybe that fearsome rock and roll band the Juggernauts might rise from the ashes of the 20th century. I went to see Deb, oh I need her, she don't need me. Oh my darling can't you see. I'm going to be a kitchen porter during this hard hard winter. I've got access to a piano but I know next to nothing about it. Well it could be better, it could be worse, we could all be riding in a hearse. We could be ailing and screaming, we could be dying and bleeding, have you never seen a witch mutter her curse. The only thing for us to do is to sit down and play away hazy man til our dying days. Love Wood.

Newport, a mining district, had a strong local branch of the Communist Party. "They wanted to recruit Joe and me and Mickey into the Communist Party," remembered Gill Calvert. "Their main recruitment method was through dope. Joe and I went along to one of their meetings, and they cooked us a meal except that it was meat, and he was vegetarian, and I don't think I ate anything either. So he smoked a lot of their dope that evening, but we didn't join the Communist Party." Somewhat enamored of a girl who was a Party member, Woody did occasionally participate in some of its more grassroots activities. "Toeing any line is obviously a dodgy situation, or I'd have joined the Communist Party years ago," Joe Strummer said later. "I've done my time selling the *Morning Star* at pitheads in Wales, and it's just not happening."

The Communist Party was not the only form of marginal entertainment in Newport. The town was ten miles from Cardiff's Tiger Bay district, a notorious anything-goes area that had been taken over by Africans and Afro-Caribbeans. In Newport docks there was a club called the Silver Sands, a Jamaican shebeen [an unlicensed, illegal bar], run by a couple named White, who were black. After paying the entrance fee to the wheelchair-bound Mr. White, it was obligatory to buy a can of Colt 45 from his wife before proceeding two floors down; here a sound system had been set up with speakers as big as packing cases from which reggae boomed. Some of the Jamaican customers took turns to "toast" on a mike to this somewhat alien music. Woody would come most Friday or Saturday nights, and it seems this was where he was first fully exposed to Jamaican music. Later he talked about how reggae's rhythms had not made sense to him until he spent an entire Christmas in Newport on acid listening to Big Youth.

In early 1973 Forbes helped Woody find somewhere to live: a friend at Newport art school named Allan Jones, also known as Jiving Al, needed someone to share his flat. The flat, 12 Pentonville, was supported by metal rods that held up the house. "The flat had an absolutely filthy kitchen," said Richard Frame, another Newport student who took over Woody's room from him. Frame remembered scouring specialist record shops in Cardiff with Woody. "He was looking for Woody Guthrie records," he said, as though John Mellor were now trying to source the origins of his nickname.

Jiving Al Jones was a significant addition to the life of Woody Mellor. He was bass player with a rock 'n' roll group called the Rip Off Park All Stars, who covered original rock 'n' roll songs with considerable dedication to showmanship. In Newport there was a big scene of teddy boys and teddy girls sporting the necessary accouterments of brothel creepers, the 1950s shoes that rose in popularity along with punk, and bouffant hair. By the time Woody Mellor arrived in Newport, the Rip Off Park All Stars had run their allotted time and the group was hardly playing. Jiving Al and Rob Haymer, the group's guitarist, decided to form another group, working with similar material. A drummer was found, a local mortuary attendant called Jeff Cooper. And who else might Jiving Al think of as front man for this new, as yet unnamed group but his flatmate? "He'd just bought a guitar and taught himself to play in three to six months. He was a really determined man," said Jiving Al. Woody was still a neophyte on guitar, and his voice was distinctly untutored, but he had a way into the group: "They had a drummer in the art-school group but they didn't have a drum kit, so I blagged [talked] my way into the group by saying, 'You can have my drum kit, or use it, if I'm the singer.' So I blagged my way into the group like that."

He was in Newport for almost a year before the musicians really began to gel as a group. In a letter to Paul Buck, he talked—among other things—about their rehearsals:

> I'm working in a cemetery filling in graves getting £15.50 a week. We've got a new band together which might be OK if I don't get thrown out for my voice. It's so futuristic. They won't let me play guitar because I can't move my fingers fast enough. But screw that, so I'm practicing at home and just singing with them whenever we get together for a practice. But you've got a bass. Every minute counts between now and next year. I'll be at the same address next month. Are you going abroad? I'm trying to save money but I'm just getting out of debt. If the band gets going OK we've got a gig in February, I think I'll hang around and pay my dues. You remember Chris? Blond Chris Payne. Last night he came up with his guitar for a go. I got my drums up here too. Next Friday I am going to take Deb to the flicks. I fancy going somewhere in Spring or Summer . . . We're 20 years old, halfway through. Love Wood. When I'm out of debt in maybe seven weeks I'll come to see you, okay. Johnny is a drum. Name and address of sender—American Sam.

The next letter to Paul Buck is dated October 24, 1973.

> Dear Pablo, great stuff about bass and it looks good too. What make is it? A Fender? I thought you had half a million saved up, to put the down payment on a transcontinental sleeper bus or something. About 3 weeks ago I had a £30 quid tax rebate and this typewriter cost £10 and as for the other fucking £20 who knows. I'll give you a quick rundown on what's been going on down here. This is how it is. This band is called Deus Ex Machina, and there's four of us. The lead guitarist is called Rob and he's an egomaniac like myself and he's OK. Then there's Al on the bass and he's a bit neurotic, you know, a bit dodgy baby, and Rob, I suppose he's the guy who makes the decisions, and he told me that he had a secret plan to get rid of him on account of his neurosis, although he's a nice bloke maybe he's not strong enough to stand the pace. Then there's Geoff [sic] the drummer who's much older than us with a bit of experience but again he gets a bit down about chicks etc. But he's bloody good but maybe he'll go too in time. So there you have it. Oh yeah, and there's me doing the sort of Mick Jagger bit and a bit of acoustic. We did four gigs last week. The first one was playing

at the student union disco which we played good although I was shitting because it was my first gig but I learnt much there. And the next day we went
to play in a party in a hotel in Shrewsbury, one of the bass player's friends'
21st. That was a rub out because the hotel manager turned the main fuse
off—ha ha. Then on the way back the van ran out of petrol and me and Rob
walked 7 miles back into Newport at 3 o'clock in the morning. The typewriter nearly broke down back there. After that it gets better and better. We
played the famed Kensington Club which is a big club where people like Dr.
John play on tours and on Monday nights where they have a crud night
where they only charge 15p and bands trying to make it play. We were the
only band on and there was 776 people there. The manager said after it was
great. There was all these teenage typists and smooth trendy guys and we
came on looking dead rough and went straight into "Tobacco Road" and "[I]
Can't Explain," etc. I was sweating like a pig and I had black nail varnish on
with me leathers. Rob was wearing an old dressing gown with an Elvis
t-shirt underneath with braces. Then we played at the Arts College Dance
supporting Good Habit who charged £100 which is a fuck of a lot. I was
completely drunk and wearing clowns trousers and we played really good.
We even whipped out "Johnny Be Good" [sic] which we'd never played before. So that's how it is. We're just practicing at the moment. Thank you for
your letter. There ain't much to do except be a rock and roller and maybe get
a little drunk and type all through the night. I'm still working sort of but I
don't go in much now. Well they won't sack me. Good pictures. Here's one
of me in a graveyard. [He encloses a photograph of himself, with shoulder-
length hair.] I'd been up the pub with the diggers and they drank 3 pints
with an empty belly in 25 minutes so I was drunk. And there was a pretty
girl with a camera so I got her to snap me and send me a print. Come on,
keep playing bass. Love from me to you. Woodrow Wilson, President of the
United States. PS I'm going to marry Princess Anne, I'm going to sing for
a big old band, toot my flute til the bird-seeds fly and I'm going to get old
and die.

Shortly after, Deus Ex Machina was renamed with the less complex
moniker of the Vultures. Richard Frame still has a poster for the group
"with a picture of a flock of vultures flying along, drawn by Woody, and
faces of the group. I had Joe's room when he moved out. He left the drum

kit and the ukulele." Later Woody came to collect his drum kit, but seemed to forget about the ukulele. When the Clash played a show in Bristol at the end of 1977, Joe Strummer spotted Richard Frame in the audience. "Hey, Frame," he hollered out in between numbers. "Where's my fuckin' ukulele?" Richard Frame also has a tape of Woody Mellor singing a song entitled "Bumblebee Blues," probably the first song he recorded, a grumbling twelve-bar blues. At the beginning of it Woody is asking someone called Martin, who also plays guitar on the tune, if he is putting his fingers in the right place on the fretboard of his guitar.

Woody Mellor wrote to Carol Roundhill about the group:

> I'm playing in a Rock 'n' Roll band called the Vultures. It's a funny sort of band, one minute we'll be hating each others guts and splitting up the band, and the next we'll be as close as brothers getting drunk together. At the moment we're in one of the former states. I'm doing a few cartoons and a bit of writing. Recently I've been taking everything about Dylan Thomas out of the library and reading till dawn. I think I know everything there is to know about him, except for one thing—I can't find a book of his poems! There's 101 books on "The Art of Dylan Thomas" or "The Life of Dylan Thomas" or "The Storys [sic] of Dylan Thomas" or "The Broadcasts of Dylan Thomas" but not one book of poems. I think they expect every Welsh home to already have one. I've got a really nice sunny room. It seems to catch the sun all through the day except for the late evening, and I spend a great deal of time with my feet on the window ledge watching nothing in particular. I did have a job but I was fired for sleeping on the job. They didn't give me a second chance! Deborah lives 10 miles down the road in Cardiff. I go and see her once in a blue moon, but she's really tough and mean now! Grr Grr!

Woody was not a great success as a gravedigger; he was not particularly strong and did not prove good at digging six-foot-deep holes in the ground. He was soon transferred to the less arduous task of clearing the cemetery of rubbish and general debris. "I wasn't strong enough to dig graves," he said. "The first morning they'd told me to dig a grave and when they came back I'd gone down about three inches. And so they said, 'Oh, that's useless.' So they set me on just cleaning up the cemetery. A really, really, really big one.

And they told me to go and pick up every glass jam jar or piece thereof. The cemetery was enormous, and they'd been leaving jam jars with flowers in them there since the twenties. In the winter of '72–'73 I was working in the graveyard. That was a really tough winter too."

Tymon Dogg drove down from London, arriving in Newport in the morning, and went to the graveyard, where "I went and had a cup of tea with these gravediggers. They called him Johnny. It was funny, they thought Johnny never really got involved in anything. I think they thought he was a bit slow or something, because he wasn't interested in stone and talking about it, so they knew he was a bit different."

The money he earned in the cemetery gave Woody greater scope for his generosity; when Gill Calvert was depressed, he bought her a pair of new trousers. At the time he was experimenting with further names; Johnny Caramello and Rooney were two of these.

On one visit to London from Wales, his cousin Iain Gillies saw Woody briefly; he felt that his time in Newport had brought about a change and was doing him good: "He was all exaggerated sideburns and flashing smashed, decrepit teeth. He had a new level of liveliness that I had not seen before. Anna, his mother, would tell us about Joe's comings and goings. She told me in 1973 they were giving Joe a year to decide what he was going to do."

This decision of Ron and Anna to let their son run with his freedom seemed to be paying off, although not every appearance of the Vultures fully hit the spot: "We played obviously the art-school dance or whatever. And we had made it to the Granary in Bristol, but we were godawful and they bottled us off [threw us out]. We were playing the Who's 'Can't Explain,' 'Tobacco Road,' and also anything that was popular at the time. I think we had a version of 'Hocus Pocus' by Focus that the lead guitarist wanted to play, because it was obviously all lead guitar or whatever. We were trying to play anything that wouldn't get us bottled off, really."

At this stage in his life Woody Mellor was not a great drinker. "He despised people on benders," said Gill Calvert. "We couldn't stand the hippies who were deadbeats. He had contempt for them too. He'd take what was going but he was fueled and driven." Gill saw a lot of Woody as she and Mickey Foote were not always getting on; she would end up going over to Woody's at 12 Pentonville: "We'd have mushrooms and toast and I taught him about Van Morrison who he didn't seem to know anything about: *Astral Weeks* was a very important record to be into, but he'd never heard it. And we became friends and sort of confidantes. I had one brief conversation with him about David. In those days it would be considered extremely uncool to admit to indulging in any sort of self-reflection. All your life was about the *now*. That was particularly Joe's thinking." Gill Calvert was known for being an extremely pretty young woman. So it is hardly surprising that between her and Woody there was often, as she puts it, "a kind of suggestion." Such a semiplatonic relationship with a member of the opposite sex fits the precise pattern of Woody Mellor's relationships with women at this time. Later, he confided to the photographer Pennie Smith that he had believed that women weren't really interested in him, and felt, as he put it to her, "like the ugly duckling." As we know, the "ugly duckling" of fairy-tale legend turned into a beautiful swan. But this would not happen for some time, and in the process Woody would undergo a complete volteface on his previous, more innocent attitudes. All the same, Gill Calvert received a shock when Woody told her that he had found a new flat: "It's next door to where you live. I thought, 'Well, that's a bit odd. Because you won't be able to sneak round to see me then.'"

This flat, next door to Gill Calvert and Mickey Foote, was at 16 Clyffard Crescent. Not long after that, early in 1974, "he suddenly didn't have any flat at all," said Gill. Woody had failed to pay the rent. "And then he lived in our place." Woody slept in the living room: "The return for him living in our place was that he'd write Mickey's thesis." Although Mickey Foote was studying fine art, his final-year thesis was on a subject familiar to Woody Mellor: pop music. "Woody sat at the typewriter with a note on the door saying, '3,000 words, 4,000 to go.' It was no problem for him to write this. We fed and housed him."

In May 1974 Woody Mellor "realized that we weren't going to get anywhere in Newport," Joe said. "The lead guitarist was wanting to go up the valleys and settle down with a woman, and everything was wrong with the group. So I left Newport, and went back to London."

9

pillars of wisdom

1974-1975

When Woody moved back to London he had to find somewhere to live. Direct from Newport, Woody Mellor arrived on the doorstep of the new house that Tymon Dogg, Helen Cherry, and Dave and Gail Goodall were sharing, at 23 Chippenham Road, on Maida Hill off the Harrow Road.

"When he came back to London in 1974 he crashed there," said Tymon Dogg. "I had two rooms, and in one I'd put a grand piano—I played all the time. It was up at the top of the house and he came and slept in the other room."

Though not a squat, 23 Chippenham Road was a "short-life" house (i.e., one scheduled for demolition because of its run-down state) acquired by London Student Housing, which found homes for people involved in higher education in the capital; as Helen and Gail were both still students they qualified. "There was a minimal rent to pay," said Helen. "Twenty-three Chippenham Road was Dave Goodall's castle," said Gill Calvert, who moved into the property at the beginning of 1975 with Mickey Foote. "He could plumb and secure leaks: we had this series of plastic sheets to stop the rain coming in. Dave—who Joe always called Larry, for some reason—was a provider. And so in Chippenham Road there was hot water, a telephone, there was always food, there was a fire." Dave Goodall was also a gardener; among the vegetable plots he grew what had the reputation of being the best weed in West London. Occasionally crashing at 23 Chippenham Road, from their hometown of Manchester, were the members of a satirical rock group of considerable and justified acclaim called Alberto y Los Trios Paranoias, a festival crowd-pleaser; Tymon Dogg played with them on one of their albums. "The Albertos were fantastic," Joe once told me, to my surprise. The Albertos were managed by two former socialist university lecturers, Peter Jenner and Andrew King, who had looked after the early career of Pink Floyd.

Maida Hill enjoyed considerable notoriety as one of London's primary squatting districts. At the time, squatting was a common means of securing lodgings in many parts of the city for young people: three hundred people lived in squatted houses on one street alone. The Greater London Council (GLC) had purchased large tracts of semi-slum housing, intending to demolish the buildings and replace them with council estates (public housing). Although many of these properties had been bought by the GLC in the late 1960s, work on most of them was yet to begin and the combination of the free housing they would provide in the meantime along with cash from unemployment benefits contributed to the British music explosion of the mid-1970s.

There was another attraction for Woody Mellor: within the very notion of the squatting movement there was something of a political act, even though it might have been only the politics of outlaw idealism.

Dave and Gail Goodall ran That Tea Room, a whole-food restaurant situated a few hundred yards away, close to Westbourne Park tube station on Great Western Road. Most days Joe would eat at That Tea Room, where he would only smoke joints rolled with herbal tobacco, himself using Honey Rose brand, which tasted like little more than air.

After he had arrived at 23 Chippenham Road, Tymon Dogg introduced Woody to some new friends, Patrick Nother and Simon Cassell. A year before Woody Mellor arrived at 23 Chippenham Road Patrick Nother, Simon Cassell and Nigel Calvert, the brother of Gill, had "opened" a house at 101 Walterton Road, which crossed Chippenham Road: Dave and Gail Goodall had pointed out the derelict house to them. Patrick's brother Richard, who was studying for a degree in zoology, had also lived there for some six months, but the chaotic ambience distracted him from his final-year stud-

Until it, too, was finally demolished, 101 Walterton Road was
eventually the last surviving house on its side of the street.
(Julian Yewdall)

ies and he moved to a room at 86 Chippenham Road: as this house was
largely occupied by bikers who regularly smashed the place to pieces at
night before repairing it the next morning, this was not the most considered relocation. "Me and Joe were over there one night," remembered Pat
Nother, "and while we were there the bikers not only destroyed the house
but they cordoned off the street. They were quite polite about it: 'Are you all
right in there?' 'Yeah, we'll be all right.' Joe and myself sat smoking dope
while the house was destroyed around us by these biker gangs who turned

up on a massive orgy of destruction. We had the door locked and just sat there. In the morning we woke up as they were banging nails boarding up the broken windows and beginning to repair the house. Mad. They just took it apart. We thought, 'This is life.'"

Dave Goodall, who had influenced Woody in political matters, also "ran" 23 Chippenham Road. As Tymon Dogg, who had tutored him in musical matters, was also living there, it made sense for Woody to move round the corner to 101 Walterton Road, evading the assessing eyes of this pair of mentors. So very shortly after moving back up to London Woody Mellor moved into the only vacant room, in the basement of the house. By now he had a collection of guitars which he had "acquired," sometimes nefariously. "In '74 it did seem like life was in black and white," he said to Mal Peachy. "There didn't seem to be any color in life. There were rows and rows of buildings boarded up by the council and left to rot—for what reason I don't know. So the only thing to do was to kick in these abandoned buildings and then live in them. And thank God that happened, because if it hadn't I would have never been able to get a group together, because you're in a situation where you're absolutely penniless. I mean, if we hadn't had the squats, (a) for a place to live, and (b) so that we could set up a rock 'n' roll group and practice in them . . ."

The basement of 101 Walterton Road had a dirt floor, which later became the rehearsal space for the 101'ers. Outside in the backyard was the property's only working toilet. In the kitchen there were no cups. "You just had jam jars for drinking your tea out of and cold water to wash in," remembered Jules Yewdall, a friend of the Nothers' from their hometown in the Midlands. This can't have affected Woody Mellor too much: as his cousin Iain Gillies told me, "Joe never liked washing. He never saw the point in having baths." But the house-dwellers clubbed together and bought a tin tub that they would fill from pans boiled on the gas stove. Bicycles were kept in the bathroom—people collecting or leaving them would walk in, say hello to whoever was bathing, and leave. The house was severely flea-infested. "You could feel them coming up to your waist," said Gill Calvert. "In the summer it got really out of control."

Deborah Kartun, who continued for the next couple of years to sporadically see Woody after he had returned to London, thought 101 Walterton Road was "squalid." Woody looked homeward when it came to hygiene.

"His mother told me that Joe would bring his laundry down from London and once she washed eighty-seven socks and not one of them matched another," recalled Iain Gillies.

Down in Upper Warlingham Woody's parents had recovered themselves to some extent from the shock of David's death. Some visitors felt that Anna was anesthetizing herself with alcohol. Disappearing to bed early each evening, Anna would miss the sight of her husband letting his hair down as cocktails were made and drank, keeping his visitors in stitches with his humor, the laughter growing louder as the hours wore on. "Ron had a really wicked humor," said his niece Maeri. "He would wind up poor Aunt Anna something terrible. He would provide these gin cocktails that were about seventy-five percent gin. He couldn't stand a gin and tonic without lemon: 'Are you sure you have a lemon?' he'd demand."

"You never knew when he was putting people on," said Joe's cousin Alasdair Gillies. "He would make mock-disparaging comments toward women about feminism to get an argument going. He was very enigmatic, but very entertaining. He was also very insecure: he felt that he'd been abandoned when he'd been sent off to school. He believed no one wanted to know him or talk to him. He was very well informed and very left-wing. A pukka [first-rate] Englishman, but also almost Marxist. Later I thought Joe was becoming like his father, an eccentric Englishman."

The contrast of 101 Walterton Road with home was clear to Woody. "No one would have lived where we lived," he told Mal Peachy. "It was an abandoned bomb site from the war. I had a guy come in. He was expert at connecting us to the main electricity. I'll never forget this: he came in, this guy with overalls on and a welder's mask, and huge, huge gauntlets. And he just advanced up the basement corridor, and thrust his power cable into the main electricity. Like he reconnected the house into the National Grid, and I'll never forget the shower of sparks was like twenty feet long—blue sparks flew down the corridor, and blew him backward. But he jammed the bloody leads into the main electricity, and then we could plug in and start playing. It was that kind of situation we were dealing with."

On July 9, 1974, Woody Mellor wrote to Paul Buck:

Dear Pablo, I got your letter and I was just trying to whip off a quick reply when I got two more. I've got the rock 'n' rolling bug again and am at this moment trying to hustle up money for some twelve-inch speakers for a cabinet I just made. I'm living in a basement too at 101 Walterton Road, W9, around the corner from 23 Chippenham. There's a drum kit in the next room and I've rigged up a stack for two guitars and we've been having a few sessions lately so we're talking about forming a group. I've been getting into slide guitar, another guy plays alto sax, and another plays rhythm guitar and another plays drums. We've got no bass or lead guitars yet. We've tried out a Danish guy on lead guitar but we really get into the music something chronic and he was very flash but a bit cold. None of us can play bass except for that bass line which goes Dum-e-Dum-De-Dum in rock 'n' roll anyway. I'm going to borrow Dick's bass off him. Talking of drums, I went to Newport and arranged to meet a Transit there, but the drum keeper left for Nottingham one hour before and his house was locked. Tough shit. I'll be down within a couple of weeks. I might have to work a week in a factory to get money for the twelve-inch speakers. Also going to buy some machine-heads and maybe a bridge for my slide guitar. See you in two weeks. Come up any time you want. Wait until I get more stacks ready. Love Wood.

On July 20, 1974, Woody Mellor went to the first one-day rock festival held in the grounds of Knebworth House, forty miles north of London in Hertfordshire. Along with 100,000 other fans he watched an impressive bill topped by the Allman Brothers Band, legendary for both their epic sets and their drug consumption, playing for the first time in Britain. Also performing, on a magically warm day, were Van Morrison, the Doobie Brothers, Tim Buckley, the Mahavishnu Orchestra and the Sensational Alex Harvey Band, whose uncompromisingly theatrical style was to be an influence on many future punks, including Mick Jones and Paul Simonon. "We saw Joe wandering through the crowd," said his old schoolmate Ken Powell, who had gone along to the event with Adrian Greaves. "His personality had changed. You couldn't get close to him: he certainly wasn't totally with us. His teeth were terrible. His speech was different. He had a pretty ordinary middle-class accent when he was at school. Now it was as though he was trying to make his speech be street-cred, like Mick Jagger did." (My take on Joe's voice change is that the influences on it were more international; the accent he came up with is an Englishman trying to emulate Bob Dylan's laconic Midwest cadences.)

Not much later Andy Ward, by now drummer with Camel, had an experience not too dissimilar. "The next time I ran into [Joe] was when he was playing a gig with the 101'ers somewhere off the Portobello Road. I was a full-on long-haired hippie by then, playing with a prog-rock band. He really scared me: he was disheveled and toothless—his teeth were awful. He was calling himself Woody. He asked me to come to the gig and I didn't go. Later I saw him at a party and he said, 'I've got a bone to pick with you.' Paul Buck told me Joe said that I'd snubbed him. But I didn't let on that the reason I didn't go to the gig was because I was too scared."

By 1974 the British music scene was splintering into factions: heavy rock—the Who, Led Zeppelin, the Rolling Stones; progressive rock—Emerson, Lake and Palmer, Yes and Genesis; glam rock—David Bowie, Roxy Music. To like one almost precluded you from liking another. This sense of division increased sharply when the American group the New York Dolls, who looked like hookers from Manhattan's Lower East Side and whose blasting, double-lead-guitar wall of sound was an amalgam of early Rolling Stones, the MC5 and the Shangri-las, burst upon the scene. An immense influence on punk rock, the New York Dolls wore lipstick, high heels, satin and leather, as though they had stepped out of the Stones' poster for "Have You Seen Your Mother." David Johansen, the lead singer, was like a clone of Mick Jagger; his songwriting partner, Johnny Thunders, similarly established himself as a cartoon version of Keith Richards. Not only were the Dolls' songs sharp and very short, but they also had suitably precise titles: "Pills," "Personality Crisis," "Subway Train," "Bad Girl," to name just a few.

Woody Mellor had watched the Dolls on their only British television performance, in 1974 on the BBC's weekly progressive show *The Old Grey Whistle Test*. Bob Harris, the program's avuncular host, had dismissed their appearance as "mock rock." "I'll never forget watching Johnny Thunders on that program on BBC 2, the *Whistle Test*," Joe told Mal Peachy. "Johnny Thunders and his crew—the Dolls—played two numbers. I remember all the musicians in Newport and all the students in the Union bar watching it on the television there, and it just wiped everybody out: the attitude, the clothes, it was different from all this earnest musician-worshipping nonsense that had come in with progressive rock. When the Dolls played that British TV show, that just gave us legs and arms, and the spirit to really get into it."

Something was afoot. A shift in the culture of the British music scene was reflected by the rise of the *New Musical Express*—soon to be known simply as *NME*—over the *Melody Maker*, which since 1967 had been required reading for music fans. Modeled on semi-underground music publications from the United States, and featuring a scathing satirical humor, the *NME*'s sales overtook those of *Melody Maker*. "It was the house rag at 101," said Patrick Nother.

An indication that change was under way came in the late summer of 1974, when the *NME* put Dr. Feelgood on its cover. This new group had had no record success so far, emerging from the grassroots movement of the London pub-rock scene: a number of pubs had turned themselves into venues at which largely unsigned groups played. A good-time scene fueled by beer, pub rock still had its star acts, among them Dr. Feelgood.

The Feelgoods, as they were invariably known, featured a part speed-freak, part intellectual guitarist named Wilko Johnson; a gruff but inspired singer in Lee Brilleaux, his skinny ties a trademark; bass player John B. Sparks; and drummer John "The Big Figure" Martin. What set the Feelgoods apart from virtually every other group in the country was that their set list consisted entirely of choppy rhythm-and-blues songs, classics and originals, that lasted no more than three minutes; they wore their hair short and dressed in tight-trousered suits with shirts and ties; and their stage act was fantastic. Wilko soared about the stage as though he were propelled along high-tension wires, brandishing his Telecaster guitar like a rifle; Lee Brilleaux grunted and growled at the front of the stage, leaning into his mike and smoking cigarettes; and the rhythm section just held it all down, anchoring the two front men so they wouldn't float away. Despite their surly appearance, the Feelgoods had an aura of approachability, one of us. Dr. Feelgood were the first steps of British punk; without them, that crucial cultural movement, still more than two years off from altering the entire aesthetic dynamic of the last quarter of the twentieth century, might never have happened. They were a very important group indeed, as noted by no less an unexpected authority than the reggae star Bob Marley; on his 1977 single "Punky Reggae Party," extolling the punk-reggae link, one line ran, "The Jam, the Clash, the Feelgoods too."

Dr. Feelgood were still a pub-rock group, but one that proved so inspirational to Woody Mellor that Wilko Johnson's Telecaster weapon-wielding was the reason that the future Joe Strummer purchased that make of guitar. He had decided that he also could form such a group. "Pub rock was going on and we sort of fell into naturally playing rhythm and blues 'cause it was easy, or we thought it was," he told me. "Although the 101'ers was really a squat band formed in a squat in the summer of 1974. During this time I held down jobs, you know. I worked for three months in Hyde Park, trying to save money for the group, trimming flower beds, cutting hedges."

With its opportunities for smoking spliffs on the job, "park work" was at that time considered desirable summer employment. "Oh, it was horrible. Yeah, horrible because the hedge goes on forever, you know that. You know, the hedge it ain't never gonna end, because Hyde Park is vast. It's like painting the Forth Bridge—you never get to the end of it. I just hated that."

At the end of the summer Woody took another job, doing general maintenance and cleaning at the English National Opera in St. Martin's Lane by Trafalgar Square: "It was kind of a much better job 'cause you could go and hide away in this huge Victorian building. I used to take my guitar into work and put my brown coat on and then disappear off up into the upper attic in these little cubbyholes so no one could ever find you, and practice the guitar. I quite liked it, but I've hated opera from hearing opera constantly, all day long, for three months. I've always hated opera since that time." At the end of three months Woody Mellor was discovered hunkered away practicing his guitar, and was fired. He managed to obtain financial compensation and walked out of the job with £120.

One morning before that Joe had commuted into central London with Jules Yewdall, who was heading for the London School of Printing, where he studied photography. "We went into town early in the morning. It was about 7:30 and he was standing on Trafalgar Square by the steps at St. Martin's church. I was rolling up a joint and saying, 'I really want to travel around the world and see what's going on out there.' He said, 'I want to be a rock 'n' roll star. That's what I want to be.'"

This would conflict with the reasons that Woody later offered for getting a group together. The 101'ers, Joe told me, "was really formed because busking had become too heavy. They started to put microphones and speakers down in the subways. I mean, at the best of times you had to run from the Transport Police. But when I saw the microphones and speakers installed in Leicester Square, or Oxford Circus, I thought, Ah . . . You know, a group of squatters trying to live over the summer. We saw it as maybe we can keep body and soul together if we can get a few gigs in these Irish pubs. I never really saw it as something to do permanently. It was like a stop-gap measure. I couldn't really see what I was going to do with my life. I stood outside the Elephant and Castle pub on Elgin Avenue, watching this Irish trio through the window—we were banned from the pub 'cause we were dirty squatters. I thought, 'I could do that, you know, me and my mates. Surely we could do that.' We put it together in the squat with just odds and ends. I borrowed money for a small PA off a drug dealer."

This last bit was not true, however. Woody Mellor actually got money for the PA from Arabella Churchill, great-granddaughter of Prime Minister Winston Churchill, whom he'd met at Glastonbury in 1971. The money was a loan: in 1997 Joe Strummer finally wrote her a check to repay it, but Arabella never cashed it. Part of this PA had formerly belonged to Pink Floyd. "For some reason Pink Floyd had like a hundred speakers in their PA system and they were selling it off—I don't know why," he told me. "And we managed to get one of the bass-bins which we used as a bass speaker from their PA. I took a drawer I found in a skip and cut a hole in it and mounted a speaker in the drawer. And I used to stand the drawer up and place a Linear Concorde amp on top."

Pat Nother shared the basement room at 101 Walterton Road with Woody, each sleeping on a "scummy, horrible" mattress. "When he was sleeping, he used to grind his teeth so much that it sounded like an underground train," Pat said. "He had this James Dean hairstyle, although at first he had fairly long hair, and he wore this tacky leather jacket with a tag on the back that read, in Latin, 'I'm No Chicken.' He picked up on the leather jacket a long time before that stuff was in vogue. I don't know if it was just a Jim Morrison influence, Joe got into everyone. Although he was into the Doors at that time, that doesn't mean that that enthusiasm lasted. He'd have stripped the carcass of everything he could get off it, he'd have eaten the head, and he'd have sucked the bones of the Doors while he was interested in them: there's a lot of meat and juice there to take on, and he'd have tried his best to get as much out of it as possible. That's what he was about everything."

There was another room in the basement, which became the musical practice room. "We used to piss on our fingertips to make them hard so that we could play our guitars. He was a huge fan of *Seven Pillars of Wisdom* by

T. E. Lawrence—Lawrence of Arabia. I had the impression it was one of the only books he'd read at the time. In the *Lawrence of Arabia* film Peter O'Toole lets matches burn down to his fingers, and Joe would do that to prove his fingers were strong enough to play the guitar. I remember Joe woke me up in the middle of the night and said, 'Patrick, I've got the new Elmore James riff!' And he played me this Elmore James riff on the record and he was so thrilled he could do it on the guitar as well.

"I'd loved rock 'n' roll as a teenager, and then I just thought it wasn't happening, although I would listen to Van Morrison. But with Joe in the basement I used to sit up late and it would be, 'Have you ever tried twelve-bar?' And he'd get out his steel-string guitar, and we'd boogie along for about a dozen songs, and go and sit on the staircase in 101. 'Do you know what?' he really did say to me at one point. 'I'm going to be a rock 'n' roll star. Do you want to be one too? We can be rock 'n' roll stars.'"

Might you not fear you were tempting fate by publicly proclaiming your imminent stardom? In the case of the future Joe Strummer, it seems that by laying his cards on the table he was seeking to motivate himself. "The guy just planked out this incredible energy 'cos he knows what he's doing, and he's got the reserves to do it, and he puts his all into it, and that's why everyone likes Joe," said Pat Nother. Pat also recalls Woody seeing the pair of rock 'n' roll movies *That'll Be the Day* and its sequel *Stardust*, both of which he found inspiring. Pat remembered him becoming wide-eyed with awe when he met Wishbone Ash's lighting man. "He was so into the whole rock 'n' roll thing, he absolutely loved it: it was an almost childish delight at the whole spectacle. He couldn't really play the guitar, but he wrote bloody good songs. He put his heart into it, which is the essence of the bloody thing."

In the basement of 101 Walterton Road, with filthy old mattresses res-cued from the trash arranged around the walls as "soundproofing," Woody Mellor assiduously rehearsed with the musicians he had enlisted to assist him in fulfilling the personal dream he had revealed to Pat. Pat himself was pulled in to play the bass borrowed from Dick the Shit, despite never hav-ing previously picked up such an instrument. Simon Cassell had an alto saxophone he had bought in Portobello Market some time before; naturally he was promptly enlisted. On drums was a recent exile from Chile, Antonio Narvaez, on a kit borrowed from someone in a nearby squat. The most ac-complished of those rehearsing was Alvaro Pena-Rojas, who had played professionally as a tenor sax player and chalked up a trio of hits before he, like Antonio, fled Chile after the 1973 coup. You may note that in this lineup of what would become the 101'ers, a crucial rock 'n' roll element is absent: that of lead guitar—sometimes it seemed Woody Mellor needed to create situations to work against.

By the end of the summer of 1974 these musicians had a set list of half a dozen songs, all rhythm-and-blues or rock 'n' roll covers: two Chuck Berry songs, "No Particular Place to Go" and "Roll Over Beethoven," Larry Williams's "Bony Moronie" and Van Morrison's "Gloria," which Woody still adored. Now they were ready to test themselves at a live show, a benefit for the Chilean resistance. Originally scheduled for September 14, 1974, the show was suddenly moved to Friday, September 6, at the Telegraph, a music pub at 228 Brixton Hill, close to Brixton prison, another outsider part of London. Two weeks before the original date, Antonio Narvaez decided to leave London on holiday. Although Richard Nother, Pat's brother, had never played drums—he owned a pair of bongos and a clarinet—he was immediately brought in on the instrument.

When the gig was moved forward, Richard Nother was left with only five days of rehearsal. "I was playing bongos, and they asked me to play the drums, which I had never played before. Then the gig was moved forward a week: my first gig!" Richard Nother acquired a new name, bestowed by Woody. When I first met him I assumed that someone called Richard Dudanski must be Polish, noting his Slavic cheekbones, high forehead and slicked-back hair. But Richard Nother is of quintessential English stock; Joe had picked up on the same features that I perceived. Proprietorially, Woody bequeathed him a second nickname, inspired by his thin and wiry appearance: Richard "Snakehips" Dudanski. This random scattering of sobriquets is very affectionate—they are almost pet names, rather than nicknames, a very honest, intimate and exclusive way of greeting friends, putting them at ease straightaway. But they are also controlling.

"People said he wanted to be a star," said Richard Dudanski. "He did, but we just wanted to get a working band together. He had strong ambition. I don't think he necessarily knew the hows or the whats, but he wanted to get there. The whole myth of the life was attractive to him."

Woody went down to Warlingham to pick up an old suit of his father's to use as his stage outfit. For the Telegraph gig the group was billed as El Huaso and the 101 All Stars: *el huaso* is Spanish for "countryman," referring to the group's remaining Chilean, Alvaro Pena-Rojas. They were the opening act for the Reggae Men, who would shortly mutate into Matumbi, one of the most influential reggae acts to come out of England. El Huaso and the 101 All Stars turned up at the Telegraph on September 6 with neither drums nor amps, assuming they could borrow these from the headline act. Joe told *Melody Maker*'s Paolo Hewitt in 1981: "We didn't know how to play, you know. None of us knew, and Matumbi lent us all their gear, and I've never come across that since. Can you believe that? And they were really late. Their

Dear Lady

I should have kissed you in the field at Windsor when I put the blanket round you Now I lost your Address.

BAND comes together better and better but how Far Can it go borrowing money left Right and centre Ha ha ha ! Send me the address of you to this one —: ME, 101, WALTERTON ROAD, W.9. Love Johnny

P.S. I LOOK LIKE A SKINHEAD (THIS IS A WARNING !)

To Anne Day, "Woody" was evidently still allowed to be "Johnny."
(Anne Day)

van broke down and they were two hours late and there was hardly time for them to do their set. But they still lent us their drum kit and their amps. I thought that was great and I've always supported Matumbi since."

"They were crap!" said Clive Timperley, Woody's old friend from Vomit Heights. "Strummer with this mad suit and shaking leg, fantastic. That was it really. No lead guitar. They were crap but fun."

Pat Nother agreed: "About four or five times we turned up with instruments. To call them gigs is stretching it. My memories are more of things like standing in a [squat that was once a] cinema in puddles of water, very worried about the effect on the electricity power supply. We played at parties in houses, which involved basements being turned into venues. I mucked around a few times with Joe—that was it, and then it collapsed for me."

As a very amused Joe said of Pat Nother to Paolo Hewitt, "He said to me in a pub, 'I can't believe that we're in a group.' And I said, 'What do you mean?' He said, 'I can't believe we are in a group. So I'm going to leave.' He said that to me!" Before he left the band, Pat revealed, they rehearsed all the time. "We would play all day long in the basement of 101 and people would come and watch us. But one day the saxophone got ripped off. This was terrible. 'It's been stolen. We need it for our group. Where's it gone?' So Joe and myself went on this two-day trip to the nether regions of West London."

Eventually they retrieved it from another squat; but the thief, clearly disturbed, killed himself two days later. Imagining you were an outlaw from society had its drawbacks. "Joe's street-punk thing was just blagging [talk]. Once Joe pissed off some teddy boys with a flick-knife [switchblade]. These guys got him at University College, London. There was a gig there, and me and Joe certainly weren't going to pay. We climbed through the loo window, and these teddy boys came in as we were climbing in, and came up to Joe. He pulled out his flick-knife, and they pulled out their flick-knives, and he does a ballet dance. I was stuck in the window watching this thing. He was very good: it was all bluff on both sides—it was as though it was choreographed. Eventually everyone backs off, and honor is saved. No one was going to knife anyone."

Following that one gig at the Telegraph, Richard "Snakehips" Dudanski went on holiday and was replaced by the original drummer, Antonio Narvaez, now back in London. In mid-October there was a benefit for the Chilean resistance at the Royal College of Art in Kensington Gore. It was a logical event for the 101 All Stars to play, and Alvaro promptly offered their services. Having started off with the rock 'n' roll classic "Bony Moronie," the group were two numbers into their set before the audience turned against them: "Get this capitalist rock 'n' roll out of here," as Joe remembered it. As though proof of that old adage that no act of kindness goes unpunished, the squat-rockers—who could hardly have lived a life more untainted by capitalism—were booed off the stage.

Pat Nother was replaced by a character known as Mole (actually Maurice Chesterton); efficient on guitar, he had never previously played bass. There was another new member: Julian "Jules" Yewdall was briefly brought in on lead vocals and harmonica, leaving Woody free to concentrate on his rudimentary rhythm guitar playing, while still contributing the occasional vocal.

But where could the 101'ers play? In November an approach was made for a residency to the landlord of their local pub, the Chippenham, a rambling rough pub popular with Irish laborers; ornately decorated with rococo plasterwork and with a central semicircular bar, "the Chip" had the ambience and character of a Wild West saloon.

The group were told that, for a rental of one pound, they could play upstairs in a room with its own small stage. Joe recalled their first gig there, on Wednesday, December 4, 1974: "We never really got off the ground until we rented that room above the Chip. Because we couldn't play, how could we get any gigs? The only thing we could do to learn to play was to start our own club up. I'd go to gigs with two bricks in a shoulder bag," said Joe to Mal Peachy, "and these bricks were to sit in the deck of a record player, upturned with a broom handle screwed in it which was the mike stand. And the mike was taped on the top, and the bricks were there to drop into the record player to keep the thing steady so the mike didn't fall over. I mean, we built our equipment, and we booked our own club. No one was going to book us. Can you imagine what we looked like? A bunch of crazed squatters. We found a pub with a room upstairs and we rented it for a quid for the evening, and that's how we learned to play, by doing it for ourselves— which is like the punk ethos. I mean, you gotta be able to go out there and do this for yourself, because no one is gonna give it to you. We clawed our way in."

The room was named the Charlie Pigdog, after a brown and white Jack Russell who lived at 23 Chippenham Road, the pet of Dave and Gail Goodall. Charlie Pigdog would from time to time wander onstage during the group's sets. As would musicians besides the core group of Woody Mellor, Simon Cassell, Alvaro Pena-Rojas, Antonio Narvaez and the new members Jules Yewdall and Mole. From time to time, Tymon Dogg would play. Clive Timperley came along to the second night, December 11. "Bring your guitar next time," Woody told him.

"It got really jumping, 'cos all the squatters from all over Maida Hill, Maida Vale, West London would come down," said Joe, "and it soon became like a real big mash-up, and gypsies would come and rip everybody off and throw people's coats out the window, and mayhem broke loose. We were onstage playing and the police raided the place. We carried on playing, and it was like playing a soundtrack to this crazy thing going on everywhere. The police rushed in—they didn't know who to search or what, with all these filthy squatters and gypsies and God knows what in this room. And like we keep playing, and I think we were doing 'Gloria'—that's when we started to extend it into a twenty-minute jam."

Around this time all the 101'ers chipped in and bought a severely beat-up secondhand hearse for fifty pounds. Now they had something in which to transport their equipment. Later it was exchanged for a van. Both vehicles were somewhat erratic, and for local gigs the 101'ers would often walk to the venues, pushing the equipment in an old pram.

The problem of no lead guitarist was about to be resolved. Clive Timperley was yet another character in the life of Woody Mellor who fulfilled a role of mentor. He had moved on from the student life at Vomit Heights and was living in the extremely well-heeled neighborhood of Knightsbridge, just behind Harrods, in a flat that belonged to his brother. A boring day job gave him the freedom to play with groups in the evening. As far back as Ash Grove he had been playing with Foxton Flight, who had once supported Medicine Head at the Marquee, a gig that Woody came to see, at Clive's invitation ("He was chuffed [thrilled] he was on a guest list at the Marquee. But he was almost overimpressed. I think it galvanized him more into wanting to become a musician.").

By the time he saw their second Charlie Pigdog Club date, the 101'ers had gotten much better, thought Clive, who found himself frequently tutor-

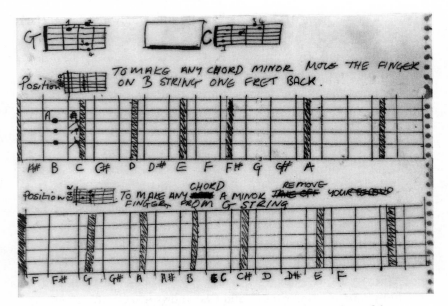

There was always a rudimentary element to Joe's understanding of the guitar. *(Lucinda Mellor)*

ing Woody. At around ten or eleven in the evening Clive's phone would ring. "What are you doing?" Woody would demand gruffly, before he jumped in a minicab for the ten-minute ride down to Knightsbridge across Hyde Park. "He used to come over with his guitars, four or five at a time, a steel-string acoustic, an electric, solid electric, and this Hoffner Verithin. We'd have a guitar workshop into the early hours of the morning."

Then Woody made Clive Timperley an offer. "He rang me up and said, 'We'd like you to join the 101'ers.' I thought, 'Good, they're gigging every week.' I'd wanted a regular gig. I joined them." As soon as Clive joined the 101'ers Woody Mellor renamed him, by reversing the letters of his Christian name: so mild, studious Clive became "Evil C" Timperley. "Clive had strong musical knowledge," said Helen Cherry, "and put a lot of it together musically for them, helping it be in tune and in rhythm and in time, to get a tough rock 'n' roll thing, which is what Joe wanted. He was after a particular sound, but I don't know if he knew how to get it."

Richard Dudanski and Esperanza Romero, his new Spanish girlfriend, returned to London before Christmas 1974 and moved into 86 Chippenham Road. When Esperanza's sister Paloma turned up in London, Richard told her of a free room at 101 Walterton Road. Pat Nother remembered her arrival at 101, when he happened to be sitting with Woody: "The first time I saw Paloma she walked in the door and he said to me: 'Agi agam aggo aging tago magake hager miagne.' All the boarding-school and grammar-school boys spoke ago-pago: 'ag' in front of every vowel sound. Joe was saying, 'I'm going to make her mine.' He fell in love with her when she walked in the door." "I had a Bolivian boyfriend called Herman," said Paloma. "We were breaking up. Joe kept asking me out. We went to see Chuck Berry in London somewhere, but he to me was nothing after seeing the 101'ers. We went to see Lou Reed and he was very boring. Before punk we were together for about two years."

Woody Mellor and Paloma Romero became an item, and she moved with him into the vacant room at 101, at the front of the first floor. With an interest in international relations, Woody even claimed to Helen Cherry that he had "figured out Spanish: you just put 'o' on the end of every word."

The two Romero sisters could not legally remain in Britain. What could be done? They would have to get married to British citizens. When it became clear during the summer of 1975 that the girls were liable to be deported, Richard Nother married Esperanza; they remain married to this day. But between Woody Mellor and Paloma there was a complication: Woody was already married. On May 16, 1975, there had been a wedding at St. Pancras Registry Office between himself and a South African named Pamela Jill Moolman, who wanted to stay in Britain; Pamela was a friend of a girl who had been living at 101 Walterton Road. For helping her out, she paid Woody £120, with which he promptly bought a Fender Telecaster. Although her boyfriend had the guitar of his dreams, the instrument wielded by Wilko Johnson with Dr. Feelgood, this was no help to Paloma. Richard's brother Pat Nother stepped into the breach and married her—with no fee involved. "People did that all the time then," said Gill Calvert. Paloma's relationship with Joe allowed him to open up, perhaps for the first time. "He told me about David—he said that his brother had chosen death and he had chosen life: he had decided to go for it entirely. As for his parents, he said, 'what a horrible thing—that shatters a family.'"

Now came a rush of creative energy. Woody Mellor began to write his first songs for the group. Was he inspired by being in love? This was evident from the words of the first song he wrote for the 101'ers, "Keys to Your Heart."

"All of us in the 101'ers were very intense rhythm-and-blues freaks— you know, really intense," Joe said about that initial effort. "We had a great knowledge of blues and rhythm and blues, and we just pulled our music out of that. And then, like in any group's life, I realized we had to start writing our own material. So I wrote 'Keys to Your Heart,' and I was just overjoyed that it came out good, and we could put it over in the set at the Chippenham. And people would still keep leaping around the room and dancing to it."

Jules Yewdall has a set of the words of ten of the 101'ers' songs, typed out by Joe on his own typewriter, accompanying a cassette recorded as the songs were played in the damp, mattress-soundproofed basement of 101 Walterton Road. The ten songs on the tape are staples of the 101'ers' live set and show the speed at which new songs had developed in fewer than six months: tunes such as "Motor Boys Motor," "Keys to Your Heart," "Mr. Sweety of the St. Moritz" and "Standing by a Silent Telephone."

These demos were specifically recorded by Joe Strummer to be placed in a bank vault by Jules Yewdall, to secure his legal status to their copyright. In that oh-so-familiar, adenoidal voice, whose tone manages both a grin and just the suspicion of a smirk, he ensures that each song is specifically identified. "That was 'Motor Boys Motor,' and this is 'The Keys to Your 'Eart,'" the "H" dropped so hard you can hear it fall.

The simplicity and directness of the songs is very apparent, and much of the material has the loose jamming feel of later Clash material. It is also perfectly clear that, despite an occasionally wobbly delivery, Joe Strummer has found his voice in the often hilarious narrative structure of the lyrics. It is evident that in 1975 so many of those creative aspects we might have believed developed only in the Clash were already present: that melodic moodiness of style, that drive of energy arrowing straight from the heart. These early songs show you that almost everything Joe would do in the Clash he was already attempting with the 101'ers: that odd discordant gruffness in his voice, the chopping rhythm guitar, the ironic asides. "Mr. Sweety of the St. Moritz" is fantastic in its lyrical, almost certainly autobiographical complexity, the sort of words he might well have written with the Clash; the song was written as a kind of note of criticism to the owner of the St. Moritz nightclub in Wardour Street in London's Soho, where the 101'ers played several times, starting on June 18, 1975.

> hey mr. sweety of the saint moritz we re cashing in all our chips
> life wont be so funny without your money but we re sick of
> playing all these hits

More personal is "Standing by a Silent Telephone." The song is disguised as Joe's lament to "Suzie": "I was living just for loving just from you." But she's not around, and doesn't call: "Standing by a silent telephone, me and bakelite all alone." "Me and bakelite all alone"—a small stroke of Joe Strummer genius.

The ability to make people smile in their hearts and on their faces was always one of Joe Strummer's talents. And many of these lyrics are frankly hilarious, evidence of a highly intelligent wit. On the "Bo Didelys' [sic] Six Gun Blues," the words are built around a perfect narrative structure: "But kettles don't boil if you watch em / And suns don't rise on demand."

Significantly, on the card inlay in the cassette tape, the man formerly known as Woody has scratched out the name "John Mellor" and replaced it with a new one: "JOE STRUMMER." Somewhere around May 1975 Woody Mellor decided to become Joe Strummer, unwilling to answer to any other name. Although "Joe" would insist that his contemporaries at 101 Walterton Road address him by his new name, it was more complex for those he had known longer: "Dave Goodall was allowed to still call him Woody," according to Gill Calvert. "In terms of the male hierarchy, the pecking order, Tymon and Dave were above Joe. Joe was a bit of a kid. He did want us to call him Joe, but he wouldn't make an issue of it with us." "Somewhere through the 101'ers," remembered Helen Cherry, "he was like, 'I'm Joe,' and you couldn't call him Woody—he'd be angry."

Things were falling into place for the 101'ers. Earlier that April, Allan Jones, Joe's old friend from Newport art school, had given the group a minute mention in *Melody Maker*'s "Hot Licks" gossip column. Tiny as this piece of publicity was, it served its purpose, as Joe later told Mal Peachy: "Dr. Feelgood came along, and there was a group called the Michigan Flyers, and there was us. And those three groups were fantastic. We fell into that scene, and we began to rock at the Elgin. 'Cos in Newport one of the students there was Allan Jones, who later began to edit *Melody Maker*, and he wrote a paragraph in *Melody Maker* when he was a cub reporter, about how the 101'ers could really rock, 'cos one day he came down to the Charlie Pigdog club, and I took this cutting [clipping]—and after I cut it out it was like three lines long and I should have left it on the page—but anyway I cut it out and it looked kinda like a postage stamp. And I took this, and some of the group, and we went around pubs in West London, and eventually at the Elgin [in Ladbroke Grove] I put this cutting on the bar, and the ginger-headed landlord picked it up and he went, 'All right: a fiver, Monday.' And that was when we first broke out of our own scene, and soon that became like a hot spot, us playing the Elgin in the back room.

"We used to push our gear there in a pram, and one night the pram got nicked while we were playing. I remember standing outside the pub going, 'This is a hard world. They've stolen the pram that we used to pile the amps up on.' And we'd push it back over the hill into Maida Vale. And then because he was doing such good business he switched us to a Thursday."

"this man is a star!"

1975-1976

One by one the houses in Walterton Road were being demolished by the council—it was as though a wartime ghetto was being relentlessly razed. Finally, the only house remaining—everything else around it a state of almost unidentifiable rubble—was 101 Walterton, tucked away down at the bottom of the street. Much as there had been problems with the property—the outside toilet, the lack of hot water, the fleas—the house and its in-built difficulties had not only bonded together a group of musicians and given them somewhere to live and rehearse, it had also supplied the name of their group. But the relatively settled existence at 101 Walterton Road was about to end. It too was scheduled for demolition.

By the middle of the summer, the Walterton crew had found a squat in a house at 36 St. Luke's Road, three streets east of Portobello Road, close to a vibrant West Indian district.

On July 26, 1975, *Melody Maker* published a full-length article by Allan Jones about the 101'ers, pushing the group up to a new level. Slanted extremely favorably toward his old friend Joe Strummer and mythologizing their underclass street existence, Jones began, "It was some time back in February that I first saw the 101'ers. They had residency in the Charlie Pigdog Club in West London. It was the kind of place which held extraordinary promises of violence. You walked in, took one look around, and wished you were the hell out of there."

Jones described the mayhem as assorted gypsies and Irishmen knocked the daylights out of each other while the group played their twenty-minute version of Van Morrison's "Gloria." "The band tore on, with Joe Strummer thrashing away at his guitar like there was no tomorrow, completely oblivious of the surrounding carnage. The police finally arrived, flashing blue lights, sirens, the whole works. Strummer battled on. He was finally confronted by the imposing figure of the law, stopped in mid-flight, staggered to a halt and looked up. 'Evening, officer,' he said . . ."

Jones's article considerably advanced the cause of the 101'ers: it helped the group secure a booking agency, Albion, specializing in alternative pub-rock-type acts; from now on they rarely were stuck for dates to play.

The dateline reads "Madrid." Woody Mellor (as he still is to his old pals) writes to his old friend Paul "Pablo Labritain" Buck:

Dear Pablo,

May the summer be with you. I'm in Espana but it is not green but brown. The food is greasy, good selection of switch-blades. Hopefully will get one for you. How is life and drums? Write me at 36 St. Lukes Road, W11. We're having trouble. Probably get kicked out. Rock 'n' roll taking a two week break. You must keep playing: that is the secret. Play for today and play for tomorrow. What this world needs is more rock. Relaxation I cannot find in fact. I'm strung out due to family [strife] here. Hope to escape to Morocco for a few days, but knowing the diplomatic relations between this country and that I'm not sure that's true. Love to Roz and your father. I think of green Sussex in this dry land. Must have another Coca Cola. Picking up the lingo a bit. Love Woody. If you get a packet for Peter Treetrunks it's for you.

"We hitchhiked to Morocco, with Richard and Esperanza, and rented a place. Joe did bring some hash back," said Paloma. "In Spain, we stayed at my parents' house in Malaga for two weeks. 'Why are you all fighting?' Joe asked, when everyone was giving their typically noisy opinion in conversation. Joe loved Spain: part of our courting was about the Spanish Civil War. The fight for freedom really interested him."

Once Paloma spent time with Joe's parents, she understood his puzzlement over the noise in Malaga: "It was stiff, and a little tense, very English. His father drank a lot, his mother read a lot. We'd watch endless TV. I'd go crazy, we'd have two separate beds. With his mum Joe's kind self would come out more. He loved his mum, who was very reserved."

Back in London it was a return to the gig circuit. The 101'ers were now a serious working band, averaging four gigs a week. "We were now making a bit of money," said Clive Timperley. "We weren't too badly off. We managed to buy a van to get to gigs, and we were getting more equipment."

That things were starting to happen for the 101'ers was a buzz for everyone involved: they all felt it. Vindicated about his belief in himself, Joe began to grow in confidence. As he became Joe Strummer, he discovered a persona into which he could inject all his abilities and fantasies of rock 'n' roll mythology, exaggerating aspects of himself, pulling other parts back, adding his own secret ingredient—himself, and that frantically pumping left leg, always a sign that things were about to getabitarockin'. Back in January the 101'ers had had three live dates, all at the Charlie Pigdog Club; in October it was seventeen. Although the last date at the Chippenham had been on April 23, the Charlie Pigdog shows were compensated for by the weekly gigs at the Elgin. The lineup had stabilized. By the end of March, Alvaro Pena-Rojas had quit, and Dudanski had stepped in. Two months later Simon Cassell had also gone. Jules Yewdall had lasted only a handful of dates, leaving the group in April. Now the 101'ers were a four-piece: Joe Strummer on rhythm guitar and vocals, Clive Timperley on lead guitar, Mole on bass and Richard Dudanski on drums. "Strummer wanted to get the band down into a useful working unit," said Clive Timperley. "We used to say we want the Shadows or Beatles lineup. We used to have these councils of war. Jules went to Germany and came back and wasn't in the band. There was this joke: 'Don't go on holiday!'" But Yewdall stayed around, taking photographs and trying to get them dates—he was responsible for the shows at the St. Moritz. Mickey Foote, who engineered the live sound and acted as unofficial road manager, also pulled in live dates for the group. By now there was a regular posse of fans, almost all of whom were reasonably close friends with the singer of the 101'ers. Among them was Helen Cherry: "I went to lots of 101'ers' gigs, probably nearly every single one. Joe was always very intent on getting more gear, getting more amps, trying to get it all together really. He had a great interest in it. But all blokes are like that around performing bands, aren't they? Just talking endlessly about the gear. He'd talk a lot about the performances afterward, being pissed off if something wasn't right or picking over a gig, picking over certain things that he felt hadn't come off.

"I used to find it intriguing when he was going on to a stage in front of lots of people and he'd be worrying about blow-drying a certain pair of trousers with a hair dryer, not worrying about the set list or the guitar strings. He liked details. I think he had this good detail with people, as well, which is why people were drawn to him as a friend—he could make people feel included."

After talking to the group following one of the Elgin dates, a roadie, John "Boogie" Tiberi, had been taken on: "I met Joe, and it was a good vibe: I really liked him immediately—Strummer was always quiet and spontaneous—and I was really impressed with the 101'ers. First time I saw them, I went up to him at the bar and said, 'I really like your group.' I started working for them with Mickey."

Pete Silverton, who had hung out with Woody Mellor and Paul Buck at the end of the sixties, was trying to make his mark as a music journalist writing for *Trouser Press*, an American fanzine. He went to see the 101'ers play on August 4, 1975, at the Hope and Anchor on Upper Street in Islington.

It was the first time in around five years that Pete Silverton had seen John Mellor, now in his new incarnation of Joe Strummer. Joe greeted him "very warmly. I had the impression that he seemed to feel he was a star—or felt the first step of being a star was to act like a star. He wasn't an asshole—and I've met lots of those who think they are stars. I felt that Joe was patently using the supposed revolutionary message of squatting, which seemed to be essentially that everybody should smoke inordinate amounts of dope and play rock 'n' roll. The political philosophy was at about that level of sophistication."

Some of Joe's exuberance of spirit was undoubtedly sparked by the presence of his girlfriend, Paloma. Not that you would have realized they were an item, according to Pete Silverton: "Paloma—very sweet, very young, but also very independent for a provincial Spanish girl. They seemed ambivalent together: it was partly the fashion of the time to pretend you weren't with someone—being in a couple was considered a bit parent-like." "Joe was madly in love with Paloma," confirmed Gill Calvert. "But Paloma was having a good and a bad time. Because there was a flightiness to Joe: he wasn't going to be there for more than five minutes, and you knew that. I never would have wanted to put myself in her position."

"The 101'ers were playing at the Hope and Anchor," continued Pete Silverton. "You would have thought from reading the music press that there was this very big vibe, but there was about fifty people and a dog there— literally, a dog. This was the first time I'd seen them and it was a transcendent moment in my life. I was absolutely blown away. By Joe. Not by the band. They were OK, but Joe . . . he had this suit on, a big off-pink zoot suit. It looked great. The way it moved, it looked like the sails on a galleon."

Pete Silverton resumed: "Joe was also wearing co-respondent shoes. He had his hair swept back and he'd got sideburns. His hair's dark, because he's greased it, I guess: his natural hair color is dishwater blond, standard English. It's the only time I've walked into somewhere and gone, 'This man is a star!' I remember them playing 'Gloria,' with him climbing all over the amps. Joe moved with a strange staccato grace onstage. It wasn't very big, the Hope and Anchor stage, but he was duckwalking across it. In the music he was playing and in his moves onstage he was obviously stealing a great deal from films of 1950s performers. My girlfriend at the time thought Joe was really sexy. I never saw him as a ladies' man at all but he had a sort of sexy appeal.

"The songs were also fantastic. It's nearly all original stuff, but derivative. Joe realized that there were a lot of great songs out there—you could just rewrite them and redo them. By now he had started to be caught up in the thrill of what he was doing, but he was faced with the problem that the 101'ers couldn't really get anywhere, so there were tensions already in the band. The conflicts in the 101'ers were very clear. Joe is not the most musically literate person in the world. But he had a fantastic rhythmic sense, even though he could barely play the guitar. He was very passionate, but he could get very depressed."

In October 1975 Jules Yewdall and Mickey Foote "opened" a new squat at 42 Orsett Terrace, a road of tall, well-appointed terraced houses with stone staircases near Royal Oak tube station. In the basement, the 101'ers set up a far more professional rehearsal studio than at Walterton Road. But at Orsett Terrace there were worries about burglaries: the next-door house was occupied by a gang of junkies. "Joe hated the idea of junkies," recalled Gill Calvert. "He thought it was a hopeless existence. I see his own depression as slightly complex, because I think some of the time he was acting: he could act the part of his depressed self. He was also able to escape from it. I know people who are depressed and don't function. So I would call him a functioning depressive."

At World's End, the unfashionable end of the King's Road, there was some cultural movement afoot. Malcolm McLaren and his wife, Vivienne Westwood, ran Let It Rock, an arcane boutique, much of whose wares were designed to shock or irritate. McLaren had managed the New York Dolls at the tail end of their careers; while he had been in the States, Bernard Rhodes, a friend of Malcolm and Vivienne's, had nurtured another scheme: a group that consisted of the shop's Saturday boy Glen Matlock and a pair of Shepherd's Bush musicians, drummer Paul Cook and guitarist Steve Jones, along with a short-lived character called Wally as vocalist. Since the previous year they had been nagging McLaren for help; all he had provided so far had been a name, the Sex Pistols—after Let It Rock had been renamed Sex.

But in August 1975 Bernard found a scrawny youth from Finsbury Park in North London named John Lydon who walked into Sex wearing a Pink Floyd T-shirt with the words "I hate" added above the group's name. Rhodes invited Lydon to come to the nearby Roebuck pub; he auditioned for the Pistols by miming to the pub's jukebox. "Bernie definitely influenced the start of the Pistols," Lydon told me in 1980. "He got me in the band."

In October 1975 the 101'ers played five times at a former country-and-western venue called the Nashville Rooms in West Kensington. In the audience one night was Mick Jones and a friend named Tony James. Jones was a guitar-playing art student who had been born in Brixton; after living with his grandmother in a high-rise off the Harrow Road, he moved earlier that year to a small flat in Highgate—though he would soon move back in with his grandmother. Soaked in pop culture, Mick Jones had known that it was his destiny to become a rock 'n' roll musician: "I'd known since I was ten that this was what I would do with my life. It wasn't so much ambition as what I knew I had to do." But even though he had devoted most of his time on a degree course at Hammersmith Art College to playing the guitar, the fulfillment of his ambition had not at first been easy. He'd been in a group called the Delinquents, followed by one called Little Queenie—though he fell out with them. Through Little Queenie he met Tony James, a bass-playing math student who had placed an advertisement in *Melody Maker* to form a group. Now Mick Jones and Tony James were trying to start up a group called London SS, one of the great mythological acts of all time, a legend only enhanced by the fact that they never played a single show.

At that 101'ers gig at the Nashville, they found that they hated the group, who seemed to this style-obsessed pair to be an archetypal bar band. But they were extremely impressed with the singer. At the gig that evening—on which there was clearly a propitious convergence of energies—they ran into a short, bespectacled man with an extremely protuberant nose. This was Bernard Rhodes.

Mick Jones was wearing a pink T-shirt he had bought from Sex that bore the legend "You're gonna wake up one morning and *know* what side of the bed you've been lying on." And so was Rhodes. "We said, 'Go on, stand over there in that T-shirt,'" remembered James. "'Fuck off!' replied Rhodes. 'I made it.'" Impressed, the pair fell into conversation with this gnomelike fellow, who gave them their first information about the Sex Pistols. Mick Jones later said: "I thought he looked like a piano player. He seemed like a really bright geezer. We got on like a house on fire."

For £1,000 McLaren had bought a rehearsal studio in Denmark Street, London's Tin Pan Alley. "Mick and I went to see Malcolm at the studio," said Tony James. "The Pistols were there. We both had really long hair." McLaren took them for a meal at which they were both entranced by his vision. "He told us what would happen," remembered James. "That a group would come along and completely shake up the music business and alter things utterly. And it all came grizzily true."

McLaren didn't recognize the potential talents before him. But Bernard Rhodes had set about looking for a group of his own, after McLaren had turned down his request for a half-share in the Pistols. So the pair arranged a more thorough meeting with Bernie Rhodes, telling him of their plans to form London SS. "Bernie made us go up to the Bull and Bush pub in Shepherd's Bush to meet him, which was unbelievably rough and dangerous," remembered James. "As soon as he got there he slapped all this Nazi regalia on the table: 'If you're going to call yourself London SS, you'll have to deal with this.' We hadn't thought at all about the Nazi implications. It just seemed like a very anarchic, stylish thing to do," admitted James.

Following their meeting with Rhodes, Mick Jones and Tony James placed an advertisement in *Melody Maker*: "Decadent 3rd generation rock and roll—image essential. New York Dolls style." Jones was still living in Highgate and it was the phone number of this address that was given in the ad. James lived in Twickenham, a two-hour trip away from Jones by city bus; nonetheless James took the trip each day to Highgate, where they would both sit anxiously by the phone.

Only half a dozen people replied—one was a singer from Manchester called Steven Morrisey, though nothing came of this. Jones and James were extremely taken with the very first response: Brian James, a guitarist with the Belgian group Bastard. As the duo deemed necessary, he was stick thin; after meeting the pair, Brian James went back to Brussels to quit the other band.

Beneath a café in Praed Street, Paddington, Bernard Rhodes found London SS a rehearsal room. "When we started working with Bernie, he changed our lives," said James. "Up to then we *were* the New York Dolls, and had never thought of writing more than 'Personality Crisis.' I remember sitting in the café upstairs with Bernie and saying I had an idea for a song about selling rockets in Selfridges. He liked it. But he was thinking of nuclear rockets and I was only thinking of fireworks. He said, 'You're not going to be able to do anything unless you give me a statement of intent.' It was art-speak. He'd give us reading lists: Proust, books on modern art—it was a great education. He also used to pull a sort of class thing: are you street, or are you middle class? It didn't seem very honest, as he was patently obviously middle class himself."

Through the door of the rehearsal studio wafted various future members of the cast of punk. Paul Simonon turned up by accident, and was auditioned for the job of singer: as a perfect David Bowie lookalike he sang "Radio One, Radio One," over Jonathan Richman's "Road Runner," for ten minutes until he was requested to stop. Both Terry Chimes and Nicky "Topper" Headon auditioned as drummers, Headon being offered the job, although leaving after a week. "I remember the audition was in some tiny little basement studio," he told me. "I got the gig, but I'd already done an audition for a soul band, and that was fifty quid a week, so I went on the road with them. London SS was very loud rock 'n' roll. It was a bad punk group, really. Although the fact that Generation X, the Clash and the Damned came out of it shows there was something there, it wasn't really very good." Having given up the hunt for a singer, London SS started rehearsing with Mick Jones on vocals and a drummer named Roland Hot. Over Christmas of 1975 Brian James left and formed the Damned with other McLaren luminaries Rat Scabies, Dave Vanian and Captain Sensible, leaving the London SS back at square one for Mick Jones and Tony James— although the Sex Pistols had unsuccessfully attempted to contact Jones to offer him the role of second guitarist.

On November 18, 1975, Joe Strummer saw the first of two shows at the Hammersmith Odeon by Bruce Springsteen. Springsteen, who had never played in London before, was promoting his *Born to Run* album, his third LP, a landmark record that saw him touted as "the future of rock 'n' roll." "When Strummer went to see Springsteen his head was turned," said Clive Timperley. "The whole idea of Springsteen doing full-on three-hour concerts. Strummer thought, 'That's the way to do it!'" The fact that Springsteen played a Telecaster was significant for Joe, who saw it as a sign. Joe even bought an excessively long guitar lead, allowing him to wander at will about the stage and even into the audience—just like Springsteen. Clive Timperley recalled that Joe Strummer's performing histrionics became even more exaggerated; at one gig the guitarist noticed as he launched into a lengthy solo that Joe had disappeared offstage and was lying on an old mattress in the wings; as the moment came for his microphone cue, he sprang up and—as though shot from a cannon—hurtled across the stage, bursting into his vocal lines with perfect split-second timing. Springsteen-like, the 101'ers' sets got longer: they would often play almost thirty songs, onstage for over ninety minutes, at a time when established high-energy acts like Steve Marriott's Humble Pie were getting away with thirty-five minutes, including encore.

Joe Strummer's invigorated stage performance was not all he took from that much-hyped Hammersmith Odeon Springsteen concert. The unique and hugely influential *Born to Run* combined an epic rock 'n' roll feel with songs that were stories of "street life" in Springsteen's highly mythologized hometown of Asbury Park, New Jersey. The Clash's similar mythologizing of Notting Hill could be seen as coming partially from here, as well as from the references to Kingston, Jamaica—specifically the Trenchtown district—in reggae records, notably those by the newly elected king of the genre, Bob Marley. "I was actually turned on to playing reggae by Mole, who was the bass player for the 101'ers, who finally made me really listen to Big Youth and feel it and I sort of saw the light," Joe told me. "I found it quite hard to step from r&b into that deep reggae style. But once it was under your skin it became almost a passion." So stirred was Joe by these profound Jamaican rhythms that, on a trip to Warlingham to see his mother and father, he found he couldn't get the "Chh-chh" sound of the hi-hat out of his mind. "I went back to London and said, 'Give me that record and put it on again.' That's when we first tried to play reggae, very early in the 101'ers." Although at the Charlie Pigdog Club, Mole would occasionally sing a version of "Israelites," the Desmond Dekker classic, Joe recalled the group's reggae efforts were largely restricted to rehearsals.

As well as the Springsteen dates, there had been another significant show in the London rock 'n' roll calendar that November in 1975. On the sixth of the month the Sex Pistols had played their first gig ever at St. Martin's School of Art. Five songs into the set the plug was pulled; among the numbers was a cover of the Small Faces' "Whatcha Gonna Do About It" in which the singer, Johnny Rotten, swapped the word "hate" for "love" in the line "I want you to know that I love you." The next day they played at Joe's alma mater, Central School of Art and Design in Holborn. They got through a thirty-minute set.

The vice social secretary at Central was Sebastian Conran, son of design guru Terence Conran, who had given him the lease of a substantial house in Albany Street, next to Regent's Park. One of those he rented rooms to was the new girlfriend of Mickey Foote. "As Mickey Foote was a friend of Joe," Sebastian told me, "we had the 101'ers come and play at one of our parties. It was good—I was really into the 101'ers. That was when I first met Joe." When the 101'ers played a Christmas concert at Central on December 17, booked by Sebastian Conran in his capacity as vice social secretary, he also designed a poster for the show.

Toward the end of 1975, however, Joe Strummer had begun to question the position of Mole within the 101'ers. Dan Kelleher, a guitarist friend of Clive Timperley, had guested with the group since the summer, until on October 7, when the group played at the Nashville Rooms, he joined the 101'ers as a full member, another guitarist. "Once, late at night," said Gill Calvert, "Joe showed me a drawing he'd done of Mole. Then he said, 'I'm gonna sack him.' He was asking, 'Is it OK to sack Mole?' I wish I had said, 'No, it isn't. You shouldn't.' There was a weakness in Joe—and I do regard it as a weakness—that he was pressured by the idea that 'Dan can play every Beatles song.' Mole was actually much more musical than Dan, much more inventive: he was totally into reggae. The thing is, he was bald, and he was not pretty. So Joe was saying, 'Well, Dan can stand onstage and look like Paul McCartney, and sound like Paul McCartney, and he can hold it all together. Mole stands there and looks odd.' Joe was obviously wanting everything to look perfect onstage. Dan was a friend of Timperley and they were sort of 'the straights.' But it was Joe and Richard who were really the driving power." On January 11, 1976, Mole played his last show with the 101'ers at the Red Cow in Hammersmith. He officially left the group four days later, when Dan Kelleher—renamed "Desperate Dan"—switched from guitar to bass. When I asked Boogie to whom Joe most related in the group, he insisted that it was Mole. Such dispensing with people would become characteristic behavior for Joe Strummer—largely in his career, though also in personal relations. Soon the 101'ers' turn would come to be so especially selected.

Joe Strummer's life wasn't all one relentless slog keeping the 101'ers on course. He stayed in touch with his old close friend Paul Buck. "Once we had a wonderful Christmas," Paul told me. "He came down with Paloma over Christmas 1975. He wrote to me, 'I've met this wonderful Spanish girl and her mum's coming over for Christmas. Can you tell me of a decent B&B, somewhere around the farm, and we'll come down there, because it's nice countryside, and maybe we can meet up for a beer or something.' I said, 'Don't worry about the B&B: just come and stay here.' He turned up, there was him, Paloma, the drummer Richard Dudanski, his girlfriend Esperanza, their mother and some guy called Julio who didn't speak any English. The whole bunch took over the house. Paloma and her mum were cooking Christmas dinner in the kitchen. My dad came back from the pub completely bemused. I'd forgotten to mention to him that they were coming."

Joe took other holidays with Paul Buck; together they went to the Norfolk Broads for a few days. On another occasion they hitchhiked down to

Bexhill-on-Sea, where, for the purposes of this trip, the young man originally known as John Mellor called himself "Rooney."

Without Joe being aware of it, though, things were moving around him.
"We used to go and see the 101'ers a lot," Mick Jones said. "He was out doing it, and we looked up to that. We never thought we could approach him.
We'd looked around and we'd seen every band going, because we needed a
singer. But there was a guy there who we knew we wanted more than anyone else. Bernie said, 'Let's ask him.' But we didn't do it yet."

While playing at the Elgin in November 1975, the group were approached by Vic Maile, who had produced the first Dr. Feelgood album,
Down by the Jetty. Maile told the 101'ers he wanted to record them, with an
eye to striking a production deal by selling the tapes to a record company. On
November 28 the 101'ers drove up with their equipment to Jackson's Studios in Rickmansworth on the fringe of North London, where Maile—an
ex-BBC sound engineer who worked at the studio—recorded six of their
songs: "Motor Boys Motor," "Standing by a Silent Telephone," "Letsageta-
bitarockin'," "Hideaway," "Mr. Sweety of the St. Moritz" and "Steamgauge
99." The 101'ers claim not to have enjoyed the experience: they didn't take to
Maile's martinetlike approach to recording. He didn't get them a deal.

But others were also interested, among them Ted Carroll, who with his
partner Roger Armstrong ran a pair of vintage record stalls called Rock On,
one in Soho Market, the other in Golborne Road, at the top of Portobello
Road, often frequented by Joe Strummer, as well as Paul Simonon. Carroll
had decided to start his own independent record label, Chiswick Records.
Joe said: "When Ted Carroll came to me after a gig at some university and
said, 'Hey, do you want to make a record then?' it was so far from my mind
that anyone could make records who were in our world that I remember
looking at him as though I was observing a lunatic, let out from a loony bin
for a day trip. I said, 'What?' And he said, 'Do you want to make a record?'
I just couldn't believe my ears—it was that far away. You know, we were under the sub-sub-sub-level of the sub-underground level. It just baffled my
head when he said that. I couldn't believe it."

But Ted Carroll was completely serious. On March 4, 1976, the 101'ers
recorded at Pathway Studios in Canonbury, with Roger Armstrong producing. They recorded a trio of songs: "Surf City," "Sweet Revenge" and "Keys
to Your Heart." Six days later Joe Strummer, "Evil C" Timperley, Desperate

Dan Kelleher and Richard "Snakehips" Dudanski returned to Pathway, where they re-recorded "Surf City" and "Sweet Revenge," and added a version of "Rabies (from the Dogs of Love)." By March 25, "Keys to Your Heart" was mixed and completed.

Under the auspices of Boogie, the 101'ers were in a different studio only three days later. Half a dozen 101'ers originals were recorded at the BBC studios in Maida Vale, where live performances were recorded for broadcast. It was not a successful session: "Joe didn't really click with studios at that stage, with the repetitious listening to the stuff that had been recorded, and the laying down of vocals, and the post-production." The songs put on tape included another version of "Keys to Your Heart," "5 Star Rock and Roll Petrol" and "Surf City."

Perhaps Joe found the recording experience difficult because—rather than resorting to drugs as did so many of his contemporaries—he needed the energy of a live performance to overcome his musical limitations. He and his cohorts were almost entirely outside the world of amphetamine sulphate, then widely used on the rock 'n' roll circuit. As Joe Strummer told Paolo Hewitt, it was absurd to claim the 101'ers' shows were the product of this cheap speed: "Used to annoy me. At [a club] one night we played this really great set, really firing on all cylinders. Then we went out into the bar to have a drink and this bloke goes nudgingly, 'Not bad that.' And he's winking and nudging me and I was going, 'What's the matter with the geezer?' And he says, 'How many lines did you snort before that set then?' And we weren't into speed. We couldn't afford speed. We couldn't afford a drink."

Something needed to change. Gigging on the pub circuit was draining, and Joe grew frustrated. "It was just a slog," said Joe. "It seemed after doing eighteen months of that we were just invisible. I started to lose my mind. I would go around the squat saying, 'We're invisible, we should change our name to the Invisibles.' You'd get back to London about five a.m., unload the gear, put on a kettle and go, 'What the fuck's that about?' And in the paper it'd be like Queen and all that. We were just shambling from one gig to the next banging our heads against the wall."

At least the 101'ers had spent five days of March in recording studios, and they had a date sheet full of forthcoming gigs. On Friday, April 2, accompanied by Tymon Dogg, the 101'ers played a "benefit dance," at fifty pence a ticket, for That Tea Room at Acklam Hall in Notting Hill. The mildly psychedelic poster—all blues, greens and oranges—sets the tone:

STARRING THAT TEA ROOM FOOD

EATEN BY

101'ERS TYMON DOGG

LOUIS THE JEEP (LATE BAR TOILETS)

CO-STARRING CLOWNS FIRE-EATERS IDIOTS MC PHILIPE 4-SPEED

RECORD-PLAYER

DOG-FIGHTERS BULLITT AND TROUBLE

THE DANCING PIRANA SISTERS FEATURING PIRANA CUSTARD AND

ROMERO——SOLO——DAVE THE VD

THE BEATLES. ROB ON INSULTS. BOUNCERS DYLAN AND WIGGIN

FOOTE AND BOOGIE

+ LARGEST FLAPJACK IN THE WORLD + A NIGEL

THE MISERABLE CIRCUS

The poster was designed by Helen Cherry. Joe, she said, "really, really liked it and I got a big pat on the back. He said, 'Helen, a lot of people came to see it and we made a lot of money because of your poster.'" In retrospect, the entire concept of the evening seems from a very specific world indeed, like a fantasy of an idealized San Francisco of 1967, certainly an event from another, more innocent time.

Which it was about to be revealed to be.

The next night, April 3, the 101'ers played what must have seemed merely another date, at the Nashville Rooms, next to the tube station in West Kensington. The opening act? The Sex Pistols. Glen Matlock, the bass player and songwriter, had gone to Acklam Hall. Backstage he found Joe Strummer trying to tune his guitar. "Ah, the Sex Pistols," he said to Glen. "We'll see how it is tomorrow night."

Joe did see. And everything changed.

1
1

i'm going to be a
punk rocker

1976

For Joe Strummer the show the next day at the Nashville Rooms was an epiphany: "As soon as Johnny Rotten hit the stand, right, the writing was on the wall, as far as I was concerned. We're top of the bill. And we're sitting in the dressing room and then they walk through it to get to the stage and they just came through in a big long line. And I saw this geezer in a gold lamé Elvis Presley jacket at the end of the line as they walked through. So I thought, I'm going to see what these guys are like. So I tapped him on the shoulder and said, 'That's a nice jacket you've got on there.' And he turned around and it was Sid Vicious. And he went, 'Yeah, isn't it? I'll tell you where I got it. Do you know that stall up at Camden? Blah blah blah.' And he was like dead friendly, he was such a nice guy. He didn't have to cop any attitude. And they looked so great that I knew this was something great. So I went out in the audience and sat down.

"There was perhaps thirty people lying around, you know. And they came out and they just, just cleaned me out. They came out, with like, I don't fucking care if you like it or not, this is it. If you don't like it, piss off.

Woody Mellor as Joe Strummer: "Letsgetabitarockin'!" *(Joe Stevens)*

It was that difference. They were like a million years ahead. I realized immediately that we were going nowhere, and the rest of my group hated them. They didn't want to watch it or hear anything about it. So I started sort of going off to the punk festivals and getting into the whole thing. Eventually it tore the whole band apart."

Nearly three weeks later, on April 23, 1976, the Pistols again opened for the 101'ers at the Nashville. I was there that night, and saw something different, the controversy meter measuring the Pistols rising several significant degrees. The venue was packed—Mick Jones, Tony James, Dave Vanian, Adam Ant and Vic Godard were all there, plus a few journalists, as well as Malcolm McLaren, Vivienne Westwood and Bernie Rhodes. Always unpredictable live, however, the Pistols did not play a good show. To liven things up, Vivienne Westwood slapped a girl's face right in front of the small stage. In the resultant uproar, both McLaren and Rotten—who had leapt from the stage into the audience—got into a brawl with the girl's boyfriend. In fear, the rest of the audience backed off; it was the strangest thing many of them had ever seen at a supposed "pop" show: there was no frame of reference whatsoever into which to fit this incident. From then on, violence would be a constant subtext of punk rock.

The same day as that second Pistols/101'ers Nashville gig saw the release of *The Ramones*, the first album by the group that was creating a mythology for itself in New York as a kind of Lower East Side set of cartoonish dunces who also happened to play some of the fastest music around. Although it contained fourteen songs, their eponymous LP's total running time was less than twenty-eight minutes. "The Ramones were the single most important group that changed punk rock," said Tony James. "When their album came out, all the English groups tripled speed overnight. Two-minute-long songs, very fast. The Pistols were almost the only group who stuck to the kind of Who speed." As the 101'ers were already, by Joe Strummer's definition, playing "rhythm and blues at 100 miles per hour," you might feel he was ideally suited for such a shift. That was the opinion of Bernie Rhodes, who again studied Joe onstage at both Nashville gigs, and talked to him briefly after each performance—though he wasn't quite ready to tell him about the plan fermenting inside his ever-active brain.

Joe had not entirely cast aside the chains of establishment rock 'n' roll. From May 21 to 26 the Rolling Stones played at Earl's Court arena, and Joe took Pete Silverton along with him. "He was a sporadically generous human being, but we had the worst seats in the house, absolutely awful. Joe says, 'We're not sitting here.' We get up and we walk down to the front, past all the bouncers, to within ten feet of the stage, and we find some seats. We were ambiguous about the Stones: this is the most fantastic band ever, but we know this is not their greatest period, and we're sneering a bit because they're not what we want. This is even before punk and the rhetoric about dinosaur bands.

"We were in front of Bill Wyman, who is poker-faced as he plays. Joe spent all the time trying to get Bill Wyman's attention, and he eventually managed. He kept calling out: 'Bill! Bill!' He was determined to make Bill smile at him. Which he eventually did."

Part of an oft-repeated myth of the formation of the Clash is that Mick Jones, Paul Simonon and Glen Matlock came up to Joe one Saturday afternoon following the second Nashville show; they were alleged to have said, "We like you, but we don't like your group." When I once asked Joe if this happened, his reply was immediate: "No, not really. I did see them in the [unemployment office] one day. They were staring at me funny, and I thought, I'm in for a ruck [fight]. But they were only staring at me 'cause they'd seen the 101'ers playing the week before at Acklam Hall under the Westway. I don't remember meeting them in Portobello Road."

Although he hadn't yet spoken to him, Joe noticed Mick Jones in the audience at another Sex Pistols show that same week as the Rolling Stones concerts, the third date by the Pistols in a regular Tuesday-night gig at the 100 Club. At the beginning of May, Mick Jones had started playing with Paul Simonon, Keith Levene, a singer named Billy Watts and, briefly, with Terry Chimes on drums, with whom he had already also tried to work the previous autumn. At this time Mick Jones and Paul Simonon were living in a West London squat at 22 Davis Road on the edge of Shepherd's Bush and Acton.

Iain Gillies, who was by then living in London, remembered Gill Calvert saying Joe was so into the Pistols she didn't think the 101'ers would continue. "I went to some party in North London at this time with Gill, Mickey Foote, Boogie, Richard Dudanski, Joe and some others. The party was in quite a straight house but Glen Matlock was there with some other Pistols hangers-on. There was a very noticeable atmosphere that came off the

101'ers and Pistols people and it seemed to me there was a new thing about to happen."

When Joe Strummer went along to that Sex Pistols show at the 100 Club, a small basement venue at 100 Oxford Street in London's West End, he took Gill Calvert with him. Gill had just helped him open another squat, in a former ice-cream factory in Foscote Mews, close to the Harrow Road. Joe's move there seemed largely impelled by his decision that his relationship with Paloma was ending, and that he should therefore depart Orsett Terrace. It was not Joe but Paloma who had set this process in motion. She was temporarily in Scotland, having had doubts about the viability of their relationship and needing some space.

"He said to me, 'Come with me and hear this group,'" said Gill Calvert. "He knew it was going to be a pivotal moment because he insisted I dress up. He had slicked-back hair, a leather jacket and was reasonably clean—he had had his trousers tapered by then."

"I met Bernie," Joe told me, "when the Pistols supported the 101'ers at the Nashville Rooms. But then I really met him at the 100 Club regular punk nights when the Pistols played."

"Joe made us walk to the 100 Club from Chippenham Road," remembered Gill Calvert. "It was a long walk, a couple of miles, and a hot night, the beginning of that long hot summer. This was where Bernard floated his interest in Joe. He bought us a drink—Joe only had half a lager—and we sat at the back at a table as he talked to Joe about what he was doing and about forming the Clash: he made a direct approach to him there and then. We were very excited. After he'd had this conversation with Bernie we left quite soon—as though it had been done, and we wouldn't want to hang around. Joe seemed very enthused."

To help him make up his mind about whether or not to leave the 101'ers for this new group, Joe consulted his copy of *I Ching*, the Chinese "Book of Changes." Throwing three coins six times to show him which of the Ching's sixty-four hexagrams to consult, the answer he was given was "stay with your friends." "He conveniently decided," said Paul Buck, "that his 'friends' were the Clash. But it was an extraordinarily hippie way to decide to join a punk group."

When Paloma returned to London, her enthusiasm for Joe rekindled, she moved in with him at Foscote Mews for a short while, unaware that he'd decided their relationship was finished. Because of this confusion, Joe felt obliged to leave Foscote Mews and he temporarily moved back to Orsett Terrace. "We were having problems between us," Paloma said, "so I went for a couple of months to a farm in Scotland, with Gail Goodall and Mole. We kept in touch on the phone. During that time punk happened. When I came back I'd seen the light and wanted to be with him. But he'd moved out of Orsett Terrace. I took a bus to the ice-cream factory. There I saw a bunch of people looking punkish. Mick Jones was one of them. They said he was in a pub. I ran up to him and put my arms around him. He was very serious and said, 'I'm going to be a punk rocker.' But as we talked he changed and we were back together. But it was never the same—I was insecure. He moved back to Orsett Terrace. Then we both went to the ice-cream factory. He said he wanted us to have an 'open' relationship."

Paloma remained there and, as Gill Calvert puts it, "formed the Slits in a rage. She'd never been into music in that way before. She took up the drums: she thought, If you can do it I can fucking do it. Then some of the Slits moved into Foscote Mews—Ari Up, the singer, and Viv Albertine, the guitarist." Paul Simonon—unusually, not Joe—renamed Paloma "Palmolive," the name by which she became known in the band. "When Joe started coming over to my mum's place," said the then fourteen-year-old Ari Up, "he never came with Paloma. When she asked me to form a group I didn't know he was with her. He taught me guitar. It was hard to learn guitar on Joe's Telecaster: it was hard to press down. He'd only speak with a joke or two. He was always fingering his guitar. Just chords. He was like a guiding star, but very quiet. He was like a brother to me. He never tried to come on to me."

Those around Joe at the time feel that his behavior toward Paloma was part of a Year Zero approach to life, as though in some form of Stalinist revision he was writing out large parts of his past.

On May 26, the day after that meeting with Bernie Rhodes at the 100 Club, Joe had gone to see Clive Timperley at his squat in Cleveland Terrace. "Strummer came round to my flat. He said, 'I want to do this punk thing and I want you to come with me.' He was talking about it as though it would be within the 101'ers. He spent the whole day with me convincing me of the direction he wanted to go in. 'Maximum impact,' he kept saying. He wanted me to make more of an effort as a performer onstage. But that's not me. So that was the end of it for me. I didn't feel bad. I realized where Strummer was going. I didn't realize Bernie had approached him already."

On May 30 the 101'ers played the Golden Lion at Fulham Broadway, with pub-rock favorite Martin Stone deputizing for Clive Timperley—he had also stepped in to help out at a show at Bromley College two days before. "Bernie Rhodes turned up at the Golden Lion with Keith Levene and I went outside and stood at the bus stop with them and he sort of said, 'What you gonna do?' And I said, 'I dunno,' and he said, 'Well, come down to this squat in Shepherd's Bush and meet these guys,' and Keith was nodding, saying, 'You'd better.'" In 1989 Keith Levene claimed to Jane Garcia of *NME* that it was he who recognized Joe's full potential: "Joe used to wear zoot suits and just go fucking mad all over the place. He was always so great to watch." Joe later declared that initially he had been convinced to leave the 101'ers by meeting Keith: "In those days people looked really boring, and Keith looked really different." Bernie Rhodes had his own viewpoint: "Nobody gave a fuck about Joe Strummer until I got hold of him."

"Bernie Rhodes came over to me the next day with Keith and said, 'Come with me,'" Joe told me. "Then he drove me down to a squat in Shepherd's Bush. They were squatting in a place above some old lady's flat: Mick, Paul and various crazies. He said, 'I think you should join this group.' We started to rehearse that afternoon."

Joe told me that the first song he remembered attempting to play with these new musical allies was "One-Two-Crush on You," a song written by Mick Jones that the group played live early on, but which was not released in the United States until it came out as part of the *Clash on Broadway* box set in 1992. In Britain, however, it came out as the B-side of the "Tommy Gun" single on November 24, 1978. "The day Keith Levene brought Joe round to Davis Road, we were all terrified," said Mick Jones. "He was already Joe Strummer, he was already somebody. We'd seen him do it, what we hadn't done. It was a big deal getting Joe Strummer. We did seem to just start straightaway. We might have had a cup of tea first. It was, 'We'll show you our songs,' and we already knew he had some songs and that was it . . . The next time he came round he was in the gear and everything, he was already part of it, he was there." "We was expecting Joe," said Paul Simonon. "We were sitting in the living room area, me and Mick, then Keith turns up with Joe. So we got into the rehearsal room, which is a box, about five foot by five foot—it was cramped. Mick played a couple of songs and then Joe played one—we alternated back and forth. The fact that he'd turned up, that made a statement: 'Well, this is it: we're going from here onward together.' That was the first day of the Clash." "'I'm So Bored with You' was the first song we worked on together," said Mick. "Definitely. He famously changed it to 'Bored with the USA.' Before we did that we played 'Protex Blue' to him, about the condom machine in The Windsor Castle, a pub off the Harrow Road. He went, 'That's pretty good. Let's get to work.' That was the first day."

Suddenly Joe felt validated. "The whole thing was really great from the beginning of 1976 when I met them and we took off, all the way through that. My dreams were like carnivals, my mind would churn over and over in my sleep 'cos of the decisions, throwing in one thing and another. Everything was being tried and experimented, it was just great. It can't be like that all the time but it's great when it is.

"We knew it was going to be good. You know that certainty when you don't even bother to think? That certainty was with us and I'm glad of it. We knew that this was it. Finally I thought, We'll show those bastards. They'd been ignoring us, and when we got big reviews it seemed like we deserved it."

When he learned that Paul Simonon was essentially a nonmusician, and that he memorized the numbers note by note from Mick Jones, Joe did have some initial reservations: "He couldn't play. It fazed me a bit at first 'cos I'd been through two years of all of us learning to play [in the 101'ers]. We couldn't really play either but we could kind of hang our chin together. When I heard that Paul couldn't play at first, I thought, Well, it slows you up. But then I got on with Paul so well and he just picked it up. In three weeks he could play as much as we needed. Well, he could play as good as me in about three weeks, yeah."

Paul Simonon brought with him another set of inspirations to the collective. "By the end of the 101'ers we were wearing drainpipe trousers," Joe told Mal Peachy. "And this might not seem significant to many people. But in a world of flares, drainpipe trousers were the equivalent of shaving your head and painting it orange—it really stuck out. If your trousers weren't flared, then you were into the new age, the new world, and so the 101'ers had a kinda grunge look. I suppose now you could describe it like that, like we were just filthy squatters. But with Paul Simonon and Mick Jones—very,

Muriel Johannes (second from left) was the mother of Ronald Mellor, and grandmother of Joe. Dorothy Johannes (far right) and Marian Johannes (second from right) were Joe's great-aunts. His half-great-aunts—after the early death of the Armenian Mr. Johannes, his wife, Agnes, married a Mr. Spiers—were Mary Spiers (far left) and Maggie Spiers (center). After the death of Muriel when he was ten, Ron Mellor and his brother and two sisters were brought up by Agnes Spiers; Mary Spiers, to whom he was close, later gave Ron the deposit for the Mellor bungalow.

With his impish facial features, the sailor-suited Ronald Mellor shows the origins of the perpetual naughty schoolboy expressions of his son Joe Strummer. The youngest of four children, brought up in Lucknow in India, Ron never knew his father, who died of pleurisy in 1917 while Ron was still a baby. With him here are his brother, Fred, and his sisters, Phyllis (second from left) and Ouina.

Left The dashing Lieutenant Ronald Mellor during his World War II service in the Indian army. His eyes have that same floating quality as those of his son John Graham Mellor.

Below When the diplomat Ron Mellor was posted to Tehran in what was then known as Persia, Anna Mellor disliked the city: she would be shouted at in the street for not covering her head. With the characteristic stubbornness inherited by her son John, she refused to compromise.

Left The Mellor family in repose in 1965 at 15 Court Farm Road in Upper Warlingham in Surrey. While younger son John takes up a position between Anna and Don, you can't help but notice that David seems distanced from the gathering, as though wishing to move away.

Right John Mellor at the age of sixteen at the wedding reception of his cousin, Stephen Macfarland, in Acton in West London. He spent much of the day with his cousin Gerry, who was struck by his charisma. Johnny went home with a gift, a guitar from his cousin Jonathan and on which Pete Townshend was said to have occasionally played. It was his first such instrument.

Below From small acorns . . . John Mellor's (second from right) part as a French waiter in his school's 1967 production of Sandy Wilson's *Free As Air* gave him only one line. Third from left is Andy Secombe, the son of the comedian Harry, from whom John later acquired a drum kit. As he progressed through the school, John became a high flier in its arts' projects.

Above John Mellor, with his schoolfriend Ken Powell, concentrating on their work at City of London's Freemen's School in Ashtead. The headmaster would regularly write to John's father, apologizing for his inability to further John's academic progress.

Right Gravedigging was an archetypal occupation for aspiring rock 'n' rollers (see also Rod Stewart). But when his seasoned workmates found that Woody was not really strong enough, they asked him instead to keep the cemetery clean of litter. He was paid £15.50 a week.

Above When the 101'ers tired of pushing their equipment to gigs in a baby carriage, they clubbed together and bought this hearse for £50. As they became more successful, they replaced it with a secondhand van. From left to right: Clive Timperley, Mole, Richard "Snakehips" Dudanski, Alvaro, Jules Yewdall, Joe Strummer, and "Big John" Cassell.

Right Paloma Romano came into Joe's life at the beginning of 1975, at 101 Walterton Road. By the time they moved to a squat on Orsett Terrace in Paddington, their relationship was faltering. After Paul Simonon renamed her Palmolive, she went off in a rage to form the Slits.

Above The Clash kicked off 1977 with a gig at the newly opened Roxy on Neal Street in Covent Garden, the punk mecca, for one hundred days. As his trusty Telecaster was in for repair, Joe played a borrowed white semi-acoustic Gretsch. Don Letts deejayed the beginning of the punk-reggae fusion.

Left The Clash's gig at London's Rainbow on May 9, 1977, marked the zenith of the White Riot tour, an extraordinary sight of massed punk. The seats that they smashed cost the group £15,000, a big chunk of their CBS £100,000 advance.

The album cover shot of *The Clash*, which came from this same London's Rainbow session, was taken by Kate Simon for a *Sounds* article in late 1976. Joe is clutching Paul's bass, with its Jackson Pollock–inspired paint drips and play-by-letters neck. Joe's hair, briefly dyed blond, was beginning to grow out at the roots.

Left A consummate dramatic performer, Joe understood the art of using every inch of floor space, hurtling himself across the stage or leaping from speakers. At this gig at Camden's Music Machine in July 1978, Sex Pistol Steven Jones joined the Clash on stage, fueling rumors he was to replace Mick Jones.

Below Driven by his unconscious, Joe was frequently in a trancelike state onstage, communing with Jah. At this Chicago show, he was moved to a state of transcendence. The gaffer-tape "Strummer guards" on his arm saved him from guitar-string cuts.

very flashily dressed people—I mean, that's what took my eye. I think Paul already had his hair dyed blond and spiky tufts. And it was so much more glamorous than the norm.

"It was Paul Simonon who really gave the look to the Clash, and kind of led us into . . . Well, we had to make our own clothes—that was one difference I have to say between the Clash and the Sex Pistols. The Sex Pistols had McLaren's boutique, and he was able to feed his clothes to the group. But with Bernie in charge of us, who'd split apart from Malcolm, we were in the situation where we had to make our own clothes. Paul Simonon was really instrumental in this, because he was an artist at the time, as he is now. It was Simmo who got into flicking the clothes with paint [inspired by the drip-painting method of Jackson Pollock], and then we started to paint words on them. I think it was Bernie who suggested putting words [on them], because he was into that situationist theory stuff, and it has to be stressed none of us were intellectuals, or are . . . But a large part of it for me was the look as well as the sound. A new world was taking over, and I mean we wouldn't stop. It was a twenty-four-hour experience, day or night, either writing songs, or making clothes, getting into records. It was a full-on thing."

"Joe looked funny when we first met him," said Mick. "He didn't look quite right. We already looked the part, committed to this new thing. We gave him some trousers and a jacket and did it up a bit for him. He started to look right straightaway. He had quite short hair at that time, dyed blond. Standing at the bus stop, opposite Davis Road, I was thinking, He's starting to look all right. But he had all this stuff that we didn't have, the stuff that we looked up to—just the fact that he was doing it and making an impression, playing to people in public. All our projects had hardly involved any public excursions. Up to that point."

For now Bernie Rhodes wanted an assurance that he had made the right decision in selecting this singer for the group. He checked out his choice with Glen Matlock. "When he got Joe Strummer into the Clash, he asked me what I thought of him. 'He's all right,' I said, 'but he's a bit old.' 'Don't you worry about that,' said Bernie, 'I'll have ten years off him.' And he did. Next time I saw Joe he looked maybe not ten years younger but certainly a totally different man and ready to rock."

"My take on Joe Strummer is this," Bernie Rhodes told me. "Before we met, Joe and I, he had a dilemma: he was dissatisfied with himself and his life. He took on the role of Woody, but then he met me and I shook his life into the future. Joe didn't want to be Woody, he wanted to be me. And that's how he became an international success."

When Joe Strummer returned home from that first visit to Davis Road, Iain Gillies was waiting for him: "He came back in the evening and was in a state of high excitement, running on adrenaline, pacing nonstop around the ground-floor rooms. The others at Orsett Terrace had to follow him from room to room. Joe and the 101'ers were supposed to be having a meeting about the state of the band. But there was no band. It was a fait accompli—Joe was leaving."

The 101'ers had one last gig to play, a show in Sussex on June 5. Although Martin Stone was again deputizing on guitar, Clive Timperley turned up to add his instrument on this valedictory performance. Then it was all over.

By now Mickey Foote had moved out of Orsett Terrace and was living with his girlfriend in Sebastian Conran's palatial house by Regent's Park. Paul Simonon and Sid Vicious replaced him in the Orsett squat. "By then Joe's new group had obviously formed," said Jules Yewdall. "The 101'ers were no more and the squat was starting to come to an end as well. Everyone was trying to figure out what they were going to do next. By then Joe had already moved. Everyone was losing touch with each other." With Joe and Paul periodically living there, 42 Orsett Terrace continued as a squat until November 1976. However, with the end of the 101'ers, the spirit of the squat significantly declined.

Joe's breaking up the 101'ers caused trouble among his squatter mates. Gill Calvert remembered him being called to ideological order one night by Tymon Dogg and Dave Goodall in the kitchen of 23 Chippenham Road, as rainwater ceaselessly dripped into a plastic bucket from the leaking roof: "Tymon and Dave were outraged with him: 'You can't do this. How can you do this?' Joe, almost asking permission, said, 'Can I go with a clear conscience?' It was painful. There was something very parental about it.

"Joe only drank in those days if it was around: if dope was about he'd have it, if drink was about he'd have it. He was much more of a drinker once he got into the Clash. I think there was a lot of pressure once he was in the Clash. [Mick Jones disagreed: "He drank loads. The 101'ers was pub rock, after all."] I think there was an awful lot of keeping up he had to do, with Mick and Paul, to prove he wasn't a hippie. So he had to become a bloke. But there was a life-support system that had been taken away from him. When he came to London, Dave and Gail were there and he met Paloma, he was anchored. I think that gave him a sense of family."

Joe had attempted to bring one member of the 101'ers into his as yet unnamed new group—Richard Dudanski was offered the drum stool: "I was in bed one night, and Joe came up with some of the guys in this new group. I went down to Davis Road, and the first guy I met was Bernie Rhodes. Bernie was not the easiest person. I just didn't want to work with him. So I said, 'We can change the name of the 101'ers, but let's keep doing what we are basically doing, and we'll be fine.' But Joe was sold on Bernie's ideas of management. So I went off to Italy—that was that. Joe had to totally deny the 101'ers and anything to do with them. After about a year I found him sleeping out in the garden one morning, where the rubbish was. He had come down to see us, but, being Joe, didn't want to wake us up at two in the morning. For me the Clash's political approach was very ironic, because the 101'ers were living political stuff—that was our existence as squatters, literally the politics of the street. We were laughing at society from which we managed to be rather separate, living another way."

Pat Nother, Richard's brother, simply said, "I don't understand why my brother didn't join the bloody Clash."

Bernie Rhodes had rented premises from British Rail in Camden Town which he named Rehearsal Rehearsals—abbreviated by its users to simply "Rehearsals." Rehearsals consisted of a large downstairs room and two upstairs rooms, one filled with secondhand pinball and fruit machines (a further sideline of Bernie Rhodes, as was selling secondhand Renaults), and another a band office and recreation area, with a jukebox.

This new group may have had space to rehearse but they still didn't have a drummer. Joe Strummer called up Paul Buck. Paul had seen the 101'ers once, at a show in Hammersmith, but he was unaware that Woody now had another name. "I called him 'Wood' and he snarled at me: 'I've changed my name.'" Although he appears in the earliest photographs of the still unnamed group, Paul lasted for only a couple of rehearsals. "The group came down to our farm in a big truck which they'd borrowed," Paul told me. "To see them all in the Sussex countryside was very funny. They were all there, including Keith Levene and other hangers-on, and Bernie.

"Unbeknownst to everybody I recorded the whole afternoon. I had a foot switch I used to flick when I was playing with another guitarist so we could ascertain our progress. I recorded the whole afternoon so I could learn the songs, if it all worked out. Unfortunately Bernie realized I'd made a copy and asked to borrow it. That's the last I ever saw of it."

T erry Chimes had been born in 1956 into a musical family in London's East End, but decided at the early age of four that he wanted to become a doctor. Still, before he settled down to what he knew would be his ultimate career, he felt he wanted to become a rock star. "You think, 'Well, it's got to happen to someone!' When you're young and stupid, you can get away with thinking like that."

Fortunately, his ambition coincided with the most radical change popular music had experienced in a decade. "I thought that punk was great because we were sweeping away all the old stuff: 'We've got a better idea than you. We're having fun and you're not!' It was a way of changing the rules. You didn't have to crawl to record companies. People at the gigs were so excited. When you'd read in the media that it was about having safety pins in your nose, I couldn't believe it—they had it completely wrong."

Terry Chimes had played with three of the lineups that Mick Jones had tried to put together, having auditioned in August 1975 for Violent Luck; then for London SS; and also for the version of this new group that had the singer Billy Watts. "I had long hair then. They had chopped their hair off and wore drainpipes, and looked pretty odd compared to everyone else in the street. We walked down the road to a [café] and it felt like a gang, only I felt that I wasn't in the gang because I didn't have the same gear. I suppose it's some male instinct, but I remember thinking, It's good for a band to look like a gang."

Chimes went along to Rehearsal Rehearsals: "Everything was the same except that Billy Watts had disappeared and they said, 'This is Joe.' He was an odd-looking character. I thought, 'He doesn't look like a singer,' and when he sang he didn't sound like a singer. I got the impression that this guy's a bit odd, and I couldn't see him as a singer of a rock 'n' roll band. But they said he was good. We had a rehearsal and I came back. It became apparent he had a different kind of charisma. He didn't look like someone from a big superstar rock band, strutting about the way they do. He didn't have the clear kind of singing voice that you would expect, didn't seem like a singer. That was my problem not his—my preconceptions.

"He seemed almost uninterested. We said hello, and then he carried on looking at the floor. When he was onstage he had more energy and emotion than you could think of but you didn't see that in conversation with him. He was a Jekyll and Hyde: offstage he was just quiet, but you put him onstage and he'd go berserk. After a couple of rehearsals I could see how it could work.

"Me and him, the drummer and the singer, we had to blast the audience with energy. He converted me to his thinking, which was if you put energy out there, then they'll feel it."

Terry was taken with the attitude of the group members. "Underlying everything was an almost obsessive sense of ambition: 'We are going to do this and we are going to get there!' They didn't care that they weren't very good yet at playing certain instruments. They didn't care about anything like that. They were going to get there."

The five musicians began frantically rehearsing, often seven days a week, from around lunchtime until about ten at night. "Only about a third of that time was rehearsing, in the strictest sense of the word," said Terry. "The rest was asking about what we should like, what we should say, what we should do, what we should dress like, and all the other things. That stuff went on for hours. There was a funny sense in which we were trying to sharpen each other up, so we'd challenge each other very much. It wasn't like having fun—it was almost a sense that we weren't there for fun. You had to be sharp, and pushing each other to be better all the time. Bernie was in the background orchestrating that attitude: that we work on everything, the way we looked, what we said, the music, the songs—everything had to be worked on to the maximum so that when we were exposed to the public they were going to go 'Wow!' Looking back, I think that really worked, but it was blooming hard."

Of the five musicians in this new group, it was Keith Levene, Terry Chimes believed, who was the most idealistically rigorous: "He was the most keen on making sure no one got too soft or too weak, the guardian of everyone's attitude. We would argue about every little detail, because it got the right attitude in the end, but it was tedious at the time."

The last member to join this group before Terry Chimes had been Joe Strummer. Where did he stand in this endless ideological struggle? What was the position here of this singer with a group whom Mick Jones certainly had been slightly in awe of? Years later, after the end of the Clash, Mick told the photographer Joe Stevens that Joe Strummer had been "like a father figure to him." An interesting remark considering Bernie Rhodes was in a similar paternal position. "Joe referred to Bernie as the headmaster—that was his humor," Terry Chimes remembered. "Joe seemed to have a certain respect for Bernie: Joe's attitude was that our job was to perform the music, and Bernie's was to do that business stuff we don't know about."

"Joe did have politics, more than Mick," said Bernie, "but it started to pull him apart. Joe was very good raw material: it was clear from the start—just be Bernie."

"Joe had a very idealistic idea of the band," considered Terry Chimes. "He wanted to share that with everyone, and genuinely wanted us all to be together. He wouldn't have had a favorite in the group. He worked with everyone trying to make everything perfect. This idea that we should be as good as we can get, this perfectionism, was rife throughout the whole thing. I found it wearing: I was always the one arguing with everyone else, me versus the rest. I thought being in a band would mean you would drive round in fancy cars, and have lots of girlfriends and lots of fun. They thought this was a shocking attitude." He laughed. "We'd have arguments, but it would all be theoretical, hypothetical and a bit pointless. It was part of the process of indoctrination we did on each other that we were going to be the greatest band in the world." (To assist them in becoming the "greatest band in the world," Bernie sent Joe for singing lessons to Tona de Brett, a vocal coach who also trained Johnny Rotten, Chrissie Hynde and Billy Idol. "I couldn't do much for that Mr. Strummer," she said later.)

"When I really saw what was going on," said Ari Up, "was when I went to a Clash rehearsal at Rehearsals. They had these paint-splattered clothes—very stylish. Back then the shape of jeans was disgusting: this was very military. It looked brilliant, compared to hippie musicians. In your eyes suddenly: *fuck!* When I saw those clothes and I was fourteen, I flipped."

As yet this potential Greatest Band in the World had no name. Several had been tried out, among them the Mirrors, the Phones and the Outsider (Terry Chimes insists it was "Outsider" in the singular—*The Outsider*, Colin Wilson's celebrated 1956 study of disaffection, was prominent on Bernie Rhodes's reading list). Two that stuck more readily with the five musicians were the Heartdrops, a reference to a Big Youth song, "Lightning Flash (Weak Heart Drop)," and the Psychotic Negatives, which seemed in the perverse tradition of Sex shop group names. It was Paul Simonon who noticed how frequently the headlines in the London *Evening Standard* carried the word "clash"; the Clash was the name decided upon. "I didn't just stumble upon it," he said. "We were so highly attuned to what we needed by then that the word leapt out at me from the pages of the paper." Which was just as well, as—after nagging Bernie Rhodes ceaselessly—the group had their first gig booked, as opening act to the Sex Pistols, at a pub the 101'ers had played, the Black Swan, 180 miles north of London, on July 4, 1976.

"It was pretty good," Joe told Mal Peachy, "because there we were in Sheffield and I think it was on a Sunday afternoon and all these people came out of the woodwork, you know, like punk types: ex–Roxy Music, like leopard-skin period, but searching on for the next thing. Lots of makeup and hair beginning to go berserk. There was a fair audience there, and that gave us a lot of heart. Because we realized that this was a nationwide thing that was just about to explode."

"One thing that didn't change from the beginning, right through to the end of the group," confided Chimes, "was that before each show Mick was always nervous, running around, very uncomfortable and really stressed. But Joe was making jokes and seemed very happy. Then we'd come offstage and Mick would be all happy because it's over, and Joe would be sitting with his head in his hands, saying it was the end of the world—and that never changed at all."

Among the numbers played by the Clash were the 101'ers' "Rabies (from the Dogs of Love)," Mick Jones's "Ooh, Baby, Ooh (It's Not Over)" and "Listen," an instrumental number. Joe's equipment included a microphone he had stolen from the English National Opera House when he worked there as a janitor. During the Pistols' set, Joe Strummer and Terry Chimes stood at the side of the stage. "I really rate this lot," confided Joe to the drummer. "They're not very good, are they?" was, in turn, John Lydon's almost predictable assessment of the Clash to Glen Matlock.

The Sheffield date only intensified the level of ambition within the Clash. July 5 saw the Clash at Dingwall's Dancehall in Camden Town, to see the revered Ramones. The following night, the Damned opened for the Pistols at one of their Tuesday-night 100 Club dates, which caused anxiety within the Clash. They should have been playing that gig: were they going to miss the boat of this new musical mood?

By now Mick Jones—in a relationship with Viv Albertine, who continued to live at Davis Road—was staying for much of the time with Stella, his grandmother, or "nan," in the eighteenth-floor high-rise flat in Wilmcote House on the Harrow Road that became part of Clash mythology. (On the *Sandinista!* album Mick would write a song about his life there. "I wrote 'Up in Heaven (Not Only Here)' about the swirl of the wind in the rubbish shaft in the tower block—'a giant pipe organ up in the air . . . when the wind hits this building, this building it tilts'—that's about Wilmcote House," he told me.) Less than ten minutes' walk from Orsett Terrace, Joe would go over there to work with his songwriting partner. "The lifts never work in those flats. That's the worst thing about them," he once complained to me. Mick Jones would reciprocate by visiting Orsett Terrace, where by now not only Paul and occasionally Sid Vicious were living, but also Keith Levene. "Joe and I had an understanding between ourselves," said Paul, "that stemmed back from when we were living together at Orsett Terrace and Mick was living with his nan. Living with someone like that, you get to really know and understand each other. So at the bottom line there was a certain separation between me and Joe and Mick."

Mick Jones and Joe Strummer began to work as a true songwriting partnership, with established methodology. "We wrote fast," said Joe. "We would fire off each other. Mick said, 'I think we should have a song called "Career Opportunities."' So I said, 'Right. You and Paul go down the Kentucky [Fried Chicken] and get some potato croquettes,' and I just banged the lyric up while they were out. When they came back, we'd bang it into a tune, or Mick would. He was a good tunesmith." "We did 'Career Opportunities,'" said Mick, "when we were sitting in Joe's squat in the ice-cream factory round the back of Harrow Road. There was the three of us. Paul was looking through the *Evening Standard*. It had a classified advertisements section: Career Opportunities. He said, 'What about "Career Opportunities"?'"

Mick had plenty of ideas for songs left over from his time with his previous groups, and Joe would write lyrics to match the music of these; on other occasions he would write out a set of words on his own to which Mick would then match music; or they would write together at Rehearsal Rehearsals. "Bernie's input was direction, not content," said Joe, "which can be one and the same thing. He said, 'Write about what's important.' He steered us away from loveydovey stuff like 'She's Sitting at the Party' [a song that Mick Jones already had written], I think because he realized it was overdone, and he steered us toward writing something that was more real. Although now and again we'd separate: like he'd come up with 'Janie Jones,' or I'd come up with 'London's Burning.' And we continued to do that throughout our time together. But quite often he'd play me a tune and I'd write a lyric, or give him a lyric and he'd come up with a tune for it. The really great stuff, like 'White Man at Hammersmith Palais' [the next year], was done like that."

"At our height, around *London Calling* or a little after," said Mick, "Joe used to sit with his typewriter, typing it straight out. I'd sit the other side of the table with my guitar. He'd whack it out like a newspaper man, hand it to me. I'd knock the tune out there and then. On the spot. There might have been a little tiny finesse, just change that, but hardly any. It was just like that, straight. A gift. That was when we were at our height. We used to sit and write together. Lyrics tell you what the tune is a lot of the time. You just read the lyrics and you hear it. It's the way the words go: if they already have that musicality, then it's a song."

In appreciating the speed with which the pair worked—Joe said that if a song took more than a day it was invariably abandoned—it is worth noting it was just over twelve weeks from the time they started before the Clash was itself on a bill at a famous venue called the Roundhouse, opening for Crazy Cavan and His Rhythm Rockers—whom Joe had known in Newport—and the bill-topping Kursaal Flyers, a semi-pub-rock group who had managed to push themselves onto the charts.

"Bernie Rhodes is a very creative man," Joe told me, after much water—and metaphorical blood—had flowed under the bridge for all members concerned. "I remember clearly he gave us direction. At the time there was a lot of discontent, because that was really the first time that a generation had grown up and realized they didn't really have any future. The sixties were a booming time in England and elsewhere, and it seemed like the future was unlimited, and science hadn't reached any kind of dead end, and pollution hadn't become a topic, and the economy was booming. By that time in the seventies the generation had realized that there wasn't going to be a lot going for it. So we were really articulating what a lot of young people were feeling."

"We liked Bernie, and he liked us," said Mick Jones. To further focus his flock, the manager contacted Joe Stevens, an *NME* photographer from New York City who had worked in the British underground press in the late 1960s. Stevens was living with another American photographer, Kate Simon, in Finborough Road in Fulham, a short distance from Sex, and he had gotten to know Bernie through Malcolm McLaren and Vivienne Westwood. Joe Stevens had been to see the Sex Pistols' gig at the Nashville at which they had opened for the 101'ers, the show where the fight had broken out. ("Sid was standing off to one side, not being Vicious at all.") "I took a couple of pictures of Strummer, and he saw me. Afterward he came over to me at the bar, the first time I met him—it bonded us. Later he introduced me to Simonon, 'This is Joe Stevens—he took pictures of me for the *NME*,' when in fact they'd run one picture, about postage stamp size."

Malcolm McLaren had recommended that Bernie Rhodes investigate Joe Stevens's sizable collection of underground publications: "It wasn't just English papers like *Oz* and *IT*. I used to get pictures in all the American underground papers, like the *East Village Other*, the L.A. *Free Press*, the *Boston Phoenix*, even Black Panther and lesbian papers. And they used to send them to me. So Malcolm told Bernie that he should get these papers and magazines off me to let his group read them and get some agitprop inspiration for songs. He came round and borrowed them from me. I never got them back. But look what it did for Joe Strummer's career," he joked.

That summer there was a sense of something new in the air, so tangible you could almost touch it, but it was not always positive. When Bob Marley and the Wailers played five nights at the Hammersmith Odeon in June 1976, the scale of mugging by black youth was a stark contrast to the evident cultural and moral integration at Marley's London shows a year before. This aggression was a mere prelude to what happened a couple of months later: on the last weekend in August, at the annual Notting Hill carnival, black youth clashed violently with the police, with running street battles in Ladbroke Grove, around the area of the Westway. "I can honestly remember standing right there," Joe said to me, "and I swear to you that stuff happened right in front of our eyes, in that small road, just under the Westway."

Also at the carnival with Joe, Paul Simonon and Bernie Rhodes was Pat

Nother. When the riot kicked off, Pat was not colossally impressed with his leather-jacketed companions' efforts to become street guerrillas. As black youth raged around them, lobbing bricks and bottles at the police and overturning cars, Joe and Paul tried to seize the rebel initiative: "They were trying to set a car on fire by holding a cigarette lighter next to the petrol cap. Luckily the lighter kept blowing out in the wind. They were hardly going to rock the establishment like this."

The outbreak of street fighting at this carnival inspired Joe to write the song "White Riot." ("Black people gotta lot of problems / But they know how to chuck a brick.") Joe's lyrics were a masterly expression of the thoughts of the disenfranchised that summer of 1976.

Pat Nother watched the growing radicalization of Joe Strummer with an amused eye. "He chased me down the road because I'd got a copy of a book on anarchy. 'Where's that bloody book? I need it!' I said, 'Joe, behave!' He was frantic to learn what this anarchy stuff was. I do think if it had been Stalinism he'd have signed up to it, and then got shot at the first trials, but he would have signed up. Because he was so into the idea of getting into the zeitgeist, the moment.

"I wouldn't say he was psychic about this stuff, but he was intuitive. Because psychic would be a message to his brain. I don't think he had messages to his brain, I think he had messages to his body—he could intuit things without having to think too much."

The story behind "White Riot" quickly became part of the Clash mythology, focusing the minds of their fans on the concept of "the sound of the Westway," a fundamental departure for Joe from what he had been singing about. "In the 101'ers," he said to me, "you'd sing 'Route 66'—in pubs people expect that kind of thing. Once we'd decided to leave that behind, we just decided to make our own surroundings the themes. In fact, I don't know if we even decided that: we just did it, instinctively, making our surroundings happen, giving them a bit of glamour or style."

By the end of August the Clash had played two more shows: one on the thirteenth at Rehearsal Rehearsals, a showcase to which booking agents and press were invited (three journalists turned up, two from Sounds, one, Caroline Coon, from Melody Maker), and the second the night before the carnival riot, on August 29, at the Screen on the Green, opening for the Sex Pistols. The Clash's performance that night was not received at all well by the *NME*'s Charles Shaar Murray. "The Clash are the sort of garage band that should be speedily returned to the garage, preferably with the motor still running," he wrote, "which would undoubtedly be more of a loss to their friends and families than to rock and roll . . . Their guitarist on the extreme left, allegedly known as Joe Strummer, has good moves but he and the band are a little shaky on ground that involves starting, stopping and changing chords at approximately the same time." The Clash responded by immediately writing the song "Garageland." "Joe was really excited about this idea of a garage band, that led to the song 'Garageland,'" said Terry Chimes. "He really thought, 'We belong in a garage.' He'd hit on something like that and get very, very excited and live off that for days. Then he'd be depressed about something else and he'd come in and say, 'We're not really a garage band at all.'" ("Joe would go into everything at a million miles an hour and then change his mind," said Bernie.) First performed at the Screen on the Green was a new song, "London's Burning," which turned an apparent pastiche of the nursery rhyme about the Great Fire of London of 1666 into a definitive expression of punk distaste for contemporary existence: "London's burning with boredom now," as well as the lines "Now I'm in the subway and I'm looking for the flat / This one leads to this block, this one leads to that." This is the only song by the group detailing the housing-project world that led to the "tower-block rock" reputation which became part of the Clash's mythology. It was a song that Joe had written almost entirely himself, in the same way that Mick Jones had come up with "Janie Jones" while riding the bus to Rehearsal Rehearsals.

Joe had been walking around the streets with Paul when the idea for the song came to him. "I wrote 'London's Burning' in the back room and I wrote it very quiet, whispering it, because Paloma was in the same room asleep." It was unusual, said Joe, to write a song on his own without Mick's input. "The best bit I like about 'London's Burning' is the intro, the guitar bit, because it's so insane," he said to Mal Peachy. "Mick was living overlooking the Westway in his gran's flat, and the very next morning I got up and I could still remember it from writing it the night before, and I took it over to him, and between him and me we sort of licked it into shape. But we ruined that number by auditioning drummers to it, and after two hundred drummers we were sick to death of that number." Joe gave credit to

Mick Jones for having come up with the line about television being the new religion—later Mick would talk to me about how his generation had been almost literally brought up by television, learning much of what it knew from the medium.

On August 31 the Clash supported the Pistols again, at the 100 Club. Early in the set, during a break occasioned by the need to replace a broken string on Keith Levene's guitar, Joe held up a transistor radio to his microphone and switched it on: a BBC news broadcast sailed out of the set, a report about an IRA bomb scare. Dave Goodman, the Pistols' sound engineer, added dub-echo effects: "It sounded like a Radio 4 discussion at the end of the world," Joe said. "I'd been lucky and bought a cheap transistor in a junk shop for ten bob and it worked quite well," he told *Sniffin' Glue*. "I'd been goin' around with it on my ear for a few days just to see what it was like. When someone broke a string I got it out and it just happened to be something about Northern Ireland."

The next Sunday, September 5, the Clash played their fifth show, one of the regular Sunday-evening performances at the Roundhouse. Available as a bootleg, this performance by the Clash stands as a testament to the extraordinary amount of work the group had done in just three months, in terms of both rehearsal and songwriting. As a rock 'n' roll performance so early in the career of an act it is remarkable, the group rising to the occasion of their biggest venue with fire, power, dynamic tension and fantastic songs, several of which were soon dropped from the group's set; these include the first live performance of "One-Two-Crush on You," "Mark Me Absent," another Mick Jones tune, and "How Can I Understand the Flies?," hardly a conventional notion for a pop song: it had been written by Joe that oppressively hot summer as insects buzzed around his mattress in the distinctly unhygienic surroundings of Orsett Terrace—Joe introduces it as "a summer song." "Protex Blue," the Mick Jones ode to condoms written before Joe had joined them from the 101'ers, concludes with a pair of bellowed words from the singer—"Johnny-Johnny"—that turn the song on its head with their humor, an example of the kind of verbal non sequiturs with which Joe would often shift Clash songs into the realm of surrealism.

After "Mark Me Absent," Joe rants at the audience. "Where did you get those denims?" he demands of one poor punter whom he has singled out as a relic from a nonpunk world. "What's that? The Jean Machine?" he sneers the name of a then-ubiquitous chain of clothing stores (started, incidentally, by an acquaintance of Bernie Rhodes) whose flared product was far removed from the sleek, aggressive look of the Clash. Then he attempts to suggest some self-determination on the part of the crowd, an early exhortation to what would become known as the punk do-it-yourself philosophy: "I've been wanting to go out and see some groups or something. But I've seen it all before. So I had to sit at home watching a TV that had no sound so I had to lip-read my way through. I'd just like to protest about the state of affairs, so any of you in the audience who aren't past it should get out and do something, instead of lying around." Although evidently acting the part of proselytizer, Joe's words are simultaneously believable and heartfelt.

The Roundhouse set finishes with a song that Joe dedicates to "the future": "1977," with its payoff lines "No Elvis, Beatles or Rolling Stones / In 1977." ("I had the lyric and Mick had the tune, and we were piecing it together. I had written in my notebook, 'No Elvis, Beatles or the Rolling Stones in 1977,' but I thought it was too silly, just to lay it on the table straight off. We were singing it through and we kept getting to a bit where we didn't have any lyrics and Mick said, 'We need something here.' I told him I had something, but that it was a bit silly. He said, 'Oh yeah, what's that?' So I went, 'No Elvis, Beatles or the Rolling Stones,' and he said, 'Great, that's really great!'") At the end of the Roundhouse set, Jeff Dexter, the venue's DJ, summarized the Clash's set by sitting on the fence: "I think that's a band that you either love or loathe, and I'm a bit noncommittal."

There might be no Elvis, Beatles or Rolling Stones in 1977, but there would be no Clash for Keith Levene any longer. This was Keith's final show. "He had gone offstage to change a string at the Roundhouse, and didn't come back for ages," said Mick. The next day Terry Chimes arrived at Rehearsal Rehearsals. "We were sitting there having a cup of tea, me and Mick and Paul. Joe and Keith weren't there yet. Joe came in saying, 'I woke up this morning, feeling we've got this phantom guitar player in the band. He just kind of comes in from nowhere and he disappears again—he's not really a part of what we are doing.' To which I said, 'Well, he's here every day. What do you mean?' He said, 'Yeah, but he doesn't feel part of it.' Paul was never very talkative—he kind of nodded in agreement. Then Mick said,

'Do you think he should leave then?' And Joe said, 'Yeah.' I was a bit out-raged, saying, 'What do you mean? One minute you've got a feeling, next minute he's leaving the band—*what?!?* This is ridiculous. We can't make decisions like this just on a whim.' But the three of them had been think-ing about it, and then they all voiced it, so it was a fait accompli. I was a bit stunned. Then Keith arrived before we had finished arguing about it, and Joe said, 'We think you should leave.' Keith was angry, and he walked off in a huff. That was the end of that.

"When he left the room we all looked at each other blankly. Then Mick said, 'I'd better learn to play the guitar,' meaning that Keith was doing the solos up until then—it was funny the way he said it. After he'd gone we re-hearsed, and we concluded that you don't need three guitars: you can do what you need to do with two guitars."

Such ruthlessness on Joe's part had been seen in his sudden departure from the 101'ers only months previously. It was behavior that would begin to be clearly seen as part of his pattern: Something's not working? Some-thing's standing in my way? Dump it. In both his professional and his per-sonal life Joe Strummer would come to be seen as operating by the same yardstick. "Joe was the one who sacked people in the 101'ers," said Paul. "He was the one who got rid of Keith Levene. He said, 'I was the hatchet man in the 101'ers: I'll do this.'"

"So now I was playing all the lead guitar," said Mick, "but Joe was rhythm guitar. And fantastic at it: the reason why is that he was really left-handed, and he played it as a right-hander. So all his dexterity was gone to waste: it was all the wrong way round. But that's why he was such a great rhythm guitarist, because of the energy he was using for fingering the chords. Both in his playing and in life, he already seemed to know what you know when you're older, as though he'd always had that in him—that older person's wise capacity. And it wasn't just that he was a few years older than us—he seemed to always have had that. We all used to learn off it."

Shows still did not come too readily for the Clash. On September 20 they played at the two-day punk festival at the 100 Club; after an out-of-town gig in Leighton Buzzard, they celebrated their first headlining gig in Lon-don, "A Night of Pure Energy," on October 23 at the ICA on the Mall. There, as proof of their sharply rising status, punk high priestess Patti Smith danced onstage with the group; Paul Simonon had no idea who she was.

The show was overshadowed by a punk called Shane MacGowan allegedly having his ear bitten off.

On October 29, a Friday night, the Clash played at Fulham Town Hall. There were only about one hundred people there, fifteen or twenty of them in assorted variants on the new punk uniforms. They were preceded by another new group, the Vibrators, who were pretty mediocre. The Clash was itself preceding Roogalator, a guitar-based group with a small underground reputation. By the time the evening concluded it was as though Roogalator's career was over. This was the first time I had seen the Clash— I was left breathless, stunned by their power and energy, astonished at the visual spectacle. Years later, when I mentioned this show to him, Mick Jones told me, "At first we weren't really bothered with what it sounded like. We just knew we'd be satisfied if it looked amazing to the audience, if they couldn't take their eyes off us." They succeeded more than amply. Jon Savage, the author of *England's Dreaming*, also went to the show, seeing the Clash for the first time. He recorded the performance on his cassette player, and you can hear what was going on. For example, when the Clash performed "I'm So Bored with the USA" it was as though they hadn't quite got used to the transition to the new lyrics, Joe having to blurt out an added "S A" after they almost reverted to "I'm so bored with you." Of course, at the time I had no idea what any of the songs were called, though I certainly noted "London's Burning," which began with its title bellowed out by Joe, and something that I thought was called "Why Riot." I really couldn't believe how great they were. For me the show was a life-changing moment, no question.

S niffin' Glue, edited by Mark Perry (known as Mark P.), was a photostatted publication that introduced the word "fanzine" to the punk vocabulary, inspiring hundreds of imitators across the United Kingdom. Its seemingly thrown-together graphic style was a yardstick for punk visuals, and for the fifteen months of its existence *Sniffin' Glue*'s unimpeachable street credentials made it the conscience and soul of the British punk movement. Issue 4, published in October 1976, with a picture of Joe and Paul on the cover, ran a four-page question-and-answer interview with the Clash, conducted by Steve Walsh only days after the 100 Club Punk Festival. More than anything, more than any stories in the weekly music press, it was this article in *Sniffin' Glue* that set the direction for the group's social stance and position. Here, for example, Joe delivered his famous anti-flares aphorism, "like trousers, like brain," and declared righteously that this was one group in which the vocals would not be delivered in a mock-American accent, the affectation of many English singers.

He also made it clear that he had digested Pat Nother's book about anarchy, and come out as a nonbeliever in the philosophy allegedly adhered to by the Sex Pistols: "I don't believe in all that anarchy bollocks!" Mick Jones agreed. "The important thing is to encourage people to do things for themselves, think for themselves and stand up for what their rights are . . . All our songs are about being honest, right? The situation as we see it, right?"

Joe Strummer also marked himself as being as much in touch with the cultural zeitgeist as Mick Jones—who in the interview often appears more as the spokesman of the group than Joe—when he dismisses almost every piece of modern popular music as "rubbish." "It's all shit!" underlined Mick Jones. Both of them agreed that the only good recent record was the Ramones album.

"How much change do you want? D'you want a revolution?" asked Steve Walsh.

"Well . . . yeah!" said Joe, railing against government secrecy and corruption. "I just feel like no one's telling me anything, even if I read every paper, watch TV and listen to the radio!"

Joe and Mick discussed their tactics at the Roundhouse gig, where they had attempted—as Mick put it—to "talk" to the audience; it is apparent therefore that Joe's haranguing of the Roundhouse crowd was deliberate, a laying out of the group's cards. When asked what effect they wanted on their audience, Joe outlined three things: to give them meaningful and discernible lyrics; to "threaten 'em, startle 'em," and to give them "rhythm." "Rhythm is the thing 'cause if it ain't got rhythm then you can just sling it in the dustbin!"

By the time this interview appeared, it was apparent that although the Clash aligned politically with some indeterminate strand of the left, the politics of this supposedly "political" group actually were those of the human condition. In Joe's opinion it was about the need to be aware—as he said, "I'd just like to make loads of people realize what's goin' on." There it was,

set in type, as early as October 1976, before they even had a record deal.
Though that was being worked on.

Through the intelligent and "conscious" statements of intent articulated in the *Sniffin' Glue* interview, the Clash was irrefutably established as
the only serious rival to the Sex Pistols; and Joe—in the inevitable manner
in which it is always the lead singer who becomes most deified—was elevated to being the only serious contender for the crown of punk king that
John "Johnny Rotten" Lydon so far had been unopposed in wearing. Moreover, the ability of both Joe and—often even more so—Mick Jones to articulate the beliefs and purpose of the Clash showed them in positive contrast
to the often mind-boggling nihilism of the Sex Pistols, especially following
the imminent arrival of Sid Vicious.

Indeed, Sid was to make his presence felt very soon at a Clash show. On
November 5 they played "A Night of Pure Treason" at the Royal College of
Art. In between "London's Burning" and "Protex Blue" something erupted
in the audience: Sid, recently out of a brief spell in a juvenile detention
home, was in a fight with some of the rest of the crowd. Joe was up for
mucking in: "Hey, you! I'm only about five foot eight, but if you've got
something then come and stand against me and we'll do it, right." With
Paul Simonon he stepped down into the audience. (Years later, Joe told the
artist Damien Hirst about this moment, complaining that Paul had left him
to it: "I realized only me and Sid Vicious were attacking the audience, so I
hit quite a big guy—he went down! Then a guy came up to me and afterward I realized he was saying, 'Calm down, calm down,' but at that precise
moment I thought he was attacking me so I hit him as hard as I could. Immediately I saw my mistake, but too late.")

Pennie Smith, like Joe Stevens a photographer for *NME*, had been commissioned to take pictures of the gig. "Backstage at the Royal College of Art
Joe had a toothache so he wasn't saying anything." But she discovered
almost immediately that the entire group had an alternative means of communication, something I, too, quickly experienced; they would think nothing of sitting with their knees touching yours, or putting an arm on your
shoulder or hand to emphasize a point. This naturally led to a greater close-
ness of feeling. "If you ever see a picture of me with Joe," said Pennie,
"there'd always be a little finger on my arm or something, just saying
there's a link. There was always a subtle, tactile bit. They were always feely-

touchy, a hug if something is wrong, a sock to the arm if something has gone right.

"At the RCA I took some shots, and after they'd seen them in the *NME* they rang up and said would I do some more pictures. It just went from there. I did a shoot in Caroline's flat, just after the Royal College of Art gig."

By now Paul Simonon had moved out of Orsett Terrace and was living in Earl's Court with Caroline Coon, the *Melody Maker* journalist and former political activist who was championing punk. Nearby lived Iain Gillies, who had got married. At the RCA show Simonon had tried to stop Iain from taking photographs backstage. "I'm Joe's cousin," he protested. "Oh, that's all right then," acquiesced the bass player. Joe would come over to see Iain; on one occasion he remembers Joe "jumping into bed with our flatmate": "One time Joe was visiting me at my flat in Earl's Court and he mentioned that Paul was living nearby, and provided a satirical account of Paul's domestic life. I don't know where Joe got these insights but he'd certainly surprise you from time to time. He would be silent with you for a while and then suddenly out of the pale blue yonder he'd say something revelatory. Uncle Ron had a bit of this quality, and Aunt Anna also seemed to me to be quite intuitive. I suppose that Joe's parents were a very interesting mix: the tail end of thoughtful British Empire and folksy but insightful Scottish Highlanders. Joe would quietly take in a lot of stuff that interested him and use this information later to good effect. Joe had the ability to get tremendously excited about some things and would act on his enthusiasms. I'd say that this energy and enthusiasm was definitely innate."

under heavy manners

1976-1977

For the rest of 1976 there was a flurry of Clash shows, at venues around London as diverse as Ilford's Lacy Lady and the Nag's Head in High Wycombe. In November the Clash had sufficiently impressed Chris Parry, an ambitious young A&R man at Polydor Records, for him to offer to record some demos at the company's studio off Oxford Street. Who would be the producer? Bernie Rhodes had a good idea: Guy Stevens. Stevens had been the DJ at the Scene, a legendary Soho mod club, where Bernie had first got to know him. His talents were noticed by Chris Blackwell, whose Island Records put out Jamaican tunes in Britain. Blackwell decided to set up Sue, an Island affiliate, to distribute American rhythm and blues, and gave it to Stevens to run; he quickly scored a number of hits by artists such as Inez and Charlie Foxx, and Roy C. When Island expanded into the "underground" album market in 1967, Guy Stevens began to produce some of the label's acts, like Free and Mott the Hoople, a particular inspiration for Mick Jones, who met him when Guy came along to check out Mick's group Little Queenie. But during the first part of the 1970s Guy Stevens became something of a rock 'n' roll casualty.

"At this time Guy was drinking a lot," said Joe, "and we went into a demo studio off Oxford Street in Polydor and cut about six songs. That was the first time we'd recorded, and the results were kind of disappointing. We were quite an energetic unit, and it sounded very flat or very dull. I think Guy wasn't really up to scratch: anyway, it didn't go off very good—it was a debacle." The songs recorded by the group were "Janie Jones," "London's Burning," "White Riot," "1977" and "Career Opportunities." "After the session we went up to Guy's flat," said Paul. "He was going on about having seen this Led Zeppelin film called *The Song Remains the Same*. It was driving him crazy—he hated it. He got so mad that he got hold of the record and chucked it up in the air and it hit Joe in the eye and of course he was all apologetic, going, 'Oh Joe, I'm so sorry.'"

"Guy Stevens was a legendary producer, but he was boozing at the time," remembered Terry Chimes. "Yet he seemed the natural producer for us. He had a feel for what we were doing: he understood the energy, he understood us. He'd pat you on the back and say, 'That's good, those drums are great, you're doing really well.' That's what you needed a producer to do. When Mick was doing guitar, he'd jump up and down in front of him, saying, 'Yeah, give it this!' He understood. Joe liked him. But there was a frostiness between him and the guy paying for the studio. Joe said to me, 'I think they've got him numbered.' When we were at the mixing stage, according to Mick and Joe, the pressure he was under was too much: he got sloshed and screwed it up. The band were behind him, the other people weren't, and they got someone else to produce it instead. We should have said, 'We believe in you, just sober up and get it together,' but we weren't used to calling the shots at that time—we were a new band privileged to go into the studio to record demos."

This would not be the last time that Guy Stevens would work with the Clash. In less than three years—as part of a seemingly ceaseless interweaving and circularity of relationships that flowed around the Clash and its individual members—he would be brought back into a fold that contained many waifs and strays; at times you felt that the Clash and their entourage was almost like a form of ongoing group (pun intended) therapy in the most select mobile rock 'n' roll mental home.

The disappointing results of the Polydor demos were not the only stumbling block experienced by the group that month. "Shortly after that," said Joe, "Terry Chimes announced he was quitting. So it was a setback on two counts: the tapes didn't come out good, then the drummer was leaving." To the amazement of the rest of the Clash and Bernie Rhodes, Chimes—who was and remains very much his own man—had decided he had had enough of the endless ideological disputes within the group, and announced that he was quitting. He agreed to stick around until they found a replacement. "Everyone kept saying that when they got any money they were going to give it away. I thought, 'Well, I'm not bloody giving mine away!' We would argue like that all the time, and it wore me out. When I said I wanted to leave, they got angry, and then said, 'OK. Will you just do these gigs until we find someone else?' But they auditioned a lot of people and couldn't find the right guy. So I carried on doing the gigs."

On November 29 the Clash stepped down a peg, to open for the Sex Pistols at Lanchester Polytechnic at Coventry. After the Clash performed "White Riot," the tune was misinterpreted as racist and the social secretary refused to pay the group. They were under the impression this was the last show Terry Chimes would ever play with them.

Ten days before the Lanchester Polytechnic show the Pistols, who had signed to EMI Records, had released their first single, "Anarchy in the U.K.," an instant rock 'n' roll classic; it not only captured the intensity and magic of their onstage performances, but actually seemed to improve on it. The record got tremendous reviews. EMI upped the ante in efforts to push the single. On the first day of December 1976 the Clash, the Damned and the Pistols were rehearsing for a nationwide punk package tour at the Roxy in Harlesden, a largely Jamaican venue; they were also awaiting the arrival from New York of the package's final component, the Heartbreakers, which featured guitarist Johnny Thunders and drummer Jerry Nolan from the New York Dolls. The Clash was playing with a new drummer, Rob Harper. In the afternoon the Pistols learned that EMI had secured them a promotional slot early that evening on an ITV magazine show called *Today* on which they would be interviewed by Bill Grundy, an experienced television journalist—Queen, another EMI act, had had to pull out of the show.

The consequences are now infamous. Grundy goaded the group into swearing on TV, which led to a witch-hunt of tabloid headlines for an entire week. The Sex Pistols became national scapegoats, convenient whipping boys for a country that had been economically emasculated and was culturally stagnating. The Clash was caught in the slipstream of this brouhaha. As the Sex Pistols' tour was set to kick off two days after the television "incident," the other acts on the package were tarred with the same brush. The dates had been booked throughout December. When the assorted musi-cians arrived in their tour bus at the University of East Anglia in Norwich for the first date on December 3, they discovered that the gig had been banned. Furious students had arranged a sit-in to protest the decision. Six other dates were canceled almost immediately. A curious pastiche of Ken Kesey's hippie Magic Bus trips was enacted as the groups were driven all around England and Wales, looking for gigs that hadn't been canceled, stay-ing in expensive hotels, bankrolled by EMI. The Heartbreakers merrily set about persuading whoever would fall for it that doing smack could be really good fun. The Heartbreakers are uniquely credited as the one single force that brought heroin into the British punk scene. "Loads of people got into heroin because of Johnny Thunders," Paul Simonon said to me. "He was the cause of huge damage in punk."

As they trundled the length and breadth of the country on the Anarchy tour bus you could almost feel from hundreds of miles away the pall of col-lective depression hanging over the Sex Pistols. It was as early as this tour that the Clash overtook the Pistols as a live act, when they played the second of two nights at the Electric Circus in Manchester; the first show was on De-cember 9, the next on the nineteenth, slotted in to give the tour one more date. For Joe, looking like the Eddie Cochran of punk, this second show was a transforming moment, a steaming, electrifying performance. "That was the night that I knew we were really going to do it," he said, "because we were better than the Pistols. They had a really hard time following us. We blew them off the stage—we beat them at it." Psychologically, this was cru-cial for the Clash, who on the tour had been very much guests at someone else's party. "We still had solidarity, but we felt pretty small just then be-cause the Sex Pistols were front-page news and we were just nothing, we were bottom of the bill," Joe told the writer Jon Savage.

Over the course of the Anarchy dates an important element of what be-came the philosophy of the Clash was established. "Because none of us had ever been on tour before," Joe told Mal Peachy, "and we were determined not to become like the stadium-type groups that were famous at the time, we didn't really have that thing where, today, backstage is almost like a monastery, protected by rows of goons, and you have to have twenty lami-nates to get to find a can of beer. It was much more open season in those days, and so the audience would kind of swarm backstage after the gig, and it was part of the times, part of the ethos of it. Because you could talk to the audience, or they could talk to you, it meant you kept your feet on the ground." It could be argued that the Pistols had first established this insistence that they were not elevated above their fans: the Pistols would always wander out into the hall after the show and mingle with whoever wanted to talk to them. But they wouldn't almost willfully insist—as would the Clash, frequently enduring arguments with theater management and even their own security—that whoever wanted should be allowed to come back to their dressing room. Ever after the Anarchy tour the Clash's dressing rooms would swarm with fans, front man Joe holding forth in passionate discussion on all manner of subjects; and then it would be back to the group's hotel to expand even further on these matters; like many musicians Joe Strummer would be buzzing for hours on adrenaline following his supercharged performances and would rarely be ready for sleep before six in the morning; if there was a girl still awake she might end up sharing his bed with him—but not until the dialectic of the night had been thoroughly dissected.

The Anarchy tour bus arrived back in London on December 23, a chilly, damp night. Joe remembered sloping up Tottenham Court Road, consciously not buttoning up his coat, as though he needed to feel the harsh wind on his body as a reminder of a world removed from a life of hotels and tour-bus travel. Some Christmas: the Clash was completely broke, having earned virtually no money for all its efforts during the year. Although Mick could usually get a hot meal at his grandmother's, Joe and Paul had been near to starving half the time—after making paste from flour and water that October to put up posters for the ICA on the Mall gig, Paul famously had gone back to Rehearsal Rehearsals, heated up the remnants on the blade of a saw and eaten them. "After the Anarchy tour returned to London," Joe told Mal Peachy, "it was pretty sad, because it was freezing and it was like the excitement was over, and we were dumped back on the street. It was all a bit of an anticlimax, though we did have something to look forward to—that we were going to sign a contract and record our songs and get them out." When Joe got back to Foscote Mews, his mood dipped even lower. While he had been away his squat had been broken into, and all his possessions had been stolen, including every piece of his memorabilia from the 101'ers. If anything, this confirmed for him that the only way was forward with his new group—but it was also a major loss for someone who had always been a hoarder of his past, and was already stuffing all manner of matter into used plastic shopping bags, out of which he almost seemed to live. Friends would say that Joe had moved so often as a child that hanging on to all that stuff gave him "a sense of permanency." For a time Joe moved into the upstairs of Rehearsal Rehearsals, sharing the place with Paul.

The group celebrated New Year's Day 1977 by playing two sets at a new club, the Roxy in Covent Garden, which had opened as a punk forum. This was the last date for Rob Harper with the Clash. Joe wore a shirt with "1977" stenciled on it and—his Telecaster in for repair—played a borrowed white semi-acoustic Gretsch guitar. "Remote Control," a new song written over Christmas on which Mick Jones took lead vocals, was performed for the first time. The Roxy, which lasted for only a hundred days, briefly became the punk mecca; it had been started by Andy Czezowski, the manager of Generation X and the accountant for Acme Attractions, the only rival to Sex on the King's Road. Running the shop for owner John Krivine were petite, pretty Jeannette Lee and her boyfriend, Don Letts, a young Rastafarian from Brixton who had been profoundly influenced by Bob Marley.

When Czezowski opened the Roxy, he asked Letts to be the DJ. Letts in turn co-opted his brother Desmond and friend Leo Williams to run the bars; Leo worked the downstairs bar. He and the Letts brothers also sold sno-cone spliffs. The ganja helped establish a cross-cultural mood underpinned by the soundtrack of roots reggae that Don Letts would play in between the amphetamine charge of the punk acts booked for each night. "There weren't enough punk records to play," remembered Letts, "so I just brought my reggae collection along." As a consequence of Letts's record choices, he helped set in motion the celebrated punk–reggae fusion which would find its most ardent interpretations in the music of the Clash and be celebrated later in 1977 in the Bob Marley song "Punky Reggae Party."

At the end of 1976 Don Letts, Leo Williams and a friend named J.R. rented the top two floors of a house in a salubrious part of Forest Hill in southeast London. After the Roxy would close the elite of the assembled multitude might well find themselves squeezing into Don Letts's Morris Minor and driving back to the Forest Hill flat, where—smoking spliffs and listening to reggae—they would watch the sun come up. A frequent visitor on such occasions was Joe Strummer; after a time he became an occupant of one of the smallest rooms. Although he was there infrequently, for close to a year he paid his small share of the rent. "It was a tiny room, like a closet," said Don. "But Joe seemed to like small rooms. Everywhere I went, even if Joe was in a big room he'd make it small by making a bunker within it. I didn't see him that often, he was moving around and going to other places, but I do remember smoking and playing different records with him and that he stole my copy of the Count Ossie and Mystic Revelation of Rastafari triple album. Which I never forgot: Joe, you bastard. Me and my brother Desmond once took him to a black wedding reception, where he was the only white man there. Joe had this way of getting involved and warming to people. He'd engage them in conversation, and in that engagement he'd make that person feel very special, as though they were maybe the only person in the world. All the way through his life he made people feel special, even though they probably weren't. Joe just seemed to like everybody. He was an equalizer. I dug that about him."

Don and Leo Williams would drive with Joe to Jamaican reggae clubs like the Bouncing Ball in Peckham or the Four Aces in Dalston, venues with tricky reputations. "He'd be the only white man in the Four Aces, and they'd kind of have to get over his look, because to the people there at first it seemed like some kind of right-wing thing. But when he lit up a spliff they realized that he wouldn't have been in there if he was like that. Once when he came to the Four Aces the guy on the microphone name-checked him while Joe was making a spliff, which seemed to surprise him so much that he somehow blew the weed out of his hand.

"It's got to be said that people like Joe Strummer and John Lydon—particularly Joe—were like the punk intelligentsia, they were the thinkers. They were the ones that gave it the depth. With Joe there was no mistaking early on that my man was deep. He knew all the cultural and literary references, all the revolutionary references, and he put it all into context: he wasn't just an angry young man stamping and screaming. As you can see in his lyrics, there's a lot more ideas in one of Joe's rhyming couplets than there are in some people's entire albums. More than anyone he moved the lyrical goalposts of what contemporary music could deal with. There had been protest songs and anti-establishment songs before, but Joe did it in a way that made it sound exciting and not overearnest. He made it humorous as well. Because it's about the way you tell 'em: you've got to capture people's imaginations before you give them the serious input, and he had a great understanding of that. I remember when I first saw the Clash I didn't actually hear what he was saying—well, no one could understand what Joe was saying—but you knew something was going on because the power and energy were so intense. It just made you want to be involved, and made you realize that you could be part of this too. Joe made me see that you should just get on with it.

"Now that Joe's dead and gone it's easy to look at him through rose-tinted glasses," added Don, "but he definitely had a bastard side to him. When Joe wanted something horrible done, when things happened that he couldn't deal with, he'd get other people to do it in a really Machiavellian way. He had a cowardly streak about him in this respect. But this is all part of Joe's humanity, the contradictions. But because he was so extreme it was more noticeable: he'd say one thing and do the opposite, all the time. If ever there was a wrong thing to do you could count on Joe doing it. I almost dug that.

"Joe was a sneaky fuck sometimes. In fact most times. Particularly to women. It must have been harder for Joe because he was supposed to be this right-on guy. But I've got to say it makes me love him more."

In his uniform of well-worn black leather jacket, circular John Lennon–like metal-framed spectacles, sprayed-on cotton trousers and blue brothel creepers, the diminutive figure of Bernie Rhodes struck an appealing gnomish posture that was at odds with his efforts to appear as an archetypal twentieth-century revolutionary, a Fidel Castro of Camden Town. It was Bernie who came up with the idea of the three- or four-word taglines with which the Clash would stencil their clothing and equipment: lumps of Clash lyrics—"Sten Guns in Knightsbridge," "White Riot," "Knives in W11"—rivaled Jamaican political slogans—"Under Heavy Manners" (the campaign slogan of the ruling People's National Party)—and mottoes from the individual members' own particular agendas—"Creative Violence" was urged by Paul, and Joe came up with "Chuck Berry Is Dead," a clear volte-face on his past, and "Hate and War," the mirror image of the hippie peace-and-love ethic. Joe, whose sixth-form ambition had been to go into advertising, took to this with gusto: in his lyrics, his economy and directness with words always delivered the message—he was almost selling the need for us all to want a White Riot of our own. The elevated, inspired amateurism of the Clash had the benefit of an extreme simplicity of approach and a shocking disregard for the accepted system of strategy and tactics. The Clash was moved, if not sustained, by abstract slogans and symbols. Like contemporary gang leaders, they had to make their authority manifest through bold, unmistakable symbols and dazzling displays of bravura elegance.

For a brief period in January 1977 it looked as though Malcolm McLaren and Bernie Rhodes might form a business partnership. Following the national outcry that had erupted after the Bill Grundy interview, the Sex Pistols had been dropped by EMI. Malcolm and Bernie had been to see Maurice "Obie" Oberstein, an American who was the visionary head of CBS Records in the United Kingdom; Obie offered the pair £100,000 to form their own punk label, to be distributed by CBS. The offer fell into a black hole. But Bernie Rhodes set up a meeting with the Clash about this possible label deal, held in the Ship pub in Soho's Wardour Street. "He said he wanted complete control," said Joe. "I came out of the pub with Paul collapsing in hysterics over those words." But that £100,000 figure had been broached by Oberstein, and Bernie Rhodes picked it up and ran with it. On January 27, Joe, Mick Jones and Paul Simonon were collected in a taxi on their way to what they believed would be their destination, the offices of Polydor Records—Chris Parry at Polydor had offered £25,000, plus all recording costs. But the cab took a different route: without their having been told this by Bernie Rhodes, they were heading farther down Oxford Street to the headquarters of CBS in Soho Square, where Bernie had managed to transmogrify Oberstein's label offer into a deal for the Clash alone. Bernie told the group members that CBS had promised them "artistic freedom"; but it was certainly better financially for Bernie that he could take his 20 percent off the top of the CBS £100,000, instead of off the Polydor £25,000—even though Bernie's percentage would eat into the money allotted for recording costs that was part of the CBS package. The deal was actually done using a Polydor contract form on which the name "Polydor" was scratched out and replaced with "CBS."

The Clash celebrated their record deal by going to see the film *Midway* in Leicester Square. Almost immediately the group members, and everyone working with them, saw a financial benefit. "Everyone was on a wage of twenty-five quid, no matter what," said Joe. "The dole was ten pounds sixty-four at that time, and now we were on twenty-five quid. I didn't feel particularly richer. We just kept on squatting."

That night the Clash went down to the Roxy, putting £500 behind the bar—a colossal amount when you consider it cost just £2 to see the Clash play. Mick and Joe were seen pouring drinks on people's heads. Paloma at the helm, the Slits stood off to one side, hectoring them for signing to a major label. There were grumblings in the columns of *Sniffin' Glue*—if only they'd known what had really gone on. Muff Winwood, the head of A&R at CBS, recalled Maurice Oberstein's instructions that his employees were to pay no heed to press reports of tension between the group and the company: this was a strategy devised by the managing director to enhance the "street" credentials of the Clash.

On Thursday, February 10, the Clash went into the recording studio, working until Sunday night, with Terry Chimes returning for the sessions. The January 1 date at the Roxy had been the group's only show of the year—virtually every day since then had been taken up with abortive auditions for a full-time replacement for Terry. They recorded in the strictly functional CBS Studio 3 in Whitfield Street, behind the record company's Soho Square headquarters, completing the album with similar Thursday to Sunday night sessions over the next two weeks. Joe and Mick were knocked out when they learned that this was the same studio in which Iggy Pop had recorded *Raw Power*, his inspirational punk blast album. "We didn't know this at the time," Joe told Mal Peachy. "It was only afterward when I knew *Raw Power* had been recorded in that room that I realized there must have been something in that very basic room."

One night in February, after an evening at the Roxy, Joe moved on to the Speakeasy, a nightclub in Margaret Street always packed with musicians, behind Oxford Circus. There a ted, a friend of Johnny Rotten's, followed Joe into the toilet, intent on giving him a beating for having faked working-class origins. In the tiled men's room he gave Joe a sound thumping, rendering even greater destruction to the Strummer dental bombsite by knocking out part of a front tooth. In an interview that the Clash did with *NME* writer Tony Parsons the next month, Joe mythologized the incident, claiming that he'd had a knife with him but realized that if he'd "stuck it in him" he'd have gone to jail. The outlaw gang image of the Clash was quickly being cemented into place. Tellingly, Joe said that the beating hadn't hurt much as he'd been so drunk. With a certain amount of surplus cash in his pockets, Joe was now drinking even more, and also hammering through lumps of hash. Like most punks he could always find a bolstering line of amphetamine sulphate, but Joe was never particularly partial to speed, hating the come-downs and the depression that followed in its wake. "We'd mainly grown out of speed by the time we were in the Clash," said Mick. But Joe's consumption resulted in increasingly erratic behavior; he could be snappy, snarling and irritable. The writer Kris Needs, then the editor of *ZigZag*, recalled that for his first year of knowing Joe he found him slightly frightening. That experience was by no means uncommon—the first time I met Joe, in May that year, we almost had a fight. These were the days when Joe was once found lying drunk in the gutter outside Dingwall's with rainwater washing into his mouth. "Many was the time we had to carry him home," said Mick. Life in 1977 was all pretty close to the edge, moving so fast there was hardly time to think—which wasn't such great news for someone like Joe, who loved to spend time on his own, thinking.

Mickey Foote, who'd mixed all the 101'ers shows and had taken on the same job with the Clash, was brought in at Joe's insistence. And Joe was adamant he produce the record ("It was a matter of go in, set up and keep the overdubs to a minimum. That album couldn't have been done any other way," Mickey said). "We were very keen that it didn't become overproduced. We didn't want to get compromised by the sound," Joe told Mal Peachy. "Mick Jones and Mickey Foote were overseeing that end of it." The mastered record was delivered to CBS on March 3. Mick Jones had dominated the sessions, translating his fascination with all aspects of the pop process to an understanding of how to transfer the group's music onto tape, which he took to with relish; although he later claimed not to remember working on the record because of his prodigious speed intake, others around the studio recall very little drug use whatsoever. "Any guitar of note on the record is Jonesy," said Joe. "I'm in there, chundering away with the bass drum and the snare, but I'd say anything you can actually discern must be Jonesy." The record was to be called, simply, *The Clash*. There could be no other title.

On March 11 the Clash played what was only their second show of the year, at the Coliseum Cinema in Harlesden. Yet again Terry Chimes was on drums—though this really was the last time he would play live with the group for five years—for a show that got great reviews across the board. In *NME* Nick Kent, who had been attacked at the 100 Club by Sid Vicious the previous summer, thereby giving him an ax to grind and a chance to get his own back on the Pistols' camp, completely "got" what the group was about: "Suddenly," read part of his review,

> Joe Strummer stopped between numbers. "Stop throwing beer at me! I don't like it," he stated in a decisively no-bullshit way . . . Strummer dead center, very, very authoritative. Strummer's stance sums up this band at its best, really: it's all to do with real "punk" credentials—a Billy the Kid sense of tough tempered with an innate sense of humanity which involved possessing a sense of morality totally absent in the childish nihilism flaunted by Johnny Rotten and his clownish co-conspirators.

"White Riot," the Clash's first single, came out seven days later, on March 18, and the album itself was released on April 8. CBS wanted to get a move on: what if this punk thing died on its feet? The picture on the front of the cover of *The Clash*, one of the archetypal images of rock 'n' roll, set the template; it had been taken by Kate Simon for a *Sounds* article in late 1976 around the back of Rehearsal Rehearsals. If you didn't know anything about them, you would have imagined the group was a three-piece—there is no drummer in this shot. (Terry Chimes was credited as Tory Crimes on the sleeve.) Mick Jones, standing to the right of the picture, has his head angled to the left and slightly down, looking vulnerable, almost depressed; Paul Simonon, to the right and a step ahead of Mick, has an air of moderate aggression and seems fed up, almost as though he is trying to fight his way out of the picture; Joe Strummer, as befits the group's front man, is behind and between both of them: his hair is dyed blond and he wears white trousers, a light-colored grubby jacket and paint-spattered shirt with a loosely knotted tie—Joe was not always the most dapper of the three, but this time his clothes are perfect; because of his position at the rear of the picture he looks as though he is shorter than he even is—he was the smallest of the trio. But the certainty of self about him is unmistakable: it is Joe Strummer who is the towering presence in Kate Simon's photograph. "He understood like Bob Marley or Patti Smith how to have a great picture taken," said Kate. And it is Joe who in that cover shot holds the three of them together.

Despite being allegedly some vision of a dark, dystopian future, from the moment *The Clash* kicked off with "Janie Jones"—recorded almost live, with none of the double-tracking or overdubbing of some of the other songs—to its finale of "Garageland," the record managed paradoxically to be warm and all-embracing, a perfect summer album, one whose fourteen songs rang out across the two sides throughout the hot months that were like part two of the previous year's heat wave. A rush of pure energy and positive feeling, *The Clash* was one of the best long-playing records that had ever been made, a stunning piece of art. Privately, rock critics would suggest that the Clash could only proceed if they employed a proper producer on their next record; and you'd think, "What are you talking about?" You just had to make a few adjustments to the different cultural parameters of the sound—like listening to a Jamaican record—and how that sound is perceived and achieved. The only variant on *The Clash* from the live set was the group's version of Junior Murvin's 1976 reggae classic "Police and Thieves," included after considerable debate—it had been used to warm up at rehearsals. "That was really the first time any white men had attempted to cover a reggae hit," Joe told me. "We used to discuss this with Johnny Rotten, because everyone was really into reggae, but especially Rotten most of all, and Paul Simonon. It was considered a little bit naff if you were trying to copy that style, but I think we did it in a way that lent something of our own to it. I remember being frightened as hell listening to Junior Murvin's feathery voice, floating high above that track, and then thinking, 'God, I've got to go sing this with my useless voice.'"

Parts of *The Clash* were often hilariously funny, a reflection of the deep absurdist vein of humor shared by all three of the group's front men. Sometimes it was the choice of phrasing from Joe, sometimes the actual lyrics themselves, sometimes simply the way he had structured the words. "Yeah, we tried to crack a few jokes," Joe said to me about that first album. "I think because of our general aggressive stance, people can only accept one kind of thing at a time and sometimes missed it. Anyway the lyrics are always pretty indecipherable because my diction isn't the best in the world. So when we shouted out about Greeks and kebabs, it was often lost in the chaos of the music. But we were excited to have our jokes in there."

The record went straight into the U.K. charts, but it wouldn't be released in the United States for two years. The Sex Pistols hadn't even got a second single out, yet already the Clash had an album not only in the shops but one that had reached the edge of the Top Ten. Now who was the underdog? Predictably Rotten sniped at them for having recorded "Police and Thieves." Joe celebrated the release of the album by taking his old schoolfriend Annie Day to see Arlo Guthrie, the son of Woody, in the film *Alice's Restaurant*.

Terry Chimes came back yet again on Sunday, April 3, to record two more new tunes: "Capital Radio," a number based on Mick's song "Deadly Serious," and "Listen," an instrumental; the tunes were featured on an EP for which *NME* readers could send off. The rest of the EP consisted of extracts from an interview with the Clash that had been held on the Circle Line of the London Underground. The idea behind "Capital Radio" was amply explained in its (relatively clear) lyrics: it was an attack on the London commercial music station of that name, which, since it first went on the air in 1973, had consistently followed a safe, dated musical policy: no punk rock on the station that boasted it was "in tune with London." Joe's contempt is great: "Capital Radio / In tune with nuffink." To underline his point, Joe went off on a mission: "As a promotional exercise I decided to spray-paint Capital Radio and the BBC with WHITE RIOT in six-foot letters in red paint. I was quite surprised when this didn't result in any airplay, but you live and learn."

The interview on the *NME* free EP was by the paper's punk young gun, Tony Parsons, extracts from the dialogue of an article that appeared in the April 2, 1977, edition of *NME*: the three Clash members appeared in profile on the cover of an issue that carried the caption "Thinking Man's Yobs." Parsons had no truck with the intellectual niceties of punk; passion and a pulp style were the journalist's all. In the article he steamed in, all preconceptions blazing, in a piece that would set the template for the general public's initial vision of the Clash. "Parsons framed them with his *NME* article in April 1977," said Jon Savage, "which fixed the perception of them as a working-class political group—and made his reputation. But really he was projecting his own fantasy onto them." Parsons's words painted the group as the quintessence of street-hip: Mick's tower-block existence; Paul's past life as a football hooligan; Joe's fight with the ted in the Speakeasy toilet. Unemployment-line doldrums. There was no mention that each of these three contenders had been to art school and were partially living out an artist's romantic vision of a "guttersnipe" existence. It wasn't all Parsons's projection: both parties were co-conspirators in a clever piece of mythmaking.

Although he didn't appear in that *NME* cover shot, a drummer who could hold down the Clash gig finally had been found. The search had begun to look hopeless: over two hundred prospective candidates had been auditioned. But on March 24 Mick had bumped into former London SS member Nicky "Topper" Headon, at a Kinks show. Topper had joined a group called Fury, but CBS executives, offering the group a deal, thought that Topper didn't hit the drums hard enough and demanded he be axed. So when he went along to Rehearsals for an audition he pounded those skins with all his might. "I thought, 'Whatever I do, I'm going to have to smash shit out of these drums,' and that was exactly what they wanted. We did 'London's Burning' and 'Police and Thieves' because they wanted to see if I could play reggae. I did the audition and I thought, 'Fuck me: this is great!'"

At the audition, Joe offered Topper a cigarette. "I said, 'No thanks, I don't.' He said, 'You will.' When I joined the Clash I wasn't drinking, wasn't smoking, wasn't doing anything. In '77 we were unknown and in '82 we were one of the biggest bands in the world, and we hadn't stopped working. It's not as if we had had time off or anything. If it weren't for the chemicals I don't know if we would have gone as long as that. Everyone was fucked up, whether it was drugs or drink or whatever. The thing was, when I joined the band it wasn't a band that was formed out of friends—the Clash were put together, really."

From the start Topper found Joe erratic and difficult. "He and Mick were running it, but you never really knew where you stood with Joe. One minute he'd be all over you, your best mate, and the next he'd be snarling at you. But all that tension made the band musically really good: it would all come together on the stage and it would be dynamite, and then it would dissipate again. Joe used to call the drum riser 'the engine room'—my hands would be bleeding after a gig." Topper paused, before sardonically summing up his time in the Clash: "I was very important onstage—although offstage I wasn't."

During the early days of the Clash Joe had only one real focus—to make the group as big as possible, as quickly as possible, a steel-hard ambition and vision he shared with Mick Jones. They were absolutely single-minded about what they were doing with their lives, with not a hint of self-doubt about where the group was going, a fact that was revealed in a lengthy interview with Caroline Coon in *Melody Maker*. Joe disputed the "political" tag that had been foisted onto the Clash, preferring the term "awareness." In fact, he told her that he didn't believe punk rock could bring about social or political change: "But after saying that—and I'm just saying that because I want you to know that I haven't got any illusions about anything, right—having said that I *still* want to try to change things." The article was revealing as to Joe's perception of the modus operandi of the Clash: "Mick's the one who's really into the sound. He's really into the music. He hears arrangements in his head. I can't. For Paul the Clash is a chance for him to strut his stuff. For me the music is a vehicle for my lyrics. It's a chance to get some really good words across." When Caroline asked if he found writing easy, his response showed what he felt was his true strength. "No—but I'm not telling you why. I learned something once: 'You can show someone what you've done but you can't show them how to do it.' And I stick to that. If I tell you how I write, when I next do it my words will haunt me and destroy me completely. For me writing is a big thing. The biggest excitement going is sitting down and writing until you get exactly what you intended to get." There was one other important issue raised in the Caroline Coon interview: for the first time Joe publicly spoke about the suicide of his brother, David, incorrectly giving the date as 1971. "Funnily enough, you know, he was a Nazi. He was a member of the National Front. He was into the occult and he used to have these death's-heads and crossbones all over everything. He didn't like to talk to anybody, and I think suicide was the only way out for him . . . Imagine! You're in the world and you're just too shy to even talk to anybody or even go into a café to have a cup of tea."

here was not much time for serious reflection on such matters of the soul. Another punk package tour, with the Clash topping the bill, was to be launched in Britain. Topper had had under a month to learn the material before embarking on this typically ambitious venture. The White Riot

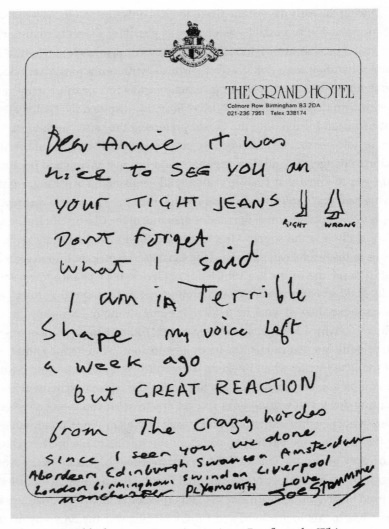

THE GRAND HOTEL
Colmore Row Birmingham B3 2DA
021-236 7951   Telex 338174

Dear Annie it was nice to see you an your TIGHT JEANS
RIGHT   WRONG
Dont forget what I said I am in Terrible Shape my voice left a week ago But GREAT REACTION from The crazy hordes since I seen you we done Aberdeen Edinburgh Swansea Amsterdam London birmingham swindon Liverpool manchester Plymouth Love Joe Strummer

Like trousers, like brain . . . Joe writes to Anne Day from the White Riot tour. *(Anne Day)*

tour kicked off on May 1 at Guildford. Also on the bill were the Jam; a hot new act from Manchester, the Buzzcocks; the Slits; and Subway Sect, another band managed by Bernie Rhodes.

On May 3 the package hit Birmingham's Barbarella's. "We'd like to do this first song for the thirty people who were here last time," Joe introduced the set. The Swindon date the next night was at the Affair club. When the Clash arrived there they discovered their lighting rig was too big for the venue. There was another hall, across a bridge, through a town square, and past the police station, where it was deemed the Clash could play. When the fans arrived at the second hall it was burning down. The equipment in the basement was rescued by some of the audience, who helped in carrying it out and back across town to the original club, where the Clash then played an astonishing set. Joe rewarded everyone who'd helped with a pint of beer.

The show in London at the Rainbow on May 9 was amazing, an extraordinary sight of massed punk. Bob Marley was backstage, at the group's invitation. ("But he never gave us tickets for his show at the Rainbow," complained Mick Jones to me.) The first thing that amazed you was that they had pulled it off and filled the three-thousand-seat venue. "That was the night punk really broke. The Rainbow was a big venue. It was kinda 'Supergroups go there!'" said Joe. "The audience came and filled it. Trashed the place as well, but it really felt like—through a combination of luck and effort—we were in the right place doing the right thing at the right time. And that kind of night happens once or twice in a lifetime."

Ellie Smith, who handled their PR at CBS, arranged for me to meet the group backstage at St. Albans City Hall on May 21. I spent time talking to Mick Jones, who was extremely personable. From time to time he would expel a thin stream of spittle onto the lino floor. This seemed to be part of the act, as though emulating the cool of street-corner black kids who constantly seemed to suffer from a similar excess of saliva. "Gob" was part of punk: every gig saw a hail of "appreciative" spit, a phenomenon started by the Damned spitting at their audience—who spat back. (Six months later, Joe implored the audience at the Coventry Locarno: "Before we play you anything we'd like to ask you one favor. Please don't spit on us. We're just trying to do something good up here and it throws us off our stride.")

Mick was open, funny, obviously intelligent and well read. In the dressing room was Paul; he too gobbed on the floor. Joe stepped into the room for a moment: he seemed wound up. He shook my hand briefly, but seemed evidently stressed—he stormed off. Joe did have something on his mind. During recent nights on the tour he had become increasingly brought down by the number of security guards: tonight Joe Strummer insisted that no front-stage security be supplied whatsoever. In midset he performed a kamikaze head-first dive into the audience. "He proved his point," pointed out Mick Jones. "They didn't trample on him and they caught him . . . Of course, if they hadn't have caught him he could have broken his neck. Joe has a very forceful way of proving a point." Joe's rage onstage was an expression of the fury and suffocating frustration felt by huge swathes of the community—there was a very real frenzied wrath on the streets of Britain, and Joe Strummer became its personification.

Later, after a couple of spliffs with Mick Jones and Don Letts, it was time for me to get back to London. On the way out I looked into the next dressing room. Joe was sitting immediately opposite me, on a bench along the rear wall, surrounded by fans. I waved goodbye at him. He snarled something at me, and it seemed to me I could pick out the word "Goebbels." I snarled back at him. He raised the fist at me that wasn't holding a can of Special Brew. I raised one back. Then I turned and left, still in good spirits, despite the oddness of that brief moment. That was my first meeting with Joe. Years later I recounted it to him. He appeared shocked: "No, no, I can't believe that." But this, it turned out, was a typical mood in which to find Joe in those times. Later I realized it was like one of those fights you'd almost have with someone at school, and then end up the best of friends.

The White Riot tour cost the Clash £28,000, over a quarter of their advance from CBS, to pay for the smashed seats at the Rainbow and the huge assortment of scene-makers they took along with them on tour. After the St. Albans gig the tour bus was raided by police, who found stolen pillows and hotel keys; Joe and Topper were charged with theft. But the Clash came back from the White Riot tour as a major English group. There was no doubt that the multidimensional Clash was the most exciting new thing in years, with real depth in their work and as human beings: their raison d'être, essentially an attack on the established order, was put over with great intelligence and a high sense of instinctive creativity. Plus, as the assorted arrests and dramas of the White Riot tour ensured, they seemed to have an almost filmic ongoing story. Their collective granitelike persona, undiminished purpose and irreducible stubbornness were delivering their cause to considerable effect. "We're anti-fascist, anti-racist, and pro-creative," said Joe, remembering the maxim: All great truths are simple.

Something else had happened to Woody Mellor in metamorphosing into Joe Strummer, singer with the Clash: he'd gained height. "I noticed that after the Rainbow show," said Gill Calvert. "Becoming successful seemed to put inches on him. He was no longer 'Weedy Woody,' as we sometimes used to call him." Joe's height, around five foot eight, seems to have veered greatly, depending on how he was faring in life. Now he was on top of the world, standing tall as a proud lion king. Later you came to realize you could gauge Joe's inner spirits by his height: when low, his neck and spine would be bent forward, and he would shrink in size.

On June 5 Joe went with Don Letts and Leo Williams to Hammersmith Palais in West London, to see Dillinger, Leroy Smart and Delroy Wilson, a trio of hot acts direct from Kingston, perform at a typical Jamaican concert, aimed specifically at expatriate islanders. Looking for an authentic reggae experience, Joe instead watched artists who had honed their stage acts on the Jamaican north coast tourist hotel circuit, and came home disappointed. "It was all very Vegas," said Joe. "The audience were hardcore and I felt that they were looking for something different than a show-biz spectacle." When he noticed a group of "black sticksmen" endeavoring to snatch the handbags of some white girls, Joe intervened. He didn't receive any thanks for his troubles. In his omnipresent notebook Joe wrote up his experiences of the evening in verse form, working up the lyrics of what would become "White Man in Hammersmith Palais." "I remember Joe was a bit disappointed," said Don, "because he expected a roots scene. I think that show was an eye-opener for him, realizing that all those people were trying to get out of the ghetto roots life."

Four days later Joe was arrested by police for spraying the word "CLASH" on the wall next to Dingwall's. Joe had to appear in court on this charge the next day at 4:00 p.m., where he was fined five pounds. Because of this he was unable to answer the case against him the same day in Newcastle on charges of stealing from the Holiday Inn for which he and Topper had been charged after the St. Albans show. The next morning he and Topper were arrested. "We were driven handcuffed together all the way up to Newcastle, and spent the weekend in jail there, before being fined on the Monday morning for stealing bedware and keys."

Early in August the Clash went into the studio to record their next single. To the fury of the group, CBS had released another single from the album, "Remote Control." Responding in an angry burst of energy, Mick Jones wrote both the music and words of a new tune, "Complete Control," referring to the absurd phrase Bernie had used. Mick's lyrics are an indictment of the way he felt CBS had betrayed the group with the "Remote Control" release; Joe added one line about an abortive visit by the group to the CBS conference in Amsterdam. "Complete Control" was produced by Lee "Scratch" Perry, the Picasso of Jamaican record producers. Joe later joked: "We wanted him to do a reggae production of a punk song, but he was trying to learn how to do a punk production." But the news they had worked with the legendary Scratch Perry enhanced the credibility of the Clash. According to Mick Jones, Scratch made "Complete Control" sound as though the record had been made "underwater." After he left the studio, the group—notably Mick Jones—went to work on the supposedly finished master.

On August 5 the Clash played the second annual European Punk Festival at Mont-de-Marsan in France, near the border with Spain; an early version of "White Man" was aired. Ten days later I joined up with the Clash on the "punk night" of the Fourteenth Bilzen Festival, in Belgium. As was now becoming commonplace, the Clash's set was no stranger to controversy.

Played before twenty thousand people, the music was extraordinary, but Joe's performance was even more breathtaking. He saw that a group of European anarchists was trying to pull down the concrete posts and barbed-wire fence that separated them from the front-of-stage pit. "Why is this space here?" Joe spewed rage into the mike. "*Venez ici! Venez ici!!!!—et maintenant . . . 'Les Flics et les Voleurs,'*" he announced as the Clash reggae of "Police and Thieves" appeared to be about to cool things out a trifle.

Joe's mike-stand slipped into the pit. Then Joe was down in the pit himself, racing for the post that was nearest to coming down, grabbing it, shifting it backward and forward, wrestling with it. No one quite saw what happened, but Joe was down on the ground. ("One of 'em took a swing at me.") He was dragged back behind a large wire shield; on his feet, surrounded by security heavies, like some very aggressive gallant young squire in a medieval battle scene.

The show continued as Joe was pushed back onstage, playing this time under a hail of cans rather than a stream of gob. Despite the adverse conditions, two new songs, "Clash City Rockers" and "White Man in Hammersmith Palais," rang out above the clamor.

Bernie Rhodes went backstage, where Mick Jones was puking. "The cymbals were too loud at the back" was his only comment. "It didn't seem like a gig. It was more like a war," said Paul Simonon, stretching the neck of his conceptually frayed sweater to show where a half-brick had landed on his left shoulder and broken the skin.

After the gig, Joe showed that, just as on stage, he was not prepared to play the game. This time it was me he had in his sights. "All journalists are swine," Joe suddenly pronounced, in front of the rest of the group. I was not too wiped out to realize that out of the blue I had been thrown into a legendary Clash debating session, the sort of thing that had made Terry Chimes leave the group. "All journalists are *complete swine*," Joe repeated.

Paul and Mick came to my aid by uttering disturbed noises. Mick declared that the press had helped the Clash a lot in the past. But Joe told Mick he was too gullible—he would never tell the press the things Mick did. Mick, however, riposted that Joe had that attitude because of a conscious need to maintain his mystique. I noticed that suddenly the discussion had struck a level of intensity on a quite personal level—it was like a group (or Clash) therapy session. "They're all swine. Journalists are people who should be kept at arm's length at all times. This is nothing personal against you, Sandwich," Joe snarled sibilantly through the gaps at either side of his upper front teeth. "The nature of what you do means you must be kept at bay."

("Joe Strummer always seems to me to be a rather tense person," Malcolm McLaren told me around this time.)

The subject thankfully moved on as we talked about the-Clash-as-political-group. Mick Jones said that he was equally appalled by the mindless bigotry of the right-wing National Front and the leftie International Socialists: "The International Socialists are always like sending us telegrams of congratulation. But we're nothing to do with either of them. We don't consider any of it a political statement. We just consider it statements of . . . life through our eyes."

"It's a load of bullshit," Joe chipped in. "We're just a group. The National Front are against us, though. They know about us. And the police."

But what had impelled Joe toward his extraordinary front-of-stage performance? "I don't think about things I do too much. I just do 'em."

On September 11, 1977, Joe went to see Mick at Wilmcote House. He was broke and hoped Mick would be able to lend him a fiver. While he was there three local teds turned up and announced that they were going to get them. One of the Clash who lived in Ladbroke Grove, they said, had beaten up a girlfriend of theirs. Mick and Joe protested that none of them lived in the Grove; and, anyway, they wouldn't do that to a girl. But the teds announced that they were coming back, with some Angels from a local pub. Then they left.

Mick and Joe turned off all of the lights and waited for Mick's nan to return. Once she did, Mick gave her some money to go to a friend's to stay the night. Sneaking out of the tower block's rear exit, they caught a bus over to Wandsworth, to watch *High Noon* on a friend's "color telly"—a detail Joe noted, a sign of the times.

Beneath Babylon's shadow, the Clash attempt abortively to play in Belfast. (*UrbanImage.tv/Adrian Boot*)

Returning to Wilmcote House around one in the morning, they found the door to Mick's nan's flat scuffed with boot marks. Above the lintel was written "PUNK IS SHIT" and "ANGELS ROOL." Despite the threat, they stayed the night there. But Joe came to a decision: "I've gotta help Mick get out of there, before they break his arms like matchsticks."

"Complete Control" was released on September 23, 1977, to ecstatic praise. The sophistication of the song's structure and the pointed satire within its lyrics showed how far they had come since recording *The Clash* at the beginning of the year. On October 20 they set off on their Out of Control tour. Belfast in Northern Ireland was ravaged by civil war, a part of Britain that no acts came to play: the Clash chose the city's Ulster Hall for their first date on the tour, but the show was banned.

At the end of the tour Joe moved into Sebastian Conran's house by Regent's Park, at 31 Albany Street; the huge property had its main entrance, hardly ever used, directly on the carriageway that ran around the park. Nobody could quite figure out how, but Bernie managed to get a foothold in the building, installing his office. The occupants of this luxury abode, among them Henry Bowles, a friend of Sebastian who became close friends with Joe, overcame their ideological conflict by pretending it was a squat—on occasions Joe actually claimed that it was—and treating it with utter disrespect. But this step up in his accommodation also brought Joe closer to his past; directly opposite the front door was the bench on which his brother, David, had died, still a tender subject for Joe.

Around this time, on a visit to Warlingham to see his parents, Joe prepared them for the mythmaking that was already under way. "You're going to be seeing a lot about me in the papers soon," he warned them. "Don't believe what you read." By now, Ron was taking the music papers—*NME* and *Melody Maker*—on a weekly basis from his local newsagent.

Joining the entourage after the Belfast gig was Johnny Green, possibly the only road manager with a degree in Arabic. It wasn't until they were back in London—and he found himself still working with them—that Johnny began to understand the inner workings of the Clash. "Fans always assumed Joe ran the band. That wasn't my perception. When he roused himself he could be extremely dynamic and forceful, but Mick was always on the case. I've always regarded Mick as being precise, whereas Joe was a man who would lift his head up and go, 'What?'

"Often it seemed that it was Mick's group. It wasn't just that he could employ bullying tactics—which he could. He was very forceful and quick to put his point of view in, in a way that Joe wasn't. Joe was more considered. There was a huge amount of energy coming off Mick. Although he was always the last man to show for a rehearsal, he always did show, and the attitude of the other three went up a gear the moment he walked into the room. Mick's behavior was tolerated because he was worth it. He could be a source of amusement: the poodle jokes about his hair, for example. But they were jokes, they weren't backstabbing. Not at all.

"But don't misunderstand the amount of energy Paul Simonon put in there. It's easy to pigeonhole him: charismatic figure, stylish, amusing. But it was energy, boundless energy, too much energy for one man to have about himself, as a matter of fact."

They would need that energy. CBS was demanding that the group begin to record their second album, and new songs were required. "That was a shock to us," Joe told me. "We had spent all year working on the songs or the sound for the first record. Once that was done we thought it was quite definitive. I remember we put it down and it was recorded, and, great, well that's it. And then the company went, 'Right, about the second LP.' And we went, 'You what? Second LP?' 'Cause to us we put it all on one, and really we should have split up there and then and gone like, 'Up yours!'" Moreover, the Clash was adamant that "Complete Control," the latest single, would not be on the long-player. "That was in the days before everything was on one LP and they bang everything off it as singles," said Joe. "It was a deliberate policy on our part to try and give value for money to the fans. The B-sides were good too: 'The Prisoner' was quite a good song. And 'Jail Guitar Doors' [an old 101'ers song, 'Lonely Mother's Son,' with revised lyrics] and 'City of the Dead.'"

On November 11 the Clash played at the Corn Exchange in Cambridge. Sebastian Conran told Jeannette Lee that he was riding the seventy miles to the gig on his motorcycle. Did she want to go? "I said yes because I'd never been anywhere on a motorbike. It was quite scary, really. We went to see them play, and we all had rooms in the same hotel." Following the show most of the group's entourage had a meal at the hotel. When some of them tried to start a food fight, Jeannette was impressed with the way that Mick Jones reprimanded them: "Oi! Stop throwing food around. It's people like our mums who have to clean it up." "I thought, 'God, that's so true.'" Joe started flirting with her; although nothing sexual happened between them that night, she and Joe and others sat up all night talking, until the morning. "I've been waiting for you," he said to her. "I thought, 'What for? How weird.' Nothing happened, except that it was obvious something was going to happen." On her return to London Don Letts sensed that something had occurred between her and Joe; this exacerbated difficulties in their relationship that were already present. "Don was not pleased, he didn't know what about, but he knew that something was going on. As a result of this we ended up having a really big falling-out." Who was there with a shoulder for Jeannette to lean on? Joe Strummer, of course. "Conveniently Joe was there to see me through in my hour of need after I'd broken up with my boyfriend. That was very complicated because the three of us were mates. It caused a lot of ruckus. It wasn't very nice, to be honest. All I can say is that we were kids. At that age you split up with people and go off with other people." "When he nicked my girlfriend," said Don Letts, "we never spoke for a year or so."

As far as Joe was concerned, however, it was on with the show. The Clash Get Out of Control tour consisted of twenty-two gigs in twenty-five days, extremely hard work. With no time to rest his voice, Joe's vocal performances were sometimes reduced to a hoarse grunt, which, oddly, audiences seemed to find attractive, as though this was further evidence of Joe's humanity. The more difficulties Joe was experiencing onstage, the more audiences warmed to him. This was also true during those times onstage when the songs' tempos would struggle to coalesce, as they frequently did about two-thirds of the way through, before they reached the finale. Especially at this point in the group's career the Clash could be really quite rough in live performance, as though held together with cheap glue—although no doubt in Mick Jones's conceptual subconscious he was appreciating the comparisons with the Rolling Stones (in the days before their slick stadium performances) and the Faces, both of whom had been similarly erratic, shambolic and even useless onstage. That was why each Clash gig was so brilliant, because every show was individual and unique, almost a literal struggle for survival. But within a year the concerts would no longer be so concentrated and the Clash would attempt to never play more than three consecutive nights on the road. From then on, Joe Strummer would spend much of the day before a performance whispering, or speaking in brief sentences; he would complain about the spliff smoke in the group's vehicle—though it never stopped him from smoking those joints. When they reached a new town, Joe would disappear on a lengthy walk. "You'd be amazed by how many problems you can sort out on a five-mile walk," he once said to me. While Joe was touring he would often appear to be extremely reticent, but in fact this was simply self-control—he was ensuring that he would be able to perform that night in his slightly odd but extremely addictive style of shouting-singing.

The celebrated rock critic Lester Bangs—to whom, at Joe's instigation, Joe Stevens had personally delivered a copy of the first album—accompanied the group on the road on this tour, writing a three-part article in *NME*. Bangs was stymied in his efforts to spend time with Joe, as the singer spent part of the time on the tour suffering from toothache and what seemed like a flu virus, finally diagnosed as glandular fever. But he noted Joe's "pure outside-of-self frenzy." "Serious without being solemn, quiet without being remote or haughty, Strummer offers a distinct contrast to Mick's voluble wit and twinkle of the eye, and Paul's loony-toon playfulness. He is almost certainly the group's soul, and I wish I could say I had gotten to know him better." When Lester Bangs told Bernie Rhodes how much he liked Mick Jones, the manager replied, "Mick is my biggest problem."

Although there were further dates in the middle of December, the final show of this section of the tour was on November 15, at the Elizabethan Ballroom, Belle Vue, in Manchester; it was filmed by Granada TV for its show *So It Goes*. "Here we are, on TV. What does it mean to me? What does it mean to you? *Fuck all!*" Joe extemporized during "What's My Name." CBS wanted a hit in the United States and a producer who understood the American market, so Joe, when he introduced "I'm So Bored with the USA," dedicated it to "Ted Nugent, Aerosmith, Journey and, most of all, Blue Öyster Cult!" For in the audience was a man who had traveled from New York to Manchester to see them perform—Sandy Pearlman, manager and producer of Blue Öyster Cult and the prospective producer for the Clash's second album. "Once," said Joe, "I found Bernie listening to Blue Öyster Cult in his car, which in those punk puritan times was a major crime: 'Bernie, are you feeling all right? Blue Öyster Cult?' And he said, 'I'm checking out Sandy Pearlman.'"

Following this show, Joe would have some time for his voice and health to recuperate. In the second half of November Bernie Rhodes dispatched Joe and Mick Jones to Kingston, Jamaica, for ten days. This was no holiday: the pair were intended to write songs for the second album. Paul Simonon, more a fan of Jamaican music than the two songwriters, was furious and up-set at not being invited: as consolation, he went to Moscow and Leningrad with Caroline Coon.

In 1977 Jamaica was riven by an undeclared civil war between the so-cialist People's National Party of Prime Minister Michael Manley and Ed-ward Seaga's right-wing Jamaica Labour Party. Joe and Mick were booked into the Pegasus Hotel, in New Kingston, a couple of hundred yards down the road from the Sheraton, the more groovy music-business location. On arrival they tried to contact Lee "Scratch" Perry, but failed dismally. Several times they went to the movies. "It was like *The Harder They Come* not on the screen but in the audience," said Joe. "I don't know how we weren't filleted and served up on a bed of chips. Me and Mick wandered around the harbor; I think they mistook us for sailors, merchant seamen, because we were walking around Kingston dressed up in our full punk regalia—they must have just let us pass because they probably thought we were madmen or something. But me and Mick didn't have a clue what we were doing there. We didn't know anybody—we were just wandering around in Kingston like lunatics."

"We went for a swim at our hotel," said Mick. "It started raining, and the two of us were in the pool. It was something we'd never experienced before: it was so hot, and we were swimming, but it was raining. I'll always remem-ber that. When we were walking through the streets to the movies, Joe told me Jamaica was just like the places he was when he was young. 'This is just like it was when I was a kid,' he said. In those days you could still really feel the colonial presence."

With some difficulty—they were ripped off on their first couple of at-tempts by the supposed dealers simply running off with their money—they scored a large bag of lamb's-breath ganja, and retreated to their hotel rooms to write songs, the edgy impressions of their Jamaican trip contained in Joe's lyrics for one of the Clash's finest, most rousing songs, "Safe European Home": "I went to the place / where every white face / is an invitation to robbery." But when he declared his intention to never return, this did cause some confusion. I heard Don Letts—by then speaking to him again—pick Joe up on this a year later in the dressing room at London's Lyceum Ballroom, where the Clash played some Christmas shows. "Yeah, but I didn't mean it," said the ever-pragmatic Joe Strummer. Apart from the lyrics, although certainly not the rhythm, of the great "Safe European Home"—of which Joe later said, "I'd put alongside anything the Clash or anyone else has recorded"—there was little evidence on the new album of any Jamaican influence. (Joe's lyrics for the song were originally some fifty lines long, shortened to sixteen by the time the song was recorded.)

As though explaining the song, Joe sent a postcard to Jeannette Lee from Jamaica, confessing that he found Kingston frightening. "I hope that Jamaica doesn't get filled with punks going down there, like Morocco was filled with hippies," Mick said to me when he returned. Less than three months later, I went to Jamaica. When I returned Joe asked me if I'd brought any weed back with me. "No," I said. "Chicken!" Joe jeered. "I brought back a compressed ounce in each of my brothel creepers."

Back in London the Clash concluded the year with a triumphant return to the Rainbow, where they played a three-night sold-out stint in mid-December. Joe and Mick went to a Christmas party at the Chelsea home of Francesca Thyssen, the daughter of a multimillionaire German steel baron who had allegedly assisted the economy of the Third Reich. Francesca was living with Philip Rambow; the Canadian Rambow was the former singer with the Winkies, a hip pre-punk group Mick Jones had rated. Phil was starting a solo career, and Mick met his managers, Peter Jenner and Andrew King. That evening Phil Rambow introduced Joe to a girl called Gaby Salter—they spoke briefly, as they did again at a Ramones concert a little later.

Then the Clash concluded 1977 with a live date in Belfast on December 20. For a group who had not even had a recording deal twelve months previously, it was an extraordinary triumph, a success story unparalleled in British rock 'n' roll. Yet it is worth remembering that most music fans and the music business still hated the very notion of the Clash, partly because they were in the slipstream of the flak thrown the way of the Sex Pistols in this year of disloyal cultural insurrection, and also because the establishment stuck to their guns in insisting that the group "couldn't play." This last view missed the point: the supposed amateurishness of punk, with all its implied democracy, had been cunningly manipulated by the leading players to their advantage. Within a month the Pistols were no more, imploding on tour in America, leaving Joe Strummer as the unrivaled King of Punk.

$$\frac{1}{3}$$

the all-night drug-prowling wolf

1977–1979

During the time that Joe Strummer and Jeannette Lee were together, he drank plenty of beer, but the only drug that interested him was hash. "He smoked all the time," she remembered, "but he didn't like cocaine, he didn't like speed. He said they made him really depressed. Joe was very depressive. He was quite disapproving of people that did cocaine." There was an anti-cocaine party line in the Clash, who took a moral high ground about the drug. "I think there was a bit of a superior thing going on: 'I don't do that time-wasting rubbish,'" said Jeannette. Which made it difficult to reconcile with Mick Jones developing a taste for coke. My personal opinion is that Mick—who had always been enamored with the pop-art aesthetic of Keith Richards and the like—simply employed the ingestion of cocaine as part of his conceptual trappings of being a rock star: snorting coke was just another part of the uniform. But such an explanation would cut no ice with Joe Strummer. "He was really disapproving," said Jeannette. "I was surprised in the last few years to learn that he was living that kind of lifestyle. But he always drank lots; I always seemed to be sitting in pubs with him and people like Mickey Foote, with Joe holding court, always about this close to being a melancholic, depressive drunk.

"There was a struggle going on between the pressure of being a great musical artist and doing the right thing according to the code of the Clash philosophy, and his ego. Joe had a much bigger ego than people realized, unless they knew him well. But there was a dark side, involving his depression. I think that was always there."

Joe's antidote to what Winston Churchill would refer to as his "black dog" was to keep working. In January the Clash had a visitor to Rehearsals, Sandy Pearlman. "Sandy came into our rehearsal to listen to the new tunes we were doing," Joe recalled to me. "And he said, 'You can't do this! It's subzero temperatures.' And we're all rehearsing in three overcoats each, and my breath was like a fog of white frost when I was singing, because there wasn't any heating—it was a large space to heat anyway. It was Sandy who first told me that it was bad for the voice to sing in subzero temperatures. We moved to another rehearsal room because it was such a cold winter."

On February 17, 1978, a new single was released: "Clash City Rockers," with Joe at his most John Lennon–like on vocals. The most self-referential of all the group's songs, it cemented their image as a leather-jacketed gang, kicking off the mythology that was to come. Except that this was incorrect. "I was talking about rockers," said Joe, "which is a certain reggae rhythm, not about people who are rockers at all. It goes, 'I want to move the town to the Clash city rockers,' meaning to the sound of the Clash. It doesn't make sense if you think it's about people in leather jackets. It was one of those things where it is obvious to you and you don't realize it's not obvious to anyone else." Joe's lyrics are out to motivate anyone ready to listen; he wants to "burn down the suburbs with the half-closed eyes / You won't succeed unless you try." It was a great record, a follow-up to "Complete Control" that urged you to do it yourself, open your head and listen. Unfortunately when Mick Jones *did* listen to the group's new single he detected something awry, something that made a mockery of the missile salvo against CBS on "Complete Control." While Mick and Joe had been in Jamaica, Bernie Rhodes had decided the single was minimally too slow. He had asked Mickey Foote to speed it up by—as Foote put it—"about one and a half percent." Mick Jones was furious: Mickey Foote never worked for the Clash again in any record-producing function.

Joe, however, was not around to promote the single. He was in the hospital. At the end of January, following low-key gigs in Birmingham and at Lanchester Polytechnic in Coventry—where Sandy Pearlman was punched out by Mick's school friend Robin Crocker when he entered the group's dressing room—Joe had been diagnosed with hepatitis, a serious infection that inflames the liver. "He was pretty ill when it started," said Jeannette Lee. "He was completely yellow: the whites of his eyes were yellow, and it affected his glands—they were swollen. He felt really ill. Because he'd changed color it was obvious it wasn't flu. The first I knew was when I got a phone call from him saying, 'I'm in hospital. Can you come and see me, and bring me some things?'"

Joe was in an isolation ward, each patient allocated his or her own glass-walled cubicle. Shortly after Joe was admitted, he was lying in bed when he heard a Clash song sailing through the glass. Investigating, he discovered that a cassette machine was being played in the next room by its occupant, a member of the Adverts, a punk group that had had a couple of hits.

When Jeannette arrived to see him, she was accompanied by Rocco, a photographer friend. "Joe said to Rocco," remembered Jeannette, "'Rocco, go into the kitchen in the basement in Albany Street, and on top of the kitchen cupboard'—he knew every single place: that was the weird thing— 'on the left, under the sink on the right, round the corner here and there, there's bottles of piss.' Everywhere there were bottles of piss. He'd come in really late at night, piss in a milk bottle, and put it up on the top of a cupboard. It was all part of this disrespect for this house they were living in that was obviously very posh. What made me laugh was that he knew where every bottle of piss was. He must have had some conscience about it—it was really infectious. Rocco had to go back to the house, and find all the piss and destroy it."

Jeannette also debunked the myth of how Joe caught his hepatitis. "Let's put it this way: I don't think he got it from people spitting in his mouth." The stock explanation for Joe's having caught hepatitis, one that he fostered, was that infected appreciative spit had gone down his throat on the last tour. But Mick Jones told me at the time that Joe had caught the illness by injecting himself with a dirty needle. He told me this not in a gossipy way but because he was angry at Joe about it—although Mick didn't mention this, Joe's almost metaphysical fall made a mockery of the stones of criticism hurled Mick's way for having spent some of his music-publishing advance on cocaine. Jeannette confirmed that Joe had shot up drugs with Keith Levene; whether it was heroin or speed she was not certain, although Mick certainly had implied that it was heroin. Joe's future girlfriend, Gaby Salter, insisted to me that it was speed. Jeannette emphasized that as far as she understood this was a one-off event for Joe: he did it because he wanted to discover what the experience of injecting himself was like. "He had been hanging out with Keith Levene and a bunch of people one night, in a spirit of let's-try-everything-once. It wasn't more sinister than that. He was a bit sheepish about it."

Lying in his hospital bed for three weeks, Joe had time to reflect on his life's recent course. Since joining the Clash his pace had become increasingly relentless as he had embarked on a giant push upward. "When he was living in a squat he was very broke and not eating much," said Kris Needs. "Then he was on speed and Special Brew right through that White Riot tour and he wasn't a nice person on it. He was very gruff and scary. The first time I saw him play live I was scared to talk to him afterward. How was this ferocious, passionate person going to talk to me? That's what Joe was like till I got to know him."

Joe came out of the hospital more focused, more resolute. And sober: alcohol was out for the next six months. As though it were a security blanket, he would always carry with him a bottle of R. White's lemonade. And his hash consumption took an exponential leap. He was also trimmed down now, the early signs of a beer paunch gone. "Here, Joe," Paul laughed at him shortly before his hospitalization, "I saw you pulling in your stomach when you were trying to chat up that girl."

Out of the hospital in March, Joe was still shaky. But he and the Clash went into Marquee studios in Soho to work on various new songs with Sandy Pearlman. The Clash's version of Booker T. and the MGs' classic "Time Is Tight" was recorded then, Paul Simonon and Topper's friend Gary Barnacle, a session saxophonist, taking the lead in a Mick Jones arrangement that dispensed with the organ solo, the original record's most defining element. "In rehearsals there were times when somebody would play one thing," said Paul, "and somebody would pick up on that and you'd nip out for a cup of tea, come back and suddenly Mick and Topper are playing it, and you'd just fall into it. That was how we started doing 'Time Is Tight.'"

"One-Two-Crush on You," the Mick Jones original, was readied for later record release. Another cover, the Clash's version of "Pressure Drop" by Toots and the Maytals, already a live favorite, was recorded at the same time. "It probably just came up in a rehearsal and then evolved into a song in the set—we used to play it as far back as the White Riot tour—into the point of being recorded," said Paul. "I suppose having 'Police and Thieves' on the first album opened the way forward for us. Not to mimic reggae, but to give our own interpretation—the version of 'Pressure Drop' that we did has got quite a different approach from the song that was very well known because of being on the soundtrack of the film *The Harder They Come*. It's a slightly faster version we did. Along with 'White Man' we were fine-tuning our reggae direction."

Already waiting in the wings, his last act before he went into the hospital, was the single Joe would always regard as his finest song, "White Man in Hammersmith Palais." As though proving a point to CBS, the tune was produced by the group—which essentially meant Mick Jones. On the "White Man" single Joe sounds possessed, buzzing on the antibiotics keeping at bay his "glandular fever." A protest ballad with a reggae beat, and as removed from the expected 120 mph punk tempo as could be, the song marked an evolutionary leap upward from the sentiments expressed in "White Riot." Now Joe was insisting that black and white youth must unite against a world in which "If Adolf Hitler flew in today / They'd send a limousine anyway." As though to assure the Clash's audience of the milieu in which the song was set, Joe delivered an attack from the heart of the punk conscience on groups like the Jam. (Later he would change his mind, describing Paul Weller as "Britain's number one soul singer.") The single would not be released for another three months. But with considerable appropriateness it would be performed at the group's next live show.

That year all over the country the National Front had been successfully recruiting youthful members. Following the Young National Front rally at Digbeth Hall in Birmingham, at which—much to Joe's pleasure—black youths had chucked the odd brick or two, there was a response from the other side: a left-wing organization called Rock Against Racism, working in tandem with the equally new Anti-Nazi League, was formed to counter this noxious influence. Given the disastrous effect that membership of the National Front had had on his brother, David, Joe had a deep-seated hatred for the NF. On a page of one of Joe's ubiquitous notebooks he drew a pair of circles; one circle, which he declared to be "Mine," showed his own ethnic origin: half of it is Scottish, while English, German, and Armenian are given smaller portions. The other circle bears the name "Mick's"; here half is English, the rest, Welsh, Russian and Irish. Joe comments on the two circles: "The National Front are hopelessly fighting one COLD fact—a GENETIC fact ask an expert—there is no such thing as a pure race. What about the half Greek fellow or the Scottish Italians are you gonna throw them out too?—where do they draw the line? Only people of a different colour? Why? For JOBS? French Dutch Swedes Germans Spaniards etc. all work here. There's room for everybody."

It was no surprise that the Clash had agreed to perform their first show for three months at a Rock Against Racism concert, a huge open-air event held on Sunday, April 30, 1978, in Hackney's Victoria Park, a working-class area of considerable ethnic diversity. The concert was the culmination of a three-mile march from Trafalgar Square in central London. By virtue of its raison d'être it was a richly emotional event; the obsessive display in Victoria Park of left-wing banners and flags, billowing under a blustery breeze, seemed like a real transcription of a willed romance. The decision to play the show had been made by the group, against the wishes of Bernie Rhodes. "It's not my idea, this. I didn't think they should do it. But some members seemed to feel very strongly about it," Bernie told me behind the stage. But the opposition of Bernie Rhodes to the group playing this concert was yet another mark among several already mounting against him.

Ideological disputes aside, to recommend that the Clash should not play this show could be seen as bad managerial advice. The eighty-thousand-strong audience was the biggest crowd the group had yet played for. The event was an opportunity to convert Clash virgins to the idea of the group, letting them be seen as a kind of white equivalent of Bob Marley and the Wailers, whom Joe loved, an act that combined an addictive pop sensibility with a larger global message. The Clash's powerful performance was a triumph. Fortunately this was captured on film; perhaps spurred on by Malcolm McLaren's efforts to make a film about the Sex Pistols, Bernie Rhodes had enlisted the services of Jack Hazan and David Mingay to make *Rude Boy*, a feature film about the Clash. The two filmmakers had had success two years previously with *A Bigger Splash*, an art-house study of the painter David Hockney; excited, theatrical impresario Michael White of-

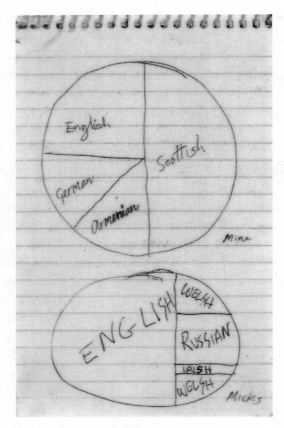

Joe provides the evidence to denounce the
National Front: "There's room for
everybody." *(Lucinda Mellor)*

fered funding for their next project. *Rude Boy* utilizes an actor, Ray Gange,
to play one of the group's roadies, a device to interweave events in the life
of the Clash into the film. At one point Gange offers Joe his can of Special
Brew. "No thanks," Joe responds. "I gave it up. It was fucking me up." The
scorn and disgust with which punk rock had been greeted had caused the
group to separate from society almost completely, and they became solidi-
fied within their own mythology, underpinned by self-referential lyrics,
military postures and the sense of a gang living by its own code. *Rude Boy*
would not document that existence, but be part of its mythmaking.

Due to the widely seen footage from *Rude Boy*, there is an assumption

The National Front are hopelessly fighting one COLD FACT - A GENETIC fact ask an expert — There is no such thing as a pure race what about the half greek fellow or the scottish Italians are you gonna throw them out too? — where do they draw the line? only people of a different colour? why? for JOBS? French dutch swedes german spaniards etc all work here? There's Room for everybody

that the Clash topped the bill at Victoria Park. This is not true: among others playing were reggae act Steel Pulse, the Tom Robinson Band, X-Ray Spex, and the Boomtown Rats. But although the Clash went onstage at around five in the afternoon, they did manage to steal the show. Joe's sterling performance as front man at this Rock Against Racism rally marked the moment when his own mythology took off, righteously opposing the National Front—the personification of positive punk.

But—as so often with Joe Strummer—there was a paradox here. He wore a shirt especially commissioned by him from Alex Michon, a girl who made the group's clothes; it bore the words "Brigate Rosse," a reference to the Italian left-wing terrorist group the Red Brigades. According to David Mingay, this was "strongly disapproved of by Mick"; no doubt the guitarist's disapproval would have been even greater had he known that in ten days' time the Brigate Rosse would kidnap and eventually murder Aldo Moro, the former Italian premier. Later in the year Joe attempted unsatisfactorily to explain away the shirt to Allan Jones, his old friend from Newport now on *Melody Maker*: "I am ambiguous. 'Cause at once I'm impressed with what they're doing, and at the same time I'm really frightened by what they're doing. It's not an easy subject." Is there a clue in a conversation that Joe's cousin Alasdair Gillies had with Ron Mellor on a visit to the family bungalow in Warlingham later that summer? "He was talking about the Red Brigades: 'Can you understand what drives these young people to commit murder? Maybe they have a point of view.'" Had Ron been having discussions with his son? Although extremely proud of Johnny Mellor's burgeoning success, Ron strove to appear cynically indifferent. "The only reason John is a singer," he would theatrically grumble, "is so that he doesn't have to get up in the morning."

Johnny Green, who was living at Rehearsals, noted that on a number of occasions the phone at the studio would ring late at night, when the group was guaranteed to have left. It would be Anna Mellor, Joe's mother. "Is John there?" she would ask. But Johnny felt she was calling at a time she knew full well Joe wouldn't be around. "'Ask him to call, would you, please,' she'd say. I had the sense that she was in her cups, waiting for when she knew he wouldn't be there, so she wouldn't have to talk to him. Joe seemed pleased that she called. I don't know if he called her back." Shortly after the Rock Against Racism concert, Joe surprised Jeannette Lee by asking if she would have lunch with his parents. She was nervous about the formality of such a situation, but Jeannette intuited that Joe wanted her to go with him to Warlingham as a measure of support. "In order for him to go he needed someone to take the attention away a bit. I said I would, although I didn't really want to."

The couple took a train down from Victoria Station to Croydon, where they caught a bus. "Joe kept teasing me that once I saw the size of the house and the swimming pool I wouldn't want to know him. He was enjoying the fact I didn't know where I was going. Once I saw how wealthy he was, he said, the bubble would burst. Then we got there and it was as ordinary as you like. Nothing special. They lived in a little modest bungalow, really nicely kept. A kind of neat couple.

"His mum was a very sweet, gray-haired Scottish woman. Very pleased to see him. I remember her being not overbearing. She was very warm and friendly, but not too much of a big presence. Dad made cheeky jokes. Joe was certainly visiting out of duty. He felt uncomfortable about it. Yet there was nothing that was awkward at all. His parents were lovely to him, and really complimentary to me. It was formal in the old-fashioned sense. More like 'How you doing, old man?' than arms around each other."

In the background to this visit were two issues that Joe never discussed with Jeannette. One was his father's past in India. "You'd think that would be something he would be bragging about," said Jeannette; more fundamentally, Joe never said a word to her about his brother, David. "He never, ever talked to me about what happened to his brother. He told me he had a brother, but he never talked to me about the fact that he committed suicide. I knew that, but he obviously didn't want to talk about it, and he never brought it up. He didn't want to talk about anything real."

Later that afternoon the pair caught the train back to London. "That was the last time I saw him as his girlfriend. He took me to see his parents and then after that he never called me again." When Jeannette next dropped by 31 Albany Street, Joe had moved, leaving no forwarding address. After her time with Joe, Jeannette became a member of John Lydon's PIL, when she

A serious culture clash: Joe takes on Rick Wakeman on the BBC "yoof" television program *Don't Quote Me. (Joe Stevens)*

formed a relationship for a time with Keith Levene, whom Joe had summarily dumped as well.

Joe had also fled Albany Street. Awkward questions had been raised around him as his new status as punk spokesman brought with it unwelcome elements. Specifically, Joe's address had been under the microscope. In the *NME* Tony Parsons railed that his choice of abode was tantamount to class betrayal. Punk audiences responded accordingly, and the sneering chant of "white mansion" became commonplace at Clash shows.

Joe moved into a one-room flat in Gloucester Terrace, just to the west of Baker Street. Although only essentially a studio, its exclusive W1 address marked it out as expensive. Wary of damaging his credibility, but also perhaps enjoying a measure of solace, Joe refused to tell anyone where he was living. Only Johnny Green knew where it was, because he would drop Joe off there. The place was tiny—a room with two single beds in it, a table and a chair. Joe loved it there, feeling it was where he should be, living off cans of tomato soup he would heat up in the lone saucepan that was provided on the hot plate. More than one observer suggested Joe liked living in academic and almost monklike ways, probably a throwback to boarding school.

"They weren't cheap, those flats," remembered Johnny Green. "He said he couldn't write, because he was too accessible in Albany Street. He wanted time on his own. He needed to be on his own, regularly. Even on tour he always had to have that space. If the space started getting closed down, he'd fuck off for a couple of hours. He could play at being the cheapskate, but then he moved into a place like that, because he knew he needed it."

In May 1978 Bob Dylan came to London for a series of dates. On the same label as the Clash, he was placed under the care of Ellie Smith, the company's press officer, who gave him a copy of *The Clash*. He loved it. At Joe Strummer's suggestion Ellie took the maestro to the quasi-illegal reggae club Four Aces in Dalston, a rough part of town. Dylan loved it, but Smith was almost fired for this.

By May the Clash was in Island studios in Basing Street in Notting Hill. The studio was renowned for the quality of work that emerged from it and had a distinctly Jamaican feel; Bob Marley recorded both his *Exodus* and *Kaya* albums there, as well as the single "Punky Reggae Party." Beginning on Saturday, May 20, Jack Hazan and David Mingay shot several sessions

The Clash in their natural habitat, beneath the Westway, in 1978.
(*UrbanImage.tv/Adrian Boot*)

for *Rude Boy*. Earlier in the month, on May 7, they had filmed a show at Bar-barella's in Birmingham, the group's performance of "Police and Thieves" that night making it to the final cut of the movie. Accompanying them was Ray Gange. "Ray was awed by Joe. If Joe would speak to him it was a big deal," said David Mingay. Not only was David a witness to the recording of much of the album, but he filmed it and—as you do when making a film—watched the resulting footage many, many times, studying the events and psychology at work.

Paul had decided he needed to get in the mood for studio work by watching aerial battles from World War II. A projector was acquired, and David Mingay went to the Imperial War Museum on South Lambeth Road and rented a number of classic war movies, including *Battle of Britain* and *Tora! Tora! Tora!* While the various members worked in the studio, Messer-schmitts and Spitfires would dive across their bodies as the films were pro-jected onto the studio wall. "They'd watch it and then play. It seemed to create the right adrenaline, and Paul would wear this militarylike uniform.

Joe pretended to go along with it, like a schoolmaster getting enormously excited by the idea of this young fellow, slightly patronizingly—though Paul didn't notice that. Mick was in favor of it." David Mingay noted that Sandy Pearlman and Corky Stasiak, his engineer, seemed like strangers in a strange land. "Pearlman couldn't deny the originality of Paul's idea, even though it invaded his lovely studio. Pearlman obviously found them difficult. He was really just sitting there as Corky Stasiak did the work, in the manner of engineers. Mick sat up there all the time with the pair of them. It was obvious that he really wanted to produce the record. But CBS wouldn't let him. There was a huge plan that CBS was trying to ruthlessly expedite to try and break the group in America. Joe was looking very worried, whispering, taking honey drinks, walking around looking shifty and a bit depressed. Bernie only came down once a week, bringing the wages from Camden. The group were worried whenever Bernie was going to show up in case he didn't like the new material."

"A lot of stuff went on behind our back," said Joe. "When we were recording we thought, 'We're in Island's Basing Street studios, this is the big realm, let's rock.' We didn't realize there was a whole crew of Yanks in the room with Pearlman, everyone putting their oar in." You wonder what might have been had Joe managed to pull off his dream of who should produce the Clash's second album: when they had been living together in Canonbury, shortly after they had released the first album, he and one of the Clash's roadies had fantasized that there was one ideal producer for the follow-up—John Lennon. Of course, this was not to be. But this wish says much about the John Lennon–like persona that Joe bore; it also provides an explanation for a remark uttered by him at a show in Leeds—to roars of appreciation. He had delivered his customary cutting comments about the Rolling Stones and the Beatles, adding the regal figure of Queen Elizabeth into the mix, following surprisingly with "But John Lennon rules, OK?" As the photographer Bob Gruen, on that tour with the Clash, remarked: "I thought, 'How come John manages to escape?'"

David Mingay noted how Joe Strummer and Mick Jones took differing roles at different times. "Joe was culturally quite limited, but also quizzically interested in culture. In the studio he'd have a beer and sit down with a pencil, and sketch out a song. Half the time he'd be an amusing, rational person, a little bit existentialist, a little bit on his own, prepared to give you a short amount of time; then he would veer off and wander into a corner, do something else. Then he would seem slightly a loner: he wouldn't really talk, and would look rather tragic. But he could be incredibly sensible and understanding of what was going on. Then there'd be these other areas where he would seem just inexplicably thick. Mick, on the other hand, seemed to be the heart of the Clash. There would be great impatience in the group, because one person would learn their parts in five minutes, and another would take what seemed like five months. They realized there are certain rules about being in a group that must be observed, as there are in a marriage. I think they realized to confront problems in a major way—to the extent that they'd have to leave the group—would entail a fundamental alteration in their lifestyle. You had the impression by now they had become a bit tired of their squat existences—they were tired of being uncomfortable.

"Joe was like a divorcee when he arrived in the Clash, and it always seemed that he didn't really fit in and was like an outsider. He was having an intense but rather embattled relationship with Mick, with whom he had teamed up for a very rational, absolutely straight-down-the-line reason. Mick was brilliant at arranging music and understood the form of pop music: he could branch off without betraying the genre that he was working in and be inventive, and seemed to know harmonies naturally. But Joe had no musical ability whatsoever of that kind, and he had this strange Brechtian-style of speaking-singing. A very odd voice."

Topper Headon—who had not previously made a record—had readily adapted to the studio. On the first day of recording he had put down most of his drum parts with absolute facility. "It was the first time I'd recorded," Topper told me. "Sandy Pearlman had a bit of a love affair with my drumming. In those days I didn't make mistakes—believe me, it changed. I was at a peak: I was contributing. If they'd got a drummer who couldn't play jazz and couldn't play funk, they'd never have got further than that second album." Unfortunately, because Topper filled his role with such expertise, he became bored in the studio; he started looking for diversions. He did have a court case on his mind, however. On March 30 he and Paul, along with Robin Crocker, Mick's school friend, the subject of the song "Stay Free," and Steve and Pete Barnacle, a pair of Topper's friends, had been arrested on suspicion of shooting at the trains that ran past Rehearsals. Topper had been trying out an air rifle of Pete Barnacle's by firing at what he thought were ordinary pigeons. They were actually valuable racing pigeons. All five were arrested and spent a night in jail. With bail set at £1,500 per man, they were released, but each defendant had to report in daily at his local police station. For a group that loved to go on the road, this was a great hassle, preventing them from touring until the case was resolved. Somewhat *au fait* with court procedures, Caroline Coon, Paul's girlfriend, took the matter under her wing, walking the defendants through the legal minefield. She secured the services of a noted barrister by the name of David Mellor (one can only imagine Joe's response on hearing this). Under David Mellor the defendants received sentences amounting only to payment of fines and damages. At least the Clash got a song for the new album out of the incident, "Guns on the Roof"—although the background to the number led to the Clash being severely castigated. The pigeon shooting earned Mick Jones's strong disapproval.

Was the worried expression on Joe's face at the Basing Street studio because he was concerned about the direction in which Sandy Pearlman was taking the second album? Quite possibly. "Obviously Pearlman had spoken to CBS and been given the brief to produce a rock LP," Joe said to me. "He probably kept it in that vein with that advice. It came up mainstream, or rockish." Years later, the sideways move of *Give 'Em Enough Rope* made more sense to him: "We changed the nature of the music. That's why we made it big in the world and the Jam and the Buzzcocks never did. Because we were willing . . . we knew that it was a journey of exploration, it wasn't toeing the line. And that's why we lost a lot of our early fans, 'cause the second album, you could almost call it just rock. I admit that we didn't know what we were doing during the second album, but we certainly weren't trying to play American. We got accused of playing American radio-friendly rock. And the producer was American. But it was the last thing on our minds. We were just trying to record the songs we had in the bag. But we got a lot of kicking for that."

By contrast a self-produced single was released on June 16: "White Man in Hammersmith Palais," backed with "The Prisoner," a song about Bernie Rhodes ("The prisoner lives in Camden Town / Selling revolution"). Although a masterly work, "White Man" got no higher in the charts than the edge of the Top Thirty.

With the court cases resolved, a nationwide tour had been set up, The

Clash on Parole. A couple of days before it began, in Aylesbury on June 28, the Clash played a warm-up show before an invited audience at Manticore, a former cinema at the bottom of North End Road in Fulham, only a few hundred yards from the hospital where Joe had recently been confined. Manticore was owned by Emerson, Lake and Palmer, exactly the sort of progressive rock dinosaurs the Clash had set out to topple, an irony commented on from the stage by Joe.

That night the Clash was on fire. I had no doubt that they were the finest rock 'n' roll group in the world. The hassles of the previous year— finding the right record producer, the constant frictions between the band and record company and, it appeared increasingly, with their management, plus Joe Strummer's hepatitis bout and the group's run-ins with the law— all appeared to have enriched the Clash with new inner strength and righteous power.

After the show Paul Simonon, Caroline Coon and I went out for Indian food and then back to Caroline's flat in South Kensington. Clearly inspired by the war films screened at the Basing Street studios by David Mingay,

The name of their group didn't necessarily mean the Clash was always in conflict. (*Sheila Rock*)

Paul Simonon told me that he had designed a new backdrop for the tour itself, police charging at the Notting Hill carnival juxtaposed against a Messerschmitt fighter plane.

I joined the group in Manchester on the On Parole tour. In the few days since I'd seen the Clash in Fulham, the change in Joe was marked; he seemed very much at the end of his rope. Driven by Joe's demonic urgency, the gigs I saw were the best, the warmest, the most involving, the most enjoyable rock 'n' roll shows I had ever seen. As the Clash had progressed to playing theater-sized venues, each with an audience of around three thousand people, Joe had risen as a performer; these larger stages offered him far more room to move around, as he performed his visionary act. But his role as front man seemed to be taking an exponential psychological, even psychic, toll on him. The moodiness and edginess I had previously observed had returned. Being Joe Strummer, which meant leading the punk masses back to the hotel each night like some anti–Pied Piper, was a twenty-four-hour job: Joe Strummer never closed, and you could see the stress that lurked permanently behind that superficially benign stoned countenance.

In Manchester, the afternoon after the regularly scheduled show and a few hours before an unscheduled gig at a nightclub called Rafters on this "day off," the Clash went to pick up some new music at HMV—Mick had bought cassettes of Peter Tosh's *Legalize It*, Al Green's *Let's Stay Together*, Neil Young's *On the Beach* and Randy Newman's *Little Criminals*, which gave a sense of how broad was his taste and the influences from his end on the group.

Later, Mick Jones and I sat up in Joe's hotel room watching a highly emotive TV exposé of the National Front, when a tense Joe Strummer walked in. For maybe two or three minutes he stood scowling at the program. "Did you talk to Bernie about all these problems with the fan club?" Mick Jones inquired. In a sudden spasm of rage that displayed Joe's ability to turn frightening on a dime, he viciously kicked a metal wastepaper basket; it flew up into the air, a broken cassette inside just missing my head, and the Clash's front man stormed out. Concerned, Mick Jones followed him out of the room and found that the reason he was so wound up was because he had been told it would be difficult getting kids into the Rafters gig for nothing.

Joe's mood swings could seem almost out of control and utterly unpre-

dictable. In the dressing room before the Glasgow performance that followed the Manchester dates, he came up to me. "Sandwich, you're an intelligent man," he said with a benign smile. "So could you tape this up for me,
please?" He produced some pieces of cotton that he wrapped around his right
wrist and about which I wound electrician's tape—this was what would become known as "the Strummer guard," Joe's own invention to prevent his
wrist from being sliced apart during his frantic chord-slashing on his Telecaster. But after the show, in that same dressing room, he grabbed by the
throat a fan who was berating him for not having done more to stop the de-
mented bouncers.

Glasgow's Apollo Theatre was notorious on the gig circuit for the excessive violence its psychotic bouncers employed. But the bouncers claimed
the audience had terrorized them over the years. "Here," said one of them,
proudly pulling up his vest. "This scar's from the David Bowie show. And
this one's from the Faces. And this"—he showed a thick welt across his
belly—"is from the last time the Clash played here."

During the Clash show the bouncers indiscriminately pummeled,
clubbed and kicked the audience, who of course retaliated. Joe—wearing a
T-shirt that read "Get tae Fuck"—backed off from the mike and shook his
head to himself after pleading with the bouncers and the kids to stop trying
to dismember each other: "Simmer down. Control your temper." Which in
the heat of the moment few probably recognized as a pair of lines from
Bob Marley's 1964 Jamaican hit "Simmer Down." When he finally gave
up, leaving the stage in tears, a whisky-fumed bouncer stepped forward.
"We're gonna have yeeew," he leered at Joe. Rumors quickly swirled that
the bouncers were heading for the group's dressing room, determined to
kick the shit out of them.

The Clash left the Apollo, me with them, glad to be away from the place.
Except that we were met outside by aggrieved fans, complaining that Joe
and the others stood by and watched while they were massacred. "Ye're jus'
big-egoed pop stars," snarled one. Exasperated, Joe slammed the lemonade
bottle he was carrying into the ground. As it shattered, police materialized
as if from nowhere, and heavy-handedly grabbed Joe to sweep him into one
of their vans. Paul Simonon stepped forward to protest and for his pains
was viciously cracked across the skull by a truncheon, before also being
thrown into a van.

Topper, wisely, disappeared. Mick and I, together with Johnny Green, raced off in the direction of the hotel to hide Joe's and Paul's drugs in case the police searched their rooms. At one point I went in search of Bernie. When I found him he showed no interest whatsoever in half his group being in jail; later Johnny Green told me that this failure on Bernie's part was a pivotal moment in his relationship with the four.

The next day Joe and Paul appeared in court, charged with breach of the peace. Joe later told me that the other punks locked up with them sang "The Prisoner" all night: "As we were leaving one of the cops on the door said to the one in charge of us, 'How come you didn't beat them up? Are you reformed or something?'"

Joe's brush with the law gave his Brando slouch in the dock real credibility. He was fined twenty-five pounds; Paul, forty-five. "What is the name of your group?" inquired the magistrate. "Vuh Clash," mumbled Joe. "How appropriate," tittered the judge.

In the street outside the court Joe Strummer turned to Paul Simonon and grinned. "Maybe it was a mistake calling this The Clash on Parole tour."

As the Ford Granada purred out of Glasgow with Johnny Green at the wheel, on our way to the next gig in Aberdeen, 150 miles to the northeast, spliffs were produced to take the edge off the general trauma of the previous night. Joe slotted a copy of *Trout Mask Replica* into the vehicle's cassette player. While this was the most avant-garde—and "difficult"—work by his beloved Captain Beefheart and His Magic Band, it was hardly the best driving music. "Eurghhh! What's that? It's horrible! Take it off," demanded Paul Simonon.

The journey through the Scottish Highlands passed without further incident, and after some hours we hit Aberdeen, then in the midst of a boom because it was the nearest port for oil rigs in the North Sea. Although it was July, it was freezing cold, a bitter wind billowing off the ocean; at a roadside stop Mick Jones took out of his suitcase a brown leather World War II German army coat he had bought in Camden Market and put it on: "Everyone said I was stupid to bring this but I knew I'd need it." With Joe sitting in the front seat, we drove straight to the venue for the sound check. I was sitting between Mick and Paul in the back. Johnny Green pulled up to open the gate in the chain-link fence that enclosed the rear entrance, leaving the engine running. As he pinned the gate open against the fence, Joe—always up for a prank—leapt into the driver's seat. Although he couldn't drive, he knew how an automatic car worked. Slotting the stick into the "drive" position, he seized the steering wheel and pressed his foot down on the accelerator, clearly intending to whiz past Johnny by inches, startling him. Except—as I said—Joe couldn't drive. He misjudged by a few inches, and pinned Johnny Green against the fence, the right edge of the car's nose lodging in the metal links. Johnny screamed in pain. The full weight of the Ford was against him. Joe was now panicking. He didn't know what to do. Although he had taken his foot off the accelerator, the automatic was still in gear and was edging slowly forward against the fence, crushing Johnny. "I can't breathe. My ribs are breaking," he screamed. Horror descended upon everyone's face as everything went into slow motion. From where I was I could see that Joe had gone white and tears were forming in his eyes— which Johnny confirmed many years later when we talked about this. Mick acted quickly. In his leather coat he jumped out of the car and ran for help. Paul raced to the front of the Granada, hopelessly trying to push it back. I could drive, and realized what needed to be done. "Joe, get in the passenger seat," I told him. Slipping through the gap between the two front seats, I got behind the wheel. I yanked the wheel to the right and put the gear into reverse. The car moved backward and off Johnny, who staggered forward, gulping for air, clutching his ribs. In shock, Joe and I looked at each other. "Thanks, Sandwich," he said, and looked away, his eyes still rheumy, his skin ashen. Mick Jones arrived with a rescue party, half a dozen thirteen-year-old kids on skateboards. But they were not needed in this story of the rock 'n' roll wars. As I said, I had already felt on this tour that Joe Strummer was a man at the end of his rope. I felt unspecifically but deeply worried for him. We never again mentioned the Aberdeen car incident, Joe and I; not that there was anything unmentionable about it, but simply because everything was happening so instantly that it somehow seemed almost quite normal.

In the Aberdeen hotel after the show, I went up to Joe's room with him. "Waterloo" by Abba wafted through the window from the hotel's disco— "That's a good one," said Joe. He told me that the occasional losses of control I had witnessed on the road were due to unrelenting pressure. But, as Joe himself admitted, in the past they were down to "the demon drink"—he said this problem was solved when his hepatitis obliged him to lay off booze. "It doesn't half make you lose your friends, though, not going down the pub," he laughed. But he also—untruthfully—vigorously denied that the hepatitis was due to any ingestion of stimulating powders.

Joe had a very powerful aura about him. Onstage, he never smiled. This hard-man stage persona, you realize, might well have been an extension of the belligerent Scotsman within him, something I hadn't known until he revealed it that night. As he leaned back against the headboard of his hotel bed, it was apparent what a very sensitive and perceptive bloke he was, though at this time he didn't strike me as necessarily a near-intellectual in the same way that Jones certainly was. All the time, he told me, underlining something that Mick Jones had said earlier in the day, he kept getting signs—whether in the form of actual emissaries or less tangible incidents—that he and the group were on the right path.

"I go in for that mumbo jumbo a lot myself," he smiled. "Like, when me and Mick went to Jamaica I was quite convinced we were going to die. At Heathrow someone dropped this ketchup all over the floor in front of us— and then we get there and we're driving through Trenchtown and I glance up at this wall and just see this one word 'BLOOD.' Mind you, nothing happened at all like that, and when I got back I thought, 'What a lot of time I wasted worrying.'"

We moved on to the contradictions within the Clash: how the warmth and positivism were hemmed in by overtly aggressive imagery—the gun logo, the militaristic stage backdrops, even the new song titles: "Tommy Gun," "Guns on the Roof" and so on. "It keeps coming up, doesn't it?" Joe nodded. "I think it's just a reflection of what's out there. I really do think we are a good force, but we're dealing with the world and those images are just a reflection of what it is."

He told me about a new song, "The English Civil War," a reworking of the American folk tune "When Johnny Comes Marching Home," which he first recalled singing as a kid in singing lessons at school. Why was the Clash's version transported to England? Because, said Joe matter-of-factly, "it's already started. There's people attacking Bengalis with clubs and firing shotguns in Wolverhampton. What really gets me is it's so-o-o respectable to be right-wing. All those big geezers in the Monday Club* will probably

*A fairly right-wing faction in Britain's Conservative party.

switch over to the Front if they start making any headway. That's what happened in Germany—they turned round and said, 'Oh yeah, I've been a Nazi all along, mate.' It's a pity, when the skins go out on the rampage, that they don't go down the House of Commons and smash that place up.

"Any time," he noted, "there's any urban disturbances they always occur in the poor areas of town. Why don't they happen in the rich areas? More things would get smashed up if they did. If it's in London it's always in either the East End or in Notting Hill: the other day I was walking along and I saw that all of Tavistock Crescent [a street in Notting Hill, which in 1978 had not been gentrified] is gone. And they used to seem to really know how to build houses fit for human beings to live in in those days. I mean, round by Westbourne Park Road these real egg-boxes have suddenly sprung up from behind the corrugated iron. Which is just brutal. I'd like to blow the head off the guy who designed those—or, better still, force him to live in it."

We discussed the paradox between his serious intent and the fact that so many Clash listeners seemed to miss out on the humor in their lyrics. I told him that there were certain tracks on the first album that made me burst out laughing every time I heard them.

"Yeah." He smiled. "I think some of it's really hysterical stuff. We all used to burst out laughing, too, when we first started playing them."

I mentioned that Mick Jones told me that he found it a strain when people tried to look on the group as evangelists: "Yeah . . . that's a bore. Just a load of old crap. I think you've always just got to be grateful for what you've achieved and then just try and achieve some more."

But why did he think the group had got to the position where people thought the Clash had the Answer? "We give 'em good stuff. That's all. There aren't that many other groups around doing it." He named, among others, Sham 69 and Siouxsie and the Banshees.

So look, I concluded, it's been two years since the group first started. How does it feel now?

"I could've told you the answer without hearing the question. We're a good group. That's the only answer. And when you're in a good group you feel good."

Causing mayhem throughout the land—there was a notable stage invasion by skinheads when the group played in Crawley in Sussex—the Clash on Parole tour continued until it wound up with four nights at the Music Machine in Camden Town. Joe made an impression on Gaby Salter, the girl he had met at Francesca Thyssen's Christmas party. Late on a hot July night when the Clash had played one of those Music Machine dates, Alex Chetwynd, a family friend of Gaby, came across her at a bus stop in Notting Hill Gate, waiting with a chum for a night bus. "We've just been to see the Clash. Oh, that Joe Strummer is so gorgeous," Gaby sighed to Alex. "But his teeth are disgusting," commented her pal.

M ick Jones and Joe Strummer were summoned to San Francisco to continue working on the tracks for the second album, this time working at the Automatt studio. "Sandy Pearlman took us to his favorite studio in San Francisco and we worked there for three weeks, just Joe and me," Mick Jones told me. It was the first time either had been to the United States. Later Pearlman suggested that San Francisco was chosen as a location by the record company to keep the pair from the confusing influence of Bernie Rhodes.

As experienced by many on their first visit to the United States, both Joe and Mick were getting plenty of input, visiting the celebrated City Lights bookstore, for example, where they stocked up on texts by the beat poets. They stayed at the Holiday Inn in Chinatown, where scenes from *Dirty Harry* had been filmed, something that impressed them. The hotel was opposite the city's only punk club, the Mubai, where they went every night. Joe and Mick also went to see a show by Carlene Carter, the stepdaughter of Johnny Cash. Through Nick Lowe, who was by now going out with her, they got to meet Carlene: Mick knew Nick because he had produced an Elvis Costello track that the Clash guitarist had played on, "for which everyone had had a go at me." But as a result Joe got to meet the stepdaughter of Johnny Cash, one of his musical heroes, and was seriously pleased.

A musical source of inspiration sat in the studio itself, a tastefully stocked jukebox, including one record that was perfect for the repertoire of the Clash. "Mick and Joe came back from working on *Give 'Em Enough Rope* in San Francisco and at the studio they'd had a fantastic jukebox that included 'I Fought the Law' by the Bobby Fuller Four," said Paul Simonon. "I'd never heard the song before. By the time they came back they knew how the song went, and we just adopted it. In some ways it became a Clash song. People even today think: 'Oh, that's a Strummer and Jones tune.' It's become more Clash than Bobby Fuller, really.

"I thought it was a great, rousing song. I liked the attitude, and the sentiment, lyric-wise, was so apt in some ways. The Bobby Fuller Four were from El Paso and played Texas rock 'n' roll. What amazed us on the original was the guitar playing, like fingers dancing like a gazelle, so in control but so light, in a Buddy Holly way. It was written by Sonny Curtis, one of the Crickets. You hear a lot of conflicting stories about what happened to Bobby Fuller: all I'm aware of was that he was in a park and they poured gasoline down his throat and set him alight."

Paul yet again had been denied the opportunity of an overseas trip with Joe and Mick. Neither he nor Topper was happy. "We were asking if Paul and Topper could come over," said Mick Jones, "and they're saying, 'Oh, I don't know.' We had a week off after we'd finished our recording—we were going to mix it at the Record Plant in New York. We insisted, 'We've got to have the other two over here, they've got to come,' and 'We'll meet them in New York.'"

To get to New York, Joe—in a typical journey of (self-)exploration— drove across the United States in a Chevrolet pickup truck with Peter Impingo, "this friend that he made there who was this very religious guy," remembered Mick—who himself went to Los Angeles with Sandy Pearlman and then flew to New York.

In New York together, the foursome linked up with photographer Bob Gruen. At the Record Plant he took a shot of Joe reclining on a couch, a replica of a picture Gruen had taken of John Lennon. After a day at the studio Gruen took them on a photo shoot on the streets of New York: "It was real late, a rainy night, and we were driving around looking for steam coming up out of the streets, to get one of those classic Manhattan shots. The thing was, there's a lot of steam in the winter, but not on a hot September night. We went down to Little Italy to try to get something to eat, but everywhere was closed. So we went to a deli and bought spaghetti and sauce and went back to my apartment and ate it and watched New York Dolls videos I'd made."

As soon as the Clash had hit New York, Joe had been on the phone with Joe Stevens, who had moved back to his native New York. The photographer introduced the punk rocker to "the Candy Store," a Lower East Side bodega whose primary function was the vending of ten-dollar bags of marijuana: Joe Strummer thought this was a great institution.

"I'd give Joe the key to my place on the corner of West Houston Street and Thompson," said Stevens. "He'd come over and hang out and watch TV and then say, 'I've got to go and be a recording artist now.' He liked going to bookstores and talking to people in coffee shops. He'd read *The New York Times* but he had a lot of half-baked political ideas, and his opinions were quite naïve. He didn't quite get it, because he was quite young. He wasn't that sharpish with the chicks. Even though I'd given him the key to my place, it never once happened for him.

"He was very awkward with girls. I'd fix him up with young honeys, but nothing happened. He was shy, not aggressive enough. He was a funny guy. I said to him, 'Did you get those teeth from John Rotten?'

"The Clash seemed to have no money, and were dependent on friends. I was buying pizza and beer for them. They were living in the Royalton on Forty-fifth Street, and very poor. Not really having a good time, all a bit miserable. [The owner of] CBGBs gave them an open tab. I especially liked Simonon, because he was funny. And Jonesy was looking great in those days. I'd see Joe and Jonesy sitting around discussing lyrics. They collaborated well. There was certainly no war going on between them."

But there was a war in one aspect of their lives. Away from London— first when Joe and Mick were in San Francisco, and then all four of the group together in New York—they discussed their increasingly fractious relationship with Bernie Rhodes. From across the Atlantic he tried to put pressure on the group to return to London by booking a date for them at the Harlesden Roxy on September 9, which would have meant abandoning their work at the Record Plant.

Matters came to a head almost as soon as they returned to London, already exhausted from their time in the various studios—"We came out like zombies," said Joe. Bernie had rescheduled the Harlesden date for September 25, but the show had been oversold—1,600 tickets for the 900-capacity Roxy. Accordingly, the Clash turned up on that night to explain to the fans why they couldn't play: they intended to reschedule a pair of shows to accommodate everyone who wanted to get in to see them. They also gave out promotional T-shirts for the imminent "Tommy Gun" single. Meeting the

Joe and Topper, working at the Record Plant in New York City. *(Joe Stevens)*

group in Harlesden, I noticed that although there was no sign of Bernie Rhodes, Caroline Coon, Paul's girlfriend, appeared to be directing operations. Afterward we drove to an Indian restaurant in Bayswater. "I can't think of any other group that turns up to a gig, spends a couple of hours talking to the fans in front of a fish and chip shop and then goes home," Mick Jones said to me. Weren't the fans pissed off, I asked? "Wouldn't you be?" said Joe. "There were kids from all over the country: Cardiff, Liverpool, Belfast, Newcastle, Glasgow. What am I supposed to say when someone says to me that they've spent twenty quid to get to the Roxy and that they're broke now?" As we were leaving the restaurant, it was arranged that I should go over to Mick's flat on Chepstow Place one lunchtime the following week to hear the new album.

With all the group, nervously rolling joints, clustered expectantly around me—the very worst way to hear a new record—I sat in an armchair as it was played to me. It sounded very impressive, I told them, but the weight of anticipation around me made it not the most easy of listening experiences. The songs that stood out were "Safe European Home," "Stay Free," "Guns on the Roof" (despite the dubious pigeon-shooting origins of the tune), "Julie's Working for the Drug Squad" and "Tommy Gun." "The English Civil War" seemed a little obvious. But the record was very different from *The Clash*—broader and brasher in both sound and themes. "There are more guitars per square inch on this record than on anything in the history of Western civilization," Sandy Pearlman had told the San Francisco–based rock critic Greil Marcus at the Automatt. The Sound of the Westway had become the Sound of the World.

By now Bernie had booked a full set of dates, the Clash Sort It Out Tour, which kicked off with the group once again in Belfast, on October 13, the day after news had broken that Sid Vicious had allegedly stabbed his girlfriend, Nancy Spungen, to death in the Chelsea Hotel in Manhattan, sending shock waves through the punk world. But the tour then moved on for a quick canter around France, Belgium and Holland.

Again, as in parts of the On Parole tour, they were accompanied by filmmakers Jack Hazan and David Mingay. What surprised this duo was that, in a typically perverse and confrontational act, Bernie had also given a green light to another pair of filmmakers, Nick Broomfield and Joan Churchill, who had a brief from Thames Television to make a documentary about the Clash.

"We went to Paris and had a wonderful time. They were so marvelous on this tour sometimes, and then we got to Belgium and suddenly Joan Churchill and Nick Broomfield were there on the plane," said David Mingay.

In Amsterdam the Clash played at the Paradiso, a potheads' haven. Perhaps inspired by the available wares, they played a show that Johnny Green regarded as "staggering," the best show by the Clash that he ever saw. "We went to some club after the Paradiso," said David Mingay. "We're by the bar with Joe, who's in a nice mood. Jack said, 'There can't be two films about you. I'm going to ring our assistant tomorrow and tell him to put all that we've filmed so far in the bin and junk it.' Joe was incredibly drunk, and he said to Jack—because he always had respect for Jack, who wasn't impressed with rock 'n' roll groups and let that be seen—and said, 'In the bin. It's all in the bin.' I admired him for that, he was great. Then the next morning we were in the tour bus: 'Hello, Joan, Nick.' The group were all gurgling with laughter in the backseat. Suddenly the bus drew up in a garage and the door was opened and the other two filmmakers were told to move out. Then all the group said, 'Hooray! Great! Got rid of Bernie! Bernie was trying to make a Communist film about us!'"

What Joan Churchill and Nick Broomfield were unaware of was that they had become caught up in a power play between the group and Bernie Rhodes. The group had decided that Bernie should no longer be their manager. The decision had essentially been made by Mick Jones and Paul Simonon, Joe reluctantly going along with it. In archetypal terms, this was a complex situation: Mick and Bernie had essentially founded the group, with—as group managers often are—Bernie as something of a father figure to Mick, and later to both Paul and Joe ("He is the master and I'm the apprentice," said Mick). Now it was as though, in a replica of real life, the father was being rebelled against. To compound the complexity, Joe didn't agree with the change. "I was the only one who realized how lucky we were to have Bernie and tried to argue against it," Joe said. "I was the only one who'd been struggling around, bashing my head on the wall since '71. It's a thankless task trying to keep a group going in those circumstances. So I realized that Bernies didn't grow on trees. But maybe Mick and Paul thought, 'Hey, anyone can do this.'" (It is worth noting that Bernie Rhodes was even more remote from the group than one might have realized. When Jack Hazan and David Mingay's film *Rude Boy* was eventually released, Bernie spoke to David Mingay. "Bernie said that when he saw the film he learned more from it than he'd ever learned about the group when he was with them: 'I'd never seen them before—I never realized what they were all about.' He had never listened to a word they said. That was it. He admitted it. He didn't understand the dynamics of the group. Mick and Bernie had invented the group. Bernie felt that he had been the person that Joe then became, the leader of the group. He'd been the person who thought he knew what the group should do, the one who had been saying: 'Don't write these love songs, write something else.'")

everal candidates were considered for the task of taking over the management of the Clash, including me and photographer Pennie Smith: Mick told me that we would have formed "the Axis of Journalists," along with Barry Miles. Miles, who wrote under his surname and had edited *IT* and worked for Apple Records in the late 1960s, had a meeting with the group, along with Ellie Smith, CBS's head of publicity. The four Clash members had suggested the pair of them should come on board as a management team, and then all proceeds would be split six ways. But Miles and Ellie backed off from the project, essentially because Miles felt dealing with Joe over business was an uphill struggle. "He just didn't seem to have a clue. He was like the most innocent schoolkid. Hopeless. Ellie and I had a meeting with them at which we went through their financial books—which amounted to about eight pages. Mick was still taking buses everywhere, and Bernie had a personalized license plate, CLA5H, a bone of contention. But Joe just sat there smoking joints, saying, 'Bernie's OK.'" After Miles and Ellie Smith dropped out of the running, Caroline Coon, Paul's girlfriend, was hired. Joe claimed to have been the one member of the group who did not favor the arrival of Caroline as manager. "Caroline's achievement at [drug-bust charity] Release was phenomenal, really amazing. But I think her ability was more organizational than inspirational or visionary. So it didn't translate too well into the weird rock world."

Besides, there was now another woman in Joe's life—although as she had just had her seventeenth birthday on October 12, 1978, "girl" is how she should properly be defined. While Joe had been in San Francisco, Topper Headon had started to go out with a girl called Dee; Dee was a good friend of Gaby Salter, whom Joe had briefly met at Francesca Thyssen's Christmas party the previous year; Topper, Dee and Gaby started to hang out. Back in London Joe saw Gaby and confirmed with Topper that this was indeed the girl he had met at Francesca's. "I'd [skipped] school to go to a press reception for *Give 'Em Enough Rope*," said Gaby. "I was at CBS with Johnny Green waiting for Topper and Dee to go to this event, then Joe arrived and he asked me out." Gaby had heard a rumor that Joe was seeing a girl named Plaxy, a presence on the Clash scene. Was this true? she asked him. "No," Joe lied. So Gaby agreed to go on a date with him. "He met me at the Roebuck pub at World's End. But it was a big punk scene and a bit too overwhelming for him, people were all over him, so we ended up with Steve Jones and Paul Cook at their flat in Bell Street.

"I found out later that Dee had ambitions to get together with Joe: Topper was the stepping-stone. She was furious when he asked me out. We fell out— she still ended up sleeping with Joe." Not that Joe hadn't provided Gaby with ample warning of the likelihood of this. "I've been to bed with over a hundred women," he revealed to her. "But you're the one." Later, she appreciated she should have heeded the latent threat that lay in his boast. "Joe was one of the most unfaithful people I could have possibly met." Such conundrums of contemporary behavior notwithstanding, this was the beginning of a relationship that—despite a nine-year age gap—would last fourteen years.

Tall, blonde and beautiful, Gaby Salter adhered authentically to the standards of what would come to be seen as Joe's female archetype. She was one of three children of Tom and Frances Salter, the very definition of groovy Chelsea hipsters, who had lived in a well-appointed house off the Fulham Road. In the 1960s Tom Salter had started the Great Gear Trading Company, which sold clothes and tourist bric-a-brac in Carnaby Street and in the King's Road. "Joe used to call me the Twentieth-Century Pop Kid," Gaby told me. "It was the swinging sixties: we had that swinging kind of life." Her father began to promote rock concerts, including the Grateful Dead at Alexandra Palace in North London in 1975. Debt followed. In 1976 the family moved briefly to the United States, where Tom and Frances split up. By the time Joe started going out with Gaby, the sumptuous house had been sold to pay the money Tom owed; and Frances, Gaby and her two brothers, Mark and Nick, were living in a council flat in nearby World's End. Gaby was at Holland Park Comprehensive, retaking her GCE O-levels.

Very quickly this seventeen-year-old schoolgirl ("I suppose the fact that Joe was twenty-six sounds shocking: our kids say he was a child molester—it sounds shocking to them but it didn't seem it") moved in with Joe into his new home, a squat at 34 Daventry Street, round the corner from Steve Jones and Paul Cook in Bell Street. As with girls, as with homes: Joe had reverted to type.

The squat on Daventry Street, off Edgware Road, had been taken over by Kate Korus, the original guitarist in the Slits, who was now busy forming another group, the Modettes. Gaby was asked to audition for them, though nothing came of this. The property, a former shop, was a long-term, established squat, and Gaby found it quite acceptable. "I can always adapt. I can live in palaces or squats. Joe did tidy up in my honor. It was quite decent: there was hot running water and electricity."

The press launch of *Give 'Em Enough Rope* that Gaby mentioned was held at lunchtime at the St. Moritz, on Wardour Street, the same nightclub Joe had immortalized in his song "Mr. Sweety of the St. Moritz." At Joe's request Julian Yewdall stood outside the venue, taking pictures of everyone leaving: "Joe said he wanted to know everyone who'd been to it."

Give 'Em Enough Rope was released in Britain on November 10, 1978, and in the United States seven days later. In the United Kingdom it had a mixed reception: *Sounds* gave it a five-star review; but Nick Kent in *NME* felt it highlighted both the group's strengths and its weaknesses; Jon Savage in *Melody Maker* came to a fairly devastating conclusion: "so do they squander their greatness." But the album leapt into the British charts at number 2, its highest slot. In the United States the record received almost universally ecstatic reviews, Lester Bangs in *The Village Voice* as passionate as Greil Marcus in *Rolling Stone*. (Marcus wrote: "The Clash rain fire and brimstone, with a laugh. *Give 'Em Enough Rope* is a rocker's assault on the Real World in the grand tradition of *Beggar's Banquet* and *Let It Bleed*.")

The Clash would become the biggest-selling import album ever in the United States, with over 100,000 copies sold before an amended release in 1979. But it was the official American release of *Give 'Em Enough Rope* that was the benchmark for an understanding of the group by the broad American public. Among the first things Caroline Coon set in motion was an American tour; she managed to wheedle $30,000 of tour support from Epic (the division of CBS that was distributing the Clash in the States) in New York, and dates beginning in early February 1979 were set.

They played the makeup shows at the Harlesden Roxy on October 25 and 26. The first date was filmed by Don Letts for a video for "Tommy Gun." Joe wore a T-shirt emblazoned with the phrase "H-Block," referring to the internment wing of Long Kesh prison in Belfast.

As the year neared its end there was a very serious trauma, of the sort that had characterized life for the group in 1978. By then, Sebastian Conran was managing Subway Sect for Bernie Rhodes, setting up shows for the group. On November 5 Subway Sect played a gig in King's Cross, and Sebastian invited along his housemate Henry Bowles, who was also Joe's friend. Since it was Guy Fawkes Day, some clown decided to set off a firecracker. "Henry, who was a little guy, was laughing at a joke or something when the bouncers came in," said Sebastian Conran. "Someone said he'd set off the firework. He said, 'Don't be silly.' So they took him and threw him out the door, and he never woke up. Horrendous."

The death of Henry Bowles deeply affected Joe; he became involved in a campaign for regulations over the hiring of doormen at music venues. It marked the final involvement of Sebastian Conran with the music scene: "Punk rock ended for me when Henry was killed. After that I got very depressed, packed it all in and got a job." Joe ensured that the next Clash album, *London Calling*, was dedicated to Henry Bowles.

The British leg of the Clash Sort It Out tour began on November 9 in Bournemouth. By the time of this tour the strongest new song in the set—apart from "Safe European Home"—was one not on the album: "I Fought the Law." When they played Manchester two weeks later, Nick Kent wrote an article in *NME* in which he claimed to detect tension between Joe and Caroline Coon. In Glasgow the next month the group heard that their two shows at Strathclyde University were open only to students. To check this allegation, Joe borrowed a motorcycle helmet: disguised by it, he attempted to buy a ticket—and was refused. "I'm in the band," he informed the ticket seller. "And we ain't playing the gig."

At the gigs the Clash did play, Joe was always extremely aware of the size of the crowd that the group could pull in. "If we play in Staffordshire," he would say, "I know we can get in about four hundred people." Like a politician estimating whether he can win a seat, Joe knew the size of the Clash's constituency throughout Britain, and—although he may always have been up for increasing it—he never exaggerated its size. (Joe liked staying in hotels on tour, and was always fond of the Gideon Bible found in most rooms: "It's fantastic, isn't it, that they put a book there for you for free, and what a great book to read." Joe's understanding of the Bible, of course, was approached from the perspective of Punk-Rastafari, and the admonition of Roots Rastas that the book must be read at the rate of a chapter a day.)

When they played the Music Machine in Camden Town on the snowy night of December 19 (a benefit for Sid Vicious's legal defense), Mick Jones and Glen Matlock played with opening act Philip Rambow. Notwithstanding the fact that Rambow had first introduced Joe to Gaby Salter, Joe was furious with Mick for this. But Gaby said Joe was otherwise extremely happy with the progress of the Clash. "He was really buzzing and very positive. He was happy. It was starting to dawn on him that it was really working. Although he didn't like the way that Caroline was managing things. He missed and trusted Bernie, the way he operated. I don't know what had gone down with Bernie. There were so many issues around the Clash I ended up thinking they were aptly named. About now Joe wanted to split the songwriting money four ways and Mick didn't—Joe later retracted this but then he wanted that. Whenever a decision had to be made, one of them was always at odds with another. For a long time it was Joe against Mick—Paul and Joe were pretty much aligned with each other."

According to Johnny Green, at this time Joe himself felt quite isolated within the group, especially as the two most musical members, Mick Jones and Topper Headon, automatically gravitated toward each other. Soon Joe had moved with Gaby into her mother's home at Whistler's Walk in World's End. "He was always very keen to get back to World's End in a way he hadn't with any of his other places," said Johnny Green. "There was an intensity about this relationship that drew him there, because you would never regard Joe as a dutiful man. I remember the staggering nature of just how besotted he was with Gaby. I was surprised, really. I never saw Paul like that: Paul had his independence always.

"Strummer worked hard to keep a private life. Even when I first met him at Albany Street, he created a private space. He'd hang around for beers in the pub, but I'd find out that afterward he'd gone to Luton to watch Ray Campi and the Rock 'n' Roll Rebels. I'd say, 'Why didn't you tell me? I'd have gone.' 'Oh, all right.' He didn't appear to be separate, but in fact he was. It's the same with him going to World's End. Different world: *bang!* Steps out of the world he's in."

By going to live with Gaby and her mother and two brothers, Joe was accepting and honoring a weighty responsibility, a sign of maturity. "Joe," said Gaby, "became the patriarch of my family. He took on me, my mother, my brothers. We'd lost our home, we'd lost everything and later his home became our family's home. In some ways we gave him that sense of family. He was very generous and giving in that way."

Joe's generosity meant he was also capable of giving extremely bad advice. "There was this time I was down the pub and I'd been with my ex-bird," said Johnny Green. "I was really proud of her. She's with some other bloke in her place across the road. Joe goes, 'Go and hit him. That's what you do if you love someone. You fight them.' I went over, smacked the bloke, kicked him in the head. The girl is screaming, and leaves with him. I go back to the pub. Joe says, 'How did you get on?' I said, 'Don't ever give me advice again.' He laughed. I was distraught. I'd lost my girl."

Within two months of starting to date Gaby, Joe took her to Warlingham to meet his parents: "I adored his dad. He was quick-witted, had a wicked sense of humor. His mother was very quiet, very stoic and seemed a bit like she'd been beaten down by life: she'd lost a son, and because she'd traveled a lot she didn't have a community of her own. She was very loyal to Ron. She seemed quite withdrawn. Anna quite liked a drink and I think a lot of that was the foreign lifestyle. Joe was charming, he was brought up as an embassy child—he knew how to fix you a drink. But he was not all charm: he was a chameleon—he was exactly what you wanted him to be. People think they know Joe but everyone got a different part of him."

Gaby, who was a couple of inches taller than Joe, noted that he looked "very much like his mother and like his father. He was the same build as his dad; his dad was slightly smaller—Joe was five foot eight. His mum was five two." The subject of David arose, but was met with almost entirely sealed lips from Ron and Anna Mellor. As to Joe's thoughts about David, said Gaby, "He felt somewhat guilty. He survived at boarding school and his brother didn't. Joe was still having a go at his mother on her deathbed about boarding school. It did traumatize them. His mother told me—and there is absolutely no reason why his brother was like he was because of this—but when they left Turkey David had lost his nanny, the first person he'd lost. He used to cry for his *yayah*.

"I'd heard Joe had been bad at school but it was worse than that: he was appalling at school. He was totally self-taught. He had a highly evolved mind and intelligence but when it came to working at school he just wasn't interested. His father had built his life on guts and determination, and Joe was totally the opposite. It was difficult for Ron, as he thought the only way you could better yourself was to be educated. Joe's marks were horrendous. He wasn't even trying. But he was really popular in school. His brother was not only not popular, he was a loner. Joe loved that there were girls at school; in some ways he made the best of it.

"David was just very withdrawn. He had a deep depression and sense of paranoia. There was depression in the family. I know Joe suffered from it."

For her own part, Gaby's schooling suffered: there was a contradiction between her life with Joe and her return to secondary school at Holland Park Comprehensive: "I would get the train on a Friday night to join him on tour, intending to go back to school on Monday morning. But it ended up being more like Thursday afternoon. I ended up mucking up my schooling again."

The Clash ushered in 1979 by playing three dates at the Lyceum Ballroom, off the Strand in central London, on December 28 and 29 and January 3. These were probably their best shows in London to date, and the January concert was filmed for *Rude Boy*. What these extraordinary Christmas shows did was to cement the reputation of the Clash as the hippest act in town.

In January they went into Wessex studios in Islington for three days to record "I Fought the Law," which had been received with such acclaim—so strong that it had been slotted in as the second tune in the twenty-odd song set—on the recent tour. Mick Jones produced the record, and the session was engineered by Bill Price, who had worked with Mott the Hoople and on the Sex Pistols' *Never Mind the Bollocks* album. At this session the group also recorded "Groovy Times" and "Gates of the West" and remade "Capital Radio"—previously only available on the *NME* free single.

$$\frac{1}{4}$$

red hand of fate

1979

On January 30, 1979, the Clash flew to Vancouver in Canada for a couple of days' rehearsal, before playing their first date of the Pearl Harbor tour—as their invasion of North America was almost inevitably named—in the town. "I flew up to Vancouver," said Bob Gruen. "I remember everyone being really nervous about whether they would be searched at the border. Would the band be harassed? They all psyched up for it."

"Everyone had emptied their pockets of millions of knives et cetera that they thought were not allowable," said Paul Simonon.

"Then no one even looked at them at immigration," said the photographer.

After the tour bus stopped for the night in Seattle, where Topper Headon paid tribute to actor Bruce Lee at his graveside, the party woke to the grim news that Sid Vicious had overdosed in New York and died. In a state of some shock they continued down the Pacific coast to San Francisco.

In an inspired move by CBS publicist Ellie Smith, Joe would record the entire trip in diary form for *NME*. He definitely now appeared the spokesman—and therefore leader—for the group.

Their first show in the United States, at the Berkeley Community Center on February 7, was an utter triumph—in fact, every concert sold out once the tour was announced. The pre-show introductory music was "There's a Riot Goin' On" by local boy Sly Stone. "There was no gobbing," said Paul. "That was a big plus, because clothes tended to last longer. I suppose people were trying to figure out what the whole thing was about from what they'd read in the press about punk groups in London." "The first show was a blast," confirmed Bob Gruen. "The place was full of happy, dancing people. The Clash was more than your average good-time band. You not only had a good time but you also thought about issues that bothered people. Things were serious and there was a lot to be angry about, but there was also a lot to have fun about. The force of the music made it sound like a battlefield, a clash. The lights were always flashing, like explosions."

The next afternoon the group traveled with the photographer to a flea market in nearby Sausalito. "I found loads of bits and pieces there," said Paul. The group purchased assorted leather jackets and vintage pieces of Americana. Afterward they drove to nearby Mount Tamalpais, where, sitting up on its heights, they could see for miles over the Pacific and back inland.

That night—much to the anger of Bill Graham, promoter of the official Berkeley show—the Clash played another date, a gig for the homeless at the Geary Temple in what had been the old Filmore West (ironically, it had been established by Graham at the height of flower power). The second show the Clash played in the United States was a benefit—right from the start, they nailed their colors to the mast. On this, his second visit to San Francisco, Joe met a political radical named Mo Armstrong, formerly a member of Daddy Longlegs, an American group that had moved to England in 1970. "He'd become very left-wing," said Joe, "and he gave us the info, which was quite hard to find, about the Sandinistas. It was the sort of thing they weren't interested in printing in *The Sunday Times*. A bunch of Marxist teenage hooded rebels oust one of your favorite dictators? The establishment didn't want to know about it."

At the request of both Joe Strummer and Paul Simonon, an opening act on the tour was Bo Diddley. "I can't look at him without my mouth falling open," confessed Joe. Caroline Coon had tracked Bo down in Australia. His fee was more than the Clash would earn on the door—initially, he refused to play any of his classic songs because he didn't own the copyright to them. Paul remembered, "Bo Diddley used to sit up all night and put his guitar in the bunk instead. Which was unusual." On the video system on the bus, rented from Dolly Parton, there were endless viewings of the first *Star Wars* movie. When the bus was pulled over for speeding, the officer demanded that everyone get down from it. "Well, I have to tell you," said the man behind the wheel, using his wits, "we got Dolly Parton asleep in the back." Reverential at the mention of the Queen of Country, the cop rescinded his order and waved the vehicle on.

In Los Angeles the Clash played at the Santa Monica Civic Auditorium, just blocks from the Pacific. Another triumph. Robert Hilburn wrote in the *Los Angeles Times* that it was "one of the most exhilarating rock shows in years." He spotted—how could he not?—the onstage strength of Joe Strummer: "The band's strongest visual lure on stage spits out the lyrics with such alarming intensity that a life insurance salesman would think twice about writing him a policy." The show was most notable for a postgig incident that has entered Clash legend. Assembled with the local Epic hierarchy for the kind of self-congratulatory photographs beloved of the record industry, the group suddenly cut and ran, walking straight out of the room, to the bafflement and apoplexy of the company employees. Joe explained this act to *Billboard* magazine: "If you let them you'll have no soul left, and if you have no soul you cannot make records. We'd rather make our records, even if they don't make the Top 100."

Despite the Clash's endless railings against CBS in London, the group's actual relationship with the company was more complex. Almost every time I went into CBS's headquarters in Soho Square, members of the Clash could be found there, having sociable chats—especially with publicist Ellie Smith. With much of their income frozen pending the conclusion of litigation with Bernie Rhodes over their management contract with him, the record company was keeping the Clash going—this even extended to the dishing out of large amounts of promotional records, knowing only too well they would be immediately sold at the nearest discount store, bearing out what Muff Winwood said of Maurice Oberstein's strategy to make it appear as though there was constant conflict between the company and the group.

Caroline Coon had an even-handed vision about the lost Santa Monica photo opportunity. "Part of the punk ethic was to refuse to be in any way gracious to anyone from the record company who came backstage," said Caroline. "My charm helped a bit, especially when we ran out of money halfway through the tour, and I had to go on my knees to the record company and ask for more cash to finish the tour. But they did it because the Clash were playing fantastic gigs that were absolute sellouts."

In Cleveland on February 14 the group played a benefit for a Vietnam vet named Larry McIntyre. "This guy called Larry McIntyre lost both his legs in Vietnam," wrote Joe in his *NME* account, "and when he went for a swim one day in the pool near his flat all the other residents banned him from the pool on the grounds that it was too disgusting . . . so we agree to play a show for him, helping his legal costs, but we don't get to meet him because, having forgot his name, I referred to him over the PA as 'the guy with no legs.'"

The tour moved on to Washington, D.C., and Boston. Joe's old friend from Newport Art College, Allan Jones, a senior features writer on *Melody Maker*, came from London to cover this section of the tour. "The sound quality may have improved slightly," he wrote, "but Strummer's vocals are still buried, the lyrics almost entirely lost. And looking at him, all criticism of his increasingly stylized performance seems so much waffling. He still can't successfully change chords on the guitar while singing; he still sings with more conviction (even when, to some ears, it's misguided or confused) than most of his bleating contemporaries; he still resorts to mere bellowing when his passion gets the better of his control."

When they arrived in the capital, Allan offered another telling vignette of life with the Clash: "Mick Jones has a map of Washington. He decides he would like to go sightseeing. Now. It is 4:00 a.m. Jones wants to go to Arlington, the military cemetery where there burns an eternal flame in memory of John Kennedy.

"'Great,' says Strummer. 'Let's piss on it and put it out.'"

The Clash hit New York the day before their Manhattan show. Joe disappeared that night with Susan Blond, the Epic publicist. The next day he whispered in Johnny Green's ear: "I've done something awful. I went out for the night with Andy Warhol." "That was the night before we all went to Studio 54: he went on his own with Warhol," said Johnny Green. "The rest of us all went to some scuzzy place. But Joe's always had a penchant for things like that, for going into a world." (Years later Joe spoke to Q magazine of this Warholian experience: "They were inspecting me as if I was an interesting coal miner they'd picked up on the highway.") On the tour was

Barry "Scratchy" Myers, formerly the DJ at Dingwall's. "The Clash played at the Music Machine in Camden, and I was the DJ. Johnny Green came up to me and said that Joe really liked what I was playing." After accompanying them on their last U.K. tour of 1978, he was brought over to the States with the group; Johnny Green remembered a quirk of Joe's character over Scratchy that seemed as off-kilter as his visit to Studio 54. "People would go to Joe with a problem. But they didn't necessarily get the response they expected." When Barry Myers bought a flight case matched to the atomic pink of the Clash's kit, and found it had been scrawled on with anti-Jewish slogans, he became very upset. Topper (whose behavior could mutate out of his benign Stan Laurel persona into something more akin to Freddy Krueger—when he was using the heroin he was increasingly fond of) and Robin Crocker were the culprits. Myers was distraught. "He went to see Strummer. Because he's the leader, innee?" said Johnny ironically. "And Joe went, 'Well, that's your fuckin' problem. Sort it out yourself.' Barry was then even more distraught about this. Joe was quite consistent in turning up that piece of advice over the years. People would go to him with a serious problem, and he'd say, 'Sort it out yourself.' They would never ask the others—always Joe. They might have done better asking Paul. But he wasn't the Leader, was he?"

Joe later outlined his laissez-faire philosophy: "Making like you've got the answers to everybody's problems—it's impossible. Everybody must sort out their own problems: that's the key to everything. You sort one problem out and get the will to go on and sort another one out. You can't expect any help, I don't think."

The New York show, the most exalted event on the entire tour, was at the Palladium. "A bit like the Rainbow," Joe wrote in *NME*. "With all the traveling we was pretty knackered. During the sound-check I overheard a Yank talking to his mate: 'Wow, these guys have had it. They can hardly stand up, never mind play!'" It was one of the most significant dates the Clash ever performed; not only was the ubiquitous Andy Warhol in attendance, but also the cream of the downtown underground: Nico, Debbie Harry, David Johansen, John Cale and Lenny Kaye were all schmoozing backstage. For the Clash this was a seriously prestigious night that set up the group for the manner in which they would springboard out of the city to national American success. "By gig-time the place was packed," wrote Joe, "and all the top liggers in town were there. We were plenty nervous. Halfway through the show I checked the audience and became convinced that we were going down like a ton of bricks. But like they say it's a tough town and by the end of the day we managed to whip it out and give 'em some of our best."

Back in Britain from their barnstorming sprint around the United States, the Clash was coming down from the high of the tour. Among other things, they were still broke. But the making of *Rude Boy* was still in progress; David Mingay and Jack Hazan realized the live sound they had recorded was not up to scratch. Accordingly, six weeks were booked at Air Studios, which overlooked Oxford Circus slap in the middle of London, in March and April 1979; Bill Price, who had engineered the sessions in January, was hired. The Clash was to be paid for this by Michael White, the film's producer: the cost of re-recording the *Rude Boy* music would more than double the budget of the film. "We were very lucky," said David Mingay, "because they had time on their hands. They were worrying about management, but they were liking it because they were on their own. Joe was thinking of going back to Bernard; I thought they should go back to him. They were short of cash; they said no one was paying them. Mick was a little awkward. He would turn up late, but when he arrived he did everything very fast—so in fact he didn't need the time that the others did."

On the sixth floor above Oxford Circus, Mick and Joe would sit out on the window ledge, their legs dangling free below them. "They were very happy there," thought David Mingay. "Kate Bush was recording in the next studio. She would make tea for them—they loved it. George Martin, whose studio it was, would be booming, as you imagined he had to the Beatles: 'Hello, boys. How are you all?'"

But tensions existed. Mick would badger Paul about his bass playing, replacing him on the instrument if he wasn't fast enough. Mingay stressed Paul's visual appeal: "Paul made the group look great: without him they would have been rather un-good-looking."

The film director thought that all was not well between Mick and Joe. "There was a jealous feeling between the two of them at that point. Joe was taking off into being something of a superstar and Mick would be worried whether he would be considered the same. Mick was always caught talking to those kids who love guitars. Joe had the press buzzing around him and they weren't talking to Mick enough, even though Mick might be giving more interesting answers, because Joe's message was fairly monosyllabic. He was considered the prophet of his generation, which is weird, because Mick had more to say of interest, was always available and calm, and he could face failure, which Joe couldn't. Hubris was a threat for Joe—he was a performer who would soak up success and manipulate his own success.

"But the real flavor of Joe was innocent and amusing. He could talk about serious matters in an original way. He would rehearse political opinions all the time, with a slightly bizarre twist. Joe was reticent, shy-appearing. He would never rush to hold forth. He did love to be like Humphrey Bogart occasionally. He'd make these sardonic statements—he possibly was being rather spiritual, but didn't put it into words. Whereas Mick seemed a straightforward, left-wingy, devoted person who was not at all insecure about his so-called working-class credentials and his aspiration to live in the best surroundings he could manage. But I don't think Mick was an anarchist, whereas Joe maybe was—rash, compulsive and self-destructive behavior and crises all were part of him."

The time in Air Studios had set the juices of the group flowing. Johnny Green and a roadie named Baker found a rehearsal room in Causton Street, Pimlico, near Vauxhall Bridge, and the group booked it for the next five months. Known as Vanilla, it was at the rear of a garage, the kind of premises you might see in American gangster films as heists are planned. With pleasure, this cinematic aspect of Vanilla was noted by Mick Jones. It was not a bad metaphor. Here, hunkered together with no visible means of financial support, the Clash would rigorously write and rehearse the new songs that would emerge as London Calling, which time would judge one of the finest rock 'n' roll albums ever made after it was released in Britain at the end of that year. Retreating into their own resources, untrammeled by management or record company demands, they would connect with their creative core, taking a leap forward in material, philosophy and image.

If the record can be seen as a harbinger of change for the Clash, a broader shift was being experienced across the country. On May 3, 1979, a general election was held in Britain and Margaret Thatcher, the leader of the Conservative Party, was voted into power as the United Kingdom's first woman prime minister, the beginning of an eighteen-year reign by her party that would change the face of Britain, with complex consequences. On election day the Clash—ever happy to act as agents provocateurs—

released *The Cost of Living* EP, made up of the tunes recorded in January: "I Fought the Law," the remake of "Capital Radio," "Groovy Times" and "Gates of the West." The EP reached number 22 in the *NME* charts. The group had a further connection to *NME*, however. What was not made public was that Joe Strummer had been the subject of a death threat from the Red Hand Commandos, a splinter group from the Protestant Ulster Defence Association (UDA), the result of Joe having written his personal election manifesto in *NME* and also of having worn the H-Block T-shirt at the Harlesden Roxy gig in October 1978. At the *NME* a letter addressed to Joe was received. Handwritten in black ink on cheap paper at odd, ugly angles, as though an attempt to disguise the writer's identity, the anonymous letter was a death threat. "It had the air of a blackmail note," said editor Neil Spencer, who opened the envelope. "I nearly chucked it in the bin but there was something about it that made me think I should take it seriously." "It all came about because Joe made a comment in the *NME*, 'Troops out of Northern Ireland,'" Mick Jones said. "Which wasn't such a terrible thing to say. The *Daily Mirror* said that." Members of Special Branch visited the group at Vanilla. They verified the authenticity of the letter: this was indeed a serious warning from an authentic terrorist organization of intent to murder Joe Strummer—the man who only a year before had appeared at the Hackney Rock Against Racism show wearing a Red Brigades T-shirt (which caused Joe's own comprehensive and substantial Special Branch file to be opened). "I think the Irish death threat is a big event, life-changing," said Kosmo Vinyl, who would very shortly be working with the Clash. "Joe was put on an assassination list by the UDA. I think Joe's militancy became more subtle after that. He put his thoughts into the writing of his lyrics instead."

As though notions of karmic retribution were alien to his way of thinking, Joe was soon back in his own role of hatchet man, something that seemed to be becoming a habit. At the beginning of May, Caroline Coon flew to New York to set up another U.S. tour for the Clash. When she returned, Joe told her she wasn't needed anymore. Joe later admitted she had advocated well for them and had been very keen; he also confessed he hadn't wanted her to do the job in the first place. Caroline had taken on the task—to which she refused to append the word "manager"—only because she wanted to help the Clash, knowing they were in crisis and their hard-won success could so easily unravel. Caroline Coon moved to Los Angeles to work in the film business before returning to her earlier love of painting.

Joe Strummer would respond to business crises by becoming a sort of Clash corporate executive, wielding his verbal ax, and then return to being the squat-king slacker. For someone so concerned about the misuse of authoritarian and governmental power, it was an extraordinary way to behave. But many things about Joe Strummer were extraordinary.

Managerless, the Clash was also broke. Their assets had been frozen pending a settlement of the conclusion of the legal wranglings over the group's management contract with Bernie Rhodes. Through the summer months they steamed on, writing and honing new material. On July 5 and 6 they played a pair of "secret" gigs in London, at the small Notre Dame hall off Leicester Square, trying out new songs. These included "London Calling" and "Rudie Can't Fail," as well as the only live performances ever of "Hateful" and "I'm Not Down." "Lovers' Rock" and "Revolution Rock" were also essayed—"appealing eulogies to reggae song styling, but both appallingly trite, lyrically speaking," carped Chris Bohn in his *Melody Maker* review.

The previous week an interview with Joe had appeared in *NME* by Charles Shaar Murray, a distinct volte-face from his "garage band" review of the Clash's "Screen on the Green" show. Joe plugged "our film. It's called *Rudi [sic] Can't Fail*. Ray Gange is the boy from nowhere." He described the attitude of the Clash to their alleged management crisis: "You could say that us and PIL are working in a Jamaican kind of way: we do what we feel like, soon come, but there's still that burning question—'What the fuck are they doing?' It's got to be answered, and that's why we're gonna get hold of some guy in America to do the American end and we'll handle things here ourselves, or maybe we'll work with someone we know.

"We're working on quite a wide front. We got all these things cookin' and we're trying to bring 'em to the boil. We've had our fill of bullshit, and now we're back to the drawing board. We're really fucked, but I don't think we're fucked enough to quit. We're way beyond that." In the interview, in Finches pub on Fulham Road, near where he was living with Gaby, Joe told the writer about the group's state of play: "I'm a man whose knees are dusty from begging on record company floors. I got no pride—but I wanna survive and I want the Clash to survive. The only thing that we got is the Clash.

"We've got some crazy ideas like . . . some LPs, like a Bee Gees LP, will

cost hundreds of thousands of pounds to make, so they're gonna cost—
what is it now?—six quid soon. Suppose a group came along and decided to
make a 16-track LP on two Teacs, which dramatically diminishes the cost
factor called 'studio costs.' Suppose you presented that tape to the record
company and told 'em that it cost just those few quid to make. So even
when they've added their mark-ups and a cut for him, you can still get a
fucking LP for two or three quid. So why can't that be cost-related?"

In another interview, with Dave McCullough and Gary Bushell of
Sounds, both of whom were willfully unimpressed with the group's new
material and with punk in general, Joe continued this theme, making a
prophetic remark that would have an adverse effect on the finances of the
Clash—although it would enhance their reputation and legend. "There will
be no six quid Clash LP ever. Why don't ya ring up the other bands and get
them to say that?"

Such paternal favor toward the fans might have been appreciated by a
surprise visitor to Notre Dame. As Joe told the audience, among them was
Ron Mellor, his father, the first time he had seen his son perform with the
Clash. (When Don Letts's *Punk Rock Movie* premiered at the ICA, Iain
Gillies learned of the pride behind Ron Mellor's cynical mask of indifference.
"Ron and Anna laughingly told me the tale of a trip of Ron's to Heathrow Airport to pick up a diplomat friend who was returning from somewhere over-
seas. The friend started regaling Ron with tales of recent diplomatic doings.
Ron hushed him and said, 'You can tell me all about this later. There's
somewhere I have to go.' Ron drove straight to the ICA, where Don Letts's
Punk film was showing. When they got to the ticket counter, they were told
it was sold out. Ron's highly ranked friend let loose both barrels of the Empire. 'Do you realize who this man is?' he demanded of the ticket seller.
'This is Joe Strummer's father!' Two ICA office armchairs were rolled into
the front row of the cinema and Ron and his friend watched the show com-
pliments of the house.")

The Notre Dame shows served as warm-up dates for a concert eight days
later, in which the Clash returned to the Rainbow, a defense fund benefit following a racist attack by skinheads on a pub in Southall in West London. The
Clash was supported by the English reggae group Aswad and the Members
(whose singer Nicky Tesco was now living with Joe's school friend Annie
Day). The political events behind the Rainbow shows bore a weighty signifi-

cance, only increasing the status of the group. Apart from a cash-raising festival in Finland the next month, the group regimen that summer was hardly ruffled. "We lost Bernie and we sort of crashed," Joe said to me. "And I think this is where we proved ourselves. We stayed in some shithole in Pimlico for five months, day in and day out, and then we just bowled into Wessex and knocked off *London Calling* in about three weeks."

Filming on *Rude Boy* was complete. David Mingay went down to Vanilla to remind the group of their promise to write a song for the end-title music. Joe pretended they'd forgotten about it. But they already had the tune, "Rudie Can't Fail," a song that used the faster reggae rhythm of the late 1960s. It was one of the Clash's best tunes, a timeless number, written especially to link up with the *Rude Boy* title. "It was written about Ray being a drunken idiot," Mingay said, "and Joe particularly put that line in— 'drinking brew for breakfast.' Myself and Jack Hazan went there to hear what they were doing. They delivered it on time, efficiently and professionally. They weren't rebellious in any way where their work was concerned."

When the two filmmakers visited Vanilla, Joe was working on the vocals of another new song, "Death or Glory." While filming *Rude Boy*, Joe had told David Mingay of his love of *Casablanca*, the 1942 cinematic masterpiece starring Humphrey Bogart and Ingrid Bergman, a regular treat on television. "Death or Glory" has intriguing lyrics, cynical, world-weary, perhaps revelatory. Joe makes both a statement of intent and a comment on the reality of that intent. Is Joe considering himself in the marvelous second verse? "I believe in this, and it's been tested by research / That he who fucks nuns will later join the church."

The song misquotes *Casablanca*, a takeoff of the film's famous set-piece song, "As Time Goes By," and its lines "It's just the same old story / A tale of love and glory." "He admitted to me that he had twisted it around from 'As Time Goes By,'" said David Mingay. "I think he was always worried—or at least romantically interested—in the idea that it should all end in an intensity that could cause death, as had happened with Sid Vicious. That for the icon of being a rock star to really work it would have to die, to die young."

The line "He who fucks nuns will later join the church"—clearly not taken from the lyrics of "As Time Goes By"—always seemed greatly significant, Joe speaking of his own dilemmas and internal difficulties: the anarchist squatter who in some way regarded himself as a failure or traitor for having broken with his past and joined the Clash—where a different form of conformity was called for. In his battle with himself, Joe couldn't win. Don Letts said, "The problem with Joe is that he sees everything in terms of black and white: always one or the other. He doesn't realize that there are all these shades of gray in the middle. He's beating himself up over that." But most of that was yet to come. It would grow much larger before it was fully visible.

With his omniscient energy, Joe Strummer is now building his separate place in the iconography of the Clash. You receive a cinematic vision when you think of his quest for a producer for the new songs, Joe trawling through the sweaty, characterless pubs filled with trashed lives spattered about late 1970s Oxford Street, a man on a mission, searching for another man with charisma: the legendary Guy Stevens, whom the group felt had been unjustly treated over their Polydor demos. Joe Strummer recalled, "I found a row of blokes sitting slumped over the bar staring in their beer. I looked down this row and I spotted him because of his woolly hat." Joe recognized that face, like a wounded puppy; he'd been there, knew that Guy was grappling with private turmoils that were never spoken of, life's ironies, like the way that this infinitely influential record producer had a son who had been born stone-deaf. "I went up to him and tapped him on the shoulder, he looked round and it was like son-finding-father in one of those corny films. He looked up at me and said, 'Have a drink.'" Joe gave him his pitch, asked him to produce the new album. "I'm just a bloke trying to get it out there," he said to Guy. "We need you, you need us. Let's do it." "OK," said Guy, downing his pint.

As he had no means of listening to the new tunes, the Clash had to buy him a cassette recorder. When he'd heard them he went up to Wessex in Islington, where the group were setting up for the sessions. A deal was struck, Mick Jones finagling the producer some percentage points from CBS. Despite considerable opposition from within his own company, Maurice Oberstein had gone along with their suggestion that Guy Stevens produce this new album. It cannot have been easy for the dapper Oberstein to negotiate with the producer. First, there was a very specific physical problem: as though you felt it could be some form of commentary on punk rock itself, Guy would spray you with a constant storm of spittle as he spoke, snowflakes of dandruff sprinkling about him with every movement of his head. "They hate his guts!" said Joe. "They said they wouldn't use him again until he was bankable. It gives me heart when Guy tells us about his business history. At least there's someone around who's as bad as us, if not worse. All the dreadful, life-wrecking things that've happened to him. People tend to be afraid of him because he's off the wall, to put it mildly. And they should be." Joe Strummer was not without a sense of perspective about an almost willful eccentricity around Guy Stevens: "There's a little bit of an act in there, but it's not entirely an act. It puts a lot of people off. They just think, 'Christ, get this man home.'" Mick Jones had his own understanding of why Guy Stevens's lateral approach to record production worked so well: "His presence in a studio definitely makes all the difference. It's like all the mess goes to him like Dorian Gray's portrait or whatever. All the messy sound goes and it becomes him, and what's left on the tape is . . . clarity."

Guy Stevens loved working with the group, as he told Charles Shaar Murray after the record had been completed: "It's been tremendously refreshing working with the Clash. They've changed a lot since I first knew them in '76. Joe is great, because he always puts you straight if you're out of order. The whole thing happened very naturally. It just worked."

Did there seem an element of Clash-Aid-to-the-Walking-Wounded over the hiring of Guy? As a deterrent to the spittle with which Guy Stevens would spray you as he spoke, Joe invented what he called "the splatter-board," which he insisted Guy hold in front of him as he spoke to them, only his eyes appearing over the top. But he was the inspiration the group had hoped for. Thanks to the DVD release in the twenty-fifth anniversary edition of London Calling, many of us have seen the footage of Guy in the studio swirling a stepladder around his head as Mick Jones tries to record a guitar part. ("Guy's methods would be considered in modern-day production a little bit out there. But he didn't actually swing the ladder at me, it was more like he was just swinging the ladder, but I was nimble enough to make space.") And heard the story of him pouring a bottle of red wine into a piano as Joe played it, to improve the sound; or the one about Guy lying in front of Obie's Rolls-Royce until the record company boss admitted how "brilliant" the new record sounded. Or the arrangement that the group had to make so that on the way to every session he could ritualistically stand in the middle of the Arsenal soccer field as a cab waited for him.

But Guy Stevens's production methods did not all hinge around confrontation: in Joe's personal archive is a copy of Patricia Bosworth's biography of the actor Montgomery Clift, a gift signed and dated "July 28 1979." "The Right Profile," a tribute to Clift, was written after that, in the midst of the sessions.

"Brand New Cadillac," a cover of the classic by Vince Taylor and His Playboys, was the first tune recorded. There was an assumption at the time the album was released that this was a tune recently picked up on by the Clash, part of their new romance with rockabilly. But not according to Paul. Even before Joe met up with them, he and Mick had loved the classic English rocker: "'Brand New Cadillac' dates back to that period when Mick and me were living in the squat in Davis Road in Shepherd's Bush. The record was lying around in the house, and when Joe met up with us there we used to play it a lot. We were trying to work out how the song went. Once we'd sussed it, we started playing it a lot more. At first it was only played in a playful way, not as a song to go in the set." The version on *London Calling*, the second song on the nineteen-tune double LP, is a recording of the first time the group had run through "Brand New Cadillac" in the studio. "It's a take," said Guy Stevens.

At Wessex the Clash pounded through extraordinary new material. Key moments were "Clampdown," a decisive and powerfully rocking statement about the never-had-it-so-good materialist thinking Joe saw at the core of the rise in right-wing thinking. Joe's faint falsetto "Who's barmy now?" is his throwaway final line, continuing that great tradition. "I'm so nervous!" is Joe's one-liner in "Lovers' Rock," the group's first love song. "Lost in the Supermarket," sung by Mick, was criticized as "another typically wimpy Mick Jones song" by those in the press who sneered at his supposed "rock star poseur stance." But, as Joe told me, he had written the song realizing it closely reflected what he knew of the guitarist's earlier life. "I thought Joe wrote that for me," said Mick. "I didn't have a hedge in the suburbs. But the people who live on the ceiling I knew all about. And the line about long-distance calls making me lonely could be about me and my mum." Perhaps the Mick Jones detractors should have listened more closely: when Joe him-

The usual suspects: the Clash at Wessex studios during the *London Calling* sessions, with engineer Bill Price (front row, left), producer Guy Stevens (in front of Joe), and CBS Records executive Maurice Oberstein (right). *(Pennie Smith)*

self sings the penultimate chorus as a counterpoint to Mick—"I'm all lost!"—the song attains a transcendent melancholy beauty.

"I'm Not Down" also tackled depression—Mick shouts the word out in the song—although Mick says that it's not something he ever brought up with Joe: "It was there. There was a point when you got right down to it and you couldn't quite go past. About his brother . . . there was something in there about that. He'd never tell anything about that. Then years later I just casually asked one day 'How's your mum?' We're in a loo somewhere, having a piss, and he says, 'She's got cancer.' There was stuff like that all inside. Really shocking to even look at."

In similar melodic vein is "Spanish Bombs," romantic in both sentiment—notably, Joe's enduring fascination and love for Spain and in particular the poet Federico García Lorca—and the kind of melody Mick Jones was so adept at producing, which opened side two. "Jimmy Jazz," set to a New Orleans jazzy-blues feel, is the story of a Rasta who has killed Jimmy Dread—what was Joe saying about his shifting interests in music? "The Guns of Brixton" had a similar theme, the first Clash number ever sung by Paul Simonon, unexpectedly creating a different dynamic in the set.

There was a version of Lloyd Price's "Stagger Lee" that cut almost immediately into "Wrong 'Em Boyo" by the Rulers. Although this felt a splendid example of Clash art-school intuition, it was a strict replication of how the Rulers had originally recorded it. "I don't know who the Rulers were," said Paul. "It was a midsixties record, with a ska element to it, before Jamaican music evolved. The original Lloyd Price song might have come from Bernie. It wasn't just Bernie Rhodes who put records on the jukebox at Rehearsals. We all did. There were things that belonged to Bernie, some were mine, and some were Mick's. I don't think Joe put any on: Joe just had lots of record covers but no records."

The album continues to build its widescreen drama with the galloping "Four Horsemen," a call to arms, another conscience shaker: "You're never gonna ride that lonely mile / And put yourself up on trial." It's a stir to action, and Joe's scolding is lessened by the heroic romantic feel of the song, reflected in its self-mythologizing melody.

Tucked away at the end of the album, as you get set to leave it, is the statement of intent of "Revolution Rock," couched in laughs, the best way of getting anything over. It was a cover of a recent reggae record, "Revolution Rock" by Danny Ray, which had a more pop sound than the rougher Clash version. "Danny Ray put out his version of 'Revolution Rock' just before we were recording *London Calling*," Paul told me. "Our version has a whole different attitude, and also you've got the element of Joe throwing in different lyrics. The horns section takes it to another point too." By the time it appears on *London Calling*, "Revolution Rock" sounds more Jamaican than the original, Joe a cool-throated badman of the microphone: "Oo-la-oo-la-oo-la-oo-la-oo-la," he half-doowops, half-chants like a mantra, toward the end. He pushes the lyrics to the max, urging them out, adding, extemporizing at length, inventing whole verses, almost speaking in tongues—and his control, his timing, is awesome, a perfect performance. "Everybody smash up your seats and rock to this brand new beat," he urges, conspiratorially—on the original Danny Ray sings "Everybody get off your seats."

"Revolution Rock" is a real statement of intent from Joe and the Clash. He popped in this message of punk-rock self-motivation, Joe, who secretly believed in hard work as much as his father had: "Young people shoot their days away." "Revolution Rock" is one of the Clash all-time greats. It was intended to wind up the album, but the last-minute addition of "Train in Vain" (Mick's urgent entrant, at first intended as a free single to give away with an issue of *NME*—"It was too good for that," said Mick) changed things. "Revolution Rock" was also a stylistic declaration: from now on the Clash entered a phase of dubbed-out, longer stage shows, rockers galore.

On an album of magnificent material, the greatest song on *London Calling* is almost certainly track 1, side 1, the title track. "London Calling," comprised of a simple chord sequence, is an ecology-in-crisis song, long before this began to be realistically feared. There were always those in the know about what was really going on in the world, and Joe was one not afraid to address the issues. In his June 1979 *NME* interview with Charles Shaar Murray he had declared, "There's ten thousand days of oil left. It's finite." Joe Strummer had been inspired to write the song riding back with Gaby Salter in a taxi from Vanilla to World's End. As the cab drove along Cheyne Walk, next to the River Thames, they were talking about the state of the world in the light of the nuclear disaster in the United States that March at Three Mile Island—an event that worried people around the globe. "There was a lot of Cold War nonsense going on," Joe said. "We already knew London was susceptible to flooding. She told me to write something about that. So I sat in the front room, looking out at Edith Grove [a street near their place]. Years later, I found out I was looking right onto the flat where the Stones lived when they started out, which seemed appropriate."

Such thinking was in tune with what he was writing in "London Calling." The lyrics for this song didn't just pour off Joe's pen, as he would suggest happened with various sets of song words. There are at least half a dozen versions of "London Calling" lyrics, some substantially different from what we hear on the final song. In what seems to be the earliest version, the lyrics of a prototype of "Lovers' Rock" are intertwined with some of what we know as "London Calling": Joe talks about the need to splash your seed on the wall—which seems to be an anti-birth-control-pill rant.

At first the song isn't called "London Calling" but "News of Clock Nine," a reference to the BBC TV news broadcast in those days at nine each weekday evening: "London calling" was the call sign for BBC radio broadcasts during World War II. What follows is from what is probably the third draft:

> London Calling News of clock nine
> Birth Control—there's a plot on it
> London Calling the past is a cult.
>
> The right kind of parka is proof of the doubt
> London Calling—the fools and the clowns
> You should be more careful—when you jeer your way around
> London Calling—kings of the south
> Hated all over—kings of the mouth

Permanently anxious to further the progress of the Clash, Mick Jones was concerned for the prospects of the now managerless group. When Mick played on Philip Rambow's first solo album, he met Peter Jenner again and they got to talking. With his partner Andrew King, Pete Jenner had formed Blackhill, the company that put on the Blind Faith and Rolling Stones free concerts in Hyde Park in 1969; the original managers of Pink Floyd, they had done the same job for Alberto y Los Trios Paranoias, who stayed with Joe in Maida Vale. Now Blackhill looked after Ian Dury and the Blockheads, whose *New Boots and Panties* was an iconic punk album. Crucially, Pete Jenner and Andrew King had reputations for being scrupulously honest. And there was a bonus: working for Blackhill was Kosmo Vinyl, a sort of conceptual publicist with energy, attention to detail and generosity of spirit.

It didn't seem a bad team. Pete Jenner and Andrew King were invited into the studio to meet the group. "Bernie has completely destroyed us," they were told. "We have no idea what has happened. We've fallen into a black hole." Jenner and King were rewarded with a management deal—a gentleman's agreement, nothing signed. With the package came Raymond Jordan, in charge of security.

Significantly, the choice of Blackhill to manage the Clash was made by Mick Jones; again Joe found himself pushed to the margins over who would care for his career. As he had started the Clash, did Mick consider it to be his group? "S'pose. To a degree." Eight years later, when I had a conversation with Pete Jenner about the Clash, I was surprised by the extent of his vitriol toward the singer. "I thought Mick Jones was fine, but Joe was a complete asshole," he said forcefully. What had happened to make him feel like this? Sitting in a restaurant on the Harrow Road, only a couple of hundred yards from Walterton Road, I reminded Pete Jenner of that assessment of Joe. "I suppose nowadays I couldn't really see him as a complete asshole," he admitted, "because actually he was really nice and really committed on all the ideas. But he failed to link things together. He wasn't stupid, but he failed to link A to B to C. There were rational problems that could be dealt with. All of their problems were solvable. But Joe would not let you solve them, and then would blame you when the further problems that you predicted did occur.

"But they really didn't get on, Mick and Joe. Joe always treated Mick like an idiot and so Mick responded by staying stoned and rock-starred-out. I could be more relaxed with Mick, and get on with him—he was fairly straight-headed. Mick didn't have the political hang-ups of Joe, who was always demanding low prices: 'It's for the kids.' With Joe everything always ended up as a compromise, with every issue unresolved.

"Joe would always have a bunch of blokes around him, Joe acolytes, random people, almost like a security blanket. So you couldn't have a serious discussion because of them. I also felt he never totally accepted me as a manager. I felt that in his eyes I was the personification of the business that they had to deal with and didn't want to, hoped it would just go away. I could outdo Joe about politics and he didn't like that. I would try to explain: 'It's not quite like that, Joe.' Went down like a lead balloon. I gave up on it because I didn't want to show up my artist in front of the punters—and there was always an audience."

Although there may have been an element of security blanket about such companions, Joe's manner of sitting around with "blokes" in front of whom your business is publicly conducted is actually very Jamaican. Aptly named "reasonings," such debates are frequently subject to the reaction and scrutiny of onlookers. During his cultural perambulations Joe must have picked up on that, and liked the position it gave him, the Don and his posse. A whole heap of the Clash street-pose came from that red-gold-and-green reggae world—in the late 1970s Joe often would wear an Ethiopian flag lapel badge.

As the years rolled on, Joe's posse tended increasingly to be characters straight off the Notting Hill spaghetti western set: professional drunks, aristocrats, actors, artists, scamsters, thieves, junkies, poets, dealers, great minds, mystics, misfits, madmen, musicians, the cream of the scum, who had worked hard to be there, the version galore of Notting Hill. They were pulled into Joe's orbit for stimulation and education and to osmose the Clash singer's energy, determination and ruthless will to succeed. In Joe's world there was only one revolutionary king: even though he took time to disguise the servant status of his basking rabble army of assorted vicarious lowlife, that is what they really were.

In the late summer of 1979 Joe is seized with a new energy. As are the whole group. At this point the Clash come into themselves: they've reached into themselves during the five months at Vanilla and the six weeks at Wessex and fulfilled themselves with what has emerged. Working on their own, they have shown extreme inner strength and know how great their new record is. They are on a far more mature high than that of the White Riot tour. For Joe, happy with both his work and his home life, it is extremely validating, only spurring him on to more. *London Calling* is a big change: this is a group in touch with its creative core, bringing to bear all the influences to which it has been subject. Ironically, it has done this by subverting the early punk notion of Year Zero and going back behind it for its subject matter. The album was now finished. Like film directors who acknowledge that they are too close to their material to edit it objectively, the group left the tracks in the hands of Guy Stevens and Bill Price, the engineer, for them to provide the final mix, then headed for California, where the Clash's second U.S. tour was about to start.

"Then we pissed off to play the Monterey Pop Festival," Joe told me. "And we left it with Bill Price. And he and Guy Stevens mixed it while we weren't there. And then years later it was voted Best Album of the Decade."

"That tells you how manic it was," said Topper. "We were doing a double album for the price of one and before we finished it we were going on tour and had to get someone else to mix it."

news of clock nine

1979-1980

O n September 4, 1979, the Clash flew to San Francisco for the opening date of their second U.S. tour, dubbed the Clash Take the Fifth: the group were to crisscross the United States for seven weeks, a rigorous work schedule leading to physical and mental strain for all of them.

That month Chet Helms's Family Dog Promotions was putting on a weekend festival, the Second Annual Tribal Stomp Potluck Picnic and Dance, on the same fairground site as 1967's legendary Monterey Pop Festival, a hundred miles south of San Francisco. Topping the bill on the afternoon slot of Saturday, September 8, above Joe Ely, the country-rock star, and the soul outfit of the Chambers Brothers, was the Clash. The presence of Joe Ely on the same bill as the Clash was significant. "Joe felt Hank Williams's music a lot," said Kosmo Vinyl, "and Joe Strummer and Ely both found something they longed for in each other: Ely wanted one of those crazy English rock 'n' roll guys and Joe wanted that authentic Southern country guy. The connection with Ely was real. Ely is authentic, he's a country singer, out of Hank Williams and Buddy Holly. He's the real thing. A spiritual connection."

The Clash was driven down to Monterey from San Francisco by Rudy Fernandez, an employee of Chet Helms, who was to become fast friends with Joe. "I'd never met anyone from England. So I picked them up, and there were these four skinny pale English guys. Back then I had long hair, like everybody. But they were cool with the short hair. I spent a week with these guys, and I saw right there that they were what was happening. When they left I cut my hair."

Always aware of his rock 'n' roll history, and the precedent set for head-line grabbing at the 1967 event by Jimi Hendrix—when the guitarist had set his guitar on fire with lighter fluid—during the set opener, "I'm So Bored with the USA," Joe collapsed backward, as though shot, into Topper's drum kit. Photographers' cameras clicked and a picture of Joe's fall put the Clash on the front page of the next morning's edition of the *Los Angeles Times*. Part contrived theatricality, part out-of-control possession by random spirits— as were so many of Joe's performances—this incident during the first num-ber of the U.S. tour proved pivotal in etching the image of the group on the consciousness of California. The first encore featured the premiere live per-formance of another tune that—as with "I Fought the Law"—the Clash al-most made their own: their cover of "Armagideon Time" by Willie Williams, a recent hit on Jamaica's classic Studio One label. Onstage the extended, dubbed-up song would develop into a set-piece production, one of Joe's most impassioned performances as he clearly felt the lyrics, the palm of his right hand firmly clasped over his right eye, a dramatic piece of mime Joe had stolen from Bob Marley but which also served to let the short-sighted singer focus on his audience. "We gave it ['Armagideon Time'] a bit more of a heavy-handed approach," Paul Simonon told me, "as opposed to the orig-inal, which is quite relaxed. Me and Joe were always amazed and thought it was fantastic, the way that in reggae a rhythm could be just lying around. It wasn't like, 'This is my song.' It could be freely used by anybody, and they'd just sing over in their own particular way, depending on what their vision was for that rhythm." Joe Ely, who would become Joe's good friend, came onstage after that number to perform on his own song "Fingernails," which the group busked through, and added his guitar to "White Riot."

Driving to the festival, in Rudy Fernandez's Ford, the group had been excitedly listening to mixes of the *London Calling* album, which had arrived by courier from London that morning. They were really up about them. During the journey to the festival, Rudy was under pressure: Chet Helms had told him the Clash had to go onstage at three in the afternoon, and time was tight. When he arrived at the designated fairground gate, the security men wouldn't let them enter: "They're like, 'No one told us.' They won't let us in. I go, 'Look, the Clash—they're English! Can't you tell? Skinny white guys—come on!'" When the stoned, long-haired security men refused to admit them to the festival, Rudy had a simple solution: he drove straight at the gate, as—behind him—the Clash delightedly sang, "Rudy can't fail! Rudy can't fail!" "The hippies go flying, and I'm racing right to the stage. The Chambers Brothers were coming offstage at that moment, and I almost ran over one of them. But I got the Clash on stage. That gate that went flying was a big gate, too." From that moment on, whenever the Clash, and later Joe as a solo act, were on the West Coast, Rudy Fernandez acted as their unofficial tour manager. According to Rudy, Joe loved being in the Monterey area. "He was getting all excited. He loved America, but they'd never seen this part of California." For the duration of their stay at the Tribal Stomp, the Clash checked into a motel-like residence in Carmel called the Mission Ranch. Joe would mutter, "This is Steinbeck country!" Apart from Mick Jones, who had finally split up with Viv Albertine, the group had brought their girlfriends with them, Topper with Dee, Paul with his new girlfriend, Debbie, and Joe with Gaby. As Joe would disappear off on his own while on the road, Mick Jones would frequently remain in his room, listening to music, watching television, smoking spliffs, playing around with song ideas.

To the delight of the group, Rudy arranged for a pot-dealer friend to bring over a duffel bag full of home-grown weed. "It was really strong, so we all had a great time." Were they stoned when they ran into the most celebrated screen policeman and cowboy star of the decade, Clint Eastwood, whose films were a staple of the group's Top Ten? Wearing a cowboy hat and carrying a guitar, he turned up at the Mission Ranch on a visit and the Clash was delighted to meet him. On a trip to Carmel's beautiful white sand beach all the group quickly burned in the California sun. Catering to the needs of both Joe Strummer and Mick Jones, Chet Helms personally checked out the finest vegetarian restaurant in the town. "I'm not a vegetarian," mumbled a somewhat miffed Paul.

Rudy was impressed with the generosity of the group, especially Joe's. "Joe was the most generous guy, more generous than I've ever been and probably ever will be. Homeless people, whatever—he'd give them all his money, and if he didn't have any money he'd give them my money. I don't mean a dollar: he'd give them packets of twenty. I'd go, 'Look, here's the guy you gave the money to going to the liquor store on Sunset.' He'd say, 'Well, he'll have a nice time tonight.'

"Joe would talk to everybody. 'Come on, Joe, we have to catch that plane.' 'I don't care. We can catch another plane.' He loved the fans. He would tell me at the end of the show, 'Bring the kids back here.' He was always sneaking people into concerts, and there was so many on the guest lists. I have opened up windows to let people in. He'd go out to the liquor store to buy some smokes, and get talking to someone, and then he'd go, 'Hey, Rudy, put him on the list.'"

When the full tour opens in St. Paul, Minnesota, four days later, Joe announces onstage: "I come over here and I switch on the radio and all I hear is the Eagles and Steely Dan." Joe is not happy with the group's performance. His guitar acts up and he performs the last half of the show without it, his hand in his pockets. "It's no good. It's a pile of shit," he grumbles after "White Man." Perhaps this is because he is very nervous: before the Clash are about to go onstage he has learned that Bob Dylan—turned on to the group by Ellie Smith at CBS during his London sojourn in May 1978— has brought his entire family, about forty people, to see them. During the performance there is ongoing disagreement between Joe and Mick, and at one point Joe bites Paul Simonon on the arm. In Detroit an empty whisky bottle just misses Joe's head. "Is that the best you've got?" he demands. Another fusillade of missiles rains down on the stage. Wayne Kramer and Rob Tyner from the inspirational MC5 are in the audience. Kramer loves the show but Tyner irritates Joe by sitting in the front row, arms folded, with an OK-show-me expression on his face. Ted Nugent, the local hard rocker, arrives at the venue with his guitar, asking to play onstage with the group. "Only if you get your hair cut first," they tell him. Ted Nugent does not play with the Clash in Detroit. When a journalist asks Joe what advice he would give to Americans, his reply is pointed: "Eat less." While being interviewed backstage by *Creem* writer Dave DiMartino, a benign fellow, Joe loses it and smashes the interviewer's tape recorder against a dressing-room wall.

Visiting the alley by the side of a Chicago cinema in which Public Enemy Number One John Dillinger had been shot to death in 1934, Joe Strummer runs his fingers around and in the bullet holes in the wall. Leaving Toronto to cross the border from Canada back into the United States, Mick Jones famously throws the kind of tantrum that later would be held very much against him. Out of weed, he refuses to board the tour bus until a spliff has been procured for him, requiring some fans to disappear to score, delaying the group's departure by some hours.

On September 19 the tour reaches Boston's Orpheum Theater and Micky Gallagher, from Ian Dury's group the Blockheads, arrives from London to add his Hammond organ sound to the group's onstage mix. He plays with them on and off for the next year and a half. The theatricality of the stage shows has become honed to perfection. At some point during the last couple of numbers, Joe always "spontaneously" slings his Telecaster to one side and it must be snatched out of the air by a waiting Johnny Green.

When the Clash hit New York the next day for two shows at the Palladium, Joe—who has lost his stage pass—almost doesn't get into the venue. Bafflingly, Bianca Jagger dances at the side of the stage. More famously, in New York Paul Simonon is pissed off by the distance between the Clash and their audience during the second Palladium show. During "White Riot" he smashes his bass to pieces on the stage floor. Pennie Smith catches the moment on her camera, and, at the suggestion of Ray Lowry, a cartoonist taken on the tour as a kind of war artist, the shot is selected as a prospective cover for the new record.

Years before, Lowry had written to Joe as a fan, and, to his surprise, quickly received a reply; a friendship grew. "I was able to see the man close up and mostly closed up, a most private gregarious fellow and quite obviously an inspiration to the vast American audiences he touched with his mixture of ferocious assault and charming vulnerability. A rounded human being carrying his fair share of demons."

Demons were circling other members of the group. In Lubbock, Texas, on the journey back from paying tribute at the grave of Buddy Holly with Joe Ely, Topper Headon nods out and turns blue. He is OD'ing on heroin. The group's vehicle is stopped and he is walked up and down a dirt path until he is out of danger. A portent of the future.

In an *NME* article, Paul Morley, on tour with the group, asks perceptive questions of Joe, who admits he is happier with his growing years. "It's a great relief for me to be twenty-seven in a way, 'cos I think the worst time of my life was when I was twenty-four, 'cos I used to lie about my age, make

Set list from the 16 Tons tour. (*Lucinda Mellor*)

JOE STRUMMER '79

Joe as seen by on-the-road Clash "war
artist" Ray Lowry. *(Ray Lowry)*

myself younger, say I was twenty-two or something, I was so paranoid
about it. It was the early days of the Clash, like 'Fuck, if they find out how
old I am that's it, I'm in the bunker, the dumper.' And then I thought,
'Fucking hell, I feel great.' I feel, like, 'cos I'm older than this lot, I've got a
little bit extra to add. Kind of experience."

What turns him on apart from rock 'n' roll? he is asked. "I like the look
of things . . . I get interested . . . I want to know about everything really.
When I'm in some God-knows-where café and I'm feeling down and I'm
having a cup of coffee, I can start listening to what they're saying at the next
table and for me it almost becomes grippingly fascinating. I almost forget
totally about myself and I start working out who they are and what they're
doing. I dunno. I get interested in any old crap."

Morley asks Joe about the new album. "Are you bothered how people
are going to take it?"

"Naah." Strummer dismisses the idea. "Y'know, I'm way past all that

'What are they going to think of this?' I don't care anymore . . . 'cos what-ever you do people are going to say 'bollocks.' "

On October 18, the exhausted group flew back from Vancouver to Lon-don. On their return they changed their look, transforming themselves into what their friend Jock Scot, introduced into the camp by Kosmo, defined as "the Mafia Beatles." The classic movie look of their new image ensured its timelessness. Fitted suits and overcoats, and an assortment of jauntily brimmed hats—the style was actually taken from English gangsters of the 1940s. Specifically, it came from the film of Graham Greene's *Brighton Rock*. Paul Simonon had loved Greene's dark tale of hoodlum lifestyle on the English south coast; David Mingay and Jack Hazan had procured the film for Paul. At weekends he would take it and the projector home to hold screenings in his flat. "I started buying clothes from that era. Everyone else then did. It was just evolution."

In Don Letts's video for the "London Calling" single, a masterstroke of image making, shot at the Festival Pier overlooking the Thames at Bat-tersea Park at the beginning of December 1979, this look is assisted by the rain that swept across the nighttime riverside set, adding a men-against-the-elements romantic timbre. Kosmo Vinyl, the self-styled consigliere of the group, had taken the Clash to Jack Geech, "the teddy-boy tailor," in Har-row, and Sid Strong, a ted barber on Camden Bridge. Not that the group al-ways went along with Kosmo's suggestions. As a rock 'n' roll purist he was adamant it was not acceptable for songs to exceed three minutes in length. Accordingly, when the group had gone back to Wessex in November to record their cover of "Armagideon Time" as a B-side for the twelve-inch ver-sion of "London Calling," Joe can be heard on the track rasping "OK, OK. Don't push us when we're . . . hot!" as the song reaches it climax: Kosmo had been signaling to bring the tune to an end at a point when Joe knew the group was absolutely cooking.

L*ondon Calling*, dedicated to Henry Bowles, is released on December 14, 1979, in the United Kingdom, and at the beginning of the next month in the United States. In Britain the record is priced at five pounds. Famously, the Clash have conned CBS by asking them if they could also in-clude an additional twelve-inch record in the album package—and then put nine songs on this bonus piece of vinyl. For once an extraordinary work is largely recognized as such by the reviewers, especially Charles Shaar Murray in *NME*. He describes it as "the first of the Clash's albums that is truly equal in stature to their legend." "London Calling: damn right," he concludes. "Now everybody here from Birmingham England to Birmingham Alabama, call 'em back. This is the one." After all the disadvantage and adversities, 1979 has turned out to be a triumph for the Clash, a major upward move, both artistically and in terms of their career trajectory. And it's not yet over.

Four days before Christmas, the Clash was rehearsing by the river, immediately south of the Thames, in the London suburb of Putney, running repeatedly through the backing track for "Rudie Can't Fail." A forty-date British tour was set to start on January 5. Although Topper Headon still had a spiky haircut, the three front-line Clash members bore little sign of their punk origins. Mick Jones sported a black slim-lapeled, drainpipe-trousered suit and pomaded black hair; Paul Simonon wore a suit of the same cut, but in brown chalk-stripe, his blond locks also plastered back; Joe Strummer's dark blue shortie overcoat proclaimed hit-man cool, though his image was softened by faded tight jeans and battered shoes. As "Rudie Can't Fail" was put to one side, Joe seated himself at a Hammond organ in the middle of the rehearsal room, pouring out his soul on a new tune, then known as "The Bankrobbing Song," a reggae blues written almost entirely by Joe that featured Mick Jones on bottleneck. As he sprawled over the notes and squeezed the mournful words into the mike, Joe invoked memories of countless anonymous bar-room bluesers, their voices husky from too many nights of booze and cigarette smoke.

Afterward, over Chinese and Indian foods brought in by Johnny Green, the group contemplated with pleasure the critical plaudits won by *London Calling*, which had entered the British charts at number 9. By contrast Joe expressed how appalled he had been that Epic Records execs had gorged down nine-course meals prior to the group's first Los Angeles show the previous winter, when the group had walked out on the corporate photo session. "What sort of person goes out and eats a nine-course meal and then goes to see some rock 'n' roll?" he demanded incredulously.

"Tell you something," Mick said, turning to Joe. "We're going to have to do something to make the album come out as cheap as possible in America.

Although self-taught, Joe was adept at the piano. *(Sheila Rock)*

That's quite important. How much is *Tusk*?" he asked me, referring to the then new double album by Fleetwood Mac.

"About fifteen dollars," I hazarded.

"But that's made of ivory, isn't it?" said Joe.

"Well, I reckon *London Calling* must definitely go for about ten bucks," said Mick. "And we'll have to stand by it, 'cos, you know, once you've said it . . ."

"Stand by your price," said Joe.

The Clash certainly were standing by their fans. On Christmas Eve they were rehearsing in Acklam Hall, directly beneath the Westway elevated highway that was such a vital symbol in the group's mythology. The next two nights found the Clash playing two "secret, cheaply priced" gigs at the hall as an antidote to the holidays and as warm-up dates for their British tour. To keep us on our toes, the Soviet Union invaded Afghanistan on December 25, 1979, catching the West in a post-Christmas snooze, except for those who had been to see the Clash at Acklam Hall. The Clash climaxed their Christmas gigs on December 27 at the Hammersmith Odeon as the "mystery act" on an Ian Dury–topping benefit for Cambodian refugees. Twenty minutes or so before the Clash was due on, I met Guy Stevens at the backstage bar. Music was precious stuff to him, he declared, deploring its bastardization by large record conglomerates. The Clash, he knew, were true to the cause. The Clash was part of what Kosmo Vinyl had dubbed "The Quest."

"Listen," Guy shouted in my ear, spraying the entire right side of my face with spittle. "Did you see Joe Strummer in the dressing room just now? Down on the floor, ironing his stage clothes on a towel? Gene Vincent would've done that! Eddie Cochran would've done that! Jerry Lee Lewis would've done that!" He had a firm hold on my arm, and a fan's passion in his voice. Then he loosened my arm and slumped down on a seat, as though in a trance, contemplating this perfect rock 'n' roll image. Midway through the Clash's set, I looked up from my seat and saw a squirming Guy Stevens carried up the center aisle by four security men. Fearful he might be kicked out of the theater or even beaten up, I went in search of him at the rear of the auditorium. He was OK. One of the guards had recognized him and was mildly scolding him for causing them bother. Carried away by the Clash's music, Guy had been dancing in front of one of the cameras filming the event. He was very drunk. We were negotiating a swaying journey down the side of the auditorium to the backstage door when someone rushed up behind us and threw his arms about Guy. It was what seemed to be an equally pissed Pete Townshend. Leaving Guy Stevens in good hands, I wended my way back to my seat.

Eight days later I was seated between Mick and Joe in the minibus the Clash had rented for their British tour. It was about midnight. We were traveling up the Ml to Birmingham, where the group would appear next morning on *Tizwas*, an absurdist children's TV Saturday show, cult viewing for alleged adults; it offered television exposure for the group that had shot themselves in the foot with their 1977 edict that they would never play *Top of the Pops*. Hard Jamaican sounds poured out of the Simonon portable cassette player, filling the rather too warm vehicle. Joe and I talked about "Lovers' Rock," an unlikely Clash song. (At the time I was unaware it had once formed part of "London Calling.") The Clash song discussed just how lovers should rock, invoking Taoism through quotes from *The Tao of Love* ("You can make a lover in a thousand goes") and decrying the Pill's subtle Babylonian oppression. "It's been misunderstood, that song, you know," Joe half-grinned, wryly self-mocking. "You have to be a bit gone in the head to try to get that over."

I asked him about "The Right Profile," the Montgomery Clift song. "I read two [biographies]," he nodded. "It's quite interesting to read two books about the same person because they both give you a completely different picture. You read one and you think, 'Oh, that's how the guy really was!' If you read another you get a totally different angle, and you think, 'Was he like this, or like that?' And you realize he was probably like neither."

Through Strummer's recent reading, the conversation turned to the *Odyssey*, Greek and Roman mythology, the Basques and Atlantis, Carl Jung, Edgar Cayce and Rasta passivity. The last topic reminded me that "London Calling" advocated just the opposite: people should step forward, get on with it and blow out their apathy. "Yeah, but it's very hard to deal with apathy. Making like you've got the answers to everybody's problems—it's impossible, of course. Everybody must sort out their own problems. That's the key to everything. You sort one problem out and get the will to go on and sort another one out. You can't expect any help, I don't think. Mainly, though, we were thinking about people accepting shit as gold. Just a little while ago we heard a record on the radio which was pure shit, and this guy goes, 'Mmm, that's good.' It's just the emperor's new clothes again and again. Of course, it ain't good. It's just a load of fuckin' shit, y'know."

The Clash was questioning everything, which is why they were so positive. They didn't believe in hopelessness; they believed we had nothing but hope. "Only the lazy ones look to us for a solution," Strummer said. "We just made our feelings clear. Other people happened to feel that way too, so they got behind it. But making your feelings clear is a long way from solving everything. That 'Bored with the USA' song has always been misconstrued. We say 'We're so bored with the USA,' having to sit at home and have it pumped into us. The second you turn on the TV you know it's in America somewhere, and there's this bird who's probably a detective, and then a car's gonna roll over a cliff—you know all the plots by heart. 'I'm So Bored with the USA' was about the importing of culture. A quick spree round the States taking in all the sights and buying all the crap you can lay your hands on—that's what we call fun. So long as we don't have to live there."

The next afternoon, arriving at the gates of the Aylesbury Civic Hall for the first date of what had been dubbed the 16 Tons tour, Joe Strummer gazed out of the minibus window at the street filled with punks and punkettes. "See," he turned to Paul, "we've sold out again. And we said we'd never sell out."

1st may take a holiday

1980–1981

It's now 1980.

So the Clash hit the new decade running. They are off on a new phase of their lives, validated. Onstage Joe's role is transformed. All the group have grown because of the success of *London Calling*, but Joe—as the onstage front man—most reveals his new authority. His onstage extemporizations grow, the spontaneity is unstifled.

The 16 Tons tour was named after Tennessee Ernie Ford's 1956 international hit. As well as being a great name for a tour, the song—an allegedly pro-Communist song about debt—precisely reflected how the group felt at the time about their financial position. But the success of *London Calling* would change that.

At one gig on the south coast, a backstage visitor overheard a pre-show argument climaxing with Mick locking himself in the dressing-room toilet: "'I'm not coming out!' He wouldn't go onstage and play. He was calling out: 'Joe, it's not fair. I've got a voice. You never let me say anything. You have to say everything. Why's it always got to be you?'"

In Sheffield on January 27, Joe and Mick had a fight in the dressing room over the choice of "White Riot" as an encore. Mick felt the song no longer represented the group and was wary of the stage invasions that its performance often incited. Joe punched him in the mouth after Mick had thrown a drink in his face. "So I hit him. Hard!" Joe said later. "It was no big deal," said Mick. "Nothing you'd linger over."

At the University of Leeds, just up the road from Sheffield, the social secretary was a student named Andy Kershaw. "I put on the Clash twice at Leeds University," he told me. "In January 1980 on the *London Calling* 16 Tons tour they were the most exciting, fully rounded rock 'n' roll group I have ever seen. The initial scratchy fury of the Clash had become something admirable and absolutely stunning. They'd paid heed to their roots— Mick with his encyclopedic knowledge of pop music, Paul who was steeped in reggae, and Joe with his love of r&b—and combined them with an incredible proficiency at playing. By this time they could play so well, and also looked so fantastic. The Clash had an élan I've seen in no other rock 'n' roll group."

Joe and Mick in Paris with Mikey Dread. To Joe's right are Bernie Rhodes and Kosmo Vinyl. *(Pennie Smith)*

Joe's vision of life onstage. *(Lucinda Mellor)*

Near the end of the month in Bradford, they were joined onstage by Mikey Dread, a legendary Jamaican DJ, toasting on "Armagideon Time." After their Manchester dates the Clash went into the studio with Mikey on February 1 and 2 to record "The Bankrobbing Song," now renamed "Bank-robber." ("That was a song Joe wrote on his own," said Mick.) The Clash plan was that "Bankrobber" would be the first of twelve singles released that year, one a month. This was immediately stymied when Maurice Ober-stein curiously declared that the lilting, melodic song sounded like all of David Bowie's records put together and played backward. He refused to put it out.

At the second of two shows at Brighton Top Rank, they were joined on-stage during the encores by Pete Townshend, proof of their status in the rock pantheon.

On the night of February 9, the Clash played Portsmouth Guildhall. They stayed in nearby Southsea, at the Queen's Hotel. As it was Kosmo's birthday, the group threw a party for him, everyone having a great time. Then the party moved on to Joe's room, where Joe sat on his bed, reading the Gideon Bible. Others were sprawled about the room, a ghetto blaster pumping out dub. Then the police arrived. Before he opened his door to them Joe grabbed assorted spliff-making paraphernalia and dumped it out of the window. Another group associate hid the residue under his hat. Joe was back on the bed reading from the Bible, wearing his favorite gray trilby, as the police came in—unbeknownst to the singer, a large lump of hash was sitting on the crown of his hat. How had it got there? No one knew. Had it bounced back off the window frame when Joe had thrown it out of the window? "I'm arresting you for possession of cannabis." Topper and four members of the group's crew were also arrested.

The Electric Ballroom shows in Camden Town, London, were power-house performances. It was snowing in the streets, extremely cold, but inside the Electric it was a steam bath. Midway through the set Joe offered refunds to punters who couldn't take the heat. Backstage after the shows Mick was sequestered in a cellarlike dressing room, away from the mayhem in the rest of the group's rooms. "I think we pulled it off," he smiled, rivers of sweat pouring down him.

By now there was another woman around the Clash camp. Pearl Harbor, a half-Filipino former member of San Francisco punk performance artists the Tubes, had formed her own group, Pearl Harbor and the Explosions. At the beginning of 1980 she moved to London to be with her boyfriend Kosmo Vinyl, but later that year Pearl and Kosmo broke up. "Kosmo basically dumped me because he was always with the Clash," said Pearl Harbor. Paul Simonon then asked Pearl out. "Go out with him, but it won't be for long because he's a womanizer," advised Kosmo. Pearl and Paul eventually married.

"I saw the pattern when I was on the road with those guys," said Pearl. "Topper was always wasted on heroin with a chick, amicable, on time, a great drummer, but a wasted dude. Paul was moody. Joe was always with important people. Mick was really selfish, always late. Everyone waited for him every morning on the tour bus, until he had a joint and egg and chips—that's all he ate. If he didn't have a joint and egg and chips, you couldn't get him out of his room. He would yell and curse at Raymond Jordan. We nearly missed all of the planes because of Mick. Mick was selfish, Joe was not. If you were Joe's girlfriend you would say he was selfish, but Joe to his mates was not. In all other ways Mick was a sweet guy, but he was selfish in that regard. Joe only showed his selfishness in terms of women and ego.

"As always with guys touring, they all cheated on their girlfriends. Poor Gaby, she had a tough one, with Joe going with so many girls. In that sense he was a true rock 'n' roller. Gaby talked to me about it. She said it was really hard for her, knowing he went with so many girls. But she was so young.

"That isn't unusual for men who are entertainers. They have huge egos. Joe is no different in that regard. He was only special in the way he treated people in general, not women. How passionate and serious he was was great, but in many senses he was an idiotic rock star. In that sense Mick Jones was no more idiotic than the others."

On February 20, Topper was stabbed in the hand with a pair of scissors while at home in Fulham. Tellingly, the altercation was over drugs: the signs and pointers to the future kept appearing. Six of the English dates had to be rescheduled for the summer. "With *London Calling* I started to be able to play the jazz and funky bits," said Topper. "By then I was starting to associate more with the crew, because I joined the wrong band in a way. I wanted that rock 'n' roll lifestyle and the crew lived it and the band didn't. But even so, the drugs were taking their toll. Even if it was only puff [marijuana], it was certainly fuzzing their ideas. We were all stoned all the time. The only difference was I was doing coke and pills. The amount of alcohol consumed was unbelievable. I never used to smoke dope, because it made me feel paranoid. Mick and Joe and Paul had to be met at the airport with it. With the three of them smoking so much dope and me running around on coke, no wonder there was paranoia."

The Clash had to maintain the upward momentum provided by *London Calling*. Following the English and French legs of the 16 Tons dates, the group returned to the United States for a brief tour of key cities. On Joe's Telecaster was stenciled a reminder of the annual socialist day off work: 1ST MAY TAKE A HOLIDAY. So how is Joe coping with all this? How is Joe doing within himself? He's off on his own a lot, very quiet, not saying much at all. He's in his own world. It's interesting in there: sometimes fantastic and joyous, sometimes crawling with specters and hobgoblins. So a certain stillness of spirit is desirable. But the time for this sifting and balancing is hard to come by. And part of Joe is still quite shy. He is at his most comfortable being gentlemanly and thoughtful.

All the same, it's good inside Joe's world. He can put a lot of interesting words together, sometimes pulling them in from the conversational action around him. Joe likes the sound of words, appreciates their texture and tone and nuances; like a modern-day Balzac searching for *le mot juste* for his tales of street life, he painstakingly tries to forever feel out the right

ones. "He was really a writer," said Gaby. "He used to work at it so hard."
Let's not forget the actor within him, the Brando-like delivery of the one-
liners dropped into the conversational mix, like surreal bullet shots, with a
killer payoff line. He's happy at home at World's End, even though he and
Gaby have an occasional propensity to break up. Joe Strummer isn't one of
the easiest people to live with.

But he wasn't going back to World's End after these American shows. Inspired by Mikey Dread's work with them on "Bankrobber," there was consid-
eration that the next album might be a reggae version-excursion with Mikey
at the controls. Straight from the American tour, the group flew to Jamaica.

Checking into the Sheraton Hotel—as featured in "Safe European
Home"—in New Kingston, the Clash had been booked by Mikey Dread into
the Channel One studio. In recent months the new "dancehall" style had
evolved out of Channel One, a rough street sound that would carry reggae
into a new era. The studio's environ was not the most salubrious in the Jamaican capital. Directly opposite Channel One was an alley known as
Idlers' Rest. There were plenty of bad men there, armed and dangerous, active participants in the ongoing undeclared Jamaican civil war. Driving to
the studio, the group narrowly missed witnessing this for real: "A youth of
fourteen was shot dead on Hope Road just ten minutes after we'd gone past
it," said Joe.

The group steamed into their first number, a cover of "Junco Partner," a
rhythm-and-blues classic originally written and recorded by James Booker,
a New Orleans keyboards player who had some minor hits in the early
1960s. "Junco Partner" had been a staple of the 101'ers' live set, and was
suggested by Joe for the new album. "That came from Joe's department, because I'd never heard the song in my life," said Paul. Playing on the tune
with the Clash were the Roots Radics' horn section: "They were the guys
that were in the studio as we arrived. There was some old bloke hanging out
outside, who had a violin, so we brought him in as well."

"We recorded 'Junco Partner,'" said Joe, "and it sounded great. All the
dreads were outside cheering. I was sitting at the piano figuring out the
chords for the next song when Mikey tapped me on the shoulder and said,
'Quick, we've got to go. The drug men are coming to kill everyone!'" It was
customary to spread cash around the local hustlers; the Rolling Stones had
done this when they'd worked in the studio on *Emotional Rescue*. But the

Clash had no money; the trip was financed by the American Express card of Paul's girlfriend, Debbie. "We had to run for cover," remembered Paul. "The mood changed as though it had been cut with a knife, and we thought, Get the fuck out—like immediately." The group hightailed it back to New Kingston in "an old Renault. I don't know where the Renault had come from," said Paul. "It weren't no *Harder They Come*–style getaway. It was more Jacques Tati," said Joe. Stuck in Kingston, Ray Jordan drove Joe and Gaby out to Hellshire Beach, very much off the map for white tourists. Joe scored some weed off one of the dreads habituating the area; but when he rolled up to smoke it he was chased away, necessitating another quick exit.

The group drove across the island to Negril in a boat-sized Cadillac convertible. In this druggy hippie haven the punk rockers "were having a spliff," said Mick, when "a cop came over to us and said, 'You're busted.' We were thinking, 'Oh God. Gun Court.' Our tour manager took him off to one side: 'Can we have a talk about this?' 'OK. I'll meet you in this field right outside of town.' So we drove out to this field and parked our car facing the cop's. He got out and we gave him some money. He seemed most amenable." They carried on around the island, visiting Bob Marley's birthplace of Nine Mile.

The time wasn't wasted on Joe. "Everyone's always saying there isn't much good reggae happening anymore," he told me. "But I don't think that's true. There's loads. When I was in Jamaica I heard ten all-time stunning classic records on the radio. There was one fantastic one called 'Rainy Night in Portland.' But I keep waiting for them to turn up here, and they don't. I heard some incredible rhythms, too. Stunningly inventive. No white group would ever play the drums like some of the ones I heard being played. Almost shuffling it. Pure invention. I heard numbers that would've cleared the floor for days, weeks, months, years. I started a couple of years ago to think that reggae had had it, but I've since found I was a bit hasty—that music is growing all the time. I'd like to hear it on the radio all night long, instead of the soothing dribble of the big band sounds."

Paul Simonon had signed up to act for six weeks in a film being made in Vancouver, *Ladies and Gentlemen, the Fabulous Stains*; the rest of the group were adamant that the creative roll needed to be maintained, and, accompanied by Mikey Dread, returned to New York. They checked into the Iroquois Hotel on Forty-fourth Street. At first they worked at the Power Station studio on West Fifty-third Street, with Mick Jones playing bass. There the focus of the new record shifted, possibly influenced by the Power Station being the creative engine of Chic, who had produced the best dance music of the era; Nile Rodgers and Bernard Edwards, the Chic main men, were in situ, recording Diana Ross's *Diana* album. The group recorded "Police on My Back," a tune written by Eddie Grant for Britain's multiracial Equals, as well as the classic "Louie Louie" and Prince Buster's "Madness," already revived as part of the Two-Tone ska phenomenon by Madness.

There were no new songs written, but Joe and Mick decided they would write them as they recorded, the most expensive way of making a new album unless the songs were pouring out—which, luckily, they were. So they took a cheaper booking at Electric Lady Studios—set up by Jimi Hendrix—on West Eighth Street in Greenwich Village.

"We were really stoking," Joe told Gavin Martin in *Uncut* magazine in 1999. "We hit New York, and we blasted straight into the studio. This is something that I must recommend to other groups. Normally after a tour

Clash Hot 100—Joe's perception of Electric Lady
Studios in the West Village. (*Lucinda Mellor*)

we used to go home and lie down for a few weeks. But we came off that tour full of go.

"We had nothing written. You don't write on tour, it takes all your concentration to make the gig—that's survival technique. Afterward you run around town to find interesting hipsters and go to all the interesting spots. You got to go to every hot spot until everything has closed down. The adrenaline is furious. You're wired as hell.

"We didn't particularly know anywhere in New York, so we went into Electric Lady. Every day we just showed up and wrote phantasmagorical stuff. Everything was done in first takes, and worked out twenty minutes beforehand. What we did was go to the core of what we are about—creating—and we did it on the fly and had three weeks of unadulterated joy. We were in New York and I never went out. But it was the most beautiful time ever, everything on a roll." (It is not entirely true that Joe never went out. Victor Bockris, a New York writer, was working on a book that consisted of him taking appropriate subjects to have dinner with William Burroughs at his home on the Bowery. As Burroughs was fully aware of the Clash—Bockris had played him their records—it was deemed that Joe would be a dinner guest. The great bohemian writer had a jaundiced view of rock stars because dealings with them invariably involved tardiness. On the designated day Victor Bockris decided he should pick up Joe at his hotel and escort him to the Bowery. There were complications. On his first visit to San Francisco, Joe had met a local girl named Damita Richter, who afterward moved to New York and became Bockris's girlfriend. By the evening of the soirée *chez* Burroughs she had disappeared with Joe Strummer again. When the writer arrived at the hotel for Joe, the Clash was being questioned by police officers over the nonpayment of some recording fees, possibly from their work at the Power Station. As though proving Burroughs's point about the habitual lateness of rock 'n' rollers, Joe turned up with Bockris some two hours late. William Burroughs considered Joe had an acceptable excuse for his unpunctuality: he warmed to Joe when he opened his jacket and showed six enormous spliffs protruding from an inner pocket. As tribute these were presented to the great man of letters, along with a bottle of whisky and a six-pack of beer. A great evening was had. However, the event was so close to the deadline for Bockris's book that it was never included.)

In those days America was a very liberal country. Joe loved the way you could climb into a cab and the driver might hand you a joint as he headed toward the studio. "Cool as fuck! I was thinking, 'This is New York.'"

It was at Electric Lady that Joe first created what became known as the Spliff Bunker. In the corner of the studio he built his equivalent of a wartime pillbox from equipment flight cases. Secreted in the Spliff Bunker, away from the mixing desk control room, Joe was free to work on his words for songs. He would even sleep in it. "Me, Topper and Warren 'Stoner' Steadman [a roadie] built it out of flight cases," said Joe. "It was a small scene, the bunker, a place to retreat and consider, for musicians and groovers only. It's a good system, which I still use today, because it stops everyone hanging out in the control room. The engineer can't work with all that background babble." From then on, a Spliff Bunker was a feature of most recording sessions in which Joe was involved.

Despite the presence of Mikey Dread, the group decided—somewhat to the Jamaican's chagrin—that they would produce the record themselves; this meant Mick Jones was in the production seat. "It was just there: we were just picking it off a tree. Sometimes it's like that. You just get that perfect moment. *Sandinista!*: we went free then and it was great. Such a lot of diversity. No rules anymore. Because even the one before that wasn't so free. It was still in the traditional structures." Bassist Norman Watt-Roy and Micky Gallagher from Ian Dury's Blockheads flew to Manhattan in early April; at Electric Lady they found themselves working on a brand-new tune with a distinctly funky backing track, one that seemed to capture the sounds, sensations, even smells of the city of New York. "There was Topper, me, Micky and Mick," said Norman Watt-Roy. "Joe was in the bunker. Jonesy says, 'We need something really funky 'cos Joe says he wants to do a rap.' So we started that riff and looped it and Joe wrote the words there and then. Totally spontaneous, a couple of hours and it was in the can." Mick Jones told the new arrivals the title of the song: "The Magnificent Seven Rap-O-Clappers," later abbreviated to "The Magnificent Seven." Joe admitted that the idea for the song came from Mick Jones, his cultural antennae alert as ever. The previous year "Rapper's Delight" by the Sugar Hill Gang had been the first hit for this new form—revolutionarily, it was a fifteen-minute record on a twelve-inch disc. Mick had visited all the shops in Brooklyn that sold rap music. "Jonesy was always on the button when it

NEW CLASH ~ "CLASH HOT 100"
LIST COMPILED AT Electric Lady land End of March 1980

1. RADIO W.J.U.B.   FUNK
2. STOP THE WORLD.   STRANGE
3. ~~FREEDOM TH SHAKEYOR WAKKER~~ WHEN ITS OVER
   3a. SAX FESTIVAL.   CLASHABILLY
4. UP IN HEAVEN.   CLASHROCK
5. FREEDOM TRAIN.   CLASHABILLY
6. THEN SOMEBODY GOT MURDERED.   CLASHROCK
7. THE STREET PARADE.   STRANGE
8. VERSION CITY.   STRANGE.
9. THE CALL-UP.   - STRANGE
10. GET UP FOR THE SUN.   CLASHROCKSTEADY
11. POLICE ON MY BACK.   CLASHROCK [COVER]
12. RUNNIN' (VERSION).   CLASHROCK STEADY [COVER]
13. ONE MORE DUB.   CLASHDISCOROCKERS
14. BLONDE ROCK N' ROLL.   CLASHABILLY
15. JUNKIE SLIP.   STRANGE
16. KING OF THE ROAD.   CLASHJAZZ [COVER]
17. J.B., KING OF SOUL.   FUNK
18. IF MUSIC COULD TALK.   STRANGE
19. LIVING IN FAME - DREAD -   CLASHROCKERS
20. ONE MORE TIME.   CLASHROCKERS

Joe's own assessment of the style of the tunes recorded for *Sandinista!*
by the end of March 1980. What happened to some of these songs?
(*Lucinda Mellor*)

came to new things," Joe told Gavin Martin. "That stuff we made the week after he came back from Brooklyn with those Sugarhill records—it all still rocks."

While the Clash was at Electric Lady a transport strike crippled the city. One night, unable to find a taxi, Mick Jones was walking back to the Iroquois when he stepped straight into Tymon Dogg, Joe's old friend and mentor, who was staying in New York for a few weeks with Helen Cherry. Mick took Tymon to the hotel and an emotional reunion with Joe. At Mick's suggestion Tymon came to the studio the next day and the group worked on Tymon's song "Lose This Skin." "It wasn't because I was Joe's mate," said Tymon, "because it was Mick who instigated that, not Joe. Joe said one of the reasons I was involved with the Clash was because when Joe left the 101'ers he came round one time to see me when I was playing at Acklam Hall underneath the Westway. He said, 'I'll carry your gear to the gig.' I said, 'You must be feeling nostalgic,' and he said, 'Well, the lads in the band, we were rehearsing, and they said, "Oh, Tymon Dogg's playing Acklam Hall tonight. Let's go and see him."'"

Often Tymon was accompanied by Helen Cherry. Before this she had not met Mick Jones, and was fascinated by what she saw. "I hadn't realized what Mick was doing in the Clash, and I don't think a lot of people did. But I was lucky enough to hear them record quite a lot of *Sandinista!*, and I was amazed to see that Mick was so much of an energy as a writer and an instrument player for the Clash. I thought, 'Mick, I can see how much Joe needs you in the Clash.' I think Joe didn't like him because he had mood swings. Yet because Mick does very quickly show his feelings, you should be grateful because it's somebody who is straightforward and you know where you are with them. You could see he was definitely an energy Joe needed, but I don't think Joe could see it. I thought, 'Wow, Mick's really firing away here.' But Joe was too—he wrote an enormous amount of lyrics. They were amazingly prolific and hardworking."

"Joe was sitting in his hotel room, writing," said Tymon. "As he said, if it moves, write it down. He was working fast. Mick was putting guitar things and sequences in. Every time I went in there a new song was on the go. The New York sessions had an openness about them, which is how I ended up on the record with my song. It was that open that some totally unknown person is going to come in and play his song."

Before the Clash headed back to Britain they flew out to Los Angeles to appear on *Fridays*, a short-lived ABC series similar to *Saturday Night Live*. They performed "London Calling," "Train in Vain," "The Guns of Brixton"— Paul was back after filming—and "Clampdown." Seizing the moment, they also played at the Roxy on Sunset Strip. The L.A. Roxy was a long way philosophically from the Covent Garden Roxy, a scene for the city's cool-and-groovy. But the Clash did play "Somebody Got Murdered," the first of the songs they had recorded for the new album to be given a live outing. Joe had written it after being approached by the American music legend Jack Nitzsche, who was providing the soundtrack for the film *Cruising*, which starred Al Pacino. "The parking attendant in the World's End housing estate, where I was living, was murdered over five pounds," said Joe. "We got a phone call from Jack Nitzsche and he said, 'We need a heavy rock number for this movie with Al Pacino,' so I said, 'OK.' I went home and there was this guy in a pool of blood out by the car parking kiosk. That night I wrote the lyric. I gave it to Mick and he wrote the tune. We recorded it and Jack Nitzsche never called back." The Clash recorded the song themselves, with Mick Jones employing a complex synthesizer arrangement.

Back in London, where they continued the sessions at Wessex, Joe and Tymon maintained their renewed relationship. When Joe learned Tymon had spotted a potential squat in an empty house close to the British Museum in Bloomsbury, he asked if he could come and live there. Some of the perpetual difficulties in Joe's relationship with Gaby had become more than usually dominant and he had decided to move out of World's End. The irony was that finally Joe's bank balance was extremely healthy and he could easily have afforded to rent a flat. Instead he purchased the most expensive pair of bolt cutters stocked by his local hardware store. "But not only did he buy the bolt cutters, which really impressed me," said Tymon, "he also said, 'Right, let's buy a can of bolts that we can practice cutting on.'"

Around midnight they drove up toward Bloomsbury in Tymon Dogg's three-wheeler Reliant Robin van. At a traffic light a police car pulled parallel with them. The pair of cops peered into the three-wheeler. "We've got the bolt cutters in the back," said Tymon, "and Joe is dressed a bit like a burglar, unshaven, and he's got a comical bad-guy look on his face. He's sitting in the van and this cop car pulls up, screwing us, and he looked so dodgy." Then Joe noticed a small Indian statue on Tymon's dashboard. "What's that?" he asked. Tymon replied that it was Ganesha, an Indian god who is the remover of obstacles. As he said this, the lights turned to green and the police car pulled off, leaving them behind. Tymon and Joe arrived at the address, a large Georgian house in Gilbert Place, and easily broke into their new home. Joe took a big room on the first floor. As he plugged in a piece of electrical equipment he noticed a previous occupant had provided the baseboard with a discreet piece of graffiti, just two words: "White Riot." "That was great," laughed Helen Cherry. But she was not so impressed with other aspects of Joe's existence. "He'd left Gaby in rather a distressed state—I thought rather meanly. Sometimes I'd see mean sides of him and find it hard to like him. I felt a bit of a strain with him living in Gilbert Place because I did feel Gaby was suffering and that was being ignored."

But another figure from Joe's past appeared at the Gilbert Place squat: Bernie Rhodes, who on one occasion had turned up at the *London Calling* sessions, and with whom Joe continued to keep in contact. "Bernie Rhodes came round," said Helen, "and was like, 'Back to your old ways, Joe, sleeping on the floor again.'"

But a crisis befell the Gilbert Place collective when Joe was away on tour: bailiffs and police appeared on the doorstep to evict the occupants. Helen Cherry phoned Pete Jenner for help. "Peter was great. He came round in a Volvo and took all the gear out and put it in the back of his office in Blackhill—as a favor, and because he was Joe's manager. He even took the curtains down for me. He got on the phone to me about a week or two later: 'Can you come round? There's Joe's washing-up to do here.' Even the dirty washing-up had been carried out."

Joe rented a second-floor flat at 109 Ladbroke Grove, which he moved into with Gaby—back together again. Mick Jones meanwhile had come up with the deposit to buy a flat in Powis Gardens in Notting Hill. Joe admitted that when he had also tried to purchase a property he had been turned down for a mortgage.

On May 13, the Clash opened the European leg of the 16 Tons tour in Berlin. Joe felt that it was already punk-revival time in Germany. "It's become everything it wasn't supposed to be," he said. "What we were confronted with was junior punks in their expensive designer uniforms with concrete heads and no ears." In a Berlin café Joe found himself in conversation with a sixteen-year-old skinhead: "He was saying he was horrified,

Much tea was always drunk around the Clash. *(Urban Image.tv/Adrian Boot)*

that he couldn't stand it, because his grandmother was grooving around to *London Calling*."

By the time they reached Hamburg seven days later the group found themselves confronted by anarcho-punk designer violence. Pennie Smith had been approached by Pete Townshend to put together a book of her Clash photographs for his publishing company. The group said they'd write the captions, so she flew out to meet them. "I arrived just as they should

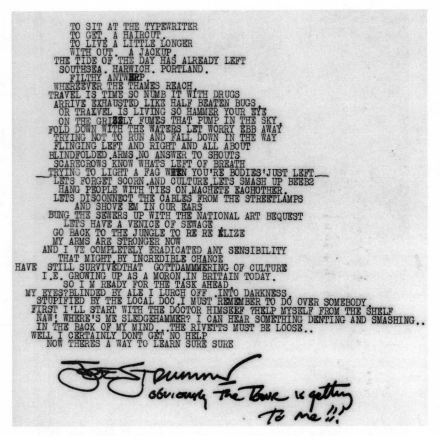

```
               TO SIT AT THE TYPEWRITER
               TO GET A HAIRCUT.
               TO LIVE A LITTLE LONGER
               WITH OUT  A JACKUP
            THE TIDE OF THE DAY HAS ALREADY LEFT
               SOUTHSEA. HARWICH. PORTLAND.
                 FILTHY ANTWERP.
            WHEREEVER THE THAMES REACH
            TRAVEL IS TIME SO NUMB IT WITH DRUGS
              ARRIVE EXHAUSTED LIKE HALF BEATEN BUGS
                OR TRAXVEL IS LIVING SO HAMMER YOUR EYE
                ON THE GRIZZLY FUMES THAT PUMP IN THE SKY
            FOLD DOWN WITH THE WATERS LET WORRY EBB AWAY
            TRYING NOT TO RUN AND FALL DOWN IN THE WAY
            FLINGING LEFT AND RIGHT AND ALL ABOUT
            BLINDFOLDED ARMS NO ANSWER TO SHOUTS
            SCARECROWS KNOW WHATS LEFT OF BREATH
          _ TRYING TO LIGHT A FAG WHEN YOU'RE BODIES'JUST LEFT _
              LETS FORGET SCORN AND CULTURE LETS SMASH UP BEEB2
              HANG PEOPLE WITH TIES ON MACHETE EACHOTHER
            LETS DISCONNECT THE CABLES FROM THE STREETLAMPS
               AND SHOVE EM IN OUR EARS
            BUNG THE SEWERS UP WITH THE NATIONAL ART BEQUEST
               LETS HAVE A VENICE OF SEWAGE
            GO BACK TO THE JUNGLE TO RE RE ELIZE
            MY ARMS ARE STRONGER NOW
          AND I VE COMPLETELY ERADICATED ANY SENSIBILITY
               THAT MIGHT BY INCREDIBLE CHANCE
        HAVE STILL SURVIVEDTHAT  GOTTDAMMMERING OF CULTURE
           I.E. GROWING UP AS A MORON IN BRITAIN TODAY.
               SO I M READY FOR THE TASK AHEAD.
        MY EYES?BLINDED BY ALE I LURCH OFF .INTO DARKNESS
            STUPIFIED BY THE LOCAL DOC I MUST REMEMBER TO DO OVER SOMEBODY.
          FIRST I'LL START WITH THE DOCTOR HIMSEEF ?HELP MYSELF FROM THE SHELF
            NAW! WHERE'S ME SLEDGEHAMMER? I CAN HEAR SOMETHING DENTING AND SMASHING..
            IN THE BACK OF MY MIND...THE RIVETTS MUST BE LOOSE..
          WELL I CERTAINLY DONT GET NO HELP
            NOW THERES A WAY TO LEARN SURE SURE
```

Joe Strummer [signature] *obviously the book is getting to me!!*

The tour is getting to Joe: "IN THE BACK OF MY MIND . . .
THE RIVETTS MUST BE LOOSE." *(Lucinda Mellor)*

have come offstage. Except that this car door flung open in front of me, with somebody yelling, 'Stop stop stop.' It was Joe, getting the driver to stop. This arm came out, dragged me in the back of the car. 'We're off to Norway.' I said, 'But I've come to get these captions from you.' So he said, 'I just got in some trouble. We're going over the border tonight.'"

An anarcho-punk element in the Hamburg audience had felt that with *London Calling*, the Clash had succumbed to marketing forces. Incessantly they grabbed at Joe's microphone to deliver political protests. Pissed off, Joe had stepped out into the audience and clattered the principal offender with his Telecaster, sparking a riot of his own. Joe was arrested and the concert brought to an early conclusion. He was taken to a local police station, where a cop congratulated him. The next edition of the local paper featured a photograph of a bloodstained and bandaged man being carried out of the venue on a stretcher beneath the headline "Last Night the Clash Played!"

The incident brought about a turn in Joe's thinking, as he explained to Paul Du Noyer in *NME*. "In Hamburg these kids attacked us, going, 'You've sold out, you've sold out.' It was like nothing you've ever seen. They were all down the front, and if they could grab hold of a microphone lead they'd pull, and it was a tug-of-war. Then it started getting really violent—and that was my fault in a way. How much can a man take, y'know? I was playing and I saw this guy sort of using the guy in front of him as a punching bag, trying to be all tough. So I rapped him on the head with a Telecaster, I lost my temper. There was blood gushing down in front of his face. It wasn't much of a cut, but it looked real horror show. The howl out of the audience—you shoulda heard it. From then on it was jump in and punch.

"After I'd been taken down the cop station and charged with assaulting a German citizen by striking him over the head with a guitar, I began to think that I'd overstepped the mark. It was a watershed—violence had really controlled me for once. Since then I've decided the only way you can fight agro [aggression] in the audience is to play a really boring song."

In Sweden an odd incident took place. When Andrew King entered Joe's hotel bedroom, who should he have found sitting there but Bernie Rhodes, giving Joe a lecture on Marxism. The Blackhill man could not believe his eyes. In the light of events that were about to unfold, it is not surprising.

As with the *London Calling* video, Pennie's book, *The Clash: Before and After*, further cemented the visual iconography of how the group was perceived. As a semipermanent fixture around the group, she had ample opportunity to observe aspects of the Clash customarily cloaked from media eyes.

"Joe always needed a posse around him, he always needed other people to keep him up. Joe was nervous. I used to see Joe gear himself up for fans when they came in the dressing room. That kicked him into his Joe Strummer personality, which meant he could leave his inhibitions behind."

Many people who spent time in close proximity with Joe were able to observe that he was not entirely comfortable with himself—that there was sometimes a tension about him, as though something didn't quite fit. Yet wasn't part of his appeal the vulnerability that that sense created, so therefore people were able to identify with it?

"I don't think he ever could believe he was where he was," thought Pennie. "Suddenly he was very big . . . in a small field admittedly—the Clash weren't the Rolling Stones. Joe still had an element about him of 'I don't really believe I'm in this situation.'

"Particularly with girls he was an emotional bully—strangely, because he's tender and caring. He had a strange attitude to girls: they were there to be used. He always thought he was the ugly boy in the class, the bloke who couldn't score with girls. There's an element of being-in-a-band-will-help-me-score. He said that to me twice. I think he needed to prove he was liked, and therefore women came in useful. Joe would be with somebody else every night. The drinking was part of this. It wouldn't even necessarily be the best-looking girl in the room. Girls slotted in for perhaps another need of Joe—they allowed him to get out of the group for a minute." Others in the group were simply getting out of their heads. "Drugs aside," said Pennie, "Topper was probably the sanest of the lot. He didn't change as much as everybody else."

Those around Topper Headon were concerned about the drummer's consumption of hard drugs. Pete Jenner had been disturbed by the powders evident in the studio in New York. "Another thing that wound me up about Joe was that while they were recording *Sandinista!* I said to him, 'I'm a bit worried about Topper. There's all these white powders. What's going on? Shouldn't we be doing something about this? I'm a bit concerned.' I'd seen him throwing up. I'm a bit naïve: I thought it was probably coke. 'Oh, we don't need any advice from you, old man,' Joe said. I was the old man because I was ten years older, and therefore didn't *understand*. Not much later he threw Topper out of the band because of drug use, which I had pointed out we should do something about."

Back in Britain the Clash played the dates that had been rescheduled due to Topper Headon's hand injury. On June 16 and 17 they played for the first time at the venue already commemorated in Joe's greatest song: Hammersmith Palais. Both Joe and Paul had had their ducktailed quiffs cropped, and their hairstyles were now more Steve McQueen than James Dean.

As though seeking light relief after the end of the 16 Tons tour, in July Joe was in Pye Studios at London's Marble Arch, producing a record for a group called the Little Roosters, Small Faces clones managed by Cliff Cooper. Cooper had asked Joe to produce their first album, and come to an unusual financial arrangement: instead of Joe receiving a fee, he would have all expenses paid for the extensive dental work he required to rebuild the postapocalypse bomb site of his mouth.

In the July 19 edition of *NME*, "T-zers," the paper's gossip column, indicated knowledge of Topper's recreational pastimes was no longer confined to those in the group's inner circle: "Clash minder Kosmo 'It's tough being a stylist' Vinyl challenged T-zers on our item last week about Topper Headon having 'bad health' problems. This was apparently news to both Topper and his mum, who rang up concerned after reading T-zers, as is her habit. Topper's mum will be pleased to hear that CBS, against what were for once their better instincts, have decided to release the 'legendary' 'Bankrobber' on August 3rd."

Why had Maurice Oberstein taken such an intransigent stance against the release of the single? "Bankrobber" had, after all, been released in Holland as the B-side of "Train in Vain." The consequence of this controversy had been a breakdown of communication between the label and the Clash. As a result, they had refused to do any further work on the tunes recorded for the next album. Only when Obie changed his position—"Bankrobber" was actually released on August 8—did the group go into Wessex with Bill Price to mix the tunes. Although "Bankrobber" rose to number 11 in the British charts, the position would have been bettered had it not been for the large quantities of Dutch import records already purchased in Britain. "They refused to put it out," Joe Strummer told me, "so we refused to record anything else. We left it at that for a while. We had a load of rough mixes from stuff in New York, but we held off from finishing them off until they put it out."

As part of that spiteful mind-set that characterized the thinking of some music journalists, the revered status of the Clash set them up as targets to be shot down. The subject matter of "Bankrobber" was perfect to sneer at. All of Joe's romantic self-delusions seemed contained within this story of "Daddy": "He just loved to live that way / Loved to steal their money." "Actually, John Mellor's daddy was a Second Secretary of Information at the Foreign Office," jibed the review in *Sounds*. But there was a fundamental misunderstanding: Joe was not writing about himself but about a character he knew whose father had been a bank robber—it was a girl with whom he had been briefly involved. Scorn was heaped upon him. As their career trajectory moved upward in the United States, the Clash discovered that their British critical honeymoon was nearing an end. But was CBS now against them? Jenner and King had examined the group's CBS contract, even though they themselves still did not have a formal contract with the Clash. They could see the CBS contract did not lock the Clash in as much as the company might have hoped. Rudimentary errors had been made: CBS had not specified, as was customary, that if an album was a two-record set, then it must count only as one of the long-players due to the label, so *London Calling* clearly counted as two albums. "The contract was the biggest mess I've ever seen," said Pete Jenner. "It had obviously been cobbled together really quickly, bits of paper stuck everywhere. They'd left out that crucial clause about double albums. But on the other hand Joe had told me that it was a five-album deal. I thought, 'That's cool: a five-year, five-album deal.' But when you looked deeper you saw that CBS at any time could ask for an additional album in any year. So in fact it's a ten-album, or ten-year, deal, with another clause that can take it up to thirteen albums. I thought that Bernie was a complete bloody twit to let this through." Due to a complex payments clause, all money earned by the Clash from their records was paid by CBS in the United Kingdom to the parent company in the United States; in New York the money was sat on for six months before being paid to the group. All the same Jenner felt the clause about the double album was a bargaining lever that could be used against CBS: "Give them double albums all the time and you can get out in no time. There was a huge contractual hole which they could have used to start walking out on CBS."

At Wessex more tunes were written, including "The Equaliser," "Rebel Waltz" and "Something About England." When they had finished at Wessex in mid-September Mick Jones announced the new album would be a triple-record set, notwithstanding that the group had only five sides of recorded material. Accordingly, in the tradition of the reggae music that so influenced them, assorted dubs were recorded: "Junco Partner," recorded in Jamaica, was complemented by "Version Pardner," "If Music Could Talk" by "Shepherds Delight," and "Washington Bullets" by "Silicone on Sapphire." Jenner and King thought that the group was committing financial suicide. Jenner also thought the six sides contained too much waffle, although "it could have been a great double album and a fantastic single album." By now Joe firmly shared Mick's vision. "That was us at a very specific time. A blast of energy over six weeks or so. It was a statement of what we were as the Clash." Looking back, Mick Jones said, "*Sandinista!* is the big reaching out. I knew we were going to make a different record every time. It had to be different. I liked that with other groups like the Rolling Stones: you knew each record was going to be different. We loved the Ramones, but we didn't want to be like them, doing the same thing."

Immediately after the group had completed working on *Sandinista!*, they set about making an album with Ellen Foley, the American singer who was Mick's new girlfriend. The record, *Spirit of St. Louis*, contained six new Strummer/Jones songs and three written by Tymon Dogg. Produced by Mick Jones at Wessex, it had the usual suspects working on it. All the Clash, as well as Tymon Dogg and Blockheads Micky Gallagher, Norman Watt-Roy and Davey Payne played on *Spirit of St. Louis*, and it was mixed by Bill Price. When released, the record received a critical thumping. The group also then collaborated on an album for Pearl Harbor.

At one point it had been mooted that the new Clash record might be titled *The Bible*: among the myriad styles essayed on the record, a great surprise was gospel, on the song "The Sound of Sinners." (Joe smiled when we discussed this later: "But I wanted to see words like 'drugs' in a gospel song. I like all the imagery in gospel like 'Going down to the riverside,' and 'hurricanes' and 'winds of fury' and all that. In the Bible," he added dramatically, "they blew the horns and the walls of the city crumbled . . . Well, punk rock was like that.") Fortunately, the potential hubris of calling it *The Bible* was evaded through the inclusion of "Washington Bullets," a song aimed at the imperialistic follies of not only the United States but also the Soviet Union and China. It concluded with a wistful sigh of a chorus line from Mick Jones: "Oo-oo-oo-Sandinista." "I was singing this song, 'Washington Bullets,'" said Joe, "and I got to a verse about Nicaragua. I just came out with it. I just shouted it out. And when I got out of the vocal booth, Mick said, 'That's the name of the album,' and I started thinking about it." ("A long time after 'Washington Bullets' came out," said Kosmo Vinyl, "I asked

Joe if he'd known there was a basketball team called the Washington Bullets, and he said he didn't, and if he'd known at the time he wrote it he would have given the song a different title.")

Joe claimed that no one was aware of the revolutionary struggle in the Central American country of Nicaragua. William Walker, a maverick American adventurer, had seized Nicaragua for Washington in 1855, and the country had remained a tool of the United States. In the mid-1970s a revolutionary movement against President Anastasio Somoza, whose family had ruled the country since 1936, began in earnest; the rebels were known as Sandinistas. But in fact, the struggle against Somoza's repressive, corrupt regime had been assiduously reported; in 1979 a U.S. television journalist was shot dead on camera there, and the footage was broadcast worldwide. Somoza fled the country later that year. The revolution won, the country became a cause célèbre for radicals.

But the Sandinistas never made three-album sets. Or had CBS to deal with. The *Sandinista!* album was an ideal testing ground for the anomalies in the CBS contract. Maurice Oberstein declared he was not prepared to release it at the price insisted on by the Clash, £5.99 in Great Britain, unless they signed an amended version of the contract that corrected the glitch CBS inadvertently had allowed to slip in—thereby locking them back into a ten-year contract. To the consternation of the Blackhill men, Joe especially went along with this. "Joe was no businessman," Pete Jenner emphasized.

Joe might have been responding to these words of Jenner's when he declared to Paul Du Noyer: "I believe in socialism because it seems more humanitarian, rather than every man for himself and 'I'm alright Jack' and all those asshole businessmen with all the loot. When I left art school, I took a dive: no future, no skills, nothing. So I just labored and doled, fucked off around the place. Took a job when I was really broke, if I could get one, got fired every time for late timekeeping [lateness].

"I made up my mind from viewing society from that angle. That's where I'm from and that's where I've made my decisions from. That's why I believe in socialism. When [my life was really down], every door was slammed in my face. Once I asked a lady outside a sweet shop in Hampshire to buy me a bar of chocolate. I'd been hitching all day and I was really hungry. I just thought I'd turn round and try society on. This lady came along and I said, 'Would you give me the rest of the money for this bar of chocolate?' She just said, 'No, why should I?' Things like that annoyed me."

Impressive though Joe's political ideals were, they were indubitably a little bit "student": he didn't seem to appreciate that even the left required certain practical economic realities to engineer a perfect society. Kosmo Vinyl admitted to me that in Joe's stance there were contradictions. "We're claiming that we're broke. But we've got quite nice places to live in, we've got taxis everywhere, we eat in restaurants three times a day, and we've always got a lot of the best drugs going."

In late September Joe was stopped and searched in the decidedly insalubrious area of King's Cross by police officers from the notorious Special Patrol Group. Finding weed in his ubiquitous shopping bags, they went to his flat, coming up with several ounces of home-grown marijuana. Joe was fined £100, and told that, if busted again, he would receive jail time.

On November 1 a playback for *Sandinista!* was held at Wessex. The record was released on December 12, and marked a sea change in the relationship between the Clash and the U.K. music press. In the issue of *NME* on the stands that week, Paul Morley reviewed "The Call Up," the single from the album, and soundly dismissed both the record and the group as "Americanized," "old-fashioned," "too wrapped up in those used-up myths." "They care so much, but seem so lost," he concluded. The *NME* review of *Sandinista!* by Nick Kent, until now a big Clash fan, was the most derogatory that anything by the group had ever received in the paper, "ridiculously self-indulgent" being perhaps the mildest criticism. He tore into Joe's singing as "simply duff" and hated the lyrics. Patrick Humphries in *Melody Maker* found *Sandinista!* "a floundering mutant." But at least Robbi Millar in *Sounds* gave it a thumbs-up.

The overwhelming negativity against the record left the Clash confused. The growing tensions within the group—"Mick and I would scream at each other in the studio," said Paul—were exacerbated by the negative reception in their own country. When highly complimentary reviews from America began to filter through—for instance, a five-star review in *Rolling Stone*—they mollified what had been said in Britain. Although *Sandinista!* made it only to number 19 in Britain, compared with that number 2 slot achieved by *Give 'Em Enough Rope*, it made it to 24 in the United States, three slots higher than *London Calling*. It was clear where the market was expanding for the Clash. Aware that the group was yet again broke, and that it was Christmastime, Obie sent a gift of £1,000 to each group member. Pete Jenner felt this was a blatant attempt to court them. For him and Andrew King, matters would soon take a dramatic turn.

he year 1980 ended on a strange note for the Clash. Mick Jones had gone to New York to spend Christmas with Ellen Foley, fueling rumors of a split. These Chinese whispers were reinforced when Joe spent New Year's Eve playing at the Tabernacle, a Notting Hill community center, with Richard Dudanski and Mole of Joe's former band, the 101'ers, performing in a Booker T. and the MGs–like group, the Soul Vendors. Joe maintained a low-key presence, sticking to rhythm guitar and keeping away from the microphone, often with his back to the audience.

I bumped into him at the bar, ordering a can of Red Stripe. I told him that the length of time needed to be devoted to *Sandinista!* had amazed me the first time I'd played the sprawling sound-system-like extravaganza. But I added that when I'd played the album at random, choosing individual songs or sides, the record seemed solidly in the iconoclastic, witty tradition of greatness set by its predecessors.

"It's a bit over the top, isn't it?" chuckled Joe. "It's supposed to last you a year, though. There's loads of bits and pieces all over it that you can just suddenly come across and get into. Mind you, we got really slated [slammed] for it in a load of reviews—just for its length alone. But that PIL album, *Metal Box* [which had recently been released], that was three records and used up just as much vinyl, even if it did play at different speed and cost more. We seem to really get up people's noses: I think it's really good. We always bring out some reaction in people."

Exactly a week later I stopped by his tiny and overpriced Ladbroke Grove flat to solve the mystery of what was happening in the Clash. We began by resuming our conversation about *Sandinista!* Staring down on us in the dimly lit room was a giant poster of Elvis Presley in *Jailhouse Rock*. Perched underneath it, Joe seemed slighter in stature than usual; his new Hollywood-like teeth, courtesy of the Little Roosters, gleamed at me. Sipping from a glass of beer, playing compulsively with a switchblade knife that almost belied a true nature that was gentle and unassuming, Joe further considered *Sandinista!*

"Some of it is very American-sounding," he admitted. "But if you go somewhere, then obviously it's going to leave its mark on you—and we did that American tour and stayed there for quite a while. If we went to Spain and spent six months there, we'd be talking pidgin Spanish by the time we came back. Well, I would be, anyway. I tend to absorb more—absorb what's going on where I am."

Although it was known that there had been occasional on-the-road rows between Joe and Mick Jones, he thoroughly dismissed any suggestion the arguments might have had any long-term basis: "It's just that Mick doesn't like being on the road at all. He really hates it, y'know. He has to get a bit pissed to go onstage. So there was conflict there in that the rest of us still really enjoy touring, and Mick thinks it's a trial and tribulation. So something or somebody has to suffer. The rest of us just think of it as a good laugh. We're not rowing at all . . . we have rows sometimes, but then you have rows with your girlfriend, too. You forget about it the next day—it's not the end of the world. It's not one row that causes groups to split up."

Joe told me he had been shocked by the changes in Jamaica since he'd last been there. "I could really tell the difference. Even the street corner guy selling herb was heavy about it—it wasn't a question of do you want it or you don't: you want it! I went into this supermarket—there was nothing in it except for 140 tins of syrup! Rows and rows of empty shelves. A big long supermarket up in New Kingston near where we were staying. Somebody was starving Manley out."

I told Joe how the International Monetary Fund and Wall Street had done a number on the Jamaican economy. "Yeah, they're like a western gang. They did that because they thought he was a Marxist, although he wasn't even really that. He was just friends with Cuba, which seems pretty logical if it's your nearest neighbor and you're a Third World country too. Not that we didn't have our own problems in Jamaica."

Suddenly Joe's attention was grabbed by a news bulletin that appeared on his volumeless TV screen. He jumped up and turned on the sound. At a post office a letter bomb had been found, addressed to Prime Minister Thatcher. As the flash ended, Joe turned down the volume again. "Letter bomb, eh?" he smirked in great amusement. "That's a bit amateur, isn't it? I can't see that doing the job. We've all got to try a bit harder than that."

Within days of my being at Joe's Ladbroke Grove flat, the crisis over *Sandinista!* had come to a head. On the main thoroughfare of Notting Hill

Gate, he had bumped into Bernie Rhodes. They had spoken for a few minutes. Calling up the other group members, Joe threatened to leave unless Bernie was reinstated as manager.

"We were drifting and I saw my chance," Joe told Gavin Martin in 1999. "We wanted some direction to the thing because *Sandinista!* had been a sprawling six-sided . . . masterpiece. You got to get out there and fight like sharks—it's a piranha pool. And I wanted to reunite the old firm, like in *The Wild Bunch*. Get the old gang together and ride again. I knew we had something in us.

"We didn't know anything about anything. We were buffoons in the business world. Even Mick wanted him back, because he's not stupid and he had to admire Rhodes's ability to make things happen and, even better, to get things over."

For once, Joe put his foot down and held to his position. "I could easily have walked out then," Mick said. "But it's like a marriage, you cling on hoping it's going to work out."

"Mick is very idealistic," Joe told me. "But I felt we had to deal with the real world. I got worried that Mick would lead us to disaster through his refusal to compromise with the real world. I do think Bernie is a very creative individual."

Andrew King and Pete Jenner were shocked, more so when Kosmo Vinyl defected to work with Bernie. For Blackhill the decision was a disaster. Due to the perpetually perilous state of the Clash's finances, they had never been able to invoice the group for their services. "We might have had a thousand pounds here and there, but that was it," said Pete Jenner. When Bernie Rhodes took over, he indicated no desire to save them from this error. "We were just dropped out of the blue. They made no effort to pay us back or make any settlement. I was furious because they were fucking stupid. They'd whine on about things, but not do anything about it, and they could have done something about that CBS contract." In 1982 Blackhill were obliged to declare bankruptcy, breaking up the seventeen-year partnership between two of the most honest, able and creative managers in the music business and causing them both hardship. The bankruptcy was directly attributable to debts they had incurred while managing the Clash.

Fans of the group who had any knowledge of its inner workings were astounded by this change in managers. It had seemed inconceivable that

Bernie Rhodes could ever reenter the fold. But there it was: he was back. "Joe's problem," Bernie told me, "was that if they got rid of me, he couldn't be me. He'd said, 'Oh fuck it, I'll get rid of Bernie.' So he became a pop star and was milking it. But he came to me and told me they were half a million in debt. His batteries had run dry and he needed to be me to recharge. Everybody loved Joe—I always had a soft spot for him. But Joe didn't like himself—so he came back to me. I made Joe great. I knew how it worked. I thought if Robert Plant is it, I know what can replace it."

Bernie's first edict? "No more hats." Bernie believed his charges were not seen in their best light in the assorted chapeaux with which they had sometimes adorned themselves for photo shoots since his departure in the fall of 1978. This was the sort of arbitrary judgment—part control freak, part willful schoolyard bully, part style visionary—that made those around him scream inside. Joe seemed to love such edicts. From now on he and Bernie had a much more hand-in-glove relationship than formerly. Mick Jones began to seem increasingly marginalized in the processes of decision-making.

Joe and Bernie had something in common. They had both had facial refits of different sorts: whereas Joe now had his sparkling set of Hollywood teeth, Bernie had had his cartoon-curved schnozz cut down to a new pert, snub nose and he had replaced the thick glass of his spectacles with contact lenses. But what else bound them together? Why was Joe so intent on remaining loyal to Bernie? As Joe's endless reading of the memoirs of World War II leaders suggested, he loved to see himself as a sort of general. At the same time he suffered huge guilt over this, believing he did not have a true awareness of the kind of heroic underclass existence that he celebrated in song: the truth, he had after all proclaimed, was only known by guttersnipes. Even though the Clash had long outlasted the Sex Pistols, to Joe, John Lydon's feral upbringing ensured he would always be far more believable. A verbally agile, witty and intelligent hustler like Bernie Rhodes possessed that tang of the street; he was an artist, something to which Joe would certainly genuflect; he was also self-made, which Joe respected, this being precisely how his own father had risen from his orphan origins.

Anyway, the deed was done: Bernie was back at the helm of the Clash. Other than the "hats" edict, his first move was to cancel a brief U.K. tour that had been organized by Pete Jenner and Andrew King. Before Bernie had been brought back on board, Joe went ahead to publicize it with an interview on Wolverhampton's Beacon Radio. He made it clear why it would have only been a brief sprint around Britain. "I'm not going to pretend that we're doing a big tour," he said. "There's a lot of things putting us off, like a group tends to believe what it reads in the press as reflecting the true mood of the country. This past year, reading the English press has been pretty depressing for me."

In an interview with Paul Rambali in *NME*, Joe said: "When I read the *NME* now, this is what I think, and this is really heavy . . . If they're teaching the readers to hate us, then I'd like to ask the *NME* who they're teaching the readers to trust? Which groups? Which ideas? I'm looking hard, and I can't see anybody."

"I don't believe it!" responded Rambali. "I thought the *NME* was supposed to dote on the Clash."

"You must have a fucking long memory. You don't notice every little pinprick—obviously not. I mean I don't care—my skin is thick enough by now, otherwise I wouldn't be able to get on stage, I'd be hiding in a cupboard somewhere. And I can deal with hard criticism. It's something I'd like to deal with, because if I'm no good I wanna know it."

Bernie Rhodes's plan was to let the negative press in Britain evaporate by keeping the group out of the country. They would tour overseas. Before that they returned to Vanilla in Pimlico to come up with more new material and to rehearse their live show. "The Clash had to get out of England," Bernie said to me, "because it was suffocating. England doesn't respect what it has."

Since the Tabernacle New Year's Eve show with the Soul Vendors, Joe had been working with Richard Dudanski on finally putting out an album of material by the 101'ers. In April 1981 they released *Elgin Avenue Breakdown* on a label contrived for the purpose, Andalusia, distributed by Virgin. The twelve songs were drawn from four different sources: "Letsgetabitarockin'" (which kicked off the record), "Standing by a Silent Telephone," "Motor Boys Motor" and "Mr. Sweety of the St. Moritz"—all written by Joe—came from the sessions with Vic Maile; their cover of Chuck Berry's "Monkey Business," Slim Harpo's "Shake Your Hips," James Booker's "Junco Partner" (showing the roots of the version recorded on *Sandinista!*), Bo Diddley's "Don't Let Go" and an epic rendition of Van Morrison's "Gloria," that particular favorite of Joe, had been recorded live at the Roundhouse on April 18, 1976, just before the group broke up; "Sweet Revenge," another 101'ers original, came from the Pathway session; and "Surf City" and "Keys to Your Heart" had been recorded at the BBC's Maida Vale studios. In contrast to the reviews of *Sandinista!*, *Elgin Avenue Breakdown* was extremely well received in Britain. Despite the return of Bernie Rhodes, supposedly a harbinger of solidity, the release of the 101'ers' record was read as further proof of the continuing rifts within the Clash. Even the Brixton Riots over the 1981 Easter weekend—in which hundreds of black people filled the streets, facing and fighting similar numbers of police—exemplified this rift. While Joe approved heartily, Mick Jones had an opposing point of view: "It seems a bit stupid burning down your own neighborhood," he said to me. For the Clash the riots only brought further criticism. Why hadn't they been manning the barricades? demanded naïve thinkers.

I n mid-April, wearing a "Clash Take the Fifth" T-shirt, Joe Strummer, the man who as a boy had been his school's cross-country running champion, ran the London Marathon. He took Gaby with him—she made it halfway before dropping out. "He hadn't trained. He just bought some shorts and said, 'Let's run a marathon.'" Even in personal relations Joe played his cards close to his chest: he never mentioned to Gaby that he had been the top runner at his school—it wasn't until I told her, over twenty years later, that she learned this. "He kept that one quiet."

On April 27 the Clash played the first date of a European tour, in Barcelona. Here the audience heard the debut performance of a song from the latest Vanilla sessions, "This Is Radio Clash," a tune that employed a riff from "Good Times" by Chic, such an influence on the beginnings of *Sandinista!* The lyrics were like the flip side of "Capital Radio"—now the group itself personified an idealized radio station. Joe's words were direct and sparse, but they seemed devoid of the humor and warmth that traditionally characterized his lyrics: they were very much the sloganeering of an advertising man. "This Is Radio Clash" always seemed an oddity, a transitional work that was not entirely successful. Yet even a substandard Clash song was head and shoulders above most pop music released that year: synthesizer pop had begun to take over in Britain.

Working with the Clash on the European tour was Jock Scot, the intelligent and very funny man whom Kosmo had introduced into the group's camp two years previously. Jock loved to don a kilt and express his love of Scotland in the most heartfelt of ways, but he and Joe rarely discussed their joint Scottish origins. "When we got back to the hotel in Barcelona," he told me, "I sang a song, a Scottish song. Joe started to shed a tear. Then he was crying his eyes out. The Scottish gypsy in him is very strong."

In Madrid the next day the Clash played at the ground of the revered Real Madrid soccer team. In Spanish Joe gave a speech in support of Bobby Sands, a Republican activist in Northern Ireland who was on hunger strike in Long Kesh prison. While on hunger strike he won a by-election as a member of Parliament after the death of an independent MP who supported the prisoners' cause. Joe said to Jock Scot: "'Get a black armband on. I've got to learn this speech in Spanish for Bobby Sands, to say to the audience. Test me on my words.' So he learned this speech, and said it to all of Madrid, wearing a black armband himself. Told them about Bobby starving himself to death in a prison in Northern Ireland. He didn't have to do that.

"He did his homework, he read up on it. He felt he had to have an opinion, or you were wasting any education you had ever had. That is what Joe made people aware of. If you were lucky enough to have been at school, and read a book, fucking use it. It wasn't preaching, it was mad! It was informed. Don't be lazy, is what he's saying. Keep applying what you've learned. At least, think of what you're doing yourself personally with your life." Bobby Sands died a week after Joe's speech.

Considering the death threat that had been made against Joe by the Red Hand almost three years before for voicing lesser sentiments, Joe's stance here was fearless. You might think that as he was broadcasting these sentiments in another country, in another language, he might have felt the hardline loyalists would not get to hear of it. Yet the Clash was not playing in the U.K. at that time; if they had, past experience suggests Joe almost certainly would have expressed the same feelings there.

Kid Creole and the Coconuts were also on the bill. One of the girls in the party fell for Joe's charm. How could she resist such a sophisticated pickup line? "I'm a man. You're a woman," said Joe. "You know what I want."

There were more Spanish and Portuguese shows—"Lisbon, that white city lying there in the sun as we crawled its alleyways like rats with hangovers," remembered Joe—and French dates followed by concerts in Sweden, starting with a show in Göteburg on May 15. That year Dotun Adebayo, a

Londoner of Nigerian extraction who had been a member of the English National Youth Theatre, was studying literature at Stockholm University. He was also writing for a Swedish music paper called *Schlager*. (When we met a few years later, I discovered he had translated into Swedish the articles I syndicated to that publication.) Raymond Jordan gave a pair of tickets to that night's show to Dotun, a huge Clash fan who had seen the group several times. After the show Dotun went backstage, where a banquet was laid out. As assorted journalists in the area attempted to dig into the food and drink, Kosmo Vinyl screamed at them: "You fuckin' greedy journalists. Leave that alone. It's for the kids, not you lot."

Topper, Dotun noted, was sitting in a corner, wearing a half-smile. Mick and Paul were swanning about, talking to the fans who would shortly partake of the feast originally intended for the group. "But Joe was just sitting there, observing, a bit like you'd find Bob Marley doing. He had a Swedish girl on his lap, in a skimpy white outfit, showing her white stockings and suspenders. I don't think she was wearing a skirt—she was the sister of a friend of mine."

Dotun had met Joe back in London, with the Slits, at a squat party in Maida Vale, so he felt no constraint in going over to speak to him. "They hadn't had an opening act that night, and I told him it was a shame that they hadn't had Mikey Dread. He said they were trying to run the tour to a tight budget. I said, 'Tomorrow in Stockholm you could have Sweden's best toaster—I know him.' 'If you get him to the gig tomorrow,' said Joe, 'he can play.' I said that I'd better be honest with him: the 'best toaster' was me. 'That's cool,' said Joe. 'Just get there and play.'"

Dotun took a train to Stockholm. Arriving at the venue, an ice-hockey stadium, he first had a fight with some out-of-town skinhead punks, then managed to make his way inside with the records he had selected to toast to: "About five tunes—a 'Satta Masagana' rhythm, an Augustus Pablo dub, Lone Ranger's 'Love Bump' rhythm, and a couple of others."

When he hit the stage, to toast entirely in Swedish, friends of his in the front rows were astonished: "Hey, Dotun, what are you doing there? Come down before you're kicked off."

Joe, who watched from the wings, loved Dotun's set. "Afterward he said, 'That was wicked!' But I didn't have the bottle [nerve] to say, 'Put me on one of your records then.'" The next edition of *Schlager* carried a picture of Swe-

SAVOY HOTEL

Malmö Sweden

SILENCE IS A VAST relief - Even the
Sound of its mighty Water Falls
can't hold me No longer......
(Tunnel Ahead" was the only Roadsign
for a thousand miles)
....Like the road that runs through
the villages of my childhood,
I cant be too sure
That it will exist.
SO BEND TO THE FIRE
STEP FORWARD TO THE FORGE
VIKING IRON YOUR BODY HAMMERED
THE ROAR AND the GLAZE
OF THE MOLTEN IRONS.
PICKED OUT AS CHIEF DEVILS
THE ASSISTANTS SECURE YOU IN PLACE.
"LET LOOSE!" THOUGHT THE MAN
AS HIS ROCKET LEFT THE EARTH,
AND US TOO. LET US NOT delay
OR CLING. PHOTOGRAPH YOUR EVIL
MOMENTS - OR TAKE NO PRISONERS AT ALL !

Joe Strummer

Gastbrevpapper

"PHOTOGRAPH YOUR EVIL MOMENTS—OR TAKE NO PRISONERS
AT ALL!" *(Lucinda Mellor)*

den's best toaster at the show, with the headline, "Schlager's Dotun Was King for a Day."

The Clash went on to Austria on May 20. "The worst city to play? Vienna. It means nothing to me," wrote Joe in 1988. A television reporter incurred the Clash front man's wrath when he asked why Topper had become ill during the journey. Is this punk posturing? asked the Austrian. "Do you think this is 1976 and you're talking to the Sex Pistols?" snapped a furious Joe. Joe seemed almost incandescent with rage at the questioning, quite the bully almost. You couldn't help feeling that the hapless TV journalist incurred Joe's anger because of the question's subtext: What really is the source of Topper's "illness"? Which was his growing fondness for heroin. But there was a lighter moment. When Bernie Rhodes came on camera, Joe observed: "That's Bernie Rhodes. He invented punk rock. It was obviously too much for him."

The next day they were in Italy, in Milan, and after a concert in Florence on May 23, their live show honed and taut, they flew straight to New York City.

$$\frac{1}{7}$$

the news behind the news

1981-1982

According to myth, Bernie Rhodes's first masterstroke upon his return to managing the group was deciding that the Clash should play seasons of gigs in significant cities around the globe. Their stint at Bond's International Casino in New York City was the first leg of this strategy. But the story omits the sixty-date tour of the United States Bernie had wanted the group to play first. Epic, however, refused to underwrite it, and the New York dates were an alternative strategy.

This was a clear case of turning adversity to advantage, for the seventeen shows played by the Clash at Bond's in Times Square in May and June 1981 marked a major upturn. In the States they already had cachet; the last two albums had made the Top Thirty and "Train in Vain" had been a hit single. But now large-scale American stardom finally appeared. The career of the Clash was definitively pre- and post-Bond's: the Top Ten U.S. success of *Combat Rock* the next year can be traced back to this springboard. And from here to the beginning of the end. When it was taking place, in the spring of 1981, it seemed like one of the most perfect times you could possibly experience. The sexy, sultry weather helped: the temperature never dropped below 90 degrees for the entire stretch of what had been planned as eight New York dates.

After the European tour, the group was back in financial shape. The new deal struck with Rhodes permitted him only a percentage of the group's net profits, so it was in his interest for them to earn wads of cash. The New York gigs were regarded as the final leg of a tour that had loosened up the Clash after nine months off the road, the longest period without live action in their career. Bond's had been picked after Rhodes and Vinyl visited New York early in the spring. Choosing the tacky former disco as the venue for an eight-night New York stint was in the tradition of the kind of sleazy venues, redolent with low-life romance, into which Rhodes had booked the Clash early in their career. It is a myth to suggest that it was the Clash that used the venue for the first time: I'd seen Burning Spear perform there that April. Still, plenty of people in New York were confused by the Bond's dates: Why had the Clash turned down Madison Square Garden, where they could have made far more money for far less effort? Here was an abysslike cultural, even ethical, gap. In the frequent words of members of the group, they didn't understand. Making far more money for far less effort was not only not the point, it was more like the anti-point.

The Clash was staying at the Gramercy Park Hotel, on whose roof Humphrey Bogart had married Lauren Bacall, midway between Times Square and Greenwich Village. Popular with musicians, the hotel was also hosting another group, a fledgling outfit called U2 who worshipped the Clash. Bono introduced himself to Mick Jones in the elevator one afternoon as I sailed upward in it with the guitarist.

This visit to New York was stage-managed with an efficiency whose machinelike momentum was cleverly concealed; the group's elite status was manipulated for maximum TV and newspaper coverage, in a quantity completely disproportionate to the amount of records the group had so far sold; you'd turn on the TV news and there would be the Clash, paying an official visit to some school in Brooklyn, like alternative statesmen—Kosmo and Susan Blond outdid themselves. Two days after the Clash arrived in New York, on May 27, a press conference was held at Bond's, in the club's foyer. A journalist pointed out that Paul Weller had accused the Clash of selling out. "What constitutes a sellout to the Clash?" he demanded. Mick Jones took up the gauntlet, to toss it to one side. "What happens," he said, deadpan, "is that all the tickets go on sale for a concert, and all the people who want to go go and buy them. And if as many go and buy them as there are tickets, that constitutes a sellout." The assembled American media thought this was witty.

Manhattan was a perfect backdrop against which a group of former art students in love with the switchblade ethos of Martin Scorsese's *Mean Streets* could perform. Just up Broadway from Bond's was Tin Pan Alley, a bar in which one of the final scenes of the revered director's latest film, *Raging Bull*, had been shot; it became Clash Central for the next three weeks. Soon new additions to the camp appeared: the graffiti artists Futura 2000 and Fab Five Freddy.

At a party Mick threw for his girlfriend, Ellen Foley, I noticed that Mick and Joe seemed inseparable, not a hint of a bad vibe, even though Joe was going through personal problems with Gaby at the time. Later he told me that because of this it had been a very difficult time for him—I didn't pick up the slightest scent of this, a tribute to a professional who knew the importance of these shows. Don Letts was making a film about the visit to New York, with a working title of *Clash on Broadway*; after each night's show he'd be handed a wedge of dollars by Bernie and told to buy more film. (Bernie placed the footage in storage in New York, forgot to pay the bill, and the film stock was thrown away.) This was the heyday of the New York after-hours bar scene: half dead from tiredness or from what you'd ingested, you'd slide into yet another dubious downtown sleaze pit at eight in the morning and find Joe Strummer and Kosmo Vinyl there, playing pool.

The temperature rose yet again, to just over 100 degrees, on Thursday, May 28, the night the Clash opened at Bond's. In the street outside black kids from Harlem were break-dancing, a riveting sighting of a then new phenomenon. Inside the packed hall it was another matter. That night's opening act, Grandmaster Flash and the Furious Five, were soundly booed—even pelted with garbage—by the out-of-town audience, a logistical whim thrown up by the Ticketron computer ticket sales outlets. (The group seemed amused by the idea of fans traveling to see them, rather than the musicians traveling to the fans. "It's the mountain coming to Mohammed," said Joe.)

That same first-night audience went crazy for the Clash, in a way I'd never seen a more reserved British audience behave, and the group seemed lifted by the applause. The group was a powerhouse, tight, tough and immeasurably confident. To the sound of "Sixty Seconds to What," Ennio Morricone's theme from Sergio Leone's *For a Few Dollars More*, they roared onstage like a thundering storm, straight into a set that lasted two and a half hours or thereabouts.

As had happened with their championing of punk, the Clash always had telescopic sights pinned on any coming zeitgeist. Dub reggae, rockabilly and then rap had been absorbed into their catalogue of material: "The Magnificent Dance," a mix of "The Magnificent Seven" by the group under the name Pepe Unidos, was bubbling on black dance stations like WBLS and KISS, the audiences probably unaware that the Clash was a white, pinko, British guitar group.

After that first night's set the problems started. Someone had called the fire department and the municipal building inspector. Bond's had been dangerously oversold; if there had been a major fire no more than 900 of the 3,500-strong audience could have escaped; the shows looked about to be canceled. The Friday night event went ahead, although only 1,750 ticket holders were allowed in, but negotiations over the rest of the dates came to a standstill and Saturday night was canceled.

A deal was eventually reached. The shows could continue if more fire exits were opened up and there was an audience maximum of 1,750. Suddenly the Clash found themselves agreeing to play seventeen dates instead of the eight they'd flown in for. "I'm very worried about Joe's voice. I hope he can hold up," pondered a concerned Mick Jones to me. Other members of the group gave perhaps greater cause for concern. Later, Don Letts showed me footage of an interview with Topper for the aborted *Clash on Broadway* movie. Topper was asked how he felt about having to play a total of seventeen shows. It was not a problem, he said, playing all those dates. But his face told a different story: he was unshaven, his voice was slurred, and he was not looking in good shape.

When the Saturday night show was canceled, there was a near-riot in Times Square by frustrated ticket holders—and more TV and press coverage. But the time spent in New York established the group in the unconscious of the city's cultural underground. Lauded by the likes of Martin Scorsese and Robert De Niro, as well as kids from Queens with aerosol cans, they became a fixture of the coolest edge of the New York art scene. They very briefly appeared in Scorsese's next film, *King of Comedy*, supposedly a test run for their appearances in his mooted follow-up, *Gangs of New York*. After the dates finally ended, they stayed on in the city, to record "This Is Radio Clash."

On a New York radio station Bernie was interviewed about the Bond's overcrowding crisis, and he gave a Bernie-type rap: "The policy of the Clash has been upheld, which is giving you the news behind the news, put to music. And we think you're more informed than any other audience there is. So that's one benefit."

Raymond Jordan, the group's minder, felt that the only person not inspired by the rarefied shenanigans in which the Clash had become embroiled was—perhaps predictably—Bernie Rhodes. It was noted that at the time he was needed, when the shows were in danger of being canceled altogether, Bernie was nowhere to be found, and no decisions could be finalized. Raymond went to the Gramercy Park hotel and persuaded a chambermaid to let him into Bernie's room. The TV set was booming out a news story about the Bond's furor. A figure could be made out under the bedding. It had the pillows wrapped about its head and ears. "What's going on here?" demanded Raymond in his characteristic booming tones. Bernie peered out from beneath the pillows: his face was wan and he was blinking even more furiously than ever. "I can't handle it! I can't handle it! Leave me alone!" whimpered his shrunken voice. "Get up, you bloody fool. Everyone needs you," chortled Raymond. And left the room.

Among the most extraordinary nights of the Bond's residency was that of June 10, when revered beat poet Allen Ginsberg came to meet the group in their dressing room. For Joe and Mick, who on their first visit to San Francisco in 1978 had paid homage to the beat writers by visiting City Lights bookstore, this had to be a seminal moment. "Well, Ginsberg, when are you going to run for president?" asked Joe immediately.

The audience at Bond's, who'd faced an array of seemingly baffling opening acts, ranging way beyond Grandmaster Flash to Lee "Scratch" Perry, the Fall and a spokesman from the Committee in Solidarity with the People of El Salvador, were now to be treated to the unlikeliest of all: the Clash was to back Allen Ginsberg on "Capitol Air," "a poem that has chord changes" as Ginsberg described it. Ginsberg himself felt honored. "I don't know of any other band that would be willing to go on with a big middle-age goose like me who might or might not be able to sing in tune."

After the shows ended, the group stayed on in New York, recording "This Is Radio Clash," which was completed at Marcus Music in London. "Epic hadn't understood at all what we were trying to do," Bernie told me. "They didn't give a fuck. So I thought, 'Let's deal with the people.' So I

booked a series of shows right in the face of CBS. After Bond's I went in
and renegotiated the Clash's contract. They wrote off the debts, and I made
sure we got promotion and that's why we got big hits."

August 29 brought the unexpected death of Guy Stevens from an acci-
dental overdose of the antidepressants that had been prescribed to combat
his dependency on alcohol. The response of the group was to record the
tribute tune "Midnight to Stevens," a sweet elegy that did not appear until
the *Clash on Broadway* box set was released in the United States in 1991.
When the new album on which the group was working would finally appear, he would be credited on the liner notes as "inspiration."

On September 24 the group kicked off the Radio Clash tour by repeating the Bond's experience with seven nights at the Théâtre Mogador in
Paris. During this set of dates the group debuted material from their next
album, with the working title of *Rat Patrol from Fort Bragg*. In April they'd
already laid down early versions of three new songs, "Car Jamming," "This
Is Radio Clash" and "Sean Flynn," at Marcus Music, off Westbourne Grove;
in August and September, using the Rolling Stones' mobile studio, the
Clash put down four more songs at Notting Hill's Ear Studios on Freston
Road: "Know Your Rights," "Inoculated City," "Should I Stay or Should I
Go" and "Ghetto Defendant." On October 5 the tour shifted to Britain,
opening in Manchester—the first time the group had played in their home
country for fifteen months. Two weeks later, it was finally time to hit the
capital and to visit the Bond's experience on London: the tour concluded
with seven nights at the Lyceum.

The Lyceum audience received the Bond's treatment, with a similar
structure. The set included a rap from Futura 2000, "The Escapades of Futura 2000." During the course of the two-hour set, Futura would spray-paint
a graffiti mural backdrop, and then leap down from his stepladder to deliver his rap. "This Is Radio Clash" was finally released as a single the next
month. There was a small lunchtime launch party for the record at a
screening room in Wardour Street in Soho; there was a showing of Don
Letts's video for the single, effectively a trailer for the *Clash on Broadway*
film he had been editing in Manhattan. "The Clash have got to have a big
single, and this is not going to be it," Jock Scot muttered to me. He was
right—the record hardly dented the Top Fifty. (Kosmo told me later: "Me
and Bernie so much needed a single after they played Bond's, and we got

'This Is Radio Clash.'") Paul, Topper and then Joe turned up for a couple of drinks before the event wrapped at 3:00 p.m. But there was no sign of Mick Jones. For those of us who knew him, this was hardly a surprise—Mick generally didn't raise his head from the pillow before 2:30 in the afternoon.

Mick, however, had declared himself to be the producer of the new record, which he insisted should be completed in New York, at Electric Lady, in the weeks before and after Christmas that year; he wanted to be in the midst of the city's sounds of urban ghettology, which so inspired him; and he also wanted to be close to Ellen Foley. When queried about this, he responded in the same way that Joe had when the others questioned the wisdom of bringing Bernie Rhodes back as manager—he threatened to leave the group. Obliged to back down, both Joe and Paul were furious: recording in New York would dramatically raise the costs of the album. When later confronted by Joe about this, Mick said that he had only been joking, but three years later his decision still rankled Paul.

Whereas Mick Jones had been thoroughly entranced by the rap culture in which he had immersed himself in New York, resulting in various experimental mixes of "This Is Radio Clash," Joe Strummer was veering back toward his love of the roots of contemporary music. "I want to do real music, not punk," he told Bernie. "Know Your Rights," first recorded at Ear Studios in London to a semi-rockabilly beat, indicated the growing rift between Mick and Joe: "This is a public service announcement . . . with guitars!" One attempt at recording "Know Your Rights" was aborted after Mick and Paul argued for two hours over the appropriate bass sound, Paul demanding a heavier reggae feel. Paul has insisted to me that the final feel of the song was entirely wrong. He's not complaining about his bass parts, but about something else altogether: "It was supposed to have been funny, but that didn't come over at all."

In addition to the tensions between the key players over the recording, the low-key but ever-present crisis caused by the extracurricular interests of Topper Headon came to a head. Flying into Heathrow, Topper was arrested for possession of heroin. On December 17 he appeared at Uxbridge magistrates' court. After his barrister had said in mitigation that he had recently been voted one of the world's top five drummers, the magistrate admonished Topper that "unless you accept treatment, you will be the best drummer in the graveyard." On the proviso that he would seek help for his drug problems, Topper Headon was fined only £500. Later he told me, "My girlfriend, Donna, had rung me up—she was ill, because there was a drought in London. I said, 'Oh, for fuck's sake. I'll bring you a bit back.' I was going to fly to London, give her a couple of grams and fly back. I used it on the plane, and when I got to Heathrow and went to collect my bag, they picked me up straightaway. 'Who ratted me out?' 'You watched your luggage go round three times before you recognized it.'"

Early in 1982 Bernie Rhodes and Kosmo Vinyl would send Topper to an in-patient rehab program in southwest London. Not only was Topper's health in jeopardy, but an imminent Japanese tour also hung in the balance—after Topper's bust the entire group came within a hairbreadth of having their work permits rescinded.

Topper's drug bust did not prevent him almost immediately returning to New York to work on the new record, and in Manhattan he returned at once to his old habits. But he was in good enough shape on December 30 when work began on a song called "Straight to Hell": this evolved not out of a Joe lyric, but a Mick Jones guitar doodle, to which Topper laid down a bossa nova beat. An epic ballad, "Straight to Hell" would become an archetypal Clash song—one of their greatest in fact—from this last period of Joe, Mick, Paul and Topper working together. "Just before the take," said Joe, "Topper said to me, 'I want you to play this,' and he handed me an R. White's lemonade bottle wrapped in a towel. He said, 'I want you to beat the front of the bass drum with it.' On the record you hear me standing in front of this bass drum swinging this towel, with this large lemonade bottle in it, whacking the front of the bass drum while the others record the backing track."

The group were back at the Iroquois Hotel. James Dean had lived there, somewhere on the top two floors, and Joe changed rooms every couple of days to ensure he would have slept in the same room as the inspirational Method actor. Back at the hotel after the "Straight to Hell" backing track had been laid down, Joe sat in his room in front of the typewriter working on the words to the new songs: "It was New Year's Eve. I'd written the lyric staying up all night at the Iroquois. I went down Electric Lady and I just put the vocal down on tape. We finished at about twenty to midnight. We took the E train from the Village up to Times Square, because the Iroquois was off Times Square. I'll never forget coming out of the Times Square subway exit, just before midnight, into a hundred billion people, and I knew we had just done something really great."

For the success of the entire album Topper Headon was able to provide his Clash pièce de resistance at Electric Lady—"Rock the Casbah," for which he wrote the music entirely himself. "Whatever my faults, I was always the first at rehearsals," Topper said to me. "I went to Electric Lady and there was no one there, and I just recorded it onto an old ghetto blaster. The others turned up and I said, 'Listen. I've just written this song.' They said, 'Leave it as it is.' I said, 'We can't. There's only two verses and a middle bit—there should be four verses.' So they just spliced the tape and doubled the length of the song. Joe wrote the lyrics and then sang on it. He just went into the toilet or somewhere, lay down, wrote it all out—it only took him about an hour. Joe said later, 'That's when I realized the true genius of Topper Headon.'"

"I saw it with my own eyes—Topper Headon's great talent," Joe told Gavin Martin in 1999. "I swear in twenty minutes he'd laid down the whole thing: bass, drums, piano. He laid them all himself. It took other people by surprise. Jonesy really wasn't into that tune when we released it as a single. We had to persuade him a bit. I think he thought it was a bit comedic."

In fact, Joe already had the first line of the song written. "We found that whenever we played a tune on the Combat Rock sessions," he said, "it would be six minutes minimum. After a few days of this, Bernie came down the studio, and I think he heard 'Sean Flynn' and he said, 'Does everything have to be as long as a raga?' From then on we called everything we did ragas. I got back to the Iroquois Hotel that night and wrote on the typewriter, 'The king told the boogie men you got to let that raga drop.' I looked at it and for some reason I started to think about what someone had told me earlier, that you got lashed for owning a disco album in Iran. So I transferred it from Bernie to these religious leaders who tried to stop people listening to music."

An occasional visitor to the studio was Jo-Anne Henry, a sixteen-year-old black girl. Noticeable at a Bond's matinee because of the stepstool she had brought with her to get a clear view of the group, she had been led backstage by Raymond Jordan. Joe had been fascinated by her experiences as a black New York girl into the Clash. Hearing that the group were recording at Electric Lady at the end of the year, Jo-Anne came to the studio most days after school and became part of the Clash entourage in New York City. She remembered when Joe and Allen Ginsberg were writing the lyrics to "Ghetto Defendant": "Somebody walked in with a tray of coke, with lines on it. Joe looked at the coke and at me, and then at the person who brought it in, and said, 'You know, you guys can't do that in here. You've got to take it somewhere else. Do it elsewhere.'"

(Years later, at his farm in Somerset, Joe and I were talking about the necessity to hide drugs from kids. I said to him, "There are people who say you mustn't be a hypocrite with children about drugs." "You have to be a hypocrite with kids about drugs," he replied. "It's too confusing for them otherwise, to be able to differentiate between the different types.")

"Should I Stay or Should I Go," a song written almost entirely by Mick Jones, assumed to be about his relationship with Ellen Foley, would ultimately become the biggest-selling Clash single ever: an international hit when it was first released off the album in 1982, it sold a further million copies in Britain when re-released in 1991 after it was used in a Levi's jeans commercial. Loosely based on the melody of Mitch Ryder and the Detroit Wheels' "Little Latin Lupe Lu," the song naturally can be taken as a measure of prescience about Mick's future with the group—although that would hardly take into account the racy original lyrics that went "around the front or on your back," which were ultimately changed to "If you want me off your back" in an attempt to ensure U.S. radio airplay. "It wasn't about anybody specific," said Mick, "and it wasn't preempting my leaving the Clash. It was just a good rockin' song, our attempt at writing a classic." But Joe certainly read it as a statement of Mick's potential longevity with the Clash—according to Paul Simonon, the Clash's principal songwriters were hardly speaking when the tune was recorded. In Joe's archive was found a satirical version of the song that he had typed out, apparently in the character of Mick: "I always whinge, whinge, whinge when the crew go on a binge." When these alternative words to the song were mentioned to Mick in 2004, he was highly amused. This customized version shows that even early in 1982 Joe was mulling over a plan to redirect the Clash onto a path he found more palatable. ("Even back in 1978 when we were going out," Jeannette Lee told me, "Joe was saying he'd like to get rid of Mick.")

By chance Joe Ely ran into Mick and Joe in New York when they were recording "Should I Stay or Should I Go." Arbitrarily Joe had decided that his section of the tune should be in Spanish and asked Ely for help. "So me and Strummer and the Puerto Rican engineer [Eddie Garcia, who was in fact Ecuadorian] sat down and translated the lyrics into the weirdest Spanish ever.

"When you listen to 'Should I Stay or Should I Go' there's a place in the song where Mick says, 'Split,'" Joe Ely recalled. "Me and Strummer had been yelling out the Spanish background lyrics and we had snuck up behind him as he was recording. We were behind a curtain, jumped out at him in the middle of singing, and scared the shit out of him. He looks over and gives us the dirtiest look and says, 'Split!' They kept that in the final version." The mix of the song featured on the original "Rat Patrol from Fort Bragg" introduced Joe's Spanish sections early in the song.

A beautiful protest ballad, "Ghetto Defendant" was Joe's expression of a commonly voiced conspiracy theory of the time—that the government encouraged heroin to flourish in the ghettos as an anesthetic: "It's heroin pity not tear gas nor baton charge / That stops you taking the city." It's easy to imagine that Topper's plight was not far from Joe's mind.

At the group's invitation, Allen Ginsberg flew in from Boulder, Colorado, and joined them in the studio. "You're the greatest poet in America. Can you improve on these lyrics?" Joe asked him. On the spot Allen Ginsberg wrote some lyrics for himself to recite on the record, including a litany of worldwide trouble spots: Guatemala, Honduras, Poland, El Salvador, Afghanistan. He also mentioned Arthur Rimbaud, his own favorite poet, a man to whom Joe bore a distinct visual resemblance. "Ginsberg wrote his own bit to 'Ghetto Defendant,' but he had to ask us what were the names of punk dances," remembered Joe, "and I said, 'Well, you got your slam dance.' He just did it on the spot. It was good."

"He wanted to get the Clash to back him on a record he was going to make, but he ended up on our record instead," said Kosmo. "People have said that he was Joe's lyric coach on that record, but I think that's a bit overplayed." "I asked Ginsberg for a word once," said Joe. "But it was just one word." In fact, Ginsberg remained in the studio for another week, collaborating with Joe not only on further lyrics but also in providing backing vocals as the Voice of God.

For the third Clash album in a row, Paul Simonon took lead vocals, this time on "Red Angel Dragnet," inspired by a topical local story: on New Year's Day 1982 Frankie Melvin, one of the red-bereted Guardian Angels, a voluntary alternative police force organized by Curtis Sliwa out of his home in the Bronx, had been shot dead by a cop in New Jersey. "It was in the papers at the time," said Joe. "The shooting of Frankie Melvin—it was a big

You're the greatest poet in America, Ginsberg: give me a word. *(Bob Gruen)*

scene. For some reason, back at the hotel I'd run out of writing paper and I only had Iroquois envelopes. I wrote the lyric down the middle of the envelope and it started to flow, so I continued to write the lyric round the edge of the envelope, in a spiral. I ended up writing round the edge of the envelope three times. The next day, I said, 'Look, Paul, what do you think of these lyrics?' I remember him moving the envelope around and around, to read the lyrics. He was looking at me out of the corner of his eye, thinking, Has Joe flipped?" The song makes reference to Travis Bickle, the Robert De

Niro character in *Taxi Driver*; Kosmo Vinyl delivers the Travis rap, "Some-day somebody will come and wash away all the scum . . . ," and at the end of the song also provides Travis's "One of these days I'm gonna get myself organized" line.

These were the big set-piece songs for the new record. The other tunes were also strong: "Inoculated City"; "Atom Tan"; "Car Jamming"; "Over-powered by Funk," which featured a rap from Futura 2000 and Tymon Dogg—who was again in New York—playing piano; and the wide-screen "Death Is a Star," the final song on the new album, which featured the lines "Make a grown man cry like a girl / To see the guns dying at sunset." As Joe explained, "It's about the way we all queue up at the cinema to see someone get killed. These days, the public execution is the celluloid execution. I was examining why I want to go and see these movies, because deep in my heart I want to see a man pull out a machine gun and go blam, blam, blam into somebody's body."

Topper was amazed at the production line that Strummer–Jones (Why not alphabetical? Mick: "It sounds better, Rodgers and Hammerstein is like that") became: "When you look at all the vinyl we released in five years: an album a year, one a double, one a triple, we didn't even take Christmas off. [Afterward] Joe said that there were only so many songs he could sing and write. He'd written himself dry. Every time we came up with a song Joe had to write lyrics for it."

There were more songs: "Cool Confusion," "First Night Back in London," "The Beautiful People Are Ugly Too," "Kill Time" and "Walk Evil Talk," a spacey piano-based free-jazz mood piece. Mick again wanted to use them all on a two-disc set, but Joe was insistent it be a single album: he had discovered that in New York record stores the sprawling triple-record *Sandinista!* was essentially unavailable, having gone out on an abortive mission to buy a copy for Eddie Garcia. When Mick Jones presented the group with what he considered to be the final tapes at the end of January, the guitarist's vision of the fifth Clash studio album ran for sixty-five minutes and contained seventeen songs. Joe refused to accept the record, calling it a "home movie mix." "Mick, I don't think you can produce," he told his songwriting partner. "You bastard. I thought you were my friend," came the reply, according to Joe.

Although Don Letts was not present in Electric Lady, his long experience of working with both Joe Strummer and Mick Jones, in film and later in music, gave him a unique insight into the way they interacted creatively: "Mick was the sugar on the pill. People don't like it too hard and direct, they like the pill to be sweetened. Mick contemporized Joe's eternal message. Mick was the melody man, the music man, and he would keep it contemporary. Joe reminds me of those guys that were on horses when everyone else was still riding around in cars, and I found that an admirable quality, but it was Mick that dragged it forward. The things that Joe says are things that have always needed to be said, but you have to say it in a way that's going to entertain the people. So I think Mick was a crucial foil to Joe. Because if Joe was doing those lyrics without that music, I think people would have turned off. Mick can come up with a melody faster than anyone I've ever seen in my life, but I guess Joe would have been quite instrumental in squashing some of what he later called Mick's middle-of-the-road tendencies and making them harder."

"I don't remember the vibe at Electric Lady being overbearingly intense," recalled Kosmo. "I really wanted a single record, because I firmly believed that a great group had to be able to do that. Everyone already knew that 'Straight to Hell' and 'Rock the Casbah' were great. But Joe could always be swayed; he could understand where people were coming from. He never had a problem seeing the other person's point of view, to his disadvantage sometimes."

With the new record still a work-in-progress, it would not meet the end of January delivery date. But there was no time for debate: Joe and Mick had to run from a mixing session at Electric Lady to a car to take them to a flight to Tokyo for their Far Eastern tour, due to begin in the Japanese capital on January 24. "Me, Mick and Joe went from New York to Japan," said Kosmo. "We got to JFK fifteen minutes before the flight, getting on the plane as the doors were closing, by the skin of our teeth. They thought it was hilarious." The others flew into Tokyo from London.

On the way from New York, Mick and Joe took a vow not to behave in the colonial manner of so many other Western music acts in Japan— specifically, they would not treat Japanese women as geisha girls. They settled back and enjoyed the long flight, their repose assisted by the relaxing hash cakes they had ingested as the plane took off. Yet it was a surprise that the reception at Tokyo airport approached Beatlemania, fans thrusting gifts

RAT PATROL OVER SOUTH EAST ASIA & AUSTRALASIA

1982

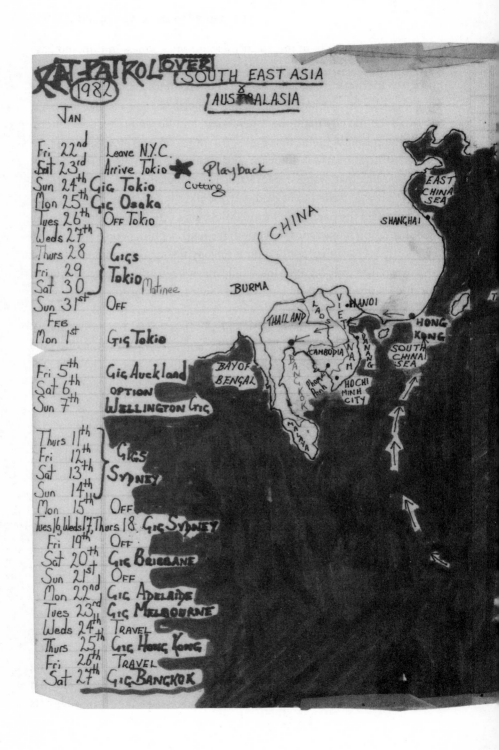

Jan

Fri. 22nd	Leave N.Y.C.
Sat 23rd	Arrive Tokio ★ Playback Cutting
Sun 24th	Gig Tokio
Mon 25th	Gig Osaka
Tues 26th	Off Tokio
Weds 27th	} Gigs
Thurs 28	Tokio Matinee
Fri. 29	
Sat 30	
Sun 31st	Off

Feb

Mon 1st	Gig Tokio
Fri 5th	Gig Auckland
Sat 6th	OPTION
Sun 7th	Wellington Gig
Thurs 11th	} Gigs
Fri 12th	Sydney
Sat 13th	
Sun 14th	
Mon 15th	Off
Tues 16, Weds 17, Thurs 18	Gig Sydney
Fri 19th	Off
Sat 20th	Gig Brisbane
Sun 21st	Off
Mon 22nd	Gig Adelaide
Tues 23rd	Gig Melbourne
Weds 24th	Travel
Thurs 25th	Gig Hong Kong
Fri 26th	Travel
Sat 27th	Gig Bangkok

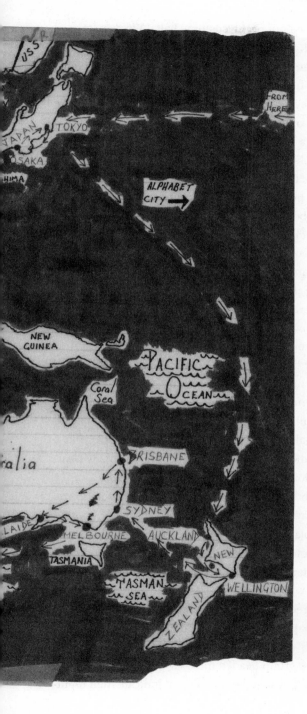

RAT PATROL OVER SOUTH
EAST ASIA AND
AUSTRALASIA: Joe's personal
map of the 1982 tour, his version
of the dates not always according
with reality. *(Lucinda Mellor)*

into their hands as they stepped out of the customs hall. "We were treated like part-time Western gods. It was a bit frightening," said Joe.

Mick's first significant memory of arriving in Tokyo was of him and Joe standing in the lobby of their hotel, asking a Japanese member of the touring party for the weed that they had expected on arrival. Instead, they were told that in the entire country of Japan, with its stringent and punitive drug laws, there was no marijuana to be found. Mick and Joe simultaneously burst into tears in the hotel lobby, prompting their aide to also start crying, in sympathy and shame at his failure to come up with the goods; he volunteered to personally take the next flight to Thailand to score weed for the group. They told him not to bother, and—probably for the first time—became a virtually spliffless operation for the eight days they toured the country. As the drama was played out in the hotel lobby, out of the corner of a weeping eye Mick observed something more disturbing: in the background Topper Headon was banging the head of his girlfriend, Donna, against a metal door. Joe received several letters from Japanese fans, among them one that began: "Hello Joe, how are you? I hope you are all right. I was very worried to see you crying in your hotel . . ."

Aside from the humor of this vignette, the response of the two Clash members to their aide's bad news tells a more serious story of the extent to which their nervous systems were frazzled by the exhaustion of their work—not only on the new album, but in general. The relentless upward drive of the last five and a half years was catching up with them, with a vengeance. This was a time when it was paramount to stay extremely clear-sighted, but the collective vision was growing increasingly muddy.

The Clash kicked off their first tour of Japan on January 24 in Tokyo. Why had the Clash never played the country before? Because of another Clash edict: they would not play in Japan unless the audience could stand up, which was expressly verboten in the culture. Even for the Clash the audience was allowed only to stand at their seats. But this compromise was enough for them to go ahead with the dates. "[The aide] liked us for having stuck out for that," remembered Kosmo. "'These are men of principle!' We got tons of coverage in the papers for that. Even the television news was there."

Taking the bullet train, the group headed for Osaka, where they played two nights. Pictures of Joe and Mick on the train do not indicate men reputedly at severe odds with each other: as the train thunders along, snow-capped Mount Fuji in the background, they look extremely happy. "There is a certain amount of concern about the new record, but I don't know if it's dominating Mick's or Joe's thinking," recalled Kosmo. "There's time to take a break. We were in a hotel room and Joe and Mick were in some dispute about the new record, but I said, 'There's a whole city out there. We should go and enjoy it.' It was fun, Japan. You're on at 6:30, 10:00 p.m. and you're done. You can go out." Back in Tokyo, they played four more dates—not a strict adherence to Bernie's edict of seven nights in a major city, but the closest they could manage.

Pennie Smith traveled to Japan to photograph the group. Just before the Clash was supposed to leave Tokyo to fly to New Zealand, Joe called her to his room. She found him surrounded by gifts from fans—dolls, carvings, clothing, even a samurai sword. "I don't know what to do," he said to her. "I can't get them all in my suitcase." "You'll have to leave some of them behind," was Pennie's solution. "How can I do that?" said Joe. "They've got them specially for me." The next hour was spent stuffing the mountain of presents into plastic bags, which were assiduously taped up and checked in at the airport, ensuring a hefty excess baggage bill for Joe. Before they left for the airport, Pennie photographed Joe with the samurai sword he had been given. Arriving in New Zealand, the Clash was subjected to a four-hour delay at immigration, a result of Topper's recent drug bust in London.

On February 5, playing in Auckland, the group were shocked by the presence of a large contingent of local skinheads, many adorned with Nazi eagle insignia. The next day, a Saturday, Kosmo was out in the town when he bumped into Joe, carrying a ukulele he had brought with him on the tour. "I've been downtown busking," he said. "How'd you make out?" "Terrible."

After shows in Christchurch and Wellington, the party left New Zealand for Australia; this leg of the tour opened with a seven-day stint in Sydney, at an art deco cinema with a tin roof, useful for boosting to a stifling degree the heat of a baking summer. The group was booked into an exclusive hotel in the center of the city. "We checked in at the same time as the Kinks, who arrived at the same moment," remembered Kosmo. "Before they'd finished checking in, we'd been checked out. We were kicked out of the hotel—something to do with girls' underwear and Charlie Parker played very loud. The cases didn't even make it to the rooms. We were told we had to leave."

A hotel was found in the funkier confines of Sydney's Kings Cross, a red-light district. In Australia Joe continued to not smoke weed. He began to speak of getting himself fit for action, and there was mention in press reports of Joe's "cult of the body": he'd get up at six in the morning and go running, and spend time in his room lifting the TV set up and down as though it were a set of weights. He had a moment of passion with a female journalist, and would absent himself from interviews to make visits to Sydney's gorgeous beaches. "While Mick was talking to *The Australian*, Joe would be in the sea," said Kosmo. "I'd be saying, 'He'll be back in a minute,' thinking I've got another journalist coming up in forty-five minutes."

Joe loved Australia, with its vast expanse of landscape, sea and blue sky—until the group came up against the downside of "God's Own Country." One night, Aboriginal land rights campaigner Gary Foley came onstage in Sydney to rap about his cause during a dubbed-up version of "Armagideon Time." Afterward Joe and Kosmo took Foley back to the hotel for drinks in the bar. Previously the bar staff had been friends with the Clash and their entourage; after this they continued to serve them but stopped engaging in any conversation. A hitherto amicable maintenance man at the venue told Kosmo Vinyl that Aborigines were "like dogs, mate."

There was another drawback. Under pressure from the record company the group agreed to work on the album in Sydney, attempting to mix the tracks at a local studio each night after the shows. But their ears were still ringing from the stage sound of that night's gig—nothing sounded right. "After the show in Sydney we'd go down and mix the album. But, of course, that sucked as well," said Joe. After a couple of nights this plan was abandoned. This lack of progress only compounded the mutual tensions over the record. The Clash made a political move, having dinner with Paul Russell, the boss of CBS Australia. It had just been announced that Russell was moving to London to replace the retiring Maurice Oberstein as head of CBS in Britain, and they needed him on board. Despite their rebel posturing, the group was ever capable of being pragmatic.

In tropical Brisbane, the capital of right-wing Queensland, an Aborigine dancer joined the group onstage; then he came back to the hotel for dinner with the Clash, his presence causing a great upset with the staff; while there he received a phone call that his home had been smashed up during his stage performance. Joe wrote a lyric about it, which was never completed; part of it ran "In Queensland state / they eat aborigine steak . . ."

After shows in Adelaide, Melbourne and Perth (so hot that Joe collapsed onstage from dehydration), they were on another plane, heading for Hong Kong. Here they were again joined by Pennie Smith. Her task? To shoot the cover for the new album. The idea was to use this futuristic Asian city's vivid locations and neon Chinese calligraphy as a backdrop. The record company had asked her to shoot in color: they wanted this fifth Clash record to be a commercial album. But the mood at the February 28 show hardly set the tone: mass fighting between Chinese and expatriate Britons in the audience broke out several times, and Joe had to stop the show twice: "We've come all this way to play and all you want to do is fight." The Hong Kong show was a downer: let's move on to the next setting, the final show in Thailand, and do the record sleeve cover there, was the verdict.

When the Clash arrived in Bangkok for their March 3 date, they were amazed that "This Is Radio Clash" was the number 1 record in the country. Soon they learned the chart position was completely bogus, an edict of the promoter.

The venue was an old cinema, with a crowd of locals and a few Westerners. All public entertainment in Thailand was obliged to begin with a performance of the national anthem. Accordingly, the Clash would have to dump their Ennio Morricone theme music and stand to attention while this was played. When Kosmo passed on this information, Joe—misunderstanding what he had heard—flew into one of those "quick rages" that those around him had seen so often. "How the fuck are we going to learn the Thai national anthem in fifteen minutes?" he demanded furiously. Nonetheless, this final date of the Clash's Asian tour was a resounding success. By the third number, "Safe European Home," the audience had rushed the stage. A great night.

Afterward the group stayed in Thailand for seven days on a rare holiday. Kosmo Vinyl had secured them a deal in a new hotel development outside the city, which created a problem for Topper Headon: after being clean in Japan, he'd started using heroin again in Australia. Now, stuck in the Thai countryside, where he had imagined he would easily score, he went into withdrawal. All he wanted to do was get back to London so he could connect

> HONG KONG
>
> ICED WATER - DAMP ROCK ISLAND
> FEEL A CHILL OR DISEASE
> PAPER LEAFLET FLUTTERS TAKES
> HOURS TO FALL TO THE FAST MOVING
> PAVEMENT—ARE WE UP OR DOWNTOWN ?
> FACTORY HERE IS A FLAT ELSEWHERE
> SAW WORK IN THE WOMENS FACES
> SAW A CROWDED HOME A ROOM
> CRAWLING WITH TROUBLE ONE DAY
> SOME RICE MORE WORK all curiosity
> about the WORLD LONG SINCE
> BURIED UNDERNEATH THE WORKLOAD
> FEEL SOME DREAD BRITISH HAND
> HERE —SOME ANCIENT REGRET
>
> HYATT REGENCY ⊕ HONG KONG
> KOWLOON, HONG KONG

The complexity of Hong Kong fired the poetry and anger
inside Joe's soul. *(Lucinda Mellor)*

with some heroin. Although others around the group recall Joe giving
him a hard time over this, Topper claimed to have no recollection whatsoever. "He probably was, but I was too obsessed with scoring and withdrawing. The humidity was horrendous: withdrawing from heroin, it was
like my arms and legs weighed a ton. I knew we were doing the photo shoot
for the album cover but I was ill and I had to get home. Joe probably was
giving me a hard time but I was oblivious to it, which probably made his
mind up even more. But the Thailand thing was really the first warning
I had."

The picture session took place the morning after the Bangkok show. It
had to be quick as Topper was booked on the next plane back to London.

SOME DEED CLOAKED IN TRADE
THAT BROKE THE CHINAMANS BACK
MY FIRST REACH IS FOR MY LONG
FORGOTTEN BOOTS AND TO PUT THEM
ON THIS I DO BOOTS FOR WAR BOYS !
BOOTS ARE FOR WAR
       PEOPLE WEAVE LIKE
FLY EATING PLANTS INSIDE
TENEMENT OF TENEMENT UNSeen
     girl combo has long
     black hair grandma's Fan
flutters Flames, chefs, dance
with NEON SEWING HANDS
TATOO CANDLES LIGHT THE PARLOURS

HYATT REGENCY ⊕ HONG KONG
KOWLOON, HONG KONG

What the drummer didn't realize was that in Thailand Joe was coming to the conclusion that Topper had to go. "I've walked into rooms where the Clash were staying," said Pennie Smith, "and thought, 'This doesn't feel right,' but I'd never witnessed open hostilities. When I saw it all break down was round the time of the shoot in Thailand. It literally somehow dissolved before my eyes. There was no longer the same clump of people I knew in front of me. It was like doing pics of a new band. I thought, 'I've got to construct this thing in front of me,' and before I never had. Something had gone wrong. It wasn't an argument. There were a few snipes at Tops." "It did start to drag us all down, Topper's drug thing," Paul said to me.

There were good times in Thailand. A group outing to the bridge over the river Kwai satisfactorily ignited the ensemble's sense of cinematic romance; there were tae kwon do boxing sessions; fueled on the local Tiger beer, Joe and Kosmo danced on a bar with the establishment's girls. Out with Pearl Harbor in the local streets, Paul bought a snack from a food cart. The next day he was in hospital in agony, diagnosed as having a twisted colon, an emergency operation suggested as the only solution. (Eventually, Paul's supposed twisted colon was established as having been a severe case of food poisoning.) As Mick sat in Paul's private room with him, he was impressed that Joe arrived with a local Buddhist monk, ostensibly to pray for Paul's well-being. Instead, the monk took off his robes and disappeared into the room's shower. Then he left. Under Joe's guidance, further monks appeared; they also took off their robes, showered, and left. Later the group learned that becoming a monk was a way of avoiding national service in the army, and the monasteries in which the monks resided were not known for their hygiene facilities. "Joe brought all these monks in. He was totally into it," remembered Pearl. "He was learning. Joe was always learning and exploring. He wasn't interested in being cool all the time. He was definitely interested in exploring."

Back in Britain, after meetings with Muff Winwood, it was decided that Glyn Johns, the stellar producer who had worked with the Beatles, the Who, the Faces and the Rolling Stones, should be asked to remix the record. Only Bernie, Kosmo and Joe were at the initial meeting with Johns; the sessions would take place at the producer's own studio in Warnford, West Sussex. Glyn Johns, who neither drank nor took drugs, had no truck with all-night studio sessions: he worked regular daytime hours. Joe was there at the kick-off on the first day, at 11:00 a.m. Mick arrived at 7:30 in the evening and was confronted with myriad changes and deletions of ideas to which he had personal attachments. Glyn Johns had the rejected tapes hanging around his neck like a tie. "That's my work," Mick complained.

Although he disagreed with all the changes, he reluctantly went along with them. The vocals for "Know Your Rights" and "Should I Stay or Should I Go" were rerecorded. "Everything about them clashed," remembered Gaby of this time. "You've got strong personalities who can't back down. Mick was very fixed. Joe could appear more charming, but he wanted it the way he wanted. Strong personalities, who lose the same vision, means trouble."

In London, the film director Stephen Frears offered Joe a substantial film role as a gunman in his upcoming film The Hit, costarring John Hurt. Frears said Joe was keen to take the part, but that "the others would kill me." Instead, he suggested an impressive new actor, Tim Roth, whom he had seen on TV.

On April 2 the news broke that Argentina's fascist junta had invaded Britain's Falkland Islands, a desolate rocky outcrop in the midst of the icy south Atlantic. The response of Margaret Thatcher was to dispatch a "task force" toward the islands. Before what became the Falklands War, Margaret Thatcher's Conservatives had been fifteen points behind the Labour Party in the opinion polls; a year after the victory in the Falklands she won a further election, setting the political tone in the United Kingdom for the rest of the decade. Joe responded to this war by personally changing the title of the new album to *Combat Rock*. After the British navy had sunk the *Belgrano*, an Argentinian troop ship stuffed with young recruits, a furious Joe wrote a poem that he called "Falkland Rock."

EXOCET! EXOCET!
TWO ELECTIONS TO WIN!
FIRE AN EXOCET!

HAWKER HARRIER! HAWKER HARRIER!
THE POLLS LOOK BAD!
SO CALL A HAWKER HARRIER!

SIDEWINDER! SIDEWINDER!
THE VOTERS ARE WATCHING!
LOAD A SIDEWINDER!

A TASK FORCE! A TASK FORCE!
GETS THE PEOPLE IN THE STREETS!
A FINE TASK FORCE!

SEVEN HUNDRED DEAD!
SEVEN HUNDRED DEAD!
WE ESTIMATE PUBLIC TOLERANCE!
AT SEVEN HUNDRED DEAD!

"Know Your Rights," the first single off *Combat Rock*, backed by "First Night Back in London," was released on April 23. Three days later the Know Your

Rights tour was to open in Aberdeen. But then took place one of the most extraordinary events in the complex history of the Clash: Joe Strummer went missing.

The disappearance was a setup, a Bernie Rhodes scam to hype up demand for tickets for the British tour, which was not selling out. Bernie issued a typical press statement: "Joe's personal conflict is: where does the socially concerned rock artist stand in the bubblegum environment of today?" Joe, said Bernie, had "probably gone away for a serious re-think." What Bernie had suggested was that Joe should disappear to Texas, to stay with Joe Ely; Bernie was adamant that Joe should go on his own, leaving Gaby behind, and call him every day. "He couldn't stand me," said Gaby. "He was weird with all women. Kosmo didn't like me either. They all knew I could be passed off on some level as a dumb blonde and I had Joe's ear— they were nervous around me. Joe always needed a sidekick and it had become Kosmo. Maybe I was in the way."

As though he had decided to show he really was his own man and not in thrall to his manager, Joe adopted an alternative strategy. He would vanish of his own accord, not telling Bernie where he was, and he would take Gaby. He really would disappear. He called his mother and told her not to worry about what she would hear about him. Then Joe and Gaby took the boat train to Paris on Wednesday, April 21.

"I had a friend who lived in Paris," said Gaby. "She had a little flat in Montmartre. As she lived with her boyfriend she gave us her place. On the third day we were at a restaurant and someone was talking to me and Joe gave me a furious look, to stop me talking about why we were there. I was pickpocketed, all our money was stolen and Joe got cross and told me I should go home—I didn't. I didn't have a passport or money. I had to go to the British embassy and they gave me travel documents. We just immersed ourselves in being Parisians for a few weeks. We went on a little tour of Paris. I had a beret and we traveled on the Métro with copies of the newspaper articles about Joe being missing. After a while he grew a beard and had an army jacket, a disguise: the Clash was well known in France, Paris particularly. Joe took me to every museum and all the places every famous writer had ever mentioned. Rimbaud was his real hero. We ran the French marathon. Both of us. I came last in the race. We had a lovely time."

It was a classic romantic act. Would a pile of Joe's clothes be found on a

Joe and Gaby after running the Paris Marathon. Gaby
finished last. *(Richard Schroeder)*

beach somewhere? (There was a brief rumor that his body had been found
in the River Clyde in Scotland.) In the real world, was Joe simply in hiding
from all the pressure, worried and angry about Topper and fearful of the reception that *Combat Rock* would receive? In Britain the last Clash album
had been savaged; now, having seized the reins on *Combat Rock*, the creative judgment of the increasingly mysterious Joe Strummer was about to
be held up to public and critical scrutiny.

On May 14, while he was still in Paris, *Combat Rock* hit the shops. To a fantastic reception. It was loved by the music press, especially by *NME*, whose earlier love for the group had seemingly turned to hate. *Combat Rock* raced up the British album charts to number 2. In the United States it was similarly adored.

A twenty-three-date U.S. tour was planned to start on May 29 in Asbury Park, New Jersey. The consequence of canceling it, with the financial penalties that would be incurred, would be to plunge the Clash into bankruptcy. Bernie Rhodes's piece of pop-manager Svengali-ism was about to blow up in his face. But the Clash was also scheduled to play a one-off date on May 20, at the Lochem Festival, outside Amsterdam. As news of Joe's disappearance was by now common currency, tickets for the event were not selling well. Through a stroke of serendipity a Dutch journalist mentioned to the Lochem promoter that he had seen Joe Strummer in a bar in Paris. The producer immediately called Kosmo Vinyl, who phoned Gaby's brother Mark. He gave Kosmo the name of Gaby's girlfriend in Paris. Kosmo immediately flew to Paris. That evening he walked into a bar where Joe stood, drinking. Kosmo looked at Joe, saw his beard. "Fidel!" he laughed. They sat down and discussed the matter in hand.

The next day, Tuesday, May 18, Joe and Gaby returned to London. Now Mick, Paul and Topper learned that Joe's initial disappearance had been a Bernie scam, one that had landed them in serious financial hot water. They were not pleased: further fuel was added to Mick's distrust of their manager. They would go ahead, they said, with the Lochem show in two days: their fee was to be $75,000, which was urgently needed to pay the British tour's cancellation costs.

Lochem was not the Clash's finest hour. The publicity surrounding Joe's disappearance meant that it was by no means sold out, but the group still demanded their $75,000, about which they were immovable. By the time they arrived at the festival site, the promoter could not help but observe that they all seemed off their heads, notably Topper. The liberal drug laws in Amsterdam were attractive to the Clash, who on the way to the festival had already spent an hour or so in the city's coffee shops, sampling the finest hash and weed. For Topper they were a disaster; before heading to the festival site he had scored heroin and coke. Prior to the show, as Joe checked out his appearance in the dressing room mirror, Topper removed it and laid it down flat, dumping a load of cocaine onto it, which he vacuumed up into his nostrils. Joe was furious.

Like a Shakespearian portent, when they hit the stage a violent storm blew up. After a few numbers Joe stopped the show, demanding the promoter come onstage. "Your security are attacking my fans," he berated him. Joe then invited the fans onstage, until the Clash was surrounded by five hundred of them. A similar number was also sheltering from the horizontal rain beneath the stage. By the end of the set the stage was sagging dangerously.

"We did the show in Amsterdam," said Topper. "I didn't know, but they'd obviously had meetings about the state I was in and said, 'We'll test Topper in Amsterdam.' What a place to test a junkie. So I got stoned there. As far as I was concerned everything was normal. When we came back to London, I said, 'Right, catch you guys later, I'm off.' They said, 'No, we're having a meeting.' I said, 'All right, tell me what happens in the morning.' But they told me I had to come to it."

The four group members and Bernie Rhodes convened in the front room of Paul's basement flat. As though it was his pattern, Joe Strummer pulled the trigger. "You're sacked," he told Topper Headon. "Mick was in tears," said Topper. "I was in tears as well, but Paul was on Joe's side. The decision had been made and that was it." When Topper asked who would replace him on the American tour, they announced they had a replacement waiting in the wings—none other than Terry "Tory Crimes" Chimes, the original Clash drummer. It was beginning to feel like an extraordinary rock 'n' roll soap opera. Bernie Rhodes had been invited back, so why couldn't anyone else be? "It was obvious Joe wasn't just a spokesman," said Topper. "He was obviously the one that had made up his mind. Which was why later on he said that was the biggest mistake he made." ("I wouldn't have sacked anyone," said Mick.)

Topper tried to throw himself a lifeline. Leaving Paul's flat, he walked round the block, in a daze. Then he had an idea, and went back. "Listen. Why don't I come on the tour? You take Terry Chimes along with us. I won't go on any pay, and I can drum, and if any of you even suspects that I'm taking drugs you can sack me and send me home."

The other group members would not go along with this. They suggested they would not formally announce that Topper Headon had been sacked: an announcement would go out that he was suffering from "nervous exhaustion" and that Terry Chimes was sitting in. "They said, 'We're not sacking you. If you've got your act together when we come back then you're back in the band.' I went away, and once the Clash went out of my life I realized how important they were to me. So I started to clean up."

But shortly thereafter Topper was devastated by an interview he read with Joe in which the Clash's singer said that Headon had been sacked from the group because he was a junkie. "I read it and I'm in London, and people saw me and thought, 'There's Topper. He's just been sacked.' Up until that point I'd never injected drugs, but then I thought, 'Well, that's it. I'm out of the group. I've got nothing to live for anymore. I might as well start injecting.' I went downhill from there. I don't think Joe could have dealt with it in any really different way. But I don't hold it against him. I admit I lost track of what was going on, but I think we all did. Everyone was fucked up, whether it was drugs or drink. Joe was singing anti-drugs lyrics and I was nodding out on the drum kit behind him."

Gaby says how adamantly against the consumption of cocaine Joe was. Yet Topper is quite clear that from time to time Joe would snort up a line or two of the drummer's coke stash, principally as fuel to keep himself going. "They said it wasn't OK for me to do heroin and cocaine," said Topper, "but they were doing cocaine, drinking a lot, smoking a hell of a lot of dope, and so it was a bit of a mixed message. By the nature of the beast, heroin makes you isolated, so I never saw that coming. It was madness. We were all knackered from nonstop working. There were so many people around the band using. Joe was anti-drugs, but he did them."

Much of the decision to chuck Topper out of the group, thereby breaking up a classic four-way partnership, seemed to come from the man whom Joe had brought back to save the Clash seventeen or so months before. In 1999 Joe told Gavin Martin: "Bernie said, 'He's a junkie, he has to go.' Ignorance ruled the day. We knew nothing about heroin." In January 1988 Joe spoke to Richard Cromelin of the *Los Angeles Times*, who asked him if Topper Headon could have continued to function in the group. "Yeah, considering what happened straight after that when everybody I bloody knew in London was on smack. I think we could have. But then we were ignorant. It was like hoo hoo hoo, the big heroin, horse. I didn't know anything about it. It was only after we fired Topper and my friends began to go down like flies. Now most of my friends in London are in Narcotics Anonymous. They can't even have a glass of wine. Just cigarettes and coffee. It's forever.

"I never liked heroin," he added. "I never even took it. I might have smoked it once in Holland. I remember the bloke said, 'Zis next joint has the heroin in it.' I took like a show puff, the one where you keep it in your mouth. And that was the only time I ever got really near heroin."

Especially in the light of the sacking of Topper Headon, you come to realize that there is something about the *Combat Rock* sleeve that seemed to reveal a fuller story. On the cover shot, with the group astride that Thai railway track, Joe is to the rear of the other three, with his hand over the right side of his face, squinting at Pennie Smith's camera lens with his left eye. People looked for all manner of meaning in this, rather like they had at the shot of Paul McCartney wearing no shoes or socks on the Beatles' *Abbey Road* cover. Joe told me he was simply trying to focus his nearsighted eyes. But perhaps this image of Joe did have a hidden meaning: could it not simply indicate that Joe Strummer was unable to see things clearly anymore?

anger was cooler

1982–1984

Topper Headon's belief that Terry Chimes was already waiting to re-place him was incorrect. It was not until five days before the U.S. tour was scheduled to start that Chimes received a phone call from Bernie Rhodes: the manager asked Terry to meet him in Marine Ices, just up the road from the Roundhouse. "Being Bernie, he couldn't say, 'Would you like to come and play drums with the Clash?' He said, 'How much are you earn-ing? Would you like to earn three times as much?' I thought, This is the man that paid me £100 to make one of the great albums of all time and he's trying to tempt me with money. 'Bernie, tell me what is this about?' He said, 'We need you to do a tour with us.' I knew nothing of Topper going. I said, 'I'll let you know. Give me a few hours.' I went home and phoned Mick. Mick said, 'Well, we couldn't have Cozy Powell with us, could we?' I said I felt more like discussing it with the band rather than Bernie. But Mick said, 'Oh no. Bernie handles business.' I think he was afraid to dis-cuss it.

"I said I would do it. Mick said, 'I bet you haven't got any of the albums, have you?' Which was quite right. I didn't know the stuff." Some twenty-five songs had to be learned almost instantly. To complicate matters, Paul had already gone to the United States. "So it was me and Joe and Mick re-hearsing. Joe played the guitar and Mick played bass. We went through the songs and I learned them roughly and in the end we got there. It was all right. I wrote it all down, had it in front of me on paper onstage—you know, how many verses each one had. Bernie complained that when I turned the page to see what the next song was, he thought I was reaching for a tomato sandwich. But it was all right. We did it."

In tune with a then new current of thought that celebrated physical fit-ness, Joe would continue to harp on throughout 1982 about the Year of the Body; when he was at home in London, he went for runs most mornings along the canal at the top of Ladbroke Grove, up the road from his new rented flat in Portland Road, Holland Park. But at the same time he was once again hammering away at spliffs, as well as spending most evenings down the pub or staying up until dawn in bars when on tour. Aside from a natural inclination toward alcohol-induced altered states, you couldn't help feeling that this sensitive—though certainly hedonistic—man was attempt-ing to obliterate something deeply discomforting within himself. In the parlance of the early twenty-first century, he was "self-medicating." Had he disliked what his unconscious had shown him when he had stopped smok-ing weed and hash in and after Japan? A consequence of the consumption of ceaseless joints is that when you sleep you hardly dream at all—your dream-state emerges instead in your stoned waking hours. When you stop smoking, however, your dreams soon return with a sometimes frightening vividness and ferocity. Dreams, of course, are necessary for psychological balance. But, as Joe admitted to Terry Chimes, you might not like what you see in them. "He wanted to give up spliffs. He told me that when you give up spliffs you dream a lot, and he hated dreams, so it was hard. He tried not smoking, but then he had a lot of dreams."

When the Clash had played at Bond's, I noticed that the Gramercy Park bedrooms of Joe and Paul each contained row upon row of Nature's Plus brand vitamin bottles, all mega-strength—the yin, presumably, to the yang of the bottles of Rémy Martin that each man also had on display. By the time Terry Chimes had returned to the group, the quantity of vitamins had only increased. "Joe was fit—he needed that for his physical work onstage. But he took a ridiculous number of vitamin pills. I'd say, 'What the hell is all that? You can't need all that.' I would say, 'If you're eating a good diet, why do you need all these vitamins?' He'd say, 'Oh, we're doing extra-hard super-work so we need extra help, and these vitamins will do it for us.'"

As he had with the Rémy Martin, Joe now was balancing out his slow-release megavitamins with large amounts of beer. "I remember him drinking a lot of beer in '82," said Terry. Although the deep depression that the drummer had observed in Joe in 1976 and 1977 was still apparent, he didn't feel that it was in any way alcohol-related. "I think that's just the way he was, with or without alcohol."

Still a vegetarian, Joe sometimes seemed to approach his relationship with his fellow occupiers of earth with the passive zeal of a Hindu priest. On one occasion he seemed to be taking his inspiration from the title of that early, unrecorded Clash song "How Can I Understand the Flies?" "I walked into his room," said Terry, "and he and Gaby were standing there with pillowcases, trying to get the flies out of the room without killing any of them. The windows were open, but every time they shooed one fly out another two would come in. They'd been doing this for hours. They said, 'We don't want to kill any flies.' They say artists have got no kind of logic."

Since the return of Bernie Rhodes something inside Joe, powerful and urgent, had pumped a driven energy back into his previously wavering spirit, and snapped life and leadership back into him. Perhaps it was the recognition of some wonderful truth within himself. Or simply a question of wanting to get the job done. But was he surrounded by the right allies? Perhaps because of the spontaneous and divisive warlordism that Joe had injected into his personal relationships within the Clash since seizing control over *Combat Rock*, he found his own allies—his co-conspirators, more like—within the group's crew, where he was far less likely to encounter dissent. "We used to get on very closely with our road crew that we had a long time, like Johnny Green and Raymond Jordan, and people like that," said Joe to me. "We didn't live above them as I've seen some groups doing. We were equals. We'd go out to drink together. When we were on tour we'd stay in the same hotel as much as possible. I think that was good because it keeps your feet on the ground. Kosmo became almost the fifth member of the group—in some ways he was its conscience."

Someone who was a true and sincere ally was Sean Carasov, an intelligent twenty-two-year-old who handled the Clash's merchandise on tour and whose father had disappeared out of his life twenty years before. "Seeing as I didn't have a dad or brother, Joe was like both to me," he told me. "I was

closer to Joe than to [Mick or Paul] and did a lot of drinking and philoso-
phizing and hanging with him. When I went to America with them on the
Combat Rock tour it was almost like he acted as my own personal tour and
pop culture guide." I felt Sean—eight years younger than Joe Strummer—
allowed Joe's father–brother role in his life to color his observations with regard to the group. "Mick doesn't have the genius. Joe was a genius. Mick
was a very talented musician, and could come up with an amazing song like
'Should I Stay or Should I Go,' but he got teased a lot."

"Joe was taking control at that stage," Terry Chimes pointed out. "I don't
know why. He'd lay the law down on certain things, and he would be bossing Bernie around, which he wasn't in the early days." Between Mick Jones
and Bernie Rhodes he noticed a different energy: "There was a bit of tension between the two of them. I just remember Mick getting angry with
Bernie now and again."

On May 29 the American tour to promote *Combat Rock*—officially known
as the Down the Casbah Club tour—opened with two nights at the
Convention Hall, in Asbury Park, New Jersey. "I don't think we played a
good gig after Topper was fired, you know," Joe said to me. "It's the whole
thing with chemistry—you've got four blokes who make a decent racket, so
don't change it. That's the moral. Don't tinker with it." He later amended
this view, conceding that maybe there had been one good show, at Asbury
Park. But he was wrong: the group was steaming.

For their new *Combat Rock* world, the Clash had adopted a stage look of
exaggerated machismo, blurring the lines between Vietnam vet and juvenile delinquent street gang; some fifteen years before it became fashionable
on the high streets, they were wearing militaristic camouflage clothes, the
sleeves torn from their jackets and shirts at the shoulders. Prior to the New
Jersey shows, the new image led to the group being mistaken for British
soldiers on their way to the Falklands War. Joe had had his hair shaved off
at the back and sides into a semi-Mohican, an adaptation of the cut adopted
by the Robert De Niro character Travis Bickle in *Taxi Driver*. "Joe wasn't interested in looking handsome, he was interested in creating an impact, so
it worked for him," said Terry Chimes. Joe unsuccessfully tried to persuade
the drummer to have the same haircut, citing how aesthetically pleasing it
would look onstage, with the drummer seated directly behind the singer.

The Clash's preoccupation with visual style earned them criticism from those unconcerned about it. "Although he might not have a lot to say," Joe said to me, "Paul certainly had a lot to do with the image of the group and the stance. He was really the physical embodiment of what the Clash was. It wasn't me or Mick or Topper, it was Paul. And he became the role model for countless thousands of young men. I think you have to come up with some type of glamour. You are stepping on a stage after all, you are putting on a show. I very much like the feeling of changing out of my street duds and the transformation from being an ordinary person on the street into a rock 'n' roll performer. I think it was really important. I don't think we'd have got across to as many people if we'd just worn cable-knit sweaters and baggy corduroy librarian trousers. To me it's all part of the glamour of it." It can't be denied, however, that there was something odd about the latest haircut: whereas Joe had always been the master of the subtle detail, this look was very obvious. Yet if the delicacy had been removed from the latest album, why shouldn't it also be from Joe's appearance? For many American fans of the Clash their abiding image of the group resides in Joe's *Combat Rock* Mohican look.

Perhaps inspired by this new militaristic tone, someone at the first show threw an M80 onto the stage. The firecracker, containing a small amount of dynamite, blew a chunk of flesh out of Joe's leg. Onstage on this part of the tour, Joe presented a cartoon version of himself, ranting to the masses, dismissing established American acts with a sneer—as he did to the crowd in this oceanside town: "How'd ya like the London fog outside? We imported twenty-two thousand tons just for you—we figured we'd show Styx and Foreigner how to do it right." In the United States such simplistically expressed viewpoints seemed to work. More than anywhere else, it was in America that Joe Strummer really did become synonymous with the Clash, boosted by his position as group singer—ignoring the fact that Mick Jones had sung on the Clash's first U.S. hit single, "Train in Vain," and was the singer on the song that would be their next hit, "Should I Stay or Should I Go," released on June 10. "Rock the Casbah," the single that followed in the U.S. market, would rise to number 8.

"A tension had crept in that wasn't there before, a tension between Mick and Joe," said Terry. "Joe was always uneasy with our success. We were playing to very much larger audiences, which is what he always wanted, but what do you do with all that money? How do you be a rebel when you've all

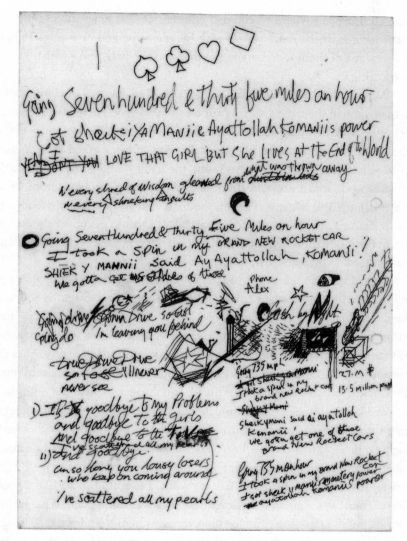

Found within one of Joe's many plastic shopping bags were these lyrics—an early stab at "Rock the Casbah"? *(Lucinda Mellor)*

this money coming in? Joe struggled with that. One of the ways he dealt with it was to meet lots of people and sign lots of autographs and hang out with normal people. But when you are on the road with a busy schedule, that wears you out, and you can never get to them all. So I think Joe had put himself in a place where he couldn't win. He wanted to be successful, sell more records, reach more people with his message, and he wanted to talk to every one of them individually, pat them on the back and say thanks for supporting us.

"Mick seemed to be enjoying the success, and Joe was uncomfortable with anyone in the band enjoying success in that way. There was a tension between Mick being a little bit more pop-star-ish and Joe feeling that the success is poisoning the purity of our mission. If Mick asked for a special meal to be cooked and sent to his room, the hairs would go up on the back of Joe's neck, and he would think that sounds like someone from Pink Floyd talking. But when you are on the road, and you want some food and you're hungry, it's OK, you can do that. But Joe would get upset about that kind of thing. Paul just got on with his job. One got the feeling that Paul was on Joe's side rather than Mick's."

Joe told me later about this hazard of touring. "That scene in *Spinal Tap*, my favorite film, where he's complaining about the sandwiches, is serious. We didn't do anything as stupid as that, but it's in the ballpark. You become so stressed out. This is why I think rock and opera singers have tantrums: so many things are demanded of you you've got nothing left to give. There's no stopping the demanding, and you overboil. You start complaining that the smoked salmon doesn't fit the bread, and throwing a fit about nothing."

Joe was simultaneously intimidated and infuriated by Mick's magnetic drift into a vortex of arcane musical and cultural information with seemingly no limit. "Musically he didn't like Mick making lots of weird noises," said Terry. "He had these boxes that guitar players have that make funny noises and it always frustrated Joe. He wanted to sound more like Chuck Berry. There was a gig in America when Mick was doing a lot of his funny sounds, more than usual, and Joe ran over and put his hands on the strings to stop the noise. There had always been a bit of tension but he'd never actually physically stopped Mick from doing it. Mick was very unhappy afterward: 'He actually put his hands on the strings to stop them.' I thought, 'Oops, that's a tricky one.' I was acutely aware of the tension between them going up a gear that night."

Not that Joe didn't have trouble with his own instrument. On tour he would always have with him some sort of singers' snake oil, usually a blend of honey and lemon, to lubricate his voice. "Anyone want to try this?" he would ask all and sundry. "It tastes like old underpants juice."

Although Joe's conscience seemed to Terry as troubled as ever, his sense of humor remained undiminished and was often at its most acute in a public arena. "Often I would be onstage, and he would say something to the audience, and it would make me laugh my head off. I remember one gig, a very big hall: off the cuff without any preparation, Joe said, 'You there at the back by the door'—and there are dozens of doors—'there's a light switch. Can you turn the light switch on?' So the guy on the lights puts the houselights on, ten megatons of houselights come on. Yet everyone's looking round, like there really is a light switch at the back. Joe has a chat with the audience, then he says, 'Turn the switch off again now.' The audience are all looking back, thinking, 'Where's this switch?' as the guy in charge of the houselights turns them back off. Stuff like that you can't imagine anyone else doing. Joe always felt very strongly that every concert should be unique. That was why we did different songs every time and he'd get guests coming onstage. He liked that you never knew what was going to happen."

The Down the Casbah Club tour headed south, playing Atlanta, New Orleans, Houston, Dallas and Austin. After the Houston show, after much drink had been consumed at a party by the hotel pool, Kosmo began giving Mohicans to beautiful long-haired girls. As he stood there with one of them, half her head sheared, clippers in his hand, her husband arrived with a gun. In Austin Don Letts filmed a video for the next single, "Rock the Casbah." "I remember when we were doing the 'Rock the Casbah' video," said the director. "There was something going on. They've all got their urban military-style combats on, and Mick comes out in a pair of red long johns. Mick's a skinny man; he had on red long johns and Doc Martens boots. He looked like a fucking matchstick. There was some problem between him and the rest of the guys, and Mick was going 'Fuck you.' And he looked really stupid. I had to pull him aside and say, 'Mick, you might be mad at somebody, but when people see this video they're not going to know that. What they're going to say is, "How come they've got a matchstick man in the band?"' I eventually convinced him to wear the combat gear, but he was still pissed off, so he wore this mask. Except it turns out that the mask looks quite cool and at the end of the video Joe whips it off him." At the time MTV was a fledgling cable network and had just started broadcasting: when "Rock the Casbah" was added to its playlist, the video assisted immeasurably in cementing the position of the group in the United States, and Joe's image as leader and personification of the group. After Austin the tour headed for the West Coast: on June 10 in Los Angeles, they played the first of five nights at the Hollywood Palladium. On opening night, Bob Dylan—always such an influence on the young Woody Mellor—and his family had a section of the balcony set aside for them; and musical progress continued as Bob's son Jakob was awestruck by the group's performance. "It changed my life. I was twelve and it was the most exciting and ferocious thing I'd ever seen," he said later. "The combat boots were flying everywhere. I knew, in that moment, that I had to be in a band."

Back in Britain there were almost two weeks off before the beginning of the U.K. leg of the tour. Joe Strummer's belief in the Year of the Body was undiminished: he insisted that members of the crew join him on daily runs. "He decided we were out-of-shape losers," said Sean Carasov. "He said we'd got to be a lean-mean-fighting-machine. Luckily I'd been on the running team at school. He would stick us all on a minibus at eleven a.m. and drag us running around the Serpentine in Hyde Park, coughing and snorting, a bunch of pack-a-day smokers." These runs were followed by re-hydration sessions at a Notting Hill pub.

On July 10 the British Down the Casbah Club tour kicked off with two nights at the 4,300-capacity Brixton Academy—the Brixton Fair Deal, as it was then briefly known. Despite the internal tensions noted by Terry Chimes, the positive energy that was being sent out remained on an unparalleled level, as the group painstakingly but painfully attempted to climb up the evolutionary ladder to enlightenment, concretizing the ineffable. In his *NME* review of the Brixton shows, Richard Cook really "got" how extraordinary the Clash had become, and why they were having such an enormous worldwide impact:

> Every one of perhaps twenty songs was dealt out with surly, scorched-earth bravado, spilling accounts of suspicion and untempered wrath; purpose in every turn. It's all overcome by Strummer's breathtaking conviction . . . The most persistent memory is of Strummer, two fingers pressed against his face, eyes half-closed in concentration, taking the hardest course through "Armagideon Time." I say we need this anger, no matter how romantic it may be. I say this antidote to romantic despair is necessary. The Greatest Rock 'n' Roll Band in the World. That doesn't sit so badly after all.

Stripped for action in a militant style, the Clash's "combat rock"
posture led to the group's being mistaken for soldiers in the United
States. (*UrbanImage.tv/Adrian Boot*)

Playing in Inverness, only forty miles from the Mellor family home at
Bonar Bridge, the Clash made a group outing to the battle site at Culloden,
where the English army had massacred the Highland clansmen. "The
Clash went to Culloden to ask forgiveness for the ancestors' sins," said Jock
Scot. When they played Newcastle City Hall on July 14, Mark Cooper was
there to write an article for *Record Mirror*. "In the dressing room there

seemed to be the usual arrogant, macho rock 'n' roll stuff going on, every-one a bit grumpy," he told me. "But in the early hours of the morning, alone with Joe in his hotel room doing the interview, he seemed this sad, lonely figure, confused with life, Hank Williams playing on his ghetto blaster in the background. I felt sorry for him." There were dates around the country, from Scotland in the north down to the south coast of England. At the Brighton gig a pair of beautiful models, Daisy Lawrence and Tricia Ronane, turned up backstage. Daisy's entire purpose was to get off with Joe; instead, she found herself going home with Mick Jones—they would be together for the next eight years. This was the first time Paul met Tricia—five years later they started going out, subsequently marrying.

The Clash played an additional date at the Brixton Fair Deal, attended by Mick Jones's father, the only time he saw his son play with the group. It was a good thing he seized the moment: when the Clash played the second of two nights at Bristol Locarno on August 3, the final night of the U.K. tour, it would be the last time Mick Jones would ever play with the Clash in Britain.

Six days after that final British date, the Clash was again in the United States, racing through the steamy summer heat of the American rock 'n' roll heartland. In late August, just after Joe had turned thirty, they were in Manhattan, playing two nights at Pier 84 in pouring rain, before crowds of eight thousand. Jamaican reggae star Gregory Isaacs opened on the first of the two nights, but didn't turn up for the second show. Allen Ginsberg performed again with the Clash, on their second encore "Ghetto Defen-dant." "Mister Allen Ginsberg," Joe announced, pointing a finger at him as he emerged from the wings and went into his section of the lyrics. "Feeling completely relaxed in the situation, Allen chanted his own verses in re-sponse, as he had done on their *Combat Rock* album," said Allen Ginsberg's biographer, Barry Miles, whom the Clash had once asked to manage them. Afterward the group spent the night with the great poet, touring the hottest clubs and bars. Also tagging along was Marc Zermati, Paris's king of punk rock. The vibe, he felt, was "good, but not as good as with Topper. There was an argument between Mick and Joe regarding Topper. Topper is the linch-pin of the Clash, an incredibly talented drummer. But there's always been a kind of little ego, maybe, in the attitude of Mick. Joe complained to me sometimes about it. I would ignore it because I know Mick from a long time. He was living his dream of being a rock star, so you have to respect that, and Joe did not understand. Joe was going, 'Me, I am a poor rocker.'

"How can you do a band without strong ego? That's like impossible. The band was a complete organic unit: you can't get people out of it and put them in just like that. I like to be their friend, because for me it was a total rock 'n' roll dream, because their attitude was a real rock 'n' roll attitude— great attitude with the fans."

This brief American tour was scheduled to end in Boston on September 8, but they were made an offer they couldn't refuse. At the end of September the Who were to undertake a tour of American stadiums, at the time intended to be their final shows ever. Pete Townshend offered them the opening slot on eight of these dates, the opportunity to perform before audiences of eighty thousand, and vastly expand their own drawing power, a consciously altruistic act on Townshend's part. "The Who were supposedly retiring at that time," said Joe's old roommate Kit Buckler, who had once worked as publicist for the Who. "Townshend was handing the Clash their mantle. He was deliberately positioning them to take over from the Who."

A number of dates were slotted in for the Clash, beginning on September 25 at JFK Stadium in Philadelphia. On before the Clash in Philly was David Johansen, once the singer with the revered New York Dolls, now a terrific solo act. He and Joe seemed cut from similar blocks of stone. "When I was a kid, I was a street kid," he told me, "and I got that same vibe from Joe. We spoke the same language, a certain kind of innate intelligence about the beast, and feeding its face. All those fuckers want to make you a star, but you're nothing more than a racehorse to them. Joe had an awareness about that corporate structure. Making music and not being co-opted by it is an art form in itself. And Joe had that art. The people who can walk that tightrope are the ones who're interesting. He did it well."

The Clash's stadium shows with the Who were short sets—forty-five minutes, on-off, all the hits. Mick Jagger was in Philadelphia, allegedly nagged to go by his daughter Jade, a Clash fan. "Mick Jagger came in and talked to us," remembered Terry Chimes. "He said, 'Guys, when you've done one or two of these it's just the same as any other gig.' He was absolutely right because when we played Chicago, about three or four gigs later, Joe said to me, 'How many people at this gig?' I said, 'I think it's eighty thousand,' and he went, 'That's nothing!' We both laughed."

"It felt a bit like miming," said Paul, "because there were so many people there. The audience wasn't very close, so you didn't get the same reaction from them. It was fantastic, but everyone seemed a bit distanced from each other—in clubs the group and audience would feed off each other. You'd get more nervous in a small club because the audience were just there in front of you."

The Clash appeared on *Saturday Night Live* the next month, great for national promotion. The group insisted on using the main entrance to the studio at 30 Rockefeller Center on West 49th Street and mingling with their fans. As Joe explained, an attempt at punk-rock situationism somewhat backfired: "Waiting around at *Saturday Night Live*, somebody had the idea to stop in the midst of playing 'Should I Stay or Should I Go' and hold a ghetto blaster up to the mike and play 'Rock the Casbah.' Remember this is live TV. So the moment comes. I press the play button. Nothing comes out. I fling the blaster through the air—thank God, our roadie catches it before it brains a hapless audience member. We carry on. Reason for no sound from the blaster? That little piece of see-through leader tape at the front of every cassette reel."

The following week, the Clash played with the Who at New York's Shea Stadium, memorably recorded by Don Letts for the video of "Should I Stay or Should I Go," not yet released as a single outside the United States. Don's footage includes the arrival of the group at the stadium in an open-topped white 1956 Cadillac. October was not exactly the time in New York for traveling in a car with the roof down, especially one without a working heater. "I turned round to Joe and said, 'It's freezing!'" said Terry. "He said, 'Yeah, but we're going to look tough—we don't worry about cold.' We just put this face on for the camera. It was funny." Terry was puzzled by Joe's headgear, a raccoon-skin cap replete with tail, of the sort that was once known as a "Davy Crockett hat"—though Joe decided that his was "a Daniel Boone hat." "He looked at me and said, 'It's called style.'" (Or was it more like cowboys and Indians?) Joe also wore an antique fur coat, of the sort he had worn as a student at Central.

To the consternation of the Shea Stadium security guards, the Clash insisted that it should be business as usual when it came to fans: Kosmo waved literally hundreds of kids into the private enclosure. But, as the photographer Joe Stevens discovered, life was not so easy for those who had not purchased tickets. "Before the show Strummer and I are in the bowels of the stadium, exploring the place. Somewhere beneath home plate we discover a prison. There were eight cells and there's a black kid in one of them. They had locked him in for trying to break into the show. Strummer went and got him water and food. But it really freaked him out—added to his ideas of what the United States was really like."

In between further stadium shows, in places like Boulder, Colorado, and Oakland, the Clash continued to play dates on their own. At Carnegie Mellon University in Pittsburgh they performed an interweaving of "The Magnificent Seven" and "Armagideon Time," which they continued for the rest of the tour. In Mesa, Arizona, clutching his guitar and microphone, Joe leapt into a water-filled moat that separated the stage from the audience. Amazingly, he was not electrocuted.

When they opened for the Who for the last time, at the 120,000-seat Los Angeles Coliseum, Jakob Dylan again came, his second Clash experience that year. Taken backstage to meet Joe, he was speechless at meeting his hero, only able to mumble, "I really like your vest." "He took it off and gave it to me. I took it home and framed it," Jakob told Nigel Williamson for *Uncut* magazine.

On November 27, 1982, the Clash was booked to play the Jamaican World Music Festival in the tourist town of Montego Bay—ensuring an audience of vacationers as well as locals—at the grandly titled Bob Marley Centre, a cinder strip of flat land off the main north coast road. Apart from the thrill of playing in their adored Jamaica, they would benefit from a five-day holiday with their girlfriends. Among the other acts scheduled were such locals as Peter Tosh—who complained that the heavy tropical downpours had failed to fall during the set by the Clash, which his followed—and Black Uhuru. Also flying in for the festival were, among others, Aretha Franklin, the Grateful Dead ("By the way, if you don't like us, I've got the Grateful Dead in the wings and I'm going to bring them on. So you'd better shape up—now!" Joe threatened midset) and the Beach Boys, whom Joe had so loved as a teenager. As Bob Gruen wryly noted, Joe was extremely happy while in Jamaica, having swapped an expensive watch for a bag of pot worth about five dollars. Familiar with the island's top-grade smoking material, Joe and Mick had been delighted to discover another local specialty: psilocybin mushroom tea of an especially cosmic strength, useful for gazing at the sky and studying interplanetary transport networks. "The night before I had a wonderful time. We sat out in the audience on mushroom tea," said Mick. "Daisy and me and Ranking Roger, the [English] Beat's toaster. The Beat were playing as well. We watched all the groups, like Gladys Knight and the Pips. Real groups and total oneness through the mushrooms. Amazing. The great thing about that festival was it went on all day and night. It was fantastic."

In archetypal Jamaican soon-come manner, the festival's schedule overran chronically. Bernie Rhodes said the Clash would pull out unless they were immediately given $20,000: "Joe said: 'That's fantastic—I thought we were doing it for free.' In fact, we were getting $200,000." The Clash went onstage at around 4:00 a.m. "Ladies and gentlemen, all the way from Ladbroke Grove, London, England: Vuh Clash," announced Kosmo Vinyl, an identity check for an area familiar to many Jamaicans. "Good morning to you, if there is anyone out there," Joe greeted the audience, "and I know you can hear me back at the chicken stall over on the very far side there. So next year if they're going to have this beano, maybe they'll let the natives in for free," he suggested, before launching into "London Calling." The group made a selection from their songs that contained the most specific Jamaican influences. Though "Police and Thieves" was not included, the interblending of "The Magnificent Seven" and "Armagideon Time" was inspired, masterly. "I think it took us years before we could jam down on 'Armagideon Time,'" said Joe. "It was like jazz. I had a few licks I'd go back to. There was no plan. A bit of singing. Jam. Lovely. That's when we were really playing."

This, finally, was the last date Terry Chimes would ever play with the Clash, a decision he had come to himself.

In London Joe, Mick and Paul, with Micky Gallagher and drummer Charley Charles, both of the Blockheads, went into the studio to record with Janie Jones, the woman who had inspired the song on the first Clash album and who had been freed from a prison term. Joe had written a song for her with Mick: "House of the Ju-Ju Queen," produced by Joe, backed by a version of James Brown's "Sex Machine," was released nearly a year later under the name "Janie Jones and the Lash." "Joe paid for that with his own money, £14,000," said Janie.

On Christmas Eve 1982 the three Clash front men enjoyed a view of the Westway: Mick's nan Stella cooked Christmas dinner for her grandson, Joe and Gaby, Paul and Pearl, Kosmo and Sean Carasov, who arrived with a black eye; he had fallen off his bicycle drunkenly riding home after an evening with Joe at the Warwick Castle the previous evening. "Joe drank a lot then," said Sean. During the English *Combat Rock* tour, he recalled, there was a day off before a date in Bradford in Yorkshire; Joe decreed that he, Sean and Kosmo would be driven to it by Ray Jordan, stopping at each pub. Sean had become used to all-day sessions at the Warwick Castle, on the corner of Portobello Road and Westbourne Park Road. English pubs then opened at eleven in the morning, closing at 3:00 p.m.: the landlord at the Warwick would let Joe and his cronies sleep off their morning consumption on the pub's bench seats before it could legally reopen at 5:30. After officially closing at 11:00 p.m., he would lock the doors and Joe and whoever remained would continue consuming alcohol into the early hours.

After one such session, Joe decided he wanted to score some weed, wandering a few hundred yards with Sean over to a council estate at the junction of Westbourne Park Road and Ledbury Road, where a Jamaican hovered at the bottom of a stairwell. Joe handed him cash and the dealer said he would be back shortly, disappearing up the steps. "He's gonna run up there and disappear down the steps at the other side," Joe suddenly realized. "Here, you'll see." He led Sean round the block to where the dealer was running down the steps, to disappear away into the night. Seeing the slightly worse-for-wear pair, the man produced a blade, brandishing it at them, and rushed off. "It was as though Joe not only knew that was going to happen but wanted it to happen," said Sean, "as though he needed to have that experience. I was confused, but Joe was loving it. To him it was worth losing the money, seeing the expression on the guy's face."

Joe introduced Sean to the Ladbroke Grove world of Jamaican she-beens—illegal drinking dens featuring roughly constructed bars, the staff protected from holdups by chicken wire in which a small slot had been cut to accept money and dispense cans of beers. In these barely lit dives (often in basements), like the one run by reggae legend Alton Ellis at the top of Ladbroke Grove, the pair would stand and sway in the corners as the spine-jerking bass rumbled out of enormous sound system speakers; invariably they would be the only white people present. By contrast with the slumming element of himself that enjoyed the down-at-heel Warwick and shebeens, Joe Strummer—who moved with ease through different social worlds— was also very partial to visits to 192, an award-winning wine bar and restaurant, on Kensington Park Road, a block west of Portobello Road. In the Warwick Joe would be public property and it would be hard to hold an indepth conversation with him; at 192 he loved to perch on a stool at the bar and talk intimately for hours about matters of the soul; lubricated by bottles of "shampoo," as he would archly refer to champagne, Joe was only distracted by the beautiful girls who visited this watering hole (part of the attraction, he admitted to me), which was frequented by local participants in the film and literary worlds. With actorly precision, he would play the gallant, offering his stool to women who attracted his attention at this spot that was a sign of the increasing gentrification of Notting Hill. The area's substantial Victorian terrace houses, each once comprising myriad hippie bedsits, were now being bought up by the well-heeled and turned back into family dwellings. Joe was beginning to think maybe he should do the same. After all, both Paul and Mick owned flats in the district; Joe was pouring rent down the drain each week.

Joe and Gaby were still living in their flat above an antique shop in Portland Road in Holland Park. From Alex Chetwynd, the Salter family friend, Joe borrowed an early video camera, eventually thrown into a bath by the children of Micky Gallagher. Joe had made a short film, starring himself, Gaby and her brother Mark. Mark played a burglar, breaking into a house as Gaby lay in bed, shaking with fear. Joe came to her rescue, fighting him on the streets. The brawl moved into the Kentucky Fried Chicken on Holland Park Avenue. Suddenly the pair of them looked up at the menu board. "I'll have a chicken burger," announced Joe, the twist in the short film.

At the beginning of 1983 Joe phoned Alex Chetwynd. He had had an idea. Could he come round to the flat? When he got there, Alex was surprised by what he saw: the living room was painted black and it looked as though it was months since it had been given a clean; as well as an armory of ghetto blasters and recording equipment, the room was piled with empty pizza boxes, the moldy contents of some of them still visible. Now, over the inevitable spliff, Joe told Alex he wanted to make a longer film: would he help him? Already he had a title: *Hell W10*. It would be a silent thriller, shot in black and white, starring the usual suspects.

Around ten on a Saturday night in the middle of February that winter, I drove east on Holland Park Avenue, heading to a party. Pulling up in heavy traffic by the tube station, I saw a clump of people on the pavement. There were film lights and someone was wielding a 16-mm camera. Then I saw Joe, and others I recognized: Gaby, Sean Carasov, Kosmo. "Park your car," Joe shouted. "I need you." This was a shoot for *Hell W10*. "Here." Joe handed me a truncheon-like implement. "Go up behind Sean and mug him." Which I duly did. Several times. It didn't make the final cut. Nor would the movie see the light of day for almost twenty years; the making of its sound-track would have a disproportionate effect on the three-man front line of the Clash. "We loved doing that film but it is actually very boring," said Gaby. "Mick was supposed to be doing the music. He was doing all this hiphop stuff, totally different from what Joe was envisaging." "Joe didn't want the music Mick was coming up with for the film," emphasized Alex Chetwynd. "Their musical tastes were completely different at that point. They seemed to fall out over this."

Mick was unaware that Joe was displeased with what he came up with for *Hell W10*. "Maybe it was a bit too hip," he laughed. "I thought it was good. It was already on the cards by *Hell W10* that I was going to leave. Or something was going to happen. In rehearsals for the next album Bernie was on my case about what sort of record it was going to be. Which was really annoying. I said, 'It's going to be a rock 'n' roll record.' 'Yeah, but watch it.' So it was all starting." Around this time one heard that tensions between Joe and Mick were so great that they were communicating only by mailing songs to each other. Mick denied this: "He'd post me a batch of lyrics, but I'd bring Joe the tape once it was done."

In March Joe and Gaby moved into a terraced house he had bought in Notting Hill, at 37 Lancaster Road, a hundred yards from the West Indian front line of All Saints Road, suitably "street." Although he didn't have a driving license, Joe also bought a car, a twenty-eight-year-old green Morris Minor with a hot-rod engine modification—its big-bore exhaust woke up the town as it roared down the street. For the time being he gave it to Gaby to drive; it was also used as a prop in *Hell W10*. He also got his father a Volkswagen camper van which—as though a comment on their relationship—had the initials "WAR" on the license plate. "That was the nearest they came to any bond between them," said Gaby. But Joe wasn't a bad son: every month, to share his good fortune and help out, he paid money by direct debit into his father's account. Spending Christmas Day with Ron and Anna was an annual ritual for Joe and Gaby.

In April 1983 Joe again ran the London marathon, for charity, despite its being sponsored by the *Sun* newspaper, whose right-wing stance he had previously abhorred. When *Combat Rock* was released, Joe—far more of a pragmatist than he superficially appeared—had been prepared to be interviewed in Rupert Murdoch's huge-selling tabloid to promote the record and the Clash; this was not something of which Mick Jones approved. "That was the only marathon where he was an official entrant," said Gaby. "Previously he would just turn up and join in. It was also the only one he trained for, and it nearly killed him." Joe finished the course in a respectable time of 3 hours 20 minutes. "He was a fit guy," said Alex Chetwynd, who ran that marathon with him, "although I personally never saw him do any exercise. But he could definitely drink a lot. It's not easy to drink as much as Joe drank."

Shortly after the filming of *Hell W10*, Joe heard bad news. Topper was £30,000 in debt to a heroin dealer; if he couldn't come up with the money he was going to get his legs broken. Joe went with Alex Chetwynd to the Midland Bank on Portobello Road where he had an account, and took out thirty grand in cash. He handed it to Alex, asking him to stuff the bundled notes in his combat jacket and take them to Topper, who lived to walk another day. (Topper sent Joe a heartfelt letter of thanks.) Considering the circumstance of Topper's departure from the group, Joe may have been motivated by a sense of guilt. But in 1983 you could buy a sizable home in London for that amount of money. The Clash was now beginning to make very good money indeed, amounts that seemed to take a quantum leap with each album release. "One thing the Clash did," said Gaby, "was to pay high tax to continue to live in Britain. Joe could have taken off and become a tax exile. It would have been hypocritical but we could have done it. But he wanted to be in Ladbroke Grove. He wanted to be at the source of the dynamism of the movement he was involved in."

The Clash was about to contribute even more to the coffers of the British treasury. Early in April they were offered a startling half a million dollars to headline New Music Day at the second annual Us Festival, promoted by Apple Computer mogul Steve Wozniak, to be held at the end of May at the Glen Helen Regional Park in San Bernardino, California. (Van Halen were paid twice that money for headlining on Heavy Metal Day.)

With Terry Chimes out of the picture, they didn't have a drummer. Accordingly, the April 23 edition of *Melody Maker* carried an advertisement requesting a "young drummer for internationally successful group." After more than three hundred people had been auditioned, Pete Howard, a drummer from Bath, was given the job. As money had not been mentioned, Pete had a friend, Falcon Stuart, once the manager of X-Ray Spex, broach the subject with Bernie. Bernie was furious—not an auspicious start. Quickly Pete Howard appreciated that Bernie's response was par for the course. "It wasn't very happy when I joined them. But I didn't see Mick being a nightmare at any point. He made overtures of friendship, and indicated to me he thought I had some musicality he wanted to exploit. Joe was busy sniffing out any hint of muso-ness. Joe had a sense of humor, but when Mick was around there was a sense of 'that cunt over there.' Joe wants to be Bukowski, and Mick is stoned with Daisy all the time. Everyone seemed to be drunk. Joe would get pissed and start ranting. You could get close to Joe, but then he'd turn and use what you'd given him as something to beat you with."

After rehearsals, the group headed for warm-up shows in Detroit, Wichita Falls, San Antonio and Tucson, before arriving at the festival site on Saturday, May 28.

There was the habitual intricate set of ironies involved with the Clash's appearance at the Us Festival that one had come to associate with the group, not the least of which—considering their huge fee—was that they played beneath a banner that read CLASH NOT FOR SALE. But what took place before the event carried almost as great a significance as the performance by the Clash itself.

Seven hours before they were due onstage, while the Australian group Men at Work were playing, the English act threw a fit: they held a press conference at which they declared they would not perform that evening unless Steve Wozniak donated $100,000 to send impoverished Latino youth of East Los Angeles to summer camp. At the press conference Joe was the spokesman; he had been infuriated when he discovered that tickets for the event, which he had been assured would be pegged at $17, cost up to $25; seizing his mood for a situationist prank, Bernie Rhodes thoroughly wound

him up—hence the press conference. ("They didn't have a fully formed political agenda," said Pete Howard. "They thought anger was cooler.")

As so often with his capricious and quite evident contradictions, it is
fascinating that yet again Joe largely should have been given the benefit of
the doubt over this, a tribute to the goodwill that he so often engendered.
For what was really clear was that this situation was full of shit. If the Clash
was receiving half a million dollars for their performance, why on earth
could they not have contributed some of their fee to the charity they were so
intent should receive a chunk of Wozniak's money? Their cash, Joe conveniently claimed, already had been earmarked for expenses in London.
While no one really fell for this argument, equally no one picked up on it as
closely as you might have expected. Perhaps everyone simply had been
worn down by the inconsistencies emanating from the group. Forced to
give in to clear blackmail, Wozniak eventually coughed up in the region of
$32,000, and the Clash moodily took the stage after having kept their audi-
ence waiting for two hours.

Immediately prior to the show there was another moment of drama.
"Bernie set up another press conference that he wanted us to do by the side
of the stage immediately before we went on to play the gig," said Mick. "He
wanted to get all the other acts to give some of their money. Joe was furious
at doing this a minute before we were due onstage. He went out and turned
his back on all the press, stood with his arms folded. So Kosmo grabbed
Bernie out to speak. Bernie held the press conference and Joe stood with
his back to them, wouldn't say a thing, completely disgusted."

The Us Festival audience of 150,000 was the biggest the group had ever
played in front of, larger than any of the Who stadium crowds. In the late
spring evening heat of southern California, irritable from the fractious day,
Joe proved anger really can be power: even though it was impossible for the
spectator to dismiss the element of corporate ritualization of rebellion, Joe
was in fine, hectoring form as he used his soapbox platform. He'd once said
that he took his energy for a show from the last person who caught his eye
as he stepped onstage, but now it was as though he had caught the eye of
an entire society. "All right then," he declared as he stepped to the microphone, "here we are in the capital of the decadent U.S. of A." Whether
from self-knowledge, masochism, or blind enthusiasm for the headlining
act, the audience responded with cheers to Joe's geographically imprecise

smear. "This here set of music," he continued somewhat ungrammatically, "is now dedicated to making sure that the people in the crowd who have children there is something left for them later in the centuries." (If that sounds an unusual preoccupation for Joe, there might have been something at the back of his mind; for Joe had a new influence in his life, something that often draws out strange undercurrents of previously repressed emotions and vulnerability in a man, something that can lead to radical decisions: Gaby had learned that she was pregnant, a child due at the end of the year.) And the Clash pounded into their first song, the inevitable "London Calling."

Joe no longer wore his hair in a Mohican, but had it swept back into a DA. He was dressed in a white sleeveless jeans jacket and white cotton pants; by contrast, Mick was in a silver-studded black jacket and red shirt; Paul wore a white T-shirt emblazoned with the first Clash album cover—available at the merchandising stand—and camouflage trousers. After the second tune, "Somebody Got Murdered," Joe returned to his theme, addressing the source of the wealth that had staged the event, and, again throwing away grammatical speech constructions, taking up the issue of American consumption. "I know the human race is supposed to get down on its hands and knees in front of all this new technology and kiss the microchip circus," he barked, before—as Joe would—delivering an unmentionable truth. "But it don't impress me over much that there ain't nothing but You Buy. You-make-you-buy-you-die. That's the motto of America—you get born to buy it.

"And," he added, with considerable prescience, nine years before the L.A. riots, "these people out in East L.A. they aren't going to stay there forever. And if there's anything going to be in the future, it's gonna be from all parts of everything—not just one white way down the middle of the road . . . So if anybody out there ever grows up . . . For fuck's sake . . . ," he snapped, before belting into "Rock the Casbah," their biggest ever hit in the United States. Does this make him a hypocrite? I don't think so. Joe was the personification of Carl Jung's view that all great truths must end in paradox—when I once mentioned that to him, he nodded with his customary sage glee, this man who, as Sean Carasov pointed out, was wired up differently to other folk.

Satire raised its head in his introduction to "Armagideon Time," with its theme of world starvation, as he referred to a faddish diet of the time—"The F-Plan Beverly Hills reggae song." A great performance, sweat running down his face; Pete Howard handled himself commendably on the reggae beat. "Lose five hundred pounds. Success guaranteed. Or your money back." Then he returned to scolding the Californian audience. "Bollocks, bollocks! You don't have to fake it. You're paying twenty-five dollars to be out there, so do what you like. Also a lot of you seem to have had speech operations: you can't talk or shout back. I need some hostility here. You know: *aaargghhh!* I need some feeling of some sort. Some collective, you know, Hey we're all alive at the same time. As it's Sunday tomorrow, I hope you'll join me in this . . ." And he ran straight into the Sunday service tones of "The Sound of Sinners," emphasizing the song's greatest line: "The message on the tablets was Valium."

Then—apart from throwing down the brief conundrum "The people on this stage . . . we're nowhere. Can you understand that?"—Joe seemed to decide to rebuke his constituency no longer. The Clash thundered through another seven songs, until they closed the set proper with an extraordinary version of "The Magnificent Seven."

They came back to play three encores. On the customarily epic "Straight to Hell" Joe seemed off-key, struggling with his breathing, as though his voice wasn't holding up. But the next song gave him a break, Mick Jones taking the lead on "Should I Stay or Should I Go"; without trying to force the symbolism, hindsight lends this an enormous resonance. But on the final song at the Us Festival, "Clampdown," with its references to the Three Mile Island nuclear disaster, Joe took off again in a stream-of-consciousness: "Nuclear power stations—don't kid yourselves—they ain't got any fuckin' idea! . . . A nation of boneheads. Bonehead has come to pass!" Back into the chorus. And off stage. This was the biggest live audience platform Joe Strummer ever had in his life. Having as so often made it hard for himself in the first place, he ended up using it very well indeed.

There was a scuffle as the group left the stage, an altercation with the DJ, who had started to play records, preventing the Clash returning for a further encore. Mick Jones and members of the stage crew exchanged punches, Mick giving a good account of himself, according to Kosmo Vinyl. "I got in a fight with some people at the end of the Us Festival," said Kosmo, "and Mick muscled in. He'd go down with you." "At the Us Festival me and

Mick weren't talking at all," said Paul. "But I saw a bloke hitting Mick, and took him out. It patched us up for the time being."

Chris Chappel, a friend of Mick, was backstage watching the show; Chris was Bruce Springsteen's tour manager and knew the requisite professional behavior in such circumstances: he hurried to find Bernie Rhodes to tell him about the incident. As at the Glasgow Apollo in July 1978, when Joe and Paul had been arrested, the manager of the Clash showed no interest. Then Bernie threw another agenda into the mix. "Anyway," he said, playing a hitherto unknown card, "Mick's not long for this group."

Meanwhile, Sean Carasov went out into the crowd with Joe, to check on the merchandising stall, Joe suggesting ways to better display the T-shirts. "There was a lot of mumbling about Mick, and you could tell that Bernie was lobbying to get Mick kicked out. Joe told me that Bernie was trying to figure out how to get rid of him. Mick was the rock star in the group and loved the festival vibe; the others couldn't give a shit. You could tell there was something going on—there was a bad vibe. Mick seemed oblivious to it. He was digging the festival thing.

"When they decided to work with Bernie again, I thought it was like that line from *The Godfather*: 'Keep your friends close, and your enemies closer.' There was immediate mistrust. I thought it was ridiculous what he was doing. The paranoia and megalomania from him was getting worse."

After the Us Festival the Clash went to Las Vegas for a brief break. "Bernie gave us a thousand bucks each and twenty-four hours to make our fortunes," said Mick. "So we all hit Caesar's Palace. I finally hit lucky on a slot machine in the airport departure lounge: fifty dollars on my way out." "I found myself walking along the Strip," said Joe. "It was pretty good. Then I started talking to Vietnam veterans who were drinking bottles out of brown paper bags. So I had an entertaining night."

That summer, Ron and Anna Mellor traveled up to Scotland to visit Bonar Bridge, the first time they had been there in twenty years. Harry and Margaret Gillies, the parents of Iain, Anna, Rona and Alasdair, went to stay at 15 Court Farm Road, looking after Lulu, a cat Joe had given his parents. Ron and Anna had a wonderful time, even managing a visit to Raasay. When they stopped at a tiny village called Clashmore near Dornoch, Ron had Anna take a picture of him standing with mischievous pride in front of the village's boundary sign, his torso deliberately obscuring the second syllable of the place name.

When Ron and Anna Mellor returned to Upper Warlingham from Bonar Bridge, Harry Gillies went to Glasgow, leaving his wife at Court Farm Road; she wanted to spend a few more days with her sister, she said. By now, Anna seemed to Joe's cousin Gerry King to have become "a quite solitary figure, and very fragile. She wouldn't cook anymore, and they would get pre-made meals." Six weeks later, back in Glasgow, Margaret Gillies died suddenly of a heart attack.

For the second time in two months Ron and Anna made the long journey to Bonar Bridge. At the burial another man, fifteen years younger and several inches taller than Ron Mellor, tried to claim Joe's father's position on the coffin. Ron elbowed him out of the way and took up his place.

But Ron Mellor was not well himself. In 1976 the Foreign Office had put him "out to pasture," as he described it, at the Public Records Office in Kew. Each weekday morning he would catch a train up to London Bridge station, then transfer to the tube for the journey to Kew in West London, a tiring, three-hour round trip every day. The work had its rewards: Ron Mellor was offered grateful dedications in the forewords of a number of books. After the extremely steep climb to Court Farm Road from the station, having poured himself a reviving glass of his favorite beer, Ron would sometimes theatrically pat his heart, parodying the effect the upward hike had had on him. Around the turn of the decade he had suffered a heart attack, but soon recovered. There was a history of coronary ailments on both sides of the family.

The Clash's inactivity earlier in 1983 had been blamed on an alleged reluctance by Mick Jones to tour. "We were just at the point when we had to give it another shove," Joe told me later. "There sometimes comes a time when you simply have to keep going." On the other hand, you might feel that the Clash's bill-topping appearance at the Us Festival indicated the goal had been achieved, and creativity always benefits from periods of lying fallow. Besides, Mick disputed the argument: "One of the things Bernie was saying was that I didn't want to tour. But that wasn't true at all. I wanted a different tour, of places we hadn't been. I thought this was a chance to go to somewhere like South America."

It seems clear it already had been decided that Mick Jones, the founder of the Clash, was to be fired from his group. But it was not Bernie who had come up with this. "Joe and I had been discussing it as far back as just after 'London Calling,'" said Paul. "I used to have screaming rows with Mick in the studio. It wasn't Bernie who wanted to do it. It was us. Bernie didn't even know it was going to happen. We knew we were cutting our arm off, but we felt it had to be better than it was."

Not that Bernie didn't play his part in the situation—in the middle of the summer he became incensed when, after presenting Joe, Paul and Mick with a management contract to sign, Mick demanded that his lawyer read it. While this may have seemed like nothing more than sensible behavior, Bernie wound Joe up about it, claiming this showed Mick thought he was above everyone else. It might also seem extremely naïve of Joe and Paul that they did not contact a lawyer for professional advice over this legal document—and that they didn't see Bernie's remarks were designed to make them feel angry. "The others signed it," said Mick, "so that put big pressure on me. Bernie said, 'Why don't you give your power of attorney to your solicitor. Then I can sort it out with him and you don't have to worry about it.' I temporarily did that. Then he went to the others and went, 'Look, Mick only wants to talk to you through his lawyers.' He got them all worked up. So they all started to get on my case. 'If he's doing that, he must have gone off his head into lawyer-land.'"

The simple fact is that one day in the last week of August 1983, Mick Jones found that—almost unprecedentedly—he had arrived before the others at Rehearsal Rehearsals, where they were attempting to write new songs. Then something strange happened. An unexpected visitor called by: Topper Headon. "It's weird," he said. "I was in Camden Town. I thought, 'I'll go and see the Clash.' I went to Rehearsal Rehearsals, and Mick was there. I saw Pete's kit, and I had a go, and we were jamming away. Then I said, 'I'd better go.' Mick said, 'Yeah, I don't know where the others are. I'm normally last.'"

Topper left. Mick went to a bookshop. When he returned ("Late as always," Paul said to me, the kind of mix-up that overstands the entire affair), Joe and Paul had arrived. "We want you to leave the group," said Joe. "What do you think?" Mick turned to Paul. "Yeah," said Paul. "I want you to go." "I put my guitar in my case," Mick told me, "picked it up, and walked out." Bernie Rhodes ran after him and pressed a check into his hand. "Like giving you a gold watch when you retire," said Mick.

"So I left," said Topper, "and after I'd gone the others turned up and sacked him, that same day. And he, like me, had no idea he was going to be sacked, which shows that Joe could be quite devious. I think the rot had set in before I went. They cut me out, but the cancer had spread."

"At the Hall of Fame," said Mick, "both Paul and Kosmo told me it wasn't Bernie who fired me. I was really surprised because I always thought it had been. Maybe it was the same thing as what happened with Keith [Levene] where there's a collective thought that everyone picks up on and goes, 'Yeah!' And then you're done," he chortled.

Mick acknowledged that he had not readily accepted the return of Bernie in 1981. "Joe delivered an ultimatum to me and the others, who were less resistant, that Bernie had to come back, or he's off. I was really in Bernie's face all the time after that. I didn't deal with it very well. I wish I'd handled it better. I was really not being nice. He was trying, and I was shouting at him. But I was so suspicious. Riddled with it," he laughed, "by that time.

"But when it happened it was horrible for weeks afterward. I felt I couldn't go anywhere. Walking around at the carnival that weekend was horrible, because everybody lived in the same area. Really fucking horrible. I grew a beard. Dyed my hair for a couple of days. I wanted to change my identity. It was traumatic. It took me ages to get over it. It took all of us ages to get over it. The whole thing. Now I look back and think it was all supposed to be. That's the way it turned out, and the way things are. Not so bad."

As the founder of the Clash, Mick acknowledged he had always perceived it as his own group. "So it was weird, being kicked out of your own group. Later I realized how pointless was the fuss and the pain that I went through over *Combat Rock*: no one really remembers now how high the hi-hat was or the cymbals. They only remember that it did really great, and everybody benefited from it. So all that pain was for nothing. The original is very contemporary. But the real record is better, so lasting. It turned out all right for everybody. I shouldn't have put myself through all that grief."

Kosmo Vinyl was in a greasy-spoon café opposite Rehearsal Rehearsals when Mick crossed the street from the studio and entered. "He said,

'They've sacked me.' It's one of those days you play around forever. I was shocked. He wore gloves, Mick, and he had his guitar in a case. He got in a taxi. Did I know they were going to sack him? No. But if Joe was here he'd say he'd been left no other option by me and Bernie. I can honestly say I did not know that Mick was going to get fired, but I would later say to myself, 'What did you think was going down?'

"My curse and my blessing is that I can understand both Bernie and Mick," Kosmo said to me late one freezing December night in the Dublin Castle on Manhattan's West 72nd Street, where he now lives. Significantly perhaps, he doesn't say "Joe and Mick." "I fall on both sides of their civil war. Civil wars have more atrocities and bloodlust than anything." As we talked "Death or Glory" came on the jukebox. "Speak of the devil and he shall arrive," laughed Kosmo, sadness in his eyes.

The news pages of the September 10, 1983, edition of *NME* carried a press release: "Joe Strummer and Paul Simonon have decided that Mick Jones should leave the group. It is felt that Jones had drifted away from the original idea of the Clash. In future, it will allow Joe and Paul to get on with the job the Clash set out to do from the beginning." The same edition carried a rebuke from Mick Jones: "I would like to state that the official press statement is untrue. I would like to make it clear that there was no discussion with Strummer and Simonon prior to my being sacked. I certainly do not feel that I have drifted apart from the original idea of the Clash, and in future I'll be carrying on in the same direction as in the beginning."

Is it not when Mick Jones leaves the Clash that the legend of the group is truly born? For now their story takes on every dynamic of life: betrayal, arrogance, art. A further problem was removed for Joe: although the egalitarian concept behind the cosongwriting credits of all members on the last two albums had been admirable, Joe had told Kosmo he regretted the Clash cowriting credit, because it diminished his and Mick's reputations as songwriters. "Joe was fiercely proud of his writing," said Kosmo.

The one fundamental flaw in the firing of Mick Jones was something no one seemed to have thought out, an indication of the corrupted thinking that lay behind this entire egregious act: with the exception of Topper's "Rock the Casbah," it was Mick who wrote almost all the music—getting rid of him was madness. "We didn't think," said Kosmo. "'Anyone can write a punk rock song!' That was our mistake." By dumping Mick, a problem may have been solved for Joe, as he perceived it, peering out of the narrow chink in his personal doorway that week. But another was about to be introduced. What the surviving members were as yet unaware of was that Bernie Rhodes believed he had a solution to this: he would take charge of the music. After all, his former cohort Malcolm McLaren had become a musical artist in his own right with hit singles like "Buffalo Gals" in December 1982 and "Double Dutch" in July 1983, as well as his *Duck Rock* album the same year.

Artistic development often comes at the expense of other areas of the personality: the requisite drive can have its roots in deep personal damage, the kind of painful experience that ultimately can deliver the gift of wisdom. As singer with the 101'ers, Joe had come to punk rock from a different direction than almost everyone else in the movement, a slightly older guy than the other players, and perhaps therefore more anxious about the passing of time. In firing Mick Jones, Joe committed one of those acts of amputation with which he seemed to have become almost comfortable. Mick was a man of the collective, someone who loved the idea of a community, a great idealist who valued loyalty. Like a lion with his pride (perhaps an apposite word), Joe also liked the idea of a gang—so long as he stood out as king. "I remember the day Joe sacked Mick," said Pete Howard. "I hadn't heard from them since we got back from America. Joe called me up. He's almost threatening—'I've sacked him. Are you with me?'"

A cross the world people were shocked by the departure of Mick Jones from a group in which they had invested a large part of their lives, and in whose apparently against-the-odds success they had taken much comfort. "When it did happen for me," said Marc Zermati, remembering when he heard about it, "it was the biggest catastrophe in rock 'n' roll history. That was the end of it, the end of rock 'n' roll. The last big rock 'n' roll band is the Clash. After that rock 'n' roll was just counterfeit. I was really fucked up and depressed about it. But then Paul asked me to choose. 'You have to choose: it's us or Mick.' I said, 'Sorry, it's Mick.'

"Suddenly everything falls apart, part of the rock 'n' roll story very often. I was expecting them to be more clever, as human beings, because Joe as a human being should have understood. But he wanted to be the leader."

When the Clash had played at Bond's, Don Letts had observed how much the emergent hiphop had influenced the group—most of all Mick Jones: "Joe could make the cultural and social connection, whereas Mick would make the musical connection, almost to the point where it was too much for Paul and Joe. Mick had a great foresight to see where contemporary sounds were going. They say he was driven out of the band for rock-star behavior, but I maintain that we need a bit of rock-star behavior. Who else is going to do it? Mick can be a difficult bastard. What did Joe say? 'Elizabeth Taylor on a bad hair day.' Though you can't fault Mick for trying to boldly go where no rock band had gone before. It was great when they did the reggae stuff and the hiphop, and the Latin rhythms coming off the street.

"In the Clash Mick didn't have any backup, whereas Joe did from Bernie. Bernie gave that madness some shape and form and made it seem like it was an intellectual decision. Joe was goaded on by Bernie, that's how I see it. It has to be said, that was one of Joe's faults—he could be directed by a manager, and also by women sometimes. He'd tell you one thing and then he'd go in the next room and somebody would say something that was the opposite and he'd be there, agreeing with them, and he'd hope that the two of you wouldn't meet."

Like Marc Zermati, Don Letts was obliged to personally feel the brunt of the Stalinist revisionism taking place. "When Mick got kicked out I was still in America working on *Clash on Broadway*. I got a phone call from Paul saying, 'We've had to get rid of Mick. If you are going to stay friends with Mick you can't really stay friends with us.' I felt really bad for Paul. Paul was obviously made to do this call. I said, 'Sorry, Paul, but the very fact you're saying that is a decision in itself. So if I don't see you for a while so be it.' We didn't speak for a while, and I stayed friends with Mick.

"It seemed like the sort of thing that Joe would always do anyway. Just as success is about to embrace him, he'd make a left turn and destroy it. I don't know what that was about."

Five years after Mick Jones was kicked out of the Clash I sat down with Joe in Notting Hill and he told me what he thought had gone on between himself and Mick. "I mean really, he was pushed out by a power struggle. Bernie convinced me and Paul that we should get rid of him. We went along with it. Because even Mick'll tell you he was being extremely un-cooperative and it was no longer a pleasure to see him. It was very difficult to get anything done. So we thought we'd try and carry on without him, which obviously proved to be a mistake."

Although the triumph of topping the bill at the Us Festival had been the zenith of the group's success, the shows opening for the Who appeared in Joe's eyes to have led to the disintegration of the Clash. "If there is a mes-sage in the music, it reaches beyond a kind of accepted gig format. It must somehow connect with the real life that people are leading. Stars do not lead real lives, and that's why I'm glad we came to a halt and the whole thing fell apart. Because I couldn't really see any future ahead of us if we were going to become like the Who. I watched very closely at those gigs at Shea Stadium and Oakland Coliseum and those places, because I could see in five or six years that would really be the only place we could expect to be at. That would be the definition of everybody's success. That's what you're doing this for. But I thought, Well, what is that? That's nowheresville! That isn't living. Standing there singing the songs while it got bigger and bigger toward the end, for some reason I began to feel worse and worse. It's to do with what those songs are saying. It was all right when we were part of the audience, part of a movement. Like in the Electric Circus in Manchester, somehow it was real. But once it became thousands of miles removed from that I began to freak out. It had become a parody of itself. Perhaps there's only a certain amount of times that you can actually play songs before it be-comes meaningless. Or kind of ridiculous."

In 1995 Joe expanded on the firing of Mick Jones in a conversation with his friend, the actor Keith Allen. "Do you regret that?" Keith asked him.

"Yeah, of course. You see I hadn't understood what the game was. The game was that Bernie had decided to become an artist. What I didn't spot that I should've spotted was that Malcolm had become an artist, releasing albums, and Bernie decided he wanted some of that. He knew he wasn't go-ing to get any with Mick Jones in the group, because Mick was the sort of musical director. Bernie stepped in and stupidly I allowed that to happen. I mean, that was the end. It's my fault about the end, definitely. But then maybe the idea had run its course."

———

On November 18, Gaby Salter gave birth to a daughter, Jazz Domino Holly Mellor. Having played the role of surrogate parent to Gaby's family, John Graham Mellor was now a father for real. But Joe himself was still being parented by Bernie, who had decreed auditions must be held to replace Mick. In October, weeks were devoted to this; at the auditions, aspiring rock stars played to rough backing tracks, a twelve-bar blues and a hiphop track. Those short-listed were called to Rehearsals a month later and their skills further tested. Meanwhile, Bernie sent Joe for singing lessons.

From hundreds of applicants a new "Clash" was formed. Nick Sheppard, formerly of Bristol punk group the Cortinas, was given the job at the end of October, and immediately found himself in the studio with Joe, Paul and Pete Howard. (Nick had met Joe many times, since they had first run across each other at the Roxy. In mid-August he had been in a pub on Holland Park Avenue when Joe had come in with Bernie and Kosmo. They had chatted. At the bar he clearly heard Kosmo saying, "He's gotta go, he's gotta go." He soon discovered whom Kosmo had been talking about.) Nick found camaraderie with Pete Howard: "Pete bridged both groups, the voice of experience: 'Wait until you meet Bernie.'" On December 10 this lineup was added to by Vince White, formerly Greg. (Bernie insisted on the more "rock 'n' roll" name. "You've a chance to reinvent yourself as a new man," said Joe, "like Gene Vincent and Vince Taylor—the bad guys.") From Southampton, Vince was a huge Clash fan, who had studied physics and astronomy at university. Insiders asked the question: Does it take two guitarists to replace Mick Jones? The intention was to take the Clash back to basics, largely performing the group's early material and new similar three- or four-chord songs. Reggae was banned, said Bernie. At first Nick Sheppard was even delegated to sing "Should I Stay or Should I Go." Most significantly, Joe would hardly play any guitar, Nick assigned the rhythm role.

"At first the second Clash was quite refreshing," said Paul. "Two new blokes. Exciting. New again through other people's lives."

"The early days were brilliant," said Vince. "We were a band rehearsing as a band, with all five members there. We'd go out drinking afterward. I went round to Joe's for Christmas. He was very warm. We got on really well. It was solid up to the point we left to go to America.

"But Joe did drag me over the café and say that Nick and Pete didn't want me in the band, and were trying to get me out. I'd just joined and they were already trying to get me out. Joe went, 'I'm rooting for you, and so is Bernie.' I imagine my arrival diminished their status in the group. I was a bit disappointed to see another guitarist as well. The relationship never got very warm between us." ("No one had said a thing about another guitarist until Vince arrived," said Nick. "Initially I didn't understand it. I found a tape of me, Paul, Joe and Pete on the new songs before Vince, an Afro-Latino song. It sounded very different because Joe was playing guitar: the force and presence that his guitar playing has, his vigor—his rhythm playing is fantastic.")

In the Lock Tavern after rehearsals, Joe justified his drinking: "Alcohol is a revolutionary drug: it makes you talk." Yet Vince noticed that at the constant group meetings ("About four a week," said Pete) Joe always would defer to Bernie: "He was basically the man in charge of everything. Joe would back up Bernie on just about anything. Paul and Bernie seemed to get on really well. But as it went on it was quite difficult for me, personally. Bernie picked on me a lot."

When Vince went round to Joe's that Christmas, he was puzzled. "There's a black boy cleaning the floor. The image doesn't sit right with the socialist rock 'n' roll star. It's like an old colonial's house. You'd get this food—fried egg and rice, some weird proletariat display. You'd eat it with champagne."

"We were involved in the sponsorship of a young Nepalese man," explained Gaby. "He worked for us for a few years, which allowed him to go to school and learn English and feed his family in Nepal."

To confuse matters, Mick Jones teamed up with Topper Headon, announcing that his lineup was the real Clash. At the insistence of Pete Townshend, Topper went into a drug rehabilitation program, though he quickly relapsed. Mick Jones's declaration that he was proceeding with his version of the Clash was little more than a scare tactic. After tickets went on sale for a brief "Strummer" Clash tour of the American West Coast in January 1984, Mick contacted promoter Bill Graham, informing him that soon he would be coming over with Topper as "the real Clash." Mick's lawyer promptly froze the earnings from *Combat Rock* and the Us Festival, which prompted Joe to write the song "We Are the Clash."

On January 19, 1984, the U.S. West Coast tour kicked off at the cozy Arlington Theatre in Santa Barbara, virtually a theme park of middle-class American values—hardly the hotbed of punk revolt and ferment you might have expected for a group allegedly returning to its revolutionary roots. New songs were featured: "Three Card Trick," "Sex Mad War," "This Is England" and "We Are the Clash." The tour included a sold-out crowd in San Francisco, a show at Long Beach Arena, and the final gig on February 1 in San Diego at the Fox Theater. In a revolt against the past, Joe—who now affected an orange crop—had opted to concentrate on his singing and performance; only on the first two numbers would he play guitar, leaving the instrument to the two new members. Like an unarmed gunfighter—or "like a frog in a microwave," as he himself described it—he would sporadically scrabble for his battered Telecaster, only to fling it past Vince's head to a waiting roadie a couple of numbers later. ("Every time he did that, I'd think, That's going to hit me one day," said Vince.) The group performed against a background of television monitors displaying video footage of suitably strident subject matter: scenes of police oppression and war movies were highlights. The shows were reasonably well received. In the *San Francisco Examiner* Phil Elwood commented: "It was a good concert although hardly of the gutsy, bombastic style of old. In his shouted, strident vocals and in his nonstop commentary, Strummer often becomes incoherent." "America loved it," said Nick. "We did forty thousand people in San Francisco. It had just come off *Combat Rock*."

Joe's interviews seemed like the rantings of someone who was slightly bonkers. In his ceaseless railings against Mick Jones, you began to sense that perhaps he did protest too much. In an article by John Mendelsohn for *Record* magazine conducted in Santa Barbara, almost half the quotes were from Kosmo, who seemed to have been selected not only to provide moral support but also to give Joe cues for his denunciations of the former Clash guitarist:

"We'd get some dates together for a tour, right?" asserts Vinyl. "We'd talk to Paul and he'd go, 'Yeah!' We'd talk to Mick and he'd just shrug."

"Or," snarls Strummer, "say he'd have to talk it over with his lawyer . . . I finally said, 'Go and write songs with your lawyer, and piss off!'"

"I had to beg him to play guitar," Joe said in another interview, "and he's supposed to be the Clash guitarist. It was like dragging a dead dog around on a piece of string. Insane!" Publicly there was an anti-drugs line. "I've smoked so much pot I'm surprised I haven't turned into a bush," said Joe. Doesn't this make you feel that Joe's railing against Mick Jones over his ceaseless spliff consumption was something of a projection? Besides, Joe had simply switched drugs, temporarily abandoning weed and hash (except when he didn't) in favor of heavy alcohol consumption. Later he confessed that this dictum over spliff consumption had been dictated by the manager: "That was Bernie's new regime. It didn't last long. After two weeks we were gagging for it."

"I went into the situation," said Vince, "thinking the Clash is a humanitarian band. They care about people. That's what Joe was always spouting on about—he's got this socialist thing going. But the reality is the complete opposite. There was a lot of bullying, and it was run more or less like any kind of corporation, with a very rigid political hierarchy.

"I don't think Joe really had a deep belief in himself. He didn't have that much strength of character. He was an artist, and absolutely brilliant. But he couldn't take responsibility, and so he passed it over to Bernie, who had complete control. Once Mick had gone, Bernie pretty much played Joe like a puppet. I'm not badmouthing Joe, because I do think he's a great guy."

But Bernie claimed to be fully aware of the fragility beneath Joe's bluster: "Joe lacked confidence in himself and I spent days and days trying to build him up. I knew the bit of Joe people loved. He wanted to be me. Later he would blame me, but he didn't own up to chucking Mick out."

Nine days after the end of the American tour, the Clash began a string of British dates in Glasgow. The fourth show in the tour was at Bristol's Colston Hall. I drove down with Billy Bragg, the opening act; his first album, *Spy Versus Spy*, and one-man Clash-type show had earned him huge acclaim—in a neat twist, he was managed by Peter Jenner. I had slightly contrived this outing in order to try to see what was going on. Bernie Rhodes had put a press embargo on the tour; when he saw me he made a wry remark about "stage-door Johnnies sneaking in." My first sighting of Joe came after Bragg's set when—shortly before the new Clash was due to hit the stage—I tried to use the backstage men's toilet. The door unlocked, Joe was in there, doing breathing exercises that sounded as though he were trying to expel his lungs through his nostrils. He seemed slightly sheepish. But the show was not at all bad, really quite exciting, even if somewhat one-dimensional. But Joe and Paul had spotlights on them, whereas the two new members were only lit from the back, making their ears stick out like Mickey Mouse's. Billy Bragg danced in the aisles during the performance. "You play those songs really loud and you can't avoid moving and dancing to them," he admitted to me. "I'd been saying rude things about them at gigs, calling them the Cash.

After their show Joe and Paul confronted me and I felt shameful. I apologized. As it was my first encounter with Joe it was very hard to do anything but show my affection and respect. I did tell him that if I didn't care I wouldn't have gone on about it.

"It's an unfortunate thing that people don't realize what his strength was. His politics were formed before punk, when he was a squatter; they came much more from that world of anarchy. He never stepped over that line to mainstream politics. I was dreadfully disappointed that the world was not changed by my buying Clash records."

The tour then moved into Europe for dates in Norway, Sweden, Germany, Belgium, Switzerland and Italy, culminating in a show on March 1 in Paris at the Espace Ballard.

The day before the concert in the French capital, Joe received terrible news.

A s Anna had told her relatives up in Scotland, she and Ron Mellor had spent a wonderful Christmas at Joe's new house on Lancaster Road. At the beginning of 1984, Ron was diagnosed with a gallbladder complication. An exploratory operation was scheduled for February 29. On the operating table, under anesthetic, Ron suffered a further coronary and died; he was sixty-seven years old. "He was a really giving man," said Gaby. "He had stopped going up to Kew by then and they used to send work down to the house. I think he lost the will to live as he needed outside stimulus and wasn't getting it." Ron Mellor's sudden death was a terrible shock to his wife. "She rang me that lunchtime," remembered her sister Jessie, "and could hardly speak. She was in such shock. It was so unexpected."

Alasdair and Iain Gillies and their uncle David Mackenzie traveled down from Scotland for Ron Mellor's funeral, losing their way in Upper Warlingham. When they reached the cemetery the service had already started. "The old man would have loved that, you coming late," said Joe with sad humor.

At the wake Alasdair and Iain separately noticed that next to a date on the kitchen wall were written three words that summed up Ron Mellor's gallows humor: "Heart attack continues." "You know what families are like," said Alasdair. "Unless you're actually in it, you don't know what's going on. Maybe Ron and Joe were so similar they were rivals. He wasn't a martinet, or Joe a rebel—it was more complex. He would take me on drives.

Any PRIVATE ROAD sign he saw he'd drive up. 'Let's have a look at this, shall we? I'm going to ignore that sign.' He'd drive in and look at the person's house. The afternoon of his funeral, in the back garden, Joe said, 'I wish I'd given him a chance to talk to me again. I lost my chance.'"

The night of the funeral the Clash was playing in Scotland. Joe left the wake to be driven to the airport, calling his mother later. "It was obviously a terrible day for him," Alasdair recalled. The grimness of the experience was only amplified by Joe's feeling that he had completely let his father down by having been away on tour when he had died, something that he expressed to me the next year. "I didn't feel good about it at all," he told me.

But why was the Clash show not canceled? "There was no leniency shown to Joe," said Nick Sheppard, "but he didn't ask for it." Joe had wanted the show to go on, taking his mind off his father's death. In his "close" way he never mentioned to the new Clash members where he had been. Like David's death, the subject was unmentionable.

I t was not going to get better. Anna was diagnosed with breast cancer. Soon she had her right breast removed and began radiotherapy at Guildford Hospital. Stricken with grief over Ron's passing, when she detected the first symptoms she had not acted as rapidly as she should have. Although halted at first, the cancer returned to her bones. She was admitted to a hospice in nearby Caterham. The hospice administrators told Joe his mother would live from two months to two years. Joe visited her regularly. He told me that to achieve parity with Anna's severely medicated state, allowing himself to communicate with her, he would smoke a powerful spliff as he stepped up the driveway of the hospice. Was he also trying to dull his own pain over her visible suffering? As though trying to return to the happier days of his own time as a small boy, Joe sometimes made an outing of his visits to his mother, stopping at an amusement park before returning home, loving its rides. But it was clear to him that shortly both his parents would be gone from his life.

O nly nine days after the death of his father, on March 8, the Clash began a five-night stint at Brixton Academy. One of the new members risked a complaint about some matter. Bernie, remembered Pete, tore into him:

"'Look at how lily-livered you are. This poor guy's father's died and he's not complaining.' Joe was in a bad way. He was depressive. My father suffered from it. I could spot it." On one of the shows they were supported by the Pogues, unique exponents of boozy, punk-powered Irish rebel songs formed by Shane MacGowan, whose ear famously had been attacked at the Clash's ICA show in October 1976. None of the group made particular contact with Joe on this occasion, but the Pogues were destined to play a significant part in his life. Backstage after one of the shows, Johnny Green ran into Joe. Having rid himself of his heroin demons, Johnny had put on a large amount of weight; he hardly fit into the only suit he had to wear. "That's a terrible suit," Joe told him. "It's not as bad as your group," replied the Clash's always plain-spoken former road manager. In the forthrightness of the Clash posse, an extension of punk's professed honesty, there was sometimes an element of "dare," incorporating a subtle mind game. But Johnny's remark cut Joe to the quick. In front of him, in the backstage corridor, Joe burst into tears.

Everything was coming in on Joe at once. His father had died; his mother was terminally ill; he had become a father and property owner. Professionally, he had seized control—or so he at first thought—of his own life and group, but there was much public questioning of his motives. When the group had played in Glasgow, for instance, a faction of the crowd had been chanting for Mick Jones; Joe offered a solution worthy of a punk Solomon: that the supporters of Mick and of himself could fight it out in an organized brawl.

The pressure must have felt enormous. The very last thing you would have thought he wanted to do was go on the road, breaking in a new group, though, as Joe could run a mile from his emotions, this might have been exactly what he did want to do. Over the ensuing months he would come close to cracking under their pressure, unable to avoid the messages they were sending him.

Ten days after the end of the British tour, the Clash was off on a three-month tour of the United States, crisscrossing the country. After the New York show at Nassau Coliseum on Long Island, Joe hung out with Jo-Anne Henry. "He initially seemed almost defiant, and certainly unapologetic. In front of his public he seemed to be saying, 'This is really the Clash, the spirit of the Clash. We're carrying this forward.' He was determined: 'Screw you if you say it's not the Clash.' The death of his father was still in his thoughts, and now Joe was beating himself up for being away while Jazz was a baby. 'I could be any bloke going off and leaving her,' he said. Jazz being born brought up tons of stuff about his childhood. He was really thoughtful, open in a way that he hadn't been before. He was offering real insights into himself and his family. He said how hard it was to be away, and was criticizing himself as a father. He didn't get there that often or that easily. Deep down he seemed to be in a really awful state.

"There was this anger that he was not able to let come out, the swirling emotions inside him that he couldn't admit to. When he would blow his top, he really could blow his top. Often people who suppress emotion and anger and hurt and pain through their lives, when you start to peel the lid off of it a little bit, there can be volcanoes' worth of stuff that starts to come up. Nobody knew what it looked like better than Joe did. It seemed to scare the shit out of him."

Perpetually upset, Joe carried on with his job. It would have been harder if he knew that—at a time when anyone with any sensitivity could see he needed supportive allies—Bernie Rhodes had forbidden members of the group's crew to speak to him. This included Sean Carasov: "I was told quite specifically on that American tour that I was banned from talking to Joe, otherwise I'd be fired. The reason I was banned was so he wouldn't realize how shitty things were. I couldn't understand how Joe wasn't able to understand what was going on. Joe should have been able to see what was happening. Obviously Bernie didn't want Joe to realize how he'd been manipulated. Paul didn't seem to care—he didn't seem to comprehend that it was all a calculated plot. There was a lot of mumbling going on among the new guys. Bernie was ever paranoid: he thought that if Joe woke up he would fire him. You had to wonder why Bernie had such power over Joe."

As Sean had already noted, Joe could be so focused on what he was doing that he missed the big picture. Was Bernie's hold over Joe exaggerated by the personal tragedies surrounding the ostensible leader of the Clash? Most probably. But also, in the "defiance" Jo-Anne Henry noted, Joe indicated he could not allow himself to see what had gone on, or to admit to his mistakes. He had made his decisions and had to run with them.

In June the Clash flew back to England from their American tour. That September they played three shows for the Italian Communist Party, which held annual music festivals. Joe went on a three-day bender, guzzling bottle after bottle of brandy. Raymond Jordan was appointed to babysit Joe through this crisis. On the tour bus Raymond and Joe would regularly harmonize together on Bob Marley's epochal "Redemption Song," a favorite tune. But now there was a different mood. Pete Howard said, "I remember Joe screaming in the hotel bar." The "group meetings" degenerated into character assassinations of at least one of the participants. "Joe always backed Bernie up," said Vince. "Usually these events ended with someone in tears," said Pete Howard. "In Italy, as though Joe was acting as manager, everyone was torn to pieces." Asserting himself, Vince—who joined the group adoring the Clash—punched Joe in the face. Joe had turned on him: "You're not a happening person. Your girlfriend, I met her in a pub. We were going to a party and I invited her along and she was up for it." Then Joe upped the ante: "What makes you think you're so good in this band?" "What do you say to that?" said Vince. "Then he says, 'I don't need you. Get out!' So I smacked him in the face. I'd had enough."

Everyone was getting it on that Italian trip. On the morning after the final show, in Genoa, Paul Simonon phoned Pearl Harbor, now his wife. "Paul says, 'Last night we all got drunk, and Joe and Kosmo told me that I had to divorce you or quit the band.' I said, 'What did you say?' I was livid. He said, 'I don't know what to tell them.' I said, 'Fuck you. Divorce me if you want.' He was like, 'No, I don't want to do that.' I said, 'Just come on home.' I was furious with Joe. Joe used to hit on me all the time, and put a hand on my leg and try all this stuff. 'Joe. Cut it out.'

"I got drunk and met them at Heathrow. I was mad, 'cos I always saw people ass-kissing the Clash. No one ever stood up for their rights, like they told you to do! First person I see coming off the plane is good old Joe. He says, 'Pearl Harbor! Hello, gorgeous!' I said, 'Hey Joe, I came to ask you something. Is it true or is it not true that you asked Paul to either leave the Clash or leave me?' He admitted it. I went, 'Fuck you,' and threw my drink on him, started punching and kicking him with my cowboy boots on the shins. He didn't retaliate. I said to Paul, 'Leave me alone. Don't even bother trying to speak to me.' Kosmo came up. I said, 'You made a big mistake. Who the fuck do you guys think you are?' The cops came, and this woman cop was grabbing me off Kosmo and Joe and she was laughing, thought it was hilarious that this loud-mouthed American was kicking these guys. She said, 'You have to continue your fight outside. We don't allow this kind of behavior in this country!' We went outside and Joe and Kosmo stood with us to get a taxi. I was saying, "You, Joe Strummer, you think it's not rock 'n' roll for Paul and me to be married, and you walk around London pushing a pram with an orange Mohican. You are a fucking idiot!'

"The next day Joe came to our house and showed me his legs, which were covered in thick scabs. He said, 'Pearl Harbor, I love you. You're the greatest, you're the smartest. I want to take you out.' We went out drinking to all the bars that night. Joe showed everyone his scars and said, 'Pearl Harbor beat me up!' He took off my high-heeled shoes and poured champagne in them and drank it."

In the words of his friend Dick Rude, whom Joe would shortly meet for the first time, "Joe was fantastic eighty-six percent of the time. But the rest of the time he could be as much an idiot as all of us."

spanish bombs

1984-1985

In October 1984 Joe Strummer walked into a bar in Granada in Spain. Punching out of the joint's jukebox was a pushy, punky tune that set the hairs tingling on the back of his neck. He became even more excited when he heard that the single was by a local group, 091—the Spanish emergency services number. Turning up in the nearby Silbar, where 091 hung out, Joe declared his intention to produce the group. When a song by another group was played Joe dismissed it: "It sounds as shit as the Clash."

Needing lyrical inspiration, Joe had absented himself from London. He had known the Andalusian city of Granada since Paloma and Esperanza Romero had introduced him to it when he went to their family home in nearby Malaga. He had taken off on his own on a personal mission: to find the grave of Federico García Lorca, the surrealist poet and dramatist murdered in the Spanish Civil War. As the years moved on, Joe's love for Lorca grew into almost an obsession; in London, he went to see a highly praised production of *The House of Bernardo Alba*. But there was always room for a detour.

Making friends with twenty-one-year-old Jesus Arias, whose brother played in 091, Joe told him: "I had a brother who committed suicide. I loved him very much, and he killed himself. If he only knew that this city existed, he would be here right now. Alive. I love Granada. How wonderful it is to be alive." Despite such protestations, Jesus thought Joe seemed in low spirits. In Granada Jesus saw a beggar ask Joe for money: Joe went to a bank, withdrew $5,000 and gave it to the man.

After a few days hanging out with 091, Joe left Granada, having not yet made it to the grave of Federico García Lorca. He had decided he must return to London.

T he anger that seemed to be pouring out of every pore of Joe Strummer in his involvement with the Clash could be interpreted as the channeling of a collective British rage. Since her reelection as prime minister in June 1983, Margaret Thatcher had taken it upon herself to once and for all break the power of the trade unions in Britain. This culminated in what was to become a yearlong strike by the National Union of Mineworkers. At collieries in south Yorkshire, the heart of the protests, striking miners were charged by truncheon-wielding police mounted on horseback, scenes that recalled murderous Cossack charges on Russian demonstrators. In the middle of the strike, on December 6 and 7, 1984, the Clash played two benefit shows for the miners at Brixton Academy. Three new songs were performed: "North and South," "Dirty Punk" and "Fingerpoppin."

Immediately after, Joe returned to Spain. "Suddenly in December," said Jesus, "Joe—now with blond hair—was back in the Silbar in Granada. He appeared when the place was empty, nobody there. He remembered Tacho, the barman and the drummer with 091, the band he wanted to produce. 'Hola, Tacho. De nuevo en Granada.' ['Hi, Tacho. Back in Granada again.'] Tacho said, 'Joe! Pepe [the Spanish equivalent of Joe]! Welcome back!' Tacho immediately phoned all of us: 'Joe's here again!' I went to the Silbar."

Jesus and his companions had a great night with Joe, booming Clash music bouncing off the walls of the bar. "He wasn't shy or angry listening to Clash records. It was more like, 'Put on Sandinista!, the first record, B-side, first track: "Rebel Waltz."' Or 'Put on "Look Here."'" Sandinista! played all night long.

Another local group, Siniestro Total, had brought out a record whose cover was a pastiche of "London Calling"; instead of Paul Simonon smashing his bass, it had a Gaelic piper smashing his pipes, a violinist smashing his violin, a techno-player smashing his synthesizer and a South American folk singer smashing his Spanish guitar.

"Joe almost died laughing when he saw it," said Jesus. "'Please, I want this record. I love it!' We gave it to him as a present. For years he had it on his front wall at home. Ten years later he was still talking about how funny the cover was."

After that night Joe again disappeared from Granada.

By the end of 1984 it was more than two and a half years since the Clash had released *Combat Rock*, an extraordinarily long time to wait for a follow-up to such a successful record. CBS was on Bernie Rhodes's case, demanding a new album as soon as possible. According to Bernie, however, he didn't believe that the group was yet ready to record: "The live thing was working, but Joe wanted to rush into the studio. He was worried when he heard Mick was getting Big Audio Dynamite together. Joe wanted to do it that moment." And when Bernie booked a cheap digital studio in Munich, he said that the German studio was Joe's idea. As he had done on *Sandinista!*, Norman Watt-Roy from the Blockheads took over on bass; Paul Simonon had gone to New York to buy paintings. Pete Howard spent most of his time in the first couple of months of 1985 in Munich sitting in his hotel room: ironically, considering Mick Jones's fondness for modern technology, it had been decided to record using a boom box, which Bernie also insisted was Joe's whim. Yet there are others, including the new group members, who disbelieved this, convinced Bernie was attempting to hijack the project.

Once Norman Watt-Roy did his thing and left, the only regulars in the studio were Joe and Nick Sheppard—Vince White was almost as marginalized as Pete Howard. In the control room sat Bernie Rhodes. "I don't know what happened to the record," said Nick. "I remember having great times recording it. 'What a night!' said Joe, absolutely joyously after one really good day's work. I had great hopes for what eventually would be released. But I went in there one day and Bernie was so intensely foul that I felt I was losing all self-belief. I left and met Joe in a coffee shop. I said to him, 'I can't stand this.' He said, 'Don't go there. Don't show any weakness. I have to keep believing.' His mother was dying, but he never mentioned it to any of us. The last day in Munich, Bernie started on me again: 'You're fuckin' useless—you let me down.' I completely lost it with him and let him have it, told him what I thought of him. On those sessions I stood back and watched as Joe let Bernie take over."

On May 1, 1985, Joe set off with the Clash on a British tour in which he unequivocally returned to his roots. The seventeen-day busking tour of Britain by the Clash Mark II, as the band had become known, was one of the most extraordinary ventures ever embarked upon by a major-league musical outfit—though there was something about it that smacked of a redundancy of thinking. Meeting in a North London pub, the five group members spent all the money they had on drinks (although Paul had a credit card for emergencies). "We started hitching up the motorway to meet in Nottingham station at midnight," Joe told me. "We just really busked it from there. That was it, no expectations, nothing, just three acoustic guitars, me singing, and Pete drumming on chairs with his drumsticks. And we had the time of our lives on that tour." The idea was that the group would literally sing for their suppers; they slept in cheap B&Bs and on the floors of fans' homes. "We had no dosh with us, so we had to earn a bit," said Joe. "Mainly people we'd meet in the pubs and clubs would put us up, but in between times we'd go to the market square in whatever town and sing until we got moved on and raise a few bob, mainly for beer and food money or bus tickets, and move on to another town. I never felt so close to the audience. I think it's absolutely important that performers should realize that they're really nothing special. OK, if they can do something great, let's get up and light them well and give them a good PA and let's be entertained or informed. A performer is no better than the person watching, and that's got to be learned. The star syndrome is completely uninteresting and boring." Bootlegs of some of the shows indicate they were a lot of fun. The set included many Clash favorites, among them "White Riot." But Joe included a staple from the sets that the 101'ers used to play, Gene Vincent's "Be-Bop-A-Lula." "I've got a photograph of Joe on bended knee giving a rendition of 'Be-Bop-A-Lula' from that period," Paul told me. "It was just a real good rouser, you know."

In Leeds they busked outside the university students' union, where a gig was in progress by Clash-copyists the Alarm. A misguided radical student—protesting against the involvement of CBS in South Africa—

poured a can of red paint off the roof in the direction of Joe, splashing his black leather jacket.

The next day the five members hitched the twenty-odd miles to York. "Probably the most exciting time was when we arrived there," said Paul. "We were playing outside this church and there was suddenly loads and loads of people, because obviously word had passed around. We were confronted by about two hundred people, and we marched through the town singing with our guitars, with this crowd of people heading toward this pub. The landlord had got wind we were in town, and said, 'If those boys want to come over and play, then we'll buy them drinks.' So it was really back to extreme basics. What was amazing was, because the audience knew all the words, it became one big singsong. You could have stopped playing, nobody would have noticed. It was bizarre."

In York the local BBC radio station interviewed Joe about the purpose behind the tour. "We feel we were becoming involved in 'release a record, go on a tour, do this, do that.' Yeah, we began to ask ourselves—What is this all about? You know? And we decided if we can't get it with three acoustic guitars and a pair of drumsticks, on a walking tour of England, then . . . We are looking for an answer. We wanna know if rock 'n' roll means anything, and this is an attempt to find out if it still does.

"We're gonna have to have an English revolution in about ten years—I think it's possible and I would like to be involved. We're not being really preachy—you know. First I like to rock 'n' roll, to hell with the lyrics. But if they come in handy . . . you know, if they're topical, if they mean something to real life, then that's extra."

"To many people, punk rock is just a noise—guitars and drums and somebody shouting," suggested the interviewer. "So what makes the way the Clash shout so successful?"

"If your song ain't good then you ain't gonna triumph," answered Joe. "It's not just a load of rubbish run together. We try and think about what we do. We gotta two-layer culture, if you like: on the top level we got the TV, Wham stuff. But underneath, underneath, there's a lot of people walking about not satisfied by that. We're trying to plug into that network—why we're on the walking tour."

An audience member expressed the gratitude with which this grassroots endeavor was being received: "Today after ten years of success, to come round places like York and Leeds and play gigs that are free really means a lot to us lot, because we're lads who ain't got a lot of cash. We're at college, we're on our own, and it means a lot to us. And I think bands like that should be top of the pops."

Although Joe's interview was only granted for the local BBC station, it was immediately syndicated nationally on Radio One. Now the nation knew what the Clash was up to. Joe was furious. But, according to Paul, there were advantages to this publicity. "By the time we got to Glasgow there was probably about eight hundred people and all we had was acoustic guitars, so if you were at the back there was no way you could hear it."

"That was fun. That's what I call fun," Joe told me. "It just gave an extra dimension to me that I need in the music."

By the middle of the third week in May, Joe had lost his voice, and—to the alleged irritation of Bernie Rhodes—the assorted assembly returned to London. It would be the last time any form of the Clash toured in Britain. There were sessions in studios in Richmond and Wood Green, where Joe walked out. A few days later there was a group meeting to answer the new members' queries about the future of the group. "Joe turned up, looking like a whipped dog," said Vince. "He knew it wasn't working. Bernie said, 'These guys here have got a beef. I thought I'd bring you here to sort this out. I understand that they've got a complaint, but the fact is, Joe, you are the hero in this group. You are the one who's sold loads of records and affected people's lives. You've changed the course of events.' From this broken-looking figure, Joe was sitting upright. His ego had been stroked and he was back on top again. It was weird to watch. I started to lose respect for him, because he just started to play this weird character. He seemed to be out of touch with his roots as a person, all over the place. You couldn't trust anything that he or Bernie said anymore."

At a rehearsal studio in Finsbury Park, Paul Simonon, Nick Sheppard, Vince White and Pete Howard began rehearsing for a planned world tour. Even though the four imagined he would reappear any moment, Joe never showed. (Joe and Paul had struck a deal with Bernie: a third to each of them. "When Joe walked out of the studio," said Paul, "Bernie said I had to sue him for loss of earnings.") "I started to get a phone call every morning from Bernie," said Nick Sheppard. "'Why are you calling me—you never have before?' 'Because there's no one else.'"

arly in June 1985 Joe turned up yet again in the Silbar in Granada, ordering a Palido-cola, his favorite local drink, Spanish brown rum and
Coke. "Tell 091 this," he said to Jesus Arias. "I want to produce their second
LP. My budget is 500,000 pesetas [$2,500]. I want to do something really
great with them." The next day he was gone again.

Two weeks later Joe reappeared in Granada with Jazz and Gaby, who
was pregnant again. They moved into a spacious house outside Granada
which belonged to the brother of Paloma. Every day of his six-week stay Joe
took Spanish lessons from Jesus, making notes in the pocket book he always carried with him. "I tried to teach him how to pronounce the sound
'q,' complicated for an English speaker. 'Shit! I can't do it,' said Joe. 'Maybe
it's because of my plastic teeth.'"

Toward the end of his stay Joe announced he would throw a Saturday-
night party at the house he was renting. He had decided there would be a
twist: at the soirée he would be incognito, playing a waiter. Joe's scheme
worked better than he might have hoped. "They're thinking I'm the fucking
barman," Joe said at one point, almost dying of laughter. If he didn't take
to someone, he would reject their order, in Spanish: "I'm sorry, we don't
have it. Ask for it when Joe Strummer comes." After a couple of hours he
changed out of his waiter role, returning dressed as Joe Strummer. Party-
goers were shocked: "Isn't he the guy who was serving the drinks?"

The guests of honor at the party were 091. That afternoon Joe had
checked out the equipment by playing Chuck Berry's "Around and
Around" for over an hour. Contrary to what the guests had hoped, he would
not play at his party, tucking himself away in a corner. At one point he advised Jesus Arias that a girl at the event was interested in him. The shy Jesus didn't believe it. "Go up to her, say hello and kiss her. If she slaps your
face, I'll give you five thousand pesetas tomorrow. If she kisses you back,
you buy me a drink," Joe told him. After Jesus had had a successful encounter with the girl, he called Joe the next morning. "I'm a guy of the
world. I know how it works," Joe told him.

"Spain was like a tonic after the Clash sessions in Germany," said Gaby.
"He didn't want to leave." Tiring of the ceaseless partying and bar life in
Granada, Gaby persuaded Joe to drive down to the coast. Finally they found

a small hamlet called San José, checking into the local hotel. In San José, Joe filled the car by mistake with diesel, which he sucked out through a hose. Afterward they caught a ferry to Ibiza, where Gaby's mother, Frances, had a *finca*. "My brother Nick was there," said Gaby, "and he was very unstable. My mother was really terrified: he was behaving very oddly, threatening to kill her, very typical paranoid schizophrenic stuff. We drove back to London with her. It was good we went there and got everyone home."

Meanwhile Joe had something else on his mind. In London, at the 1985 Royal College of Art degree show, where Esperanza, the wife of Richard Dudanski and the sister of Joe's former girlfriend Paloma—the Granada connection—was exhibiting, Joe talked with his cousin Iain Gillies. "What am I going to do with Paul?" he asked, worried. "I've been with the Clash for years and it's all come to nothing." "Are you serious?" said Iain. "Yeah," Joe nodded, resignedly. "Look, cousin, Paul's my brother. What am I going to do?" "He was really concerned," remembered Iain. "He knew it was over and done with, but Paul didn't."

"It was a special relationship that Joe and I had," said Paul. "We were like brothers. I didn't have an older brother, and then I did. I could tell how much what happened to his real brother cut right into him. Rather than press him on it, I tried to make it easier for him not to talk about it."

Mick Jones had long abandoned any ideas of an alternative Clash, and instead was in the studio with his new group, Big Audio Dynamite (aka BAD), with Don Letts on keyboards, bassist Leo Williams and drummer Greg Roberts. On a hot Wednesday lunchtime early in August I was in Edgware Road, near the tube station, when, like a sudden gust of wind from out of nowhere, a leather-jacketed figure going in the opposite direction walked almost straight into me. It was Joe Strummer. Joe said that he had had a meeting that morning with his accountant and had decided to head home on foot to "walk off a hangover." All the same, he suggested we go to a pub on the opposite corner and he got in a round of beers. We made small talk about what had been going on with the Clash; after half an hour or so Joe said, "What are you doing tonight? Meet me at nine o'clock in 192 on Kensington Park Road."

Just before nine I found myself sitting on one of the bar stools in 192, nursing a glass of red wine. About ten minutes later I was looking in the other direction when I felt someone slide onto the stool next to me. Joe had on the same clothes—leather jacket, off-white jeans—he had been wearing that afternoon, and he looked in good shape. He ordered a bottle of "shampoo." Yet despite his expensive choice of drink, there seemed that day to be a humility about Joe that had not been present the last few times I had seen him on and off stage. His energy was very easy to be around. He appeared younger; his skin looked healthy, with a light tan, and the tiredness lines had disappeared from his forehead; he seemed tender and very open and rather alone. He was angry about women, distrustful, cynical, felt they'd always let you down, believed they always fucked around, that they behaved exactly as women say men behave. "They always do, all of them," he said, his voice rising almost into anger, when I said I thought this wasn't always the case. He seemed a man at a point of change. He told me he was putting his house on the market, suggested that this was Kosmo's idea; said he was going to buy a flat above the Tesco supermarket on Portobello Road, by the junction with Westbourne Park Road (and conveniently, no doubt, only about a hundred yards from the Warwick). "I only bought it because it reminded me of the places I used to squat in," he said of his house, an argument that to me did not sound entirely convincing. He was clearly very conflicted about his new wealth. I told him he didn't need to sell the house; he'd worked hard for it and he had a child now, he needed some space. Joe told me how when a real estate agent came round to measure up the house, he had showed her the features of his bedroom. "The estate agents are always out to fuck us. I bet I'm the only person you know who's fucked the estate agent," Joe told me, proud of his act of revolution. Joe's political act of fucking the real estate agent—about which he didn't exactly keep quiet— earned him considerable kudos as well as much chap-on-chap mirth in the local watering holes: it was generally considered one of the funniest things he had ever done. Whether Gaby would have laughed is another matter. (Eventually he decided not to sell the house. I was glad—I thought the flat-above-Tesco's idea was crazy.)

He talked about the Clash a bit. I told him that I used to think that it must have been very hard being the ever-on-duty public figure of Joe Strummer, always expected by the fans to have a ready sage-piece-of-wisdom. "Yes, it was," he said simply. "Drove me nuts sometimes." He said that the Clash had been making a new album, that he hadn't heard it yet, that they had recorded it in Germany; in those days there were considerable tax advantages for musicians from recording out of Britain, but Joe didn't seem at all aware of this when I mentioned that this surely was why they had made the record overseas. He had already told me that the new album did not have a title. But now he came up with one. *"Fuck Britain!* That's what we should call it. *Fuck Britain!* That would say it all." He seemed very pleased with his idea.

It was some time around a quarter to midnight when Joe ordered a further bottle of "shampoo"—the third or the fourth—and made a surprising declaration: "I've got a big problem. Hang on, I'll have a wazz [piss] and come back and tell you about it." Joe went to the toilet for a minute and returned to his stool. "Mick was right about Bernie." I couldn't believe my ears. I didn't know what to say. "Well, I did think that was always the case," I spluttered. Then he told me that Bernie had hijacked the latest album, demanding to write the songs with Joe. He said that he'd walked out on the project earlier in the year and had hardly spoken to Bernie since; he told me he'd only recorded guide vocals for the new record [later I checked with both Pete Howard and Vince White, both of whom knew nothing of this] and those were what Bernie must have used: "What do you think I should do?" He wanted to see Mick Jones and tell him what he had realized. I told him to go and see Mick or at least call him up; I gave him his phone number, which he didn't seem to have. He didn't call him, though—I didn't appreciate that at the time Joe was one of those people who was leery of the phone and quite uncomfortable making calls. Afterward we went back to his house, to drink into the night. On the kitchen table I noticed a well-thumbed copy of the *I Ching*.

A couple of nights later I went up to Basing Street studios, where an exhausted-looking Mick Jones, unshaven for over a week, was putting the final touches to the mix of the first Big Audio Dynamite album; I told him about my evening with Joe. He was finalizing the first steps in a new career he had been forced into by Joe having kicked him out of his own group. Mick seemed to be trying to prove himself with BAD—as Kosmo Vinyl said, "Joe would have to acknowledge that Mick was the only one to have commercial success following the breakup of the Clash." Almost immediately afterward Mick had a holiday planned in the Bahamas with Daisy and his daughter Lauren; with them went Tricia Ronane. As they waited at

Mick's flat, the doorbell rang. Through the frosted glass could be discerned a man in a trilby hat. "I've come to offer a spliff of peace," said Joe, when it was opened. Mick and Joe went into the kitchen together for five minutes. But then the taxi arrived to take them to the airport.

I was concerned about Joe, and felt his energy had disappeared from the area. And in Portobello Road I ran into Gaby, who had been in L.A. with her dad; she was evidently pregnant. She said that Joe had had to go away somewhere.

Then it was the last weekend in August, the time for carnival in Notting Hill. On the Sunday, out in the claustrophobic crush of Portobello Road with my three-year-old son, Alex, I sought some kind of safety for him by slipping up Lancaster Road. On the pavement outside number 37 was Joe, a bottle of dark rum in his hand. "Come in. Go in the kitchen and get yourself a drink." There, in the back of the house, he told me where he had been. "I went to Nassau, to see Mick. I landed in the early evening. I went straight down to the dodgiest part of town, full of crackheads, and scored an ounce of weed. The next day I rented a moped and tracked down Mick's hotel and took it up to him." A couple of days later I saw Mick Jones, who told me of his surprise when Joe had knocked on the door of his room in the Bahamas. He told me that he had played Joe the BAD album. Joe had said, "It's no good. You need me." "Which was hardly the most tactful thing to say in the circumstances," laughed Mick, who to his credit had resisted giving interviews railing against Joe and the new Clash: perhaps he remembered the early dictum he had expressed to me about not dismissing other acts in interviews because it drew you closer to them. Anyway, it was great at Joe's that carnival Sunday; there were quite a few other people with kids. Micky Gallagher was there with his family, as well as several others. The children were an important part of the mood: they softened the vibe, one of those things I used to like about the kids and adults hanging out together. I talked to Joe about this. "The 'adults' stop being so full of shit when the kids are around, they are more like human beings," he said. This became an integral feel of the times I would spend at Joe's.

I went back to his place with my girlfriend the next day, a Monday holiday, early in the evening, the second and final day of the Notting Hill carnival. That year there was a nine o'clock curfew to close it down. A few minutes before that a lot of people were outside the front of the house, moving and sway-

Joe in repose at 37 Lancaster Road, taking a respite from the
Notting Hill carnival raging outside. (*UrbanImage.tv/Adrian Boot*)

ing on the pavement and the steps to the last tunes being played by Saxon
sound system, set up on the corner of Lancaster Road and All Saints Road,
with its shuddering rhythms and especially insightful toaster.

Suddenly there was a flurry of movement. "Get in the house. Now," Joe
muttered at me, motioning with his eyes to a posse of youth rapidly gathering on the opposite side of the road. "I was sitting on the front steps and
this hand came and whipped Jazzy off my lap, and it was Joe, also pulling
me back," remembered Harriet Cochrane, a young friend of the family.
"What's going on? I'm thinking. And Joe pulled us in the front door."

Before the safety of the house could be reached by all of Joe's crew, their brains befuddled by the day's consumption, the property was being steamed by five or six youths who slipped up the front steps and through the front door like quicksilver, almost unnoticed they moved so fast. As I slammed the front door shut I saw an empty whiskey bottle arcing through the air toward it. It shattered against the wood as the lock slipped shut. But then I was in the dark hallway with my back to the door. Directly in front of me was Joe, punching it out with one of the youths. I stepped past him and grabbed another one of them, trying to pull him toward the door. He landed a fist in my face, knocking my sunglasses onto the ground. Then it was more fists flying all around—everything in slow motion—and Joe opening the front door, and the two of us shoving them out. At the rear of the living room, menacing all the partygoers, was the last of these home invaders, strutting around. The owner and I told him to get out. He sulked toward the front door and was gone. I then noticed that in his hand Joe was now brandishing a wooden machete, a weapon whose zenlike qualities are worth considering. "I was so frightened. It was really heavy. But I always remember the wooden machete," said Harriet. In the great tradition of the last hours of the Notting Hill Carnival the entire area now seemed to be going off. In Westbourne Park Road, parallel to Joe's road a block south, more than one thousand youths were hurling missiles at around one hundred police.

Two days later my phone rang in the early evening. "All the pussy-men ran to the back of the house, but you stood with me. Thanks," breathed a familiar voice. "No problem, Joe," I said, pointing out that as I was pinned by the front door I didn't have much choice. "It doesn't matter," said Joe. "You stood alone with me." Several times over the years, Joe recounted this story to people to whom he was introducing me. On one hand it always slightly embarrassed me; but on the other, I was very touched that he was so touched. I remember when he told the story to my new girlfriend. Then he looked at her tits. "Gosh," he said, rather spoiling the moment.

On August 27 at the Olympic Stadium in Athens Joe played another festival date. Before and after the show he argued furiously with Bernie Rhodes. Topping a bill over the Cure, the Style Council, Culture Club (whose white dreadlocked singer Boy George had become a particular bête noire of Joe), the "dodgy" Clash played before sixty thousand people; the initial forty thousand tickets sold were bolstered by half that number again when the promoters gave in to radicals' demands that people be let in for free. It was the kind of gesture Joe might have approved of, for what was destined to be the final show by any form of Clash lineup.

September 30, 1985, saw the release of "the last great Clash song" (Joe's description), "This Is England," an impassioned semi-epic protest song that could have been on *Combat Rock* if there was a greater fluidity in the music against which the words were set. The single made it to number 24 in the charts. *Cut the Crap*, the title ordained by Bernie Rhodes for the new album, was released five weeks later. The fact that Rhodes had not consulted a single member of the last Clash lineup about the title was significant: whatever happened to *Fuck Britain!*? The significance took a quantum leap when you saw that the songwriting credits of the record were attributed to Strummer–Rhodes. "That's not to say he didn't write anything," said Joe, "but I wouldn't have said it was half-and-half."

The production of the opening song, "Dictator"—all cut-up radio broadcast samples and boom-box rhythms, ironically like a pastiche of what BAD turned out to be doing far more effectively—set the tone for *Cut the Crap*. Although it had a few good moments—"This Is England," "North and South" (a tune about the geographical divide in Britain) and the vaguely acceptable football song chant of "We Are the Clash"—the sound of the record was jarring and virtually unlistenable. Hard as one might have tried to like it, *Cut the Crap* was mostly a terrible din, and dreadfully disappointing. It spoke volumes about the contempt felt by Bernie Rhodes for the legacy of the Clash and for the group's really quite musically sophisticated audience; it also said much about his misguided concept of himself as a musical artist. With one or two exceptions—*Sounds* gave it a good review—the record received a critical kicking. And rightly so: although it made it to number 16 in the U.K. charts, *Cut the Crap* was a disaster.

What must have been even more dispiriting for Joe was the extremely positive reception given the first releases from Mick Jones's Big Audio Dynamite: there was a trio of classic singles, "The Bottom Line" ("That tune had lyrics Joe had written when I was still with the Clash," said Mick), "$E=MC_2$" and "Medicine Show," the last two British chart hits. The excellent album *This Is Big Audio Dynamite* was released a week after *Cut the Crap*, largely to critical acclaim, which also was how the group's first tour was received. When they played their first major London date, at the Town and Country Club in Kentish Town, there was a full-scale turnout of the groovers who in the past would have been at a Clash show. Tracy Franks, a long-standing fan of the group, would regularly see Joe around lunchtime as he had his breakfast at Bites café on Westbourne Park Road. Joe's Bites breakfasts enjoyed an unswerving routine: a sardine sandwich and a "special" coffee into which was injected a slug of brandy from a bottle stashed beneath the counter reserved for this one customer. On the day of the Town and Country Club BAD show, she noticed that Joe seemed in a particularly low frame of mind: "Joe was obviously feeling gutted. He said, 'Are you going to go and see Mick play tonight?' I said I'd like to go, but I didn't have a babysitter. Joe said, 'I'll do it.' I thought, 'Oh shit: Joe Strummer? Babysitting for an old fan while I go and see Mick Jones play his first big London gig since the Clash?' I left and went home, thinking, I can't believe this. But at about six o'clock Joe was ringing on my doorbell. 'Tracy, I don't think I can make it. The wife thought it was a bad idea.'"

Round at the new house at 53 Oxford Gardens shared by Paul Simonon and his wife, Pearl Harbor, Joe was a frequent visitor. "For some time Joe had been coming round regularly," recalled Pearl. "Joe was really confused about it all. He wasn't convinced things were going well. I think he and Kosmo had had a falling-out." Kosmo might have had good reason. At the time of *Combat Rock* he'd been promised a percentage of the group's profits; because of the subsequent litigation everyone seemed to have forgotten about this.

"Joe and Paul were together a lot at that time," said Pearl. "The other guys in the group never came around. But it was Joe who was feeling completely negative about the group, not Paul. Paul always liked Bernie. In fact, Bernie really loved Paul, and always wanted to give him lots of advice. He was probably trying to talk to Joe, but Joe wasn't buying it.

"No one ever seemed to address the fact that Joe's father had just died and his mother was dying. I think he was in hell. But I found all those guys so internal about their feelings—they wouldn't talk about how they felt. Even though Joe was obviously in this state, he wouldn't come over and say that he felt terrible. Later, when I'd moved back to San Francisco and I'd sometimes see him, he didn't even talk then: the most vulnerable he'd get with me was trying to be sexual. But you have to remember that at that time blokes weren't supposed to talk about their feelings. It was the current of the time. For Joe to start talking, he'd have to be very low, with drink in him. With all of those guys, my favorite thing was being with them drinking, when they'd be very open."

By the time that *Cut the Crap* came out, Joe Strummer was no longer really a member of any form of the Clash. Out of the blue he turned up at Vince's place in Finsbury Park. "He came up and had a cup of tea. It was really weird. What was he doing there? It was the first time in nearly two years that he just turned up. He stayed for about half an hour and then he disappeared again."

In the period building up to the release of the record, Joe had disappeared to Madrid to produce 091, the group from Granada. But life was not much better in Spain. He had immediately run into the kind of difficulties that had plagued the Clash: the record company worried about his presence, to which Joe only added with his habitual absences from sessions to bars or gigs. The record company wanted a cute pop record; they had no truck with Joe's fondness for using a distortion pedal on the bass guitar, or recording the slamming of doors. The inexperienced 091 were largely too timid to speak up for Joe.

Joe's already precarious spirits were wobbled even more. He was very dispirited. He felt he should be in London with Gaby, by now very pregnant, and he was running out of money. Joe made a phone call to a friend, the singer with Radio Futura, Spain's top group. Joe asked if he would lend him 150,000 pesetas, around £600. When he came up with the cash, Joe bought what he called his "Spanish-American car," an old silver Dodge Dart with a black roof. Then he headed off to Granada.

In Granada he met Jesus Arias. "Look what I've bought," said Joe. "Ain't she a beauty? My Spanish-American car. I've always wanted to have a car like this." "At stoplights," remembered Jesus, "he would address people: '*Es mi nuevo coche, amigo. Tu gusta? Coche Espanol-Americano.*'"

Joe announced that he wanted to finally visit the burial site of Federico García Lorca, referenced in the lyrics of "Spanish Bombs." His adoration of Lorca's work can be explained by a simple line of the great writer: "At the heart of all great art is an essential melancholy." They headed to the town of Viznar, nine kilometers from Granada. Driving through the countryside, Joe dropped his guard. He told Jesus of the difficulties he was having in

Madrid. "I'm not having a good time. I don't know what to do, because I really love this band. I just want them to put into music the ideas I'm having. Guy Stevens did the same with the Clash, and it worked. The first time we met Guy Stevens we thought he was crazy. Look what happened. I feel like the poor Guy Stevens of 091."

The road along which they were driving was that on which Lorca had been taken to his execution. This information shocked Joe. "I can't believe that. This landscape is the last thing his eyes saw." Jesus had to dissuade Joe from buying shovels to dig for Lorca's remains: along with two thousand other death squad victims, the writer had been dumped into the ground without a commemorative marker. His final burial place was close to a pair of olive trees.

When they reached the bald terrain on which Lorca was murdered, Joe immediately felt the intensity of the setting, as well as its characteristic somber mood. "I can hear them," Joe suddenly whispered. "I can hear the screams of the dead."

He stepped over to the olive trees, sat down and remained in silence. "When I turned back to Joe," said Jesus, "he was silently crying, his face full of tears, while he made a joint."

"I promised myself," said Joe, "that if some day I visited Lorca's grave I would smoke a joint in his honor. When I was writing 'Spanish Bombs' on a plane, I made that promise." "This is for you, Federico," he said, lighting the joint and saluting the sky.

The next morning Joe climbed into his "Spanish-American" car and drove for four hours straight to the studio in Madrid, offering the record company money out of his own pocket for further recording time—which was rejected. As soon as his work was completed he flew back to London. The record company remixed the record, *Mas De Cien Lobos* (*More Than a Hundred Wolves*), losing Joe's effects and idiosyncrasies. Joe was not having a good time in recording studios in 1985.

Back in London he hung on with the Clash, characteristically equivocal, until the disastrous reviews of *Cut the Crap* appeared. Then he wrote a tract denouncing the role of Bernie Rhodes in the record, declaring he would take out full-page advertisements in the music press to broadcast these views. But he never got round to that. Meeting with Pete Howard,

Nick Sheppard and Vince White at Paul's house, he told them it was over; in a bar in Soho the next day he handed them each an envelope containing £1,000 and told them it was the end. Then he was gone.

The split was reported in the November 23 issue of *NME* in a communiqué credited to Joe Strummer, but actually put out by Bernie Rhodes: Bernie was insisting Joe and Paul would continue as the Clash, citing the imminent release of "Shooting Star," a song Joe had written. In the same way Malcolm McLaren had kept the Sex Pistols' brand name going after the departure of John Lydon, so Bernie Rhodes believed he could keep the Clash name alive. Having had to accept that Joe had departed for good, for a time he pushed the idea of another group called the Clash in which Paul Simonon would be the front man. Of course, it was not to be. However, it was at the suggestion of Bernie Rhodes that Paul soon moved to the United States, basing himself in El Paso and later Los Angeles. Havana 3 A.M., the group he led at the end of the decade, derived from this move. When Paul bailed out, Bernie even tried to keep the Clash going with Nick Sheppard, Vince White and Pete Howard.

But what was Joe Strummer to do? In the middle of 1974 he had set off on his journey to becoming a rock 'n' roll star, first with the 101'ers and then with the Clash, with whom he unequivocally achieved his goal. Now, eleven years on, he was effectively without a gig.

man of mystery

1985-1987

"Those five years, from '77 to '82, were very intense.
Yak-yak-yak, nonstop yak. I didn't have any more to
say, because we'd done eight slabs of long-playing
vinyl inside a five-year period, and that's a lot of
yakking for one man to do in terms of lyric writing,
as opposed to gassing on generally. So I think it was
pretty cool of me to shut up for a bit. I think I was
exhausted: mentally, physically, every which way, you
know?"

—JOE TO CHARLES SHAAR MURRAY, 1999

With his 1984 film *Repo Man*, Alex Cox had signaled his intent as a Young Turk of independent cinema. His first feature-length film, *Repo Man* was a surreal film noir as well as a critical and box-office hit. On the strength of that, he had started working on his second feature, *Love Kills*, produced by Eric Fellner, who until recently had worked mainly on top-end videos. *Love Kills* was the tragic story of the doomed lovers John

"Sid" Ritchie (played by Gary Oldman) and Nancy Spungen (played by Chloe Webb), whom he had allegedly stabbed to death in the Chelsea Hotel in Manhattan. The film soon would be renamed *Sid and Nancy*.

The film had already been denounced by much of the punk elite. Why was this man who had never been around the Pistols coming over from L.A. and making a film about them? But this didn't stop Joe Strummer from turning up on a wintry night at the end of 1985 at the wrap party for the English section of filming.

The shindig was being thrown at the top end of Ladbroke Grove, at a club on Kensal Road. The venue was therefore comfortably within Joe's fiefdom as King of Notting Hill; as soon as he heard about it he assumed right of entrance. But he discovered he was expected to pay a tithe to the robber baron who was behind the event. As soon as Alex Cox learned that Joe Strummer was at the party, he sought him out. "I said, 'Right, if you've come to the party you can write some music for the film.' Joe didn't want to know at first. He reacted as most people did when they heard about the film. I persuaded him to see a rough cut."

That December Joe also went back to Granada. He seemed unconcerned about the 091 record. On December 19 he called Jesus Arias: he wanted to visit Lorca's birthplace with some friends and refreshments. "I've got the joints," said Joe when he met up with Jesus.

At Fuente Vaqueros Joe had photographs taken of himself by the room in which the poet had been born. After visits to several bars, he drove to the killing fields of Viznar. In very good spirits, Joe sang an a cappella "Spanish Bombs" for his friends as he sat under the olive trees, firing up yet another joint.

In Madrid the next month Joe drunkenly parked the silver Dodge Dart in a parking lot and forgot where it was. He then spent several days searching every parking facility in the area, to no avail. Joe's "Spanish-American car" simply vanished from his life. It is possible that here Joe was being offered a lesson about the losses that could come from drunken driving. Evidently he ignored it; soon he would pay a stricter penalty. While he was in Spain, Gaby went into labor. On January 14, 1986, Gaby gave birth to a second daughter, Lola Maybelline Mellor; the girl's first name was taken from a suggestion the previous spring by José Antonio García, the 091 singer, her second from the celebratory Chuck Berry tune.

Birth and death are interlinked. As well as the traumas of the Clash breakup, Joe had learned at the beginning of the year that his mother's cancer had developed further. But that wasn't all. "I had this foreboding," said Gaby. "I knew something was going to happen." Nicky Salter, Gaby's brother, had been suffering from paranoid schizophrenia. On January 24 he committed suicide by hara-kiri. "It tore the family apart," said Gaby. "Joe was so supportive because he'd been there with David." When I heard the news of Nick's suicide my immediate, unchivalrous thought was for Joe. How much more mental turmoil, I wondered, must be thrown up for someone who had never really recovered from another family suicide?

When he was back in London, Joe was shown a rough cut of Alex Cox's available footage. Possibly because he wasn't doing much else that month, Joe quickly became, said Alex Cox, "very attached to the *Sid and Nancy* project. He came and wanted to hate it. But didn't." Cox's appealing energy and charismatic certainty would have attracted Joe Strummer; at the time, that was something Joe certainly needed.

Keeping up a public face, Joe agreed to write and perform the title tune for Alex Cox's movie, a song that had to have the title "Love Kills." "He became part of the post-production music department," said Alex. For a time Alex and Joe discovered each other to be kindred spirits, the film director's guerrilla approach corresponding to the musician's attitude: both believed in the energizing, edifying effects of an artist throwing his entire essence into a project. Also, they both had a fondness for the occasional refreshing drink. Under the terms of his contract with CBS Records, which would become more niggling and constraining as the years wore on, Joe was only legally permitted to write and perform a pair of songs for the film. Falling back on that old music business standby of the *nom de disque*, he wrote another six. "Quite soon after we'd met, he was doing me tapes," said Alex Cox. "Twenty different tracks that he thought I should listen to—reggae, or other types of music he thought I didn't know enough about. He'd start out making the tapes at about six o'clock in the evening, and the writing would be perfect, very musical-looking handwriting, and it would start to go scribbly about halfway through the bottle of wine, and by the end it was a spider walking all over the tape box."

Almost immediately Alex discovered how enigmatic Joe was. "He was a man of mystery. He would appear and disappear like a character in a spaghetti western. He'd be there and then he'd be gone. Because this guy had been in the Clash, and had gone through experiences I couldn't possibly imagine, to be not really weird was impressive. A lot of rock 'n' roll people act as though they are encased in a strange glass bubble of celebrity and protectiveness. He didn't feel like that: he seemed a really vulnerable person, a tough person, but a person who wasn't immune to what was around him. He was very empathetic.

"He was like a boxer who'd been smashed back onto the ropes. He was trying to stake out a new part of the arena. I think movies were great for him in that way. You sign on and put in a period of time. You go to some very exotic locations. There's camaraderie. There are opportunities for *amour*. I think he wanted to sign on for somebody else's trip, as opposed to having to create another, even more sensational version of himself."

Being around Alex Cox also meant being around his producer, Eric Fellner, who had a heroin habit. "Joe was the first dissenting voice toward me about that," said Eric. "He was the guy who said: 'Don't do that stuff. Have a smoke but don't use that shit. Stay off it.' He always gave me shit about it."

"This was a pivotal time for Joe," said Alex. "Big Audio Dynamite were kicking off and he was frustrated, not in a great state. Very fragile. He seemed idiosyncratic and brilliant. He always had an opinion about everything, and would try and weave this opinion into what you were saying, in quite a forceful but always jokey way, and was very funny about it. Even if you thought he was talking complete shit, you couldn't really go up against it because it was such fun hearing what he had to say."

During post-production Joe Strummer met a friend of Alex Cox from Los Angeles. "The first thing he said when he heard my name was, 'Dick Rude? That's great!'" As with many punk sobriquets, Dick Rude's nickname was singularly inapposite for this polite, well-mannered fellow. "We've met before," Dick said to Joe on that first meeting. "I saw the Clash show at Santa Monica Civic. You spat on me the whole night long. I think you owe me an apology."

"He got red-faced and embarrassed," Dick Rude explained to me in his apartment in the Los Feliz section of Los Angeles. "But that started our friendship. I wasn't afraid to be outspoken, and had a sense of humor about it. So right away we bonded."

Contrary to popular myth, and perfect as the poetry would have been, Mick Jones did not produce "Love Kills" and its B-side "Dum Dum Club"— a simple glance at the single shows that production is credited to Joe Strummer. These two songs, the first Joe had worked on in a studio since any form of the Clash, were recorded at Regent Park Recordings in Primrose Hill in North London. Mick did turn up to the sessions, adding guitar parts to both of them, a big-hearted gesture on his part. When remix wizard Eric "E.T." Thorngrun added his efforts, he mixed out virtually all of Mick's playing. For Mick this must have seemed like a reprise of his last studio work with Joe, Glyn Johns's mixing sessions on *Combat Rock*, when so many of his ideas were jettisoned. "It seemed ridiculous, this vintage moment of the two of them back playing together, and it ends up unused," said Chris Musto, present at the sessions as both drummer and general brethren to Joe. But he noted, "The vibe was fine. It was really easy as soon as Mick arrived." He could perceive Joe's synergy with Mick, and what Joe brought to the session: "What he managed to do was energize it to the point where you couldn't play badly. He was so up, incredibly up." In 1977, like most drummers in London, Chris had tried out for the gig with the Clash at Rehearsal Rehearsals, being asked back for a second audition. Drumming with former Clash roadie Welsh Ray Jones on "some boisterous country tunes" in a Brixton studio in the autumn of 1985, Chris Musto had been surprised when Joe turned up to produce Ray's music. Joe told Chris he loved his drumming. "Which was great. I'd waited a long time to prove a point to him." As soon as "Love Kills" had received a green light, Joe asked Chris to work with him. The other tunes Joe wrote were recorded for the album at a small studio—"a closet," according to Dick Rude—off Kilburn High Road; among others, there was a reggae dub tune, credited to the Dynamiters, a blues tune with Joe trying to impersonate Howlin' Wolf to disguise his voice, and "2 Bullets," a country song sung by Pearl Harbor.

There had been some old-timer punk controversy over Joe recording "Love Kills"; Glen Matlock, who had been hired by Alex Cox as the film's music supervisor, had also written a song entitled "Love Kills," and was reportedly miffed that Joe won out. Perhaps with justification, for "Love Kills" is a hesitant, plodding song, with a sense of A.N. Other Joe Strummer Track about it; it feels like early steps; but from E.T.'s sessions an excellent dub version emerged. The B-side, the driving "Dum Dum Club," is a great tune, much more powerful, used to terrific effect in a scene where Sid crashes through a plate-glass window. Although "Love Kills" is stylistically fairly ordinary, its blues feel was the direction in which Joe felt he should be going. He and Chris Musto would take long drives around West London in Chris's tiny Fiat 500—with which Joe was very taken—or in Joe's Morris Minor. Joe would talk endlessly about the blues, and his love of artists like Bukka White and SunHouse, and how he wanted to get a three-piece blues group together. "His vision was that the blues was the future," remembered Chris. "From what he was saying he wanted to do really dirty, grungy stuff—years before people were doing that."

Before Joe Strummer could put his dreams about blues bands into practice, there was more work on the current project. A video had to be shot for "Love Kills," and Joe persuaded Alex Cox that it should be filmed in the stretch of country north of Almería in southern Spain, where so many spaghetti westerns had been made; no difficulty in persuading him to do this, as the director was an expert on the genre. What Joe didn't know was that his favorite film, *Lawrence of Arabia*, had had its desert scenes shot in the wild natural film set of the region; he was knocked out when he learned that the camels used in the video had a direct lineage back to the animals used in David Lean's great film. A specialist was brought in to construct flies for a scene in which Joe sits at a desk, interminably swatting at them: the flies were made out of strawberries; as Joe swatted away at them everything turned red. As Joe had a live chicken on his desk, a chicken trainer was brought in to hypnotize the bird.

Joe came up with the video's story line: "He decided the song was about what would have happened if Sid Vicious had escaped," Alex Cox said. "He hadn't stuck around to get arrested, but took off to Mexico. Joe says, 'We'll do it as Sid Vicious goes down on the Mexican bus, goes to a saloon, meets a young girl. But this young girl's boyfriend is the local cop, so he gets in trouble and thrown in jail.' Joe plays the cop, and Gary Oldman plays Sid Vicious. That night the Mexican girl comes to see Sid, and then in the morning, invigorated by her, he dresses up as Sid Vicious, puts on all his rock 'n' roll gear, kicks the door of his cell down, liberates the prisoners, and they all run off into the desert. That was Joe's script."

When the single was released in late July, the record reached only 69 in the charts, and the video was hardly shown. Changing the name of the film to *Sid and Nancy* hadn't helped. "I spent days trying to get the words to fit in properly with the song," Joe laughed to me, "and then they changed the title to *Sid and Nancy*."

But the trip to southern Spain had set an idea gestating within Alex Cox, one that would soon come to fruition. Dick Rude remembered what happened. "I was going back to L.A., and Alex said, 'Fuck it, come to Cannes, let's go to the film festival.'" In May 1986 Alex Cox, Joe Strummer and Dick Rude convened at the annual film festival, having convinced themselves they were needed to promote *Sid and Nancy*, all sleeping in the one room Alex Cox had been allocated in a small hotel back from the seafront. They attended the official screening of the film. "There were some guys from Duran Duran there, as well as Jack Lang, the French minister of culture," recalled the director. "The lights go down and the film starts. Then when Gary Oldman appears one of these pop guys calls out, 'Johnny Thunders!' Strummer just stands up: 'Shut the fuck up!' That was very funny. Cannes seemed like mindless bullshit to me. I imagine he thought it was bullshit too." The assembled troupe went to only two of the festival's films, Jim Jarmusch's *Down by Law* and Spike Lee's first feature, *She's Gotta Have It*, a pair of movies that between them established a new genre of New York independent cinema.

The morning after the *Sid and Nancy* screening, they staggered down to sit in the shade by the poolside, nursing their hangovers. Hunkered down by the water they dimly recalled the scam they had drunkenly hatched the previous night: a spoof thriller, the exploits of three hapless deadly killers, shot as a modern spaghetti western. "I had to go off to a *Sid and Nancy* promotional event," said Alex Cox. "I came back, and outside the hotel in the bright sunlight, still in their evening wear, black suits, white shirts, black [bow ties] were my roommates, like characters in a film, sweating, drinking coffee, trying to get over their hangovers. That was the origin of *Straight to Hell*. We were full of the energy of the video in Almería, and really wanted to go back."

There had been a plan for Joe Strummer, the Pogues and Elvis Costello to tour Nicaragua in the late summer of that year. Alex Cox would have filmed it for a documentary, but the scheme, a trial run for a feature Alex wanted to shoot in Nicaragua, fell apart. Eric Fellner was convinced such a collection of names, with the addition of further stellar billing, was an easy-to-sell package for a movie. He approached Chris Blackwell, Guy Stevens's mentor at Island Records, who came up with £900,000 for *Straight to Hell*, the feature that had been drunkenly mooted at Cannes—named, of course, after one of Joe's greatest songs. The film, it was decided, should be made at the same urgent pace at which it was conceived; the cast and crew agreed to work for next to nothing, with a profit-participation plan. Shooting was scheduled to begin in the middle of August, again on one of the spaghetti western film sets.

When things are not going well, the only thing you can almost guarantee is that they will get worse. As though emphasizing his time of inner crisis, Joe Strummer had a run-in with the law. He had finally taken and passed his driving test—which suggests that when he was driving around Spain he was not legally entitled to be behind the wheel of a motor vehicle. Six weeks after obtaining a driver's license he spent the evening with Elvis Costello at the latter's home on the edge of Holland Park. When he left, he jumped into his Morris Minor hot rod and hurtled down Kensington Park Road. The extraordinary racket from his car's big-bore exhaust caused Joe to be pulled over by the police as the car reached the junction with West-bourne Park Road; he was given a Breathalyzer test and found over the alcohol limit. He was banned from driving for eighteen months. He had failed to pay heed to the warning provided by the vanishing "Spanish-American car."

From now on—in England, anyway—Gaby did all the driving; although the noisy Morris Minor was parked on Lancaster Road, and she would occasionally drive it, it was supplemented by a distinctly nonpunk but eco-friendly Renault people carrier. (When Joe had been stopped on his way back from Costello's place, the police had immediately recognized him, referring to him throughout his time at the police station simply as "Joe." This would also be their greeting when they would stop and search him on the street—"Come on, Joe. Turn out your pockets"—as they regularly did. That Joe's home was so close to All Saints Road, with its regular army of drug dealers, brought with it both an up- and a downside.)

After the "Love Kills" sessions, Joe Strummer and Mick Jones had continued to see each other. Paul Simonon, who was starting to reimmerse himself in the painting in which he had trained, also returned to the fold. At the video shoot for the third BAD single, "Medicine Show," in a Thames-side studio in Battersea near the "London Calling" location, both made cameo appearances as Southern cops, Joe—his mouth stuffed with cotton wool—looking a bit like Rod Steiger in *In the Heat of the Night*. This was the trio's first creative work as a unit since Mick had left the Clash. But there was another, darker side of Joe that carried the taint of walking disaster; at the final edit, at a facilities house in Covent Garden, I found Joe shuffling around, swallowing the dregs from abandoned cans of beer, like a park bench wino. Was he so knocked sideways by the internal tensions created in him by the situation he found himself in that he was desperately trying to anesthetize himself? In the mid-1980s tales of Joe Strummer's alcohol consumption were legion: once when he paid one of his regular visits to Mark "Stan" Eden, who specialized in late 1950s rock 'n' roll haircuts at the hip hairdressers Smile in World's End, Joe arrived with a magnum bottle of red wine, which he polished off during his haircut, before disappearing up the pub with a gaggle of cute junior cutters.

At lunchtime on June 26, 1986, Mick Jones's thirty-first birthday, Joe ran into Don Letts in Wardour Street in Soho; Don was on his way to Trident Studios, where BAD were making their second album. On a nearby wall

John Lydon and Don Letts with Joe and Paul at the shooting of BAD's "Medicine Show" video. (*UrbanImage.tv/Adrian Boot*)

was a poster for BAD. As though Don was a total stranger, Joe grabbed passersby, pointing at him. "Look! It's the man in the poster!" Stricken with embarrassment, Don fled into a nearby tobacconist's. Joe followed him in, continuing his rant. Together they turned up at Trident, where the sessions were into their third week. Joe never left, taking on the role of co-producer and helping out on lyrics. "We need some rock 'n' roll," he told me at Trident. Suddenly Joe looked an integrated, whole human being as opposed to the man torn apart by internal crises that he had been a few months previously. Having told me a few weeks earlier that he had given up smoking joints, he now had a large chunk of hash in his pocket and was rolling up continually. "There's some link between working long stretches in studios and smoking big amounts of hash," he said. "They just fit to-gether." In the studio itself, beneath a grand piano, he had built a spliff bunker out of the usual assortment of metal flight cases, where he often slept. Joe approached his task with the obsessive, loving dedication of old, working thirty-six-hour stretches—as Mick Jones was—and sleeping on the floor under the piano. "Once the rest of BAD realized that I don't get in-volved in anything unless I do it to the max, it worked out fine," he said. The rest of BAD were concerned. Were Mick and Joe getting back together? About the Clash, and its main players in their subsequent incarnations, there was often an intense sense of unexpected drama and poetry, a roman-tic, mystical quality worthy of a South American novel.

The situation was mutually advantageous: Strummer's creative block vanished, and songs started to pour out of him, in his delightful phrase, "like spunk in a whorehouse. Ever since I hit that BAD studio I just started to go. It's got to be truly bad, this record," he insisted. "Hard. You know," he joked, "I've figured out why all the BAD songs are a minute too long: be-cause so many of the parts are programmed onto tape, and no one remem-bers to stop them. I'm getting them to roughen up the sound and lose that Radio 2 tendency Mick has. Mick isn't going to know what happened when this record gets going in the mix."

The mix was done in New York. Afterward Mick said this had been "Joe's revenge" for his own insistence on recording *Combat Rock* in Man-hattan: using the expensive Hit Factory, *No. 10 Upping Street*—as Joe de-cided the record should be named, a play on 10 Downing Street, the residence of the prime minister—cost a small fortune, the most expensive record Mick ever made. "We flew in," said Joe. "Got a cab. Hit the hotel.

For BAD's second album, Joe came on board as coproducer, once again writing songs with Mick Jones. *(UrbanImage.tv/Adrian Boot)*

Threw our stuff in the room. Walked seven blocks to the studio. I was in there for twenty days and nights before I went to a bar. We did it in New York because we wanted it to be like good vegetables—fresh."

"Everything's gone as it should have done," Mick told me two days before the record was completed. "It went even greater once Joe was on board. I always felt great about this LP, right from the very start. I can't remember a time when I felt so overawed, or was so happy with what I was doing." *No. 10 Upping Street* is a magnificent and underrated piece of work, probably BAD's best record, with a tough, contemporary production. With Mick, Joe cowrote five songs: "Beyond the Pale," a beautiful, melodic tune with an epic sweep that talks about the immigrant mix ("Immigration built the nation" runs a key line) that has built Britain—one of the best ever songs involving the Strummer–Jones combination; "Limbo the Law," a story of Latino gangsters; "V. Thirteen," a view of a dystopian future; "Ticket," on which the lead vocals are taken by Don Letts and bass player Leo Williams; and the superb "Sightsee MC," a thundering tune in the style of contemporary New York rap with lyrics specifically about London.

What was Joe's purpose in this work? Unquestionably he was guided into it by the magical meeting with Don Letts, and he went with the flow; he didn't have another agenda. But when you looked at him in the studio, there was still that great hurt in his eyes: it seemed like he might burst into tears sometimes. Working with Mick Jones and his simpatico posse was reminding Joe how great it could be, what a fantastic team had been ruptured. At this time he really wanted to get the Clash back together, even though he knew it was impossible. He admitted to me later that he invested a large amount of "psychic energy" in that direction, trying to will it to happen, for a substantial amount of time.

On August 5 Joe flew back to London from the New York *Upping Street* mix, and the next evening he traveled on to Almería for the beginning of the *Straight to Hell* shoot. Eleven days later, at three in the morning Spanish time, he called me. He was standing looking at Africa eighty miles away, he said. No, he insisted adamantly, he had not joined BAD, as the rumors insisted. "Are you kidding? The BAD LP's brilliant, because me and Mick were involved. But I'm going to make a record of my own when I've got something really good.

"I'm just about ready, and I'm looking forward to working with Mick again, because we're going to do it together. It'll be called *Throwdown* and it'll be completely the opposite of everything else that's being made now: just three instruments and the cheapest studio. Everyone'll hate it except the hipsters and flipsters. I just promise to make a good record when I can, and not to tour, and not to foist any shit on the public. And never to make another video. It's the performance and the content that counts.

"It ain't rock 'n' roll anymore. It's just wallpaper. Now is the time when you've got to look for things, as it was in the days of beatniks existing in straight society, when the good stuff was hard to find. But was even more valuable when you discovered it."

The story of *Straight to Hell*, which had been written by Alex Cox and Dick Rude very quickly (if not in the claimed three days), was like a *Mad* magazine parody of a spaghetti western. Joe Strummer, as a character called Simms, Dick Rude, and Sy Richardson, an L.A. actor, played a trio of hapless, hopeless "deadly killers" who had pulled a bank heist and were on the run. "I'm bad energy, man," Joe's character Simms declared. "That's his own line, his self-knowledge thing," noted Alex Cox. The film also featured the Pogues, Elvis Costello, a young newcomer named Courtney Love, and a member of Alex Cox's informal repertory company, Zander Schloss, who became a firm ally of Joe. Alex Cox's idea was to litter the film with cameo parts: Dennis Hopper, Grace Jones, John Cusack and Jim Jarmusch were among those flown in.

In Spain Joe was more closed down than I had seen him in London, more I felt from being Joe Strummer on public display than from trying to stay in character. As the male lead, Joe was surrounded by conceptually correct details—an acoustic guitar, a switchblade knife, a pack of man-sized Commando cigarettes ("H.M. Government warning: cigarettes can seriously fuck with your health!"), a moldy prepackaged pizza. He was wearing a black suit that he had not removed since filming began two weeks previously, after having first dived into the hotel pool wearing it. He spent all day on set in a beat-up '71 Dodge. As he also sported a barely concealed shoulder holster and revolver beneath his dust-ingrained jacket, this caused a measure of consternation among the customers in the bars he was prone to visit until six in the morning.

It had got to the point, Joe said, where he was no longer able to discriminate between life on and off set. "Acting requires concentration," he offered as an explanation as to why he appeared so enclosed, so within himself; and why half the crew suspected him of temporary insanity, particularly over such crucial matters as the necessity of allowing himself to be covered in flies without flinching. "This," he announced in the Dodge one day, "is a film for everybody, a film that people all around the world can understand. A Bolivian tin miner can take his señorita to see it on a Friday night and know that he's getting his peso's worth."

Frank Murray was manager of the Pogues. As he was also a walking character actor, almost a stage Irishman, he naturally had a part in *Straight to Hell*. "Joe stayed out in the desert at night a lot," Frank remembered. "Joe likes bonfires and they had bonfires out there and played guitars. It was a very, very unique and magical experience."

In a drinking session Joe told Frank what he had decided he should do. No longer was it a blues band he was after—now he wanted to form a semi-acoustic group, like the Pogues. "Joe started talking about an acoustic project he wanted to get involved in. In a roundabout way he was asking if he could poach Terry Woods from the Pogues. I did like the idea that Joe wanted to play acoustic music, or semi-acoustic. I thought it was the right road to go down." When Zander Schloss suggested he and Joe play together, Joe replied, "Zander, I don't want to play music. I'm an old man, Zander." Joe had turned thirty-four a few days earlier.

Frank Murray walked out of another cantina with Joe. "He started looking up in the sky and identifying things like Ursa Major. I thought he was taking the piss. He said, 'No, Frank, I can identify them all.' I could understand why he stayed in the desert in Almería, because you looked at beautiful stars at night. Then when he moved to Somerset: same thing, beautiful skies at night."

But Joe had a day job. How was he doing? "He would come up with inspired ideas for lines," said Alex Cox. "When he and Dick Rude are on their

Starring in a heist film shot on the sets of spaghetti westerns: what better way to spend the summer for Joe Strummer? (*UrbanImage.tv/AdrianBoot*)

deathbeds, Dick is lying there, groaning and moaning that he's dying, and Joe comes up with: 'Still, mustn't grumble'—his last words in the film. He improvised them, the words written in the script were probably something like 'Adieu, *hombre.*'"

Down in Almería Joe also encountered another member of the ensemble: Jem Finer, the banjo player and engine room of the Pogues. While the gnarled visage of Shane MacGowan was the public persona of the Pogues, Jem Finer—who wrote much of the material—was the real leader of the group. He had come down to the set with his wife, Marcia, and their two daughters, Kitty and Ella, roughly the same ages as Jazz and Lola, there with Gaby; later, Joe's treat for all four girls would be to make them fish finger sandwiches. Gaby became tight with Marcia Finer, an intelligent, interesting artist. "After Spain Gaby and Joe invited us over to Lancaster Road," said Jem. "I knew him primarily through the family connection. I didn't know him through music at all. There were a few times when we'd all go and do stuff with the kids and Mick and his daughter Lauren would come along. Joe always seemed a very no-bullshit person, good company, good fun, good at setting up things for kids to do, making dens. We'd get pissed and stoned in the evening. I felt there were two people there, John Mellor and Joe Strummer. The person I knew was John Mellor; Joe Strummer was very much a construct.

"The Joe Strummer character would emerge after a period of sustained activity which seemed to involve staying up very, very late, getting more and more obsessed, being destructive, and being a control freak. As time went on when we were working together it took longer and longer until he was Joe Strummer the whole time—which was not always pleasant.

"The singer is the focus of attention. Joe was a front man in a very different way from Shane, our singer: there's an element of a showman about Joe. Interlinked with that was his position as Joe Strummer, saving the world, and he'd try and figure out how to do that role. But there were weird contradictions. There was a side to him that was decidedly totalitarian, poised on the precipice between the extreme left and the extreme right. I'm not saying he's a fascist, but just somebody who has that control tendency. One of the last times I saw him he was talking about [Field Marshal Bernard] Montgomery. He was saying how brilliantly he'd done."

Jem and Gaby, Joe and Marcia: people used to joke that they were like two pairs of brothers and sisters. Not that it always stayed so platonic: "There were the odd times," said Marcia, "he'd come on a bit amorous to me and I'd think, 'I don't believe this for a minute.' Sometimes he'd do that 'You understand me' routine and I said, 'You say that to all the girls, come on.' There was that thing about the depression, and being in love, or having a fling, was a move away from it. He had that duality. I wasn't very girly and he wasn't really totally macho—that construction, that masquerade of a person's sexual persona and type. He could relate to people who had that duality."

"I wouldn't say he seemed depressed," Jem added. "He seemed very positive, not cheerful—that's not the right word for Joe. There was a time the Pogues were recording round the corner from his house. I bumped into him and it seemed obvious he wanted to be in a band again, making music again, out in the world rather than his basement. I felt he wasn't totally happy not being a working rock 'n' roller. He definitely wasn't an uproariously happy person. He was seriously engaged with the world, and the world's not the nicest place, and any sensible person isn't going to be uproariously happy." (Later Mick Jones echoed Jem's thoughts: "Maybe Joe did fall into depressions. Because he was grounded in reality.")

The film director Jim Jarmusch, who had met Joe briefly in Cannes, quickly became part of his posse and returned to New York from the *Straight to Hell* film set via London. "I stayed at Joe's house on the sofa for a few days and often after that. Once Jazzy and Lola came downstairs dressed in feather boas with strange lipstick marks on their faces and started jumping up and down on the furniture. Joe said, 'What's all this then?' They said, 'Daddy, we're playing punk rock olden days.' And the expression on Joe's face . . . He sat down in the kitchen and poured himself a brandy and Coke and poured me one. One time we were walking in London and we passed a guy younger than us in a suit and tie, a businessman guy, and he had a Walkman on. Joe said, 'He's probably listening to *Sandinista!*' That remark, even though it was funny, was probably born out of that depressive side of Joe."

After *Straight to Hell*, more film work for Joe came up almost straightaway. Through Alex Cox, Joe met Rudy Wurlitzer, who had scripted Sam Peckinpah's *Pat Garrett and Billy the Kid*; Joe was a big fan of Bob Dylan's soundtrack for that film. With Robert Frank, who had made the Rolling Stones' banned *Cocksucker Blues*, Wurlitzer was codirecting *Candy Moun-*

Paul Simonon's painting of Joe's ancestors' home at Umachan
on the isle of Raasay amply conveys the vigor and rigor of life on
the Inner Hebridean island. Children at play would be tethered
to trees, to save them from tumbling down cliffs and ravines.

Everyone needs a hobby, and Joe Strummer and Mick Jones certainly shared one:
Joe specialized in passing spliffs via an under-arm lob, which the recipient was
obliged to catch.

Left Although Joe had had an expensive dental refit the previous summer, it appeared his bridgework had vanished for this show at Bond's in Manhattan in June 1981. "There were a couple of teeth situations," said Mick Jones. "Once, we were in the studio and Joe couldn't sing for weeks because he'd had a big dental session just before we started."

Below With Pearl Harbor onstage in Tokyo performing Wanda Jackson's Fujiyama Mama, Joe is deliriously happy. The Clash had refused to play Japan unless the fans were allowed to stand, the first act ever to be granted this concession. "For this they were considered Men of Honor," said Kosmo Vinyl.

Joe's fingers were permanently in shreds while the Clash were on tour. Joe approached life like a warrior monk, which was greatly appreciated in Japan on their only tour of the country, in 1982. The shining clarity in Joe's eyes is perhaps attributable to the absence of marijuana on the tour.

For their arrival at Shea Stadium on October 12, 1982, the Clash rented an open-topped 1956 Cadillac. As the vehicle's heater was malfunctioning, the group was freezing. The image of Joe with his "Mohawk," part *Taxi Driver*, part *Mad Max*, is the defining memory of him for many American fans.

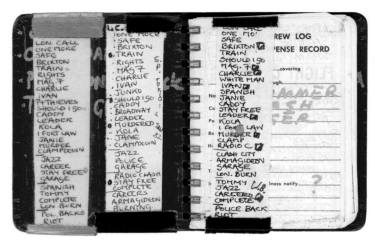

Every night on tour it would be Joe who chose and wrote out the set lists. He compiled two versions, a larger one for the crew, and—as here—three narrow ones to be stuck on the top side of his and Mick's guitars and Paul's bass. This trio of lists was found in one of Joe's personal diaries.

On the May 1985 busking tour, Joe would drop to his knees during his performance of Gene Vincent's "Be-Bop-A-Lula." Although the experience bonded together the Clash Mk II after a miserable time in the recording studio, the end was nigh. From left to right: Vince White, Paul, Pete Howard, Joe, Nick Sheppard.

Joe happily feeding Jazz, his firstborn daughter, in 1984 (*above left and right*). He was never one to forget his priorities. Joe's children, Jazz and Lola (*below*), were soon pulled into his cowboy world. Here they are with Gaby, their mother, and Joe at a fancy-dress party at the Tabernacle in 1989. Wagons ho!

Right Joe with the author at the Hard Rock Casino in Las Vegas on November 7, 1999, following the Mescaleros' show in the venue.

Left On May 31, 1995, John "Joe Strummer" Mellor and Lucinda Tait were married at Chelsea Registry Office. From then on, Joe's career finally began to take an upward curve: the days of "the Wilderness Years" were behind him.

Below After being given a pair of tickets to Glastonbury as a wedding present, Joe rediscovered his love of the festival lifestyle. Central to this were the campfires he would always create, great levelers of the playing field. Later, he felt his true legacy might not be the Clash, but the campfire experience.

The complex simplicity of the Mescaleros, coupled with the affecting wit of Joe's lyrics and vocals, soon found them selling out concerts around the world. In the second lineup of the group, Joe was reunited with his old mentor Tymon Dogg, who spars with his visionary multi-instrumentalist Martin Slattery in this photograph.

Despite his age, Joe frequently would perform with the Mescaleros as though he were a twenty-year-old. Joe—here at an instore performance at HMV on London's Oxford Street to promote the *Global a Go-Go* album—is yet again thundering through a set that frequently contained a high percentage of Clash songs.

The final lineup of Joe Strummer and the Mescaleros. From left to right: guitarist Scott Shields, drummer Luke Bullen, Joe, violinist Tymon Dogg, and bass player Simon Stafford.

On Friday, November 15, 2002, there took place one of the great moments of rock 'n' roll. Billed to play a benefit at Action Town Hall in West London for the striking workers of the Fire Brigades Union, Joe Strummer and the Mescaleros were joined onstage by Mick Jones, the first time Joe and Mick had played together since 1983. The poetry of the event was lent an even greater poignancy by the death of Joe Strummer just over five weeks later.

Joe and his spar Sean Carasov at the bar of 192, the Notting Hill
restaurant that became a part of Joe's scene. *(Sean Carasov)*

tain, shot in Canada in the autumn of 1986. Wurlitzer offered Joe a small
part, as Mario, a security guard. "It was frustrating that Joe had only a small
part, because he was very exciting—one wanted more of him," said Rudy
Wurlitzer. "He could be a great star, a major leading man."

Returning to London, much of Joe's time was dedicated to his mother.
Anna Mellor, whose cancer had reached a terminal stage, was in the last
throes of her life at the hospice in Caterham. Paradoxically, said Gaby, this

"withdrawn" woman "only came alive when Lola was born—the day after Anna's birthday. She was besotted, the only time I saw her really animated. She had bone cancer. It was painful for her to touch anything—yet she'd let Lola crawl all over her." Anna Mellor did not leave this world without a considerable fight; twice she was moved out of her ward at the hospice and taken to a room where she could die on her own; twice she packed her things and moved back into the ward.

This was the time when on so many occasions I'd walk round a corner in Notting Hill and find Joe walking straight into me, tension sparks almost visibly flying off him, his head bowed, his face drawn. He seemed hardly able to bring himself to speak, not even looking entirely comfortable in his habitual black leather jacket, as though the uniform no longer fitted. After the great success of working on the second BAD record, he now seemed desperately unhappy. On such chance meetings I would want to put my arms around him and tell him it was all right, he was going to be OK. But the defense mechanisms learned young within John Mellor, and certainly frozen within the complex Joe Strummer, would not permit such thinking from others. You felt his antennae were so alert that he would second-guess your every attempt to console him, and he would traipse off on his way. Later Jim Jarmusch would describe him to me in such moods as "Big Chief Thunder Cloud," an apt description of the dark aura that Joe seemed able to summon up at will to surround him like a shield.

The final end of Anna Mellor, on December 28, 1986, led only to more introversion. "After Ron died," said Joe's cousin Iain Gillies, "Anna was dignified and gracious. When she became ill herself she didn't complain or even want to talk about it. From Ron going until her death in late 1986 I saw her regularly, once a month or so." When his mother finally died, Joe stopped going out, stopped drinking, stopped smoking spliffs. Late in January 1987 I was walking up Portobello Road in the early evening winter dark to the Gate Cinema, where I was going to see Jim Jarmusch's *Down by Law*. Suddenly a long-haired, bearded scruff walking in the other direction barged into my shoulder. "Don't you recognize me?" asked a familiar voice. It was Joe. I was amazed. His new look was for his part in Alex Cox's forthcoming film, *Walker*. He told me that he had been staying in since his mother had died, but that he was looking forward to going to Nicaragua to make the film the following month. Now he seemed fragile and open again.

"*Down by Law's* good," he called out over his shoulder as he set off on his way. "I've seen it twice."

"When his mum died," said Dick Rude, "it was incredibly traumatic for him. He felt a lot of guilt for not having been closer to her, and not having been there when she died. I imagined his mom was the carrier of that depression and he had some rebelliousness toward her because of that. He was the child of an alcoholic. I think at some point after she died he found forgiveness by looking outward, not inward. The way he treated Gaby was the result of his relationship with his mother. I remember him going to the funeral, and he was really at odds with Gaby. He's sitting there going, 'How did I get here?' That was his truly dark night of the soul. It was his period of deepest brooding, and he was very introverted. Your mom dies, you've gone from hero to zero, and you're off acting in little movies around the world."

2

1

soldiers of misfortune

1987–1988

**The *Walker* film set, Granada, Nicaragua,
late March 1987**

William Walker, played in Alex Cox's movie by the excellent Ed Harris,
was a figure little known in his home country of the United States. In
1855 he shipped an army to Nicaragua and had himself proclaimed president, though he was overthrown after a year. "He's a complete puzzle," a
still bearded, still long-haired Joe Strummer told me when I arrived on the set.
Like those humorous roles Shakespeare wrote for the alleged "groundlings,"
Joe was playing Faucet, a cook in Walker's army; Dick Rude played his partner-
in-cuisine. "Even the book he wrote, *The War in Nicaragua*, he wrote in the
third person. He was a megalomaniac, and in the end he went bonkers. He
even shot his own brother," he concluded, describing what for Joe might
have been the very worst of mortal sins. Joe's face was smeared with mud:
"Sunblock," he announced. "That's all that Walker's men had to use. So I'm
using it too."

In a cantina to one side of the set, he was thoughtfully sipping a *cerveza*.
"They released *Sandinista!* here," he suddenly announced, slightly oddly. "I
don't think it sold any copies, though." Contrary to what I had expected, in

Who was the Man of Mystery? Joe Strummer (center) in character for his
part in *Walker*. *(Daniel Laine/CORBIS)*

a land which had a deep resonance for him, Joe did not seem to be exactly
having a great time. In the cantina he snapped at me for not knowing that
the Spanish for "beer" was *cerveza*. As though taking his lead from those
family sojourns in far-flung parts of the Empire, and despite his film cos-
tume, Joe seemed more like a white-suited Graham Greene character than
a member of *The Wild Bunch*. (All the same, Joe Strummer was offered
Nicaraguan citizenship, which he respectfully declined—he thought it
might prevent his family from being given U.S. visas.)

Spider Stacey of the Pogues was the only member of the group to have
been given a part in the film. This was the first time he had seen Joe Strummer since being on the set of *Straight to Hell*. "He seemed troubled, at least
distant. I know he was acting in a film, and his appearance had had to
change for it, but it made him look very strange. He didn't seem the Joe I
had met in Spain the previous summer."

The spiky aura I had observed around Joe on the streets of Notting Hill
had traveled with him on the plane to Nicaragua. He again seemed not in a
good state, awkward, visibly uncertain. He was suffering a lot from his
mother's death, yet in that traditionally Highland "close" manner, Joe had
omitted to mention this to those involved with *Walker*. Alex Cox had no idea

that he had gone through the experience of losing his mother shortly before leaving for Nicaragua.

Rather than live in the crew hotel in Managua, Joe and Dick Rude moved into a house in the smaller city of Granada, where Dick observed Joe's angst firsthand. "There is no man that was ever better at brooding and isolating than he was. You could be in a bar with him having a laugh and everything is fine, then you turn around and he's left without saying good-bye. He could isolate better than anyone, he could make you laugh better than anyone, he could be there for you more than anyone. He did it all to his fullest."

So isolated was Joe that during his time in Nicaragua, he refused to get in touch with Gaby and the girls in London. Dick Rude was astonished: "It used to blow my mind. I would say, 'Did you talk to Gaby?' He'd say, 'No.' I'd say, 'Why not? Aren't you interested how your wife and kids are?' He would say, 'She'll call me.' But it was not because he didn't care. He cared so much it hurt. I'm sure that's the same as he was toward the Clash. 'I can't talk to you right now. I can't talk about this. I can't deal with this. I just need to walk away from it. If it means I have to get drunk off my ass to not think about it, then that's what it's going to take.'"

What really had happened in Joe Strummer's life was something that often comes as a surprise to people when they grow older: he had fallen in love. At a party for *Sid and Nancy* during the New York Film Festival in October 1986 at the Milk Bar on Houston and Broadway, he had been introduced to a twenty-year-old drama student called Danielle von Zerneck. She had just finished playing the part of Donna, the girlfriend of the singer Ritchie Valens, in the well-received Valens biopic *La Bamba*. As Gaby was, Danielle was blonde and beautiful. She had grown up in Los Angeles, where her mother owned a bookstore, in which Joe had been known to peruse, while her father was a film producer. The next day Danielle met Joe at the same bar where the party had been, and Joe went home to Danielle's brownstone apartment on Thirteenth Street in the West Village. "We probably both thought it would be a one-night stand, and I don't know why it wasn't. I'd go to classes every day, and he'd be there at night when I got back. He stayed there. He'd just dump his clothes on the bed. We'd sometimes be with Jim Jarmusch and Sara Driver and Bob Gruen. Joe was polite and gracious and gentlemanly. He enjoyed being like that, displaying what he had learned in his father's diplomatic life."

Joe went back to London but a fortnight later returned to stay with Danielle for another two weeks. "I never asked him to leave Gaby, who I subsequently met and think is really great. I was really young and quite comfortable with his situation. I didn't want to settle down. After those two weeks he went home. He said he'd come back. Then his mother died. Jim and Sara told me how devastated he was. Because of it he decided he must put his life back together with Gaby and the girls. So he never called."

In the house that he shared with Joe in Granada, Dick Rude inadvertently made a serious faux pas one night, crossing a line with Joe that he hadn't even realized existed. On his guitar Dick had written a song, which he told Joe he wanted to play to him. "I said, 'You gotta hear this.' It was called 'The Ballad of John Mellor' and it went something like: 'Once there was a man called John Mellor / Then he changed his name to Joe Strummer.'

"He did not like that song, man. He turned to me and scowled. When he looked at you the wrong way, it was one hundred percent. He scowled and shot daggers at me, and said, in that voice, 'Don't you ever play that song again!' He meant it. I knew I had pushed a button, and I knew then that he did not want to be reminded of who he was and where he was from, of anything outside of having the experience of being there and acting in this movie."

Zander Schloss, who was also in the film, noted: "When you would see early footage of the Clash, you would see this kind of small man, but his aura was huge. It made him look like a giant. But at the time of *Straight to Hell* and *Walker*, it was as if his aura had crumbled in on him, and he was hunched over, and would look up and look back down and was very reserved and controlled about what he would say. There was this bubbling undercurrent that would never really surface."

Whatever his frame of mind, Joe's improvisatory skills seemed undiminished, as the director noted. "In one scene Joe had to walk past a group of bare-breasted women doing their laundry, and it was Strummer who put in the line, 'I think some of us should go in the water and get them.' It was his idea."

As was often the case with Joe, he had his own agenda: to write the soundtrack music for the film. "Joe manipulated that situation in a very nice way," said Alex Cox, whose plan was for Joe to work on the soundtrack with Nicaraguan musicians. But Joe said, "I've been thinking. The music for *Sid and Nancy* and *Straight to Hell* is a bit of a mishmash because you've got so many bands. It would be better if the music for *Walker* is all written by one person."

"I said only if it was as good as the soundtrack for *Pat Garrett and Billy the Kid*. He said, 'All right then.' We stayed in Nicaragua for a few weeks. He composed most of the score there. Then we went to San Francisco and recorded the music there and did the mix."

Before Joe could begin to install himself full-time in the recording of the *Walker* soundtrack, he returned briefly to London to publicize the release of *Straight to Hell*. The finished film that had emerged out of the four weeks in Almería was baffling. It held your attention as a cultural curio—appearances of its various musical and cinematic icons ensured that. But it was not a good film, and was critically savaged.

I saw Joe a few times while he was back in London. I interviewed him for the BBC Radio One program hosted by Andy Kershaw, who had been Leeds University social secretary in 1980. Joe threw in a memorable line: "*Straight to Hell* is like good cheese: it improves with age." Then we left. Joe needed to get up to the Dome, a bar in Hampstead where he was to be interviewed for a television program. He asked me to come along. We bought a couple of cans of beer each and caught a tube up to Hampstead. On a packed Northern Line tube train up to Hampstead, both of us standing, swigging on our beers, Joe seemed to be recognized though not acknowledged. I saw him again the next week, at the launch party for the film, held at a dance hall on Tottenham Court Road. It was June 11, election day. As though proof of that old adage that the better the party, the worse the film, the *Straight to Hell* launch was fantastic: every groover in London had been invited and there was endless free drink. Joe was there with Gaby. At one moment, quite late, I saw him and Mick Jones deep in conversation, their mouths turning down in disdain at something. "What's up?" I asked. "The election results have started to come in," said Joe. "We've lost," grimaced Mick decisively, as we braced ourselves for another term of Conservative Party rule under Margaret Thatcher. I saw Joe with Frank Murray, manager of the Pogues: "Frank really wanted to manage Joe," Gaby explained, "but Joe wouldn't go for it." Eventually we all staggered off to a bar, ending up back at Joe's house, eating toast, smoking spliffs and drinking even more as the sound of people going to work sailed into the house from the street. As photographer Bob Gruen would say: "When you go out with Joe for the evening, make sure you take your sunglasses. Because you'll need them when the sun comes up."

Then Joe Strummer went to San Francisco, continuing his battle to save his soul through his own creativity.

The film production company had booked time for Joe at Russian Hill Recordings, where Sam Lehmer was the resident engineer. Sam's introduction to Joe Strummer was not the most conventional. "Joe came by the first day. He had been out drinking with Alex the night before. He was completely wasted. He brought in a boom box, sat it down on the recording consul and said: 'Right, listen to this. This is what we're going to do today.' On the b-box were strummed sketches of a song. 'Right, let's try to do this. You guys try to work something up. I'll be back in an hour or two.' He went off to get some breakfast at three in the afternoon."

Lehmer remembered how Joe got back on course during the recording. "He got completely back to normal. He had something to focus on. It was productive. Joe was a pretty private guy. He was hard to read; he didn't share a lot of what was going on inside. He liked to fool people. He liked to keep you off balance and not know whether he was telling you the straight story or not. You had to guess."

Joe's disappearing for breakfast on the first day marked the almost Warhol-like way in which he approached the entire record, leaving the musicians and studio staff to work on ideas he had given them before returning to hear the results. His vision was that the soundtrack would incorporate native Nicaraguan sounds along with American hillbilly music of the 1850s. Despite his hangover, he had been on time for his meeting on the first day, as he would be every day for the five weeks it took to make the record, when there was a 10:00 a.m. start. "Joe knew what he wanted. There was no doubt about that," said Lehmer, who quickly empathized with his client and became part of the Joe Strummer West Coast posse. Joe needed all the allies he could get; working on his own was frightening. As he admitted to *Melody Maker* the next year, "I was a bundle of nerves when *Walker* was recorded. I thought it would be a fucking disaster. I tell you, I've only realized now what pressure I was under."

At Sam's suggestion they brought in Dick Bright, the leader of the house band at San Francisco's Vermont Hotel, with access to the kind of seasoned popular orchestral musicians who could match Joe's perception of the *Walker* music. Bright could write the musical charts from which they would play.

It was as though the ideas Joe had been mulling over for an acoustic-based group in Almería with Frank Murray the year before had come together. Yet he was recording far more music than was needed. "We did all these Latin tracks," said Sam, "and we kept saying, 'Joe, we only need so much for the picture.' Joe kept saying, 'Yes, but we're making a soundtrack album. They can just cut it up and use it in the movie.' So we would make various versions of all the songs. He didn't really feel Latin music because it wasn't his roots, but Joe would let the guys experiment and see what came together."

Joe had immediately built a spliff bunker in the drum booth at Russian Hill. "Joe got our runner to go and get all the empty two-inch-tape boxes and pile them up so he could go in there and make it his office. This was a great idea because people were constantly coming to see Joe and Joe didn't want people hanging out where the work was going on. They would sit there and smoke 'English,' as he called those half-tobacco and half-pot joints. When there weren't visitors, Joe would be there drawing a lot of cartoons." The spliff bunker: you don't exactly have to be Freud to perceive its various resonances, the primal nature of the child's den, and its secure back-to-the-womb element.

Frequently in the studio, offering moral support, was Rudy Fernandez, who had driven the Clash through the Monterey festival gates in 1979. Once Joe asked Rudy to canvass the local Mexican restaurants to find a mariachi band that employed a guitarron, a fretless six-string bass guitar, to use on a song. But Rudy also experienced the idiosyncrasies of Joe's needs. Despite his hangover, Joe called Rudy on his first day there. He said, "I want to get a Cadillac. I've been singing about these cars for years. I want one of my own." What Joe was looking for was a mid-1950s Cadillac Seville, a beautiful classic of the marque, the image of the Brand New Cadillac. After spending Joe's first weekend in California looking for one, the pair gave up and went back to Rudy's home in San Carlos. Walking out to the local liquor store, "there it was, a 1955 turquoise Cadillac," said Rudy. "It had been sitting there for years in this guy's driveway and it looked like the FOR SALE sign had been there for years too. It was $5,000. We drove around for a while. He didn't have a license, but it didn't matter to him. People would stop in the street, and kids would point at us: 'Look at that car!'" Rudy then learned what was at the back of Joe's mind: this was to be his car for Californian visits. "I can take the kids to the zoo in it in L.A. Oh, Rudy, I couldn't keep it in your garage, could I?"

Zander Schloss received a call from Joe, asking him to come to Russian Hill, "and bring your Spanish guitar." Joe was well on his way to finishing the "Nicaraguan" side of the album; Zander added overdubs and textures. "When it came to the second side of the album, which was a little bit more organic and folky, we started to build the tracks from the ground up." On three of the tunes, the only ones featuring singing, Joe took the vocal lead; following straight on from the beautiful melody of the instrumental "Latin Romance" comes "The Unknown Immortal" (there seems an especial poignancy in Joe's line "I was once an immortal"); he also sings on "Tennessee Rain" and "Tropic of No Return." "When Joe wasn't feeling good about himself," said Alex Cox, "he would mix his vocals right down, so you could hardly hear them. But on those three songs his voice is clear and strong. He was enjoying what he was doing."

Alex Cox was working on the edit at the Napa Valley ranch of Francis Ford Coppola, the director of *The Godfather* and *Apocalypse Now*. Joe drove the fifty miles in the Cadillac. "It takes hours to get there," said Rudy, "because Joe's so slow—he's loving every minute of it. It's just like in a movie. We're going through the dirt roads, kind of like in *East of Eden*, driving through the fields. We get to Coppola's place, and no one knew we were coming. The assistants thought we were migrant farm workers. 'What are you guys doing here?' The Cadillac didn't have any window wipers. It started sprinkling. Joe was driving, and I was cleaning the windshield with my hand.

"Coppola was real nice to Joe, so was Sofia Coppola, his daughter, a young girl then. She knew who Joe was, and she would hang out with us, riding in the Cadillac."

Joe Strummer's soundtrack for *Walker* was artistically a great success. It proved to him that he could do something on his own in his own way, revitalized him, bolstered his spirits, got him great reviews. Had he been restored by *Walker*? asked *Melody Maker*. "Yeah, though I do have a manic depressive side that I've only just been able to conquer. You know, I spent the last four years not doing anything, just sitting at home trying to understand what I'd done or perhaps what I should do. And it was a very depressing four years." When he saw the completed *Walker* film, however, the movie was a great disappointment. "What am I going to say to Alex?" Joe asked Gerry Harrington, his new agent, as they exited a screening in Los Angeles. "Tell him," said Gerry, "it's going to scare the shit out of them. Let's see how the establishment handle that." This was exactly what Joe told Alex Cox. (After running into Eric Fellner at a screening of John Hughes's *Pretty in Pink*, Gerry Harrington had learned that Joe was working in San Francisco and had tracked him down, giving him his pitch. Joe went for it, appreciating Gerry's earnestness and innocence, and they began working together. Quickly Gerry realized that Joe "gave himself such a raw deal most of the time, then it became a self-fulfilling prophecy.")

Gaby had visited him in San Francisco, but once the work was done, Joe returned to 37 Lancaster Road to be with her and the girls. Some four weeks later, at around midnight, Rudy Fernandez heard a knock on his front door. To his amazement, Joe was standing there. "I gotta get to L.A. Give me the keys to the Cadillac." Joe had flown to California for a meeting the next day in Los Angeles with Virgin Records, who were releasing the *Walker* soundtrack, but he had decided to come to San Francisco to pick up the Cadillac and drive overnight the four hundred miles to L.A. Rudy pointed out that they were in the middle of a storm and the Cadillac had no windshield wipers; to drive that distance would be suicidal. "Joe goes, 'I don't care! I don't care! I've gotta get down there.' He was freaking out. Eventually I say, 'I'll drive you down there. We'll take my car.'"

After a frantic eight-hour dash through the rainy night the pair arrived in Los Angeles, making it to the Virgin Beverly Hills headquarters and squealing into the parking lot. "Park there," said Joe, pointing out an empty space. As they did so, another car aimed at it, Rudy beating him. The reserved space belonged to the company's president, and it was he they were pushing out of his place. But when a red-eyed Joe emerged from Rudy's car, due deference was shown by the record company boss. The meeting, about Joe's part in promoting the *Walker* soundtrack, ran smoothly, though not as much as Joe had hoped. He had wanted to use the record's release on Virgin to somehow lever him out of his Sony deal, but found he was strapped in too tight by all that small print in the ten-year-old Clash contract.

Since last seeing Joe Strummer at the end of 1986, Danielle von Zerneck had got on with her life. She'd acted in a pair of "terrible" movies, had a couple more boyfriends, and stayed friends with Bob Gruen, Jim Jarmusch and Sara Driver. "OK, that was great!" were her only thoughts about the romance with Joe. She heard Joe was in Los Angeles, staying at the Sunset Marquis, and called, left a message and then went out. "When I came back I had a message from Joe on my machine, singing the song 'Donna.' It was one of the most romantic things. He'd gone into the bathroom to make the call so Rudy wouldn't hear. We talked. It was nice." Then she went to bed.

At 7:00 a.m. the door buzzer rang at Danielle's New York apartment. "I go downstairs and Joe is standing there with a bouquet of flowers. It was so lovely. It started up all over again. He'd got off the phone and caught the red-eye. He stayed with me for about a week. I was now in L.A. quite a bit. Back and forth. He was too. When we started seeing each other again that September, it was much more serious.

"When we were together he was not depressed. Later I broke up with him and he was depressed in front of me. Mine is a very odd perspective— his relationship with me was like how going on holiday will kick people out of depression. It was like a holiday romance. We enjoyed eating in restaurants in malls because no one eats there who might know us. In New York David Johansen was developing his Buster Poindexter set at the Bottom Line and Joe took me along."

In Los Angeles Joe linked up with a film music supervisor named Kathy Nelson, whom he had met during *Sid and Nancy* post-production. One day she drove him to the airport to catch a flight to London. Arriving back at her one-bedroom house off Laurel Canyon, having made some stops on the way, Kathy was surprised to find Joe sitting on her doorstep.

"What's going on?" she demanded.

"I didn't feel like getting on the plane, so I caught a cab."

"How did you know my address?"

"I had your address."

"At the time I thought he was an oddball. But he was probably completely out of it. I was about twenty-five years old and I thought 'How odd.' I remember going up the street, thinking, 'Oh my God. What's he doing here?' He was kind of aimless. He just said, 'I didn't want to go home.'"

Late in October 1987 Joe did go back to London, but not for as long as he had expected. "After *Walker* I wanted to go back to London and think," he said. "Then the phone rings. I had just looked at my horoscope. It said, 'You will receive an interesting call.'"

It came from Frank Murray. In less than a week the Pogues were due to set off on an American tour. But a long-standing ailment of Philip Chevron, the guitarist, had been finally diagnosed as a stomach ulcer. So Frank came to a decision. "I rang up Joe to ask him to join the Pogues. Phil wouldn't survive a U.S. tour. 'Do you want to be rhythm guitar player?' Joe said, 'You're not trying to get rid of Phil?' I then rang every member of the Pogues and said Joe had offered to do it. Which wasn't true. They all said OK. Then I rang Joe back and said the group were all into it. He had one day's rehearsal. He taped the set to his guitar, and made a note of the keys. Three days later we hit New York and did two nights at the Ritz. Nobody knew Joe Strummer was playing with the Pogues in America until people saw him walk onstage at the Ritz that first night. Half the audience didn't even know Joe Strummer—and I mean no disrespect to Joe. He had the time of his life. He got that hunger back, you could see it up on the stage in how he played. It gathered momentum as we crossed America."

So Frank Murray's wish to manage Joe Strummer had almost come true. Scottish Joe fitted in well with the mostly Irish Pogues, a union of Celts; their world seemed comfortable for him. Onstage with the Pogues Joe subsumed himself into the group, rather as he had done with the Soul Vendors, the reconstituted 101'ers. But at the end of the set he would return for the encores as front man, performing "London Calling" and "I Fought the Law." "When Joe was with the Pogues he just liked being with the band," said Frank. "What he was getting was crazy sold-out audiences, and I think that floored him. He had to sing during the encores. But the rest of the night he was there enjoying himself. He was a total professional. He was conscientious about everything he did. He thought that the hour or two onstage was the most important thing. He made sure he was there when he was supposed to be there."

The Pogues' shows at the Ritz Ballroom coincided with the New York Film Festival. Gaby was in town for the event and went with Joe and Bob Gruen. "I was standing on the sidewalk with him," said Bob, "and Spike Lee saw Joe and just bee-lined over: 'Hey, how you doing?' They had an instant, great conversation. So many people like that were thrilled or impressed to meet him. I think his innocence was one of the things that kept him normal. In the sense that he didn't really think he was that different from anybody else." After the show at the Ritz, Joe went out drinking in the East Village with the usual gang, including actor Matt Dillon, who had grown up listening to Irish folk music. "When I heard the Clash I got a little bit of that sense," said Matt. "Sure enough, Joe was into that music. I thought when he joined up with the Pogues that was a great move. Great call, a total natural move for Strummer to come and step with them. I thought it was great the way the Pogues invited him in. That was a great period for Joe. Because certainly there was a part of him—I understood it creatively—that was having a little trouble finding his niche. He did that great score for *Walker*, which was beautiful, but musically he was like a soldier without an army. He didn't have his cannon. But he seemed more at ease with the Pogues. You know who he reminded me of? He looked a bit like Alec Guinness. I remember busting his chops once, telling him that he looked like Margaret Thatcher. Because he kind of did."

"At a party for a charity Paul Newman and Joanne Woodward were involved with, they were interested in what Joe had to say," recalled Gerry Harrington. "But Joe Strummer would never think that Paul Newman had ever heard of him. In fact, everyone from Paul Newman to hot girls in clubs, to the hiphop gods of the day, all had time for Joe in New York. But he would hunker down with some quite depressing guys. He'd sit up all night with them. They drag you down, reduce your self-esteem, then your ambition."

Danielle was also at the event: "We'd been together for a while by the time he came back to do the Pogues: the New York Film Festival coincided with that. Gaby was there, so it was very strange for me and my New York friends, who knew what had been going on. He was trying to work on a broader canvas, and was full of ideas. He had a new spurt of energy. He'd get rolls of paper and write and write and hang them from mantelpieces and other places, and create his own world."

In the course of the tour Danielle found that she often had great chats with James Fearnley, the group's accordionist. At the end of the dates James asked if he could write to her. No one had ever asked Danielle that before.

The Ulcer Says No Tour, as it became known, crisscrossed America and Canada for three weeks. "There's something about thrashing an instrument to the limit," Joe said later, "and what really appeals to me about the Pogues is the sheer physicality of the music. I loved the way we could really rock the house with a tiny little thing like a mandolin, rather than bludgeoning the audience into submission with a huge wall of sound. On 'Medley' we'd all gather round Terry Woods and he'd raise one eyebrow, which was the signal to go double time. It was scary enough just to learn all that stuff, let alone try and play it at nine hundred miles per hour."

Although Jem Finer did notice the increasing tendency of his friend John Mellor to metamorphose into the character of Joe Strummer, the long journeys across the United States gave them plenty of time to talk. "Joe did sometimes talk about problems, the politics of a band, especially when things were getting difficult in the Pogues," said Jem, referring to the well-known propensity for drinking and drugging by Shane MacGowan. "He'd talk about the Clash, he'd talk about difficulties he'd had with Mick. He'd say it with a trace of regret. He called both Mick and Shane 'poobahs,' and went on to define it: 'poobahs' are people who believe that the world revolves around them to such an extent that the whole world *does* revolve around them. Their opinion of themselves is so strong that it creates a vortex in which things do spin around them, which can be quite annoying, destructive and difficult. But it seemed to me that he was beginning to realize what Mick had been trying to do musically. Mick was into more adventurous musical development, taking on board dance and hiphop. Joe was a bit conservative. In the end Joe realized that Mick was on the ball and he hadn't been."

Marcia Finer, Jem's wife, had had similar conversations with Joe. When I mention to her that sometimes you didn't exactly know where you stood with Joe Strummer, she suggests, insightfully, "Wouldn't you say that's because he didn't know where he was? Mick Jones was a really dignified man, one who really knew that about Joe. I always had this feeling that Joe really loved Mick and he would say every now and then, 'I've done damage to people.' Big Audio Dynamite was brilliant. Jem was going, 'Ha-ha, look what they threw out.' Mick was a person brought into conversations by Joe with respect and reverence."

The Ulcer Says No Tour crossed the Atlantic. In March 1988 Joe played with the Pogues at the Town and Country Club in Kentish Town in London, a low-key return to the stage in his hometown. Joe did promotion for the *Walker* soundtrack—tied to a flop film, the record sold only fifteen thousand copies ("He was incredibly proud of the *Walker* soundtrack, but maybe he didn't appreciate that soundtracks don't sell," said Danielle von Zerneck), nothing compared to the sales of *Combat Rock*. In a *Melody Maker* interview he described an insight that had come to him at Russian Hill Recordings: "I do remember thinking, 'Rock 'n' roll is better than this. Rock 'n' roll's much better than this.'"

In April, Joe was back in L.A. With Danielle he went to a screening of a film, *Permanent Record*, directed by Marisa Silver. It had been suggested that Joe might be interested in writing the film's soundtrack. Joe was after more work in this area. Already he had been offered the soundtrack of Martin Brest's intelligent chase movie, *Midnight Run*, starring his old New York compadre Robert De Niro, but curiously had turned it down. Perhaps that was an example of Joe's lack of confidence: in a big-budget movie like *Midnight Run* his work would leave him exposed to criticism. Although it was backed by Paramount, *Permanent Record*, which starred Keanu Reeves, had the feel of an independent film, including a cameo performance by Lou Reed. But as a study of teenage suicide, it was a subject to which Joe would feel close. "We went to Paramount to see a rough cut," remembered Danielle. "During the film Joe was crying, tears pouring down. He said, 'I'll do it.' It really resonated with him. What was so memorable was the level of emotion he showed. But when I tried to talk to Joe about his brother, the tension was like a nuclear bomb."

The four songs Joe wrote for *Permanent Record* that were included in the soundtrack—"Trash City," "Baby the Trans," "Nefertiti Rock," "Nothin' 'Bout Nothin'"—were much more in the vein of those he had come up with for the Clash. "Trash City," in particular, has such a terrific rhythmic melody it has even been described as "the last great Clash song"; it hinges around the lines "In Trash City on party avenue / I've got a girl from Kalamazoo," a lift from the Glenn Miller song title "I Got a Gal in Kalamazoo." Joe sounds freed up, at ease with himself, confident, his vocals mixed clear and positive. He also wrote a particularly plangent score for *Permanent Record*; he had assembled some musicians to play on the recording. "He was really enthusiastic," said Marisa Silver. "He didn't write to time. But he'd have a feel for the scene and would write to that. It was somewhat improvisatory. In the studio he brought in a little grocery cart and played that at one point. He was in great spirits and into it, so enthusiastic and happy with the result. It was a great experience." Predictably, the executives at the studio hated what Joe had done. "It was way too obscure for them," believed Marisa. "It felt too much like an independent film for them."

The musicians Joe brought together to record the soundtrack formed the heart of the first group Joe had established since the demise of the Clash. He found them through Jason Mayall, the younger brother of Gaz Mayall, who ran Gaz's Rockin' Blues, a shebeenlike club in London's Soho of which Joe was very fond—he had even taken his friend Bobby De Niro there a couple of times. They were the two eldest sons of John Mayall, the British bluesman. In 1976 Jason had moved to Los Angeles to live with his father at his pretty hillside house in Laurel Canyon. On return visits to London he would see Gaby, a family friend, and through her met Joe. "This was at the end of the Clash, so I didn't meet him as a big punk figurehead. He was just 'Joe.' I was never in awe of him. In subsequent years I saw him grow into a fantastic human being."

Jason was managing a group called Tupelo Chainsex, a cult punk-jazz act. Joe hit it off with a couple of the group's musicians, Joey Altruda, who played stand-up bass and a guitar made out of a bedpan, and Willie McNeil, the drummer. Joe was looking to put together a group that incorporated Latin, jazz and rock 'n' roll. With Joe adding Zander Schloss to the mix of Joey Altruda and Willie McNeil, they formed what would become known as the Latino Rockabilly War. This was the team of musicians Joe took into the studio to work on the *Permanent Record* soundtrack.

The soundtrack was recorded at Baby O Recorders, located on Sunset Boulevard behind the Hollywood Athletic Club—and opposite an English-style pub called the Cat and Fiddle, which Joe already had discovered. Although Gerry Harrington had disliked *Permanent Record*, he had recommended Joe take the project. Use the studio time that Paramount will pay for, he suggested to Joe, and work on your own stuff.

Contrary to the clichéd punk-rock view of Los Angeles as a superficial city which is where you went when you were Rod Stewart, Joe Strummer felt at home in this vast urban conurbation, where the furthest extremities of the West collide with those of the Third World in a largely idyllic setting. The still calm and serene confidence of the vast, palm-fringed metropolis offers a reassuring, creative cocoon for artists. Paul Simonon and Sex Pistols guitarist Steve Jones were already in residence; although Paul would soon return to Britain, Steve Jones lives there to this day. These English punks were the kings of a gang whose members owned vintage Harley-Davidsons and prowled the city in leather-jacketed packs—the actor Mickey Rourke was an honorary member. So Joe was not alone there: he had a scene to fit into—when he wanted.

When Joe was recording *Permanent Record*, Kate Simon's husband, David Johansen, had a part as the Ghost of Christmas Past in the Bill Murray vehicle *Scrooged*. "Joe was living in the Sunset Marquis," said Kate. "Everyone's stayed there, but only Strummer would take this pretty nice-sized room and make it like that place on Albany Street in Sebastian's house. Everything was on an angle, and the light was completely covered. His aesthetic sense hadn't changed."

Joe had taken the advice of Gerry Harrington, and had tried to work up material during the *Permanent Record* sessions at Baby O. But he didn't really have time; there were only a couple of songs and a few outlines. On "Turnpike" he had got the secretary from Baby O to sing the vocal, and then there was a tune called "Sleepwalk," which he entrusted to Gerry, saying he had written it for Frank Sinatra, and giving his agent the task of placing it in the hands of Nelson Riddle, the arranger of Sinatra's great 1950s material. Trying to get a tune to Sinatra alone suggested a returned self-assurance. And now, his confidence bolstered by his work on the *Walker* and *Permanent Record* soundtracks, Joe was insistent he was ready to make his own record.

But his appetite for live performance had been whetted by the live dates with the Pogues. So first he had something to do.

Unsurprisingly, Joe Strummer's return to fronting a rock 'n' roll group began at a Saturday drinking session in the spring of 1988, at the Warwick in Portobello Road. The notion unveiled contained the usual set of complex paradoxes that one might associate with Joe, especially as these dates would be billed as the Class War "Rock Against the Rich" Tour.

Class War had started out as an anarchist group (with a publication of the same name), its think-globally-act-locally credo appealing to the punk and anarchist movements. With the miners strike that began in 1984, Class War took on a larger mantle, which really appealed to the natural trouble-maker in Joe, although as one of Class War's targets was the yuppification of areas like Notting Hill, where he had bought his house, he was obliged to do more fence straddling. But he had been sold on it that Saturday afternoon in the Warwick, when Ian Bone, the Class War "leader," told Joe about his plan to hold a free festival on the Isle of Dogs in the Thames, then being transformed from abandoned wasteland to prime real estate. The Class War organizers vowed that they would "start a riot and burn every fucking yuppie flat to the ground." As the pints flowed in the Warwick that afternoon, it must have sounded fantastic. Even better, who would be playing onstage as the Isle of Dogs burned? None other than Joe Strummer, with the Latino Rockabilly War, the musicians he had put together for the *Permanent Record* tunes. On such a vast stage, as Babylon flamed all about him, he would make his return as a headlining act for the first time since the final show by the "dodgy" Clash in Athens in August 1985.

Except that it didn't happen. The offer of land for this festival on the Isle of Dogs was withdrawn: "hopefully he now rots in a grave and will go down in history as a traitor to the working class," read a Class War missive on the individual responsible. Instead a national tour was arranged, one intended as the biggest rock 'n' roll threat since the Pistols' Anarchy dates at the end of 1976. Joe was totally up for it, enthused by the local protest issues at each different venue, as well as the potential for mayhem. Class War put him on the cover of their flagship publication.

Playing with the Pogues on tour had made Joe realize what he had been missing. Since making the two movie soundtracks he had a body of work of his own, separate from anything he had done with the Clash. He had material to promote—"Trash City" was released as a single in June, to strong reviews, though it didn't sell. "There were a few posters around and stickers and patches, and some press," said Gerry Harrington, who came to England for the dates. "But it didn't feel like there was anyone pushing it, because it was on Epic Soundtracks. Then it became a self-fulfilling prophecy of 'No one wants to hear my music anymore.'"

Joe Strummer and the Latino Rockabilly War kicked off the Rock Against the Rich tour on June 17 with the kind of "secret" gig with which the Clash had often set off on tour. The show was at the Tabernacle in Powis Square, where Joe had played with the Soul Vendors, a home ground gig, only a few hundred yards from 37 Lancaster Road. It was a benefit for Green Wedge, a Green Party fund-raising venture. Joe's introduction to the audience by the show's emcee conjoined the inspired amateurism of squat-rock with a reference to his position as a rock 'n' roll deity, in a manner that may have calmed Joe's pre-show nerves and given a fillip to his ego. "The old fuckin' technology is playing us up a bit," the man said, "because the confetti has got in the fuckin' amps. Let me welcome a neighbor of mine, local boy makes God: Joe Strummer and the Latino Rockabilly War."

"Thank you for coming here and supporting this cause. And we'll start now," confidently pronounced Joe. The group plunged into a slightly hesitant version of "Police on My Back." The choice of material for the opening song set the tone: of the fifteen numbers in the set, seven were tunes that the Clash had played, but six of these were covers—"Police and Thieves," "Brand New Cadillac," "Armagideon Time," "I Fought the Law" and two versions of the set opener. Only "London Calling," the Clash original that Joe had sung with the Pogues, was a Strummer–Jones composition. Joe was at first unable to remember the chords of many of the Clash's songs, and Zander Schloss, his new guitarist, had to painstakingly teach them to him. Although all the group wanted to play "White Riot," Joe adamantly refused.

Unsurprisingly, this first public performance by Strummer's new outfit was pretty rough. At the end of the show Joe admitted that he couldn't hear anything he had been playing. Of the new *Permanent Record* songs "Nothin' 'Bout Nothin'" sounded terrific, as did "Trash City." There was something stubborn about his performance of "Love Kills": "You didn't like this? Fuck you!" Forty-five minutes after it had begun, the set concluded with a further rendition of "Police on My Back." Though the performances frequently may have sounded scrappy, Joe had made his public debut as a solo artist. Job done; on to the next venue.

Which was in a much larger setting altogether, an outdoor festival the next day at the National Bowl in Milton Keynes, fifty miles north of London straight up the M1, before an audience of fifty thousand. Here Joe Strummer and the Latino Rockabilly War, scheduled to play late in the afternoon, were part of a benefit for Amnesty International. Serendipitously, topping the bill was Big Audio Dynamite, who had just released *Tighten Up Volume 88*, their third album, another of those strokes of poetry that almost visibly hung in the air at any conjunction of Joe Strummer and Mick Jones. The previous evening Don Letts had filmed the Tabernacle show.

How had Joe styled himself for this tour? He wore his hair in an exaggerated rockabilly quiff. ("It was huge, and disgusting," said Zander. "He would use the heaviest pomade and wouldn't wash his hair for weeks—you

would see white flakes in it, crap that had gotten in there from the street.")
He seemed fit and in shape; as Gaby said, by then Joe's booze consumption
had begun to show on his body, especially his belly, but he'd made an effort
for this tour, getting rid of his slight beer paunch: consciously he moved
over to drinking red wine.

Milton Keynes seemed stressful for Joe, struggling again with a bad
sound and largely grim-faced throughout his set, pushing a stone up a hill
at the start of his solo career, visibly willing it on. But his mood was hardly
assisted by an incident that occurred as the Latino Rockabilly War were
about to go on. Suddenly Joe had angrily pushed a stranger down the ramp.
"We are getting ready to go onstage, standing at the side," said Zander
Schloss. "We are all dressed in these rockabilly suits and some guy comes
up to us. He looked like bad news. He whispered something in Joe's ear
about Topper Headon." The previous year Topper had hit rock-bottom, and
was now coming to the end of a fifteen-month prison sentence he had received after returning to his hometown of Dover, where an acquaintance
died from an overdose of heroin the former Clash drummer gave him. The
man turned out to be one of Topper's heroin dealers. Zander said, "What
the hell was that all about?" Joe said, "Never mind, let's play." "I got up
there and played, and Mick Jones started running up when we kicked off
with 'Police on My Back': he heard the first guitar line, and ran onto the
back of the stage thinking he was supposed to go on."

Mick and the assorted BAD members stood watching Joe as if they were
willing him to succeed. It wasn't a great show, seeming rushed. But in a
backstage trailer afterward, jammed with both BAD and his own group, as
well as Dammed drummer Rat Scabies and a visiting Joey Ramone and Stiv
Bators from the Dead Boys (who would be fatally knocked down by a taxi
two weeks later), Joe Strummer finally managed to relax; it seemed like a
1977 reunion package, even down to the low clouds of preoccupation that
would suddenly seem to encase him, as though a dart of unease had flashed
into his brain from the spliff he was smoking, for the post-show depression
that Terry Chimes had observed continued to accompany Joe after gigs.

"We would sit around Joe's kitchen table, drinking and smoking English joints," said Zander. "Mick Jones and Paul would come over and reminisce about the early days of the Clash, and it would inevitably end up in
some violent story: 'Do you remember when we were walking down the

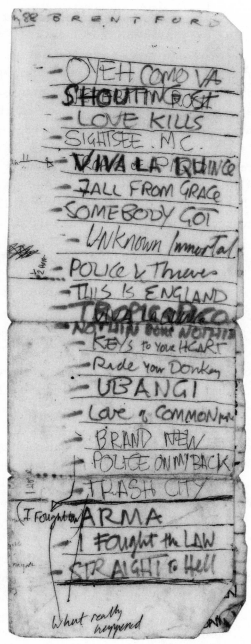

Latino Rockabilly War set list, 1988. What really happened? (*Lucinda Mellor*)

road, and the coppers came up from behind and hit you on the back of your head with a truncheon and you were bleeding all down your shirt?' And Joe goes, 'Good times!'"

For the next couple of months Joe and the Latino Rockabilly War were out on the road, all over the British Isles, even taking a foray into Sweden for the Hultsfredsfestivalen on August 13. As they played on, the repertoire expanded. At the Electric Ballroom in London's Camden Town on July 7 Joe announced, "I'd like to dedicate this next one to the guys in Big Audio Dynamite," before "Sightsee MC," cowritten with Mick for the second BAD album. Half a dozen songs later he declared, "I'd like to rip another one off the Big Audio Dynamite catalogue. It's called 'Sodom and Gomorrah/Let the Deejay Play,'" and with those two lines from the song he dove into "V. Thirteen." Joe had bolstered his twenty-three-song set with a pair of the best BAD tunes on that superb album. ("When he was announcing the next song," said Gerry Harrington, "he wouldn't say, 'This one's called "Trash City,"' he'd give the first line: 'In Trash City on Party Avenue I've got a girl from Kalamazoo,' or 'This one's called "Midnight to Six for the First Time from Jamaica,"' and then the band would start into 'White Man in Hammersmith Palais.' I said, 'Why do you do that?' He said, 'Because I've got to remember how to start the song.'")

There was possibly some prescience in Joe's unexpected decision to perform the two BAD songs: had he intuited that Mick Jones might shortly need a spiritual leg up? By early July Mick was in the intensive care unit at St. Mary's Hospital in Paddington: after catching chickenpox from his daughter Lauren, the infection had spread to his lungs, putting him into a coma for ten days. "Gaby made Joe come to see me," Mick told me, "and going to hospitals was the last thing he wanted to do." At the Nottingham Rock City show on August 8, referring to a news story in that morning's edition of the *Daily Mirror*, Joe dedicated "Sightsee MC" to Mick, saying, "I think he's got over the worst."

At the Glasgow Barrowlands show on August 7, "This Is England" became, inevitably, "This Is Scotland." In March that year Sony had released a twenty-eight-track Clash double compilation album, *The Story of the Clash, Volume One*, which was a Top Ten hit. Joe preceded the Glasgow show with a record signing at the local Virgin Records. Unannounced, Alasdair Gillies, his cousin, who lived in the city, turned up. "Alasdair, you must hang out with me," Joe said, grabbing his cousin. "Although there were queues down

Union Street he wasn't at all sure of his position," remembered Alasdair. "Don't press the cousins to come if they don't want to," Joe emphasized to him. "As it was during the day, I was wearing my suit for work," said Alasdair. "He was saying, 'What's it like being a lawyer? Isn't it heavy? I think you should give it up. How much hassle do you get?'"

After watching Joe carry out his traditional post-show routine of hand-washing his shirt, Alasdair realized something. "Everyone was reticent about telling Joe how great his show had been," said his cousin. "The end result of that was a disaster, really, because he didn't realize how good he had been or was being."

The commercial success of the Clash compilation should have helped convince Joe of his worth. Finances were not really a problem, but at this point he could have had a lot more money. Muff Winwood, in charge of A&R, told me there was "an enormous amount of money waiting for the Clash from royalties from all the various records. But because they had all been suing each other, and it still seemed unresolved, we didn't know who to pay it to."

In between shows Joe hung around in Notting Hill. One afternoon he and Gaby, along with Jem and Marcia Finer, took their daughters on an expedition to see the grave of Karl Marx in Waterlow Park in Highgate in North London. Although they arrived not long before the gates in the park closed for the evening, there was sufficient time for all concerned. As soon as they left, the gates were locked behind them. "We were milling about, waiting for our next move," said Marcia, "and we saw these young Japanese tourists, a pair of them, who were locked in. Joe immediately went into campaign mode, telling the guy to lift his girlfriend up, so she jumped into Joe's arms. There was this amazing moment where she looked at Joe, and she nodded at him, like 'Yeah.' The boyfriend scrambled up and thanked Joe. The recognition was unspoken, which he particularly liked. Unlike the times when people would come up to him and say, 'You changed my life.'"

At the end of July Joe came with Gaby, Jazz and Lola to the sixth birthday party of my son Alex, in the garden of a restaurant on the Thames in Hammersmith. Daisy, Mick's wife, was there with Lauren. The kids had a great time and Joe and Gaby seemed happy together, a rock 'n' roll nuclear family. "I can't leave Joe alone with the kids too much," Gaby grinned. "All he'll feed them is cake." Joe's methods of child rearing were always unconventional. "Leave them alone to get on with it and they'll figure it out for themselves" was his philosophy. Which presumably explained the outrage created in the hotel in which the Pogues were staying in Glasgow for their Christmas shows the previous year: Jazzy and Lola, tiny little girls, danced in the crowded lobby completely naked. "When I stayed with him at his house," said Dick Rude, "Gaby left him in charge of the kids, which she didn't do very often, and he said, 'Come on, let's go for a walk in Hyde Park. The kids are supposed to be in school, but I'm just going to keep them out and let them eat sweets.' When I saw those kids when they were sixteen and eighteen, and saw how well behaved they were, how grounded and centered, I thought, 'What happened? Did his experiment work? Or did Gaby really do a great job?'"

In Notting Hill I would run into Gaby almost daily, and couldn't help noticing the sadness that seemed often to reside in her blue eyes. As the years went on she had more and more reasons to be critical of Joe. Although she felt he was not an especially sharing partner with regard to bringing up the girls, she respected the attitudes with which he imbued them: "I loved his spirit toward them. I loved what he did with the girls. He told them they could be whatever they wanted, nobody could stand in their way. There was that inspirational, powerful side to him." Although quiet that afternoon at my son's birthday party, Joe seemed content within himself. In a corner of the garden, over a bottle of pink champagne, always a favorite tipple, he told me that he was about to have a part in another film, the next work by the increasingly revered Jim Jarmusch. After that, he said, he was going to make an album of his own.

The friendship between Jim Jarmusch and Joe had grown deeper since they first had met in 1986. When in London, Jim continued to stay at Joe's house. "He loved his girls: wonderful. I realized his circle all knew the same people, but we all know each other through Joe, so many people. What a strange character . . . he's almost magical. It sounds silly. I don't know how you could explain that to people, but it's so evident to me. His imagination, and his love for ideas and expression, was so strong.

"I became close with him during a period when a lot of the time he was really down. It was a hard period for him. He had a dark cloud over him. I used to call him Big Chief Thunder Cloud. But he was still generous and spirited and uplifting to be with. He could be funny, but it was also a depressed period."

Budgeted at $2.3 million, *Mystery Train* is a masterly work. Jim Jarmusch's script is divided into three different yet parallel and simultaneous stories, taking place over twenty-four hours in Memphis. Each of the three sequences focuses on a different group of people and their relationship to the city that was the home of Elvis Presley. Although he was in Memphis for three of the five weeks of shooting, in the film Joe did not appear until the final tale, entitled "Lost in Space," as "Johnny" (aka "Elvis"), who has lost both his job and his girl. Late in the film he puts a gun to his head before the weapon goes off, wounding his brother-in-law, played by Steve Buscemi. "I had no idea suicide had such a personal meaning for him," said Steve.

"I wrote that part only for Joe," Jim said. "I wasn't going to cast that character. Joe was interested. One of the main things, I think, was that it was set in Memphis. He loved Memphis, and that really sold him on it. When it was time to leave, he canceled his flight four days in a row, just to stay one more day. He was having a good time. I think he was very happy.

"On the set Steve would be joking around and other actors with more experience would snap right in when it was time to roll. But Joe would stay off the set, off with himself always. He said to me, 'I feel like I carry a basket of eggs to the set. I don't want to drop any on the way. I have to prepare them in the basket, and then just come get me and I'll bring them over.' That was such a great metaphor for his way of approaching a character. He really worked on getting himself into the right frame of mind to be that guy, accentuating the parts of himself that were Johnny, repressing parts that weren't. It's a subtle performance. The other actors, like Steve Buscemi, really respected him. He was very, very focused and took it really seriously. He did a beautiful job."

When Jim Jarmusch and Joe Strummer spent time together, one subject inevitably came up: "He talked a lot about the bad times that ended the Clash. He seemed to feel guilty. He felt really bad about *Cut the Crap*, said it was crap. I said, 'You only learn from your mistakes. You can't learn things without fucking up.' We had a lot of discussions about mistakes and accidents, how circumstance and fate affects our lives, how if you want to find your dream lover, you'll never find it, but as soon as you dismiss the possibility, then it arises again. I was trying to relate that philosophy to him when he was down. I was throwing back his own attitude, because he was very good when people were down—just give them a few little words. He was very good at picking you up again."

While they were shooting *Mystery Train* in Memphis the Australian hard-rock group INXS came through on tour. Joe had met the group; when he learned they were staying in an adjacent hotel he went over with Jim to say hello. When they found Michael Hutchence, the singer, he was in all his leather-trousered rock-star glory, surrounded by fourteen-year-old girls in miniskirts. "Wow, it must be really strange to be a sex symbol," said Joe to him. "Well, you're Joe Strummer," replied Hutchence, "you should know." Joe had the perfect response: "No, I was never a sex symbol. I was just a spokesman for a generation."

Joe's character of Johnny was riven with angst; his girlfriend had walked out on him. Life at this stage was certainly imitating art. Sara Driver, the director girlfriend of Jim Jarmusch, had had conversations with Danielle von Zerneck about her relationship with Joe. "She was very important to Joe, but she was never allowed to call him. It was a one-way thing: he would come to town and they would have this very intense, heavy thing, and he would go home and she was cut off again. This went on for two or three years."

As often happens in such matters, Danielle's life eventually took another turn. James Fearnley of the Pogues had been writing her, as promised, and on the group's next U.S. tour (without Joe), they met again, clicked and fell in love. "I loved Joe," said Danielle, "but I knew there was no good ending. There was no way I could give up James. Joe was the perfect man for something wonderful and romantic, but not real.

"Joe called me from Memphis when he arrived there for *Mystery Train*. I said, 'I have to tell you that I'm seeing someone.' It was hard to be such a grown-up. Joe said, 'Fine. Of course.' Jim told me later that it couldn't have been better timing, because his character's girlfriend had just left him. Joe was devastated."

"Joe came up to me," related Sara Driver, "and said, 'Why didn't you tell me?' He'd gotten off the phone with Danielle and was clearly upset. I said, 'Joe, it was really inevitable this was going to happen. It was too one-sided.' He looked at me and went, 'Inevitable. Inevitable.' All night he kept coming up to me: 'Inevitable. Inevitable.'"

"Joe called me back in the middle of the night and was crying," said Danielle. "He said, 'This isn't OK.' I think he was really surprised that I was falling in love with James. I think it was a surprise to both of us. But I had to go back into the real world. I don't think either of us realized how much we cared until we broke up. We stayed friends and would have dinner together."

"Fuckin' bollocks," Joe's first line in *Mystery Train*, could be seen as a summation of his life perspective at this point. Not that everyone around Joe was similarly affected. Steve Buscemi ("He used to call me Bushbaby, his nickname for me") had long been a fan of the Clash, having seen the memorable Bond's show at which the audience hooted at Grandmaster Flash: "Joe reprimanded the crowd: 'That's not cool—give 'em a chance!' I loved that. I loved that he was trying to bridge those two worlds. It really hit me how epic and personal, at the same time, that band was.

"Most of *Mystery Train* was a night shoot. To unwind, everybody would go to the hotel pool. We wrapped at five, we'd get to the pool by six, and stay there until nine or ten in the morning. It was so funny to see families on vacation, coming down to the pool at ten in the morning, and seeing us [laughs] with bottles of tequila. They'd turn right around and leave. I went to see live music with Joe. He was so disappointed at the state of the counterculture at that time. We had fun going out, but our expectations were high."

"He was a hard worker, really conscientious," said Sara Driver. But she remembered an evening when Joe was very much wallowing in darkness, as the legendary Screamin' Jay Hawkins—who played a hotel clerk in *Mystery Train*—was playing "Constipation Blues" on a piano in the middle of their hotel lobby. "I asked him if Gaby and the kids were coming out. Joe said, 'No, no. How can I concentrate and think with the kids and Gaby around?' But he was very broken up about the Danielle situation. He seemed very lost." Over the weeks of the shoot, Sara was increasingly impressed by Joe. "He was interested in being an actor. He was a very good actor, and I never understood why more people didn't put him in things. He had a wonderful presence."

on the other hand . . .

1988–1989

I n November 1988 Joe moved to Los Angeles with Gaby, Jazz, and Lola. As he had told me that summer, it was the moment to make a record of his own. He booked three months at Baby O Recorders, where he had made the *Permanent Record* soundtrack. The musicians were a version of the Latino Rockabilly War: Zander Schloss on lead guitar and vocals, Lonnie Marshall—a new recruit—on bass and vocals and Willie McNeil on drums. It must have been a hard decision for Joe to finally stop putting off the inevitable next step, but it was also a logical one; things had been successfully building ever since the *Walker* album; there had been *Permanent Record*, the Pogues tour, the Lone Star Rockabilly War tour, and the small detour into acting in *Mystery Train*. While making *Walker*, followed by the spurt of *Permanent Record* songs, Joe had rediscovered his voice. He had learned how to write songs on his own, without the musical input of Mick Jones.

Contrary to what he had vowed in 1986, Joe Strummer's first solo album would not be called *Throwdown* or be produced by Mick Jones. Its name was *Earthquake Weather*, with Joe himself at the production helm, though the title, which carried its own in-built sense of brooding, dangerous power, was still to come to him. Working in Hollywood on his own record was a move to virgin territory for Joe. The Clash had never recorded in L.A.; there were no memories, good or bad. There was a freshness in the step of his broken boot when he was in the city, touched like everyone by its seductive, warm whispers of fecund possibilities.

Joe and his family rented a small house off Fairfax in the Russian section of West Hollywood. He had decided—for the meantime, at least—he was going to make his home in Los Angeles. (A year later he told *Sounds* about his experiences of life in L.A.: "There are people that successfully go out there and live, but they always look like an expatriate colony. And there's always something a bit sad about standing in an English pub on Sunset Strip where everything has been carved deliberately trying to look like a boozer.")

While recording, Joe confided to Mark "Stebs" Stebbeds, the engineer, that he was thinking of moving permanently to New Orleans. "Gangsterville," the song that opens the record, contains the line "I'm going to New Orleans—gonna buy me a prayer." "He was still giving himself a raw deal most of the time," said Gerry Harrington. "We were having breakfast at the Chateau Marmont. I'd bought a copy of Q magazine which had a feature, 'The 100 Dumbest Things Ever Done by Musicians,' which included Joe doing a runner from the Clash and going to France. They wrote: 'Joe Strummer always spoke in capital letters.' He read that. He goes: 'Yes. I DO ALWAYS SPEAK IN CAPITAL LETTERS.'"

The Clash and its spin-offs were temporarily out of fashion. BAD's record sales were dwindling, though they would pick up in the next decade. Yet this was the climate in which Joe would release his first solo album. To try to tune him in to contemporary sounds, Gerry Harrington had a tactic: "Every time I found a great new record, I'd want Joe to hear it so he could see he could be better himself. When 'Fisherman's Blues' by the Waterboys came out, I thought it was a great song. I played it to him. He said, 'The problem is he's saying what he feels. Bob Dylan doesn't say, "I walked through a door." He says, "There was smoke in the air." He doesn't say the obvious. This guy's hitting it on the head. It's just not interesting.' I'd never thought about it that way. Joe always cut right down to the essence. Except when he didn't. I also wanted him to hear Lou Reed's *New York* album. But he didn't want to be daunted while recording by a great work that he was going to have to equal. He goes: 'Lou Reed? Is it really great?' 'It's fucking great.' He goes: 'I don't want to hear it.' I said: 'This guy's ten years older than you. He's found a way to write older, more mature rock music and get a lot of people to listen to it. You should check it out.' 'I don't want to hear it, man.'" It is worth noting that for much of the end of the 1980s Joe's favorite record was Paul Simon's *Graceland*, a clear influence on the way he was to integrate more ethnic sounds into the rock 'n' roll structure of the Latino Rockabilly War. *Graceland* was an interesting choice, for here Joe was taking a politically incorrect line. Simon had gone out on a limb, using South African musicians when there was a ban on working with artists from the apartheid-riven nation. But Joe felt that through Paul Simon's record people in the Midwest became acquainted with the true art of South Africa, gaining information about the iniquities of apartheid. (In a more pronounced politically incorrect moment, Joe declared to Stuart Maconie in *NME* that a rush of pride secretly ran through him when English soccer hooligans ran amok attending overseas matches; he himself admitted that he had overstepped the mark and contacted Maconie to tell him this.)

Through an advertisement in the *Hollywood Reporter*, Joe and Gaby found another rental more in line with an English rock 'n' roller's idealized view of life in southern California: a beautiful wood-framed house with a swimming pool on Ridgemount Drive off Laurel Canyon, with a fine view of the vast sweep of L.A. The place belonged to Luke O'Reilly, the English manager of Al Stewart, whose *Year of the Cat* album had been a big hit in the United States in 1976. Joe bought Gaby a racy 1963 blue Ford Thunderbird. He passed the test for a California driver's license; Joe would take Gaby and the kids on family outings to the desert in the T-bird. Later he and Gaby drove down in it to New Mexico for the Santa Fe film festival, where *Mystery Train* was being screened, hanging out there with Mo Armstrong, the friend who'd clued him in about the Sandinistas and who had moved there.

Rudy Fernandez drove the Cadillac down from San Francisco to the lot at Baby O, where it sputtered to a halt, its power finally dying. "Joe came out and saw the Cadillac and was incredibly happy. The car stayed there the whole time he made that record." In the studio Joe arranged a security camera to permanently show a shot of the entire car, parking the Caddy back in the same spot on the few occasions that he ventured out in it onto the roads. When he tired of being in the spliff bunker he had built, Joe would go outside with his guitar and sit for hours in the Cadillac. One night there was a shoot-out in a drugs heist in the parking lot—Baby O was not in the most salubrious part of then extremely sleazy Hollywood—and a bullet went through the door of the Cadillac, leaving a clearly visible hole in its turquoise skin. Joe couldn't have been happier. "It made it even more perfect," said Rudy. "He loved it even more." When the first single—"Gangsterville"— was released from the album it was in a sleeve adorned with an image of Joe Strummer's beloved Cadillac, bullet hole in clear view. "He didn't want to drive a new car, or a flashy car," said Dick Rude, who came up to the studio most days. "He wanted to fix the Caddy so it would run right, but he didn't want it to be new. He didn't want to be above his station. He felt that he was a worker among workers. He liked to keep his feet on the ground, he liked to keep a sense of humility about him. It was really key to him not losing his shit. He was very obstinate about one thing: 'Gotta get the beat-box message back out on the street.' He meant the stripped-down roots of rock 'n' roll. He was really into his past and how the 101'ers had got started: his humble beginnings and where his roots of music came from, and the roots of rock 'n' roll—Buddy Holly and Gene Vincent."

When the sessions began, much of the material for the record was not written. Joe solved this problem by moving on his own into a small motel, the Sea Tour on Ocean Drive, above the beach in Santa Monica, and writing feverishly. "I'd get these calls," said Gerry Harrington. "'I need you to meet me. You know where Cora's Coffee Shop is? I need you to come out. I'll tell you when you get here.' I'd get there and it'd be, 'I need a jump-start for the Cadillac.' One of those times he took me into his room at the motel and played me 'Leopardskin Limousines,' which he'd recorded, hand-miked, playing a child's toy piano and singing the song. Then we had to jump-start his car and I had to follow him into town in case it broke down again."

"Leopardskin Limousines" was a song Joe had written about Danielle von Zerneck, his voice as loving and caressing as a tropical breeze, but as sad and tearful as a fantasy falling to pieces, Joe so evidently talking about himself, Joe who didn't like what his dreams told him: "Suppose I should drag my stuff on out / But I don't like the memories / Found a pint of brandy on top of the fridge / And it's working like an antifreeze." You were certain that he really had found that pint of brandy.

Mark Stebbeds had a distinct memory of Danielle's visits to the studio:

"I knew he was very fond of her because he was holding her hand very affectionately the few times she came round. I didn't really think anything of it until one day the phone rang in the control room and someone said, 'Danielle's on line one for Joe.' He came back after the call and said, 'Please don't announce it when she phones.'"

There were other visitors: the Red Hot Chili Peppers came by, and Flea played trumpet on a track. Jesse Dylan stopped in with Sean Penn. Jesse's dad, Bob, dropped by, once leaving a tape of a song he thought Joe might like to try out. For his usual complex set of reasons, Joe never listened to it. "I think it was Joe not wanting to deal with it," said Zander. "It stayed in the drawer."

Josh Cheuse, an art director and photographer from New York, had become friends with both Mick and Joe, and worked with them. He was staying at Joe's house on Ridgemount Drive, without a car—in L.A., a problem. Sometimes Joe would drive down to Baby O without telling him he was leaving, "almost as though he was saying, 'Let's see how he gets to the studio on his own.' It seemed a bit of a public school thing." Joe started renting cars, cool vintage vehicles: one a kind of Batmobile, another a Ford Mustang. Once, leaving the studio in the Mustang, Joe jumped a red light and was immediately signaled to stop by a police car. Instead, he decided—possibly ill-advisedly considering the trigger-happy reputation of the LAPD—to lead the cops on a chase into the Hollywood Hills. "We're going to outrun them," he told Josh, who was sliding lower into the shotgun seat. "Let's see if we can outrun the cops in L.A." "What? Suddenly you're in this film. He thought he knew those winding roads so well, that he was going to lose the cops. We made it to the top of the mountain, but the cop car was already up there. He charmed them. The cop said something like, 'Well, I know you got a nice little ride there.' That was a time in L.A. when you could still charm the police."

Joe experienced four earthquake tremors while making the album, once in the Santa Monica motel and three at Baby O. The studio turned out to be built on a fault line: "So I thought I'd call it *Earthquake Weather* rather than making any heavy comment on the state of the world."

An intense routine was established. The only break was for an evening ritual of Italian food, everyone sitting in a circle and eating pasta out of delivery containers. Songs were still being written in Santa Monica, remembered Mark Stebbeds, but soon "Joe had pretty much all of them worked out in the crudest form on a cassette. He would strum the melody and a rhythm on a cassette, and it might be incomplete, but he would take this cassette into the bunker, show the guys the song and everybody would try to work up ideas on the spot."

Joe's production method was pretty much the same hands-off approach he had used on the *Walker* soundtrack. Although he was credited as the producer of the record, the songs were arranged—often in Joe's absence—by Zander Schloss. "Joe was involved with the structure of the songs, but after the basic tracks were cut he left it to the band to finish them," said Mark. "I think in doing that the guys in the band who weren't as experienced as Joe, and didn't have the same history of recording, became a little self-indulgent. Some of the songs were great in the way they came out, but I think other ones took a wrong direction and perhaps could have had a little more Joe Strummer influence. We wouldn't see him for hours at a time, and he didn't really know what was on the record until it was time to mix it."

Joe's customary disappearing acts often concerned his need for input for his lyrics. "When it was time for him to sing and the lyrics weren't written," recalled Mark Stebbeds, "he'd have a favorite cabdriver he would call, and the driver would drive him round the city for a couple of hours. I can't tell you how the lyrics he wrote related to what he saw out there on the street, but somehow it would obviously stir up his juices. Joe kept a mild state of mellowness going on, smoking English joints, which weren't heavily laced with pot. He had two kinds of pot: he called them 'work pot' and 'after pot.' But the stuff in the studio was quite weak. He didn't drink much. Sometimes he would get some brandy. He was very much into the whole Latino thing, so he would get Mexican brandy, horrible stuff, but he would drink it because the owner of the studio was Mexican and he figured it was the least he could do."

A few times Joe slept in the studio, locked into the building, until it was opened up again the next morning. "He would take the couch cushions and throw them on the floor and sleep in the studio," Stebbeds remembered. Life at Baby O was not dissimilar to that at 101 Walterton Road. "He had these motorcycle-type boots," Stebbeds continued, "the heel was falling off. People would bring him replacement boots: 'Here, have a pair that actually work.' But he wouldn't wear them because they weren't comfortable." Joe's personal hygiene, recalled Gerry Harrington, also suggested someone still coping with life in a squat. "He'd be in the studio all the time, so he'd shower there, and put soap in his hair to slick it back. You'd see coagulated soap in his hair all the time. But he wasn't neglecting his brain: he was always a great reader, and he had a history of the New York Yankees and then started talking knowledgeably about Joe DiMaggio. He was like a little book warehouse."

"Let's rock again!" Joe's opening words that almost fade you into *Earthquake Weather* do not hint at the epic struggle with himself that Joe had had to make the record. The volume of that declamation is at a lower level than "Gangsterville," which bursts open immediately after it, the first song. Are those three words muted and uncertain, as has been suggested? Or do they emerge like an Apache war cry ringing down from atop an Arizonan butte? I know which I think. I never had any problem with the way Joe's voice is allegedly hidden away in the mix on this record—after a time, and with the aid of the lyric sheet in the record, all the words were perfectly clear to me. You've simply to listen to Joe's vocals on *Earthquake Weather* via a slight adjustment in your hearing and thinking, like you would the first time you hear how the words and music are layered around each other on Studio One records. The way Joe Strummer's voice is mixed down on *Earthquake Weather* is often taken as proof of his inner doubt about the project, and it could be diagnosed that way. Yet there is a simpler explanation: "Joe was not in good voice when we recorded this record," recalled Mark Stebbeds. "He wasn't physically ill but he hadn't been singing a lot. His voice had largely been sitting idle for several years, so it wasn't that powerful."

"One day," said Zander Schloss, "I was sitting in the control room, and he started barking out his words, and I got so excited. But it turned out his bridgework had fallen out, and because he'd lost the bridgework he was overpronouncing and -enunciating. I said, 'Let's keep the track.' But he put his bridgework in and did it all over again, that same mumbling fashion.

"But there was one time when he was doing things like turning on a transistor radio and recording the static. One day I was in the equipment room and heard this train whistle. I mentioned something about it. Joe said, 'So you don't like my train whistle?' I'm like, 'No, I don't.' He picked up a chair, threw it against the wall and said, 'Well, it's staying.'

"At the end of the working day Joe and Dick Rude would go out to Dick's Dodge convertible in the parking lot and play that session's music on its shitty little car stereo, to hear what people were gonna hear. That was his concern: how will it portray itself in the real world, not in the studio."

In Joe's real world there wasn't much reality. Things with Gaby were up and down, not assisted by Joe's tendency to vanish for days. "For all his faults he had the most incredible spirit," said Gaby. "He believed anything was possible. He inspired people to go off on a track with their life, through listening to the Clash. Quite a thing to achieve. He really listened to people. In men that is quite a talent. But everyone wanted him. The kids found that hard. On an emotional level with Joe, I'd had enough. As someone said: 'Joe was a great person to be friends with, but who would want to be part of his family?' I was fed up with him. On some levels he was brilliant with the kids, but I expected him to muck in a bit more. I stopped giving him attention. I think that was the most hurtful thing I did. I think I was quite blocked and damaged myself. I knew his childhood hurt, but I didn't really know him."

"Gaby was unhappy during that time, and was confused and despondent about Joe's behavior," Zander said. "It was apparent he had lost any kind of zest for the relationship. He was out of control. I seriously think that Joe had a bit of a sexual addiction. Sitting in an airport once Joe came up with this justification for his need to have sex with lots of different women: he said if John F. Kennedy didn't have sex every day he got a headache."

Gerry Harrington would not agree with Zander's assessment of Joe's love life. "Musicians check out girls, but Joe was always busy talking about important issues. I never saw Joe looking at a great-looking girl unless she was some unfortunate woman he wanted to make feel good. It was more, 'Señorita, what a ray of sunshine!' He never seemed terribly driven by libidinous pursuits."

In the studio Joe was driven by a blinkered ruthlessness. One night Willie McNeil, the drummer, made a classic error: when at four in the morning Joe asked him for one more take, he protested he was too tired and would do it the next day. That was it. "You're fired."

They were more than halfway through the album; who could they get in as a replacement? Ginger Baker, stalwart former member of supergroup Cream and recently playing with John Lydon, was in Los Angeles, up for a gig. Joe had concerns that, as Ginger was an even more seasoned professional than he was, there were possibilities for strife—and he'd had enough of that in groups. But there was an even more unlikely candidate: a former drummer with the Red Hot Chili Peppers, who had suffered a nervous breakdown after the group's guitar player, his best friend, had OD'd on heroin that summer. More than anything, Joe was taken by his name: "Mr. . . . *Jack* . . . *Irons!*," as Joe would introduce him onstage.

"I told Joe I was impressed by Jack Irons," said Lonnie Marshall. "I had gone to an audition once, and the Chili Peppers were rehearsing there. Jack Irons was rehearsing on his own, playing all the grooves by himself. I thought that was impressive: I'd never seen a drummer practicing by himself. I told Joe that. He kept saying, 'Jack Irons! What a name for a drummer. Jack-Irons-Jack-Irons.'"

"I got a phone call in the hospital from Dick Rude, and he says, 'Joe wants you to play with him,'" said Jack. "I said, 'I'm not doing too good, but I love Joe and I love the Clash.' So I got a day pass from the hospital and I got my girlfriend at the time to drive me to Hollywood, to Baby O."

Jack's problems with his own reality seemed even greater than Joe's. "The first time we got together," said Zander, "Jack's eyes were rolling back in his head, like he was hearing voices or something. He gets up and says, 'I'm going to go in the bathroom and look in the mirror and see if I'm still here!'"

On his return, Joe said, "Let's try a song." "Two takes later I cut the song: 'Jewellers and Bums,'" said Jack. "Joe said, 'You've got the job, whenever you're ready. Whenever you can get out.'" "Jewellers and Bums" moves along to its own internal rhythms, a very Clash driving rock song, a Death-or-Glory-like insistence, with added melody. Addictive stuff.

The *Earthquake Weather* sessions took more than three months, with a brief break for Christmas. How was Joe functioning in the studio? He seemed to see his role more in the tradition of a movie producer than a music producer. "He does this great record, in the studio every night for almost four months," remembered Gerry Harrington. "He's doing everything from buying guitar strings to taking the petty cash and getting it reimbursed."

In the Clash, apart from *Combat Rock*, Joe had taken a backseat to Mick Jones. Josh Cheuse believed it was harder without Mick. "For Joe it was hard to not have Mick to fight against, I think. When everyone's deferring to him, it's a very different situation."

As the record neared completion, an official delegation, headed by Muff

Winwood, arrived from the record company in London (CBS had become part of the Japanese giant Sony). Joe ran off in response. "I couldn't find Joe anywhere, so I came home," said Gerry Harrington. When Gerry arrived at his place, not far from Baby O, he found a sheet of yellow legal paper nailed to the door. "Dear Gerry, I've gone to the desert. I'll be back on: Sunday, Monday, Tuesday, Wednesday, Thursday, Friday, Saturday. Sorry if I've inconvenienced you. Joe." Around the word "Thursday" Joe had drawn a circle. "He could have just written: 'Gone to the desert—be back Thursday.' He had to write the other six days. That's why you've got *Sandinista!* being a three-disc set. Joe could not even edit himself."

"He did run away," said Muff Winwood. "I've had other artists do the same thing—just run away. I understood it." But Tricia Ronane, by now living with Paul Simonon and having been given charge of the Clash's business affairs, felt there was a subtext: when Joe had declared to Sony his intention to make *Earthquake Weather*, Winwood immediately had asked to hear demos of the songs Joe intended to record. "He was offended," said Tricia. "Joe's attitude was that he was one of the songwriters with the Clash who had had a big-selling album with *Combat Rock*. So why was he being asked to play demos? It had a profound effect on Joe and dented his confidence."

When Joe did return from the desert, on the Thursday, for his meeting, it seemed he had never heard of the golden rule: when presenting any idea to "suits," never indicate a single shred of doubt, because if you do, that is all they will pick up on. Joe's deference and humility were not what was required at that point. "Here it is. I'm not sure that you'll really like it," he undersold his work to the record company execs, immediately before pressing Play. They said they wanted to hear more Joe guitar on the record. And went back to London.

Muff Winwood was given a copy of the tape. He listened to it; whatever bothered him about the record, he expressed to Mark Stebbeds. Then he received a letter from Joe: "Muff, only you, me and the Stebbeds know this stuff. I've been a bit of a hermit of late. Love to the wife. You're a rock. Down with Bros [Sony's biggest English act of the time]. Love Joe." Then Joe listed the twenty quibbles that Muff had with the record, and rebuffed every one of them. "Joe was sensitive about his music," said the A&R man. "He has no idea what the world is going to think and it's a frightening experience. In the letter he says to me, 'The drummer on the sessions was in and out of a mental hospital. The doctors were experimenting on him: the drum tracks on this album were derived from eight or ten mikes. I can't help feeling you disrespect me to think I haven't thought of this.'"

Whatever the view from Sony, by the middle of February 1989 *Earthquake Weather* was completed. A rock 'n' roll record, it is the work of a basic combo getting as close to the feel of 1948 as possible forty years later, with all that has been learned since. The lyrical imagery is often very extreme and surreal, a statement of Joe's mental frame at the time—though his warmth and innocent joy at the world still pour out of it. The album kicks off with "Gangsterville," a complex song "about the Mafia electing the President," as Joe explained it. "Gangsterville" is both Joe's world and the world to which he is opposed, one that is very attractive, but also confusing, one that Joe can see both sides of—so, in one of his most deft songwriting moments, Joe turns the song on its head halfway through with a simple phrase at the beginning of a line, "On the other hand . . ." Let's look at the other side, he's saying. Another Joe Strummer contender for one of the best and funniest lines in rock 'n' roll? It ends with a message from the Luddite in Joe, the man who still wrote on a portable manual typewriter: "Stop writing things on screen." Also a hit on the album is the thundering "Highway One Zero Street," a sort of West Coast treatment of a Bruce Springsteen song, another of Joe's best tunes, with a beautifully insidious chorus melody, specifically set in Los Angeles: "I can't believe I'm feeding cockroaches in the biggest jungle known to man / Right where the heart of Chinatown cuts in to old Siam." "Boogie with Your Children" is like a musical expression of life at 37 Lancaster Road, one of Joe's great parties; he loved Jazz and Lola deeply, and wanted to celebrate these feelings for his daughters in this song. It is like a tune that Prince might have recorded; or the Clash, if Mick Jones had had his say. "Island Hopping," a lilting semi-calypso, a paean to the fine art of Caribbean-style idling, is a sunny joy, an expression of what part of Joe seems to really want to be doing, taking off all the pressure. And on their affecting version of the Tennors' rock-steady tune "Ride Your Donkey," the Latino Rockabilly War show they can acquit themselves well on Jamaican rhythms. Both tunes remind you that Joe is never frightened to be corny, aware of the strength of simplicity. In a similar elegiac vein to the lovely, heartfelt "Leopardskin Limousines" is "Sleepwalk," the album closer, the tune first worked up at the *Permanent Record* sessions that Joe had asked Gerry Harrington to get to Frank Sinatra. With its first line of "Matchbooks of lonely places I'll never find," it reminds me of Joe's superstition that you must never use the last match in a matchbook: the homes of serious tobacco smokers like Jim Jarmusch had drawerfuls of matchbooks that each contained just one match.

Over the next few months until the record was released, for most of which Joe remained in Los Angeles, Jim Jarmusch came out to the city. Hanging out with Joe, the grateful film director thanked him for the acknowledgment on the song "Shouting Street," a version of the song Bernie had wanted him to record with Paul for yet another version of the Clash, which had been played live on the Class War tour. "I said, 'Joe, you namechecked me in the song. I'm honored.' And he said, 'I wouldn't be too honored. I couldn't think of anything else to rhyme with "garbage."'"

But then Joe made one of his whimsical changes. Gerry Harrington was fired. "In L.A. I kept getting calls from promoters who'd seen the Clash at the Santa Monica Civic, and they all wanted to see Joe again. We'd get offers of $100,000 for three nights at the Universal Amphitheater. He wouldn't even think of it: 'No man, I'm not ready. You've got to understand.'

"He calls me to go to lunch with him at the Café LA, on Sunset Strip. Joe was never on time. I get there five minutes early; he's already there, mulling something over. There was a mean, threatened sheepishness about him. He starts yelling. He made me the villain before I'd sat down so that he could let himself off the hook for what he was about to do. 'You're not ready for it,' he said. I replied, 'Joe, I'm more ready than you are. I'm dealing with people. You're hiding from them. I'm paving the way for you. You're running backward.'

"I was very upset about it, devastated. The good by-product was I didn't have to be nice to those wanker hangers-on, guys that would bring out the worst in him because he would have a bunch of losers supposedly as his equals. Which would reduce his self-esteem."

What Joe had decided was to take on his landlord, Luke O'Reilly, as his manager. "Joe kept experimenting with different people," said Gaby. "He had taken on Gerry Harrington, and Gerry pissed him off about something. Joe fumbled around for a long time. He might have been having a crisis, age-wise."

Luke O'Reilly was involved with Joe's management for around a year. I remember him backstage at Joe's show at the Town and Country Club in autumn 1989, seeming confused by Joe's edict that whoever wanted could come backstage. "Luke tried to come on board but it wasn't successful," said Gaby. "Joe never gracefully extracted himself from the situation. It was left to a bad conversation between me and Luke."

"Joe had very silly reasons for incorporating people into his business or his life," said Zander Schloss. "One time we played in San Francisco. I had a friend who was a pot dealer up there and had his own group, More Than Beautiful. But another band was supposed to [open for us]. I said, 'Joe, my friend has offered to give us an ounce of the best kind of bud in order that he do the opening slot.' Joe was like, 'Really?' He calls the promoter and says, 'You know that first band? They're shit. I want More Than Beautiful to be the openers.' They canceled the first band and More Than Beautiful got the gig. These guys had only been together a couple of weeks. We got this bag brimful of beautiful crystal buds, and me and Joe split it."

Joe needed a video for "Gangsterville," so he formed WFN—We're Fucking Nuts—Productions, with Josh Cheuse, and the pair shot it themselves in L.A., giving Sony two videos for £10,000. "The A&R guy was like, 'What? You only need ten thousand? I'll get the check right now.'" The videos cost even less: "We made the two videos for almost nothing, so we could pay a Chateau Marmont hotel bill," said Josh. When Sony rejected Joe's collage for the *Earthquake Weather* cover, Josh Cheuse photographed him, standing at sunset fully clothed on the diving board of Luke O'Reilly's pool, Telecaster in hand, cigarette in mouth, head held high, an iconic Strummer image ironically much better known than the music inside the record it was intended to herald.

Earthquake Weather was scheduled for release on September 29, 1989. Everything was put in place to push the record, including live dates on both sides of the Atlantic. "*Earthquake Weather* didn't do a thing," remembered Muff Winwood. "The tide had gone out for Joe when he did that record. He wasn't a good self-promoter." Such a bad self-promoter in fact, that he kept a BBC film crew waiting for three days before they gave up. "We would have loved it to succeed," said Muff, "but it was such a failure. There was tremendous respect for the guys who'd been in the Clash. No one was thinking: 'Those wankers. Let's drop them.' Mick knew how to deal with problems in the studio. But Joe was more of a poet and artist than a musician. He didn't really know what to do, and went into panic mode."

The critics were not hip to Joe's trip. Very typical was the sniffy review of Robert Christgau, the self-styled "dean of American rock critics," in his column in New York's *Village Voice,* into which he mystifyingly dragged Mick Jones's ex-girlfriend: "A man without a context, Joe digs into Americana up to his elbows, up to bebop, up to Marvin Gaye, cramming obsessions and casual interests into songs as wordy and pointless as Ellen Foley's. Foley's absence is a relief, but with Joe emulating Gaye and Bird— crooning and murmuring instead of screaming and spitting, cramming in the syllables—not that much of a relief. New guitar sidekick Zander Schloss does what he can to make things worse."

Christgau gave the record a C rating; even worse, he put a "Must to Avoid" symbol next to it. BAD's fourth album, *Megatop Phoenix,* reviewed in the same column, got one grade better, a C+—by the end of the year, however, the original BAD would splinter apart, and Mick Jones would form Big Audio Dynamite 2. In London *NME* was up to its usual tricks, Andrew Collins calling Joe's big shot "a minefield of duff moments," and berating his "penchant for weedy Latino tinkling."

In an interview published in *Sounds* on October 8, Joe said, "I'm definitely not someone who's worth worshipping. We shouldn't really worship anybody. I mean, everyone's fucked up . . . I just say to myself, It's a good job you're a rock 'n' roller, because people expect you to be nuts and a bit flakey. But if I had to do something really proper, it'd be a disaster. I'm useless for anything except what I do—that's what I've come to realize, which is no bad thing. I don't want to put across any romantic notion that it's a gang, or anything like that. We're just four guys, y'know." Another volteface from this former member of the Last Gang in Town.

In London to promote *Earthquake Weather,* Joe would often be at Paul and Tricia's house at 53 Oxford Gardens, a hundred yards from the intersection with Ladbroke Grove. "Joe was the sort of person who would go off for a while on a tangent," said Tricia, "but you knew he would be coming home. The doorbell would ring one day and he'd be there." From their friendship Tricia gained valuable insights into the relationship between the two men who had lasted the longest in the Clash. "Joe and Paul needed their camaraderie: they were so close because it was like a band of brothers. Joe and Paul found that in each other, that need for a sibling. Paul had a brother but they were separated when he was ten; Joe had a brother, but they were separated by his death. I think because Mick was an only child and never had a sibling, he didn't even begin to know about those relationships. Maybe that was something Joe and Paul found in each other, but couldn't quite find with Mick."

One night at Paul and Tricia's, Joe opened his heart to her. "Joe wanted to have a talk and a drink, he said. He did—all night long. We talked about so many things. I didn't know who Iain Gillies was, who was often at Lancaster Road. I said, 'Is he your brother?' He said, 'I'll tell you about my brother, and I'll tell you this once and never again.' He said, 'Look, I became a bully at boarding school. That's how I survived. My brother wasn't like that.' He said his brother was too soft, too weak, and that boarding school had got the better of him. Joe explained that by becoming a bully he covered himself up to the extent that no one was going to get to him. A lot of the resentment toward his parents was based on what had happened there. He felt that if his parents hadn't packed them off to boarding school, his brother wouldn't have died. Of course, by another extraordinary coincidence, Gaby had a brother who committed suicide. Gaby and Joe were tied in so many ways, and that was significant, I felt. The death of his brother seemed to have formed Joe into what he was, some sort of warrior: everything had to be some sort of fight or mission. He almost admitted that he had become very selfish afterward. His brother died when Joe was at a really impressionable age, when it's hard to get over things easily. I don't think Joe did get over it."

I told Tricia of the tension coming off Joe when I had talked to him about the death of his brother; how I would walk into him on the streets and almost bounce back from the static coming off him. "Yes, you'd feel that he wanted to hit you. He'd walk around seething. But he was a deep thinker, and he needed his space. Sometimes he was in a chain of thought, and didn't want to be interrupted. He needed his head space to think. He liked to be alone. That night he talked late into the night. I was thinking, How am I going to get away from him? I want to go to bed: It's 4:00 a.m. I want you to go. Sometimes you couldn't get rid of him. I loved him, but sometimes you'd want him to leave."

That autumn, despite the iffy *Earthquake Weather* reviews (he'd had those before), Joe was justifiably in good spirits. His imminent tour was getting good previews. "Judging by his floor-shaking gigs last year on the ill-starred Rock Against the Rich tour and his new LP—the best Strummer work since '82's classic *Combat Rock*—these gigs should be fuckin' memorable," said *Sounds*. "With a band who brilliantly realize the multicultural rock 'n' roll the Clash ached to achieve, and a canon of songs (both his own and others) that's vast, well-aged and still relevant, Strummer's a modern electric folk-singer par excellence. His hand is still welded to the old Telecaster and he's got as much hog-wild, brandy-fueled energy as any young upstart, and then some. Bollocks to the rest of them—Strummer is the only name left from the punk era with more than a light and less than a tedious career." Now it was on with the shows, beginning at Barrowlands in Glasgow on October 6. Before "Island Hopping," four songs from the end, Joe gave a plug for "Simmo's" new group, Havana 3 A.M., who were scheduled to play Glasgow a couple of days later. The set was a real move forward. Thirteen of the twenty-three songs had been written since the end of the Clash.

The relatively brief U.K. tour—only ten dates—hit London six days later, for two nights at the Town and Country Club in Kentish Town, opening the shows with theme music from *Walker*. The Clash had stepped onstage to music from Ennio Morricone, but now Joe and his group were walking out to his own music—a subtle but significant advance. I went to the second London show, and they were a real driving group. I preferred them to the previous year's version; some of the crowd were confused by the Latino Rockabilly War's changed lineup—but at least that indicated they had registered them the first time round. After the show Joe seemed exaggeratedly businesslike, a bit tense, but he invited me back to Lancaster Road and he relaxed, sitting at the round kitchen table, with Gaby and some bottles of wine. He did complain that the tour was costing him a small fortune; he would discover his personal shortfall on the dates was £24,000.

In an interview with Carol Clerk for *Melody Maker* on September 30, Joe claimed to be cutting back on booze, something that was rather a regular rap. "Who wants to be fat and wrinkled apart? I still get drunk if it's someone's wedding, or those days when you just have to go on a binge, which I think is quite therapeutic. But you see a lot of casualties around, I suppose, and that's the biggest way to warn anyone off." Carol Clerk commented that she'd give Joe the benefit of the doubt over the large amounts of red wine he consumed during their talk. When Carol asked Joe how he would like to improve his life, the man who played everything so close to his chest did utterly the reverse; it all came out, in the confessional with a female priest: "I'd like to be able to not take things so seriously that I get frantic. I've had times in these past ten years where I've been really unhappy, really at the end of my tether, and when I get into that I'm just awful. Moody, sullen, aggressive. I like to smash things, but I don't think it gets you anywhere." He described to her how he had whirled a chair over his head and smashed it into a floorboard while talking to his manager at the other end of a phone line. (Rock 'n' roll tantrums become very tedious. It is a surprise that Joe Strummer had not figured this out.)

As a nondrinker, Lonnie Marshall watched Joe from a different angle. "The shows were getting great responses. Joe was really up. He was excited. The whole experience was incredibly entertaining. He was just real playful and curious. He related to people: he'd meet somebody one second and next thing you know he'd be off on some philosophical conversation." Lonnie learned to follow Joe's every move closely: "If we were playing too fast or too slow we would watch his foot, and that would show us where the beat was. Or if there was a change, he would maybe give us a nod for the change part. On the sections where we were vamping out and grooving, we were all together. I'm an improvisational player, so I loved that excitement of not really knowing what to expect."

"His boot would lead the way," confirmed Mr. Jack Irons. "Sometimes you couldn't even hear where he was going to start. He'd be talking to the audience, and we'd be watching his boot. You'd keep an eye on that boot, because sometimes he would change things. He would go in different directions, and you'd have to really follow. He'd always signal a change with a wave behind his back if something different was coming—if he wanted to rap to the audience and had something he wanted to say. He wasn't too anal about it having to sound perfect. He was just, 'Let's do it. Let's rock.' He really was into communicating. He'd talk and rattle the audience a bit.

"He burned the candle at both ends. I remember thinking, 'God! Take it easy. Get some sleep.' I don't know how he kept it up, because Joe did the roll call at eight or nine in the morning, and he wouldn't have got to bed until six or seven. You'd just avoid it when he was hungover and grumpy. If he was like that, he'd apologize." When they hit San Francisco, Jack met the woman he would make his wife. At the San Diego show he encountered and became friends with a guy working with the crew called Eddie Vedder; by 1994 Jack Irons was the drummer with Pearl Jam, one of the biggest groups in the United States, with whom Vedder was singer.

Following dates in Paris and Italy, a short American tour began at the Palladium in New York City on November 11. It was here that Joe later maintained he made a major decision. A fan told him that at Tower Records on Fourth and Broadway, in the middle of the allegedly hip Village, they didn't have *Earthquake Weather*. "I just realized that if I couldn't get my record into Tower Records in Greenwich Village the very night the tour hit New York—never mind Poughkeepsie or Oswego—I thought, 'Well, you better retire yourself, boy!'"

You can feel in those words the withdrawal from emotion, the setting in of a freeze of the soul. When you live in a habitual state of depression, fighting to keep above it, fragile from its ceaseless presence, the smallest thing can send you slithering all the way down the snake. A healthy mind's response to habitual record company incompetence might have been to laugh about it, or even be driven by fury, and go out and make another record and then another, and prove a point. A little like Mick Jones had done, in response to Joe's actions. But small things could knock Joe off-kilter—it had been such a struggle to get even to this seemingly pointless point. Now again it seemed hopeless. Everything did.

The tour was a success, but no one bought the record. Worldwide, *Earthquake Weather* sold only just over seven thousand copies, less than half the fifteen thousand that *Walker* had moved, a paltry figure blamed on its being merely a film soundtrack. The excoriatingly disappointing *Earthquake Weather* sales figures were a staggering blow to Joe, supposedly setting off on his solo career. He took it personally, thought it was a judgment on his own work. He didn't appreciate that it was simply not his time, and that the solution would have been to make another record and keep playing live. But Joe, disillusioned, dissolved the group. "They were great," Joe said of the Latino Rockabilly War to his friend, the actor Keith Allen. "It was fun. They were all good players. But I understood at the back of my mind that we weren't doing anything new. So I let it drop. Thankfully, I think." If Joe had kept going in this vein until March 1991, when—thanks to its use in a Levi's commercial—"Should I Stay or Should I Go" became the Clash's first number 1 hit in Britain, he might have been in a position to capitalize on a new wave of credibility that swept upward the reputation of the group and its members. But he didn't do that. His state of mind didn't help. "This decade has pissed me off," Joe confided to Carol Clerk in that *Melody Maker* interview in September. "It's been a waste of fucking time, apart from the kids. Music's got shit, Thatcher became God, ninety percent of the papers are right-wing and brown-nosing."

But would Joe Strummer find the next decade to be much better?

the reckless alternative

1990–1991

As a matter of fact, the eighties wound up far finer for Joe than he might have expected. Out of the blue, in November 1989 *Rolling Stone* voted *London Calling* "Album of the Decade," which immensely raised the stature and position of the Clash. (Although *London Calling* had been released in Britain in the middle of December 1979, in the United States the official release date was January 15, 1980.) Joe told me about this award in December 1989, standing on the pavement outside his house where I'd bumped into him. He was very excited, animatedly positive, spluttering with laughter at the confused release date. The *Rolling Stone* acclaim was a story picked up internationally, and the immense influence and inspiration of the Clash was carved into the rock. Almost inevitably there was also a downside: the same edition of *Rolling Stone* that lavished such praise upon the Clash carried a postage-stamp-sized, lukewarm review of *Earthquake Weather*. The acclaim for *London Calling* failed to translate into increased sales for Joe's first solo album. But the next month, January 1990, brought more good news: Jim Jarmusch's *Mystery Train* was released to great acclaim, an art-house hit.

But Joe wasn't capitalizing on this new status of the Clash. He wasn't really doing anything at all. Mostly he was going to the pub. There was another problem: despite his position as front man for the Clash, rallying the faithful to the barricades, Joe was not the most logical person for such a role. "Even though he'd been the lead singer in the Clash, Joe wasn't a leader," said Tricia Ronane. "He was so passionate about everything, but I could talk to Joe about work and his mind would be changed by the next person he met. On the other hand, both he and Mick had this incredibly seductive manner of draining and taking everything from a situation." It had been his front-man role that had tipped the balance in Joe's relationship with Mick Jones, when the confusion engendered by Bernie Rhodes's return meant Joe started imagining he was in charge. But Joe had come to mistrust that side of himself. So in his productions of *Walker* and *Earthquake Weather* he had merely issued his instructions and disappeared. Such apparent ordaining from on high was probably all that Joe could manage at the time, as he grappled with who he was and where he stood, psyching himself into a new career of some sort. If *Earthquake Weather* had been a success, Joe might have persevered. "I spoke to Paul Simon about this," he told me the next year, "and he said, 'Hey man, before *Graceland* I was dead in the water. Nobody was checking my stuff.' So he's a realist. He had some barren years after stuff like *One Trick Pony*, and out of the hat he pulled *Graceland*. So life is interesting: anything can happen. But you've got to be tough enough to take a spell in the wilderness, instead of hoping to be in the spotlight the whole fucking time. People get sick to death of you."

On April 6, Good Friday, I saw Joe at the funeral of Sean Oliver, the stylish bass player with beatnik group Rip, Rig and Panic and a pioneer of warehouse parties, who had died from sickle-cell anemia. A lovely, great-looking guy, Sean was the father of Slits bassist Tessa Pollitt's daughter Phoebe, and there was a big turnout for his funeral. In his black leather jacket and tight white pants Joe had a clean, just-washed look about him that day; he seemed both slight and sprightly, almost elfin; but simultaneously the diminution of his size was like that of someone vanishing into the ether. It was odd that you could still feel his energy as strongly as ever: angry, powerful, a raging whitewater current beneath apparently stoic rocks. You had to hold your ground sometimes: the stuff coming off Joe could be so potent it could knock you off your stride.

Around lunchtime we left the crematorium together, walked along Harrow Road and down Ladbroke Grove, in that sad shock that characterizes departures from funerals. When we reached my place, close to the tube station, he came in for a cup of tea. I played him a couple of "cumbia" tunes I had picked up on my visit to a festival on the Colombian north coast. Joe also had discovered the joy of this rhythm-drenched Latin music. Jason Mayall had made up a tape of its pulsating sounds for him—Joe rarely took it out of his ghetto blaster, he loved this stuff. My IBM computer stood in pieces on my desk. The hard drive had died and this expensive investment was now useless. Joe was adamant I should not buy a replacement computer. "Get a typewriter," he insisted. "It's more economical for your writing. You'll edit yourself in your brain before you type it down."

Perhaps because he wasn't doing anything else, Joe went on holiday the next month with Gaby and the kids, to St. Tropez. They were joined by their friends John and Amanda Govett and their young son Will. Back in London, Joe acted in *I Hired a Contract Killer*, a film by the Finnish director Aki Kaurismäki, a man with a reputation for alcohol consumption that would have impressed Joe. His role was brief, a one-day job; Joe strums onstage with a percussion player in a corner of a pub. Nicky Tesco, formerly of the Members, had written music for Kaurismäki. Now he had a part in the film, in the same scene as Joe. Nicky had lived for seven years with Annie Day, Joe's old friend from school. "Because of that he was always a bit wary of me. He was very protective of Annie." On the day of filming, all suspicion on the part of Joe Strummer toward the Members front man had evaporated. "Bright and early at nine o'clock on a Monday morning Joe turned up and passed me a huge joint and we spoke properly for the first time. Aki recognized him as a guy with a lot of integrity. They liked each other a lot."

Joe was also to record a pair of songs for the soundtrack of *I Hired a Contract Killer*, "Burning Lights" and "Afro Cuban BeBop," the latter a reflection of Joe's recent musical interests. Both tunes were credited to Joe Strummer and the Astro Physicians, although they featured only Joe and a bongo player. He opted to slip in the recording at the end of a lengthy set of sessions he was about to undertake. At the instigation of Frank Murray, Joe had agreed to produce the next album by the Pogues, a record that would be called *Hell's Ditch*.

Working with the Pogues would entail a different production route. Far from adopting the hands-off approach of *Walker* and *Earthquake Weather*, this time Joe would prove himself extremely hands-on. Shane MacGowan, who had recently discovered a fondness for LSD, and had returned from a visit to Thailand, declared he was not "in the mood" to write Irish-sounding material. Joe encouraged him to come up with more traditionally rock-sounding songs with a Latin tang. All the tunes were written and there had been lengthy pre-production prior to heading down the M4 from London to Rockfield residential studio in Wales, near the market town of Monmouth in the beautiful Wye Valley, a gorgeous part of Britain. Joe drove down in his Morris Minor hot rod; as he did with most of his friends, he had given the vehicle a pet name, the "Moggie" Minor.

"At the end the recording got quite messy," remembered Jem Finer. "When you're making a record and there's eight people in a band, they've all got ideas. And Frank was saying, 'You don't want to put that track on. You want to put Terry's track on.' There were all these politics going on. That happens in bands, but with eight people in the Pogues there would be more politics than there were group members. To deal with this, Joe'd become quite psychotic, destructive and obsessive. He'd smash things, not a lot, but more than necessary. In the context of the record he didn't have to go into that persona every night, but something gradually overtook him during the process. I saw this interesting, weird split going on within Joe. That said," added Jem, "I was impressed by how hardworking he was, how meticulous. He worked his ass off. He kept us all on our toes."

Recording took place during the three-week run of the 1990 World Cup in Italy. Many involved, including Joe, took time off from recording to watch the matches. Throughout the sessions, vibing himself into his role, Joe Strummer wore a straw Stetson he had brought back from Nicaragua; it was his turn to be handed a moniker, the Pogues dubbing him "Strumboli." Joe would pace himself during working hours, small amounts of hash in his joints, no excessive boozing. During the mixing of the record he moved into his own established pace, working half the night. After work Joe would head out into the summer dawn mist to drink brandy and Coke and watch foxes chasing mice on the hills through binoculars. Somewhere around nine in the morning he'd fall into bed. For a couple of weeks Josh Cheuse, then a partner-in-crime when it came to consumption, was at Rockfield, designing the cover for *Hell's Ditch*: "During the actual session, the spliff bunker was always a good way of keeping people out of the control room. Once the actual recording was finished and the mixing had started, we built a kind of art studio in the recording studio, and then we built a bar, using tape to make a beaded curtain. That created a place where everyone hung out and talked and got drunk and didn't interfere in the control room during the mixing." "We set up the *Hell's Ditch* lounge, and made good music," Joe told me. "Me and Josh are very good at creating scenes to hang in. You must have a place for humans to relate. That's what these scenes are about: a cool-out place. Then you eventually talk about your ideas, when you're ready to."

What Josh found was that in this atmosphere he could readily participate. "For example, when they were doing that one track on the album about Lorca, 'Lorca's Novena,' we'd been listening to these cassettes of mad flamenco singers, and we were worried about copyright. So I said, 'Let's play it backward.' So they did it: it's on the record, this backward flamenco thing that sounds great." As he had with the train noises for *Earthquake Weather*, Joe sought out appropriate found sounds: howling dogs were recorded, as well as the sound of the "Moggie" Minor revving up.

Joe needed all his abilities to bring out the best in the group's singer. Shane MacGowan was so off his head for much of the time, his voice accordingly slurred, that Joe was obliged to oversee the way in which much of the *Hell's Ditch* vocals were recorded, not line by line or word by word, but often literally syllable by syllable, the vocals assembled like a jigsaw. "Shane wasn't at his best," said James Fearnley. "He walked into the studio well turned out in a gray suit, but as you looked upward from his shoes, by the time you got to his head he looked terrible. There was a lot of work needed on the vocals."

"Shane was my artist," Joe told me. "If you're in the producer's chair, he's your singer. You've got to understand what his spirit is feeling, and when to record him. You're dealing with an artist. I know Shane well." "Joe did a brilliant job," recalled Spider Stacey. "Given the state Shane was in, he saved what could have been a nightmare and turned it into something very good, by doing the vocals word by word. It was a great idea to use Joe."

James Fearnley agreed: "*Hell's Ditch* was not as belting as our previous albums. But it was a reflection of what was happening in the group. Shane was on his way out. It was manifestly hard to work with him, and him with us. I think he wanted to go. A lot of the songs on the record—like "Sayonara"—are saying goodbye. The ones about Thailand are to do with

Shane's disillusionment. Joe did a fantastic job. He got us to play instruments we hadn't used before, like finger piano and electric sitar. The Thailand feel fit in perfectly."

"The only way it went wrong," said Jem Finer, "was the ultimate choice of the tracks on the record, which ended with an all-night session in my house with him and I arguing about it."

Until almost dawn phone calls crisscrossed North London about the final listing of tracks on *Hell's Ditch*. Several hours were spent on the subject of whether or not to include "Six to Go," a Terry Woods song about the "unsafe" conviction of the alleged IRA bombers of a Birmingham pub in 1974. "It's all about the Birmingham Six," Joe justified its inclusion to Jem Finer. "Have you ever spent fifteen years in prison for something you haven't done?" he said to Spider Stacey on the phone. Although both Jem and Spider appreciated Joe's argument—"I liked that ferocity he had. But the song wasn't good," maintained Jem—they were both against its inclusion. But the tune stayed on the record.

"Joe decided that was the way it was," said Jem. "We had a very long night and in the end I just gave up and said I wanted to go to bed. I told him he was wrong and an idiot, but hoped he'd realize he was a twat one day.

"Later—I think we were at the Electric Ballroom—he came up to me," remembered Jem, "and said, 'You were fucking right, man.' I said, 'Too late now. Listen to me next time.'"

Joe's work with the Pogues was not over. In L.A. in September, Joe rang James Fearnley, who was living with Danielle von Zerneck, his old flame. "Do you fancy a beer?" "Sure," said James. The pair met in the Powerhouse, a bar on Highland in Hollywood. A few weeks later Joe told me the surprising information that James Fearnley presented him with. "He said, 'I'm sorry to have to do this to you, but we parted company with Shane three days ago, and we've got tours booked until March around the world.'"

Joe knew that he was being asked to stand in for Shane MacGowan. "I had a glass halfway to my lips, and I went, 'Uhhh?!?' I nearly spat my beer out. I went, 'You what?????'"

After an acrimonious few days in Japan, Shane MacGowan had left the Pogues. With a world tour to be completed, and no manager—Frank Murray was no longer there—they were in a spot. Until James Fearnley had had his brainstorm.

"I couldn't believe what he'd said. To me it was another normal day in my life. I didn't expect this. I thought about it for maybe three long seconds, and all my intelligence was screaming, 'No, no, no. You don't know what you're letting yourself in for.' And then I said, 'Fuck it. I'm in.' I like to make instant decisions, and go the whole hog with them. Because when I was young I remember reading about the Cherokees, how when a Cherokee is faced with a decision, he always takes the more reckless alternative. That briefly flashed through my mind, and I thought, 'Go for it. What's life for but to make reckless decisions?'"

James Fearnley recalled this pivotal moment differently: "He wouldn't give me an answer. The next day he called me and said, 'OK.' It must have come to him as an insane idea."

So Joe had a new job, singer with the Pogues; the next leg of their tour was kicking off in under two weeks in New York City, on September 26 and 27, at the Beacon Theater. Shane MacGowan was reported to have been upset at being replaced by Joe Strummer.

In Los Angeles the Pogues played at the Wiltern, a beautiful art deco theater in Korea Town on Wilshire Boulevard. Joe's presence on the bill pushed up ticket sales; they ended up playing three nights. "Me and Joe had a competition," said James Fearnley, "to see how many we could get on the guest list. When we used to play 'London Calling,' 'Straight to Hell' and 'I Fought the Law,' he very much directed us."

As opposed to the anti-front-man role that belonged to Shane MacGowan, Joe stamped his authority from the first. A typical set was studded with Pogues' favorites: "If I Should Fall from Grace with God," "Dirty Old Town," as well as "Sayonara" and "Sunnyside of the Street," both from *Hell's Ditch*. Halfway through he stuck in "London Calling," followed a couple of numbers later by "Straight to Hell," with "I Fought the Law" and "Brand New Cadillac" bringing up the rear of the show. The lead singer's onstage pronouncements increasingly took on the sneering nasal intonations of his hero John Lennon—as though the origins of many Pogues had caused the character of Joe Strummer to mutate in the direction of Irish-dominated Merseyside.

"He jumped into the audience at a show, and we kept on playing," recalled James Fearnley. "I didn't know what was happening. Having worked with Shane, we knew it was best to let things like that carry on. Then he got on at me for not helping out: a girl was being given a hard time in the audience by some bloke. Was he being romantically cavalier in the extreme? Was he really angry at something else? Or was he testing us?"

In the bar of the Chateau Marmont one night, Joe found Bruce Spring-steen coming over and putting an arm around him. "I really like what you're doing, man," said the Boss. "I loved Joe's stories about his encounters with the big boys of rock 'n' roll. They were always full of the same enthusiasm as a fan," said Marcia Finer. "I think it was to do with his school experience. He's been accepted. There's something nice about that." In L.A. the Pogues opened for Bob Dylan. "I hope you don't meet him, he might be a disappointment to you," Joe suggested to Marcia. "What he was suggesting wasn't a put-down of Dylan," she considered. "People were always wanting to meet Joe and from that he understood what people wanted from other stars. He knew I would be looking to find something that might not be there." Once when Joe phoned Jesse Dylan, he was told, "Sorry, Dad. I can't talk right now," and Jesse hung up. Joe was amused that Bob Dylan's son had mistaken him for his father.

"The start of the tour was really relaxed," said Jem Finer. "But there's always a weird routine in touring, where you've got all this adrenaline after the show, so then you have a bit of a party, and so you're a bit tired the next day. And you get tireder and tireder. As the front man, Joe had to psyche himself up into the character of Joe Strummer to do the gig. After the gig he'd slowly become John Mellor again, but as the tour went on it look longer and longer for him to come down after the show, until he was Joe Strummer the whole time—which was not always pleasant.

"Joe turned up for rehearsal with this bag full of Hawaiian shirts. He was trying to stamp some collective identity on the band. Control, power. He would create his own environment wherever he was, a lot of which was to do with sound. He'd always have a ghetto blaster playing his choice of music. If you're playing music you're making a whole atmosphere, another kind of power. When we would be getting off the bus waiting for the bags, Joe's ghetto blaster already would be out on the street playing. For a few minutes even that section of the pavement would become Joe's world. He was creating this bubble to travel round in, to isolate or insulate himself in."

At the end of November, after the shows in the United States and Europe, the Pogues hit Britain for an eleven-date U.K. tour, ending on December 12 back at London's Town and Country Club. On the blustery night of November 29, I went up to the first date, at the Corn Exchange in Cambridge. I had been commissioned by the arts pages of *The Daily Telegraph* to write an article, a simple pitch: the singer with the Clash becomes the singer with the Pogues. In March that year the Clash had had their first number 1 single in the U.K., "Should I Stay or Should I Go," on the back of that Levi's commercial. "Rock the Casbah," re-released as a follow-up two months later, got to number 15. But Joe's status wasn't hip and the piece was never run, which I found embarrassing. I had, after all, sat in his dressing room with him for ninety minutes or so before the show and conducted an interview with him.

He had been in chirpy spirits, singing Brian Wilson's "Vegetables" to himself as I entered. Even though he would only be there for a brief time, he had customized it to his liking, putting gels over the lights, and establishing a mood through the tape of Bobby Darin songs that he began to play on his ghetto blaster. Before we began talking, he hawked up a lump of phlegm into the sink. Then he rolled a spliff.

Q. **What's going on with Shane?**
A. Maybe Shane needs a rest—he's entitled to one. These guys work, in the flicker of an eye they tour and tour and tour. They walk it like they talk it, the Pogues.

Q. **How does it feel doing Shane's songs?**
A. It's not the singer, it's the song. Now these songs are great material. I love getting my teeth into them. They'd already parted company with Shane, there are seven other men, trying to scrape and make ends meet. I felt I could do my mates a favor, so they didn't have to cancel a tour, because it costs you money to cancel. It'll take everything you got. So I felt righteous. I realized after a while that the public didn't see it like that sometimes. They thought, "Oh, they've got Strummer in instead of MacGowan." I can understand if people want to shout abuse. But I feel completely honorable, and his material is great to sing.

Q. **You knew what you were letting yourself in for: you'd been on that previous tour, and now you're the singer in the group . . .**
A. I had five days notice on that one. To learn twenty-four numbers, and 1,000 chord changes. I was just concentrating on the rhythm guitar. I never thought about fronting the outfit.

Q. **How do you feel about the live experience these days?**
A. We are proud of it being live. The more stuff that gets pre-recorded— backing tapes and all this stuff—the prouder we feel that we're the real

thing. Even when you're all feeling knackered and it's a bit shabby, I'd rather live with that because at least it's human. Life is unpredictable. If everything is pre-recorded, then everything is monotonously the same, whether you're up or down.

Q. Have audiences been surprised to see you singing with the Pogues?

A. In America the Clash are still really enormous, but the Germans never took to the Clash and they didn't really know who I was. So I had to win them by dint of making great art, now, on the spot. That keeps you sharp. They are very free there, man. It showed up again how people like to restrict us in England: they don't want you to have fun in England.

Q. How's your voice these days?

A. Raspy. Two or three gigs and it starts to tune up. Just like a car, you've got to fill it with gas to make it down to The Smoke tonight. Hey, there's four lines coming up with no breaks, so you fill every cavity within you with air before that, and you feed it out gradually, hoping to get to the last syllable with enough juice to grunt out that last syllable. There are no clear notes required from me. [*Laughter*] Who can say what singing is? People understand that you're out there, and you're going to come back with some strange murmuring or whimpering from where you've been in your thoughts. That's what singing is. You're relating some emotional experiences you had—that you shouldn't have had if you wanted to retain your sanity.

[At this moment, a member of the road crew knocked on the door to present Joe with a tumbler of brandy, a pre-show ritual. "Exactly half that would be fine," he said. "It's like being in the British navy before the battle. This is the Pogues' cannon room. He serves one out to everyone in the group and crew—everyone gets a tot, even the people who don't need one."]

Q. All the projects you've done since the Clash have been interesting . . .

A. A long time ago I realized my stuff was never going to reach a wide audience. So that's a hard thing to realize, and to come to terms with, especially after you've been big. The Clash had massive record sales and reached a lot of people. After that broke up some years have to pass before you get perspective on it, and then pieces drop into place, and you understand that you're never going to get that surge again, because youth, adolescence and rock 'n' roll, combined with people doing the right things in the right place at the right time, is a rocket-propelled jet-fueled mix that's going to last you into the stratosphere. After that you realize you've got to approach life differently, that it's another stage. So I just decided that I would try and do interesting things. I'd try and keep my lifestyle at a low enough level so I could coast along for a while on Clash royalties and not have to go and drive a cab.

I instinctively knew there'd be a long period where I'd have to go into the wilderness. After it broke up I never had the will to form a supergroup with God knows who. I realized we'd had a great crack at it. So I've always tried to do little interesting things down the years. I knew they'd never reach any audience. When *Walker* came out 15,000 people bought it. And rather than say, "What a downer," my attitude was: "This is great. There are 15,000 hipsters out there tuning in, and they are the people who'll always be with you."

Q. I know that *Earthquake Weather* sold badly, but you seem very sanguine about it. I'm impressed with your cold realism.

A. I am coldly real. It's OK. I've beaten myself with the biggest stick. [*Pause*] When you're in the Clash it's very clear. Here's a new group. Dig this sound. They're coming at you: *Booooom!* But when that disintegrates it all gets murky and people have to get to move on and have wives or partners and children and buy and sell Ford Cortinas. I understood I could never hope to command their attention like that ever again, because the world is so full of things and there's not time to check everyone out. I just had to make do with the ones that have drifted into Tower Records. Life is interesting. Anything can happen. But you've got to be tough enough to take a spell in the wilderness, instead of hoping to be in the spotlight the whole fucking time. People get sick to death of you. But I was able to become a human again after being in Shea Stadium.

Q. Have you anything left to give?

A. That's another good thing about being on the road for almost twenty years. I was sitting backstage in some gig in Germany the other day, and I knew we were going to go out and do a great set any second. And I was destroyed beyond the frontiers of endurance, at the end of everything. But I still had it and I could walk to the stage and rip it up.

But that's as much as I had. Afterward a German youth came up to me, with a cool analytical mind. He said, "The gig was really great." I said, "Thanks." But he said, "Of course, I expected that." I said, "Why?" He said, "Because you are a singer without a band and they are a band without a singer." It seemed very clear why it worked after he spoke. I hadn't thought of it like that.

After the British and Irish dates there was an ecstatic response to the addition of Joe Strummer to the Pogues on further Japanese dates, where his legend lingered strongly. When they had been playing in Germany, Joe and Jem had had talks about writing and recording, either together or with the Pogues. Jem gave him "a load of half-finished songs." But these plans would never come to fruition.

By the time that the English tour was halfway through Joe had made a decision. "I've got a letter he wrote to me," said Jem. "He didn't want people to think he was letting them down. But he didn't want to carry on." "I've helped you out three times, man," Joe wrote. "But this time you gotta let me go. I gotta go out on my own and find it."

But where was it? Not in Notting Hill any longer. A big change was about to take place.

It's a good thing Joe never put down that notepad: "THE FUTURE IS UNWRITTEN?" *(Lucinda Mellor)*

the cool impossible

1991-1993

DAMIEN HIRST: What's the biggest thing you've
ever killed?
JOE STRUMMER: My career.

Joe had told Jem Finer he'd "gotta go out on my own and find it." But he would need to look hard. For Joe Strummer nothing seemed to be going quite right.

To the external world Joe appeared a wise man, almost a Solomon figure, whose knowledge had been honed by overcoming external and internal challenges with honesty and insight. With the apparent philosophical overview that came from long experience, he would listen deeply, watch closely and speak last. In the end, his apparent evenhandedness and objectivity had earned him the respect he received, and those who could not work out their problems would come to him voluntarily for advice—although they might not always like what they heard.

Wherever he went, supplicants would clamor to hear Joe's "message." But what exactly was it? Joe had a series of instinctive complaints about society—against racism, inequality, oppression, corruption—but there was never anything especially specific in his satirical grumbling, apart from "Get on with it!" The vision of Prophet Joe essentially derived from what was projected onto him by those who came to genuflect before the sound of his hurt vocals. This "wise man" craved reassurance and validation.

Death had relentlessly shadowed him throughout the previous decade—first his father, then the suicide of Gaby's brother Nick, then the lingering end of his mother—and these tragedies were all overshadowed by a further ending that held an equal significance: the death of the Clash. Joe needed to always surround himself with a posse, but now he pulled the wagons into a circle and barricaded himself against the world. This high plains drifter was floating, not only in his career but also in his personal life. For reasons that seemed to have most to do with his own state of mind, his relationship with Gaby left him troubled, which he attempted to overcome by seeking solace in the arms of whoever was available.

What would happen to him over the next ten years? Things would go wrong, even become worse at first. But they would pick up later. And he would meet a new world.

"I don't remember him being actually depressed until after Clash Mark II split up," said Gaby. "I think he was disappointed in himself for believing in Bernie. He spent a lot of time and energy trying to get the Clash back together. That he couldn't talk Mick into doing it frustrated him incredibly, on top of that feeling of 'What the fuck am I doing?' He'd been on a career in a certain direction, and it all falls apart around you.

"When we went to L.A., he lightened up, and the times we spent in L.A. were a lot better. But that was because when he was there he was always working on a project. At Lancaster Road he used to say, 'I'm downstairs writing.' After a couple of years I started to think, 'Well, he's down there all the time, but I haven't heard anything!' But I was just getting on with the kids. I think we were beyond caring what anyone was doing. If he was in his room writing, that was fine. But it did strike me that he stayed there for a very long time and no music came out of it. In retrospect.

"Everything had gone wrong. I think there is depression in his family. Because he never talked about it, it wouldn't be something that he could go and seek help about. In quite a lot of pictures of him, the girls say, 'Oh, it's Dad's angry face.' There were these manic, almost demonic faces he would pull that were quite frightening."

Later in the decade, when he met and became friends with the artist Damien Hirst, he found someone to whom he was able to unburden himself. "He talked about his mum," said Damien. "About the fact that she was an alcoholic. He talked about sitting on the stairs as a child and hearing her shouting and screaming and said, 'I didn't understand what was going on.'"

(Although others would not agree, Iain Gillies, Joe's cousin, has an opposite view: "Aunt Anna was not an alcoholic. I would stay the night at their house and there was never any sign of hard drinking on her part: I would have spotted it, as my antenna had been up for those kinds of antics for a long time, and if it were true I would have no qualms about confirming it. Joe himself was a Mickey Mouse drinker until he was in the Clash. In the early seventies he was down on drinking: I remember a couple of times being surprised by how little he could drink or even wanted to drink, so he construed his mother's one daily gin as hardened addiction and his extravagant imagination took over and he had to run with this theory all the way up to Damien Hirst.")

"I tried to talk to him about his brother," added Damien, "but he didn't want to go there at all. I bought a book for him: *Night Falls Fast: Understanding Suicide*. But he wasn't interested in the least. He'd shut a door that couldn't be opened."

As in the manner of these things within families, and despite Iain Gillies's view, it seems as though the drinking of Joe's female archetype (as well as that of his father, of course) had been passed down to him. Gaby said to me she had once been told that Joe had for a brief time attended Alcoholics Anonymous meetings—though he never got round to telling her that himself. This seems to have been not long after the death of his mother, when I remember him telling me that he had stopped drinking.

Solomon to the fans, Genghis Khan at home, Joe was a suitable candidate for therapy or psychoanalysis. "I don't think he really believed in things like that," said Tricia Ronane, reminding us of the eternal Luddite within Joe. "Although his staying up all night drinking and talking was his own form of therapy." Gaby felt that she also was dealing with the psychological detritus of her own upbringing, something that she thought probably was part of the unconscious bond between herself and Joe. "A lot of his behavior I would not put up with in a relationship today," she said. "He put me on a pedestal and I didn't have to partake in the world. I lived in a cocoon. I guess that was the payoff for the support and security. I didn't realize that.

"But after losing my brother Nicky, my life changed. Joe sometimes would disappear for days and wouldn't call and I never knew where he was. He'd just go off on benders. That was Joe. The thing that pissed me off about him most was that he would disappear. I didn't know if he was still alive when he did that."

Because he was always so distant, Joe never wholly revealed to Gaby his full frame of mind, including the depression in which he was frequently mired. ("Joe used to go on about people needing to communicate," said Paul Simonon. "But he was the worst at communicating." "I really tried to get through to him," said Mick, "but you'd get to a certain point, and that was it—no further.") Ironically, Gaby says of Joe's depression, "I read about it in a newspaper, where he was talking about it—I think it was an article by you. It was the Scottish thing: you don't talk at all about your emotions, or about pain. In Spain once he somehow got a third-degree burn on his hand. Obviously it was very painful. He just said, 'I don't think I'll come out drinking tonight.' Took a painkiller and lay down. He didn't make a fuss and didn't want any fuss from anyone." When ill, Joe would refuse to submit to his sickness, encouraging his children to do the same. Gaby believed he took a similar approach to his depression, not really admitting it was there.

There are of course always at least two sides to every story, and Alex Chetwynd, Gaby's old friend, had a different point of view: "Gaby's a beautiful person, but she's never had to work." ("Gaby had never worked because Joe had never wanted her to," Tricia Ronane countered.) "I think there was nothing really wrong in the relationship, except that Joe liked his women," continued Alex. "He'd always had loads of women, and Gaby says she didn't know about it. You could tell he was a rascal: he tried it on with every one of my girlfriends. He stuck his tongue down a couple of my girlfriends, and it well pissed me off. But I know Gaby as well as him, if not more. He loved Gaby, and Gaby held the purse strings [in 1988 Gaby took over the day-to-day running of Joe's business affairs, setting up an office at 37 Lancaster Road] and was allowed to do whatever she wanted. She didn't have a bad life, the kids got everything they wanted, she had the big house, plenty of holidays, and he always had his private time. He was a funny guy. He snuck in and out and threw big parties or whatever and had good things to say. He made you feel like you were boss, and that he was there almost as your servant. Life's hard, and people like that make it better and easier, and if you can learn a trick of how to do it from someone like Joe, it's a good thing." Perhaps Joe had learned from his studies of the copy of the *I Ching* that I had seen on the table at Lancaster Road: is not one of its most memorable edicts that to learn how to rule, you must first learn how to serve? But his dilemma now was: what was he supposed to be serving?

P at Rodger, the daughter of a Scottish academic, had first met Joe and the Clash in 1977 while working for an Edinburgh music promoter. When Pat moved to London, buying a small flat in Notting Hill, she was hired as nanny for Mick Jones's baby daughter Lauren. As a rapprochement took place between Mick and Joe, she would sometimes moonlight, taking care of Jazz and Lola for Joe and Gaby.

In December 1990 Pat returned to London from six months in India to discover that the man she had been seeing before her trip abroad had killed himself. She was so devastated, in such pain, that—as she put it—people would cross the street to avoid her. But early one afternoon the first week she was back, she ran into Joe Strummer on Portobello Road. She told him what had happened and he responded in an archetypal Joe way: he took Pat to the Warwick Castle and they spent the afternoon getting drunk, Joe seemingly creating a shield around both of them to ward off his usual drinking cronies. "We went to the pub and virtually the first thing he did was to tell me his brother had killed himself—which I didn't know about. He was the first person who understood what I was going through. Without laying his angst on the table he gave me the lessons. He said his was a different situation, because he hadn't got on that well with his brother. 'But he was my brother, he was my flesh and blood,' he said. 'When somebody decides to actively remove themselves from life you feel as though part of you has been taken away.' I felt great guilt: would this guy have done it if I'd been around? So there was a real 'Wow!' there with Joe that afternoon. I think anybody who has suicide close to them will be haunted by it. 'Use this as an opportunity to empower yourself, to do something you wouldn't do otherwise,' he recommended. Joe said how alienated people are by suicide. When you share that experience you are drawn together, which must have happened to Joe and Gaby after her brother died.

"Joe was so easy to talk to that afternoon in the Warwick. He made me see things within this tragedy. 'It's not just about losing somebody, because there's also always guilt,' he said. 'But it tells you you have only one life, and if you're going to do something with it you should start now. Because you might not be around one day and not leave anything behind you.'"

Pat took a job at the Globe, a shebeenlike nightclub off Powis Square, near where she lived. "Joe knew I would finish at five in the morning, and he would come and knock on my window around then and come in for a spliff. We'd talk about a lot of things: how when cultures come together there can be collaboration, conflict or celebration. In that context he talked about bringing punk and reggae together. And also how when we first lived in Notting Hill it was the front line but now it had become gentrified. He hated the way that capitalism had made us consumers. He hated apathy and the way that people demanded to be fed on tap, and how people didn't have responsibility when they had the power. He had seen how powerful a conglomeration of people could be, but at that time they seemed to be doing nothing. He would get very angst-ridden about Topper's heroin. But we would also talk about Scotland. He talked about how it was a tie from his heart. I said that my heart was there, in Scotland. He said, 'My heart is when I'm onstage.'

"He acknowledged that he'd made bad decisions. He didn't say he'd lost the plot. But he said that he hadn't been in a place where he could listen to his own voice. And he'd listened to the wrong people. Bernie had been important in getting Joe to talk about politics. But everybody looked up to Joe and he had no one to look up to. When there were tensions between him and Mick, Joe didn't have a father figure—maybe that was the role that Bernie took on for him. Because he'd had such a disastrous upbringing there was a real need for structure, and because it was so lacking you hold on to other established things to have your frame of reference.

"I remember us talking about the film *Clockwork Orange* and its very manipulative use of Beethoven's Ninth Symphony. He said that when he saw it he worried about what people were doing to his own music that he couldn't control—the enormity of what he was putting out there and how he definitely needed to feel he could control it. His songs are so unequivocal and intense, and onstage with Mick—who was similarly dysfunctional—there was the possibility for either greatness or great conflict. Paul was a traditionalist in his painting style and had found an anchor there, and

I think Mick and Joe didn't have that. Joe was jealous of Mick's musical abilities. He almost replaced his brother with Mick, that element of sibling rivalry: 'How can you do that and I can't?' But Joe had an ability to relate to people, perhaps more than Mick in those days. Mick used to hide behind his dope smoking."

A few days before Christmas 1990 Joe and Gaby threw a party at 37 Lancaster Road. A really great night, as usual. Joe touched me deeply by retelling the story of the carnival home invasion and how I'd stood with him. There was not the slightest hint of domestic discord; you would have thought that these two people were very happy together. This also seemed to be the case four months later when they arrived with the two girls at my house for a party; Joe—who had been battling with booze-related weight fluctuations, his face sometimes seeming puffy from alcohol—was drinking only red wine; he had given up beer, he said, because it put too much of a belly on him. "We were both very good at that," said Gaby. "We'd have a party, or people to stay, and everything would seem very jolly. Then afterward we'd just return to our separate ways." Some might feel that since time immemorial that has been the way of many relationships—it's why men have a shed, or in Joe's case a studio, except that in the textbook of love written by Hollywood, to which most recent generations subscribe, that wasn't what we were told to expect. And Joe is in his own movie, which at this time seems to involve a lot of hitting on other women, almost as reassurance. (It was almost literally "hitting" on them: one of Joe's favored pickup techniques involved a sort of mild shoulder charge into his object of seduction.) But he pissed off people close to him through this behavior. "Look at him. He's pathetic," grunted Raymond Jordan at a party as, over in a corner, Joe mooned like a teenager over a girl. Such secretive, sly behavior leads to feelings of guilt which burden the mind, the last thing needed by Joe, who already had a brain close to imploding. At the very least, such conduct often leads to a fractious attitude to one's main partner.

There are few words more poignant in the English language than "longing," and Joe was endlessly longing for love. Life seemed to work well for him when he was in love: the love affair with Paloma coincided with the 101'ers; Gaby came along just before the beginning of *London Calling*, a golden phase; the Danielle von Zerneck affair was no bad thing—the Pogues, the *Permanent Record* soundtrack, *Mystery Train* (just about . . .), all came to fruition while he was in love with her. His next relationship would involve a creative rebirth.

A t Easter 1991 Joe, Gaby and the kids, with their friends John and Amanda Govett, went to Andalusia, staying in Mojacar, a base to find somewhere to rent for the summer months in nearby San José. They discovered an apartment in San José at 1 Los Genovese.

A great time was had in August in San José, to which Joe would now return every year, to the same property, always going back to London in time for the Notting Hill carnival. When Joe and Gaby returned to England, a momentous decision was taken: although they would keep 37 Lancaster Road, they would move out of Notting Hill and set up home close to Andover in Hampshire, in a farmhouse owned by the Govetts. Joe always maintained that this was his idea, that Jazzy one day had picked up a used hypodermic syringe in a playground in Powis Square and he realized it was time to make a move. But this shorthand explanation was typical Joe romanticism.

The reason did involve the children, but was about the education of Jazz and Lola, in a way that Joe could not reveal in interviews. Adamant he would not send his children to private schools—knowing it would be contrary to everything in which he professed to believe—Joe had enrolled Jazz and Lola in Coleville Primary School, the state school closest to Lancaster Road. He and Gaby were disturbed to discover their children weren't progressing at school. Here a real moral dilemma opened up, familiar to parents of liberal persuasion.

"I think the move to the country was definitely from Gaby's end," said Tricia Ronane. "She wanted to do that. But Joe felt the children's education in London was not great. With their edicts about 'No private education' they made a rod for their own backs. Then they've got their own children going to the state primary round the corner and the education isn't that great. Joe is realizing that and is finding that really hard to cope with. Lots of times I had conversations with Joe where he was battling with that principle and the actual reality of it."

Accordingly, in September 1992 the children were placed at Thorngrove, a private day school not far from the farmhouse. As headteacher

Connie Broughton recalled, "Joe was fantastic, always very helpful and generous. He would take all the children under his arm. He would do recordings of the Christmas carol services—but only on the condition that he was provided with a glass of wine. He was a very kind, likable man, so different from the impression you got from him onstage." On one occasion, drinking wine in the kitchen at Thorngrove, Joe made an announcement: he had decided the name of any new group he formed—it would be the Mescaleros. What inspired this? Connie Broughton didn't know. To the school he donated an electric guitar and amplifier, and he gave a copy of *The Clash on Broadway*, a box set released in the United States in November 1991 and in Great Britain almost three years later, to Connie's fourteen-year-old son. Both Jazz and Lola left Thorngrove in July 1997. Jazz went as a boarder to Bedales, a celebrated public school in Hampshire, and Lola soon joined her there.

"Getting his mother to apologize for sending him to boarding school— that was one of our points of difference when he sent his own children to boarding school," recalled Marcia Finer. "He said he wanted the best for his kids, and I said maybe he should have been a bit more sympathetic toward his mother." Marcia was also concerned about what she saw as needless self-inflicted suffering: "Come on, maybe it would be nice to have an easy time of it now. You've worked hard, actually suffered quite a bit."

Not that everyone seemed to appreciate Joe for who he simply was. "I got detoured on a train back down to Hampshire," he said. "I had a long wait until my connection. I went to get a drink in a pub. Some bloke said, 'You look just like Joe Strummer.' I said, 'I am Joe Strummer.' He said, 'You wish!'" Down at the farmhouse in Hampshire Joe set up a home studio, trying to grapple with modern technology, never his strongest point; he began to work on songs for the soundtrack of Sara Driver's *When Pigs Fly*. But matters between Joe and Gaby had hardly changed. Sometimes they seemed worse. To Paul and Tricia, Joe complained about living in what he said was spelled the "c-u-n-t-ry." He was miserable that he couldn't hear the excellent music programs on BBC Radio London—eventually he erected a tall aerial behind the house to pick up the station—and that he couldn't buy the London *Evening Standard*—despite that publication's right-wing slant, both Joe and Mick Jones were avid readers of the capital's daily paper. "Down in the country there was no coffee shop for him to go to for a breakfast sardine sandwich and he'd have to drive to the pub," said Tricia. "He had to work round that. When we stayed down there, we'd come down for breakfast, and Joe would be sitting outside in the Moggie Minor with his coffee and newspaper while everyone else was inside having breakfast. That's the coffee shop he's created. He's got to get out of the kitchen and have a bit of peace and quiet. I was allowed to sit in it with him once and have a chat." The "c-u-n-t-ry" wasn't all boring: one night, on the way back from an evening out in Winchester, John Govett rolled his car, Joe gripping on to his seat belt in the front passenger seat as the vehicle tumbled over. But such fun aside, this was the beginning of what Joe would later define as "the Wilderness Years." His frustrations were building up and the problems between himself and Gaby were coming to a head.

Shortly before he went on tour as singer with the Pogues, Joe had taken Gaby to Pisa and Florence for a long weekend, to celebrate her thirtieth birthday, on October 12, 1991. In characteristic manner, as though—you might feel—to prevent the need for any unpalatable intimacy between himself and Gaby, Joe had also invited along John and Amanda Govett. Alcohol was consumed, especially by Joe. After their last evening out, back at their rather sumptuous hotel, Joe lost it. "He verbally attacked me. He came out with so much venom," said Gaby. "He told me I was a dreadful mother. He told me I was terrifying for the kids. He was projecting onto me about his childhood and his relationship with his mother, and it was the final straw. I said that was it: it was absolutely over between us. We discussed splitting up. He wanted to take the kids—I said that wasn't even an issue. We came back and lived in separate rooms, as complete strangers."

Perhaps as compensation—at such times the delusion that you simply need a change of scenery can be strong—there were more holidays. At Easter 1992 Joe went with Gaby and the kids to Barbados. They had booked into the Cobbler's Cove Hotel, a former plantation house on the west coast of the Caribbean island. Clearly needing his habitual social backup, but on another level operating from altruistic feelings toward his old spar, Joe called up Paul Simonon in London. Paul was grieving over the recent death from cancer of Nigel Dixon, with whom he had formed Havana 3 A.M., the man Paul had regarded as "his only friend." It didn't take much persuading before Paul, Tricia and their young son Louis were on a flight from London to Barbados. At the airport, they were greeted by the sight of Joe sitting at the wheel of a rented Mini-Moke, a pair of cocktails that he had bought for

Joe and Paul Simonon with Eddie Grant, whose "Police on My Back"
the Clash covered on *Sandinista!* Joe and Paul ran into Eddie in
Barbados, where he was a resident. *(Lucinda Mellor)*

his friends melting in the tropical sun on the dashboard. "Come on. I've
come to get you," said Joe, as they set off on the forty-minute drive to Cobbler's Cove. "He was looking after Paul in his way," said Tricia. "We had a
bag hanging out of the Mini-Moke, a baby hanging out the other side, Paul
and I hanging on. 'Come on. Let's stop and have a drink,' says Joe. Joe was
on his best efforts to cheer Paul up and give us a good time. It was really
nice. Eddie Grant, who lives there, saw us one day at this bar and we got to
know him. Joe was drinking a lot."

On August 21, 1992, for Joe's fortieth birthday, he, Gaby, John and
Amanda Govett and their assorted children drove up to Granada from San
José. This significant birthday was to be celebrated in considerable style, at
the ritzy Alhambra Palace Hotel. As a present Amanda and John bought Joe
a top-of-the-range Spanish acoustic guitar. What had been intended as a two-
day stay turned into five nights. There was a pair of reasons: check-out time

at the Alhambra Palace was 11:00 a.m.; each morning everyone would still be in bed then and their stay at the hotel would roll on to an additional night; and then it was learned that during the day the kids had been raiding the minibars, meaning their parents didn't have enough cash to pay the bill, and they had to send to San José for more money. Joe's reluctance to use credit cards was sometimes an obstacle to the smooth running of his life.

So Joe had hit forty, the signpost of middle age. You know that that chapter marker in his life hit him like a sledgehammer. His depression and self-recrimination only intensified. All the holidays in the world couldn't anesthetize that.

"He was very depressed," said Tricia Ronane. "I don't think it was even about him and Gaby—although I think he thought it was. When you're depressed, you take it out on the people closest. Paul and I would go to see them, they'd shout a lot, there was a lot of tension if she turned up in the pub, and they would be arguing all the time. I think Joe loved Gaby a lot, in spite of his philandering, and he adored his children. He did tell me once that in a row—when you do say horrible things—she'd told him he was no good and useless. That's not what a guy like that wants to hear. Joe always needed someone he could talk to, and he didn't have anyone like that down in the country. He'd try these different people he'd bump into. He was down there with not a lot going on, very depressed."

Part of Joe's solution to his state of internal bewilderment was to spend more and more time in London, crashing with Paul. "Paul and Joe would sit up all night in our living room," said Tricia. "But they weren't doing drugs: they drank bottle after bottle of red wine, Joe would smoke some spliff. I'd come down at seven in the morning, because of the kids, and the turntable would still be turning, ashtrays full of cigarette stubs, Joe asleep in the alcove by the window, Paul lying on the sofa, and I'd be: 'You two, can't you even drag yourselves up to a bed?' Night after night. They stayed up on conversations which were sometimes useless and sometimes enlightening, but they were always intense and fun. They would listen to music, and they would laugh their heads off. Smoke, drink, stay up all night."

Joe's parenting skills were demonstrated just before Christmas, when he was in London for the Notting Hill pantomime, an annual event held at the Tabernacle in Powis Square, with cameos from local celebrities. Joe gave my two-year-old son Cole such an endless supply of sweets—involving much licorice—that the boy threw up. Down in the country, as 1992 slid into 1993, Joe and Gaby threw a New Year's Eve party. First party-goers congregated, in fancy dress, at Paul and Tricia's house in Oxford Gardens to travel to Hampshire in a bus. The usual suspects were involved: Don Letts and his family, his brother Desmond, and Leo Williams, formerly bass player with BAD, were all on the bus, as was Gordon McHarg, a pop artist from Canada who had met Joe through Paul. Gordon took down several packets of king-sized blue Rizlas for Joe. "You can't go to the shops in the country and ask for king-sized Rizlas: it's a dead giveaway," Joe had advised Gordon. "It seemed a fair exchange," thought Gordon, who partook of Joe's omnipresent golfball-sized lump of high-grade hash. The coach taking everyone back to London departed at 1:00 a.m.—a little early, it was generally felt.

Gerry Harrington, who, despite no longer working with Joe, had remained friends, went to Hampshire. "I was in the living room on a Sunday with Simonon in the middle of winter. All the women were in the kitchen. Suddenly Joe says to Simonon and me, 'It's pretty cold out there. Do you reckon you can run a hundred yards in this kind of cold?'

"'Yes, of course. But what are you getting at?'

"'It's just that if you fall it's very icy . . .'

"'Joe: where are we going with this?'

"Paul doesn't need to figure anything. He's heard this a million times. Joe says, 'It's one thirty. We only have an hour's worth of drinking before the pubs shut, if we leave now on foot and get there in three minutes. So we've got to go. You don't have time to get your coat. Gerry, I'm begging you.' He doesn't want Gaby knowing that he's going to the pub. This is a guy who's forty and he behaves like he's fourteen."

"I told Gaby, 'You two have got to confront this situation and do something about it,'" said Tricia. "'Or one or the other of you is going to fall in love with someone else. Not even because you want to, but because it's unavoidable when there's no love going on in the relationship.'"

Over the 1993 Easter holiday there was a big country picnic at the house of the artist Charlie Baird. Gordon McHarg took a photograph of Joe Strummer cheerily holding aloft a Roy Orbison CD, an artist whom Joe always loved. But later, walking in the fields, Gordon overheard Joe, pacing the grass in evident angst with Frances, Gaby's mother, say to the woman who was effectively his mother-in-law: "I don't know what I can do. I don't know how to make her happy."

The Clash on Broadway box set, which Joe had gifted to the son of Connie Broughton, was an iconic, intimate and highly satisfying example of a then new form that enhanced the legend of the Clash—people who hadn't listened to the group for years pricked up their ears again. It had brought Joe back into contact with Kosmo Vinyl; the two had not really spoken since the end of the Clash. Out of the blue Tricia Ronane called Kosmo, asking him to work on the *Clash on Broadway* project. He flew over to London and reacquainted himself with Paul and Mick. "Of course Joe was being elusive. I got him on the phone one day and he said, 'Just fucking get over here!' He slammed down the phone. I can't finish it without him, so I go over to his house in Lancaster Road. He does everything I need in about twelve minutes."

Kosmo was known for looking sharp. When he arrived at Lancaster Road, Joe also was dressed to the nines—"great shirt on, jacket, pegs. He said, 'I don't always dress like this anymore, but you're here.' He looked fantastic. We renewed friendship. He was completely on board with the *Clash on Broadway* thing. Fantastically cooperative." Kosmo threw an offer in the direction of Joe: "If you need any help on anything . . ." Some time later Joe called him: "'If you want to help me, help me sort out this film.' I said, 'What film?' He said, 'I've agreed to do this soundtrack for Sara Driver. They've got no money. We've got to do it fast. We really have got to do it: I've booked time at Rockfield and haven't got any musicians.'"

Kosmo came back to England and went to see Joe. "He's out in Hampshire with Gaby and it seems to me that the situation is very bleak, very heavy there. Not in a combative way, but you can feel it in the air. That awesome quiet. There's not much being said in the house."

When Pigs Fly, an Irish ghost story starring Marianne Faithfull, was the second film made by Sara Driver. "One of the reasons I wanted Joe to do the music for my film," said Sara, "was not only because of his knowledge of Irish music, but because he was like an archaeologist with music. He had such a love of different kinds of music that would influence his work. He would layer them, like an archaeologist.

"Joe had an enormous ego, but he was also someone who was very sensitive. Insecurity often goes with big egos. Joe was more and more internalized. Big Chief Thunder Cloud was eating him up. He really did have a cloud over his head, a dark cloud."

The dark cloud allowed him to reject Sara's suggestion, which Kosmo had tried to get him to go along with, to sing a duet with Marianne Faithfull. But Joe was absolutely ready for studio work—especially when the director, who could offer only a small fee, gave him the music publishing rights to the movie.

Contrary to what Joe secretly feared, everyone jumped at the chance to work with him. Kosmo called Danny Thompson, the masterly English jazz stand-up bass player who had worked so memorably with John Martyn, another eccentric genius. "Strummer's name seemed to be good with everyone. Danny Thompson said, 'I'll be there.'"

"I knew and loved his stuff, but I didn't know him," said Danny. "I'd loved the Sex Pistols and the Clash. To me Joe seemed more of an intellectual with an outlook beyond music. He said, 'I'm doing a film.' I said, 'Who's doing the arrangements?' He said, 'It's not like that. We're just doing it. It's only E and A—there's no grammar-school chords.' I said, 'Can I play to what's on the screen and respond accordingly?' He said, 'That's how we're going to do it.' I met him down at Rockfield and fell in love with him. But we were talking F-sharp minor and B-flat—it was more complex than he'd had me believe. He had great ideas. He would suggest things and gave me more freedom to express myself."

On drums was Terry Williams, who was in Rockpile with Nick Lowe and Dave Edmunds, the latter the owner of Rockfield. Joe and Kosmo brought in some Irish musicians Joe thought would understand the material. "I tried to get really good players," said Kosmo. "I figured the best thing to do was get in some guys who could really play, who he'd never really been around. But Joe didn't really like that. I think it put too much pressure on him, but I wasn't quite aware of that at the time."

"Joe's boys' club felt very male: as soon as these musicians would arrive, they would always ask me for a cup to tea," remembered Sara. "Joe would get a gleam in his eye and go, 'She's the director.' It would make him really happy to stick it to them a little bit."

Although there was no formal arrangement between the two men, Sara was under the impression that "Kosmo was organizing and helping manage Joe. He was my main contact when I was organizing all the music stuff. The money and the administration, it all went via Kosmo."

Joe went down to Wales on March 19, 1993, for a day's pre-production at Rockfield, but the sessions proper started on April 27, lasting until the thirtieth, with a day of post-production on May 2. As soon as they began, Joe steamed ahead. "From the four days at Rockfield he gave me nine hours of music," said Sara. "What am I going to do with all this music? It was the ac-cumulation of all those years of not being in the studio. He was writing fu-riously. He had so much to show me when I arrived that was already sketched out. I have these napkins of Joe's lyrics: his brain was so active that he was always doodling, always writing."

There were three songs with vocals—the title track "When Pigs Fly" (which ultimately was not used in the film), "Pouring Rain" and "Rose of Erin"—and one, "Free at Last," on which Joe extemporized a scat-style, free-form spoken-word rendition. Among the pieces of instrumental music in the film were "Ellis Island Line," "Phantom County Fair" and the thunder-ing instrumental "Storm in a D-Cup." On "When Pigs Fly," a meditation on the thorny subject of romance ("No one knows if it comes and goes / it is a difficult thing, this thing called love"), his voice is buried even deeper than it appeared to be on *Earthquake Weather*. But still, no more so than on "White Riot."

"I'm a Moslem, and it was Ramadan," recalled Danny Thompson. "It got to one o'clock and he'd offer me sandwiches and tea. But I'd have some-thing to eat at 4:30 a.m. and then when the sun went down. After about the third day he asked me why I wasn't eating. I said, 'I'm a Moslem. I fast for a month.' He said, 'Blimey, that's hard. All right, I won't have a joint until you break your fast. At sunset I'll skin one up.' He showed me he knew what I was doing and was understanding and courteous.

"I knew from the word go that I loved this bloke. Whether I played with him didn't matter. It would have been all right to just have a picnic. He was a cartoonist with his words. I laugh when I think about him, that grin of his—he was a naughty boy."

As opposed to his previous work at Rockfield with the Pogues, when Joe had rigorously overseen every note, he now reverted to the hands-off method of the *Walker* soundtrack. "He would show the musicians just a lit-tle something of how the song should be," said Sara, "and then let them dance with it."

"He was very positive and impressive as a producer," said Danny Thomp-son. "Very nicely in control. He was aware he had a budget and had to match it. He wanted it right. He had a project to do and it was fantastic. He wasn't drinking much, a person in complete control getting on with the project."

Sara did observe that Joe seemed somewhat hard of hearing, an occupational hazard for musicians: "We went to dinner and he couldn't hear a word the waitress said. That's when I realized. A lot of times he would say, 'Oh, right!' to things that really shouldn't get an 'Oh, right!'"

Accompanying Sara Driver at Rockfield was Jim Jarmusch, partially, she thought, because he was aware of Joe's perpetual propensity for mischief. "I told Jim that I was going to be there for four days of hard work. After three days, I said, 'See Jim, all we're doing is working.' He said, 'Yes, you're working very hard.' Jim absolutely adored Joe. I think Joe had that effect on men: it was like they were in love with him, not in a sexual way but in an intellectual way, because of everything he stood for. It's really interesting how the whole 'family,' from near and far, would show up to things he was involved in."

Almost as soon as Joe returned to Hampshire from Rockfield, something unexpected happened. "I had gone down to stay with Amanda Govett with my daughter Eliza for the weekend," said the then Lucinda Henderson. "It was a miserable, gray Saturday, and Amanda said there was a fair in Andover, and suggested we take the kids because there was nothing else to do. We got in the car, and she said, 'I'm going to go and see if Joe wants to come, because I know he's alone.' So Amanda went into the house and asked him. It was strange. Joe was enjoying the house: Gaby had gone up to London with the kids. He was just thinking, 'Phew, I've got the house to myself and some space.' But something made him say, 'I'll come.' He got in the front seat. I was in the back. She turned round to introduce us, and our eyes met and that was that.

"We went to the fair and it was drizzly and cold. We walked round the fair together and he shot all the bull's-eyes and got all the ducks and all the teddies—Eliza had a mountain of this stuff. We just got on really really well.

"I was into Dexy's Midnight Runners and Blondie. I knew the Clash, but I wasn't a fan—I wasn't cool enough. But I just felt at ease with him. We just talked and he amused me, and flattered me, I suppose, but not in a flirty way but in an intellectual way. He made you feel you had something to say and were interesting and great to be with. He made you feel you were the most important person in the world. I loved being with him. We saw each other over the weekend. Two weeks later I was again staying with Amanda—I was a godmother at a local christening. I took Eliza for a walk and Joe rang up the house and asked where I was—unheard-of, this was about ten in the morning. Amanda said I'd gone for a walk. Joe came and found me. We'd had no physical contact at all. And he just went to hug me, and it was completely, utterly electric. And I knew that something was going to happen. He wasn't predatory, and he wasn't greedy. I just completely fell under the spell which is Joe.

"But he was down. He said he'd put his heart and soul into *Earthquake Weather* and had had no tour support from CBS. And that he'd come back home after the tour and felt like a failure. He was really down."

Born on June 15, 1962, Lucinda Tait grew up in West London; her father was an architect who'd been an officer in the British army and her mother had been a model. Joe was forty. "That's not too old for you, is it, baby?" he asked her. Not too old for a single woman, but this was not what Lucinda was: she had been married for ten years to James Henderson, who, almost inevitably, had been one of the two hundred drummers who auditioned to take over from Terry Chimes in 1977. They had a daughter, Eliza, born on January 5, 1992, and had been the previous tenants of Bransbury Cottage, rented for five years as a weekend retreat from their London home in Fulham.

"Joe didn't talk about the past," said Lucinda. "I don't think it was because he was hiding or covering anything up. It was because he lived in the day. There were never any war stories. He'd never say, 'Oh, I was hanging out with Ronnie Wood . . .' It was never about famous musicians, but what people had to offer you as a person. He was on a constant thirst for knowledge. And he didn't use that ever to belittle people. He would listen, like he'd heard it for the first time. The stories that he told were about interesting people he had met. 'I met a baker. I sat up all night with him. And he told me how to cut bread, that you always put a loaf on its side.' Or, 'I met this guy and he worked in a factory and made nuts and bolts, and he told me . . .' He told me, 'I've learned never to have opinions.' He was genuinely open-minded. I think he'd learned to be open-minded. So many things that he'd been taught by his parents, or that he'd learned in the early days of the Clash, didn't hold water. Everyone was different and there were always two sides. And he'd always say, 'Think it through, think it through.' I'm a hot-head when I get cross. But he'd always say, 'Think it through.'"

Joe and Gaby and Paul and Tricia had been invited to the British Grand Prix on July 11 at the Silverstone racetrack; when they returned to London, Gaby went back to Hampshire while Joe stayed the night at Paul's. Tricia had noticed that recently Joe had arrived on their doorstep more frequently. He needed an alibi, as his journeys to London had one purpose: to see Lucinda Henderson. Very soon after he had met Lucinda Joe had confided in Paul what had transpired in his life. "Don't tell a living soul, not even Tricia," he had admonished. Paul kept his lips sealed. The day after the Grand Prix, Joe asked Tricia to have lunch with him. "We went to 192. When he wanted to say something, he liked to buy you a bottle of champagne in 192. Walking there with him, he said to me, 'Everyone's staring at us.' I said, 'That's because of you, you silly ass.' At lunch he told me about Lucinda. He said he was thinking of bailing out from Gaby. He was worried I was going to judge him and fall out with him. I said I was not judging anyone's relationship, because there but for the grace of God goes anyone's. It's not my business, because no one really knows what goes on between two people. It was as though a weight had come off his shoulders. We had a good chat."

A couple of days later Joe drove over with Gaby in their Renault Espace to Winchester, where Danny Thompson was playing with his group. "Afterward he came up to me and gave me a big cuddle and said, 'I think it's a bit too clever for me.'"

Within days, Joe and Gaby were at Paul's place, to go to a party in Fulham. They went with Paul and Tricia, driving over in Paul's Mitsubishi jeep. At the party was a blonde with a bobbed haircut, wearing a hat. "That's her, isn't it?" Tricia said. "How did you know?" said Joe. "If it's that obvious to me, you've got to tell Gaby," said Tricia.

The four of them left the party, Paul at the wheel of his jeep. "Joe decided to tell Gaby about Lucinda in the back of our car on the way home from the party," remembered Tricia. "They were both staying at our house. Thanks, Joe! I didn't mean *now*, in the back of our car. He's a coward—he did it because we were there. Poor Gaby. She wasn't even in her own home. We got back to our place, and she went to bed. I wanted to give them privacy, but Joe doesn't want you to leave the room—he wants you to stay. I think Gaby knew. It wasn't the first time she had heard such a thing about Joe, so she took it better than some people might.

"She went back to the country the next day, and Joe stayed. I said, 'Go home. You can't drop a bombshell like that and then stay in London for the weekend with us. Go home now, and fuckin' sort it out.' I forced him out of the house."

"I didn't go to the party with the three of them," Gaby recalled. "I had been for a psychic reading that afternoon where I was told he was having an affair, which could account for his sudden interest in doing laundry. I arrived at the party alone and confronted him. After his admission I left, stunned, and went to spend the night with friends, still oblivious to the fact that it was Lucinda. Joe would not let on to her identity, as he was protecting her, as she had not yet decided if she would leave James. He turned up later that night at my friend's house and slept on the floor next to me. We agreed to meet the next evening for dinner to talk. It's amazing other people's recollections: I think in this instance I would remember what happened."

But a Strummer family summer holiday in San José had already been arranged. Nothing was going to get in the way of that, not even such an impending guillotine chop as their breakup.

Joe's own actions in San José rendered any reconciliation impossible. Although Paul and Tricia had not been scheduled to go on this vacation, Joe phoned them incessantly, insistent they come to Spain, telling them he was spending all his time finding them somewhere to stay. Having such a job to do rescued Joe from having to spend time with his family. "Paul and I went out with little Louis, our eighteen-month-old son, and Joe was hanging out with us a lot," said Tricia. "There was lots of alcohol. It was always, 'You lot are OK here. Me and Paul are going to see my friend in such-and-such a bar. We'll be back.' He'd take Louis with him. Is that some sort of security blanket?

"There were times when you'd go down in the morning and one of the kids would say, 'Look what Joe gave me for breakfast: a lollipop.' Anything for a quiet life is really what it was. It doesn't matter that it's seven in the morning: 'I'll give them lollipops.' The man was incapable of saying no to children. But don't do that to my kids."

Despite his behavior with the children, Joe himself didn't immediately get into the spirit of beach life. At first he would lie on the sand, tightly buttoned up, dressed in black jeans and black shirt; as time wore on he relaxed more about this, taking off his uniform and swimming and splaying out in the sun. Gaby was largely oblivious to Joe's machinations. Resigned to the end of their relationship, she tried to largely ignore him in San José and make the best of her time there with the girls.

Jem and Marcia Finer would be in San José each summer, having been going there even longer than Joe and Gaby. "I was there at the split-up," said Marcia. "Right after it had all come out, I was having a meal with them and Gaby went to the lavatory. I was left with Joe. He said he was worried she'd get involved with some deadbeat and he'd have to pay—very practical. I said I very much doubted it. I said to Joe, 'Don't feel too bad. She's been sick of you for years.' He looked both relieved and hurt. She came back, and then he went to the loo. I told Gaby I'd said a terrible thing to Joe, but she thanked me and said she *had* been sick of him for years. After the split I talked with Joe about coping strategies and noncoping strategies, and he said, 'I've got to survive.' I don't think he had such an easy time loving himself. I remember something he said, when we were talking about depression, that that stock line about having to learn to love yourself first is narcissism."

While Joe was in San José that summer of 1993, the Pogues—who by now to all intents and purposes had split up—were surprised to find they had a hit record. Jem had to fly back to London to appear on *Top of the Pops*. When he returned three days later, he learned of the splintering relationship. "It all sounded pretty mad. But separating was probably much better for Gaby. I don't think it was better for Joe. It was quite destructive. He threw himself to the wall in a sense."

A few days after this complex Spanish sojourn, Joe was in New York, conferring with Sara Driver. *When Pigs Fly* had financial difficulties. While in Manhattan Joe visited Kosmo, not breathing a word about the romantic developments in his life. Kosmo had been stimulated by the success of the film music sessions to consider there could be further trips by Joe to the recording studio. "I wanted to keep the momentum going. Joe seemed a little revitalized. *When Pigs Fly* had gone fairly smoothly, so I was thinking we could exploit that. I thought the film-jazz and the beat thing might be a way to go, if we could also get a contemporary remix. Joe was very dubious about remixes, but I was thinking of getting someone from Sting International, the Brooklyn reggae studios."

To play on these new sessions, set for another four-day period at Rockfield at the end of September 1993, Kosmo again enlisted Danny Thompson; he also brought in Aaron Ahmun, a session drummer with a strong reputation. Kosmo wanted to use only these two musicians at Rockfield, to maximize the minimalization. Joe spoiled Kosmo's plan, pulling in a couple of musicians who'd played on *When Pigs Fly*. "If it had been the bare thing I wanted," said Kosmo, "Joe would have been more involved. I think Danny was too much pressure for Joe. His reputation was such, just being there was hard for Joe. There was pressure for him, seeing Danny Thompson sitting around waiting."

It was evident to Danny Thompson that, after the success of the April sessions, these September recording dates were "anticlimactic." "We turned up and there was nothing planned for the second sessions. It was a pity after the first sessions, which were brilliant."

Joe did have one new song, "Forbidden City," but couldn't work out a satisfactory arrangement. He was not focused, disappearing for twenty-four hours as another domestic crisis exploded. Even when he was in the studio, said Kosmo, "it was fairly obvious that Joe wasn't really there. There was a lot going on on the home front. The sessions didn't really work out."

But on one song they came close to Kosmo's movie-jazz beat template. "The Cool Impossible" was a tune Joe worked up in the studio, a meandering, moody, piano-based tune, a song about a past success: "Because they're sick of hearing about it all / So rev your motorcycles and piss against the wall / I know about a man who lost it all / Suddenly it all becomes probable / possible / a certainty surely / When you're riding on the crest of a wave / You're riding to the top of the world / You're throwing cool shapes and you're letting it spin / When you're riding on the crest of a wave / To the stone cold cool impossible." He keeps repeating it: "When you're riding on the crest of a wave / You're riding to the top of the world / You're throwing cool shapes and you're letting it spin / When you're riding on the crest of a wave." These last lines conclude the song. For Joe knows that when the wave crests it must fall. "I thought 'The Cool Impossible' sounded very where he was," considered Kosmo. "The lyrics are amusingly telling. I was very keen on him writing in that vein. I don't think he was keen to go down that path. We did half a dozen tracks but 'The Cool Impossible' was the only one that we really got. I was applying the wrong pressure and we ended up with this music that Joe didn't really want and I didn't really want. He left me on my own one afternoon. He said, 'I've got to go somewhere, so you do it the way you think.'"

the excitement gang

1993-1997

J oe and Gaby had now split up. "I wasn't necessarily prepared to leave James, because I knew James loved me, and we'd been together since we were sixteen. I was thirty at the time," said Lucinda. "So it was a helluva risk. Joe said, 'I'm moving out of the house anyway.' He rented a house nearby on the Guinness estate, Ivy Cottage, in Heckfield, near Basingstoke in Hampshire, which Hugo Guinness [scion of the Irish brewing family] had available. So the onus wasn't, 'Let's leave our respective partners and set up home.' He was going to do it anyway. And he did. And about two days later, I joined him. I literally walked out of the house with Eliza and a few clothes. That was it. It was in September—late in September. When he moved in to Ivy Cottage, I said, 'Where are all the suitcases?' There weren't any: just plastic bags. I arrived and there were plastic bags everywhere.

"Also, he was adamant that he wanted to marry me. Which was lovely, because I knew he hadn't married before. I definitely felt there was a commitment there. He said that right from the beginning. So I didn't feel I was just flavor of the month. Or being used to get out of an unhappy relationship. I knew that he genuinely loved me."

With the stipulation that he could keep his archive of shopping bags from the basement, Joe gave Gaby 37 Lancaster Road, although she had to take on the remaining mortgage on the property. Some considered this unrealistic: Gaby had never worked and didn't have a job. No lawyers were involved in their separation. Some years previously Micky Gallagher, who had played keyboards onstage with the Clash during their middle period, had taken legal action against them, claiming that he had contributed toward the songwriting on the *Sandinista!* material that he and Blockheads bass player Norman Watt-Roy had worked on in New York. "Joe was so upset about that," said Gaby. "It meant endlessly paying out to lawyers. We decided to keep away from the legal profession when we were breaking up and do it ourselves."

There were small signs of a return to a creative life. On April 16, 1994, Joe Strummer performed live for the first time since he had played with the Pogues; the show was in Prague, a Rock for Refugees charity event; Joe played Clash songs with a local group called Dirty Pictures. Largely, though, Joe was lying fallow. "We had a year of him doing absolutely nothing, work-wise," said Lucinda. "He took me to New York to meet Kosmo, who he introduced to me as his manager. And to L.A. to meet Gerry Harrington. But apart from that we were just living totally quietly in Hampshire. We had a few friends down from London. And we'd go to London, for dinner and whatever. But he didn't really work at all. He said, 'Enjoy it. Because when I start, I'm really going to start.' He said he was recharging his batteries and he would start again. It was almost two years really, but he was always scribbling. Always a notebook, and always a constant stream of plastic bags. But I think it was random. There wasn't anything specific.

"He'd take the dogs for walks for hours. At Ivy Cottage, and in Hampshire at the Govetts. He loved walking, loved it, loved the dogs. I would certainly say that I never met anyone like Joe, who knew their own mind in the way he did, was comfortable in their skin in the way he was, and was completely happy the way he was. I'm sure he had regrets, and he definitely did harbor resentments about his parents and the school they sent him to. I said to him, 'If you put yourself in their position and you think, we have an opportunity to send our sons to a decent public school which will get them a decent job, or we drag them round Malawi and Persia, I said I'm sure I would do the same thing.' And he said, 'No, it was the wrong decision.' He was adamant about that. I think the parents did it for the right reasons. But he was miserable, he was unhappy, and obviously it was completely devastating for David. But I think Joe worked through all that."

Over Easter 1994 Joe repeated his previous Barbados holiday, taking Lucinda and Eliza with him this time, again staying at Cobbler's Cove. As before Paul and Tricia accompanied them. They spent more time with Eddie Grant. During a discussion as to the true worth of the Clash not being fully appreciated, the Guyanan musician had a simple solution: "It's not old enough. When the material is twenty years old people will start to realize how great it is." "That's exactly what happened," said Tricia Ronane. "When their music was twenty years old, almost to the day, offers started to come in from everywhere—films, TV, ads—all wanting to use it."

In early 1994 a story swept the show-business sections of the British media: that the Clash had been made a multimillion-dollar offer to re-form. In fact the sum involved was more like $50,000 a show, as part of the alternative Lollapalooza Festival that toured the United States annually. The offer came from the head of the William Morris Agency; Perry Farrell from the group Jane's Addiction, which had been involved with starting up Lollapalooza, was a William Morris client. "Perry really wanted the Clash to get back together," said Peter Kinnaird, who worked at William Morris in Los Angeles on the projected reunion. "Mick was calling him, and then Joe was calling him separately. When the rumor went out, all these young punk bands were dying to get on the bill. The story I heard about why they didn't ultimately do it was that Joe went to an Elastica show at the Roxy on Sunset and some kid came up to him and said, 'Are you going to rock the cashbah?' and I heard that that really put him off the idea."

That may have been the case about Lollapalooza, yet ever since Joe had become involved with Lucinda he had been almost obsessively determined to get the Clash back together. He needed a job and a source of income and inspiration. "Paul was extremely cautious about these endless conversations," said Tricia. "They seemed to be going on and on and on every time we went down to stay with them. Then suddenly it's apparent that no one has spoken to Mick yet."

When Mick Jones—still the leader of BAD 2—was contacted about Joe's scheme, he was not against it, but he said that he would be involved only if this reconstituted Clash was managed by Gary Kurfirst, his own manager. "The others were against that," said Tricia. "Joe says we'll get Kosmo, and you, and have Gary Kurfirst as well. And we'll all have some sort of representation. Which was quite unrealistic. Joe wanted to do it, but he also stopped it happening. Because he managed to throw a spanner in the works always, at some point." All the same, Tricia Ronane started having unofficial discussions with record companies to give her financial leverage with Sony, who would have been involved with any new work by the group. "They still hadn't been in a room together. Whatever you said, Joe would say the opposite. 'Well, Trish, I think I've got to retreat from the battlefield. Mick is going to want Kurfirst, I don't want him.' It was all done by fax. Joe wouldn't talk to me on the phone," Tricia added, recalling that the fax machine was adored by Joe for its ability to convey handwritten sentiment.

Finally there came an evening when Joe and Paul went to the Kensington Hilton for a meeting with Mick and Kosmo Vinyl, who had flown over from New York. "Within half an hour," remembered Tricia, "the phone rang. It was Joe: 'Can we come back to the house and do the meeting there?' Sure. They came back and we sat in the living room at Oxford Gardens and had a conversation there."

Joe's first action was to apologize to Mick for having kicked him out of the Clash. Unexpectedly, at this moment Paul Simonon literally put his hand over Joe's mouth. "I'm not apologizing," he said to Mick. "We were right to get rid of you."

"I feel like I've been taken down an alley and beaten up," said Mick.

"He heard a lot of home truths. It was like get-it-out-on-the-table-time," said Tricia. "But Mick was really ready to have a chat and Joe suddenly announces, 'I'll mix some cocktails. You lot get on with it.' Then he spends twenty minutes over getting the drinks. Joe was avoiding Mick, because deep down he never wanted to have that conversation. Mick and Kosmo left together."

"Joe had said, 'Come on, let's get the Clash back together' on several occasions," said Mick. "In the Bahamas he had said it, but that was the wrong time. But when we were talking about getting back together in the first half of the nineties, he suddenly said, 'Perhaps we shouldn't bother.' He was sitting there in the Union Chapel in Islington. There was a rave going on there: he'd just discovered raves—a bit late: suddenly he was like 'Wow!' We were sitting in the pews next to each other and we'd been talking about it. He just came out with it suddenly: 'Perhaps we shouldn't bother.' I said

'OK,'" Mick laughed. "And that was the end of that. That was probably the last time we were about to get back together again—maybe, possibly . . .

"One good thing about that was that we remained close friends. We never got back together again, but our friendship remained. If we'd got back together, we probably would have rowed again. Although maybe not. Because we'd grown up and realized things. Maybe we'd have been able to keep it together." "I don't think that Joe was ever jealous of Mick, but there might have been something of a sibling rivalry," said Lucinda. "Mick could drive him mad, though.

"When Joe and I got together, this whole idea of re-forming the Clash started. Kosmo came over, and we had a meal in an Indian restaurant to discuss it. Before that we had been round at Paul and Tricia's. Then Joe and I went over to Mick's flat off the Harrow Road so Joe could talk to Mick. Joe was definitely quite nervous, because he wasn't just going to hang with Mick, he was going to talk. We got round there—and I thought Mick was lovely. But Mick just sat there watching telly, smoking spliff after spliff, in a room surrounded by stacked-up videos. And he offered us endless cups of tea. I don't smoke, but I could hardly stand, and was feeling ghastly. Joe was just sitting there in this fog, and nothing was discussed. When we left I knew that Joe was disappointed: he turned to me and said, 'The problem with Mick is that he doesn't drink enough.' Just tea. Joe always maintained that if we'd gone out to the pub and had a few beers, it might have been different. Smoking weed and drinking tea it wasn't going to happen. But he loved and adored Mick."

At this time Daisy Lawrence, who had split up with Mick Jones in 1990, threw a summer party at her home in nearby Queen's Park to which Paul, Kosmo and Joe came together, Joe accompanied by Lucinda, the first time I had seen her. Joe was all over his new love, edged into a corner of a room and kissing and cuddling, not speaking to anyone else. To the assembled throng it seemed very teenage lovey-dovey. But that evening in Joe's face you could see something of his perpetual hurt; his new emotional release had broken down the defenses of his façade and he had reverted to a shy, nervous, young boy; you could see that part of him almost wanted to cry, as though he was overwhelmed with gratitude for being loved and allowed to love. It seemed to me Joe returned to the frightened and needy young boy behind the wheel who almost killed Johnny Green in Aberdeen: unguarded, almost shockingly vulnerable, and—here, now, with Lucinda—

grateful. He looked about sixteen years old. Which, not to put too fine a shine on it, was the age of John Mellor when his brother David ended his days. You felt that night that you could see that part of Joe's emotions were frozen at that age, in trauma: part of his neediness, part of his ambiguity in all its forms, even when he was in love. *Prove to me that you really love me!* his joy was screaming, even in the prettiness of his adoration.

For their first summer holiday together, Joe and Lucinda had reached a compromise. They would spend two weeks on the beautiful Spanish island of Majorca, where Luce had vacationed since she was ten, followed by another fortnight in San José. But a holiday with Joe always involved his crew. Accompanying them were Paul and Tricia Simonon, Jazz, Lola and Eliza, and the two Simonon boys, Louis and baby Claude; also along, helping out with the kids, was Luce's mother. And a newcomer, Dave Girvan, who had been present at that White Riot tour date in Swindon when the venue had burned down and the equipment was moved by fans to another venue. "From the first time I met him that evening Joe was shockingly delightful: a present, helpful, all-round great geezer," recalled Dave, whose surname, Girvan, had briefly been Joe's mother's when she was married to her first husband. In attendance at most Clash shows in the south of England in those years, he had even paid to take three unemployed friends to Paris to see the group.

"But then I didn't see Joe for a few years. In 1990 I was at Harrow art school studying ceramics. I went to a party in Notting Hill, and he was there and we had a chat. I said I wanted to get pictures of people with some ceramics I was making and he gave me his number. I went round a couple of days later to Lancaster Road and took some pictures with my pots on the hood of his Morris. He was up in London from Rockfield, where he was producing the Pogues. We went for breakfast in a café, next to Nu-line builders, and sat there going through a mountain of newspapers looking at pictures of Paul Gascoigne crying after being sent off in the World Cup.

"In London when we were meeting for a pint in a pub he was quite chipper. But I think it was different when he was living in Hampshire. The home situation was difficult. On top of that he had his post-Clash depression. His major occupation then was being depressed: the days of treacle, as he called them. He was unaware at that point how many people he had affected. People would come up to him and say 'You changed my life,' and his mind-set seemed to be 'You're just being polite.'

Olé! Joe in the streets of Granada, Spain. *(Lucinda Mellor)*

"It's a tricky area to be in, summed up in that fantastic lyric, 'If they tell you you are the chosen one / I defy you not to believe them, my son.' I love that not the least because he is aware that is happening to him and he is trying to do something about it by recognizing it. He obviously wasn't stupid."

Shortly after Joe and Lucinda had moved into Ivy Cottage, they went to visit Hugo Guinness. Hugo gave the pair a tour of his property, and took them into a building that had become a pottery. He introduced them to a man at work there. Before Hugo could finish his sentence Joe demanded, "What are you doing here?" For it was Dave Girvan, who through a set of tangential connections had wound up working in Hampshire. Dave Girvan was himself living only a few hundred yards from Ivy Cottage. Usefully for a friend of Joe Strummer, Dave has a large appetite for consumption, and is warm and intelligent, more easily able to be open than his pal. At Ivy Cottage he watched as Joe emptied out a small brick woodshed. He saw Joe transform it into a miniature recording studio, a double-glazer brought in to install two sets of glass dividing doors. "A percussionist might sit in one section, while Joe would be playing his guitar in the middle section. It was

Artwork by "Art Dog," faxed to Bob Gruen. Note the "Moggie" Minor in the background. (*Bob Gruen*)

very Joe Meek style." The studio remained known as the Woodshed. Joe made an effort to live more conventional hours, going to sleep at the end of the evening with Lucinda, but his nocturnal habits soon returned. Sometimes with reason. One night Joe came to the pottery, holding the body of a wire fox terrier to which Joe had given the name of Chaka Demus, after the Jamaican deejay. "Chaka Demus had got run over," said Dave, "and Joe buried him at the back of the pottery. It was perfect funeral weather: full moon, and trees, and one elongated cloud sliding past the moon slowly, Joe with a long black coat on outside the back window of the pottery, with a spade digging a grave, and me handing out slugs of brandy. Joe was digging the grave in floods of tears, talking about working in the graveyard in Newport, and how he didn't actually dig graves there, but knew how it was done.

"The tears didn't seem to be just about the dog. He'd go off on these flights: 'I loved this dog more passionately than anyone could ever know, and now I'm burying it.' I'm sure that would have related to other stuff. To his brother, David, of course. And his parents. Joe said to me and various people: 'Families: you don't need families. Families hold you back.' That's bullshit. That he bothered to say it shows he doesn't mean it."

On May 31, 1995, John "Joe Strummer" Mellor and Lucinda Tait Henderson, looking radiant, were married at Kensington and Chelsea Registry office on the King's Road. After telling Gaby for years he couldn't find Pamela Moolman, he'd finally divorced the South African woman. The actual ceremony was a small event. "I stole her," Joe later explained. "I had to keep it quiet." Josh Cheuse was Joe's best man; also present at the wedding were Jazz, Lola and Eliza; Lauren Jones, the daughter of Mick and Daisy; Kosmo Vinyl and his wife, Jennifer; Lucinda's sister Arabella and her husband; and Tricia Ronane. The girls clutched small bunches of flowers. On the wedding certificate Joe listed his occupation as "producer."

A sumptuous lunch followed at the elegant Belvedere restaurant inside Holland Park. Among the score or so of guests were Mick Jones, Paul Simonon, Jim Jarmusch and Sara Driver, Don Letts and his partner, Audrey de la Peyre, the actress Patsy Kensit, Bob Gruen and Hugo Guinness. "It was really nice, a lovely day," remembered Don.

The meal at the Belvedere was followed by a more rootsy party at the

Earl Percy pub on the corner of Ladbroke Grove and Chesterton Road. In between the events Joe and Lucinda retired to their hotel suite. Unusually for a newly married couple they were accompanied by several members of Joe's close posse: Mick Jones, Kosmo Vinyl, Josh Cheuse and Dave Girvan, among others, who ransacked the minibar with Joe while Lucinda changed and freshened up.

At the Earl Percy no food was provided, only large amounts of alcohol. Everyone present quickly became very drunk. When Alex Chetwynd attempted to make his excuses and leave, the groom would have none of it: Joe grabbed an unopened bottle of tequila and a pair of beer glasses and divided the liquor between them, handing one glass to Alex and downing the other himself. (On his distinctly unsteady journey home Alex would fall, knocking out all his front teeth on the pavement.) Following the bash at the Percy, there was another shindig on the agenda. Gerry Harrington was staying with a member of Duran Duran, who had volunteered his house as a location for an afterparty. Alex Chetwynd was not alone in suffering from excessive alcohol consumption.

Something that at first must have seemed almost incidental to Joe's life came in the form of a wedding present. Masa, a Japanese promoter, gave the couple a pair of tickets to that year's Glastonbury Festival, the twenty-fifth anniversary of the event. Masa's act of largesse would help transform Joe's life and restore his career as a musical artist. But this was not immediately apparent.

Joe had been to Glastonbury in between the 1971 and 1995 festivals. In the early nineties he had gone to the festival on a couple of occasions, once with Gaz Mayall. Joe and Gaby had set up their tent in the late evening on what seemed to be the perfect site, only to be woken by security guards, telling them they'd camped in a prohibited area. But the visit he and Lucinda made to Glastonbury in 1995 became another adventure altogether. As the film director Julien Temple told me, "You confront yourself when you go to Glastonbury: and each time it's different." For Joe this personal confrontation would have an extremely positive consequence.

"Joe was so excited," said Lucinda. "This was before Glastonbury had really got big, and we drive down with Jason Mayall, and we've got a shopping-trolley [cart]. We drove in on the Thursday night, and all the lights were up, and we drove straight to this corner of the field backstage, which was where the Mayalls always camped. But Joe said no, he wanted to camp up near the stone circle. We dragged everything there in this shopping-trolley and it was really hot. Blood was coursing through his veins, he was so excited. We got there, but there was trouble: the fence was smashed down and it got a bit nasty. So we moved back—Jazzy and Lola came the next day—to Jason. And Gaz had the campfire going, and that's kind of where it all started. Backstage it was very quiet, so he could sit round the campfire and talk. We did have our first 'E' there. When Joe did drugs like that, he did it as a sort of ritual. He said that years and years ago you would literally have a blowout every month. You'd take your magic mushrooms and dance around the stones, but they were administered by the druid or whoever. And everyone just got completely [wasted] and then they were over again. He adhered to that: he thought that was good. That's what he liked about festivals: that you got together annually and just had a complete blowout.

"He totally believed in God. He just hated religion. Hated any form of organized religion. He said to me, 'Do you believe in humankind?' I said, 'What do you mean?' He said, 'Do you believe that humankind will survive?' I said, 'No, because I think we are inherently greedy: we will devour the planet and we will devour each other.' And he said, 'You're wrong.' And he never said, 'You're wrong.' And he said, 'No, I believe that mankind is inherently good, and that good will always triumph.' But he believed that man was good. He believed in the goodness of people."

In cahoots with his friend the actor and comedian Keith Allen, Joe plotted up in the backstage area, getting all his mates together, bedecking the area with flags of all nations, and playing choice sounds nonstop for the duration of the festival. The centerpiece of his Glastonbury scene was a large campfire, in the construction of which he was tutored by Masa. To this flaming circular entity were attracted like moths those seeking a more rarefied entertainment than that provided by the nearby hospitality tents. "Joe set up backstage because there were a lot of people who had young kids, and Glastonbury then wasn't safe for toddlers to be [wandering] around," said Dave Girvan. "We just had a cool corner to camp out in. Within the beams of the fire was where it was happening—everything else going on around it didn't matter. Jason and Gaz Mayall would turn up with vehicles and build a wall around us. Masa was there with a Japanese contingent. Bands would come over and hang out. Joe would just sit there. While he was being quiet he would figure out which people were smart and which were idiots, or which ones were smart idiots or idiots with smarts. Half the time Joe wasn't even there."

After Joe took his first ecstasy that Glastonbury weekend of 1995, he finally understood the attractions of dance music for Mick Jones. Soon he also returned to that love of other psychedelic drugs that had nurtured him during his squatting days with the 101'ers. Magic mushrooms were high on the menu, but also LSD, and the immensely powerful DMT, in the form of ayahuasca. Influenced by some of his co-conspirators, who were very partial to cocaine, Joe became a more regular consumer of "gak," a street term of which he was fond. But in his drug consumption Joe was really caught up in the bombardment of illicit substances that swept Britain during the nineties. The beginnings of his own upward curve could similarly be seen as a reflection of an increasingly creative national mood: thanks to Britpop, U.K. music was once again on the upsurge. Oasis, Blur, Elastica and Pulp transformed the charts.

Playing at Glastonbury in 1995 were both Oasis and Pulp, a particular favorite of Joe's. "Somebody that Joe was very much a champion of, before they were famous, was Jarvis Cocker and Pulp," said Marcia Finer. Also on the bill were Elastica. Getting into the Glastonbury spirit was their guitarist, Antony Genn; possibly influenced by the acid he'd ingested, he divested himself of his clothes midway through the set. At that point, Joe's daughter Lola was sitting on his shoulders; Joe leaned up and covered her eyes.

For Joe Strummer Glastonbury 1995 was an epiphany. "They came back from the festival and Joe took me to the pub for a pint," said Dave Girvan. "He got halfway through his beer and spanked the glass down on the table and said, 'We're going back. I can't stand these walls.' We went back to the cottage and Joe shouted up the stairs, 'We're going back.' I was amazed Luce did this without question. When we got there they'd already started taking the fences down and we drove into the darkness across the fields. Suddenly we heard a booming sound and found some sound systems and food stalls and fires burning."

As rekindled as one of his campfires, Joe then went with his Glastonbury crew to the annual T in the Park festival in Glasgow, and then to the Womad world music event organized every year in Reading by Peter Gabriel. I was not aware that he had gone there. I drove out to Womad on the second day, as the masterly Senegalese musician Baaba Maal was topping the bill that night. That morning I had been about to put on a favorite T-shirt, a rare one that bore the sticker for the Don Drummond single "Cool Smoke" on the Jamaican Treasure Isle label, but had changed my mind. Parking my car at Womad, I stepped out straight into the path of Joe; he was wearing the very same T-shirt. We spent a moment discussing this. When the ticket office couldn't find the pass supposedly waiting for me, Joe slipped me one of his own, and we were through the gate. He took me over to his campsite, where a fire was burning and cumbia was sailing out of a ghetto blaster. Jason Mayall and Keith Allen were in attendance. Then someone stepped over: "Hello, I'm Damien." "I was introduced to Joe by Keith at Womad," said the artist Damien Hirst. "At about four in the afternoon at Womad I was twatted on all manner of stuff by the campfire and I lay down. Joe put a pillow under my head and a duvet over me. Joe turned into a hero. He was the only one who lived it like he talked it, through and through. My first question to Joe was, 'Why aren't you doing something?' He avoided it."

Long after it was due, Joe finally renamed Dave Girvan as "Pockets," which required no explanation. "At Womad," said Pockets, "we met this guy who christened the Joe campfire scene Strummerville. Strummerville never really existed. But this guy got a load of T-shirts done, a black shirt with an orange print and a logo that said: 'Strummerville: where the past mixes with the future.'"

Also at Womad was Glen Colson, a friend of Keith Allen and a resolute nontaker of drugs. This stance earned Glen a scolding from Joe. "'There's something wrong with you if you don't do drugs, Glen,' Joe said to me. They all began to look like people from a Hunter S. Thompson book, melting on psychedelic drugs."

"Womad was when Joe realized he had started something really," said Lucinda. "We had this fantastic campfire, with netting and fluorescent lights. We had been invited there by Donovan, who had the Master Musicians of Joujouka over for the festival. The Donovan connection was through his daughter, who was married to Shaun Ryder [formerly of the Happy Mondays]. We all went and watched everything. Keith Allen arrived with a Hammond organ. First of all we had the campfire with the musicians. At about one or two in the morning, Donovan was sitting around the campfire singing 'Mellow Yellow,' when this voice breaks out, 'It's all right for you if you don't have to work. Some of us have got to get up at eight o'clock in the morning.' Little sweet Donovan sitting there with the Master Musicians—all very gentle. And the following night at five o'clock in the morning Keith dragged the Hammond organ out into the middle of the field and started playing and nobody said a thing."

At Womad (in one of the subsidiary stage tents), Joe caught a set by vocalist Gary Dyson. Joe was taken by his spectacular light show and spent time talking to Gary afterward; he told Joe that the following week he was heading to Peter Gabriel's Real World residential studio in Wilshire for "Recording Week"—an annual event in which musicians from around the planet play together in a spirit of global creativity. Why don't you come down? Gary suggested to Joe.

Among the eighty or so musicians in residence to play at Real World Recording Week that year was Van Morrison. Also there was Richard Norris, the computer wizard behind the Grid, which he had formed with Soft Cell's Dave Ball in 1988, earning success and credibility for their adventurous techno-dance music. At the beginning of the week "Norro," as Joe would rename Richard, was hanging out on the grass outside the Real World main studio when "a van-load of reprobates with rather loud voices and loads of flags and instruments turned up. Joe was one of them. Suddenly he demands, 'Is there anyone here who can program a drum machine?' I said I could, introduced myself, and started programming rhythms into the drum machine.

"The Real World studio management were fairly vexed by the fact that Joe and a kind of floating posse had turned up. It was like, Here comes the freak show, with tents and flags—you know, usual scenario. But Peter Gabriel came over and appeased the studio manager and really welcomed Joe into the thing.

"I hooked up with Joe and we cobbled together bits of recording, got some eight-track recorder from a studio, nicked some microphones from somewhere else, and then found a little cubbyhole to work in. I'd be playing acid house in one corner, there'd be the bloke from Living Colour on guitar, some Bengalis singing, and Joe with some shaker percussion shouting in the middle. We recorded lots of madness. Nothing came of it. At Recording Week it can get quite loose. We met, mucked about and had a laugh.

"I realized Joe hadn't really understood techno or dance music, hadn't got his head round it. But now he was starting to understand it. When he did get it, he really got it, and we wrote a song, 'Diggin' the New,' which is pretty much about that, saying when you get it you don't forget it. 'Diggin' the New' was about him going to Glastonbury and the various other places he'd been, like Real World."

Shortly after Recording Week, the Grid was scheduled to film a video in the hills above the Spanish resort of Malaga. Joe, Luce and Eliza, who had moved on to San José for their summer holiday, came over to join the shoot. "Joe and I kicked off straightaway, and spent a bit of time together, chatting," said Pablo Cook, who played percussion with the Grid. Along for the holiday in San José were Paul and Tricia Simonon and sons, the Govett family, the Finers, and some new additions to the Spanish seaside throng, Don Letts and his partner, Audrey de la Peyre, and their children, Jet and Amber. And, amazingly, Gaby with Jazz and Lola. "Only Joe could get away with the new and old there at the same time," said Don Letts. "What a geezer. In public it seemed remarkably cool. I couldn't see an ounce of tetchiness from anyone. But then because Joe is there everyone is on best behavior. But if he had been in that situation, Joe would have been the exact opposite."

"I remember," said Audrey, "that Don and I were more worried about how you dealt with this situation with these two women, Gaby and Lucinda, than they seemed to be. They were perfectly fine about it. Gaby was open and friendly. Joe was in superb spirits: he was in love. It was very hot and laid-back. Joe seemed incredibly at home. He insisted he take us high up in the mountains along a precarious coast road to this old hippie colony, where there was a bar. There was guitar playing and good vibes. Wherever we went Joe always offered everyone a drink, and even called the people from the back of the bar to see what they wanted."

"Joe's place was built around a communal swimming pool, about four hundred yards from the beach," Don recalled. "Not ostentatious. The only other people around there were Spanish. A reasonable location, with a big Rasta flag flying above it. I couldn't work out how to get there, because of the winding roads, but you could see the red, gold and green flag in the distance. A two-story red terra-cotta house, very unassuming, not pop-star business, but normal bloke business.

"When he wasn't doing the family thing, down on the beach with the kids, he'd be doing the Joe thing. He'd set up the spliff bunker in the garage, where he had four-track recorders and tape machines. He got loose in the garage and would come on to the beach, do half an hour of the family thing, then run away. Joe took us to a bullfight: Oh dear!

"The morning we were leaving I got a note through the mailbox from Joe saying it was so hot the tarmac had melted; my plane was canceled. It wasn't true. I missed that plane and got a later one. He didn't realize to spend the money for that extra flight was a major deal."

"We came home," said Lucinda, "and the summer of campfires continued. We had met Pablo through Norro, and he started to come down to Hampshire, and the idea of making music started around the campfire." The philosophy of Glastonbury had really captured Joe's soul. In future years at the festival, said Lucinda, "we would pitch an extra ten tents, just in case people didn't have anywhere to stay. We were known for our stockpile of spare Wellington boots, because Joe liked to be hospitable. 'I know what it's like to turn up cold and hungry,' he'd say. So we had to have plenty of water and booze, and it was always to give away. And Joe used to buy a lot of tickets for the hardcore posse. But he didn't want them to know he had bought the tickets. Because they all had a thing about bunking in for free on principle. But Joe just said, 'We've got a job to do here, to set this thing up.' Joe wanted the hardcore posse there, so he used to say we had the tickets for free, which we didn't. The hardcore posse evolved initially from Bez, when he was in Black Grape. Actually, Kermit was the first one we met. We went to a Black Grape gig in Portsmouth. Kermit became a friend. Then we went to T in the Park and we met Bez. And Bez said to come up and stay and we went up and met Debs, his wife, and his sons, who got on with Eliza. They lived just outside Manchester in the Pennines. So we became family friends, if you like. Then they came to stay for a weekend, and we had a very gentle campfire. I think Norro was there. When we were in Manchester with Bez, we went to the Hacienda, and we got taken to all the Manchester places with the Manchester posse. They understood Joe, and Joe loved them. The Manc posse were very important to Joe. We used to go up there a lot, and they used to come and stay a lot. And again, not all drugs and going out: the kids got on."

That autumn Johnny Green, the former Clash tour manager, came to visit Joe at Ivy Cottage. Johnny wanted to see Joe over a book about the Clash he was writing. Joe had called late one Saturday morning. "You coming over tonight?" he demanded, as though this had been planned for weeks. "I wasn't planning on it. But I can," replied Johnny, getting into his car and driving to Hampshire.

"I can't quite figure what is going on. There is this shed, about thirty yards from the little cottage. The door is open and I see a portable typewriter and that black homburg he used to like to wear, covered in dust and spiderwebs. 'What good's that, Joe?' I ask. 'You never know,' he mutters. But that is the tip of the iceberg. I take a look in the shed. Everything is there, suitcases and black bags of stuff. I always knew he was a collector, but I didn't realize he was a hoarder."

Joe announced they needed to go on a wood-foraging expedition. He wanted to build a campfire. "They're good, these fires. I'm into them," he declared, collecting his ax. Johnny Green noticed something. "If Joe's so into his fires, how come his ax is so crap and blunt?"

When Johnny Green arrived at the house, Pockets was at the cottage; Joe introduced the two men. The three of them wandered over to Pockets's pottery kiln, which lay on a slight rise. In view was a wide, tall mansion house. "It's the fuckin' Guinnesses," barked Joe, dismissively, like a bit player in *The Great Gatsby*.

Apart from Joe's spliff accoutrements, there was no evidence of any greater drug consumption. "He doesn't have any coke," said Johnny. "Just a load of booze—which I was off by then."

L ate in 1994 the pop artist Gordon McHarg decided that at the end of the next year he would stage a major exhibition of his work. To complement his pieces he asked musicians he knew to come up with a tune based on the title "Sandpaper Blues." "The idea was: 'Sandpaper Blues—starts off rough, ends up smooth.' I was trying to move the art and music worlds closer together. By the time of the exhibition a year later I had thirty-six songs, and turned it into a double CD on sale at the exhibition." Included on the record were Maria McKee, John Mayall and Wayne Kramer. Joe Strummer was the only musician who used studio recording facilities from the off, writing his song with Richard Norris and Gary Dyson. On McHarg's CD the tune, which had a working title of "Another Fine Piece of Madeira," a line from the song, was credited with the *nom de disque* Radar (Joe was fearful of the response of Sony, to whom he was still under contract). Joe's "Sandpaper Blues" was a successful melange of African and Latin influences; it contained the line "From the Yukon comes a cowboy," a reference to the Canadian Gordon McHarg's Stetsoned persona.

As so often with Joe there was a subtext concerning his recording of the song. He was using finances from his friend Masatoshi Nagase, who played a Japanese rocker in *Mystery Train:* Masa had commissioned Joe to record a song for *Vending Machine,* an album of new material for Japanese release only.

Booking all-night sessions for several weekends at Orinoco studios in South London, Joe decided that he would use Nagase's money, around £15,000, to make an entire album with Richard Norris. "He's got the money to do this song with Nagase, and he goes into the studio and records 'Sandpaper Blues.' There was a giggle over that," remembered Gordon, who went to the sessions. "'Sandpaper Blues' is an attempt at a cumbia beat," said Joe later. "It's way off beat, but it's another cayenne pepper in the pot."

"In the studio he had flags and bits of material set up and draped around the recording booth," added Gordon. So some sort of spliff bunker was in place, an auspicious sign for Joe's return to recording. "When Joe and his mates arrived at the studio, they turned it into their home," said Ian Tregoning, another computer wizard who worked with Richard Norris. "The first thing Joe did was get his flags up. He said we should live like bedouins. He thought bedouins were really cool—you make your home wherever you are. So we knocked up this vocal booth with flags on it: a real homemade job, but something that felt like Joe."

"I was renting a place in Devon at the time and Joe and Luce came to stay," said Damien Hirst. "After ten nights of conversations with him not saying what he was doing, and me demanding, 'Why aren't you doing something?' he finally pulled out a cassette. He played me four or five tracks—'Diggin' the New' and 'Sandpaper Blues' were among them. We were all on MDMA at the time. He took so long to play me this cassette. Maybe he couldn't get a word in: I used to talk my ass off on drugs."

Between September 1995 and March 1996 Joe recorded half a dozen new songs; the weekend sessions at Orinoco produced "Sandpaper Blues," "Yalla Yalla" and the bones of "The Road to Rock 'n' Roll." "Diggin' the New," Joe's celebration of his psychedelic summer, was developed at Sarm East studios on November 12; at this same session Joe and his fellow workers devised "Boom or Bust," a near-instrumental on which Paul Simonon played bass, deemed the correct offering for Nagase's *Vending Machine* project. "Yalla Yalla" was worked on again at Berwick Street studios in Soho on December 15. "The Road to Rock 'n' Roll" was completed at the same studio early in February 1996. ("The Road to Rock 'n' Roll" had been written when Joe first met Luce. He had heard from producer Rick Rubin that Johnny Cash was looking for songs to cover for his *American Recordings* album. But when Rubin later introduced Joe to Johnny Cash in Hollywood, the great American archetype simply remarked, "You really confused me with that song, boy." Joe said he used it to woo Lucinda; in that context you can see the lyrics of the song as Joe laying out the route of his future from that point. And he's doing more than that: Joe takes the notion of "rock 'n' roll" to a higher place, a journey toward a mythic, but attainable, quest.) Around St. Valentine's Day there was a weekend of recording at Joe's Hampshire Woodshed, dedicated almost entirely to overdubbing, with the completion of "Yalla Yalla" a priority. Integral to this reimmersion in music for Joe was the manner in which Norro took him out on the techno and dance scenes. "He was always very aware, listening to radio and reading the music papers. He had that band mentality of wanting to be involved in stuff. He realized the generation of dance people weren't anti him at all: they thought he was fantastic. He loved Leftfield, a big fan. I went to a studio off the Harrow Road with Joe: Leftfield were there so we went and had a chat with them and heard some stuff. Joe was, 'Play it again.' They were like, 'Who's this bloke making us play and rewind our tunes?' They didn't realize until we left that he was Joe Strummer."

Often Joe would not arrive at Orinoco until late in the evening; other times he would turn up around lunchtime, bringing Lucinda as well as Jazz, Lola and Eliza to the studio. Revealing their business acumen, the girls spotted a moneymaking opportunity. There were two studios at Orinoco, a smaller one used by Joe and his crew, and a larger room, in which the Chemical Brothers were ensconced. Accordingly, plenty of people passed through the building. In a vestibule the girls set up a stall, selling sandwiches and cups of tea. "His kids were great mileage," recalled Ian Tregoning. "Joe was handling them really well. He was working with a lot of people, but the girls got all the attention they needed, without a drop more.

"Dave Stewart did a little guitar overdub on 'Yalla Yalla.' 'Yalla Yalla' was a big success. I love those lines: 'There's a mirror in your soul / You should turn it to the sky.' When we'd finished 'Yalla Yalla' and were packing up in the studio, Joe kept listening to it over and over again. When it stopped, he'd take it back and listen to it again, for hours. He was in this delirious state, so happy with it. Almost like, 'It doesn't matter if it doesn't come out. I'm happy with it.'"

"The first thing Joe said to me was, 'I want that loud, banging, relentless techno-drumming that is real rock 'n' roll,'" said Richard Norris. "So it was easy to build up on that excitement. But when it came to recording vocals it was a lot more difficult. At Orinoco we'd start at ten in the morning. Joe would arrive at ten in the evening and listen to what we'd done. He'd get into it, have a drink, and get ready to record about midnight. Then we only had a very finite time between recording a good vocal and the partying started—he'd arrive with various people. This was a shame because it was difficult for Joe to realize what he wanted. He had a big confidence problem. He was beating himself up about not being as good as he wanted to be. It took a while for him to be full on a hundred percent. He'd be re-recording the vocal, but he'd be hoarse by the end. That he couldn't really get what he wanted was very problematic.

"We were each coming from very different disciplines. Computers slow things down. It's not four blokes in a room; it has a different energy. There'd be me and Ian, the engineer, and a couple of other people, huddled round the computer, but Joe would be playing Telecaster like he was at Shea Stadium. Two cultures colliding, but when it worked it worked.

"He's writing lyrics as he goes along, enthusiastic and really up for it, meeting a bunch of new people and seeing there's another way of doing things. 'Yalla Yalla' and 'Diggin' the New' were particularly good examples of what was going on, what we were doing."

There were moments of stress during the sessions. Richard Norris saw Joe punch Ian Tregoning. "It was play-fighting," the engineer insisted. "I'd work on the vocals with him. I'd kid him, saying we should get a real vocalist. When it was going really well once, he came up and hit me. There was a lot of bashing each other about the chest and shoulders. It wasn't about being pissed off. If he wanted to do a vocal he would come up and whack me round the shoulder. Richard witnessed it one time: 'My God, are you guys not getting on OK?' No, this is us getting on. When we wanted to do 'The Road to Rock 'n' Roll,' one of my favorite sessions, we were punching each other out. Joe was really straightforward to work with: no arsiness, no star stuff whatsoever. Just Joe.

"I wouldn't announce I was recording. I'd just set it up, knowing the strength of Joe's voice from hearing it, and I wouldn't fine-tune it while I was doing a take. At the end of the track I still didn't tell him. He'd come into the studio and I'd say, 'Listen to this, it's great.'

"Joe had painstakingly written lyrics. Some of them were on sandwich packets, although he would always have a notepad. He copied them out for me by hand, because the studio photocopier had broken down. I thought the poetry in his lyrics was stunning. I remember that line in 'The Road to Rock 'n' Roll': 'There's a lot of wreckage in the ravine'—the way the words just roll along. You'd see this phrase and you'd have a movie there."

There were discussions over the group's name. "What about 'Sausage'?" recalled Ian Tregoning. "I think that was one of Damien Hirst's suggestions—either 'Middlesex' or 'Sausage.' I remember how the name of 'Sausage' came up: 'Which came first—the chicken or the egg, or the sausage in the middle?'" Later Joe said that the final name decided on for what he described as his "acid punk group" was Machine, "but no one ever heard the name since it crashed before we got anywhere."

The name was strong, not necessarily a reflection of Joe Strummer's state of mind. Tricia Ronane recalled Joe coming round one evening with Richard Norris to see her and Paul. "He took us out to dinner, and Richard's attitude seemed to be that he was hip-and-cool because of his work with the Grid and this was a great opportunity for Joe. When Joe asked me what I thought, I said, 'Don't forget who you are. I don't give a shit if he's just had a dance hit. You're Joe Strummer, and don't forget that. It's fantastic to do this project, but make sure you are in control and respected. Don't let that go.'"

On November 2, 1995, Gordon McHarg held the opening of his Sandpaper Blues exhibition. On sale was the *Sandpaper Blues* album, which included Joe's song. The sleeve of the record was made of sandpaper, which tickled Joe. "You can put it next to CDs you don't like," he said to Gordon at the opening, "knowing it will scratch them and you won't have to play them again."

George Best, the soccer star, opened the exhibition by signing a soccer ball. Behind him was a large Union Jack background, along with a shot of the crowd from 1968 when Best's team, Manchester United, won the European Cup. George's mike kept cutting out and he suddenly declared, "Oh fuck it, let's have a drink."

Joe introduced Gordon to Damien Hirst. Gordon learned that Joe was working on a song for a short film that Damien was making. When the movie was shown at a film art exhibition the following year, the song was credited as "Another Fine Piece of Madeira"—it was, of course, "Sandpaper Blues."

Early in 1996 Joe involved Richard Norris in a project that involved several of his friends and Euro '96, the soccer championship of the European nations, being held in England that summer. Black Grape, the group formed by former Happy Mondays main men Shaun Ryder and Bez, had had a number 1 British album in 1995 with the ironically titled *It's Great When You're Straight . . . Yeah*, a melange of funk, house and rave sounds, with a melodic emphasis on heavy reggae bass. They had decided they would record an anthem for Euro '96. Shaun Ryder asked Joe to be involved and came over to Norro's place one evening, when the shape of the song was established. "We finally get to play the tune, really loud, and then my neighbor comes down from upstairs, knocking on the door: 'It's three in the morning. What are you doing, playing this so loud?' Joe answered the door with half a bottle of Martell brandy in his hand: 'But it's for England.' 'Oh, all right.'"

Time was booked at Real World. Black Grape arrived, along with Joe and his friend Keith Allen. The Black Grape ensemble included Danny Saber, an L.A.-based guitarist, producer and huge Clash fan. "When I met Joe he was nothing like I thought he was going to be. I thought he'd be really angry. One day he took me shopping to record stores. He started talking about dub and reggae: 'What do you think about this one?' He gave me a great crash course on Jamaican music and how to appreciate it. There's a certain type of person—there's not a lot of them around—where everything they do, whether it's smoking a cigarette, writing a song, or pouring a drink, it's just pure. Keith Richards is like that. Joe had that."

With such a congenitally anarchic crew, the Real World recording of the Euro '96 single did not flow too smoothly. "You know you're in trouble when Keith Allen is the voice of sanity," recalled Danny Saber. "I remember going to bed one night, leaving Joe and Shaun Ryder," said Richard Norris, "and getting up in the morning and coming to see Joe, and he was still with Shaun—they'd just sat up all night talking. Joe was suddenly, 'Where were you?'" In the vast studio Joe had not only created his habitual spliff bunker but had set up a tent into which he had moved Lucinda and Eliza. At first Joe did not want to sing on the record—did not want anyone to sing on the record—insisting the tune be an instrumental. "Me and Shaun were up in the studio trying to mix this thing," said Danny. "Joe was driving me fucking mad. He got really weird about the whole thing. He was freaking out about shit that was totally fucking irrelevant. I think he'd lost his confidence. But I think the song helped him regain it."

After three days Danny Saber had prevailed upon him sufficiently for Joe to feverishly start writing lyrics, all night, for several nights. "He was forty-three years old and he'd discovered ecstasy and was up for several days. He had big pieces of paper all over the floor and was writing endless lyrics. He decided he wanted to use ninety percent of it. We couldn't, of course." Did Joe have so much material stored up within him from his years of inertia that he was unable to stop writing it down? Or was such overwriting a sign of his uncertainty? Eventually Keith Allen added to the lyrical mix. "Keith was the one who pulled the whole thing together because Shaun was off doing his thing. Joe was at a tangent with all his lyrics and stuff. Keith really came up with the bulk of that, the body of it. But the song did all right. It came out really good."

It was called "England's Irie," the juxtaposition of the Jamaican term for "all right" with the name of the soccer team's country presumably being the point. The lyrics bubbled with double entendre. But also with wit. "Flying saucer rock 'n' roll," Joe, taking happy lead vocals, dropped in at the end of remix three (Suedehead Dub).

"Joe was a bit of a flirt," reported the journalist Jane Cornwell, then working at Real World, indicating that though Joe might have been true to his new wife, his essential demeanor had not shifted. A friend of Joe's cousin Gerry King was working at the studio and was concerned that Joe was so consistently out of it, relaying to the family that their relative was not in a good state. There was concern.

On March 5, 1996, Joe and his cohorts came up with another tune, "War

Cry," a moody, driving, machine-head instrumental that almost could have been by the Happy Mondays. You could not hear it without conjuring up the image of Joe cutting out the chords onstage, head hanging down, mouth wide open. By now new songs were needed: Joe's film-music supervisor friend Kathy Nelson in Los Angeles asking him to submit material for *Grosse Pointe Blank*, a comedy-thriller starring John Cusack, whom Joe had met when making *Straight to Hell*. The invitation was from Cusack himself: "John Cusack called me and said, 'Hey, we're writing this movie listening to very heavy Clash tracks like "Sean Flynn" and "Armagideon Time." Do you want to write some bits of score?' I basically wormed my way in on that," Joe explained his involvement in *Grosse Pointe Blank* to John McPartlin. "*Grosse Pointe Blank* was very interesting," said Lucinda. "Kathy Nelson was his great friend. At the time she was head of music at Disney and was doing the music for the film. Several people connected with the production, including John Cusack, were big fans of Joe. Johnny had said to Kathy, 'Do you think you could get Joe to do the music?' Kathy said she would try. So they flew us out first-class. Joe always loved L.A., so it was a very attractive proposition. But after he'd said he was interested, he got complete and utter cold feet about it. He got scared.

"We were staying with a friend named Hein Hoven who had a recording studio in his house and made commercials. I think Joe suddenly realized what was being asked of him was not to come up with some music like he did for *Walker*: Hein had a whole picture-to-sound-synch system, and Joe saw him digitally putting in music at certain sequences. So he was looking at Hein's studio and he's thinking, 'Oh, my God: there is just no way I can deal with this.'

"So he gets Norro out, to bolster him really. He didn't understand that they wanted Joe. They didn't want Richard Norris, or Hein, they wanted Joe. And Joe simply couldn't handle it. He got Hein to do some stuff and had this meeting and they came to hear Joe's work, but in fact they got Hein's. Joe was saying, 'Here: there's your man.' Kathy Nelson politely watched what Hein had done, and then she said, 'Joe, you don't get it, do you? We want you to do it. We want your music and vibe.' I think Joe was terrified. I think he was really scared. It was a different way of working, and he wasn't really ready for it.

"But in the end he agreed to it, and Kathy Nelson booked him into Westlake Audio in West Hollywood. He set up the studio with the flags. Joe lived under the piano. The whole place became his home. And Joe's great friend was the tramp, a hobo, who lived in the alleyway behind Westlake. Joe would feed, clothe, and talk to this hobo all the time. Joe made him a bed in the seating area in the loading bay.

"He needed to be reassured, but he wrote the most incredible music. And I think he got disheartened that a lot of the music didn't make it into the movie. But by the time Joe agreed to do it, they already had a lot of music in place, and they were used to hearing those tracks. So when the Disney producers heard what Joe came up with, they were like, 'We kinda like "99 Balloons,"' and Joe was, 'Urrrhhh . . .' He got quite down, but Cusack explained to him, 'When we write a script, it's something that we're immensely proud of, but when we sell it we have to let go of it. We wrote *Grosse Pointe Blank*, but the finished movie is not the way we wrote it. But we've sold it and we have to let go of it. You've been employed to score the movie: you provide the music, and whether they use it or not is not your problem. You have to let go of it.' And Joe found that quite hard. There's a lot of unused very good stuff from those sessions. But I should think it was quite expensive to install Joe in Westlake for three months. We were there a long time. We first went out at the end of March and didn't come back until September."

In America there was goodwill and a good feeling toward Joe. "It was always very chaotic, working with Joe," said Norro. "We wouldn't ring up people's management to see if they wanted to work with us, it would be like, 'Let's go and see them at this club, and maybe we'll talk to them.' It had a strange sort of chaos all of its own, which made it work or made it not work. Joe went to L.A. to do *Grosse Pointe Blank*. He was there for a day, and calls, 'Norro, it's brilliant, we are staying at this bloke's house, get the next plane over. Come on, we can do this. We've got a new studio to do something.' So I got the next plane."

Hein Hoven's house was on Mulholland Drive in the Hollywood Hills: as well as being a commercial and video director, Hein had produced the Stray Cats, and was married to Melissa Modette. It was a good-sized house, resplendent with Mexicana. While Joe was there, he would take Lucinda and Eliza to the Chateau Marmont for the afternoon to use the swimming pool; Gerry Harrington remembered coming across Joe and family there, playing with Courtney Love's daughter in the water. Some evenings, he and Lucinda would go off to exclusive L.A. show-biz parties, suitably suited up. Recording at Westlake Audio, Joe pulled in his punk contemporary, Rat Scabies, formerly of the Damned, visiting L.A., to play on drums on the soundtrack. Rat moved into the property on Mulholland. On bass was Seggs, formerly a member of reasonably successful Clash copyists the Ruts. Joe sent a plane ticket to Pockets, who moved into the pool house. "Joe would work at Westlake during the day, come home for some food, and then shut himself in the garage all night where he'd set up another studio," recalled Pockets. When Hein Hoven put the property on the market, Joe, Lucinda and Eliza moved to the Chateau Marmont, "which was our favorite place in the world," said Lucinda. "Then we moved to a house at the top of Mulholland and Laurel Canyon which was rented by a writer friend, Mel Bordeaux, from Rupert Everett. It had views over the Valley and over Hollywood. Really lovely. We were there for about six weeks. He liked to work, Joe. He liked to be involved in something. I think that's where all the energy came from when he wasn't working. If it wasn't being poured into a studio or something actually taking place now, it still had to come out somewhere. He'd have two days off, and it was like, 'Let's get in the car: you've never been up the Pacific Coast Highway north. Come on: jump in the car—let's go. Jump in the car—let's go to Mexico.' 'Joe, we've got two days off—let's relax.' 'No, I want to go to Mexico.' He said to me, 'All we have is today.' He lived every day."

They went to see Black Grape play in Tijuana, Joe driving Shaun, Bez and Richard Norris the ninety miles to the Mexican border town in his '55 Cadillac, which he had taken out of mothballs for his stay in L.A. (Richard Norris: "Because it was L.A. people would be driving around in sparkling pristine new things but the drivers would be shouting, 'Hey, is that a '54 or a '55?'") On the way back Joe managed to become completely lost, the two-hour drive back to Hollywood turning into six, all to the soundtrack spinning out of a ghetto blaster—perhaps the giant spliffs being consumed for the entire journey on the vast backseat by Shaun Ryder had something to do with Joe's navigational difficulties. "The vibes, man," Shaun uttered incessantly as the Caddy wandered its peripatetic course across southern California. That was all he said. In the inappropriate location of Los Angeles, at Westlake Audio, another remix of "England's Irie" was worked up, very ragamuffin.

Playing with Black Grape was a twenty-year-old multi-instrumentalist called Martin Slattery, from Hebden Bridge near Manchester. Much he was experiencing was from way outside his parameters of expectation. When Shaun Ryder attacked Ged Lynch, the group's drummer, at a show in L.A., Martin felt disturbed. "Joe just went, 'Oh, don't worry about it. It'll be fine tomorrow. I've been in this situation a thousand times and I guarantee it will be fine.'"

At Westlake, Joe employed beer crates and camouflage netting to quickly erect a spliff bunker. Assorted Red Hot Chili Peppers would drop by. "Joe was incredibly sensitive," said Kathy Nelson. "On *Grosse Pointe Blank*, because he didn't really know what he was doing as a composer, there were many times he would start to shut down. He required positive reinforcement when he entered an area where he was a little bit insecure. I don't think he thought he wasn't really good, it was more that he didn't want to disappoint anyone. He would many times say, 'Oh, I robbed you. I didn't do a good enough job. Mrs. Kathy, I always give her piece-of-shit songs.' He was very mindful of wanting to come through for you."

One night in a bar Gerry Harrington and Joe had a big falling-out, Gerry telling him he should remain true to his roots of reggae, ska, jazz and gospel. "I said he was doing himself a disservice by writing these little ditties for movies. I said, 'Don't do it with people who are lucky to be working with you. Work with people that are to their art what you are to yours. That is the only way you should be giving music away on film.' Joe said, 'You could stack up on that table all the records I've sold in the last ten years.' I said, 'I know, I've bought most of them. But I'm telling you, your way isn't working. Trust me on this.'" After a few moments, fired by the general consumption of the evening, they were shouting at each other. Joe stormed off. "I come to the office the next morning," recalled Gerry, "and there's this really charming message from Joe, apologizing in the best possible way."

In Los Angeles Joe also recorded a song titled "Generations," working with Rat and Seggs, under the *nom de disque* Electric Doghouse; the name was the suggestion of the engineer. "We're not going to think of anything better than that," said Joe. He had been contacted by Jason Rothberg, working as executive producer on a project called *Generations I—A Punk Look at Human Rights*, a charity project founded by Jack Healey, who had been behind the Amnesty International benefit concert at the Milton Keynes Bowl.

Joe respected Healey, and signed on to record the *Generations* title track. "When Jason Rothberg called, I was inspired to put pen to paper," said Joe. "I was really taken by the concept of a punk album benefiting human rights, and doing this for Jack Healey. I wrote the track in a couple of hours, and with the help of Rat Scabies and Seggs we produced and recorded 'Generations' in a day." The song was recorded on downtime at Westlake, with Seggs's cabdriver waiting in the studio to take him to LAX for his flight back to London. (For a short time Jason ended up as Joe's manager.)

Joe's time in Los Angeles in 1996 was not at all unproductive. He also recorded a song, "It's a Rockin' World," that was used in an episode of the iconoclastic cartoon series *South Park*; a cartoon Joe was featured in the show. Recording the tune with Joe were Flea from the Chili Peppers on bass, drummer D.J. Bonebrake from X, and Nick Hexum from 311 and Tom Morello from Rage Against the Machine. "It's a Rockin' World" was great, a fast-paced archetypal rock 'n' roll tune, with some of Joe's most witty lyrics. The line "the laws of chaos left us all in disarray" reminded me how Joe complained that chaos theory was an exposition of what he believed he had personally come up with, tripping on acid. The tune was produced by Rick Rubin.

It was at the instigation of Tim Armstrong of Rancid that Joe had gone to the *South Park* sound studio. With Green Day and Offspring, Rancid formed a triumvirate of very successful 1990s U.S. punk bands who owed much to the spirit of '77. Now Joe forged a useful link with Rancid's main man, even singing with them on an unreleased ska version of Nick Lowe's "[What's So Funny 'Bout] Peace, Love and Understanding."

There was a downside to the work Joe did in southern California. In *Grosse Pointe Blank* the studio used only two new Joe tunes, the already written "War Cry" and "Yalla Yalla." Kathy Nelson also got a couple of Clash songs into the rather good film, as well as "Lorca's Novena" by the Pogues, which Joe had produced. It must have seemed like a consolation prize; such blanket dismissal of those weeks of work at Westlake must have been deeply dispiriting. When you are trying to climb out of a low period, it sometimes hangs on tight enough to strangle you.

Joe argued with Rat over the dread subject of money, the drummer feeling that although Universal decided not to use Joe's material he should still be paid as a session musician. At Joe's wake at the Paradise bar, Rat Scabies changed his mind: "It was ridiculous. I should have gone with it. Working with Joe was immediately free, much, much looser than anything I'd experienced."

More significantly, Joe Strummer and Richard Norris fell out, and their working collaboration ended. According to Norro, someone in L.A. told Joe that the Grid man considered him over the hill. Which, he insisted, could not have been further from the truth. But it was enough for their relationship to end in metaphorical tears. "All I could say was, 'I didn't say that. It's not how I feel. I want to get on with doing the music.' So that was pretty much the end of it. Which was a shame. Fuck 'em!" Norro laughed resignedly. "But I think what we did was a bridge to him getting back together and getting out there and making records. So something good came out of it."

When "England's Irie," the Black Grape soccer song, was released toward the end of June 1996 to coincide with the Euro '96 kick-off, the single reached number 6. The song was credited on the record's label to Black Grape featuring Joe Strummer and Keith Allen. The success of the song finally obliged Joe to appear on *Top of the Pops*. Joe was still in L.A. and flew over to London for the taping. "I met him at Heathrow," said Pockets, "he did *Top of the Pops* with Shaun, and then went back to L.A. the next day."

Joe was not constrained by any necessity to get to Glastonbury: Michael Eavis, the festival organizer, had suspended the event for that year. And back in L.A. Joe had a big party to attend, for Gerry Harrington's thirty-fifth birthday, at his sumptuous house in Belair. Gerry wanted to introduce Winona Ryder, a Clash fanatic, to Joe. But it didn't happen. Gerry said sarcastically, "If you were a big enough loser or offensive enough or drunk enough you could go up to Joe and live in his house for the next couple of weeks."

Joe returned to London for a second *Top of the Pops* appearance and again went back to L.A., where he, Lucinda and Eliza remained until early autumn. Later in the year, back in England, he went with Luce at Gerry Harrington's instigation to Paris to see the Rolling Stones' Bridges to Babylon tour, afterward having dinner with Mick Jagger.

When Joe went to London from Hampshire, he and Lucinda stayed at the new house Paul Simonon had bought that year in Aldridge Road Villas, off Westbourne Park Road in Notting Hill. In the basement of the tall house, Joe set up camp, renting the space for seventy pounds a week. "But he'd be upstairs the whole time anyway," said Tricia. "If you let him he'd come back with loads of people, drink up all your wine, leave the place in a mess, and push off. We had nice times at home with him, and when Richard Norris was still around it was fine. But Paul and I wouldn't let him abuse the situation."

Back at Ivy Cottage Joe called up percussionist Pablo Cook, who had played on the Norro sessions. "I knew him and Richard had had this falling-out. But on the phone Joe suddenly said to me, 'You're a good man—remember that.' I thought, That's a very Joe Strummer thing to say, but I wonder what that's about? Then he asked if I wanted to come down to the Woodshed. We were right bang into the cumbia. At the early campfires it was mostly cumbia being played, although you got a lot of reggae thrown in there. The first thing we did was the music for a black-and-white short film called *Tunnel of Love* featuring Eddie Izzard and Tamara Beckwith.

"Somebody heard it and Eric Cantona got in touch. Eric Cantona said, 'Will you write the theme for this film I am making?'" Joe flew to Paris for a meeting with the great soccer star, who had just retired as striker with Manchester United. Although he thought a driver would be picking him up at Charles de Gaulle Airport, he was impressed when he stepped out of the arrivals gate to find Cantona himself waiting. It was the sort of thing Joe might have done.

"Cantona was making a film called *Question of Honour*," said Pablo. "It involved Eric and his three brothers pretending to be actors in the docks somewhere. They'd got Jake La Motta, who Scorsese's *Raging Bull* was about, to play a part. I put together the theme and the score for it. Joe was doing guitar parts, with little bits of vocals here and there. I did most of the music and Joe did the words. He did a beautiful bit at the start of *Question of Honour*."

In Chile that year Joe took part in what he insisted would be his last acting job. The film, a chase movie entitled *Docteur Chance*, was made by F. J. Ossang, a French director with his own rock 'n' roll group and another career as a poet. "F. J. Ossang and his producer contacted Joe by letter about three years previously to ask him if he would be interested in this film," recalled Lucinda. "Joe said no, but they persisted and we agreed to meet them in the Osteria Basilica in Kensington Park Road to talk. Joe just adored Ossang as he was so unbelievably enthusiastic and crazy and he said yes to the film." Although Ossang had considered Joe to be "rather fragile" the first time they met, he noted that by the time filming started he seemed much stronger within himself. Joe was to play a character called Vince Taylor, an arms trafficker; the real Vince Taylor had, of course, written and recorded the original "Brand New Cadillac" and had been approached to play the part before suddenly dying in 1991. Joe's main role in the film was not until the final ten minutes, speaking entirely in French. "I was a rock 'n' roll star," he defines his past. Earlier in *Docteur Chance* his image had flashed up on the screen for a moment as he delivered the cryptically mock-profound line *"Victory Lane—c'est un anagram de Vince Taylor."* (The film is rather French.)

"We flew to Santiago on October 12, 1996," said Lucinda. "We spent one day there and then flew up with the rest of the crew to Iqueque in the north. It was amazing. When we landed at the tiny airport our luggage was carried from the plane by porters and put on a weeny carousel. As Joe went to retrieve it, the porter whisked the bags off again and said he would carry them to customs for us. He was completely in awe of Joe and asking him for autographs and saying he was a hero in Chile and his dream had come true now he had met him." (When *Docteur Chance* was screened at the London Film Festival in October 1997, F. J. Ossang and Joe Strummer appeared at London's National Film Theatre, to answer audience questions afterward. "Ah, fuck it. Let's go to the bar. Anyone can talk to me there," Joe decided after a few minutes.)

Although nothing had come of it, Joe had had an exploratory management meeting with Tim Clark and David Enthoven, music business old hands who between them had formed IE Management. IE managed Bryan Ferry, Massive Attack, Faithless and—fresh from Take That—Robbie Williams. Massive Attack worked with the legendary London-based Jamaican singer Horace "Sleepy" Andy, whose career IE attempted to guide when they could pry him away from the ganja chalice.

Searching for material for a prospective new Horace Andy album, Clark and Enthoven called Joe: Did he have any ideas? The number Joe came up with, cowriting with Pablo Cook, was titled "Living in the Flood," a suitably apocalyptic world vision to match Horace's strict Rastafarian beliefs. "With the fire of truth / we will evaporate," wrote Joe. So effective a tune was "Living in the Flood" that it had become the title track by the time the new set of Horace Andy songs was released in 1999. "Horace Andy came over," remembered Pablo. "That's when we started to get to where I thought we were going with the music. I wasn't sure how seriously Joe was taking it, if he was really trying to come out of the long silence he'd had. But I thought 'Living in the Flood' was a beautiful piece of music with amazing lyrics by Joe."

"Horace came down to the Woodshed," said Pockets, "and liked the demos they had done there so much that he wanted to do his own vocals there. I was introduced to him as Pockets. I said, 'Actually my name is Dave.' He said, 'Every man needs a nickname. Mine is Sleepy.' A few hours later Joe asked me to bring him into the studio. Horace was in the sitting room, lying asleep on the sofa, half an enormous reefer in the ashtray and the *Dumbo* cartoon playing on the TV."

Bez was a frequent weekend visitor, often arriving with a crew of friends from Manchester. Invariably the garden of Ivy Cottage would glow with the light of a campfire. A close friend of Bez was Dermot Mitchell, who often accompanied him. "He was younger than we thought," said Pockets. "Which was why he was so quiet. But he was someone who Bez, Shaun Ryder and Joe trusted, and there aren't many of those around. He'd gone from being a Manchester teenager with a rough upbringing to hanging out with some cool guys. He became one of Joe's closest friends."

From time to time at the Woodshed there were impediments to musical progress. "We were trying to write songs," said Pablo, "but a lot of the time we were too out of it to actually put them together. This West African hallucinogenic turned up—I didn't get involved in it. The point was to try and record, but it would end up with Bez in tears beside the campfire because he thought a plane had crashed into his head, and Joe trying to find a cigarette machine out in the woods. I'd send him off: 'Joe, can you try and find me a microphone?' 'Yeah, man, I can find anything.' I'd see him wander into the wood, and you wouldn't see him until the morning when he'd come back. I'd say, 'Where have you been for seven hours?' 'Oh, I've been in the wood, man, looking for cigarettes.' Fuck knows what was in that stuff."

Pablo observed Joe's state of mind. He could read the cloud of depression that overhung him, and felt this was why Joe was creatively blocked. "The actual picking up of the guitar seemed a big problem. I've seen it with other writers before: there's always some little thing getting in the way. But one afternoon we decided, 'We need to think of another style, man.' I told

Joe and his good brother Bez, at the Fuji Rock Festival in 1999, where the Mescaleros performed. *(Gordon McHarg)*

Joe that everything had been done—violins had been mixed with hiphop, for example. What did he say? 'Yeah, but nobody's done heavy metal with prog rock. Let's do that.'"

"I'm not sure about that, Joe."

"Fucking let's do it."

"So I programmed up this piece of music, which went from 14/8 to 13/4, and then Joe got the guitars plugged in. 'The guitar's got to be as loud as possible.' I got him up to eleven, and he hit this chord and goes, 'Oh man, that's the worst idea we ever had.' So we went to the pub."

The customary lines of legal copy on the "England's Irie" packaging had declared that Joe Strummer appeared "courtesy of Epic Records." But this was the last time such deference would be needed. On March 25, 1997, Joe was released by Epic's parent company, Sony, as a solo artist, although he remained signed to the label in the event of any Clash reunion. Later Joe said he had been "waiting out his contract" as an explanation as to why he had not released any of his own records since *Earthquake Weather*. Though there was an element of truth here, it was also a good cover-up for the personal creative inertia and confusion of the proud lion during his "wilderness years." Yet it can't be ignored that the moment Joe was free of his old contract, the upward arc of his creative trajectory grew markedly steeper. But there was something else taking up Joe's time in 1997. He was moving house.

On a chilly January day in 1997 Joe, Lucinda and Eliza had driven down to Devon and Somerset. They were looking to buy somewhere. To help pay for this, 15 Court Farm Road, which Joe had kept intact ever since his mother had died ten years previously, had been put on the market. Joe and Luce found a house tucked away in a red-soiled valley in the picturesque Quantock Hills to the northwest of Taunton that was what they were looking for. "We were the first people to see Yalway," said Lucinda. "It needed a lot of work and we continued to live at Ivy Cottage while the work was being done, making frequent visits to oversee the work. We actually moved there in December 1997." The work was done but there was still lots to do and it was very basic. "We had started again," said Lucinda. "We couldn't buy a house at the beginning. Ivy Cottage only cost £100 a week. Part of the reason we moved to Yalway was because the rent was going up. We knew we had to buy something because what we were spending was the same as a mortgage. So we sold Warlingham, which gave us enough to put down on the house. Initially Joe didn't want to move. He didn't like change. He loved Ivy Cottage. But once we were in . . . I remember we spent our first night there. We were sleeping on the floor in the downstairs sitting room, because the bedrooms still had missing floorboards, and he said, 'I'm so happy. I'm so excited. This really feels like home.'

"He loved Yalway. It's funny, if you do feng shui, it has all the aspects that are right for a house: flowing water on the left, the kitchen faces south, all the things which you don't actually notice unless you are aware of it. But then maybe that's why he loved it. He loved the walks. The only thing he missed was a good pub. But he used to read a book a night. He read everything from the Koran to biographies, books about the war. When we first got Sky TV, he used to watch the History Channel a lot—he used to call it the Hitler channel. He used to love all that. Mick and Paul used to like all that too. Joe used to devour books.

"He'd wake me up and say, 'It's a sunny day: the kid's not going to school today.' I'd go downstairs and he's made a picnic. We used to go to the Isle of Purbeck, a ferry ride from Poole. He'd say, 'I had a friend at school here, and I know it well, and it's great.' Whenever the bluebells were out, we'd go and have a picnic."

Realizing that her closest friend from childhood lived nearby, Lucinda got in touch. "I called Amanda and said we had found a house which I thought might be near them," said Lucinda. In April 1997 Amanda Temple invited Luce and her new husband to stay for a weekend. Amanda lived with her husband, the film director Julien Temple, and children near Bridgwater in Somerset, a more rascally, anarchic town than Taunton.

As a film student, Julien Temple had chronicled the Anarchy tour as well as early Clash rehearsals. Later he had made *The Great Rock 'n' Roll Swindle*, the fantasy story of the Sex Pistols, and *Absolute Beginners*, a musical based on Colin MacInnes's trilogy of novels set in Notting Hill; Julien had also directed top-end videos for artists like the Rolling Stones and Neil Young. He had been told by Amanda that her friend Lucinda would be

Joe on the rear wall of 15 Court Farm Road at the time he decided to finally sell the Mellor family home. *(Lucinda Mellor)*

bringing her new husband, some sort of musician. "They come through the gate and there's Joe behind her, the last person I thought to see. I'd never thought about him for years, and I'm sure he'd never thought about me. It's always going to be uncomfortable, meeting someone you haven't seen for that long, with strange parameters around your mutual experience. But we became good friends after that."

On Joe and Lucinda's second visit to the Temples' beautiful old country house, the two men bonded over the kind of rudiment of life which had always entranced the musician. When Joe arrived in the evening Julien had been laboriously assembling a hot-air balloon for his son Leo. "We got stuck into putting all these strips of paper together. The project had to happen. We had to finish it. We had to get this hot-air balloon up, whatever happened. So into the early hours of the morning we tried to put this thing together. We finally got the hot-air balloon flying, and kept the kids up to watch it. Spending a night doing some mad thing like that kicked us off again together.

"The whole Campfire idea came out of that country thing and going to these very straight country pubs, sitting there having these amazing evenings just talking."

Joe, Julien noted, seemed in very good spirits. "He didn't seem down. My daughter Juno was doing a Victorian musical play at school: we used to drive around in an old Land Rover, steaming down these country lanes, me and Joe in the back with the kids, singing the songs from the play—'Daisy' and 'Burlington Bertie' and 'Champagne Charlie,' a great vocal roar of 'Champagne Charlie.' We had this great, mad summer of singing these songs. He knew all the words, which surprised me, because I'd only just learned them.

"I think Lucinda opened up another side of Joe. He loved her deeply. There was a huge liberation in being with her and starting again. Although they did lead different hours: Luce's life ran on school hours because she'd have to get Eliza up and off in the mornings, about when Joe would be going to bed."

The town of Glastonbury is only fifteen miles from Yalway; the music festival takes place at nearby Shepton Mallett. Glastonbury—whose legend includes a visit from Jesus Christ—is said to have been the site of the first Christian church in England, and is claimed to have connections with the court of King Arthur. These rich mythological associations hit a deep nerve with Joe Strummer. "He was obsessed with King Arthur, and with the Bronze Age and ancient British culture," said Julien. "At night he would look up at the stars in the clear sky and speak about how this must have been precisely what people in ancient civilizations had seen. Joe was remarking that the one thing that hasn't changed since the first people were alive is the stars. I think he was finding and liking the sense of being grounded in himself. He was a very spiritual person, although he wasn't a religious person." As well as these spiritual connections, the region had a radical past. It was the site of the last rebellion in England; in 1685, using Taunton and Bridgwater as a base, the Duke of Monmouth had attempted to usurp King James II; savage reprisals only strengthened the characteristic local mood of rebellion, and a freethinking point of view persists to this day.

The area was partial to unexpected rituals. Each year at the beginning of November Bridgwater hosts its own carnival, the oldest in Britain. "I took him to Bridgwater to the carnival, which is an extraordinary event in that town," said Julien. "He was pretty amazed by the number of people watching all these crazy floats. The first thing that came round the corner was a 'Rock the Casbah' float. Then there was a 'Should I Stay or Should I Go' float. So it was like he'd come to this place to forget, yet they were doing this kind of Aladdin strobe dance to 'Rock the Casbah.' After he overcame that shock he got totally into the Black Friday, the mad aftermath of carnival in Bridgwater, where they have to drink in each bar. That is a hard thing to do; he did it very well. He was very good at sips of drinks."

Damien Hirst was living not far away, at Coombe Martin in Devon. Accordingly, Joe and the enfant terrible of British art spent much time together. "Damien was very important to him," said Lucinda. "I think he really recognized himself in Damien. He adored him. He loved him and [his wife] Maia, loved them both. Damien challenged him, he stimulated him. He provoked him, he inspired him. Damien was irreverent and is hugely talented. Joe loved him. He loved being with him and Maia. We had lovely times there in Devon. Endless days on the beach. Lovely lunches and long walks. Interesting people were always there. They're a good crowd. Joe needed to spend time with peers, not mates. I remember once meeting him from somewhere at Heathrow. We got the train down to Somerset. He had just come off tour, and he said, 'Give me the phone.' He hated mobile phones, but he rang Damien and said, 'I want to come down.' I said, 'No, you're exhausted.' He said, 'No, I'm going down to see him.' Because he was still buzzing and he knew he could decompress with Damien."

"Damien had a big impact on him," thought Julien. "There was a real energy that Joe got from Damien that helped him feel he could put all this back together and be a different version of Joe. Joe could be so supportive to people like Damien. Joe would sit there and Damien would get off his head. You know, it's bullshit when people make the accusation that too many late nights killed Joe, because Joe never got out of it like Keith or Damien or me. He was always in control of the situation.

"He did give me some weird joint one night, when we were on our own, that was laced with PCP or something, and I was projectile-vomiting. He did sometimes do a lot of weird strong stuff that you can't do unless you've got five days to recover. But he was the one who was in control of the pacing of things, while other people were losing it. He wouldn't lose it. Joe was slow-burn in terms of consumption, but he did it all the time. There are few people like that. He did love altered states, but he had it down to a fine art, where he was always slightly altered, but not so much as to be out of step with reality around him. Joe approached drugs as very spiritual things, in the same way that Mexicans or Indians would smoke tobacco, as a spiritual and ritual bonding exercise."

A characteristic of Joe's that impressed Julien was his stripped-down approach to life: "Joe needs very little to have a good time. He didn't need material things or designer drugs: a pint that he didn't drink was enough, if he was with someone who he's getting something from. A very simple way of living was enough."

Joe had a 1930s book, *Campfire Leader*, rules on getting a good campfire going, which wood to use, what songs to elevate the spirits. "He read it," affirmed Julien. "He took the Campfire very seriously. It's a hard place to be. You have to be strong enough to get out of it, and lose your worldly bullshit. An important part of what he saw in the essence of the Campfires is you have to be able to live with nothing, under the stars, so when the electricity goes off in your house you can deal with that. He was a very wise person."

I've been to those Campfires. The first thing I noticed was the democracy: everyone is equal in the circle around the flame. In a way, the Campfire symbolized the circular nature of Joe's life; the student from Central, best friends with the biggest names in contemporary art, has his own shows in

the dipping Somerset hills. "If you see it in a Damien kind of way, the Campfire was his art statement," said Julien. "The Campfire was about surviving
without all the other shit, preparing you to survive without material goods.
All you need is other people, which in the end was Joe's big thing. You and
someone else can do much more than you can on your own. When one gives
up, the other doesn't. It takes place at night in the open, night becomes day,
an old thing but Joe was bringing it into a modern context. 'Club Dawn,'
that's what he used to say: 'You and me and Club Dawn.'"

A diatribe against the modern world was never far from Joe's thoughts.
"We're forming a new country called Rebel Wessex," he told me a couple of
years later. "We want Cornwall, Devon and Somerset to secede from the
union. All we do in Rebel Wessex is drink cider all night and plot revolution. We're so far into it we've opened up a website and designed a flag: red
and black with a burning skull and flames of change blowing in the wind.
We're making a virtual country on the Internet. We want a place where
there are rave parks and where we can decriminalize marijuana for personal use. All we do down there is talk about how crap these giant super-
markets are, spraying pesticide all over the land. It's like an abattoir out
there. There's no joy when the harvest comes in, it's just a giant machine
with poor animals caught in it, run by the lunatics who're going to fuck up
the gene pool."

Before retreating to San José in Andalusia for his traditional summer
sojourn, Joe went that July of 1997 to Japan to the first Fuji Rock Festival, organized by Masa, who had blessed Joe and Lucinda with Glastonbury
tickets as a wedding present. He had booked Joe and Bez to deejay in the
dance area on the second night—in Japan Joe Strummer was, and is, considered like a fusion of James Dean, Elvis Presley and Bob Dylan, and bigger than any of them. Although staged in a perfect setting, a spectacular
national park on the side of Mount Fuji, the festival was devastated when
struck by a full-force typhoon. As tens of thousands of blankets were air-
lifted in, the dance area was turned into a hospital, Joe and Bez unable to
fulfill their task. Joe was overawed by the power and ferocious energy of the
typhoon, entranced by its elemental command of mankind. He vowed to return as a performer.

But his past was pursuing him. Tricia Ronane had talks with Sony to promote the group's back catalogue. It was agreed that a Clash live album would finally be released, and that Sony would fund a definitive biographical documentary, to be directed by Don Letts. "Joe needed money with his house move, and Paul and I had two kids and needed to get in cash," said Tricia.

In April 1997 Joe had appeared on a Jack Kerouac tribute album, *Kicks Joy Darkness*. He played music, recorded at Ivy Cottage in his makeshift studio, behind a tape of Kerouac giving a live reading of the poem "Mac-Dougal Street Blues, Cantos Dos." Joe was no stranger to occasional side projects: in 1995 he'd gone to Brighton to work with the Levellers on a single, "Just the One"; he had even, through Danny Saber, worked on a song with Michael Hutchence, who'd clearly forgiven him for his cheeky, but insightful remark back in Memphis.

The year ended with another death in the Mellor family, that of David Mackenzie, Joe's uncle. "Uncle David was very pally with Johnny. They spent a lot of time together," said the sprightly Uncle John, whom Joe had defined as "the original punk rocker." For his own part Uncle David had the kind of credentials that thrilled young Johnny Mellor—a distinguished war record, with one especially harrowing experience: as a member of the RAF's Coastal Command, scouring the drink for surfaced U-boats, he had been forced to ditch in the rough North Sea, floating for three days in a raft with one other surviving crew member before being rescued.

For his uncle's funeral that December, in the churchyard next to Bonar Bridge, Joe made the long journey up to the heart of his mother's family in northeast Scotland, his first visit there for more than thirty years. Pockets Girvan went with him on the sleeper from King's Cross station in London to Inverness, where they completed the last stage by taxi; not that for one moment on the train from London did they lie down in their berths, choosing to pass the entire excursion in the bar. "It was very nice of Johnny to do that: a long, long journey," thought Uncle John.

As the bagpipes wailed in the graveyard on the chilly edge of the choppy firth, Joe stood hunched in his black coat. Then he detached himself from the cluster of thirty or so relatives and friends and wandered off, close to the Mackenzie family communal headstone, where he was observed wiping his eyes. "The funeral was classic," said Pockets. "As the coffin was lowered into the ground, with the bagpiper playing, sunlight suddenly blasted through the pine trees, producing these pointy shadows. Perfect. Then we went to various homes of various family members. Neither of us were whisky drinkers, but—realizing it would be rude not to drink it—we were obliged to have a tumbler of whisky everywhere we went."

Later Joe, Alasdair Gillies and Pockets went to the Caledonian Hotel, next to the bridge, where they drank pints of "heavy"; Joe loved the Scottish term "heavy" for what in England is known as "bitter." "With us later was another younger cousin," said Pockets. "He was too young to be a Clash fan, a young 'un with a pronounced London accent. Joe loved that this guy wasn't into the Clash. He was just into the fact that Joe was another family member. They didn't know each other, except they were cousins. Joe always liked talking to people who didn't know anything about the Clash." The taxi driver scheduled to drive them over the Struie to Inverness was worried, he said: the night was getting stormy—they should set off. First Alasdair was instructed to get Joe moving; then it was the turn of Anna Gillies. "Just have another drink," Joe kept saying. When they eventually got him outside the Caledonian to the car, Joe was asked, "Where are you going to sit?" "On the bonnet," he grinned beerily. "I'll help you," said Aunt Jenny. Joe finally climbed into the car. On the return journey to London, he and Pockets again spent the entire trip in the train's bar, dining on eggs on toast when they finally reached the capital.

let's rock again!

1998-2000

> Like a modern scientist, the Mescalero knew that
> there was power in every atom of nature. It could
> be tapped and channeled, for good or bad. He could
> tap the power in nature for his own and others' good
> if he had the right revelation and could acquire a
> ceremony from another Indian or from some supernatural
> power.
> —*THE MESCALERO APACHES*, BY C. L. SONNICHSEN
>   (UNIVERSITY OF OKLAHOMA PRESS)

Despite Joe's extracurricular musical activities, it seemed as though he, Bez and Pablo Cook were the nucleus of a group. Further names were discussed: after the Hand of God ("Joe decided that was too arrogant," said Damien Hirst), Longbow was temporarily settled upon. "I put some more tunes together," said Pablo, using the Depot, a studio near where he lived in Camden; Joe would come over and stay with him. Bez would also come to the studio.

That year Joe had performed on "Vindaloo," an absurdist song written by Keith Allen as an unofficial anthem for the 1998 World Cup. Released under the name of Fat Les, "Vindaloo"—a celebration of the British love of curry—reached number 1 in June that year as the World Cup was staged. Joe again appeared on *Top of the Pops*. Wryly, Pablo Cook gave him a hard time: "'You're fucking out of order. How come you've gone from being a punk legend to being a fucking comedian, dressing up to do *Top of the Pops* with Keith Allen? Never do that again. I'm not in this business with you to write football songs. That's a bad mistake, a bad move.' That really got his goat. He said, 'I can't believe I've done that, fucking comedy music. I've never done comedy music.'"

Through a set of associates, a number of meetings with record companies had been set up for Joe, to strike a deal. Unfortunately, these were put in the diary for the week following that year's Glastonbury festival. "This was before I knew that Joe would go off on these five-day parties," said Pablo. "I go to Glastonbury on the Saturday. We've got a meeting the following Thursday, so I keep an eye on Joe. On Monday morning I shoot off to make sure the meetings are in hand. On Tuesday I call up Luce; she hasn't seen Joe. Jason Mayall says, 'Joe said he was going out of the festival to buy a couch, to sit beside the campfire.' On the Thursday morning, after the meetings have been canceled, someone finds him on the far side of the Glastonbury site. He's sitting on a couch with these old-school crusties and travelers. He's been there for four days. Fantastic."

Ironically, considering his criticism of Joe, Pablo now found himself working with him on another sports song, a tune for Manchester United, the biggest brand name in soccer. There was a comedy element here too, even in the title of the song: "Man, Man United." Because all of Joe's "Manc posse"—as they became known—were United supporters, Bez was involved, as was his close friend Dermot. A weekend was booked at Hook End studio, thirty miles west of London. Joe soon was scurrying about the woodland, gathering kindling for a campfire. "Sitting at a campfire for forty-eight hours getting hammered—what a brilliant idea," mused Pablo. "Why do you want to sit in your flat and watch TV when you can sit with your mates and get fucking trolleyed? Joe got out what was supposedly a box of damp fireworks, which he thought he'd use as ballast for the fire. How we didn't kill ourselves, I don't know. There's fireworks flying everywhere."

The "Man, Man United" song seemed to similarly blow itself up, never to resurface.

Pablo Cook had met the guitarist and keyboards player Antony Genn, who'd run onstage naked with Elastica at Glastonbury in 1995. "Ant," as he was known, was the archetype of the groovy viber, a particularly rarefied breed of musician, a blend of talent, charisma and energy whose very presence is capable of moving a creative endeavor upward. A consummate scene-maker since moving to London in 1995, he had become friends with Damien Hirst and Keith Allen, bankrolled by a song he had written on the first Robbie Williams solo album. "His enthusiasm and understanding of music is fantastic," said Pablo.

Following his naked appearance onstage with Elastica, in 1995 Ant had briefly met Joe at the campfire. "The next time I met Joe was in the Depot in Camden, with Pablo and Bez. They were working on a tune. The chorus was minor and the verse was major. I said, 'You want to try changing that around.' Joe would have been quite in his rights to say, 'Who the fuck is that wanker?' But Joe is the kind of guy who doesn't miss a trick. For some reason he must have thought something of that."

The next time that Joe and Ant met up was again in a recording studio, the Fortress, off Old Street in East London. It was September 1998. Flush with the success of "Vindaloo," Keith Allen was now making a Christmas single. "Really shit, called 'Naughty Christmas,'" said Ant. "Total bollocks. But somehow I got roped in, and so did Joe."

As a six-year-old Ant Genn had been indoctrinated with the spirit of punk by his thirteen-year-old brother. "I stood outside Sheffield Top Rank on the *London Calling* tour to get the Clash's autographs. I knew who Joe Strummer was: he'd changed my life. That was what I grew up on. I'm not a fuckin' Britpop nancy boy, I'm a kid off a council estate whose life was changed by punk at a very early age. By that token I have total irreverence for anyone. So while I have respect and love for Joe Strummer, I don't give a fuck he's Joe Strummer. Hence I said at this session, 'I ain't being funny, mate, but you should be making your own record.'

"He said he'd been doing stuff with Pabs. I'd heard some of this. Damien had played me a version of 'Diggin' the New,' off our heads at eight in the morning. The song had an electronic backbeat and when he came up with the lines 'You gotta live in this world / Diggin' the new' I went,

'That's the chorus there, mate. That's the fuckin' money shot. You want to be repeating that.' Which of course I ended up doing when we made the record."

A s a struggling young promoter, Simon Moran had first met Joe Strummer in 1988 at the Rock Against the Rich Electric Ballroom date. Through linking up with Joe then, Simon had put on several Rock Against the Rich shows. Ten years later, Simon was a highly successful promoter and co-owner of the annual two-venue V Festival. Seeking a headline act for V the next summer, in December 1998 he made Joe an offer he thought he would probably refuse: re-form the Clash for the two dates and he would pay them a million dollars. To Simon's surprise, Joe said he would think about it. A few days later Joe called him back, asking him to come down to Somerset in early January. "I went to Yalway. We had a nice meal, there were lots of dogs, and it was a lovely place. But then Joe said, 'I've got you here on false pretenses. I don't want to get the Clash together. But my powder's dry and I want to get out there and do my own record. I've got all these songs ready. I want you to manage me.' I said, 'Yeah, great. This is exciting.'"

Joe already had an offer of a record deal from Hellcat, the pet project of Tim Armstrong of Rancid. When Simon Moran spoke to the label, he was impressed. "They wanted to do it for the right reasons, and they were offering really great royalties." The initial contract was for one album, for $250,000, out of which Joe would have to pay recording costs. Simon excluded Europe from the worldwide contract, striking a deal with Mercury.

But who would Joe be playing with? "The next time I see Joe is the important meeting," said Antony Genn. "It's in Damien's restaurant, the Pharmacy in Notting Hill Gate. This is January '99. We're with a bunch of people, including Joe. We got talking and talking—about music, about everything. That's when I said it again, about making his own record. 'You're Joe Strummer, for God's sake. The world needs you.' To which he said, 'OK, man. I'm going to go in the studio with you.' And he knew who I was."

That Joe did know who Antony Genn was and still made a decision to work with him verges on the extraordinary. For Ant was a full-blown heroin addict of long standing. "I was an addict, not a kid off his head. I'm a big geezer from up north: two grams of heroin a day kept me normal, along with the fourteen pints of cider and a gram of coke. That's what I worked on every day. I didn't understand that I might be just a greedy fucker who should never take anything." In the light of the demise of the Clash following the sacking of smackhead Topper Headon, and the subsequent lengthy self-recriminations over this on the part of Joe, his choice of new co-worker had an almost cosmically bewildering significance. Joe Strummer had knowingly taken on a musical collaborator who was a junkie? Well, he would, wouldn't he? And you can't help finding yourself wondering: In the unmistakable paradox of his action was Joe thereby making some sort of unformulated penance to the errant Topper?

"He's already seen this movie. He knows how it ends," said Ant. "But we had a great conversation that night. At the end Joe says, 'OK, man. I'll call you tomorrow and I'm going to fix it so you and me can go in the studio for a few days.' I thought, 'Yeah, whatever, mate.' The next day I got a phone call. We booked some time at Battery Studios in Willesden."

Joe had had a further meeting with Simon Moran. "I've got this guy who's a bit of a wild card," Joe told his new manager. "He's a drug addict, but I think I can do something with him." "I'd met Ant and he was dead keen," said Simon, "and he understood that Joe needed to make a proper rock 'n' roll record with a proper group. I didn't want Joe to go down that route he'd been trying and become a dance group."

Once Joe and Antony Genn started work at Battery, on St. Valentine's Day 1999, matters moved apace: "Two days into starting we'd written this song, 'Techno D-Day,' and he said, 'Let's book the studio for three months and make a record.'"

Joe was concerned Ant should never be without his requisite daily survival kit. "Joe would always make sure I had money for drugs. 'Hey man, you all right there? You need any money for that thing?'" For his part Ant thought Joe seemed in great shape: "Excited. We were in the studio and writing. I just wanted to see Joe back playing."

The atmosphere at Battery felt like a horse-racing stable, everything about to go off with these pure thoroughbreds. Joe and Ant wrote and recorded four new songs: "Techno D-Day," "Willesden to Cricklewood," "Tony Adams," and "Nitcomb." (Who else but Joe Strummer would start an ode to his sweetheart with the unlikely metaphor "Gonna take a nitcomb / To get rid of me"?) "X-Ray Style," a new song written almost entirely by Joe, was recorded at Battery. "Forbidden City," written by Joe much earlier in the decade, was re-recorded, as was "Diggin' the New." "The Road to Rock 'n' Roll" was reworked. The versions of "Yalla Yalla" and "Sandpaper Blues" produced by Richard Norris were added to the tunes recorded in Willesden.

The song "Tony Adams" was quixotically named after the former England and Arsenal soccer captain—even though the lyrics only contained a reference to him tucked away in a mixed-down vocal coda—after Joe had read *Addicted*, Adams's then newly published autobiography. As much of the book recounts the battle with alcohol of this master of defensive play, it is hard not to sense significance in the story having had such resonance with Joe.

The song presents Joe's image of a dystopian world, presumably New York: "All the neon blew down funky Broadway." The opening verse signified that time certainly had not withered Joe's lyrical abilities, as well as displaying a new fondness for the effectiveness of alliteration: "Stroboscopic snowflakes fell from the stratosphere."

Joe's voice was strong. "Joe was not a master of tuning, but that's not his forte," Ant said. "He's a singer. He'd choose performance over perfection any day of the week, and I think his vocals sound good on that record. We'd usually do four or five takes. Occasionally he'd drop words in later, but generally that would be it."

In typical Joe Strummer mode, the entire studio was reinvented as a spliff bunker. Although they would sometimes sleep at Damien Hirst's houseboat on Cheyne Walk in Chelsea, Joe generally rested up in the vocal overdub studio ("Hotel Overdub," as he named it) while Ant Genn got his head down in the drum booth. It was a simple life that the pair lived, aided and abetted by Richard Flack, the in-house engineer. Joe and Ant would crawl blearily out of their pits around one in the afternoon, stumbling over to a nearby Irish pub. After three or four pints ("Joe would always have a bit less. Joe was a very steady drinker"), they would leave at 5:00 p.m. At the package store on the way back to Battery Studios, Joe would buy half a bottle of brandy and several bottles of red wine; Ant would pick up a dozen cans of Strongbow cider, as well as a pack of Stella lager for Richard Flack. Back at the studio Joe and Ant would watch the double episode of *The Simpsons* that aired every night on Sky at six. ("With *The Simpsons* you can go back to work with a keen heart," said Joe later. "I'm kind of Homer, you know.") "By then all the phones had stopped," said Ant. "Joe didn't like anyone to contact him. I would very rarely see Joe with a phone to his ear. Then we'd work until we weren't inspired any longer, which was usually somewhere around five-thirty in the morning. Then we'd sleep in our respective havens."

One day early in the sessions, as they walked down Willesden High Road, Joe turned to Ant. "I've decided that this record is by the Mescaleros," he ordained, recalling that at Jazz and Lola's school Christmas carol concert he had declared this would be the name of his next group. "He had decided then this was the name of his new group, even though there were only the two of us at that time," said Ant. "Then he started to get guilty about it, wondering if it was disrespectful to the Mescalero Apaches."

When Joe arranged for Bill Price, who had worked with the Clash on *London Calling* and *Sandinista!*, to come to Battery to mix the record, the sessions didn't work out. "Joe never fucking spoke to Bill," Ant recalled. "He daren't call him. He's a fucking girl. He's a pussy, really. He used to have this thing going, 'We're men! We're men! We've got to behave like men!' But he didn't exactly live up to it."

In the pub, Joe would open up. "We got down to honest stuff. He talked about his brother killing himself. He didn't know why his brother had killed himself. He talked about his mum and his dad. He was a loner, Joe. That's why he didn't give much away. I don't think Joe ever dealt with his brother's suicide, what it meant to him. It was too painful. It was a massive thing. He didn't know what it was about. The reason he didn't know was because that family didn't talk."

That year Amanda Temple's brother also committed suicide. "She was very close to her brother and it was a horrible thing, his suicide," said Julien. "Joe was so impassioned toward her about it: 'Don't hold on to the past. Live now. Don't invest everything in the past. You've got to move on.' The way Joe dealt with the death of his own brother is on one level clinical: the situation didn't exist, and he never talked about him. But on another level it's probably the best way to deal with it. Joe's thing was you can't grieve all your life. You've got to deal with the future, and where you are now."

"You learn more about Joe Strummer from looking at the things he loved," said Ant. "The guy loved music. He loved art, he loved excellence, he loved brilliance, he loved a man that could mend a shoe. That was the poetry in Joe for me: the tiny detail. As much as Joe could focus on the big things, his attention was always on many little things."

More than might ordinarily have been the case, Joe's mind was wandering over specific aspects of the Clash: Don Letts was making the documentary Sony had commissioned and Joe gave the director a long interview, conducted by Mal Peachy, formulating his thoughts on the group. Could his on-camera metaphorical confession have helped free him from his creative past, allowing him to move forward at last? "Joe spoke very highly of Mick, what a great arranger he was," emphasized Ant. "I think that Joe had probably bullied Mick a bit, reading between the lines from conversations I had with Joe: Joe seemed intimidated by Mick's ability. I said to Mick, at a Mescaleros' Brixton Academy gig: 'I never realized until I worked with Joe what a genius you are.' Mick looked embarrassed, like I'd insulted Joe."

Every Friday afternoon Joe would walk over to nearby Cricklewood to gather supplies for the end-of-week "blowout." On Friday, March 19, 1999, while Joe was on his peregrinations through the lanes of northwest London, Ant came up with a tune. "This was never going to be a Joe Strummer song—it's a 3/4 waltz with strings and all this gentle stuff. Of course, Joe comes back and goes, 'Right, man, right. I like that. Keep going on that.' So we started that song and Joe wrote the lyrics and we mixed it and finished it at eight-thirty the next morning." The lyrics, like a pastoral ode to the joys of the area, were essentially Joe's musings as he wandered on his mission to score cocaine. "I was working with Joe Strummer," said Ant. "But I think 'Willesden to Cricklewood' is very John Mellor—those words in that song: 'Thought about my babies almost grown / Thought about going home.'

"I would love the way he would let you talk and then fly one in. I was talking in the studio with Richard Flack about how we'd like to run the marathon, how we'd been not bad runners in our day. Joe suddenly goes, 'Yeah, I've run three marathons.' What? How long did you train? 'I didn't fuckin' train. Not once. Just turned up and did it.' That was Strummer, man.

"Often I think with Joe, I had moments when I knew who he was," said Ant. "But it was still very fragmented. The reason for that is simple: he was fragmented, as a human being. He was an alcoholic. For many years he drank too much. He shit himself when I got clean and then—worse for him—Damien got clean. Meeting and hanging out with people like Damien who gives as good as he gets and is also the fuckin' king of his world had been very important for him. Because often Joe liked to have people around him who were lesser beings.

"When we went into Battery he was lost and I was lost. One thing about Joe in his ruthlessness and diplomacy and wisdom is that he's got his eyes open, all the time. For what he can get." Antony Genn laughed loudly.

After writing the songs, it became Ant's task, in his role as producer, to assemble a troupe of musicians to formally record the material with Joe. When the Mescaleros were revealed, it was apparent Joe had cherry-picked much of the finest young talent in Britain. Pablo "Pabs" Cook came in immediately on percussion. The next person in was Martin Slattery, the versatile musician whom Joe had met when he was in Black Grape, a favorite of Ant's. Bass player Scott Shields was from Glasgow; he and Martin Slattery had already played in a group together. "With Joe there was a lot of 'Are we men or are we mice?' talk," said Martin. "Joe was our friend, but it was more a work relationship. I think it would take a very long time to be connected with Joe. He would be guarded with his emotions, and he would only let you in when he truly, truly thought you wouldn't let him down. Because I've seen people let him down, and I've seen how he was with them: *Chop!* No matter how tight you were, once you'd gone, that was it. Quite ruthless."

Yet, said Martin, it was easy working with Joe at Battery. "Joe was really relaxed, and it was good fun. That's when we started to learn about Joe's working methods. I've been involved in late-night sessions before, but not where your whole life gets turned on its head. Joe was amazing at that alternative existence, just walking through Soho with him, with his blaster playing, sat outside some bar, smoking a joint. He had this invincible feeling that was a big '*Fuck you!*' to everybody."

"We were making the record and we'd be in there for days," said Ant. "Richard Flack had been going out with this girl for seven years. Working these hours, Richard's not been seeing much of her. She rings in, he picks up: 'Hi, how you doing?' 'What do you mean, how am I doing? Haven't you been home?' 'Oh, I stayed in the studio the last couple of nights. Sorry I haven't been home.' 'I haven't been there. I left you two days ago.' 'Oh, right.'

"He puts the phone down. 'She's left me.' Strummer goes: 'It was bound to happen.' Straight off the bat: 'It was bound to happen, man. Don't worry. These things happen in life.'

"There was this girl, Hayley, who worked on reception. An Irish Harlesden bird. Joe says: 'Don't worry. You're going to get together with the Harlesden girl downstairs, and make babies. That's what you're going to do.' Richard has just had twins with Hayley, his second and third child with her. The man was a prophet."

Also brought up to Battery was Ged Lynch, formerly with Black Grape, who played drums on many of the songs. When he quit the embryonic Mescaleros to tour with Marianne Faithfull, he was replaced by Smiley Bernard, who had played with Martin with Robbie Williams. Arriving at Battery for rehearsals, Smiley immediately found himself playing on "Forbidden City," soon recording the song.

In terms of Joe's lyric writing, the strength of the words of the new songs shows he had had this stuff thoroughly stored up in his unconscious, ready to flow. With the tunes added from the Richard Norris sessions, Joe had an impressive body of work set to go. And that is what he did. At last, ten years since the release of *Earthquake Weather*, Joe Strummer had a solo album waiting in the wings. The days of lack of productivity had silted into weeks and months and then years. And now—what a return, what a handsome payoff.

As the recording began to wind up, the assorted musicians started to rehearse an onstage set in Battery's live recording room. Not too assiduously, however: Joe liked rough edges.

Back home in Somerset, Joe's life continued as before. Damien Hirst was a frequent visitor to Yalway, as was Joe to the artist's home forty minutes away. In May that year the pair of them got drunk and decided to play a kind of written question-and-answer truth game. Some things Joe said were flippant, some revealing:

DH.   what is money?
JOE.   money buys the radio.
DH.   yes but what is money?
J.   money = FM network, FM network = dissemination of ideas,
       dissemination of ideas = art
DH.   what is money in one word
J.   power
DH.   what is power

J.	realizing things that you thought should be realized
D.	how much do you love luce?
J.	more than anyone else
D.	is money important to you?
J.	yes because we couldn't pursue good tunes at battery studio without paying
D.	what else is there?
J.	only social interaction when friends exchange ideas in ideal circumstances and communication on the upper levels is achieved.
D.	what do you want? (in one word)
J.	to groove.
D.	why don't you ask me what I want?
J.	because I know you want to be loved.
D.	do you care?
J.	yes 'cos you and I are the prow into an ocean of ideas or even shadows and ghosts of ideas, nevertheless sail we will.
D.	in truth who the fuck rattled your cage?
J.	my mamma never gave me no nipple
D.	what do you hold dear to you?
J.	I like feeling good
D.	can you sing?
J.	no
D.	can anyone?
J.	technique is not where it's at
D.	I know you're talented why don't you?
J.	because the oldsters were better! lets not delude ourselves!!

"Joe was very excited by the Mescaleros," said Lucinda. "He had real, proper musicians. I think he quite liked being the elder statesman. I think he felt he had earned that position and he was comfortable with it. He definitely thought about being the elder man. And he worried about having a bit of a belly, and he worried about not being slick onstage anymore and being able to do leaps and jumps. But the energy was still the same. Yet he definitely worried about being an old man with a young band. Stupidly. But on the other hand he quite enjoyed it, I think. When they toured, they toured on buses, and they didn't stay in plush hotels, and they always traveled economy. They would arrive and Joe would have to do press all day. Then they would do gigs. Then it would be up in the morning and on to the next place. The younger band members could at least [sleep late], but he would have to do interviews. He never complained once. I remember once in Toronto he did press all day and he did the gig, and I said, 'I'm going back to the hotel,' and he said, 'I can't, babe: there's all these people here.' And he came back at three in the morning: and that was just signing records, and talking to people. And we were up at six-thirty the next morning. But you could never tell Joe not to work so hard. He seemed to thrive on it: I remember saying, 'Surely you could delegate?' No: he knew he had to do it all."

On Saturday, June 5, 1999, Joe Strummer and the Mescaleros played their first show, at the Leadmill in Antony Genn's hometown of Sheffield, the same city where the Clash had played their very first date in July 1976. The set opened with "Techno D-Day" and concluded with the Clash's "Tommy Gun." Although the show was—hardly unexpectedly—a little scrappy, Joe was heartened: he was touring again, he had his own group, and he had a great record waiting to come out. Then they crossed the Pennines to Liverpool, to perform at the Lomax club the next day. If Joe needed reassurance, the Merseyside show was a critical hit; the *Guardian* reviewer wrote, "Strummer has a clutch of new material and a new skin-tight band. He leaves us with a 'Tommy Gun' so startling I drop my can of lager and grown men are seen to weep into the streets." It was working.

"He loved it when he got that first great review in the *Guardian*," said Lucinda. "He loved all that. He would say, 'I'm not reading it, because I'm not going to believe the good and I'm not going to believe the bad.' But if you went up to him with a good review, he'd be, 'Go on: show me!' He had prepared himself to be completely and utterly battered. He really wasn't expecting anything at all."

Then it was on to a date in Glasgow at King Tut's, where Joe linked up with Alasdair Gillies. "I asked them to get in a couple of bottles of malt whisky, because I knew you were coming," Joe told his cousin, before making a grand admission: "This is only the third show of the tour and I'm already exhausted." Stuffing Kit-Kat chocolate bars in his pocket from the backstage catering, Joe was then back on the bus for the all-night ride to London.

The next day was one off for the rest of the group, but Joe and Ant went straight to Battery, stripping down "Yalla Yalla" for release as a single. The

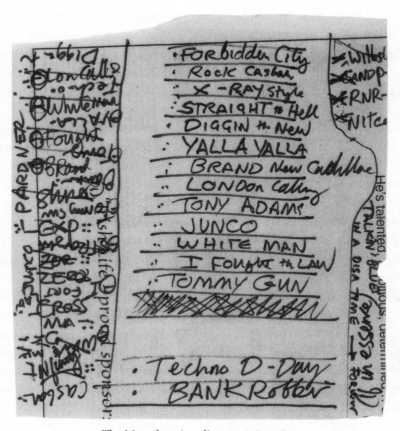

The Mescaleros' set list. *(Lucinda Mellor)*

following afternoon they drove to Portsmouth to play at the Wedgewood Rooms. What is surprising is the number of Clash songs that Joe had in the set: "London Calling," "White Man," "Straight to Hell," "Rock the Casbah," "Bankrobber" and "Tommy Gun"; soon he added "Safe European Home" and—a perennial crowd-pleaser—"Rudie Can't Fail." But, as on the Latino Rockabilly tours, the Clash tunes were often covers: "I Fought the Law" and "Brand New Cadillac" were the only examples on this first brief tour, but soon "Armagideon Time," "Pressure Drop," "Junco Partner" and "Police and Thieves" were added.

After Portsmouth Joe and the Mescaleros sprinted through European summer festivals and club dates: a Tibetan Freedom Concert in Amsterdam on June 13, the Elysée-Montmartre in Paris the next day, the Brussels Botanique on June 16 and the Markthalle in Hamburg right after that. Joe was ever anxious to cater for Antony Genn's pastoral interests. "'We can get you heroin anywhere, man,' he said to me in Brussels. 'That guy in that van—he's definitely got heroin.' Then I went off on my own to score in Brussels and came back having been sold a bag of mud."

Two days later they were in Sweden at the Hultsfredfestivalen, before a crowd of twenty-five thousand; on June 20 they were in Finland, at the Provinnsirock Festival, in the backwoods of the country. Gavin Martin, a former *NME* journalist, was there. Joe invited him up to Battery to write an in-depth article for *Uncut* magazine. "I've never seen anyone drink as much as Joe," Gavin said afterward.

They were back in England by June 26. That Saturday marked Joe's first and only appearance at the event he had transformed into his own spiritual home—the annual Glastonbury Festival, where he had established himself as a kind of king. Unfortunately this performance, on the main Pyramid stage, was not the great triumph he had hoped for. "Until then the dates had been fantastic. The group had been really steaming," said Simon Moran, his manager. "But it all fell apart at Glastonbury, just when Joe didn't want it to."

The show was great, really. There was just one problem, which happened at the end. The late-afternoon set on this muggy day started off fine, even though Joe griped at having to play before nightfall. Joe was in great voice on the crowd-warming opener, "Techno D-Day," after he declared how he had realized that Tony Blair reminded him of Cliff Richard, and he had concluded, he said, that Britain was being governed by Cliff. ("There's a picture of him with Mick Jones at Paul's first gallery opening, just after Tony Blair got in," said Lucinda. "He's wearing this white T-shirt that says 'TLF—the Tony Liberation Front: We've got to get rid of Tony Blair.' He felt totally betrayed by this Labour government. When they got in, he was so ecstatic, and he really felt betrayed.")

Not wishing to test the patience of the crowd—the material he had written and recorded with the Mescaleros would not be in the shops for another four months—and aware of what they really wanted to hear, Joe played "Rock the Casbah" as the second number, dedicating the song to "Mr. Topper Headon," and following it up with "Yalla Yalla," with its heartfelt opening lines: "Well so long liberty / Let's forget you didn't show." After the end of the next song, "London Calling," Joe delivered a rap from the center of his soul, one that included an explanation of his approach to life in recent years: "Going to festivals is one of my favorite things to do. And I'm always thinking, 'This is not meaningless!' There's something about getting together, which we have every right to do, and they're going to fuck us up on that right. You see this coming and we're going to be kept away, separated. This is a new song. It's called 'The X-Ray Style.' God help us."

Following a joyously received "White Man in Hammersmith Palais," Joe introduced the next song. "Although I'm a Chelsea fan myself, I just felt that Tony Adams had to have a eulogy as great as anything that Keats or Byron wrote," he declared with commendable lack of modesty. "And I came up with this: it's called 'Tony Adams.'"

Joe and the Mescaleros then flew into "London Calling" and "Brand New Cadillac," followed immediately by "I Fought the Law" before returning to new material with "Diggin' the New." The line "I've got no time for Luddites, always looking back" rang out with especial irony from someone who for years had been dictated by his inability to move on and adopt new recording techniques.

But during the middle of "Straight to Hell" there was a sudden eruption onstage: Joe swung his heavy mike-stand at a BBC cameraman as he came too close to him. The cameraman was in his fifties, assiduously attempting to do his job and extremely unimpressed by the incident. Luckily Joe missed him, but did catch his extremely expensive camera lens, all of which was shown later in the evening on national television, with remarks from the host about how Joe had not been in the Glastonbury spirit. "The crowd was screaming, 'Go for it! Smash it all!'" Joe later remembered.

After introducing the group, with a reference to Antony Genn's naked appearance at a previous Glastonbury, Joe and his musicians dropped in a thumping "Tommy Gun" before winding up the twelve-song set with another Clash classic: "Bankrobber."

Still, his moment of irascibility had ruined for him what should have been the finest hour so far of his comeback. "Because Ant, Martin and I had stayed up until seven in the morning doing a remix of 'Tony Adams,'" said Scott, "Joe was saying, 'Don't worry, man. I'll carry this, just watch me.' But the cameras were really in his face, and I don't think he was comfortable enough with the situation for that to be happening. The crowd was great

Writing up the set lists for his group, overseen by a young fan.
(*Rudy Fernandez*)

and the reaction was great but it was quite overwhelming for everybody, Joe included."

After the TV broadcast, the phones of those who knew Joe were red-hot, several people having the opinion this was a classic case of Joe Strummer showmanship, an endeavor to hijack attention to himself. But it was more a consequence of extreme nervousness and anxiety, and indicated Joe was still fully capable of shooting himself in the foot. The first person to whom Joe spoke when he came offstage and dived into his dressing room was Alan Yentob, an extremely senior figure at BBC Television, someone who could mollify the matter, who told Joe how fantastic he thought that his performance had been. Mark Cooper, who had written about the Clash and interviewed Joe on the *Combat Rock* tour for *Record Mirror*, was now in charge of the BBC broadcasts and saw Joe's performance. "That incident on stage was so typically Joe," he said. "Because you got the two sides of him: the on-stage lout who then goes through some apparently magical transformation and writes this extremely humble and very long letter of apology to the cameraman."

Furious with himself for his lack of control, Joe disappeared off into the vastness of the Glastonbury site, tears slithering down his face, before he threw up violently. He made his way over to the campfire where Amanda Govett and Jem and Marcia Finer were plotted up. Also there was a comedian who had been booed offstage. "He was quite hurt, being booed off the stage," said Marcia. "Then Joe comes along. He's crying. Jem was pouring him drinks and he nestled in Jem's lap for a while. I said, 'Joe, I wouldn't be too upset. Just a bad day at work. This poor guy's been booed off stage.' Joe came to life. 'Were you, man? Which stage?' I said he was a comedian. Joe said, 'How intelligent.' Then he gave a master class in comedy, ending with that joke about the piece of string that goes into a bar." "I do think there was suddenly a lot more pressure for him to be Joe Strummer," thought Jem Finer.

F ollowing Joe's controversial performance at Glastonbury—far less a failure for those who watched him than for himself—there was little time for maudlin self-recrimination. Beckoning was the group's first tour of the United States. Two days later, they were flying to Washington, D.C., the capital of a country then under the semiliberal auspices of President Bill Clinton. There was an ominous moment as the group arrived at immigration at Dulles airport. Andy Boo, the guitar tech, was stopped by customs; he was carrying Antony Genn's guitar case, inside which—unbeknownst to Andy—were twenty morphine capsules. "We'd come from Glastonbury. When I was there I'd put them in the case and forgotten about them," admitted Ant. Andy Boo was hauled off for questioning, where it was accepted he had had no knowledge of the drugs. Luckily there was nothing to identify Ant Genn as the owner of the guitar.

On Tuesday, June 29, the group's brief, water-testing American dates began at the 9:30 Club on D.C.'s V Street, to positive local press response. Shows followed at Irving Plaza in New York (where Joe and his group filmed a video for "Yalla Yalla"), the Cabaret Metro in Chicago, the Milwaukee Summerfest, the San Francisco Fillmore and the Palace in Los Angeles. Throughout this brief tour the "young musicians" in Joe's new group were especially commended, while Joe received reverential reviews worthy of his status as a British national treasure. To the group, their singer seemed a strange one. "The first American tour we did, I didn't really know what was going on," said Martin Slattery, "but Joe was a really angry person. He distanced himself from us, wouldn't come into the dressing room. It was hard to know what was going on in his head."

Arriving back in Britain, they returned to Glasgow to play the T in the Park festival on July 8. Following a three-week summer break, they flew to Japan for their slot on August 1 at Fuji Rock. When ZZ Top, who were headlining that day, realized that as the bill was running late they might miss their flight out of Japan, they asked if they could swap slots with the Mescaleros. "Fuck off," said Joe.

On Friday, August 13, the group played in France at the Free Wheels Festival at Clermont-Ferrand. All but Joe were concerned about how he would respond after a sixteen-hour journey and saw how their performance was being sold at the site: "A tribute to the Clash: Joe Strummer and the Mescaleros." The posters were hurriedly taken down before Joe got to see any of them.

One week later they played before twenty thousand people at the Two Days a Week Festival in Wiesen, Austria, then crossed the border to Germany to play at the Bizarre Festival in Cologne, where the group's set was shown on television. Much of the audience was there for the American metal bands on the bill; some responded to Joe's appearance by throwing razor blades. Joe picked out a member of the audience who was wearing a T-shirt celebrating anarchy: "Who gave you your anarchy T-shirt? Was it your fucking mother?" "The guy was giving the finger," said Scott Shields. "Joe's like, 'Come up here and do that!' He gets him up on the stage, and the guy's about six foot six. The bouncers are holding the guy back, and Joe's going: 'You fucking pussy!' Then he walks away from it, thank God. There was the potential there for Joe to get crucified. It was really scary. There were a few of those moments." Back in his hotel room, Joe watched a documentary about the Beach Boys and burst into tears.

After a date in Portugal, there were shows in Dublin and Belfast. In the group's history the Dublin show became legendary. "The whole place literally wouldn't leave," said Ant Genn. "The promoter came into the dressing room and said, 'You've got to do another song.' But we'd played every song we knew. So Joe said he'd go and tell them they had to leave. As he left, I said, 'Let's play "London Calling" again.' Just as he got out there the tour manager said to Joe, 'Do "London Calling" again. The whole band's behind you.'"

In Dublin Joe was joined by Charles Shaar Murray, who was writing an article for *The Daily Telegraph*. Hunkered over the hotel bar at three in the morning, Charles found Joe to be reinvigorated, with the strength to look back on his past with clear eyes.

When Charles discussed the notion of the-Clash-as-political-group, he suggested that Joe had always come more from an anarchist tradition than one of strict socialism. "I'm more of a Merry Prankster type of person than a committed anything," Joe immediately agreed. "I realized that I didn't know anything about anything. What I'd like to do personally is to start all over again. If I had a red button here and if I pushed it everything in the world would vanish and we'd be nomads walking the grasslands, I'd push it straightaway. I wouldn't even hesitate. Because money runs this nonsense, and they're gonna feed us gasoline and oil until the world is a dead shell. I'd like to think the Clash were revolutionaries, but we loved a bit of posing as well. 'Where's the hair gel? We can't start the revolution till someone finds the hair gel!' We were revolutionaries on behalf of punk rock.

"I've never envied U2. I often thought, 'Thank God we didn't have to do that, that huge circuit,' because I wanted to be a person. Also, I stayed at home when my kids were growing up. I've got two children from my first marriage who are fifteen and thirteen now, and I'm glad I can remember 'em when they were one, two, three, four, five, six, seven. It was the best career move I ever made, not releasing any records, because you're not letting people down with crap albums. You're still in with a shout, and that's why I'm rocking here and having a good time, because I didn't put a record out. If I had, I think I'd have been rowed out of here already.

"I had a crisis of self-confidence around '85, when all that went down. But I outlived 'em. It's like a Vietcong maneuver: go out in the bushes and wait it out. Dig a few tunnels."

When Charles asked Joe about his new material, his reply was succinct: "I only realized what it was about the other night when I typed all the lyrics out for the new record. It came to me that, without getting too pompous, the record's about freedom—although I never planned it. They're anti-democratic, those politicians, they want power for as long as they can hold it, and it's going to take an earthquake to get rid of 'em. And then we got nothing to replace 'em with. We're fucked. They've got us in a real half nelson."

"So where would you put yourself politically these days?" Charles asked him.

"In the DMT universe! I'm in the Psychedelic Home Rangers."

Although he probably knew what the answer would be, the needs of journalism required Charles to ask the sucker-punch question: "What's the single worst decision you ever took?"

"Could I have two for the price of one? Firstly, to fire Topper Headon, and secondly, to fire Mick Jones. Topper was a heroin addict, but at the time we didn't really understand what that was. We could have been more intelligent and gone, 'OK, he's strung out on heroin, but so was Charlie Parker. So was Miles Davis.'"

The group drove on to Belfast, Joe stashing his weed in the bottom layer of a tin of biscuits as they crossed the border. After two more European dates, Joe Strummer and the Mescaleros came off the road for six weeks, until the beginning of another British tour.

A lthough the working title of the Clash live album had been *On the Road with the Clash,* by the time it was released in October 1999 it had been named *From Here to Eternity.* A fifty-minute cut of *Westway to the World,* the documentary commissioned by Sony from Don Letts, was aired on BBC 2 the same month. Already the eighty-five-minute feature-length version had been screened at the Notting Hill Coronet, followed by a party at the Cotton Club on Kensal Road in Notting Hill. Joe, Mick, Paul and Topper, who resolutely ignored the musical instruments optimistically set up on the stage, had been swamped by media figures anxious for association with these legends. The film, for which director Don Letts was awarded a Grammy, is a definitive look at the career of the Clash; each of the four members gave Don customarily frank interviews. As so often Joe played both sides of the park, comparing Mick to "Elizabeth Taylor on a bad hair day," but then admitting, "Sometimes genius is worth waiting for." Mick was remarkably forthright. "I didn't understand about self-control," he admitted. In many ways the film was more illuminating than the live record it was intended to promote. Don Letts told me that when putting together the footage Joe was by far the most narcissistically finicky of the group: he wouldn't let Don include a clip from a TV show—he no longer liked the Davy Crockett hat he was wearing in it.

Busy with his new record, Joe had given over the project to Mick Jones and Paul Simonon, offering virtually no input. Unexpectedly, *From Here to Eternity* had something of a museum piece feel. The live album was made up of seventeen songs from nine concerts; the disparity between the different performances meant that the record lacked the fluidity that would have come from a single show. It crept into the U.K. Top Ten, but curiously failed to sell in the United States, previously the biggest market for the Clash.

Although this affected Joe's bank account, he personally had bigger fish to fry. *Rock Art and the X-Ray Style,* as the Mescaleros record was titled, was released on November 2. It could not have been a better time. The release of the live album and the presence of *Westway to the World,* along with a barrage of related publicity and interviews, ensured the profile of the Clash and its individual members was as high as it had been since *Combat Rock.* The record's title came from a chapter title in a 1930s book Joe had found; "X-Ray Style" was a genre of cave paintings in which animals were painted with the bones of their skeletons showing. Nowhere in the packaging of *Rock Art and the X-Ray Style* were there any pictures of Joe or of the Mescaleros. The artwork was by Damien Hirst; the front sleeve was in vivid pink, adorned with extremely primal sketches of people and animals which had been photographically lifted from cave paintings. "Every figure on the cover was done sixty thousand years ago. Every animal and picture is from beyond history," said Joe, emphasizing his belief in the timeless continuity of existence, a belief that had been reinforced by lying on his back at Yalway, gazing at the stars with the likes of Dermot Mitchell (once they had clearly watched a UFO), and the ingestion of all manner of psychedelics.

Rock Art and the X-Ray Style got great reviews. "Triumphant return by former Clash legend . . . an album brimming with hope and optimism, that looks forward both musically and lyrically . . . mesmerizing," read some of the review in *Uncut.* "A joy, worth spending both time and money on," said *Q.* "He was definitely pleasantly surprised and really happy that people liked the record," said Lucinda. "He thought he would never be forgiven for breaking up the Clash. It had weighed heavily on him. He'd got over it, but he was aware that was what people were going to think. But he obviously got to a stage where he said, 'I don't care: I'm going to do it. Fuck it: I'll give it a go.' That's why he did it."

Before the record could hit the shops, Joe and the Mescaleros embarked on a full British tour. Damien took Joe to Harrods to buy a suit for onstage wear—but Joe chose one on sale, "a half-price, simple suit." Nottingham Rock City on October 18 and Leeds Town and Country Club the following night were sellouts. The London dates followed after a day off: a pair of packed nights at the two-thousand-capacity Astoria, a venue by Tottenham Court Road tube station with seriously sticky carpets. For Joe this was the big return, London dates always pulling everyone—family, friends, fellow conspirators, a few unbelievers (mainly in the media)—out of the woodwork. The second night was one of the best concerts I had seen in years. "I thought I'd never see another rock 'n' roll show like that," said Rick Elgood, the producer of *Westway to the World*. Before the first Astoria show, Joe was on the local television news, worryingly seeming a rather puffy-faced talking head. But now in front of the heaving crowd he looked really good, almost glowing as he belted through a set of new material and old Clash hits.

The Astoria was rammed with men of a certain age in black leather jackets. Even though the show was superb—passionate, profound and intimately personal—there were moments when I thought Joe might physically explode onstage from the ferocity of his performance, sweat pouring in visible rivers down his face, veins bulging out on his forehead and neck until you thought they might pop. Though I loved the evening, I thought I detected something forced about the singer's act, as though he was willing himself on, pushing himself into the part of Joe Strummer the Rabble-Rousing Rocker.

(My suspicion that Joe was playing a part was correct. Sixteen days later in Las Vegas he told me in his gravelly voice, "I've only just begun performing in the last two or three days, and really getting to it. I was uptight since June 5, when I started, acting it. But then you realize you've got to jump that and get over it. I like to be a performer when I get up there. I'm at machine-pace now.")

Joe's penchant for sprinkling his speech with oddities remained; two-thirds of the way into the set, Joe introduced the next number: "Here's a Toots Hibbert song, a long-time favorite with the peeps: it's called 'Pressure Drop.'" ("The peeps—he'd call people the peeps," explained Damien Hirst.)

"This is going out to Paul Simonon and Mick Jones!" was his introduction to a rapturously received "White Man." Topper naturally received the "Rock the Casbah" moment. The audience did not seem to have any trouble with the new material, which hardly anyone had yet heard. But I couldn't identify any of Joe's onstage musical cohorts; I didn't remember seeing any of them before. It felt like a party with unfamiliar faces, slightly odd.

The next day I turned on the local BBC radio station, Joe's favorite, and an announcer was describing it as one of the shows of the year; the review in the *Guardian* said something similar.

But the London dates were not without an ominous rumble within the soul of one of the musicians. "We played two nights at the Astoria and it was fantastic," said Ant Genn. "I think after that was probably when I lost interest."

Joe Strummer—never without a pen or a notebook.
(*Lucinda Mellor*)

The British tour carried on to Norwich, Cardiff, Manchester and Glasgow. Scott Shields was happy to be playing in his hometown at Barrowlands. In this Scottish city there was controversy. When Scott woke up in his bunk in the bus as it arrived in Glasgow, he found the driver telling everyone to get off the vehicle and not return, threatening to call the police. "One of the Manc posse had been doing heroin at the front of the bus, and there was tinfoil everywhere," said Scott. "Joe was hanging off the front windshield wiper of the bus and shouting at the guy as he was driving it off. We checked into a hotel in Glasgow where there was a police convention. We'd commandeered the lobby and Joe was passing round joint after joint, trying to get one up on the police. Joe loved to push it: make sure that he had his last joint at the airport in New York before he was about to leave in the plane, turning up at four in the morning smoking weed with music blasting out of his ghetto blaster. Causing absolute chaos was like a hobby."

Three days later Joe Strummer and the Mescaleros were on the West Coast of the United States for a nineteen-date tour of significant venues, beginning at the Seattle Showbox on November 1. As the tour bus wound its way to the next date in Portland—Joe also played a solo acoustic set at the same city's Music Millennium record store—he felt a need to drive home some cold realities to the Mescaleros. "I'm so glad I'm not you young guys, because you're going to be disappointed. People in America won't listen to us. I'm glad I'm not one of the young guys that are really hungry for success and fame because you're not going to get it."

"He was trying to resign us," said Scott, "to the fact that we weren't going to be liked, we weren't going to be played on the radio. I think he genuinely felt bad for the young guys in the band. But the good thing was that Joe had this whole ethos of why he was doing it: 'I have to promote this record, because if we don't break even on this record we will never get a chance to make another record.'"

Rock Art and the X-Ray Style not only broke even, but went into profit, selling around 150,000 copies worldwide. Within a couple of years Joe was receiving royalty checks.

On the bus it was largely a professional relationship, the group members occupying the lounge at the rear of the vehicle while Joe would hunker down at the front, often with Andy Boo, his guitar tech. As in the days of the Clash, Joe would hardly speak during the daylight hours before a show, sucking lozenges and sipping herbal teas. A bolstering glass of pre-show brandy aside, alcohol hardly touched his lips until after his performance. At sound check he would leave the group to play on their own, joining in only if there had been a problem he was anxious to rectify. "The only time we really spoke was after the show, at night when we were back on the bus," said Scott. "It was a bizarre relationship really. Sometimes he was like your father, sometimes he was like your devil, sometimes he was somebody that you just couldn't understand. Onstage Joe always let you feel there was an edge, so you didn't know what was coming next, and you'd be caught off guard. At first I was quite nervous in this band." As with the Latino Rocka-billy War, Joe—unseen by the audience—conducted the group with hand signals behind his back. If a cue was missed it was not unknown for the of-fender to find an object whirling his way.

After playing in Portland's Roseland Theatre, the group moved on to San Francisco, another sellout date at the Fillmore on November 4. Here Joe linked up with Rudy Fernandez, who traveled with him to the next dates, in southern California. On the tour bus, sitting at a table at the front of the bus at five in the morning, with everyone else on the bus asleep, Joe put a Dexter Gordon CD on his ghetto blaster. As the beautiful music sailed out of the speakers, Joe turned to Rudy. "This is the good life," he said.

After a November 5 show at the Sun Theater in Anaheim, the home of Disneyland, the tour moved to Los Angeles proper. The next evening was a date at the House of Blues on Sunset Boulevard. I had flown out to write an article for the *Daily Telegraph*'s Saturday magazine. When I turned up around 5:00 p.m. for the sound check, I found Joe in his dressing room, en-gaged in a series of interviews as Lucinda busied herself in a neighboring room—she had flown out for the show with Damien Hirst and his wife, Maia. "Grab a beer," said Joe. As I waited for him, I talked to a friend of Alex Cox. A DVD of *Straight to Hell* was scheduled for release and Alex had asked his mate to interview Joe on camera for the DVD extras. I mentioned this to Joe, who immediately postponed everything else he was doing, posi-tioning himself at the rear of the House of Blues to talk about *Straight to Hell*. As he was supposed to be promoting *Rock Art and the X-Ray Style*, this caused controversy; an MTV crew had to wait, which kept Joe happy— when he had turned up earlier that year at the offices of MTV in New York, wired for sound with his ghetto blaster, Joe had been shocked that he had been asked to turn down the volume.

Although more hesitant than at the Astoria, the show was still a stormer, with a phalanx of celebrities in the audience, including actor Robbie Coltrane, Sex Pistol Steve Jones and even Kiss's Gene Simmons, who had once soundly denounced punk rock to me. Afterward there was a party at the Viper Room, so packed that it was claustrophobic. Joe and I were supposedly scheduled to do an interview while he was in L.A., but there was no way this was going to happen. The next day I flew to Las Vegas, where he was playing the Joint, inside the Hard Rock Hotel.

Early that evening I sat down with Joe and Lucinda at a table in the Vegas branch of Nobu, the chic Japanese restaurant. They seemed very easy together, very comfortable to be with.

A discussion of the finer points of magic mushrooms led to me asking if Joe's move to the country was the final proof that punks had always been hippies with short hair. "Not really, because I started out a hippie, and I ended up a punk. So I'd say the difference was, hippies were trying to believe in the illusion of an alternative world, and punks knew that to create that alternative world something had to be done.

"I've gone through both trips, and my only conclusion is that we were better out on the land. When we were hunter-gatherers we were happier people. You had time to express yourself. That's when people are happiest, when they are expressing themselves, being in the creative universe. Instead of spending ten hours a day pumping the job. For what? So you can build these malls and buy these shitty goods here? To desecrate the world for this? It ain't no bargain. The world is going to turn against all this. This world we're in, especially here right now, is the equivalent of genetically modified tomatoes. The Disney experience and the mall is hollow—it looks good, but there's nothing there. The hash browns look great but they taste of nothing. From A to Z, it's a brilliant scam. If you raise your voice you're going to be fined. If we rolled up some marijuana and smoked it, we'd be in jail. But we're only smoking the herb that grows in the earth. Everybody is out of their fucking minds here anyway."

It was this distaste for modern existence, Joe told me as we ate our exotic sushi, that had led to his fondness for festival life. "The only reason I hang on the festival scene is that I've been to a few free ones and they were the ones where you felt, This is getting there, everyone pitching in together. I'd like to get involved with some of the free festival throwdowns and help bring them about."

I asked him about his itinerant, tramplike existence. "Me and Bo Did-dley are the same: you can't keep us out of dumpsters. It must be a disease. Have you seen those shopping bags in my room? Now all I need is a shop-ping cart: a few bum records and I'm away with my cart. It must be a dis-ease, this cart, shopping-bag-itis. It's universal, isn't it? You see cats in Holland, cats in Vegas, women in Helsinki."

And here we discussed one of the central elements in the life of Joe Strummer: his fondness for placing things in plastic bags. "Because they hold things and you can put things in them. And come back to them later, sometimes many years later."

A full moon had peaked on the night that Joe and the Mescaleros had played in Anaheim. Now, on the wane of the moon, the Vegas show was not a sellout, with only maybe 500 people there out of a 1,500 possible capacity, the energy dipping. ("Darling, it was a Sunday," Lucinda said to me after-ward.) But the smallness of the venue and the crowd gave the evening an intimacy lacking at the House of Blues. "A lot of people have come here tonight from L.A.," said Joe. "So let's get on with it." Yet, later on, there was an onstage contretemps. Joe chinned "a cunt" who'd jumped on the stage before the last verse of "Tommy Gun," knocking drink into the micro-phone. "Do what you like, but don't fuck with me here," Joe bellowed, al-most a statement of his existence.

In the dressing room after the show he reintroduced me to Damien Hirst and his wife, telling them the story about the carnival and the house invasion, embarrassingly complimentary. Then Joe told me something that startled me: his dentist had recently informed him he had had a hairline fracture in his jaw from when the rude boys steamed his house fourteen years previously.

"Thanks for coming. Now we're going to cross over and lose all our money. It's a cruel world," Joe had uttered at the end of the group's set. Joe and I agreed gambling was pointless, but we wanted to go to "old Vegas," where Frank and Dino would have hung out. We stopped for a couple of drinks in Caesar's, but the bar staff's requests for ID rankled with the older members of the party. We ended up in the Golden Nugget, original old-style, down-at-heel and laden with atmosphere, where a gnomic, wizened figure in his eighties who looked like he might have been a *consigliere* of Meyer Lansky assiduously counted and recounted the chips and—you felt—possibly controlled the hookers who regularly approached us. Joe loved it. "I remember Joe saying, 'Check out that old bloke over there, the overweight kind of husky guy,'" recalled Chris LaSalle, the Hellcat Records publicist, in town for the show. "Joe was sitting there writing out his bits of ideas about the place on a napkin. One from that night always struck me: 'The shards of America.'"

Around 4:30 in the morning the assembled company stepped into the street for a spliff. It suddenly dawned on me that we were in Las Vegas. "You can bet your bottom dollar we're on closed-circuit TV right now," I muttered to Joe. We decided to go back to the Hard Rock and jumped in some taxis. As we drove off a pair of police cars cruised up to precisely where we had been standing. I shared a cab with Damien and Maia. Damien explained how he was considering an art piece that would be a forty-foot-high pile of shit, which he would call "Untitled Number 2." Which I did think was potentially very funny. But—as Damien explained to me later—Joe didn't: "He said, 'Don't do it. It'll be bad for your career.' I said to him once, 'I can do anything. I've got more freedom than a musician.' He said, 'You couldn't go to your opening in a fez.'

"I think he used to like my work. I'd come up with stuff like, 'I'm an artist. I'm prepared to die for my art.' Then he gave me a plastic lighter— 'Artists—hah!' he'd written on it. He'd always goad me. At first I thought he was looking down on me as an artist. But he was encouraging me.

"When he was round at my house and people were wittering away on drugs, he'd throw in, 'You can't talk about the past or the present, only the future.' That shut people up when they suddenly went, 'You know, when I was fifteen . . .'"

I staggered off to bed and the next lunchtime, a day off from the tour, we went to a shopping mall where Joe had a shoe shine and we did a formal interview. Returning to the Hard Rock, food was ordered on the patio. "Can sour cream go off?" Joe inquired of the waitress. "Oh, I'm not sure. Is there a problem?" she asked, worried. "No," said Joe, "it's just a philosophical question."

"When we arrived in New York for the Roseland date, which was being filmed for HBO," said Ant Genn, "I got off the tour bus at 8:30 a.m. and found at the front of the vehicle Joe was lying on the floor, red wine stains all over his mouth. I go, 'You all right, man?' He whispers back incoherently. His voice is fucked. But what he would always do would be to not talk all day, and take loads of lozenges, and have his honey and lemon and just get through it. At that Roseland gig he started some bollocks with the bouncer, and there was tension there, and he knew I didn't like him getting like that." But at the Roseland show there was also a problem within the group over Antony Genn himself. "I turned up to the gig a minute before we were due onstage. I'd been in Queens scoring heroin," he admitted. "I had a bruise over my eye and only one shoe, track marks all over my arms, and we're in front of HBO cameras."

During the last days of this second Mescaleros U.S. tour, Ant Genn's heroin addiction took hold. Before leaving Britain for America he had gone to a clinic and had the drugs pumped out of him. "As soon as I got to San Francisco I was getting homeless people to score for me. Wherever we were, I'd get a cab to the needle exchange and find some junkies: 'You get me mine, I'll pay for yours.' Or get in a cab and say, 'Take me to the worst part of town, where all the junkies and prostitutes are.'"

Ant's personal crisis did not interfere with the customary afterhours celebrations. "We'd be in some bar and there'd be John Cusack and Matt Dillon and Joey Ramone and Debbie Harry and Tina Weymouth and Chris Frantz and all these legends. But Joe would be talking to Justin the barman, and going, 'Hey, Joey Ramone, didn't you once go to Hawaii? Yeah, this guy's bird lives in Hawaii. Hey, Cusack, come here. You've got to meet Justin. You'll love this guy.' He was a great puller-together of people. I loved that about him."

After their gig in Philly, Joe and the group played "Tony Adams" and "London Calling" on *The Conan O'Brien Show*. Then they flew home to London, and three dates in Europe: Barcelona on December 2, Milan on the fourth and Paris on the seventh. That was it for the year, the most productive for Joe Strummer for at least a decade. In Las Vegas he had had a whim to have run off a set of millennium-themed T-shirts bearing the slogan "Same Shirt, Different Century." Such an item of apparel could almost have been a testament to the utter shift in existence that had taken place for Joe in the previous twelve months: Same Man, Different Life.

———

At least Joe hadn't stolen this microphone from the English National
Opera . . . *(John Zimmerman/Proper-Gander)*

A s ever, Joe did not stand still for long. Since August 29, 1998, he'd been broadcasting a weekly show on the BBC World Service, the short-wave radio station which had an estimated global audience of 40 million. Music he played varied from Woody Guthrie's "This Land Is Your Land," performed by Trini Lopez, the Chicano star of the late 1950s and 1960s, through the Senegalese-Jamaican fusion of Baaba Maal and Ernest Ranglin, to yet-to-be-released tracks by the Mescaleros. Joe's style—his first gig as a radio deejay—was terse and to the point: "Dig it!" he demanded of his audience following the Trini Lopez track. "That's a train you have to ride all the way to the end," Joe said, after playing a seven-minute track by Cornershop.

"Joe came up with the idea for a show," said Andy Norman, Joe's first producer. "He grabbed a pen and paper and wrote down 'Cross-Cultural Transglobal Show.' 'We need another title,' I said. 'We should call it Joe Strummer's London Calling.'"

At first, Joe found the rigors of BBC schedules and working from a script tough. "He didn't get back to me when I faxed him a script," recalled Andy Norman. "Then I discovered that someone had sent him a fax asking to use a Clash track as a dog-food commercial. He had been so furious that he tore it up, along with my script, which he hadn't even seen."

Making it clear that his life was now a family business, he would be accompanied to the studio by Lucinda, Jazz, Lola and Eliza. "There was a really odd mix of radio team, family, fans and Joe all milling around outside the studio," said Andy Norman. Joe had fans in high places, such as the head of the World Service, Mike Byford. "Mike was a rampant Strummer fan, and came down to the studio to meet him," said the producer of the second series, Simon Barnett. "I think Joe was delighted that this important man had come down to see him."

Joe would gather his week's playlist from many sources. The Radio One deejay Andy Kershaw had a late Sunday evening show. From time to time he would receive phone calls from Joe, asking for the names of tunes he had played. "Joe had one of those plastic battery-operated record players," remembered Simon Barnett, "marketed at children. He'd come up with his kids, and get a black cab and drive round and round London in it listening to the records."

"Joe loved the idea of retro technology. The cheapest and the tinniest was always best as far as he was concerned," Simon Barnett said. "He played more U Roy than anyone else, and Bob Dylan, a bit of bangra, cumbia, and loads of African music. He insisted on playing vinyl. 'I can get you the CD.' 'No, let's play the scratchy vinyl. It'll sound better on short wave.' All he tried to do was capture a mood and it would always flow nicely, a great half hour."

Joe may have objected to a Clash song being used in a dog-food commercial—he of course had not complained overly in 1991, when "Should I Stay or Should I Go" had given the group their first number 1 in Britain after being employed in an ad for Levi's. But he was not so squeamish about more upmarket, noncanine products. In the spring of 2002 "London Calling" could be heard on U.S. television in an advertisement for Jaguar's new X-type model. For their participation the Clash received $50,000. Joe's share of the cut from such an ad could help finance the Mescaleros for a few more weeks. "I agreed to that," Joe told the Mescaleros website. "We get hundreds of requests for that and turn 'em all down. But I just thought, Jaguar . . . yeah. If you're in a group and you make it together, then everyone deserves something. Especially twenty-odd years after the fact. We've turned down loads of money. Millions over the years." That same year "London Calling" also was used as part of the soundtrack in the James Bond film *Die Another Day*. Also in 2002 on the MTV Video Music Awards, former New York mayor Rudy Giuliani made his entrance to the chorus from "Rudie Can't Fail," also from the *London Calling* album. "Should I Stay or Should I Go" was revived that year as part of a Stolichnaya Citrona vodka campaign.

In the middle of January 2000 Joe and the Mescaleros returned to Japan. Lucinda and Eliza went with him. For the first show, at the Zepp in Osaka, Joe taught the Mescaleros "Police on My Back," the Eddie Grant song on *Sandinista!*, by playing it in the van on the way to the gig. Joe probably needed something to keep him awake. Jet lag took a far greater toll on his forty-seven-year-old body than in the days when touring with the Clash; the nine hours' time difference between Britain and Japan would take it out of him. "At the beginning of that tour Joe was really stressed out," Scott recalled. "Joe would get very bad jet lag. He'd get really fucked up by it, especially going to Japan. He'd get run-down and he'd get a cold. You could see it was hard for him, just to get to the gig and do the gig. One show, Joe was actually lying on the floor in the dressing room curled round my legs. Then he stood up and said, 'Hey guys, let's go outside and take a break—it's so hot in here.'"

Once Joe's body became adjusted to the time difference, it was business as usual. "We'd take it in turns to stay up with him all night," said Scott, "because somebody had to. In Paris we were out once and it was nine-thirty in the morning and I was like, 'Joe, I've got to go to bed,' and Joe said, 'If you go to bed, you're sacked.' But I think the Joe that I knew was a very different character to the Joe a lot of people knew from the Clash days, based on what I've heard. By contrast, I knew a very chilled-out Joe."

Things had certainly changed since the old days. Having spent at least two decades pursuing casual sexual encounters with what seemed close to neurosis, had this drive been extinguished since he had married Lucinda? "No, mate, Joe wasn't chasing skirt," Ant Genn replied. "He was chasing booze." "Joe just didn't strike me as a very sexual person at all," said Martin.

Scott added, "I don't know if I would necessarily have liked the old Joe. I have seen him being [aggressive], but very irregularly. I saw him kick a record company A&R guy up the ass in the streets of Tokyo when we were there in 2000. The guy was taking it, because he knew Joe was right. People had told Joe they couldn't find the record in the shops. 'I can't believe it!' he's bellowing. 'You're useless!' The guy's going, 'I know, Joe. I'm so sorry!' 'What's the point of me doing six or seven hours of interviews every single day if they can't buy the record?' He worked so hard, though. It wasn't apparent to us, but when there was an album campaign he'd always be doing interviews, busting his balls to spread the word."

Following three Japanese dates, the group flew to New Zealand for eight Australasian shows, part of the annual Big Day Out touring festival. The first was in a forty-thousand-seat stadium in Auckland. On the package's bill were the Foo Fighters, Primal Scream, the Chemical Brothers, Beth Orton and the Red Hot Chili Peppers. With the Chili Peppers was Dick Rude. In the first half of the 1990s Dick had had his own battles with heroin, falling off Joe's radar, but now he was clean. "I loved his new band," he said, "but I could sense the lineup wasn't right. I could see where it was wrong, the drug addiction thing. The word was out this was a very druggy group, and that image was being reflected onto Joe, even though he was never a great participant. He probably learned from his experience with Topper. He seemed to be handling the situation with Ant in a pretty cool way, but I could see it was bothering him. There was an effect on the unit as a whole."

"For us, not so much for Joe, the Big Day Off—as we called it—was a total drug-fest," admitted Martin Slattery.

Joe was otherwise engaged during the Big Day Out. Some of the Manc posse had followed them down under, and gone on a spree. When questioned by a suspicious hotel manager as to one of their identities, Joe feigned confusion. "We just call him 'the Boss,'" he replied, nodding to himself. Joe, Lucinda and Eliza drove with his Manchester mates down the Australian coast to Sydney for a warm-up date at the one-thousand-capacity Sydney Metro on George Street, followed by the Big Day Out proper at the RAS Showground on January 26. "People would come up to Joe and say: 'You really changed my life with that song,'" remembered Scott. "They're still harboring all these thoughts and feelings that they've had since the first time they heard that Clash song. I think it was hard for him when he wasn't feeling particularly comfortable with himself. His self-confidence really flourished over the time I knew him.

"At first onstage he was edgy, tetchy and generally pissed off. It wasn't a nice vibe to be around. You didn't know whether he was going to go off at you or at somebody else. You'd just wait for him to snap out of it."

"In the smoking breaks between rehearsals," said Martin, "me and Scott would jam a lot, and Joe started taping us on this little Fisher-Price plastic tape recorder. Somewhere he realized what me and Scott could do. We started to feel a connection with him, and realized it wasn't us creating the bad energy. It all filtered into this moment where Ant almost imploded."

Yet not everyone observed negativity in the relationship between Joe Strummer and Ant Genn. Early on the Big Day Out tour Jack Notman, who worked with Primal Scream, had been complaining he couldn't find any weed. A few minutes later he walked past Joe, with whom he had shared "no more than three words." "Hey, Jack," Joe called out. When Jack turned toward him, surprised that Strummer even knew his name, a grinning Joe chucked him a packet of grass. He realized Joe was either psychic or had very big ears. In Australia Jack noticed how Joe and Ant Genn would go and sit by the side of the stage for the first four numbers of Primal Scream's set, to get energized for their own show. "Joe would go to watch the Primals to get vibed up for his show, and then the Primals would go to watch Joe, to come down from their own set," said Jack. The Mescaleros watched as Joe psyched himself up before he went on stage. "Prior to the shows Joe had a little Zen routine," said Martin, "almost working himself into a near-trance, to get the energy so the foot didn't stop pumping the ground. This trance-like state was part and parcel of the show. Occasionally if he turned around you'd get a wry smile. 'It's still me. Don't worry.'"

In Melbourne Ant was mugged scoring heroin. After a date in Adelaide, the Australasian tour finished on February 6 in Perth, where they had four days off. Living there in Western Australia was Mick Jones's replacement guitarist, Nick Sheppard; he and his family linked up with Joe, Luce and Eliza. "We went to the beach one day, and there was no baggage. One evening in a bar Joe turned to me and said, 'I'm sorry.' I said, 'No problem. I got a lot out of it.' Later Joe said, 'I'm going back to the hotel—I can't keep up with these guys.'"

"Luce's influence on him was great," said Damien Hirst. "She kept him on the straight and narrow. Which some people didn't like." Then the group flew home to the United Kingdom. "When we checked in for the flight," said Lucinda, "it was virtually empty: four seats each at the back of the plane. As we walked onto the plane, Eliza said, 'Why can't we ever sit in first-class?' Joe said, 'That's for famous rock stars, Eliza, who make lots of money. Not for the likes of me.' And as we walked past, I heard one of the stewards say, 'That's Joe Strummer.' He was the uncle of Richard Ashcroft [of the Verve]. He came up to us, and said, 'Would you like to be upgraded?' Joe said, 'No, no, we're quite happy.' I said, 'Bloody right we would.' And we flew first-class all the way back to England from Perth. Which was great."

On March 31 Joe and the group were in New York City for a one-off show to celebrate the fifteenth anniversary of *Spin* magazine. The gig was at the Bowery Ballroom on Manhattan's Lower East Side. The afternoon before the show Joe and Josh Cheuse took a subway ride out to Queens, to the headquarters of VP Records, the U.S. distributors of some of the finest Jamaican music. Ushered into the storage vault, Joe was in ecstasy as the assorted vinyl treasures were unveiled: "Oh my God, this is too much." Finding a room rammed with cassettes upped Joe's joy level. "Wow, this is great. I always wanted a cassette of that." Joe and Josh returned to Manhattan each weighed down with a huge box of reggae, for which—despite the protestations of the VP owners—Joe insisted on paying.

On April 4 Joe and Pablo Cook appeared at the Royal Festival Hall in London at the "Poetry Olympics," playing an adaptation of "London Calling/London's Burning" dedicated to the beat poet Michael Horovitz, Britain's answer to Allen Ginsberg, for his sixty-fifth birthday. Among others on the bill were the renowned dub poet Linton Kwesi Johnson and the Mancunian punk poet John Cooper Clarke.

In May, beginning in Dublin on the first of the month, Joe and the Mescaleros undertook a short tour, concluding with a Saturday-night show at a sold-out Brixton Academy, where Joe had played with both the Clash and the Pogues. Standing a third of the way back from the front of the stage, I watched Joe's show with Mick Jones, noticing how he unselfconsciously mouthed his own backing vocal parts on the Clash songs Joe played. There was something indefinably profound as well as almost achingly humble about Mick's doing this, just one of the audience, still a pop fan even when it was half his own work. This London show—which had a rapturous reception—also included the only performance by Joe Strummer and the Mescaleros of "Sandpaper Blues." Afterward the dressing room was packed to the gills. I saw Joe in a corner, tucked away on his own, no one speaking to him. I hugged him and said I'd just come to pay my respects, but he pulled me to one side: "What's it like in the bar?" I told him it had cooled out considerably. "Good," he said. As though he really wanted to get away from the dressing room madness, he slipped out with me to the bar. We each had a brandy. Then Joe was swamped by people. I made my excuses and left.

The Monday and Tuesday of the next week were taken up with rehearsals and recording of a slot by Joe and the group for the *Later with Jools Holland* BBC 2 TV series, produced by Mark Cooper, who oversaw the Glastonbury recording at which Joe had attacked the cameraman's lens. Although Jools Holland accompanied the performances of the inevitable "London Calling" and "Yalla Yalla" with his trademark boogie-woogie piano, Joe immediately went to the mixing booth to request this be removed for the actual broadcast. (This didn't stop Joe from writing and recording a track with Jools, "The Return of the Blues Cowboy," for his 2001 release, *Small World Big Band*, a compilation album with assorted luminaries.)

Martin Slattery announced that he and his girlfriend, Kirsty, were getting married in their hometown of Manchester on June 2, an opportunity for another Big Day Off. Following the wedding ceremony in Manchester Town Hall, a party was thrown in the building itself, featuring the Manc posse. At a nearby Ramada Inn the postnuptials continued, Joe still buying bottles of champagne for the assembled crew at ten the next morning. "Someone went down for breakfast at about eleven o'clock and Joe was still at the bar," said Martin.

At the end of the month, the group was booked into an open-air event in Italy, the Jesolo Beach Bum Festival in Venice, with Eels, Gene and Reef. Ant Genn, whose narcotic hobbies had taken precedence, did not turn up. "It was bad behavior to miss the gig," he admitted. Conflicted about what to do, Joe was unable to come to a decision. "When I spoke to Joe about it," said Pablo, "Joe said, 'Well, we can't do anything about it, because that's what happened with Topper, wasn't it?'" "Ant was my mate," said Damien Hirst, "but I said to Joe, 'Throw him out.'" Finally Joe did come to a decision about his writing partner; he made a phone call to Antony Genn. "He called me up in late July and said, 'It's time we parted company.' I thought he was saying we should split the band up. I said, 'I think you're right.' I then realized he was saying that he thought I should leave the band. But I did say that before I went I would like to play the two festivals we were booked in for."

"The Ant sacking," said Lucinda, "came sort of out of the blue inasmuch as although it was on the cards, Joe seemed to put up with him for an awfully long time, when as far as a lot of us were concerned he should have been given the push. Joe certainly said to me that Ant's addiction was his cross to bear and as long as it didn't affect his musicianship Joe wasn't going to sack him. He didn't really discuss it with me. Just said one night that it had to be done, and he did it. He said on more than one occasion he had always regretted sacking Topper, and I'm sure that played a large part in his thinking."

"Before he was going to sack Ant—which I didn't realize he was going to do—he just went into a quiet space. He sat up all night, running through all the permutations of the arguments—he could predict what he was going to say, and the counterarguments that he would come up with. If you had an argument with Joe, he always won: he'd say, 'I'm always right—except for when I'm wrong.' But he would think it through, and had an answer for everything without squashing you or belittling you."

On August 19 and 20 Joe and the Mescaleros were set to play the two legs of that year's incarnation of the V Festival. There was a warm-up date at a club in Leicester, at which, although Antony Genn had taken steps to control his heroin intake, everything else was on the menu, making even-keeled Martin Slattery declare Ant "an embarrassment." Ant promised he would not drink more than five pints before he went onstage for the V Festival shows.

Although Ant had promised he would limit his pre-performance drinking, he said nothing about how much he might consume onstage. During the course of the first V Festival show, he downed another six pints: "That was between numbers in a forty-five minute set, so there was only about a second for each one: straight down the hatch."

"Joe came up to me on the bus," said Martin, "and said, 'I want you and Scottie to produce the next album.' When he said that, Ant was upstairs. I thought, 'Hang on, Joe, I'd love to do it, but let's sort the situation out first.' Joe was a strong man, and a great guy, but not good at tying up loose ends."

Yet Joe did not permit Ant's behavior to sway him from his habitual course. The second V Festival date was in Essex, twenty miles east of London. The previous night the group had checked into a nearby hotel. "In the morning," said Pablo, "I thought, 'What's that smell? I know: it's wood smoke.' I could see Joe in this tiny bit of woodland in the hotel parking lot. He's sitting by a fire and he's got a bottle of red wine and a spliff on the go. So I went and sat down there. Then Scott and Marty came over, and we were sitting there, pissed before lunchtime. By this time the hotel security has come running out—we've got a full-on campfire: 'You can't do this. What are you doing?' Joe went: 'I'm Joe Strummer. We're doing a video. They said: 'Where's the crew?' 'They're coming later. We've got to set it up.' 'What video?' Joe goes: 'Oh, it's a cover of a Paul Weller song. It's called "Wild Wild Wood."' 'Oh, OK, all right.' Then Joe adds: 'They said they were going to send some drinks over for us.' The next thing, the security guys are bringing drinks over."

"What happened with Joe and Ant," considered Pablo, "was a sort of love affair. But within the love affair they got a bit bored with each other's behavior."

By the time the tour bus trundled back into London, it was August 21. It was the early hours of Joe's forty-eighth birthday. One chapter of his life had ended; another had just begun.

campfire tales

2000–2002

L ater on the day of his forty-eighth birthday Joe flew to Spain, to his regular holiday spot of San José. Lucinda picked him up at the airport. In San José, Joe would worry he might run over some of the local children playing in the streets. Accordingly, he drove everywhere extremely slowly, his warning lights permanently flashing. But that year the waggish Damien Hirst decided to play a prank on him. Hiding behind a bush, when Joe approached in the vehicle the artist sprang out and leapt across the hood, tumbling over the other side. Until he realized who it was he had "knocked down," Joe was horrified.

Joe and Lucinda returned to England at the end of August. On September 11 Joe went up to London to record his final series for the BBC World Service. Ten days later he and Lucinda flew to New York for Damien Hirst's first major American opening. Afterward Joe, Damien, Keith Allen, Jim Jarmusch, Bob Gruen and many others spent the night busking on makeshift instruments around SoHo's chic restaurants; in the repertoire was an almost-nursery-rhyme version of "White Riot." "In 2000 and 2001," said Lucinda, "there was lots of hanging with Damien and Maia, either at theirs or at Yalway, and the diary dates seem to merge into one continual campfire."

"I associated Joe with taking loads of drugs, though it was only in the nineties he'd really been into them," said Damien. "He loved 'E.' But I've given him one and found him palming it and putting it in his pocket, saying he'd keep it for later."

Although "differences of musical opinion" is a standard music-business euphemism for "sacked," in the case of Joe and Ant there genuinely were creative divergences. Many of these hinged around "modern" notions of recording and stagecraft: Joe was uncomfortable with the onstage tape machine used on "Yalla Yalla," one of the very best Mescaleros songs, and with the devices required for "Techno D-Day" and "Tony Adams." "Joe wanted it to be much more organic," said Martin Slattery, who operated them during live work.

That autumn Joe and his group returned to Battery Studios in Willesden to begin recording what would become *Global a Go-Go*. "It must have taken us less than a week to get into starting at eight in the evening and leaving at nine the next morning," recalled Martin Slattery. "I want a gang mentality in the studio," Joe ordained. As Joe had suggested, Martin and Scott seized the reins and—with Pablo Cook on percussion and Smiley Bernard on drums—drove the sessions along, aided and abetted by engineer Richard Flack. "We'd throw some stuff down," said Martin, "then each of us would have half an hour or so to see where it would go. That album is an experiment from beginning to end."

Attempting to return to his musical roots—those of busking, perhaps—Joe iconoclastically insisted the songs be based around guitars and keyboards rather than the rhythm section. "I don't want any drums. Hit a waste bin instead," Joe demanded. Drumming on the songs was generally added on after the number was near completion. "That's why the tracks go on for so long," said Martin. "'Shaktar Donetsk' is based around a wacked-out sample that Richard found, which me and Scott jammed to for over thirty minutes. A lot of the playing on the record is a first take." Joe frequently left the musicians to their own devices. "Joe's not there a lot of the time," remembered Martin. Joe would sequester himself away in his spliff bunker, writing lyrics or meditating on life. Lyrics occasionally came about in an organic way. Walking down Willesden High Street on a break from the studio, Joe was approached by a young New Zealander who had just stepped out of a taxi from Heathrow. He asked Joe if he knew anywhere

where he could buy some "mushy peas," the side dish of mashed processed peas that is a staple of fish and chips. Unfortunately this connoisseur's favorite is a northern specialty, a rarity in London. This led to "Bhindi Bhagee," a song that was a meditation by Joe on the ethnic mix of the capital as seen through its stomach. When the New Zealander realized who he was talking to, he was staggered. Joe, the perpetual gatherer of waifs and strays, took him to the studio, inviting him to return on another day. When he did, he was more staggered to find Joe had written a song in which he had become the protagonist.

Joe would record the musicians' sessions on his Fisher-Price tape recorder before stealing away to write the lyrics. "It sounded really chunky and analog on that machine," said Martin. "It allowed him to sometimes say, 'It sounded much better three hours ago.'" Every night he would roll in at about 5:00 a.m. to see how things were going. "Almost always he would walk in and stick his thumbs up and be really pleased and very encouraging. 'I'm so happy, guys. This is the greatest music I've ever made. Do whatever you want and I'll sing on it.' We were willing to do anything for him."

Would they have been so willing if they had known that Joe had an alternative scheme for the new album? He had sent Mick Jones half a dozen sets of lyrics, asking him to turn them into songs. "I did it in about a week," said Mick. "He'd sent me some before and I hadn't got on with it, and he'd been pissed off. What he wanted to do, he said, was make an alternative album with me. He said he wanted to do it when Martin and Scott had gone home— they mustn't know about it. I told him he'd better think about the logistics. I sent him the songs—they were really good. Then I didn't hear any more."

On Sunday, October 8, Joe enjoyed a diversion from the recording sessions at Battery. Michael Horovitz was promoting a further Poetry Olympics, at the Astoria. What Joe was not expecting was that as he walked through Soho he would run, as though apparently by chance, into the man who had introduced him to live playing, as a busker—Tymon Dogg.

After Joe had worked with Tymon Dogg on several of the *Sandinista!* sessions, he had then gone into the studio with him, financing a Tymon solo album, *Hollowed Out*, recorded with producer Glyn Johns. Tymon decided not to release the record: "I move on." The tapes languished on Joe's landing. The pair did not link up again until 1998, when Joe went to a memorial evening at Acklam Hall for Maurice "Mole" Chesterton, the bass player with the 101'ers. "When I met Joe at Mole's thing, the first thing he said to me was, 'Have you heard that album again yet? You might like it.'"

Now Joe asked Tymon, "Where are you going? Come with me. Where's the violin?" "About a mile away in the back of the car," said Tymon. "Go get it!" said Joe. As at the Poetry Olympics six months previously, Joe had turned up with Pablo Cook to provide percussion and backing vocals. He immediately enlisted Tymon and his violin into his act. Unexpectedly, after a backstage conversation, the lineup was augmented by another performer on the bill: Martin Carthy, the celebrated British folk guitarist, a friend of Bob Dylan during his British sojourn in 1962.

"That event displayed Joe's open-hearted stance and brilliant group-feel musicianship," said Michael Horovitz, "in the way he brought others, notably Martin Carthy, onstage and created a spontaneous jam session, which for my money compared favorably with the one filmed by Scorsese in *The Last Waltz*. He was always terrific fun to be with. We were soulmates, and fellow cultural revolutionaries from different genre places."

Joe performed a short set, only three numbers: "Island Hopping," off *Earthquake Weather*, "Silver and Gold" and an acoustic version of "White Riot" on which Keith Allen and his daughter Lily joined in. "When Joe came offstage at the Astoria," Tymon told me, "he said he had enjoyed singing that night more than ever before. I said, 'Why?' He said, 'Because I could hear everything I sang, and I felt like everybody else onstage was listening to me.' He'd always worked in electric rock, so he'd never realized how much he could enjoy the vulnerability of an acoustic performance. Joe had always been a singer-songwriter, like those performers in the early seventies, and I think he was beginning to realize that's what he was."

Following this performance the assembled company then retired to the nearby Colony Club, a tiny members-only bar that had once been a favorite of the painter Francis Bacon and the poet Dylan Thomas. In the Colony, watched by a packed crowd (including Mick Jones), Joe, Pablo and Tymon played for a further forty-five minutes. But this was just the beginning: when Joe returned to Battery the next day, it was with Tymon Dogg, now a member of the Mescaleros.

The arrival of Tymon significantly shifted the demographic of the group. Whereas previously Joe Strummer and the Mescaleros had signified an-older-bloke-with-a-bunch-of-young-blokes, now Joe had an ally of his own age, someone who literally knew where he was coming from. As though indicating the various archetypal roles on offer, Martin Slattery's father had once studied in a Catholic seminary with Tymon. Like Martin and Scott Shields, Tymon was a consummate multi-instrumentalist: on what was to become *Global a Go-Go* he would play violin, electric guitar, Spanish acoustic and mandolin. It seems no coincidence that in its loose and complex sprawl *Global a Go-Go* is the Joe Strummer solo record that is closest to the feel of the Clash's *Sandinista!*, on which Joe also worked with Tymon. Yet—as with *Sandinista!*—the tone had already been set before his arrival. "In its roots of music and variety," said Dick Rude, "*Global a Go-Go* was the only other time, after *Sandinista!*, where Joe spoke of a recording coming from absolute spontaneity."

After Tymon had been with Joe in the studio for a week, out of the blue Joe tossed him a request: "Can you come on tour with us?" Like a flashback to the U.S. stadium dates of 1982, the Who were to tour Britain, and the Mescaleros had been booked to open. Almost immediately Joe began to change his mind about playing the shows. "We're writing a song a day, I don't want to break the spell," he said, concerned. Late on a Sunday afternoon, Joe, Pockets and Tymon retired to an Indian restaurant on Willesden High Street. Joe was restless and awkward as he mentally sifted through the reasons for playing the tour; the fact that he was legally contracted was weighing on his mind, but there was also something else: "I've got to get up and play 'London Calling' for the fifty thousandth time when I'm coming up with something really great here in the studio."

Tymon had a suggestion. "Why don't you go on the Who tour and use it as a rehearsal space for these new songs?" After a moment, Joe came to a decision. "OK, we'll do that. But we start the gig with you playing the violin on 'Minstrel Boy.'" That first week at Battery, Joe had got Tymon to join in on violin on this traditional Irish tune, as he had taught a version of it to Martin Slattery, Joe throwing in scat lines. The version they played was at least twenty minutes long; Tymon began to add experimental effects. When Joe suggested the song as a set opener, Tymon was concerned. "I thought, You're kidding. You want me to play that old tune in front of a load of punks waiting for 'White Man'?"

But that was precisely how the show kicked off on Thursday, October 27, when Joe Strummer and the Mescaleros played a secret warm-up gig at the 100 Club on Oxford Street. Initially I was as perplexed as Tymon had predicted the audience would be as he stepped with his fiddle to the front of the stage to start the set, Joe standing to the back of the tiny stage, mouth familiarly lolling open as he chopped out rhythm chords on his trusty Telecaster. "Minstrel Boy" stirred you to your bones: like many old folk tunes, it was fabulously rousing. It was followed by a quartet of new numbers: "Bhindi Bhagee," "Bummed Out City," "At the Border, Guy" and "Gamma Ray." As often when an act introduces previously unheard songs, they were initially baffling. But after a few bars their rhythms and beats were moving your body and feet. It felt like there was sunshine everywhere. In addition to his version of Jimmy Cliff's "The Harder They Come"— which Joe had recorded for an American benefit for the West Memphis Three, a trio of teenagers dubiously convicted of a triple homicide—he shifted gear through a clutch of old Clash favorites, including the "Folk Riot" version of "White Riot." Condensation dripped from the ceiling onto the packed crowd like a chorus to the sweat pouring down Joe's face. The 100 Club was as hot as if it were August, fans stripping down to their bare chests as Joe pounded out the songs. "It was one of the most amazing gigs I'd ever done, standing on people's heads to play," said Martin Slattery. In the dressing room afterward, the toll that the heat and lack of oxygen had taken on Joe was manifest: he lay down on the floor for a quarter of an hour to recover his breath. Lucinda looked worried. I was concerned. For the first time it really dawned on me that Joe was not as young as he had once been.

Not that Joe was as full-on in his drug usage as other members of the group. "We'd have to have a week or two off after about every three weeks," said Martin. "It was too hardcore a lifestyle. But Joe's smart—he didn't take coke every time it was offered, hardly at all. Once when we were doing the mixing, Joe had just one line and went absolutely mental. We left him at 5:00 a.m., and when we got back the next afternoon you couldn't see the studio for the paper he'd been writing on on the coke. It had a massive effect on him, so he didn't do that much."

Scott Shields was in such bad shape that he was subbed for the Who tour. It began three days after the 100 Club, in Birmingham at the National Exhibition Centre. The next day Joe was back in London, appearing at the Park Lane Hotel at the annual awards ceremony of Q magazine; he received the "Special Inspiration" award. After Manchester the tour moved to Glasgow, where there was a day off. By now Joe had acquired a driver who, in what seemed as Zen as the wooden machete, had only one leg. Joe had an idea. Calling up "One-Legged Tim," he asked if he would run him "up the road," the suggestion being that this involved a distance of some ten miles. "Just drive," said Joe. What Joe actually required was that One-Legged Tim would drive Joe's rented Mercedes the 250 miles northeast to Bonar Bridge. Joe suggested they take the longer scenic route, but as it was pitch-black this was pointless. The first anyone in Bonar Bridge heard of his imminent arrival was at around eight in the evening when Joe briefly called. He phoned again, concerned he would not be welcome as it was so late. On their arrival at the farm of his cousin George he instructed One-Legged Tim to remove his prosthetic limb in order to engage sympathy so they might be asked to stay the night. Joe and George then sat up until 5:00 a.m. drinking bottles of rum that Joe had brought with him. George introduced Joe to the music of Alasdair Fraser, considered the finest modern Scottish fiddle player, by repeatedly playing him Fraser's CD *The Road North*. After George had gone to bed, needing to rise in a couple of hours for his farmwork, Joe wrote a note for him on a children's shoes catalogue: "Dear George!!! This Alastair [*sic*] Fraser CD is unbelievable!! My blank tapes I don't have with me otherwise I'd muck in with your big system and try to copy. Love Joe!! P.S. Thanks for being such a good sport. Warning, Georgie! Frazer [*sic*] CD in my machine in kitchen. High nick-a-billity factor." (In a drawn heart Joe added two words: "The Rebels.") Before he turned in, Joe tended to a domestic task, lopsidedly changing the nappy of George's baby son Duncan.

At lunchtime Joe had One-Legged Tim drive him the couple of miles to Carnmhor to see Uncle John. "He stayed here an hour or two," said John. "He was still here at three o'clock, and said he was supposed to be in Glasgow at two-thirty. He was quite happy." As Joe set off on the journey south, "he was standing up in the Mercedes, his head sticking through the sunroof, like the Pope."

By the skin of his teeth Joe made it back for the Glasgow show that evening. The Who tour concluded with three nights in London, the last show on November 16. After this date drummer Smiley Bernard left the group.

B ack in London the sessions at Battery continued apace from November 20 until Christmas, Scott Shields returning. A result of the Who dates was that Roger Daltrey came to the studio to provide additional vocals on "Global a Go-Go," the tune that became the title track of this second Mescaleros album. "Roger began to hang out with us," Joe told journalist Fred Mills. "He knew we were recording, so one night he said, 'Hey, if you want me to come by I'd be more than pleased to do that.' I said, 'Sure, come on down, and let's get out the mikes and sing.'"

After the Christmas break, work resumed on the record all through January, but without Pablo Cook—strapped for cash, he had begun playing percussion with Moby, hoping to juggle that job with his Mescaleros work. One evening an added measure of social realism overhung the sessions. Arriving at the studio, Joe and his driver heard a shot ring out, and in the far distance they saw a man crumple to the pavement as another figure ran off: a Somalian had been shot in a drug turf war. In shock Joe entered the studio, wondering whether he should approach the police. "Joe came into the studio and was like 'Fuckin' hell. You won't believe what we've just seen,'" said Martin. "He was really torn about what to do." Joe decided that as he had not seen the person who fired the gun there was no point in volunteering his services.

But there was a lighter note to these New Year sessions. So many disposable lighters vanished into the pockets of visitors to the studio that Joe would arrive bearing literally dozens of them, which he would proceed to turn into what he termed "unstealable" lighters, customizing them with stickers and logos, gluing three together, or making them too long to fit into pockets by gaffer-taping them to pen bodies. It was good to have a hobby.

The studio was a very private male world. "There was a no-birds-in-the-studio philosophy," said Scott Shields. "Every time Luce would come up to the studio Joe would go out with her. She'd never be around as we were recording." At the end of the sessions, Joe assembled the assorted wives and girlfriends of the various participants, and apologized for having so disrupted their lives.

But it wasn't over. Joe announced he had been asked to write the soundtrack for *Gypsy Woman*, a comedy directed by Sheree Folkson. The process took a further six weeks; the film went straight to DVD.

Bob Gruen called me. The photographer was working on his book of Clash photos; Joe had suggested I should write the text. In late April 2001 Bob, his wife, Elizabeth, and I took a train down to Taunton. Joe picked us up at the station. He was hobbling around with a walking stick, his foot in plaster. "Joe broke his ankle playing soccer round about March 26, so that was a few months of plaster and crutches," said Lucinda. He still managed to drive: had he been taking lessons from One-Legged Tim?

Sitting against the wall at the kitchen table at Yalway, with Luce to his right, reggae playing on a ghetto blaster, Joe seemed extraordinarily at ease, doodling on a pad of paper. From time to time one of his three dogs would push their way into the room, tails wagging, muddy paws over everyone. Opening a bottle of red wine for us, Joe at first drank tea. During the course of the evening he gave me a copy of *Straight Life*, the harrowing autobiography of Art Pepper, the great jazz alto saxophonist, a book he told me he loved. It was not for at least a couple of hours, as Luce served up supper, that he poured himself a glass of wine. But Joe was pacing himself. Although Luce went to bed not long after midnight, at around four in the morning Joe was making toast and honey for us and pouring me a glass of what he was consuming, a shot of brandy in a tumbler filled to the top with water. "I recommend it," he said. "It'll keep you going." In five days' time it would be May Day. Mass anti-capitalist demonstrations were planned for London. "Let's go up and get stuck in," said Joe, his patent naughty-boy grin spreading over his features. It was like a moment from "Cool 'n' Out," one of the songs recorded for the new Mescaleros CD, which he played us: "I especially like the line in that song about putting LSD into the gin supply at the G7 summit," he said. I went to bed around five. Down in the kitchen Joe was still going for another couple of hours.

On May 24 Joe was back at the Park Lane Hotel for the Ivor Novello Awards (selected by the British Academy of Composers and Songwriters), this time with all the Clash—including Topper—who were honored for their "outstanding contribution to British music." It was the first time all four members had appeared onstage together in nineteen years. "I know the Ivors is a bit 'establishment,'" Mick Jones told the BBC afterward, "but the reason we came is that it's a recognition of our craft—and for the laugh!"

That day was a busy one for Joe, as it also marked the sixtieth anniversary of Bob Dylan's birth. He had been called to BBC studios early in the morning as a pundit for the *Today* current affairs program; remarkably, he was partnered with Stevie Wonder, also in London for the Ivor Novello Awards. Michael Horovitz enthusiastically listened to this Dylan birthday segment. "I loved hearing Joe on the *Today* program, on which both he and Stevie Wonder enthused about Dylan's contribution and, told there were only a couple of minutes left to name a song they liked best, Joe instantly started chanting, and urged Stevie to do so too, 'Blowin' in the Wind,' on which they achieved perfect harmony and euphoria. Immediately after the orgasmic climax, the presenter James Naughtie picked up the cue to state something on the lines of '. . . and now, for once in a lifetime, from Joe Strummer with Stevie Wonder, to Steve May with the sport.'"

On July 24 *Global a Go-Go* was released. "This album was inspired by Michael Horovitz and Nina Simone and is dedicated to Joey Ramone," read Joe's final line on the sleeve notes insert. The death from cancer of Joey Ramone—whose group had so enormously influenced the Clash—the previous September had deeply upset him. The album opened with "Johnny Appleseed," originally written in the *Earthquake Weather* sessions, thirteen years previously. "The song is a yell from the heart," said Joe, "a howl for some kind of truth in our lives."

The title tune was directly inspired by Joe's BBC World Service program and reflected his belief in a world community free of borders and nationalist prejudices. But it specifically hinges around the liberating force of global radio bringing the planet together: motivated by the same mood that had driven the anti-globalization demonstrations, *Global a Go-Go* concerns itself with Joe's anarchic preoccupations and sense of fairness toward those less fortunate. "Shaktar Donetsk" (a Ukrainian football team) is the story of an illegal Macedonian immigrant to Britain. And "At the Border, Guy" is about Mexican migrant workers. But it wasn't all about suffering; "Gamma Ray" turned this on its head—"There's nothing but bad news in the newspapers to make us live in a constant state of paranoia, which is what they want"—while both "Mondo Bongo" and "Bummed Out City" were love songs, Joe Strummer style. The final tune on the record is a seventeen-minute version of Tymon Dogg's crowd-pleaser, "Minstrel Boy."

Before the official release, at Joe's instigation he and the Mescaleros had been booked to play a free tour of record stores to promote the album, in both the United Kingdom and the United States. The dates began at Virgin in Leeds on July 16, with a London show at HMV in Oxford Street the next day. "It was Joe's idea to do that tour," said Martin Slattery. "It was a good example of his passion for just getting in there." The plan was to play a forty-five-minute set; afterward Joe and the group would hang around for as long as necessary, talking to fans and signing autographs. Apart from "The Harder They Come," the set consisted entirely of new material. At the show in Oxford Street, the problems of in-store performances were highlighted—or not, as the case may be, for there was little lighting and amid the racks of CDs it was hard to see the group, set up at the back of the store. But considering that *Global a Go-Go* would not be out for another seven days and hardly anyone had heard the material, the show received a rapturous response. The Mescaleros' lineup now consisted of multi-instrumentalists Martin Slattery and Scott Shields, Tymon Dogg on violin, and two new players, bassist Simon Stafford and drummer Luke Bullen. Luke, who had played with a group called Adict, met Joe at rehearsals: "I was nervous of meeting him. He was much quieter than I expected. He kept himself in his own world. I couldn't gauge him really. Quickly I found out if everything was going smoothly, Joe would change it, even the songs themselves—he'd add in another chorus. I think he fed off the energy of the friction. Joe was really like a shepherd. He'd go along with whatever was suggested, and then subtly change it. He went where he was feeling."

Tucked away upstairs after the HMV gig in an office that served as a dressing room, Joe played a couple of classic reggae compilations he had picked up at the date in Leeds. He came over and sought me out, apologizing for not having made a further contribution to Bob Gruen's book—although I knew he had been smothered with advance promotion for *Global a Go-Go*. "You shouldn't let down your mates," he said. Afterward we retired to the nearby Groucho Club, a members-only media hangout that seemed a strangely rarefied location in which to find a fellow like Joe. Yet since the middle of the 1990s he might often be seen there, in the company of the likes of Keith Allen or Damien Hirst. "There was an upstairs room that was a bit of a Britpop hangout," explained Martin Slattery, "where Keith, Damien, Joe and a few others had a little scene. I don't think it was so much that it was the Groucho, I think it could have been anywhere that was central and private and had a snooker [billiards] table. They ruled it as kings—Ant Genn was very much involved in that scene. The bar at the Groucho is tab-based, which left Joe with some fuck-off bar bills. 'Another round, everybody?' He must have spent some money there. No wonder they put up with their behavior." As an out-of-town member of the Groucho, Joe would receive very generous room rates when he needed somewhere to stay in London. One night a waitress came up to him: "I think you know my father." She was the daughter of Richard "Dick the Shit" Evans. After not seeing each other for a quarter century, their friendship resumed.

On this visit to the Groucho, we hunkered ourselves away in a corner of the downstairs restaurant. Lucinda was there, along with a few others. A couple of bottles of red wine were ordered. Joe seemed subdued, quiet, doing what he was so fond of, sitting at the edge of the table and watching the conversation unfold in front of him. He was smoking Cutter's Choice rolling tobacco, which he decreed to be "the Courvoisier of rolling tobacco"; we were both on the same tip, smoking hand-rolled cigarettes because the hassle ensured we smoked less. "You've got to stick at it," insisted the man who'd moaned "There's no smoking anywhere" on "Mega Bottle Ride," on the new album.

A few days later Joe and the Mescaleros were on their way to New York City. On July 24, the day that *Global a Go-Go* was released, they played at

Mescaleros? Punk rock, mate! (*John Zimmerman/Proper-Gander*)

Virgin Megastore in Times Square. Later that evening there was a TV performance on *The Conan O'Brien Show*, playing "Johnny Appleseed."

Dates followed in Toronto, Chicago, San Francisco, and Tower Records in Los Angeles, on Sunset Strip. Leaving a bar after playing at Tower, Joe encountered a street musician he had met the last time he was in L.A. Then the busker had serenaded him—inappropriately, as Joe had pointed out—with a version of "Train in Vain." "I hope you know more than 'Train in Vain' this time," said Joe now. At which point the man burst into "Should I Stay or Should I Go." Smiling, Joe pressed a twenty-dollar bill into his hand. "You're so nice," he told Joe. "Prince wasn't that nice." But then Prince hadn't been a busker—as Joe had.

The next night, August 2, Joe and the Mescaleros stepped across Sunset from Tower to play a show in the tiny Viper Room. Although he had played only a few dates with the Mescaleros, Luke Bullen already detected tensions between Scott Shields and Tymon Dogg. "Tymon and Scott would wind each other up: Scott was very progressive and Tymon was completely old school. It made it difficult. Also, Joe didn't really like to rehearse. We'd say we'd want to start rehearsals at 2:00 p.m., but Joe would say, 'The smart money is on 4:00 p.m.,' and it would end up being six."

Whenever a hot new group was in L.A., Gerry Harrington would go to see them. Gerry told Joe he was going to see the Strokes play at the Troubadour the day after the Viper Room date, just over three weeks before the release of the acclaimed New York act's first album, *Is This It?* This time Joe was up for a night out. "Let's go," he said. "It will be terrible. We'll just go and drink and tell them they're no good." But Joe loved the group. Standing at the front of the venue up against the stage, he pummelled the air with his fist throughout the Strokes set. After, he and Gerry went upstairs to the dressing room bar. Julien Casablancas, the singer, could not believe Joe was there. Grabbing and hugging him ecstatically, he demanded, "Why did you come to my show? You're so great, you should just listen to your own music." This sort of moment would always perk Joe up.

But there is no silver lining without a cloud. On August 4 Joe and the Mescaleros had agreed to play as support to his friend Brian Setzer, on whose 1996 album *Guitar Slinger* Joe had contributed. The show was at the open-air Greek Theater, in the shadow of Griffith Park. Also in L.A. was Pablo Cook, who had played in the city with Moby the previous night. Attempting to juggle both loyalties, Pablo agreed to play the Greek Theater show with the Mescaleros. Out of the loop since the beginning of the year, he was surprised when he turned up for the sound check. "There's acoustic guitars everywhere. In my absence there'd been this weird transformation, and one I don't like: with someone like Joe it's got to be fucking nailed down and loud. I thought, I don't quite know what to do here." For the show Pablo adapted to the moment. Following this date Joe and the group went along to the bar at the Standard Hotel on Sunset, where Danny Saber often deejayed.

"In those situations," said Martin Slattery, "he would often have a word with the bar manager and pull rank, and before you knew it he'd have the guy wrapped around his finger and the place would be ours. He had that down. No place would ever close with us in it."

As they partied into the night, with assorted Mescaleros dancing on tables, Joe advised Martin in a worldly manner that a particular girl was there for the musician's taking. Information of this nature emanating from Joe would always rather surprise "Slatto": "In the same way you don't see your dad as a sexual character, I never saw Joe that way either." Satisfied he had imparted this knowledge, Joe leaned over toward the bar, to support himself on his elbow. But his alcohol-impaired brain misjudged the distance. Like a cartoon character, Joe Strummer, Punk Rock Legend, splattered sideways onto the floor.

After playing with the Mescaleros in Los Angeles, Pablo Cook was uncertain about the group; he realized that Martin and Scott were effectively now running the music, and that they were adamant the previous tour-bus alcohol and drug consumption should cease. "It's bad enough being on a tour bus if you can't get off your head a bit," thought Pablo. When a Mescaleros tour was suggested for later in the year, he asked Simon Moran for a raise. "Joe's tours tended to be Thursday-Friday-Saturday tours—a man of his age didn't want to do seven-month stints. I was fine with that, but when you've got a home and a family to support, that's not going to help financially." When Joe's manager wouldn't up Pablo's rates, the percussionist decided he had to accept the offer he'd been made by Moby. But he wanted to tell Joe this himself. The next time he saw him was on Wednesday, September 26, at the launch party for Bob Gruen's Clash book at the Proud Gallery in Greenland Street in Camden.

Having contributed to the book, I went along to this absolutely packed event, filled with journalists and camera crews, but also with the presence of Mick Jones and—far more controversially—Bernie Rhodes. Joe came over and hugged and kissed me. "I love the book," he said. Not unreasonably I presumed he was talking about the tome we were there to celebrate. "No, no," he said, almost irritably. "I mean your reggae book," referring to the also just published *Reggae Explosion*, which I had put together with the photographer Adrian Boot—I had sent Joe a copy. (Joe was always great about my writing. A year previously I'd published *Rude Boy: Once Upon a Time in Jamaica*. Joe called me at three in the morning to tell me it was "a masterpiece." Lucinda told me that *Mick and Keith*, my next book, was "probably" the last book Joe read.)

I noticed Joe seemed in a very odd state, half in the midst of events, half hiding in corners of the dark parking lot; even when he was in the center of matters he seemed very alone. Pennie Smith said Joe seemed unable to look her in the face that evening. I assumed the evening's emphasis on the Clash was stirring up all manner of debris within Joe's mind. But I did not know what had transpired.

Shortly before Joe arrived at the Proud Gallery, Pablo had phoned him. "I said, 'Listen, I can't do it anymore. Simon ain't got the price right, and I think the power thing is a bit wrong.' He said, 'OK, man. All right.' He sounded a bit angry." At the book launch Joe and Pablo still hung out together, putting away a fair amount of booze. When a film crew appeared in front of them, eager to grab a few sound-bites, Pablo stepped away, feeling he should not participate. But Joe grabbed him by the arm and led him into the parking lot. "He just broke down in front of me," said Pablo. "I've never seen Joe cry before, except one time when he took too much of that funny stuff. But this seemed to really break Joe. I said, 'Joe, I have to earn money, and I've got to get out and I've got to graft.' He said, 'Yeah, but you can't do this.' It wasn't an argument; it was more, 'What can we do to resolve it?' I said, 'It's not going to resolve itself. I've accepted the tour. I've got to earn more money.' 'OK, man.' I thought that was the end of it, so for the rest of the evening we proceeded to live out a weird façade. Later in the evening, after more drinking, there was a bit of 'you fucker' and some friction, but I thought we got through that."

To add to his traumas, Joe himself was dragged to one side, along with

Mick Jones, by Bernie Rhodes. All evening Bernie had wandered around clutching a sheaf of papers in his hand, a speech he intended to deliver to the assembled multitude. But no one wanted to hear it, so he'd decided to give a personal reading to Joe and Mick. "'Oh, go away,' we both laughed," said Mick. When signing an autograph book, Mick saw Bernie had beaten him to it. "I started it all," Bernie had appended to his signature. Mick chose the moment to ask Joe what had happened to the songs he had sent him, supposedly for what had become *Global a Go-Go*. "No, they weren't for that," Joe corrected him. "They are the next Clash album."

"At Bob Gruen's book launch," said Bernie, "Joe started to blank [ignore] me. But I thought, 'I'm a dignified person: I'll wait.' He got me in a corner and put his head in my lap and started to weep like a baby. He said, 'Bernard, you're the only true one.' I saw that night he was surrounded by insensitive takers, all going, 'All right, Joe!' Joe died of a broken heart. He needed me, to be me."

As the event at the gallery wound down, a move was made to the Groucho Club. Again, the atmosphere around Joe seemed strained. "A few of us were sat round a table," said Pablo, "and I looked at Joe, and he had his head in his hands, and when I looked again he was crying again. That really, really upset me." Also in the bar at the Groucho was Paul Simonon. Joe was reputedly angry with him for not having turned up at the Proud Gallery. "Our fans were there," he told him. "You should have come and given them your time." It was said that as a consequence a falling-out took place, and Joe and Paul never saw each other again.

But this was not quite true, and Paul had his own remembrance. "I didn't go to the Bob Gruen thing because I thought he'd got us all to con-tribute to it but I wasn't going to go and wave the flag. I saw Joe in the Groucho and we wanted to talk, but he was surrounded by all these drunken blokes who followed him around. We couldn't talk because of those oafs. So I left—I was a bit pissed off.

"We saw each other briefly outside the Groucho a month later. I was get-ting into a taxi with Gaz Mayall. Joe got in with us. Gaz said to him: 'You'd better go back to your wife. She'll wonder where you've gone.' He did. Af-ter, Joe and I still communicated by fax."

———

Fifteen days before Bob Gruen's book launch in London a pair of hi-jacked planes had smashed into the World Trade Center in Manhattan, introducing the planet to the fragmented reality of the twenty-first century. Joe had spent time at Bob Gruen's party that evening asking former *NME* editor Neil Spencer, wearing the hat of astrologer, for his prognosis on com-ing events in the wake of 9/11.

"He was absolutely devastated by 9/11," said Lucinda. "I was in the kitchen and I heard it on the radio—a plane had flown into the World Trade Center. I went to put on the telly. So we had it on before the second one hit, and I ran and got Joe up, and funnily enough he was supposed to be having his eyes tested that day. He was finally admitting he couldn't read the writ-ing on the CD boxes. He was going to get some glasses so he could read the CD cases. But he sat in his dressing gown and didn't move all day. He just sat there, watching it all."

On October 3 Joe Strummer and the Mescaleros were scheduled to be in New York, plugging "Johnny Appleseed" on *Late Show with David Letter-man*, the first salvo of a series of American shows. Joe thought of canceling the dates: was a Mescaleros tour what the United States needed in the after-math of 9/11?

"Everyone was canceling their tours," said Lucinda. "He said, 'I'm not canceling.' I really didn't want him to go. He said, 'I'm going to New York and I'm doing it for the firefighters.' Because his great friend Steve Buscemi used to be a firefighter. 'I'm doing it for the firemen. If no one turns up but the firemen, then that's good.' He insisted on going ahead with the tour. He was devastated by it."

"After the Twin Towers incident Joe was very opinionated in an almost shocking way," said Dick Rude. "I expected this live-and-let-live political point of view. But his response was, 'We've gotta go in there and take care of this. If they had to kill every person on earth to fulfill their religious dogma, they would gladly do it.' He said, 'Look at Hitler. In the beginning he wanted to take over his country, and we in Britain said, "Go ahead." Then suddenly we were bombed for four years straight. You can't let these people take an inch, because they will take the whole mile.'"

Dick Rude had visited Joe in Somerset for a few days at the end of the summer. "One night we sat around a campfire, just me and him, until four in the morning, and practically didn't say a word to each other. That was unusual. It seemed he wasn't sure in his own head what was going on with the group. Then he called me up and said, 'Hey, come on the road and film us.'" The result was Dick Rude's critically acclaimed documentary *Let's Rock Again*.

On October 6 the group played at the Trump Marina Hotel in Atlantic City. On a whim and for the benefit of Dick's camera, Joe wandered out into a shopping mall, handing out flyers for that night's show. He also knocked on the door of the largest local radio station: "It's Joe Strummer. I was in a band called the Clash. I've got my new record. I wonder if you could play it?" The program director played a song from *Global a Go-Go* and to Joe's delight plugged the show. "He would do whatever it took," said Dick. "He had no lack of humility about what he was doing. He was all about turning people on. That was his role."

The tour headed across the United States, dipping into Canada before the climax: four nights in the last week of October at the Troubador in West Hollywood. When he learned that Gerry Harrington had bought full-body anti-chemical-warfare suits for his children, Joe became nervous about a rumored pending Al Qaeda attack on Los Angeles. "They're not going to hit here as well," Scott Shields told him. "What do you know?" demanded Joe. "You've only got a dog! We've got families!" The acid test, Joe decided, would be to drive out to LAX airport and see if a disproportionate number of Afghani-looking people were boarding planes to leave the country, as though they had been tipped off. Accordingly, he and Dick Rude went to the airport to scope out the scenario. Not noticing large flocks of men with beards lining up to leave the United States, Joe decided Los Angeles was safe. The Troubadour gigs went ahead triumphantly. "Few artists could walk this world music tightrope as effectively as Strummer," wrote John Lappen in the *Hollywood Reporter*. "Nothing is forced or seems out of place as Strummer moves easily between these musical cultures; his audio passport allows him certifiable access to wherever he seems to want to go."

From L.A. the Mescaleros flew to Japan for five dates before returning to London via the Womad festival on Gran Canaria on November 11. At Womad a "jet-lagged" Joe, looking "pale and tired," was interviewed for the BBC by Martin Vennard, who noted that he "may surprise a few people with his views on the war in Afghanistan. The forty-nine-year-old, who once sang about the Nicaraguan Sandinistas fighting the American-backed enemy, says: 'I think you have to grow up and realize that we're facing religious fanatics who would kill everyone in the world who doesn't do what they say.'"

Vennard asked Joe about *Global a Go-Go*. "'We got all the influences for it from Willesden High Road,' he says, referring to the multicultural London street where they recorded the album in a studio. 'When you go out for milk and cigarettes you go through three countries because all the shops and cafés are playing their own music,' he says. He describes the songwriting process as 'like going through hell.'"

But Joe wasn't too weary to stand up proudly for the future of the Mescaleros: "We'd like to be known as one of the good groups from London . . . I haven't even started yet."

The Womad date was a bridge into the U.K. and European tour that followed, beginning on November 15 at Brighton Concorde 2, a funky venue on the seashore. Down for the gig was Johnny Green; backstage after the show Johnny detected "a certain distance" between Joe and the group members: "It seemed like nervousness on their part." He also observed that there was "lots of coke around. Also good-looking women of a certain age, dressed like rock 'n' roll chicks, with studded belts and leather."

Tracy Franks, the fan whom Joe had not babysat for, also went along to the show. "It turned out to be the last time I saw Joe. But my first thought was, 'He's drinking too much.' He couldn't look me in the face. I think Joe knew that he wasn't very well. He was very tired. He was trying: 'How you doing, Tracy?' But he wouldn't look at me, his face almost away from me. I'd never seen Joe like that before."

The tour cantered through Birmingham, Dublin, Bristol and Brixton (filmed by Don Letts), before crossing the Channel to Paris. Then the group flew to Thessaloníki in northern Greece, the tour winding up at the Sporting Club in Athens on November 30, the city that had seen the final date of the last lineup of the Clash. The night after the Athens show Joe found himself embroiled in a controversial discussion. "These guys took us back to their penthouse flat," said Martin. "As dawn broke over Athens, Joe started berating the Greeks, taking the piss. He said you had to fight, and that he was into Alexander the Great and those kind of conquerors. I'd just seen the film *Gandhi*, and was saying, 'I'm really into pacifists.' The conversation ended with him saying, 'Well, if I had my way I'd just nuke the whole fucking planet. But everyone has to have the opportunity of having children. I wouldn't want to take that away from you.' "

When Joe and the Mescaleros had played at the Troubadour in L.A., his old friend Kathy Nelson brought the film director Ridley Scott to the first show. Scott was looking for music to include in his new movie *Black Hawk Down*, the story of a firefight involving U.S. troops in Mogadishu, Somalia. Impressed with "Minstrel Boy," the stirring set opener, the director asked Joe to record a version of it that included the lyrics from the original "Minstrel Boy" poem by Thomas Moore, the story of a musician-warrior gone to fight, destined never to return. "I'd always wanted to work with Joe," said Hans Zimmer, the composer of the score, "because I think there's an intelligence to his music. There's nothing false about it." Accordingly, at the beginning of December 2001, Joe, Martin Slattery, Scott Shields and Richard Flack were booked into the Chateau Marmont. In a studio they drew the vocals out of Joe line by line. Although the recording was supposed to take three days, Joe twice postponed their return to London. At the end of a week he was trying to persuade his musicians to spend another day in L.A. "Don't you want to stay? What does your Dr. Jekyll say and what does your Mr. Hyde say?" Joe was demanding, even as the exhausted musicians were dragging him into the limousine to take them to the airport. As the limo pulled onto Sunset Boulevard, Joe called out: "Hey, driver! Stop the car!" With the limousine stopped in the middle of Sunset, with cars and trucks backing up behind it, Joe endeavored to open a debate: "Don't you want to stay? We could get some bongos and some girls and have a party! Let's get on the phone and get some drugs." Joe climbed out of the vehicle to direct the congested traffic.

Eventually they got Joe onto the plane. He turned to Martin Slattery, seated next to him. "He gets something out of his pocket and goes: 'There's two lines left in this. Me and you, in the loo. I'll put it out for you—I'll put a little piece of tissue over it!' We're on a plane with a bed and he wants a line. We have a little drink, the plane's about to take off and I look at Joe and he's fast asleep, gently snoring. The one and only time I've ever seen him wipe himself out." The version of "Minstrel Boy" recorded for *Black Hawk Down* was used to great effect behind the end credits of the hit film, and the fee paid to Joe and the Mescaleros and to Hellcat resulted in *Global a Go-Go* quickly recouping its costs. It also led to a philosophical shift in Joe's thinking. "Me and Scott had been arguing about something in the studio," said Martin, "and I was saying, 'Look, it's just a matter of opinion.' Joe came up to me at the airport as we were leaving and said, 'It's just a matter of opinion.' I've been thinking about that all week." There was yet another spin-off from the tune. Early in 2002 the same team flew to New York to Electric Lady studios to record a new take of "Minstrel Boy" in which the group hummed the melody for use in a television commercial for MCI.

bringing it all back home

2002

The impetus from recording the film version of "Minstrel Boy" led to Joe, Martin and Scott deciding to record a new album as soon as possible. In February 2002, along with Simon Stafford, they began working on fresh material at 2KHZ, a tiny studio they rented in West London. In L.A. the "Minstrel Boy" vocal had been extracted from Joe with assiduous attention to every syllable, Martin and Scott having consciously set out to stretch Joe's abilities. "We got this incredible vocal from him," said Martin. "Me and Scott thought he was really into the method of how we did that. We thought we could really get him singing on this next album. We didn't talk to Joe about it—it just felt like he was into it. Joe would potter about, make himself a little room, get flags up and posters all over the place, and get some lyrics down. The idea was to get a contemporary-sounding album, made together as a band."

After half a dozen rough arrangements had been worked out, Joe was brought into the studio to try out vocals on an all-night session. "We hammered him, and got too carried away. We'd be literally three or four lines in and we'd go, 'Hang on, Joe. Can you go back a line.' He'd go, 'OK, OK.' It was tough, man. We did this 'London Is Burning' song, which has quite a lot of melody for Joe. We definitely over-egged it."

Joe did not turn up for the next session. Nor the next one. Nor the one after that. Then they got a phone call: "I need to come in and talk to you. I've gotta come in. I'm fuckin' losing my mind." The pair of Mescaleros wondered if Joe was having a domestic crisis. But no. "This is how I see it, guys," said Joe. "I love control freaks. I'm one of the few people that has respect for control freaks. It means you've got a path. It means you've got a vision. But you two do your thing, and you're so quick and you're so good at your thing that when you get that done you then want to come and get on my thing. Martin's great, Scott's great, but then there's this other guy called Martin-Scott, and that guy is hard to deal with. When one of their arguments fails, the other one steps up and helps him out. It's really fucking difficult to argue against you guys. It's really difficult to get my point across."

"He felt we were a threat to his process," said Scott. "It was obvious he liked being in control. During the *Global a Go-Go* thing he was in control because it was out of control and he had made it that way."

"I straightaway realized," said Martin, "that we'd completely overstepped the mark of what we'd set out to be—a band where each individual does what each individual does and gets respect from the others. Now we'd taken it to this place where we were going, 'Joe do this, Joe do that,' and it had blasted his mind. He was really beat up. He didn't know what to do and he didn't know how we would take it. He was worried it would split the band up.

"We said, 'We're not trying to fuck with you. We thought after *Black Hawk Down* that was the way you wanted to go.' It was discussed and sorted, and ended up with a 'See you at the next session.' But it was incredible to get so close to everything falling apart. That's why *Streetcore* took such a long time."

Early in February, Joe, Brian Eno and Andy Kershaw found themselves propping up the bar at the World Music Awards in Hackney, where each was presenting an award. Andy Kershaw was relating his experiences in Iraq, which he had visited twice the previous year. "It was already the phony war. Brian and Joe were asking me what my trips had been like. I was telling them that the Iraqis were wonderful people, brought to their knees by the sanctions. We cooked up this harebrained idea that Brian and Joe would each get some sort of band together, and I would approach the authorities and see if we could do an open-air gig in Baghdad the next year."

Lucinda told me that Joe was very committed to this idea—which of course never came off.

In the middle of March Joe took a sideways step into a different role. Through the auspices of his friend Dave Stewart, who had taken on the interests of the legendary Jamaican singer Jimmy Cliff, Joe was selected to sing with Jimmy on his *Black Magic* album of duets. The idea of doing this excited Joe so much he couldn't sleep for the week before going into the studio. By the night before the sessions he had become so wound up and anxious that he got drunk and stoned, then became "double-happy," as he put it, that he was going into the studio the next day with Jimmy Cliff. The tune they recorded was "Over the Border," written by Joe. "He turned up one day with some lyrics," said Jimmy Cliff. "He said, 'I thought of you, Jimmy, when I wrote these.' I asked him how he wanted to record it, and he said, 'I dunno. I just wrote these lyrics.' It was such a great feeling to record that song with him, so spontaneous. He looked so great." The great reggae singer found it very rewarding to record with Joe: "It was great working with Joe because we have sort of the same outlook—the same rebel stance, revolutionary outlook against the system, so it just flowed."

Work at 2KHZ was halted at the end of March. In a similar manner to that in which the four nights at the Troubadour in Los Angeles recalled the residencies around the world that the Clash had begun with their stint at Bond's, Joe Strummer and the Mescaleros had been booked at the beginning of April to play five nights in New York City. This time the dates were not in Manhattan but in now-fashionable Brooklyn, at the six-hundred-capacity St. Ann's Warehouse at 38 Water Street beneath the Brooklyn Bridge, beginning on April 1 and running through to April 6, with one day off. Lucinda was over for the week, and assorted Mancs were in attendance. Mick Jones came to one of the shows, Steve Buscemi and Jim Jarmusch showed up, and Barry "Scratchy" Myers was on the decks, spinning his habitual superlative sounds. "We stayed up partying till dawn each night," said Bob Gruen. The entire crew would end up in Rocky Sullivan's, a bar on Lexington Avenue; Joe was a long-standing friend of the owner, Chris Byrne, once a bagpipe player.

"We're fresh out of the airport to tell the truth, but that never stopped us before," Joe opened the set on the first night, April 1, as they moved smoothly into "Yalla Yalla." "Lose This Skin," sung by Tymon Dogg, was recorded "in this city" twenty-two years ago to that very night, declared Joe, a memory of those epic and momentous *Sandinista!* sessions. There were only four Clash songs—"London's Burning," "White Man," "Rudie Can't Fail" and "Bankrobber"—but a host of Clash covers: "Police and Thieves," "Armagideon Time," "Pressure Drop," "Police on My Back" and "I Fought the Law" as well as Joe's version of Jimmy Cliff's "The Harder They Come." The penultimate encore was Joe's tribute to the deceased Joey Ramone, "Blitzkrieg Bop." Otherwise it was Mescaleros tunes. The Five Night Stand, as the dates were billed, was a raging success, cementing Joe and the Mescaleros in the soul of the city, Joe even paying tribute to New York's underground with his cover of Lou Reed's "Walk on the Wild Side." Slotted in toward the end of the main set (later it became the first encore) was a new tune, "Get Down Moses," recorded at 2KHZ, very loosely based on the Louis Armstrong song of the same title (one of Joe's lines ran: "Carve the message on the tablets of LSD"), a copy of which Joe and Pockets had found on a cassette in a service station near Taunton. Who was Joe referring to in his lyrics for the song that ran: "in the eagle eyrie gotta make a new friend out of old enemies"? Every review of the Brooklyn shows mentioned the extraordinary and sophisticated dexterity of the musicians, how every time you looked up they seemed to be playing a different instrument. More than one drew attention to Joe resembling an old prizefighter who just couldn't be knocked down.

After the Five Night Stand, Joe, Lucinda and Eliza flew out to Los Angeles for what had become a habitual Easter break on the West Coast. Staying at Gerry Harrington's house in BelAir, Joe was soon involved with his old friend Rick Rubin, still touting for songs for Johnny Cash. Getting one of his songs recorded by Cash had become an obsession with Joe Strummer. Written with Smoky Hormel, the hip session guitarist, the song that he came up with, "Long Shadow," was one of the finest, most insightful and most beautiful songs Joe ever wrote: even if you have to crawl up a mountain, Joe says, so long as you finally reach the top, you'll cast a long shadow.

Surely Joe is talking about himself? He wrote the lyrics in a sudden burst of creativity, on a piece of cardboard torn from a box found in Harrington's garage, where Joe leaned over the table-tennis table with his pen and spun words of such a valedictory nature that they were like his own "Redemption Song," the masterly Bob Marley tune that marked the end of the Jamaican master's work recorded in his lifetime.

Yet again Johnny Cash did not click with this tune that Joe brought to him. But the Man in Black did end up at Rick Rubin's house recording two versions of "Redemption Song" itself, one a solo recording and one a duet with Joe, who also recorded a solo vocal of the tune. Finally, from out on a tangent, Joe had got to fulfill his ambition of working with the great musical icon.

Joe had a reason for being in Los Angeles. Kathy Nelson had suggested he might write a song for a new action thriller, *xXx*, starring Vin Diesel. Joe immediately enlisted his musical *compadre* Danny Saber, who had a studio in his house in Laurel Canyon. "Joe takes these things really seriously. So I wrote this track and he came over and sang on it." But Danny felt that Joe was miscast in trying to write for this explosion-packed film, and the song, "All in a Day" (as well as another tune, "Secret Agent Man"), was never used in the movie. Joe had spent a week driving around the more arcane areas of L.A., gathering imagery for the lyrics; as he was writing a song for a character whose adventures are set in Prague, this may be why it was never used. "The great thing about doing it—and it's my last memory of being in the studio with Joe—is that his vocal performance is one of the closest things I've heard to what I grew up listening to in the Clash. To see him in that state in the studio was incredible. He was bossing me around: 'Go back. Do that bit again!' He knew what he wanted to do." Had Joe come to appreciate a different way of working during his rigorous time with "Martin-Scott"? He was so nervous of introducing "All in a Day" as a tune for the new album that he couldn't bring himself to play it to Martin-Scott for a month.

After Joe came back from California there was another stint at 2KHZ. On June 8 Joe and the Mescaleros played at the Fleadh, the annual Irish festival in Finsbury Park in North London. Disappointingly, it was one of the weakest performances from the group, who had not played together for three months. When Luke Bullen missed a cue signaled by Joe from behind his back, Joe flung a microphone at the drummer's head. Luke was furious. Following the set, a worried Joe Strummer came and sat beside him. "We're still mates, aren't we?" he asked, troubled. Martin strongly disapproved of Joe flinging the microphone. "I should have said something to Joe about it, because he could have split his skull open."

At Glastonbury that year Joe again was in residence with his campfire. Fuji followed on. Then he was straight to the West Coast, where Joe appeared at the eighth annual Hootenany rockabilly festival and car show.

That year festival organizer Bill Hardie expanded the California-based Hootenany: in addition to hosting the bash at its long-time home in Orange County, he also took the event to San Francisco and San Diego. That year Joe and the Mescaleros headlined each of the three shows after having warmed up with a date on July 5 at the Las Vegas House of Blues. Joe's old friend Sam Lehmer, who had engineered *Walker*, came to the Orange County show with Rudy Fernandez. "Joe had been sick that day," said Sam. "The night before he ate something and got food poisoning. He was out of it until the show started. But the band sounded great. Really excellent. Joe saved himself during the day and just put out complete energy." "Joe always seemed to believe in the romance of the traveling troubadour," said Luke Bullen. "He turns up to the show and plays the part of Joe Strummer." Lola, Joe's sixteen-year-old daughter, came along with a school friend on that short West Coast tour, and Joe wrote a song about her, "Coma Girl," one of his greatest final songs ("I was crawling through a festival way out west," runs the first line). "Lola didn't play on the fact that she was Joe's daughter," said Martin. "She didn't stomp about, she was totally cool. She's got Joe's artistic talent: she drew me a brilliant little cartoon—just like Joe would have done." On the final show, during a great version of "Yalla Yalla," Joe began to cry onstage during his performance. "He was letting all his emotions out in front of everyone," said Martin Slattery.

Onstage at the final Hootenany show it had been Martin's turn to feel Joe's wrath. "I was supposed to come down a bit but I held on into it a little bit, and he turned round and went, 'Shut the fuck up!' That was the only time he'd been derogatory toward me onstage. It really fucked me off. I would never have gone to him, 'You're singing in the wrong place, you cunt!' I was pissed off and I spoke to him about it afterward. He was taken aback: he went all humble. 'I get really emotional onstage.' He was really apologetic, and he spent the rest of that night coming up to me going, 'Sorry, Marty.' I wished I hadn't said anything."

Back in England, Joe and the Mescaleros played a date at London's Shepherd's Bush Empire on July 11, before the MOVE festival the next day at Manchester's Old Trafford Cricket Ground, sharing the bill with Ian Brown and Paul Weller, and one on July 13, that year's T in the Park in Scotland, playing with Oasis, Badly Drawn Boy and Primal Scream.

On August 3 Joe and the Mescaleros played the Cambridge Folk Festi-

Joe with Rudy Fernandez (left) and Tymon Dogg (right), invaluable friends and supporters. *(Rudy Fernandez)*

val, an unusual setting. That day, Martin recalled, Joe seemed "quite crazy," citing a BBC television interview in which his sound-bites seemed especially manic. Before the show Pockets found Joe hiding under the steps to the group's caravan, smoking a spliff. Perhaps he was only obeying his own edict: after Martin and his wife, Kirsty, arrived with Isabella, their baby, Joe put up a large cardboard sign announcing: "ABSOLUTELY NO SMOKING: THIS IS THE CRIB."

A backstage guest at Cambridge was Richard "Snakehips" Dudanski, the former drummer with the 101'ers: "Joe was great. He was fantastic, very friendly." Joe insisted that Richard play with the Mescaleros on the encore, the first time that they had worked together since the Soul Vendors at the Tabernacle on New Year's Eve, 1980. As the group played in pouring rain, Joe introduced his old musical and squatting partner: "Hey, Richard from the 101'ers is in the house!" Dudanski appeared onstage armed with a tambourine, and Joe almost immediately bellowed at him: "*Play in time, you cunt!*" "Having just sold this guy as a soulmate from back in the day," reminded Martin. "Snakes" was not fazed by this: "It was nice we played together after so long."

While Joe and Tymon were hanging out at the Cambridge Folk Festival, Joe noticed a BBC mobile broadcast studio. He told Richard, "What I want to do is to buy one of those, and drive it down to Mali in West Africa to record there." He wanted Richard and Tymon Dogg to come with him. He told Richard about his visit earlier that year to Essaouira in Morocco. "He said that he'd once gone overland with his dad in a car, from Haifa, through Syria, and then through Iraq to Tehran when his father had been stationed there."

Had Joe's thinking been directed by the journey he and Tymon had made to Cambridge? "Just me and Joe went on the bus, and I said, 'Look, I never joined the band. I was in a relationship with you.' We were questioning how we could do something that was valid, not just how to make another record, but moving on what we were doing as an art form. The art form was vital, and Joe still had that fire about it."

Not unusually Joe had two life situations, ones that were entirely contradictory, but he was managing to make them coexist: he had his global radio deejay world with Tymon and Richard Dudanski and his desire to buy a broadcast truck; and he had the young, thrusting Mescaleros, ambitious to put out a hard rock 'n' roll album—which Joe was also up for. Joe wanted both these situations, loved them both.

However, he had some uncertainties about the group. He had learned that, without telling him, Martin Slattery and Scott Shields had agreed to spend the summer working on a new album with Paul Heaton, the former singer with the Housemartins and the Beautiful South; they already had worked on a remix of a tune by former Spice Girl Mel C. Following the defection of Pablo Cook the previous year, Joe—whose antennae over such matters were always raised—was not at all pleased; he was questioning where the loyalties of his musicians lay. If he had considered that that loyalty mainly lay with their bank managers, Joe might have gained a different view.

The conversation with Richard Dudanski at Cambridge Folk Festival was soon taken up again. Eighteen days later was Joe's fiftieth birthday. As usual he spent it in San José, along with Damien and Maia Hirst, Jem and Marcia Finer, and John and Amanda Govett. Richard and his family drove over from Granada, where he now lived. "We were in Joe's bar, run by these biker guys in a place called Escullos, three hundred yards from the sea."

"There was a weird German bloke playing amazing old-fashioned r&b all night," said Jem Finer. "They had this drink there called *toxico*, made from tequila and infused with marijuana. '*Hola*, Joe!' He was knocking back the *toxicos*, round after round, all night long. But I wouldn't say Joe was drinking more than anyone else." For Joe's fiftieth birthday present Jem Finer had made him a potato tortilla: "I didn't expect him to eat it and it was no surprise when Lucinda said it was still in the corner of his garage in Spain, where he just liked to look at it."

Jazz and Lola, Joe's two daughters with Gaby, were in San José and spent Joe's birthday night with him. "They came back with him and had gazpacho for breakfast," said Marcia Finer. "They were saying what a lovely time they'd had with Joe as they hadn't seen him for a while. Definitely he could handle the kids. He had more of a problem with adults."

"The following night," remembered Richard Dudanski, "we agreed to meet up on the beach at midnight, a full moon. We were there until 6:00 a.m., with bongos and tents. He told me that world music was the direction he was going in. He was talking about taking the sound of the Mescaleros and stripping it away. Tymon's tunes were a direction he wanted to go in. In the 101'ers days we'd try and dig out obscure Cajun music—'Junco Partner' was a good example. When he started in the Clash he was always having a dig at me for being a folkie for doing stuff with Tymon. From what he said now it seemed his Scottish side was bringing this out of him, but you don't have to go further than *Walker* to see how rooted that view was. I said, 'If you ever end up with just Tymon, there's a drummer here.' 'I really appreciate your support,' he said. He was really buzzing with everything going on. The last time I saw him he was taking out the rubbish from the back of a café in San José where he knew the people."

In September Antony Genn and Damien Hirst went out for a night at the Groucho Club. Unexpectedly Joe also turned up. He walked straight over to Ant. "I've got a bone to pick with you. I thought we were going to do a track together. You called Luce about it. You never called me back." Ant, who had called Joe when he was in California, was surprised by Joe's vehemence.

"Two hours," grunted Joe.

"What do you mean?" asked Ant.

"I live two hours from you. You call me, day or night, any time, and I'll be there in two hours. Anything you want me to do."

"That was Joe's way of saying, 'It's gone. All the past is over.' We hung out for hours, talked about all sorts of things, hugged and said goodbye, and that was the last time I saw him."

At the end of September Joe and the Mescaleros returned to Japan for three dates, a festival, for which they were being paid good money, one in Fukuoka, and a final show in Tokyo at the fifteen-hundred-capacity Liquid Room. Before the dates Joe sent an e-mail to Dick Rude at his home in Los Angeles. In itself this was extraordinary, as Joe still had not fully adapted to computer culture, far happier with faxing. The e-mail was an invitation to Dick Rude to go with them to Japan: "You've gotta come with us. We're doing a cover of Iggy's '1969,' you've gotta film it!" In Japan Joe told Dick Rude how disturbed he had been by Martin and Scott's summer job with Paul Heaton, but he was still up for playing with the group and really making a mark with them. When Dick said that Tymon Dogg and Scott Shields hardly saw eye to eye about anything, Joe had a simple, and very characteristic, solution: "Leave them to it. They'll figure it out between themselves."

"Joe wanted to test new material like 'Get Down Moses,'" said Dick. "They performed like I'd never seen them before. They had really started to take it to a different level. Joe was rolling around onstage, jumping off the amps, or over the drum kit, or out into the audience. He was everywhere. He was so alive he didn't know what to do. Like a kid.

"Especially the last night in Tokyo, there were no pretensions about what he was doing whatsoever. He was performing with all his heart, with absolute reckless abandon. There are people that are artists because they have to be. He was so happy, so smiley, so full, so shiny. He really was reaching something there at the very end." When fans would ask Joe about Dick Rude's camera, he had a ready reply: "Dick's making a movie. Don't tell anyone, nobody's going to want to watch it!"

The shows had been set up by Masa, in conjunction with Jason Mayall. Jason also was in Japan, and after the Tokyo gig was severely reprimanded by Joe. Waiting for the star performer were around 150 Japanese fans. Not only did they all want a personalized autograph—always replete with some Joe artwork—along with signatures on every piece of memorabilia they had brought with them, but they all expected to have their photograph taken with Joe. After Joe had dealt with about a third of these supplicants, Jason had a word in his ear. "I think you could slip away now," he said.

Joe rounded on Jason in fury: "I'll stay to the very last person. This is my job. This is what I do!" Ninety minutes later he finally left the building.

On the final day in Japan a typhoon struck the country. "I hope the typhoon sticks around so I can spend another day here," Joe said to Dick, who suggested he change his return flight to a later date. But he had noticed that even in front of him, Joe would be on the phone every day to Lucinda, blowing kisses down the line. "He said, 'I can't do it. I gotta get back to Luce.' Coming from Joe, that was something else, man."

At the end of October Dick Rude received a phone call from Joe. He had a meeting in New York on the afternoon of November 4, he told him: VH-1, the music cable channel, had offered Joe a show, to be called *Joe Strummer's Global Boom Box*, a TV version of the BBC World Service *London Calling* series. Joe would do it, he said, only if Dick would cohost the show. "I was so flattered," said Dick. When they went to the meeting, Joe had with him a boom box he had had covered in reflectors, stickers and flashing lights, as well as a torn plastic shopping bag. He was in great spirits: earlier in the day he had been driving around Manhattan in a convertible Cadillac, scouting out locations for that evening's fun. "Everyone came by to say hi," said Dick. "The CEO of Viacom came down. Everyone came to shake Joe's hand. Everyone was thrilled to have him in the building." It was agreed the show would be broadcast in the new year.

A very happy Joe with his wife, Lucinda. *(Lucinda Mellor)*

Joe stayed in New York for another three days. Unusually he had some time on his hands, a chance to hang out and relax. "We were in Starbucks in the Village," said Dick, "just sitting there looking out of the window, and he turns to me and goes, 'This is so great! Just drinking coffee, staring out the window, looking at New York City. It's so beautiful.'"

There was a gathering of the usual suspects. Bob Gruen, Josh Cheuse, Jim Jarmusch—when Jim and Sara Driver decided to stay in one night, Joe broke into their apartment in the early hours and dragged them from their beds. On the last night, however, it was the turn of Dick Rude, now a teetotaler, to feel Joe's wrath. At five in the morning Dick neglected to save a drunken companion from falling off a bar on which he was dancing. Joe, himself very drunk, was furious: "At Glastonbury we stick together and look after each other. What were you playing at?"

Something else had occurred that evening, something that had perhaps raised Joe's level of irascibility, something even more fraught with subtext than the Bob Gruen Clash photo exhibition had been. Chris LaSalle brought the news that the following March the Clash would be inducted into the Rock and Roll Hall of Fame. If they accepted the award, it was very likely that the group would be expected to perform. "We talked about the Rock and Roll Hall of Fame that night," said Dick, "and even though he knew it was a load of crap, he did recognize that it still meant something. It was his peers who were the people who had voted them in, so it really was an honor, like the Ivor Novello had been—that's how Joe saw that. The irony was that now his other band was taking off and performing in a way that had never happened before, and he loved it in a way he'd never loved it before, and was really happy to just be the ordinary guy, playing his stuff, without all the bullshit. Joe used to make a joke about musicians being on the level of crossword puzzle writers.

"That night in New York we went back to the hotel as the sun was coming up—we'd got over our differences. Me, him and Chris LaSalle were talking about the awards show. At first he didn't want to do it. Then he said he'd definitely do it. He was trying to figure out which song to do. Should it be 'London's Burning' or 'London's Calling'? He couldn't figure out if Simmo would do it."

"Joe was very excited about the Hall of Fame for five minutes. He was in the middle of recording and touring and all that," remembered Lucinda.

"He said the Clash had to play as how awful it would be to have other people playing your songs while you sit and watch. He did also say that he wouldn't do it if Topper didn't do it, and he knew that Paul had said a definite no. On the other hand he did also call Mani from the Stone Roses and Primal Scream and ask him if he would join them, and Mani was on standby."

"I thought it would be absolutely wrong to play the Hall of Fame," said Paul. "I wanted to explain to Joe that the tickets were twenty-five hundred dollars. There'd be no ordinary fans there. I was threatened, 'We'll get Mani.' I said, 'Go ahead.'"

Back home Joe had slotted in a short British tour, the Bringing It All Back Home Tour, taking in assorted small towns and unexpected venues. They were the sort of dates the Clash would often play, taking their music to parts of the country that rarely see quality live acts. There were murmurings among the Mescaleros—some felt they should not be playing such deadbeat venues. "That was the hardest tour," recalled Luke Bullen. "Joe thought it was a good idea, but I remember him apologizing to Scott and Martin: 'I should never have booked this.'" At the beginning of December the Mescaleros were scheduled for a two-week stint at Rockfield residential studio in Wales. Did they not appreciate that Joe liked to be at peak match fitness when he went into the studio?

These shows opened at a decidedly prestigious venue. Through the auspices of Louise Aspinall, a school friend of Lucinda, Joe had been added to a bill that included Michael Palin and Bryan Adams for a benefit for the Dian Fossey Gorilla Fund at the Royal Opera House on November 10. Since he had worked at the English National Opera as a cleaner in his early twenties, Joe had hated opera. "Joe could carry a chip on his shoulder," said Dick Rude, "and one of the chips was the fact he had had to clean out the toilets. He told me how he loathed those people because they would piss in the stall and throw their cigar butts down. Joe would have to pick them out."

"It was a great evening," said Lucinda, "the first time rock music had ever been played there. They had a great sound check and then Joe told me in confidence what the real running order was. The last tune was 'White Riot.' He thought it would be a fantastic buzz to play that in the Opera House, and it was."

The next night Joe and the Mescaleros played the Liquid Room in Edinburgh. The *Edinburgh Evening News* gave the show a review that can only be described as ecstatic. "A hero's welcome awaited Joe Strummer when he took to the stage, the sort of spontaneous uproar that speaks volumes about the respect in which he is held in Edinburgh," ran the first line. "Strummer is obviously reveling in one of the most fruitful periods of a remarkable career . . . The Joe Strummer of late 2002 is every bit as vital, vibrant and unmissable as the man who fronted the Clash in 1977. The crowds will keep coming out for many years to come."

Shows followed in Newcastle and Blackpool before a move back to the west of Notting Hill for a gig on November 15 at Acton Town Hall, a benefit for the striking workers of the Fire Brigades Union. While in Japan, Joe had been approached to play the benefit; he immediately agreed.

But the major significance of this show, what makes it a historic rock 'n' roll event, was that it marked the first time that Mick Jones played onstage with Joe Strummer for nineteen years, since the Us Festival outside Los Angeles. As it was, Mick nearly didn't make it to the show. Someone who'd said he'd go along with him let him down at the last moment, but he caught a cab on his own to Acton Town Hall. "I'm glad I did," he told me afterward. He also said he had not meant to necessarily play with the Mescaleros at the FBU benefit. He simply grabbed a guitar at the side of the stage and found himself playing with Joe.

Joe Strummer's audience already knew Mick Jones was in the building. "Mick Jones is here tonight," Joe had declared after "Bhindi Bhagee," the second number. "And more than that, Mick Jones and his lady Miranda have had a baby last Sunday morning. And the baby's called Stella. And this is going out to Stella." Joe and the Mescaleros sloped into the reggae beat of "Rudie Can't Fail."

It was a set of extraordinary music, a steaming punk-rock performance. Just like Joe: to have thought of doing one thing, and then done the complete opposite. As Dick Rude said of the Japanese shows, Joe Strummer on the Bringing It All Back Home tour was performing at a peak of his abilities, his voice honed and sinewy with catarrh, his improvisations from the top of the pile—in the way, for example, that he segued "White Man" into an unexpected verse of "Last Train to Skaville" with such utter aplomb. His ad-libs were as rich as ever. Before "Mega Bottle Ride" he announced: "Ladies and gentlemen, for the next three minutes we are going to try and bring everyone in Acton Town Hall into the fourth dimension. The bar's still open in the fourth dimension."

Before the eighth number Joe requested, "If you've still got vocal chords, give us some assist on this one, thank you. This one's going out to those other two cunts in the Clash. That's affectionate, of course. Namely, Paul Simonon and Nicky 'Topper' Headon." Into a historic staple of Clash material, their version—with arrangement by Mick Jones—of Junior Murvin's "Police and Thieves," the tune that cemented on vinyl the punk–reggae alliance. "This one's entitled 'I've Been Running, Police on My Back,'" announced Joe, introducing the Eddie Grant song with the first two lines, a prompt to his memory, as he had done with Clash songs. There were the first performances in London of "Get Down Moses" and "Coma Girl," a fantastic version, creatively muscular.

As soon as Mick Jones heard the opening chords of "Bankrobber," the first encore, he felt "compelled" to join Joe onstage, finding a guitar to borrow. Mick seemed joyous up there, dapper in a fitted three-button jacket and white shirt; the chemistry and interaction between him and Joe—as band-leader more consciously in control of the moment—was instant and spontaneous; it was as though no one else was on the stage. "All right, baby, play that guitar now—for the baby," Joe scatted to Mick during "Bankrobber," a laugh in his voice, as though he was immediately freed up, as though something had fallen away from him. The Spinal Tap–like cliché of this onstage reunion only added to the innocent joy. "That was for the Harlesden and Willesden Fire Companies," said Mick Jones after "Bankrobber." "In the key of A," Joe bellowed to his group. "Look at him," he gestured to Mick. And the group pounded into a stupendous "White Riot."

"Thanks for being a great crowd. Honestly, we're with you," said Joe after the Clash classic. "And this is the last tune of the night. Specially requested by Andy. And this is called [pause]: 'London's Burning.'" What more perfect choice for final number could there be for a benefit for the Fire Brigades Union? What did you think they were going to play? Mick Jones onstage multiplied the inspiration.

At the end of "London's Burning," Joe finally introduced the man who had appeared onstage: "Mick Jones, ladies and gentlemen. And thank you very much. Good luck with everything, everybody."

The poetry of the occasion—not all of which could immediately be recognized—was compounded by the event itself, a nonprofit righteous act of defiance, unsullied by ego. That Mick Jones should have gone onstage with Joe at his last London gig before he died is a testament to the magic that overstrode the Clash (and those around it). That always overstrode it.

"When he saw Mick, Joe's face was like a kid," said Luke Bullen. "He was genuinely delighted." David Mingay had gone along to the show. After the gig he told Joe how great he thought the Mescaleros songs' were. "He said, doing his Joe Strummer voice, 'Can you get any money for movies? This is my e-mail.' My daughter asked Joe what his politics were now. 'I'm still a man of the left,' he said. 'But I'm not against America. I have a lot of American friends.'"

Gaby Salter, the mother of Jazz and Lola, was also in the audience. "I stood at the front of the stage when Joe and Mick were onstage together and it took me back to being a teenager. It was really powerful seeing them there together. A real deep feeling."

"I asked Joe in the cab leaving the gig how he felt about Mick jumping up onstage like that," said Lucinda. "He turned round with a big grin on his face and said, 'Bloody cheek!' He loved it."

There were more shows that weekend, on Saturday at TJs in Wales in Joe's post-art-school stomping-ground of Newport, and on Sunday night, on home territory, at the Palace in Bridgwater, Somerset, a benefit for the Engine Room, a media center. "Joe's gig provided the last bit of finance needed to complete the project," said Julien Temple, who was involved with the Engine Room.

After a day off Joe Strummer and the Mescaleros were at the Wedgewood Rooms in Portsmouth. Joe was approached by a fan who showed him his "Combat Rock" tattoo on his arm. "Great," said Joe, signing his name underneath it. When they made it to Hastings the next day, the fan turned up: he had had Joe's signature permanently tattooed onto his arm. Johnny Green caught up with Joe there. "We walked in the rain up the esplanade in Hastings. He's having his stroll before the show, gazing out at the sea, away from the pier. He stopped and put his hand on my arm and said, 'You would tell me, wouldn't you?' I said, 'Yeah, course I would.' The truth, he meant, of course." During the show Johnny noted the strength of the new songs, "Get Down Moses" and another new number, "Dakar Meantime." "Barry Myers, who was working as deejay, said they were changing them every night in the set. These songs really weren't finished. Barry told me they did 'Dakar Meantime' very differently to how they'd been done in Portsmouth."

Then there was a show at the Leadmill in Sheffield, before the Bringing It All Back Home tour wound up at Liverpool University, on Friday, November 22, 2002.

Back in Somerset Joe heard devastating news. Damien Hirst, his companion in the excessive consumption of drugs and alcohol, had made a life-changing decision—to give them up. "I decided it was time to stop. Even Joe would tell people to ignore me because I was getting so out of hand I'd be climbing up the chimney at home and taking Joe up there. I'd have two- or three-day sessions and the house would be wrecked afterward.

"All that consumption starts having a negative effect. If you're using it to hide something, don't do it. I think he should have stopped drinking, sitting up consuming as much as we could. I think Joe was afraid of losing something." Joe got Lucinda to make a phone call to Damien. "This stopping drinking," she had been instructed to ask by the man clearly unable to ask this painful question himself. "Is it for good?" Damien replied in the affirmative.

The next weekend, Joe was in Bonar Bridge for the wedding of his cousin George to Fiona, his longtime partner. "On November 29 we took the sleeper to Inverness and hired a car and drove to Bonar Bridge for a family wedding," said Lucinda. "Joe loved the wedding and he reeled away all night—last to bed, I think. The following day he had lunch with his aunt Jessie in her beautiful croft high in the hills and then a dram or two with Uncle John in the farmhouse where his mother was born. Then we drove to the cottage which his cousin Alasdair was renting with his wife, Deborah, and son, Harry. Joe didn't want to leave and tried to persuade me to change the tickets and fuck the cost. I said it wasn't about the money but he had to be in the recording studio in Wales as it was all booked. So he very reluctantly left with me to catch the sleeper back. He absolutely loved being in Scotland with his cousins and family again."

Joe was supposed to have arrived by then at Rockfield, where the Mescaleros were already ensconced. The lineup consisted of Martin, Scott, Simon and Luke; Tymon was due for the next sessions, in the new year. "Joe was late getting to Rockfield," said Luke Bullen. "'Coma Girl' and 'Get Down Moses' were the most complete of the songs when we got there. A lot was being pieced together still. By the time we left we had a lot of material, but not always the lyrics."

The residential nature of Rockfield inclined Joe to behave as if he were at home, wandering around in his slippers—which in Joe's case were a pair of Native American moccasins. The Acton Town Hall show seemed to have drawn him back to the past. Finally, Martin had learned that many of the musical aspects Joe brought to the Mescaleros had originally been learned in the Clash. "He was really into backing vocals, for example. He was always getting me and Scott to do backing vocals. One night at Rockfield he was really candid about who did what in the Clash. He was really respectful of Mick, saying, 'I was into the songs, but it was Mick that was into the sonic picture. It was Mick's idea to put the backing vocals on and it was Mick's idea to overdub some great guitar line there.' Another thing I realized he'd got from the Clash was this thing of just throwing a tune down, not overrehearsing it, so everyone's still sharp. It takes you to that place a little bit quicker when you're not sure what's going to happen."

At the end of the fortnight that had been booked at Rockfield, the group went their separate ways. "See you after Christmas," Joe bade them farewell, with a hug.

On December 15 Joe went back to Scotland for a few days with Lucinda's mother and stepfather at their home in Blairgowrie. Back at Yalway on the evening of the nineteenth, Joe drove around Taunton with Pockets Girvan, who was leaving the next day for a family Christmas. Joe was searching for an ATM with money in it. Finally they found one. Joe withdrew one hundred pounds and handed it to Pockets, who he knew was broke. "I'm worried about you," said Joe.

The next morning Joe, Lucinda and Eliza traveled up to London, to the annual pantomime treat that Luce's father organizes for Eliza. "This year it was *Grease*. Poor Joe had seen it before," recalled Lucinda. Staying at the Groucho Club, Joe had late-night drinks with Mick and Miranda.

"The last night Joe spent in Groucho, those two together, it was just lovely to see," said Lucinda. "Really lovely. Mick and Miranda arrived and I said, 'Oh Mick, Joe's here.' And Mick's whole face lit up. Then they found each other, and it was great. They really loved each other. Joe adored him."

The next day, Saturday December 21, a Christmas lunch had been organized by Joe, with Jazz and Lola, Eliza, Luce, Gaby, Frances, and Tom Salter.

Gaby had slept strangely the previous night, waking from a troubling dream. Then Lola had told her she had had a premonition that she was going to die that weekend. Gaby put it to the back of her mind, as she buried herself in practical details, booking a table for them at Kettners, an upmarket pizza restaurant in Soho—Joe had forgotten to make arrangements for the meal. "There were eight of us there, at a huge table in the middle of the room with a light shining over it. We had a three-hour meal, with the girls telling him what they wanted to do with their lives and Joe really listening. I made a decision to stop the uncomfortableness between us. I thought, Why don't I try and be more easy with him, and able to communicate. It was so much easier to be with him that day. He had been to Scotland and seen all the family and reconnected with them. Mick had been with him the night before, and later that evening Tricia had a phone conversation with him. But Joe and I tidied up everything between us over that lunch. It was as though he knew everything needed to be sorted out."

"After lunch," said Lucinda, "Joe, me and the girls walked to Covent Garden, where we did some Christmas shopping. Joe was totally exhausted but still in wondrous form. He laughed and joked with Eliza on the train home, chasing her up and down the empty carriage."

When Joe, Lucinda and Eliza got back to Yalway, there was a message on the voice mail, not exactly what he needed that night. Tricia Ronane was pointing out that the deadline was on them for the track listing for a Clash compilation, *The Essential Clash*, being rush-released by Sony in time for the Rock and Roll Hall of Fame event in March. Joe called her back. He stayed up all night working out his choice of songs for the record.

Waking early on the afternoon of Sunday, December 22, Joe sent a fax to Tricia with the tunes that he suggested. He appended a note to his old friend "Simmo," suggesting he reconsider his refusal to play at the Rock and Roll Hall of Fame. "Try it. You might like it," he suggested. Then Joe went for a walk with his three dogs.

Back home, at just after three in the afternoon, Joe sat down on the living room sofa to read *The Observer*.

$$\frac{2}{9}$$

coda (the west)

2002–2003

The autopsy revealed that John Graham Mellor had not died, as thought, of a heart attack. Although he had never known this, he had been born with a congenital heart defect: a main artery that should have run around his heart went through it instead. He could have died suddenly at any point during his fifty years.

"I woke Joe up on the morning of the twenty-second," said Lucinda. "The night before he had said he wanted to come with me to do the Christmas food shopping, but he was too tired so I left him in bed. When Eliza and I got back he was still in bed, very sleepy, so I didn't hassle him. I told him we were going to look at a pony we were going to buy Eliza. We got back at around 4:00 p.m. and there was no sign of Joe. I could tell he had been up as the dogs had obviously had a good walk and his car was still there. I searched for him, and Eliza and I found him sitting on the sofa, apparently asleep.

"I tried to wake him. Then I realized something awful had happened. His body was already going cold in places. I gave him mouth-to-mouth resuscitation and was screaming hysterically. Eliza got the phone and I told her to call the ambulance, and to go and wait for the ambulance in the road. She didn't even put her shoes on and rushed outside. She went to our neighbors, who were having a drinks party. One of the guests was a nurse. She took over from me in the resuscitation. I could tell that he was gone when I saw the look on her face."

A lmost immediately, some were apotheosizing Joe. But those who knew him, that international group of interconnected old souls who had formed his and the Clash's posse, knew he wasn't Saint Joe. No, he was much more interesting than that. If you knew him you'd love him. But you'd be mad not to realize what a piece of work he could be.

Regardless, Joe showed how, if you lock yourself into a great truth, however apparently implausible (that man might be able to live with man, for example, as he articulated in "White Man in Hammersmith Palais," or that you should get out of bed and motivate yourself), it can resonate around the world with a loving spirit. Despite the endless contradictions that seemed to fuse him together, there was no doubt who he was. "I'm a good guy," he said to me in Las Vegas. "That's how I see it, somewhere in my mind." In his work with the Mescaleros, Joe had transcended all those questions in the Wilderness Years about what he was doing, and had become a genre of his own.

That genre had a final act needing to be played out. As Joe lay in his open casket in Taunton, Martin Slattery had been struck by how his features resembled nothing less than those of an American Indian chief. From out in the ether this chief led his braves on. Martin and Scott Shields immediately set about finishing the record they had worked on with Joe at Rockfield. At Unit 21 in Hackney they put in another month's work—often using Joe's guide vocals—with Cameron Craig, the engineer who had recorded and mixed it. *Streetcore*, which contains ten songs, was released on October 20, 2003. "Coma Girl," the first single, had come out two weeks before. Martin and Scott, who never quite understood why Joe wanted to play so many Clash songs onstage, did superlative work, turning in a thundering record that was the closest Joe had come to the Clash since the demise of the group. Worldwide it had great reviews. On December 15 "Redemption Song" was put out as the last single from Joe Strummer. The duet of the song that he had recorded with Johnny Cash received a Grammy nomination.

The ten *Streetcore* songs included two the group had tried on that last

British tour—"Coma Girl" and "Get Down Moses." "Arms Aloft" and "Ramshackle Day Parade" had been recorded with them at Rockfield. "Long Shadow" and "Redemption Song" were brought in from the sessions Joe had done in L.A. in April 2002, as well as "All in a Day." "Burnin' Streets," to which originally Joe had mischievously given the title "London Is Burning," had been worked up for a TV program about firemen. "Midnight Jam" was cobbled together by Martin and Scott from samples of Joe's World Service broadcasts. "Silver and Gold" covered and renamed Bobby Charles's 1952 classic "Before I Grow Too Old." The artwork, which included a picture of his studio at Yalway, had already been decided on by Joe, who left ample notes about it.

In the grounds at Yalway, as a tribute to her husband, Lucinda erected a circle of twelve standing stones, installed in a druid ceremony; she also had planted 1,300 trees in what was named Rebel Wood, overlooking the house. On the isle of Skye, eight hundred miles north in Scotland, a further wood grew. In May 2003, at the suggestion of Michael Eavis, the organizer of the Glastonbury festival, the same head druid oversaw the unveiling of a memorial stone to Joe in a far corner of the Glastonbury site. No plaque was put up: people could learn the significance of the stone for themselves. Eavis gave the area immediately in front of the stone, behind the surreal Lost Vagueness area, for use as what became Strummerville, a physical representation of a charity established by Lucinda to assist underprivileged musicians. With a big campfire, surrounded by sofas and chairs, permanently blazing during the days of the Glastonbury festival, an equally hot sound system, and flags and bunting fluttering, Strummerville has become an established feature of Glastonbury, where those in the know—up to one thousand people sometimes—congregate for all-night sessions after the rest of the festival has died down. "Joe told me he thought his real legacy might not be the Clash, but his campfires," said Julien Temple. "He thought he'd found a way for people to communicate with each other in a very easy way. The campfire at Fuji was an example of how he wanted it to spread around the world."

Globally, websites growled with news of local tribute nights to Joe, which time did not appear to diminish. But almost immediately there were larger versions of these. On February 24, 2003, at the Grammy Awards, like the ultimate tribute group, Bruce Springsteen and E Street Band guitarist

Shot by the pool of the house he was renting in the Hollywood Hills, this image became the cover shot of *Earthquake Weather* and was later taken up as the iconic logo of Strummerville. (*Josh Cheuse/WFN*)

Little Steven joined Elvis Costello, Dave Grohl of the Foo Fighters, and No Doubt bassist Tony Kanal in a rousing rendition of "London Calling." At those Grammys Don Letts earned an award for *Westway to the World*, belatedly released in the United States. "What concerns me," he considered, "is that Joe is starting to be taken out of the context of the Clash and placed on a pedestal. I don't think he'd have wanted that."

No form of the Clash played at their Rock and Roll Hall of Fame induction two weeks later. But Joe's death had removed the controversy for Paul, and he went with Terry Chimes and Mick Jones, who said he was accepting the award on behalf of all the garage bands out there that might never have thought a moment like that would be possible. But, to his derision, his mention of Robin "Banks" Crocker having gone to Baghdad as a human shield was edited out of the televised broadcast.

Sifted from Joe's dusty shopping bags, Gordon McHarg curated an exhibition of Joe's work in London and Tokyo. In a sweet ceremony at Bristol train station, a railway engine was named after Joe. That night Elvis Costello, at the city's Colston Hall, played Elvis Presley's "Mystery Train." "That was for Joe Strummer," he said. Joe would have loved that, but not as much as when Bob Dylan kicked off his encores with "London Calling" in a season of concerts at London's Brixton Academy in November 2005.

J oe always had a twinkle in his eye," said Lucinda. "He was fun, the Pied Piper of happiness. You knew you were going to have a good time with Joe, and that life was going to be great. He said to me, 'I promise you life will never be boring.'

"I'd say he was very happy at the end. But I think he was very, very tired. Very often he only had four or five hours' sleep. A punishing and hectic schedule. He was very excited about what was going on down at Rockfield. He had the most incredible time in Scotland. He was really moved by all of that. Those plans to come back were not empty promises made as you leave a party. He was saying, 'I'm going to make Jazz and Lola come back at Easter. I'll drag them up there if I have to.' I loved him. I loved being with him. I loved the life he made. He was alive. So alive and vibrant. Intoxicating and exciting."

On August 21, 2003, on what would have been Joe's fifty-first birthday, there was a celebratory concert in the hills above Granada. Mick Jones, Tymon Dogg, Jem Finer and Richard Dudanski were among those who played into the warm night.

Afterward, down in San José, Jazz and Lola took their portion of their father's ashes along the coast to a cliff of gnarled white rock, a beautiful, perfect spot. Behind it, in the desert, was the bikers' bar where Joe would enjoy *toxico*, the marijuana-infused tequila drink. As well as his two daughters, there was a small party present, including Jem and Marcia Finer, Lauren Jones and assorted children.

They were responding to a dream that Gaby had had. From a pottery urn made by Pockets, Jazz tipped Joe's ashes over the cliff toward the sea. "I'd never seen them before," said Jem. "I was amazed how fine they were, like particles. It was beautiful to see them drifting out in the breeze, like white, sandy rock. They dispersed toward the sea, the mountains in the background. That's my last memory of Joe, drifting off across the sea and mountains. Very beautiful."

Jazz still clutched the urn. "Shall we keep it?" she asked Lola. As Lola was replying in the affirmative, it flipped out of Jazz's hands, as though grabbed by a gust of wind, and hovered in the air above the cliff edge before smashing down onto a rock below. The urn's broken fragments were gathered and thrown out to sea.

"It was very weird," said Jem. "Mischief from the other side. You don't stop, Joe, do you?"

"*Get on with it!*" Joe would have barked.

Ahoy, me hearties. *(Lucinda Mellor)*

acknowledgments

Over the three and a half years that it took me to write this biography of Joe Strummer, I met or talked to more than three hundred of his relatives, friends, work partners and acquaintances.

The company of women that John "Joe Strummer" Mellor kept was of the very highest. So first and foremost I must give my deepest thanks and appreciation to Lucinda Mellor and her daughter and Joe's stepdaughter, Eliza Henderson, and to Gaby Holford.

Lucinda introduced me to Joe's fascinating family tree. On his mother Anna Mackenzie's side I met the uncle who was—according to Joe—"the original punk rocker," the late John Mackenzie, who sadly passed on just as this book was being completed; and I had absolutely invaluable support and assistance—way beyond the call of duty—from Iain Gillies, Alasdair Gillies, Anna Gillies and Rona MacKintosh, Jessie and Ken MacKinnon, Jenny Mackenzie, Chrissie Nicholson, Sheena Yeats, Maeri MacLeod and George MacLeod, whose wedding in Bonar Bridge Joe had attended just over three weeks before he left us.

On Ronald Mellor's side, I met or corresponded with Joe's equally gracious and helpful cousins Gerry King, Phyllis Netherway, Jonathan Macfarland and Stephen Macfarland.

Of course, this book could not have been written without the absolutely heartfelt support and access to the most personal and honest reflections of Joe's fellow members of the Clash: Mick Jones, Paul Simonon, Topper Headon and Terry Chimes. Thanks so much, guys, and serious respect. And though the Clash Mark II was a controversial issue for many, Pete Howard—who on the drum stool bridged both groups—and Vince White and Nick Sheppard proved highly intelligent, sensitive and perceptive interviewees. As did Bernard "Bernie" Rhodes, and Clash *consigliere* Kosmo Vinyl, seemingly permanently on call for questions of small detail or large philosophical overview, a role he shared with former road manager Johnny Green.

Joe's later success with the Mescaleros came as a consequence of his linking up with some of the finest musical talents in Britain; I especially thank Antony Genn, Martin Slattery, Scott Shields, Pablo Cook, Luke Bullen and Smiley Bernard, as well as Tymon Dogg, Joe's former musical mentor, who bookended both ends of his life as a musician and artist; and I must not forget Joe's great on-the-road sidekick, Andy Boo. In the years building up to the launch of the Mescaleros—that time that Joe would refer to as his "Wilderness Years"—he worked with a number of spirited individuals whose energy and creativity helped impel him on the next stage of his life: the inimitable Bez, and the redoubtable Richard Norris and Ian Tregoning.

Both in Britain and in California during that time Joe worked with supersession-man Danny Saber, whose understanding helped move along the narrative, linking up with the days of the *Earthquake Weather* sessions: Zander Schloss, Jack Irons and Lonnie Marshall filled in key areas of that period in Hollywood as well as providing the background to the Latino Rockabilly War. Zander had also worked with Joe as an actor on the Alex Cox films *Straight to Hell* and *Walker*, as well as the soundtrack to the second film—he gave key insights to a crucial time, as certainly did Alex Cox himself. A serious big-up to all the aforementioned, as well as to Sam Lehmer and Mark Stebbeds. And Kathy Nelson, Queen of the Soundtracks, thank you so much. Gerry Harrington gave selflessly of his knowledge: Gerry, I loved your tour of Joe's L.A.

But going back in time to Woody Mellor's days before the Clash, numerous individuals have splendidly given time above and beyond the call of duty: Gill Calvert, Helen Cherry, Carol Roundhill, Clive Timperley, Richard Dudanski, Pat Nother, Julian Yewdall, John "Boogie" Tiberi, Kit Buckler and Paloma Romero, as well as Ari Up, all of whom get a special thanks for having been not only such insightful interviewees but also such great company. In this context I particularly thank Deborah van der Beek, whom Joe arranged—via his friend Paul Buck—for me to finally find as the allegedly completed manuscript was sitting by my front door, waiting for a bike messenger. So a very big thanks to Paul "Pablo Labritain" Buck as well as to Richard "Dick the [he's no] Shit" Evans, for wonderful reasonings and heartfelt friendship.

Equally good raps came from several school and art-school-era friends of Joe: Celia Pyke, Anne Day, Ken Powell, Adrian Greaves, Andy Ward, Andy Secombe, Dave Bardsley and Desson Thomson, as well as excellent overviews from Derek Boshier, Pete Silverton and Steve White—cheers, guys.

From the days of punk rock and beyond, I didn't come across a single person without a deep understanding and love for Joe Strummer. These include, in no particular order: Jeannette Lee, Tony James, Keith Allen (who gave me access to a lengthy interview he had conducted with Joe in 1995), Robin "Banks" Crocker, Sebastian Conran, Barry "Scratchy" Myers, Jock Scot, Marc Zermati, Kumari Salgado, Jo-Anne Henry, Nick and Connie Broughton, Amanda Govett, Suzi McKewan, Tracy Franks, Audrey de la Peyre, Jesus Arias, Harriet Cochrane, John Shearlaw, Pat Rodger, Dave "Bimble" Parsons, Michael Horovitz, Michael Eavis, Sabrina Guinness, Nyle Shepherd, Alex Chetwynd, Alfonso, Desmond Letts and Spencer Style. And there were eight filmmakers of exceptional ability who poured their hearts into memories of someone who for them had been a close and sincere friend—Don Letts, David Mingay, Dick Rude, Jim Jarmusch, Sara Driver, Marissa Silver, F. J. Ossang and Julien Temple, who, with his wife, Amanda, helped Joe and his wife, Lucinda, find a new place in the world. Also, thanks indeed to superproducer Eric Fellner and to Mark Bedford, fireman-filmmaker.

Two people who also assisted Joe Strummer to move into the next phase of his life were the artist Damien Hirst and his wife, Maia, who both gave unstintingly of themselves, above and beyond the call of duty. Thanks so very much to both of you.

And the same to the following: Jem and Marcia Finer, for more deep reasonings, Spider Stacey, James Fearnley, Danielle von Zerneck, Frank Murray and the great Rudy Fernandez.

Inspirational throughout my writing this book were a number of deeply creative and cultural individuals who were very close to Joe: Gordon McHarg, the pop artist, Dave "Pockets" Girvan, Gaz Mayall, Jason Mayall, Tricia Simonon, Patti Paladin, Michael Wojas and Josh Cheuse. Oh, and Steve Kirk: I couldn't have done it without you, man—your magnificent collection of concert material kept me on the vibe from the moment I met you. Coming from very different worlds, a quartet of musical artists gave me inspiration at precisely the right moment. So hats off to Pearl Harbor, Danny Thompson, Rat Scabies and Billy Bragg. Other musicianly fellows who have been there for me include Jerry Dammers, Glen Matlock, Andrea Oliver, Chris Musto, Nicky Tesco, Leo Williams, Dan Donovan, J.C., Jesse Malin and Sting, as well as those top-notch treaders of the boards Steve Buscemi and Matt Dillon.

How could parts of this book have existed, moreover, without the great, great help of Anthony Davie and Sukwoon Noh—guys, you helped it go up several levels. I am so indebted to you. Similarly to the Mescaleros website, and to Don Whistance of Black Market Clash.

Meanwhile, back in Manchester, chapeaux aloft to Simon Moran, Kev Nicko, Graham Jones, Tommy Dunne and the always splendid Dermot Mitchell. And for London uptown banking business, thanks to Anthony Millar.

In the photographic and illustrative world, huge, huge gratitude to Jane Ashley, George Binette (and Tammy, of course), Adrian Boot, Paul "Pablo Labritain" Buck, Sean Carasov, Josh Cheuse, Anne Day, Jill Furmanovsky, Bob Gruen, Sho Kikuchi, Tony Lyons, Ray Lowry, Gordon McHarg, Sheila Rock, Richard Schroeder, Kate Simon, Paul Simonon (this time for the use of the art form that was his first love), Pennie Smith, Fiona Spear, Joe Stevens, Justin Thomas, Deborah van der Beek, Julian Yewdall and John Zimmerman. And I must not forget the phenomenal heartfelt work of Chuck Sperry: thanks, pal.

Many denizens of the music business have been extremely helpful and giving: Chris LaSalle, Hein van der Rey, Rob Partridge, Tony Linkin, Kit Buckler, Ellie Smith, Muff Winwood, Peter Jenner, Andrew King and Glen Colson, as well as Mo Armstrong, Peter Kinnaird and Raymond Jordan. Serious thanks also to Raoul Shah.

In the world of the Fourth Estate, thanks to Dotun Adebayo, Simon Barnett, Victor Bockris, James Brown, Mick Brown, Richard Cook, Mark Cooper, John Dillon, Pip Dunn, Jamie Ferguson, Pat Gilbert, Marcus Gray, Paolo Hewitt, Boris Johnson, Andy Kershaw, Gavin Martin, John Mendelson, Barry Miles, Paul Morley, Charles Shaar Murray, Andy Norman, Mal Peachy (for the *Westway to the World* transcripts), Kris Needs, Paul Rambali, Tresa Redburn, Ira Robbins, Jim Shelley, Dave Tate, Adrian Thrills and the venerable denizens of *Trouser Press*; and especially to Vivien Goldman, Jon Savage and Neil Spencer for their ceaseless support and advice; and to Alan Card and Nick Daganbest for celestial musings. Also, for companionship and a good kip at just the right time, thanks so much Damien Love and Alison Stroak.

In the publishing world, I give heartical thanks and respect to Trevor Dolby of HarperCollins; Denise Oswald of Farrar, Straus and Giroux; and Humphrey Price—without you, mate, I'd still be drowning at the bottom of the well. Also in the world of U.K. publishing, a big cheers to Monica Chakraverty, Caroline Hotblack, Bartley Shaw, Terence Caven, Dominic Forbes, Jane Beeton, Jill Crouch, Rose Harrow, Iain

Chapple, Eve Fernandez, Clive Kimtoff and Elspeth Dougall. And of course special thanks to my agents Julian Alexander and Sarah Lazin (without whom . . .), not forgetting Lucinda Cook for tolerating my endless questions.

Sam, Steve and Jill Eade all helped. And I could not have written this book without the support, companionship, and love of Alex Salewicz, Cole Salewicz and Pamela Esterson. Thanks also to Versa Manos.

I'm sure there are people I've missed out: so to all and any of you—apologies and a very big thanks.

And Joe . . . cheers, mate: I'm sure you're doing fine. Big kiss. We all love you. As Mick said, "It's maybe a good job Joe's there first: he can get us all in on the guest list."

index